Encounter
on the Narrow Ridge:

A Life of Martin Buber

Also by Maurice Friedman:

Martin Buber: The Life of Dialogue
Problematic Rebel: Melville, Dostoievsky, Kafka, Camus
The Worlds of Existentialism: A Critical Reader
To Deny Our Nothingness: Contemporary Images of Man
The Philosophy of Martin Buber (chief Editor)
Touchstones of Reality: Existential Trust and the Community of Peace
The Hidden Human Image
The Human Way: A Dialogical Approach to Religion and Human Experience
The Confirmation of Otherness: In Family, Community, and Society
The Healing Dialogue in Psychotherapy
Contemporary Psychology: Revealing and Obscuring the Human
Martin Buber's Life and Work: The Early Years — 1878–1923
Martin Buber's Life and Work: The Middle Years — 1923–1945
Martin Buber's Life and Work: The Later Years — 1945–1965
Martin Buber and the Eternal
Abraham Joshua Heschel and Elie Wiesel: "You Are My Witnesses"
A Dialogue with Hasidic Tales: Hallowing the Everyday

Encounter
on the Narrow Ridge:
A Life of Martin Buber

Maurice Friedman

PARAGON HOUSE

New York

BB 921 F3

First edition, 1991

Published in the United States by Paragon House

Paragon House
90 Fifth Avenue
New York, NY 10011
Copyright © 1991 by Maurice Friedman

Library of Congress Cataloging-in-Publication Data

Friedman, Maurice S.
    Martin Buber's encounter on the narrow ridge: a life / Maurice Friedman. — 1st ed.
        p.   cm.
    Includes bibliographical references and index.
    ISBN (invalid) 1-55778-795-0
    1. Buber, Martin, 1878-1965. 2. Philosophers, Jewish — Germany - Biography. 3.
Philosophers, Jewish — Israel — Biography. 4.Zionists — Biography. 5. Philosophy,
Jewish. I. Title.
    B3213.B84F726   1991
    296.3'092—dc20
    [B]   90-44502
                                                      CIP

10 9 8 7 6 5 4 3 2 1

Manufactured in the United States of America

The paper used in this publication meets the minimum requirements of American National
Standard for Information Sciences - Permanence of Paper for Printed Library Materials,
ANSI Z39.48-1984.

For Eugenia

CONTENTS

Preface   ix

Part I   The Road to I and Thou (1878–1923)

CHAPTER 1   Childhood and Youth (1878–1900)   **3**
CHAPTER 2   Zionism (1898–1904)   **21**
CHAPTER 3   Mysticism: The Discovery of Hasidism (1904–1914)   **37**
CHAPTER 4   Prewar Teachings of "Realization" (1909–1913)   **55**
CHAPTER 5   The First World War and the Breakthrough to Dialogue
(1914–1918)   **73**
CHAPTER 6   Communal Socialism and Revolution: The Murder of
Landauer (1906–1919)   **99**
CHAPTER 7   Postwar Zionism, Education, and Politics
(1918–1922)   **116**
CHAPTER 8   Ascent to *I and Thou* (1916–1923)   **125**

Part II   The Weimar Republic and Nazi Germany (1923–1938)

CHAPTER 9   Franz Rosenzweig and the Buber-Rosenzweig Bible
(1921–1929)   **155**
CHAPTER 10   The Weimar Republic (1922–1932)   **178**
CHAPTER 11   Nazi Germany (1933–1938)   **208**

Part III   Prewar Palestine and the Early Years of the State (1938–1953)

CHAPTER 12   Ascent to the Land: Prewar Palestine (1934–1939)   **235**
CHAPTER 13   The Second World War (1939–1945)   **257**
CHAPTER 14   Jewish-Arab Rapprochement and Conflict
(1939–1949)   **268**
CHAPTER 15   Biblical Judaism, Hasidism, and Adult Education
(1943–1959)   **285**

**Part IV   Postwar Germany and America: Replies to Critics
(1945–1963)**

CHAPTER 16   Dialogue with German Christians (1945–1961)   **315**

CHAPTER 17   Dialogue with Americans (1951–1956)   **333**

CHAPTER 18   Encounter with Psychotherapy and Paula's Death
(1951–1958)   **355**

CHAPTER 19   Replies to Critics: Buber versus Scholem (1956–1963) **377**

Part V - Hammarskjöld, Ben Gurion, and Last Years (1949–1965)

CHAPTER 20   Buber and Dag Hammarskjöld: The Covenant of Peace
(1952–1963)   **409**

CHAPTER 21   Buber versus Ben Gurion (1949–1964)   **420**

CHAPTER 22   Surfeited with Honors (1958–1964)   **436**

CHAPTER 23   On the World's Edge (1959–1965)   **447**

Sources   **461**

Annotated Bibliography   **467**

◆

PREFACE

All true teaching derives from and points back to the concrete lives of the persons who have shown others the way. Martin Buber was a great philosopher, a consummate stylist, a world-famous scholar of the Bible, Hasidism, and many other fields and disciplines, a genius with an inexhaustible store of creativity. But above all he was, in the words of his friend Hermann Hesse when Hesse nominated him for a Nobel Prize in literature, "one of the few wise men living in the world today." "It is not true that wisdom comes of itself," Buber once said. "It begins in learning and fulfills itself in true teaching." A true teacher points the way. For Buber, this pointing took place through his personal response to each situation, and his words were the product and expression of this response. The true greatness of Buber's writings and the seriousness and responsibility with which Buber uttered each word can only be grasped in relation to Buber's life itself. It is in Buber's encounter with the persons and situations of his time that his active presence is revealed, and it is to this presence, above all, that I should like to point. In its human significance, Buber's presence transcends his worldwide influence and illuminates his writings. In the deepest sense, the whole of Buber's works, even his translations and interpretations and his retelling of tales, may be understood as words addressed to the time: they grew out of situations and speak to situations.

The first part of this book describes Buber's road to *I and Thou* because *I and Thou* is the classic work that Buber himself saw as the first mature expression of his thought. This description is not just a matter of intellectual and philosophical development but of Buber's response to events and meetings in many different spheres of life — the loss of his mother as a child, his Zionism, his encounter with mysticism, the impact of the First World War, the murder of his friend Gustav Landauer, his work in postwar education, community, and politics, and his maturing from the "easy word" to the "hard word." The remainder of this book shows Buber's application of his philosophy of dialogue to many spheres of life and his continuing "encounter on the narrow ridge" in the face of the cruel demands of the hour.

Although Buber was a great worker for peace, controversy seemed to surround him his whole life: his opposition to Theodor Herzl in the name of a democratic and cultural Zionism; his marriage to a non-Jew who converted to Judaism; his espousal of a decentralized, federal socialism; his more than forty years of fighting for Jewish-Arab understanding; his leadership of the spiritual resistance to the Nazis in Hitler's Germany; his acceptance of the Peace Prize of the German Book Trade after the Second World War; his refusal to take sides in the "cold war"; his advocacy of nuclear disarmament; his attack on Heidegger, Sartre, and Jung for contributing to the "eclipse of God"; and his many conflicts with Ben-Gurion for the sake of the "covenant of peace." Martin Buber's significance for us is not that he was a saint or even one to whom the life of dialogue came easily, but rather that he was a person who embodied the contradictions and ambiguities of modern existence and yet was able again and again to reach personal wholeness and integrity in faithful response to the persons and situations of his time.

For the scholar, I have listed my sources in the back, instead of using footnotes that might get between the reader and the text. The list includes reference to the relevant sources from the three volumes of my *Martin Buber's Life and Work,* on which this present book is largely based, plus the additional sources used in writing this book. It is my hope that the serious reader will have recourse to these three volumes, which are available in paperback from Wayne State University Press.

Although I called the three volumes a "dialography," I found that I could not, in fact, capture the two-sidedness of most of the events that I narrated, but, rather, had to deal with them mostly from Buber's standpoint. This does not mean, on the other hand, that I have given up my emphasis upon Buber's thought as a response to the events and meetings of his life or my strong feeling that the ordinary conception of biography represents a linear and process distortion of what are really dialogical events.

The difference in the title of this present book does not imply a new emphasis. On the contrary, I wanted to call *Buber's Life and Work* "Encounter on the Narrow Ridge" when I imagined it would only come to one volume. The "narrow ridge" is a phrase of Buber's himself, and, even more than "holy insecurity," it is the central metaphor of his life. He told me that he would be happy to have my book about him carry this as its title. I had it in mind, in fact, even when I wrote *Martin Buber: The Life of Dialogue* (1955), the opening chapter of which I entitled "The Narrow Ridge." I began this chapter:

> "I have occasionally described my standpoint to my friends as the 'narrow ridge,'" writes Buber. "I wanted by this to express that I did not rest on the broad upland of a system that includes a series of sure statements about the absolute, but on a narrow rocky ridge between the gulfs where there is no sureness of expressible knowledge but the certainty of meeting what remains undisclosed." Perhaps no other phrase so aptly characterizes the quality and significance of Martin Buber's life and thought as this one of the "narrow ridge." It expresses not only the "holy insecurity" of

his existentialist philosophy but also the "I-Thou," or dialogical philosophy which he has formulated as a genuine third alternative to the insistent either-or's of our age. Buber's "narrow ridge" is no "happy middle" which ignores the reality of paradox and contradiction in order to escape from the suffering they produce. It is rather a paradoxical unity of what one usually understands only as alternatives — I and Thou, love and justice, dependence and freedom, the love of God and the fear of God, passion and direction, good and evil, unity and duality.

I am grateful to my friend Susan Charnow Richards for suggesting a one-volume abridgement and to my editor, the late Bill Whitehead, for encouraging me to go ahead with this work, which he would have published himself had he lived. In deciding to focus the single volume on Buber's life, I also decided to emphasize the life more than the works and therefore to add what I could to flesh out the life. For this purpose, during the academic year 1987–1988, when I was Senior Fulbright Lecturer at the Hebrew University of Jerusalem as well as on sabbatical from San Diego State University, I did research on Buber's unpublished letters at the Martin Buber Archives of the Jewish National and University Library at the Hebrew University, and I have added the results of that research to the abridged text. I am grateful to the Jewish National and University Library, to the Hebrew University of Jerusalem, and to San Diego State University, all of which made possible this research. I am also grateful to Martin Buber's literary executors for permission to publish quotations from the unpublished letters, to Professor Haim Gordon of Ben Gurion University of the Negev in Beer-Sheva, Israel, for permission to publish quotations from his book *The Other Martin Buber,* and to the late Miriam Beer-Hoffman Lens and the Houghton Library of Harvard University for permission to publish selections in the last chapter of this book from the two documents pertaining to the relation of Martin Buber and Naemah Beer-Hoffman. I also wish to acknowledge my friend Dick Huett, who was freelance editor for the three volumes of *Martin Buber's Life and Work*; Dr. Grete Schaeder, who gave me invaluable help in preparing those three volumes; and my literary agent Georges Borchardt, who became my agent in connection with what evolved into the three volumes and has remained my agent in the quarter of a century since. I should also like to acknowledge the part played in the formation of this present book by my editors at Paragon House, Don Fehr and Jo Glorie, as well as by Laura Greeney, who performed the final cutting.

I must also express my indebtedness to the Martin Buber Archives of the Jewish and National University Library at the Hebrew University, Jerusalem, and to Rafael Buber, Alfred Bernheim, Max Braun, Inez van t'Hoff, the National Fotopersbureau of Amsterdam, David Rubinger, and Miriam Beer-Hoffman Lens for permission to use the photographs that appear in this volume.

The Road to
I and Thou

(1878-1923)

❖

CHAPTER

◆ 1 ◆

Childhood and Youth

(1878-1900)

More than any other single element in his physical appearance except his gentle but penetrating eyes, it was Buber's beard that gave him the appearance of the "Zaddik [Hasidic rabbi] of Zehlendorf," as he was jokingly called even by his family when he lived in that suburb of Berlin. Still later, it was Buber's beard that made many speak of him as a biblical prophet. Buber was photogenic, and he knew it; he was not shy about having his picture taken. His appearance, indeed, was an integral part of the impact he made in his lectures. But Buber did not wear the beard because he wished to appear to be a *zaddik,* still less a prophet. Nor did he wear it out of identification with traditional Jewish forms. The real reason for Buber's beard, which he wore from his youth, was that the doctor had to deliver him by means of forceps, and he thereby received an injury on the right side of his mouth, which produced a disfigurement in the otherwise exceptionally handsome youth. This disfigurement he covered by the beard, and though it was not kept a secret, it was known only to relatively few.

Mordechai Martin Buber was born in Vienna in 1878. He lived with his parents in a house over the Danube River, and he watched the moving canal with so intense an enjoyment that even toward the end of his life he could close his eyes and still see it flowing. Bound up with that experience was the certainty that nothing could happen to him. But this certainty was soon shattered. Martin Buber's mother literally disappeared without leaving a trace, and the home of his childhood was broken up. This had a depressing effect on all the family, and particularly on the young Martin, who, even though he

3

never spoke of it, bore signs of mourning and bereavement throughout his youth. The three-year-old child was sent to live with his paternal grandparents, while his father later remarried with the permission of the high rabbinic court of Lvov. Only much later was it discovered that Buber's mother had gone to Russia and had remarried there.

Martin Buber's grandfather, Solomon Buber, and his grandmother, Adele lived on a large estate near Lvov (Lembert), then the capital city of the Austrian "crown land," Galicia. Buber describes his grandparents as people of high rank, "noble persons in the exact sense of the term and, in a special manner, suited to and supplementing each other." This nobility of character placed an indelible stamp on the life of the child, for his grandparents became both parents and teachers to him. However, the effect on him was to intensify his sense of isolation and abandonment. They were not people who talked over their personal affairs even with each other, much less before the child. They said nothing in his presence about the separation of his parents. Nor did they prepare him in any way for what he might hope to expect in the future. Since no one told him that his mother had disappeared, he assumed that he would see her again soon. But in the atmosphere of his grandparents' house, he did not even dare ask if this were so. His unasked question did receive an answer, nonetheless, from an altogether unexpected source.

The house in which Buber's grandparents lived had a great rectangular courtyard surrounded by a wooden balcony extending to the roof, on which one could walk around the building at each floor. Once, when he was not yet four, the boy stood on this balcony with a girl several years older, the daughter of a neighbor whom his grandmother had asked to look after him. They both leaned on the railing, and here there took place the dialogue that had not taken place with his grandparents. "I cannot remember that I spoke of my mother to my older comrade," Buber related. "But I still hear how the big girl said to me: 'No, she will never come back.'" He remained silent, but he had no doubt that she had spoken the truth.

This was the decisive experience of Martin Buber's life, the one without which neither his early seeking for unity nor his later focus on dialogue and on the meeting with the "eternal Thou" is understandable. The fact that he could accept unquestioningly what this diminutive authority had said did not lay his problem to rest. On the contrary, it marked its true beginning. It brought realism but not resignation. It moved him into a new situation that was to be the touchstone and testing point of every other situation into which he entered. The words "She will *never* come back" remained with him, and over the passing years they became indelibly fixed. After more than ten years, he began to perceive that what had happened to him—unusual though it was—concerned not only him but everyone. In connection with this experience, he later coined the word *Vergegnung*—mismeeting—to designate the failure of a real meeting *(Begegnung)*, between persons. This mismeeting was present even when his mother, Elise Brock, came from St. Petersburg with her two daughters to visit him around 1911:

> When after another twenty years I again saw my mother, who had come from a distance to visit me, my wife and my children, I could not gaze into her still astonishingly beautiful eyes without hearing from somewhere the word "*Vergegnung*" as a word spoken to me.

Anyone who has looked at a picture of Martin Buber's mother as a young woman will not think his reference to her "astonishingly beautiful eyes" the product of sentimentality or nostalgia. It would have been more than understandable if he had clung throughout his life to the dream image of the mother he had known, as Marcel Proust clung to his mother and Franz Kafka to his father. The remarkable thing is that, for all the strength of his longing, he did not. "I suspect," Buber concluded this autobiographical fragment, "that all that I have learned in the course of my life about genuine meeting had its first origin in that hour on the balcony."

The corollary of Martin's "mismeeting" with his mother was his meeting, in the deepest sense of the term, with his grandparents, and in particular with his grandmother, Adele. Adele Buber was the daughter of the rich Mr. Wizer, the owner of a paper factory in Sasov, near Zlotchov. Among the Jews in this small Galician town where Buber's grandmother grew up, the reading of "alien" literature was proscribed. The education of girls was still more limited. For them, all literature, with the exception of edifying popular books, was held unseemly. When she was fifteen years old, Adele Wizer set up for herself in the storehouse a hiding place in which stood the German books she had secretly and thoroughly read. When she was seventeen years old, Adele brought these books with her to her marriage and, with them, the custom of concentrated reading. She was one of the Jewish wives of that period who, in order to create freedom and leisure for their husbands to study the Torah, managed their businesses for them. Each day, she recorded income and expenditures in large-size, similarly bound copybooks. But each day, too, in between these entries, she registered, after she had spoken them half aloud to herself, the passages that had become important to her out of her reading. She would also set down her own comments, as her part in her dialogue with these great spirits.

With her, Buber tells us, immediate experience and reflection on experience were not two stages but two aspects of the same process. Both in her speech and in her writings, the thoughts Adele communicated always seemed like something immediately perceived.

> When she looked at the street, she had at times the profile of someone meditating on a problem, and when I found her all alone in meditation, it seemed to me at times as if she listened. To

the glance of the child, however, it was already unmistakable that when she at times addressed someone, she really addressed him.

Adele Buber did not send Martin to school until he was ten years old. Instead, she had him taught by private tutors; humanism, with particular stress upon languages, was for her the royal road to education, and the child's own inclinations and talents lay in the same direction. On the other hand, she pampered him so that he never learned to be dexterous with his hands.

Martin Buber did not begin to speak until he was three. When he came to live with his father's parents at the age of four, he found himself in an environment in which very different peoples lived next to one another and a great many languages were spoken. In his grandfather's, as in his father's, house, the German language predominated, but the language of the street and the school was Polish. "Only the Jewish quarter rustled with the rough and tender Yiddish, and in the synagogue there resounded, alive as ever, the great voice of Hebrew antiquity." But Buber owed his special relation to the German language to his grandmother, Adele. She reared her sons, and later Buber himself, to respect the authentic word that cannot be paraphrased, the integral unity of word and thought that this age has lost sight of. Everything she wrote down was in a pithy and firm German, and her oral utterance was the same. Buber's grandfather was a true philologist, a "lover of the word," but his grandmother's love for the genuine word affected the child even more strongly, because this love was so direct and so devoted.

Buber saw the wonderful variety of human languages as the prism in which the white light of human speech at once fragmented and preserved itself. But already in his boyhood he realized that this variety came at a price. Time after time, he followed an individual word or even structure of words from one language to another, and in the tracing found that something had been lost that apparently existed only in a single one of all the languages. What was lost was not merely nuances of meaning but the meaning itself. This precocious *Wunderkind,* undoubtedly a very isolated and lonely little boy, devised for himself dual-language conversations between a German and a Frenchman, later between a Hebrew and an ancient Roman. Through these conversations, he came "half in play and yet at times with beating heart," to feel the tension between what was heard by the one person thinking in one language and what was heard by the other person thinking in another. "That had a deep influence on me," Buber testified, "and has issued in a long life into ever clearer insight." Indeed, it is here that one can find the essence of dialogical understanding not as precise definition, technical communication, or subjective empathy, but as "inclusion"—experiencing the other side of the relationship while not losing the awareness of one's own and of the polar tension between one's own and the other.

Why then did this essential insight, central to Buber's developing philosophy of dialogue, disquiet him? The answer is known by anyone who has ever tried to translate from one language into another: the difficulty of remaining faithful to the original while literally re-creating the meaning in the second language. For example, Buber's knowledge of languages as a boy of fourteen or so made it possible for him at times to provide his grandfather, Solomon Buber, whom he went to visit daily from his father's house, with a little help at his work on the Midrashim. Occasionally, it happened that in reading "Rashi," the great Bible and Talmud exegete of the eleventh century, Solomon Buber found a text explained through a reference to a French turn of speech and asked young Martin how this was to be understood. At times, Martin had to deduce from the Hebrew transcription the old French wording and then to make this understandable first to himself, then to his grandfather. Later, however, when he sat alone in his room in his father's house, he was oppressed by the question: What does it mean and how does it come about that one "explains" something that was written in one language through something that one is accustomed to say in another language? The world of the Logos and of the Logoi—the world of the word and the world of words—opened itself to him, darkened, brightened, and darkened again.

Buber's favorite language as a child was Greek, and his philosophical education was established in particular on a thorough reading of Plato in Greek. When Buber took his *Abitur*—the examination given on leaving his gymnasium—the instructor questioned him about a speech of the chorus in Sophocles. Buber recited the passage from memory and thereby ended the examination.

Buber spoke German, Hebrew, Yiddish, Polish, English, French, and Italian and read, in addition to these, Spanish, Latin, Greek, Dutch, and other languages. This polyglot background was of importance for Buber not only as a translator, but also, as Hans Fischer-Barnicol has pointed out, as a predominantly German author. Even in conversation, Buber knew how to express differences of meaning simply and surprisingly, not because he used individual words in unusual senses or coined new words, but because he employed long-familiar turns of speech with especial attentiveness and lent a customary grammatical function a fresh, deeper significance. This entirely unself-conscious quality of attentive listening characterized his writing as well.

By comparing the way things were said in German with analogous uses in other languages, he had become particularly aware of the possibilities of expression in German.

French, however, was one language that the child Buber learned only reluctantly, as he recounted after he had received an honorary doctorate from the University of the Sorbonne in Paris. Buber's grandparents had written for a Frenchman to come to their estate in Galicia; he not only had to teach grammar to young Martin and introduce him to the French classics but also had to be concerned about tutoring him in French conversation suitable for salons. This chatter finally annoyed Martin so much that when the chance presented itself he gave the pedagogue a hefty push at the edge of a fish pond. The poor man landed in the water and finally had to be fished out, drenched to the skin.

Abraham Joshua Heschel has suggested that Buber's style cannot be really understood without recognizing the great impact of Yiddish on it. Although Buber preferred to speak German rather than Yiddish and spoke a pure, classical German rather than any form of dialect, his early fondness for the color and warmth of Yiddish never left him and did, indeed, influence his style and with it his way of thinking. In 1904, Buber translated, from Yiddish to German, David Pinski's *Eisik Scheftel,* "a Jewish workers' drama in three acts," and published it in the Jüdischer Verlag that he and his friend Berthold Feiwel had established. The man who was to write within the next two years two German books that were on the very highest level of cultural German, and who had to work for years until he could simplify and bring down to earth the overly ornate style of his youth, was delighted by the popular ethnic qualities that he found in Yiddish.

Yiddish did not cease to be of central importance for Buber. Practically all of the Hasidic legends and tales that he worked over for a lifetime and many of the Hasidic teachings were originally in Yiddish. Almost sixty years later, Buber reaffirmed his statement of 1904: "Yiddish is that spoken idiom of the popular masses of East European Jewry that has continually delighted me as the popular itself become speech." One single difference, indeed, between Buber's early rendition of the legends of the Baal-Shem and the legendary anecdotes that he later developed as the best form of rendering Hasidic tales is that the former tend to be exalted and romantic while the latter retain the rough, humorous, and down-to-earth quality of the Yiddish original. By the same token, the former, even when they take the form of long stories, are usually lyrical or epic, while the latter, no matter how short, are invariably dramatic.

Buber's grandfather, Solomon, was, as Buber himself described him, the last great scholar of the Haskalah, or the Jewish Enlightenment. He was unusual in his combination of business and scholarship. Although a self-taught man, he learned languages and their interrelationships so well that he is to be thanked for the first, and today still, *the* authoritative, critical editions of the Midrash—a special class of Talmudic literature made up of interpretations of the Bible, wise sayings, and rich saga. In his civil occupations, Solomon Buber was not only a great landowner but also a corn merchant and the owner of phosphorite mines on the Austrian-Russian border. An experienced man with independent judgment, he belonged to the leaders of the Jewish community and to the town's chamber of commerce. He never neglected his honorary offices, but he left much of the management of his business to his wife, Adele (she conducted it most capably, although she made no decision without consulting him).

Contrasting his own more modest reputation with the fame of Buber's grandfather and the eminence that marked Martin Buber even in his twenties, Buber's father, Carl, is reported to have gently complained: "I am only the son of my father and the father of my son." Solomon Buber was one of the leading Jews and citizens of Lvov, beloved by and loving his fellow men. He was also honored near and far by Jews of every branch of Judaism, even by the zealots among the Misnagdim—the opponents of the Hasidim—and by the Hasidim of Belz and Zans. His many articles and his arrangements, introductions, notes, and explanations of the Midrashim led Jewish writers and rabbis from all over the world to enter into correspondence with him and to send him their own works. The most learned Jewish scholars and rabbis of his time honored him and spoke of him with respect, even though in his outlook he saw himself not primarily as a Jew but as "a Pole of the religion of Moses."

Despite the many activities of business and scholarship that absorbed Solomon Buber, he found time to be something of a companion to his gifted grandson. If it was his grandmother, Adele, who taught him the true love of reading and of language, it was his grandfather who, even after Martin had gone back to live with his father, introduced him to the world of scholarship and, what was more important, to the task of Hebrew translation, which was to occupy Martin throughout his life.

While Buber saw his mother only once again, his father reentered his life from his ninth year on. Carl Buber had remarried, and the boy went to join his father and his stepmother every summer on his father's estate. At fourteen, he moved from his grandfather's house to his father's townhouse.

Although in his youth Buber's father had strong interests in the issues that Darwin's *Origin of Species* and Renan's *Life of Jesus* had made current, his influence on his son was not an intellectual one. What struck the child, rather, was his father's devotion to agriculture, which made him a phenomenon among the East Galician landed property owners. He was far in advance of those around him in his scientific farming, working for thirty-six years to heighten the productivity of his soils through careful testing of all kinds of implements. Once, he even brought with him from the Paris International Exhibition a great packing of breeding eggs of a type of hen still unknown in the East, holding it on his knees the whole long journey to protect it.

What made him still more exemplary was that he combined this mastery of technique with a direct concern for the animals and plants with which he worked. When he stood in the midst of his splendid herd of horses, he greeted one animal after the other, not merely in a friendly fashion but each one individually. When he drove through the ripening fields, he would halt the wagon, descend, and bend over the ears of corn again and again, finally breaking one and carefully tasting the kernels. He was not some English nature poet but a practical farmer: "This wholly unsentimental and wholly unromantic man was concerned about genuine human contact with nature, an active and responsible contact." From accompanying his father at times in his work on the estate, the boy Martin learned something that he could not have learned from any book. In his own person, Carl Buber anticipated one of the most fundamental aspects of his son's later thoughts: that the man who practices immediacy does so in relation to nature just as much as to his fellow man—the "I-Thou" relation to nature is a corollary of the "interhuman."

Carl Buber, his son later reported, took part in the life of all the people who were in one way or another dependent on him—the laborers attached to the estate in their little houses built according to his design, which surrounded the estate buildings; the peasants who performed services for him under most favorable conditions; and the tenants. He concerned himself with their family lives, with the upbringing and schooling of their children, and with all who became sick or aged. This solicitude was not derived from any principles, Buber asserted, but was directly personal. This same way of acting in relationship to people carried over into the town. He was fiercely averse to impersonal charity. "He understood no other help than that from person to person, and he practiced it." Even in his old age, he accepted election to the "bread commission" of the Jewish community of Lemberg and fulfilled his responsibilities himself, in direct contact with those in need. He constantly visited these people in order to discover their real wants and necessities.

The last thing that Buber has told of his father is particularly significant for the development of the son. Carl Buber was "an elemental storyteller." When he spoke about the people whom he had known, he always reported the simple occurrence without any embroidery—"nothing more than the existence of human creatures and what took place between them." Perhaps the most remarkable achievement of Martin Buber was that, in the course of a long lifetime of retelling Hasidic and other legends, he himself became "an elemental storyteller" in just this sense.

One of the earliest memories that remained with Martin Buber in his old age was the red riding habit that he wore as a child. But his love of horses was not confined to riding. When he was eleven years of age, spending the summer on his grandfather's estate, as often as he could do it unobserved, he used to steal into the stable and gently stroke the neck of his darling, a broad dapple-gray horse. This was no casual delight for him, but a great, deeply stirring happening. When he wrote of it many years later, the memory of his hand stroking the horse was still fresh, and with it the sense of friendly contact, "the immense otherness of the Other." This otherness did not remain strange for him, like the otherness of the ox and the ram, but rather let him draw near and touch it.

> When I stroked the mighty mane, sometimes marvelously smooth-combed, at other times just as astonishingly wild, and felt the life beneath my hand, it was as though the element of vitality itself

bordered on my skin, something that was not I, was certainly not akin to me, palpably the other, not just another, really the Other itself; and yet it let me approach, confided itself to me, placed itself elementally in the relation of *Thou* and *Thou* with me. The horse, even when I had not begun by pouring oats for him into the manger, very gently raised his massive head, ears flicking, then snorted quietly, as a conspirator gives a signal meant to be recognizable only by his fellow conspirator: and I was approved.

If it was experiences such as this that made Buber unwilling to relinquish his concept of an "I-Thou," or direct, open, personal relationship with nature, this particular experience became for him a concrete example of "reflexion," the basic movement of "the life of monologue." As "dialogue" did not mean for Buber two speaking, so "monologue" did not mean one. It meant turning toward oneself and away from the particularity of the other person. In "reflexion," the other is allowed to exist only as "a part" of oneself. Once, when young Martin was stroking the horse, it struck him what fun it gave him, and suddenly he became conscious of his hand. The game went on as before, but it was no longer the same. The next day, when he gave the horse a rich feed and stroked his mane, his friend did not raise his head. Aware of how his relationship to the horse had changed, he felt himself judged. Later, when he thought back on the incident, he no longer imagined that the horse had noticed his lapse into monologue.

If Martin Buber's parents had remained together in Vienna, his education undoubtedly would have been entirely different from what it was. It isn't likely that he would have been kept at home with private tutors, studying languages, until he was ten. Even when young Martin did go to school (it was called the Franz Joseph's Gymnasium, after the emperor) it was really in most respects a Polish gymnasium, not an Austrian one. Since the Ruthenians had their own schools, by far the largest number of the pupils in Buber's schools were Poles, with a small Jewish minority. The language of instruction and of social intercourse was Polish, but it was not, of course, a Polish national school. Individually, the pupils got on well with one another, but the two groups as such knew almost nothing about each other.

At this school, Buber received his basic instruction in a variety of subjects, the report cards on which can still be seen in the Buber Archives at the National and University Library in Jerusalem. There he learned the excellent command of Polish that remained with him even when he no longer had occasion to use the language and that once enabled him more than fifty years later, as Abraham Heschel has related, to address a group of Poles in perfect Polish. Even when he had gone to the University of Vienna, he kept contact with the Polish student movement, probably in particular with the socialists. His uncle, Rafael Buber, was himself a prominent Polish socialist. Some months before the outbreak of World War II, Buber went as an emissary to Lodz, Poland, from the Hebrew University.

Martin Buber spent his first year of university studies in Vienna, the city of his birth and earliest childhood. "The detached, flat memory images," he wrote of Vienna sixty years later, "appear out of the great corporal context like slides of a magic lantern; also many districts that I could not have seen address me as acquaintances." The return at this point in his life to Vienna had a profound effect upon Buber, which, in his own words, established something "that in later years could not be shattered by any of the crises of the age." What this was Buber again described in terms of mutual contact, contact with otherness. "This original home of mine, now foreign, taught me daily, although still in unclear language, that I had to accept the world and let myself be accepted by it; it was indeed ready to be accepted." In the rich and exciting Vienna of the turn of the century, Buber found a unique culture in which south German, Jewish, and Slavic influences were mixed.

> Nowhere at that time was there so much openness to the cultural contacts of the Scandinavian north and of the Romance literatures as in Vienna, but here all these influences which had arisen in firmer, harder forms, nearer to reality, seemed transformed by a warmer, feminine nature.

But the Jews in Vienna were the patrons and exponents of culture in a way that in former ages the nobility had been. Writing at the beginning of the 1940s, Stefan Zweig claimed that "most, if not all, that Europe and America admire today as an expression of a new, rejuvenated Austrian culture, in literature, the theatre, in the arts and crafts, was created by the Viennese Jews."

During his two semesters at the University of Vienna, Buber attended lectures that left little impression upon him. Even the significant scholarly lectures did not have the same impact as the seminars into which he had prematurely flung himself. Nor was it the content of the seminar that strongly influenced him but the form, the seminar itself: "The regulated and yet free intercourse between teacher and students, the common interpretations of texts, in which the master at times took part with rare humility, as if he too were learning something new, and the free exchange of question and answer"—all this disclosed to Buber, more directly than anything that he read in a book, what makes the human spirit actual: the reality *between* person and person.

While Buber was studying at the University of Vienna, he adopted the Viennese style of speaking and writing, particularly of those in the forefront of Vienna culture who were developing a language of great richness and beauty, though often overcultivated and somewhat affected. Overlying his love of Yiddish and his childhood experiences with Polish, German, Greek, and Latin was the impact on the young Buber of his total immersion in the exciting but chaotic artistic and intellectual atmosphere of Vienna at the turn of the century.

Hugo von Hofmannsthal was the Viennese poet whose work initiated and virtually seduced Martin into availing himself of "the primordial gold of speech" in the Vienna of his day. "Let the heir be a squanderer": so began the "Song of Life," the magic and bewitching poem by Hofmannsthal, that became Martin's siren call. After young Buber had purchased on a Vienna street the issue of *Wiener Rundschau* in which this poem appeared, he sat down on a bench in a public park and read. "A shudder (not of enjoyment, but truly a 'holy shudder') overcame me: this verse there had been written only a short time ago." It was Buber's first penetrating experience of the contemporary, and it remained so vividly present to him that half a century later he chose this poem as one of three that he contributed to an anthology of favorite German verses.

When the eighteen-year-old Martin came to Vienna, he discovered a whole world of living theater, whereas before "theater" was merely drama read in books. What affected him most strongly was the great Burgtheater, which was in many respects the central cultural institution in prewar Vienna in a way that was hardly possible in any other city. Into the Burgtheater at times, day after day, the young Buber rushed up three flights after several hours of standing in line in order to capture a place in the highest gallery.

> When far below in front of me the curtain went up and I might then look at the events of the dramatic agon as, even in play, taking place here and now, it was the word, the rightly spoken human word that I received into myself, in the most real sense. Speech, here in this world of fiction as fiction, first won its adequacy; certainly it appeared heightened, but heightened to itself.

What Buber learned here about living, spoken speech, the speech that "takes place" in the "between," was not and could not be restricted to the artistically detached sphere of the theater alone. Living speech illuminated for him human existence as such, and as such became for him one of the highways leading to *I and Thou*. This reality of speech-as-event was particularly connected for Buber with Vienna. Having learned this in the theater, he could now hear it in the street:

> Since then it has sometimes come to pass, in the midst of the casualness of the everyday, that, while I was sitting in the garden of an inn in the countryside of Vienna, a conversation penetrated to me from a neighboring table. (perhaps an argument over falling prices by two market wives taking a rest), in which I perceived living, spoken speech, sound become "Each-Other."

As a student, Martin was fully supported by his affluent parents and grandparents. In his first year as a student at the University of Vienna, Buber occupied himself with literature, the history of art, and philosophy. In the winter semester of 1897–1898, Buber studied at the University of Leipzig, and in the summer of 1899 he studied at the University of Zurich. In Leipzig and Zurich, he attended lectures on philosophy, the history of art, the history of literature, psychiatry, Germanics, classical philosophy, and national economy. His philosophy at that time was particularly oriented to the natural sciences. He attended the lectures of Ernst Mach, Austrian physicist and philosopher, Wilhelm Wundt, German physiologist and ethnopsychologist, and Carl Stumpf, German philosopher and psychologist, and was an enthusiastic student at the psychiatric clinic.

An incomparable portrait of Martin Buber as a university student is given us by a friend of his youth, Ahron Eliasberg. Even before Eliasberg met him, Buber's name was familiar to him. The families of the two youths were related, and Buber's father and stepmother often came to Eliasberg's home city of Pinsk, where they spoke of Martin's rare gifts. As a result, Eliasberg was overjoyed when he heard one day during his first semester at the University of Leipzig that Martin Buber had been invited to dinner along with him at the house of some relatives. Before he actually met Buber, he found his name in the student register and tried unsuccessfully to imitate Buber's already distinguished signature! When the eagerly awaited day finally came, Buber exceeded all his expectations. Martin told of his two semesters as a student at the University of Vienna, of his meetings with writers and scholars, and of the contents of the courses he took there. He expressed a very strong interest in Wundt's ethnopsychology, which he had read for the first time, and recited whole stanzas from the old and the very newest poets. "I saw at once," Eliasberg reports, "that his knowledge was genuine, and I tumbled from admiration to admiration, from enthusiasm to enthusiasm."

From then on, the two youths met frequently and had much to do with each other. It is difficult to express, says Eliasberg, how much instruction, stimulation, and even elevation he owed to young Buber, only six months his senior, whose many-faceted personality was already at that time essentially formed.

Together, they read philosophical and poetic works, among which were the writings of the great sociologist and philosopher Georg Simmel, who was later Buber's teacher at the University of Berlin. The young Buber gave Eliasberg glimpses of his extensive acquaintance with great literary figures. He was an enthusiastic supporter of Peter Altenberg, who at that time was almost unknown in Germany, and Eliasberg was much impressed when in his presence the newest work of the poet arrived with a dedication and an accompanying letter for Buber. The latter had an acute ear for the voices of the time. He was one of the first to notice and recognize Walter Rathenau, later a great German-Jewish statesman and man of letters in the Weimar Republic. Rathenau's antithesis of "not knowing yet creating" expressed Buber's own feeling about life. When, with the close of the winter semester, Buber left Leipzig, he sent Eliasberg Schopenhauer's works and inscribed in them:

Content yourself with the world as it is—the wise men teach.
But I call to you boldly: Create for yourself a world!

Buber's tirelessness was stupendous, Eliasberg reports. Once they rode to Berlin—fourth class, of course—in order "to rescue" a Zionist meeting, and they came back the same day. The train left Berlin at one in the morning, and they arrived in Leipzig at dawn. As always in such cases, Buber did not go to bed but went instead to a meeting held that morning. Then he returned to the house, where he donned a frock coat in order to take part in a banquet, which was followed by a ball. Buber, at that time a passionate devotee, danced the whole night through and then proceeded directly from the ballroom to his classes at the university.

In addition to his regular courses at the university, Buber worked in the psychological seminar of Wundt and—as the only nonmedical student—in the physiological institute. He also took part in the seminar on art history run by August Shmarsov, who, hardly known to the wider public, surrounded himself with an esoteric circle of respectful admirers. Along with these activities, Buber found time to participate in whatever social and artistic groups Leipzig offered. It goes without saying that he missed none of the premieres of the "Literary Society" founded by Hans von Weber, the evenings with authors, and above all the performance of new theater pieces.

Buber quickly became prominent in Leipzig Jewish society. The rabbi Dr. Porges, whose house he much frequented, called him "a lad of genius," while his wife, who had formed around herself a circle of "beautiful spirits," championed Buber with a vigor that was possible only in a "salon." Through the Porges family, Buber joined the "Ethical Culture Society," to whose closeted existence he lent an unaccustomed splendor with two lectures on Lassalle and probably felt himself to be destined for a life similar to Lassalle's. He prepared himself thoroughly for his first lecture. The effect of the not yet twenty-year-old was staggering—because of the fullness of his research, the independence of his judgments, and the force of his delivery. The public was immediately overcome. "I have never again," attests Eliasberg, "so experienced youth triumphing." It is striking that this was the very lecture whose success so profoundly shattered Buber by forcing him to see the problematic aspects of Lassalle that he had formerly chosen to overlook.

When Ahron Eliasberg and Martin Buber walked home together after their first meeting, Buber called attention at one point to the opposite side of the street. "Beyond good and evil therefore," Eliasberg remarked, and Buber asked, "Have you too read Nietzsche?" "No," answered Eliasberg timidly, "and you?" "Oh, for two or three years I was a passionate Nietzschean," the teenage boy replied, "but now I see in him only just another pathfinder...." Poor Eliasberg was crushed.

Precocious and even affected as these words must seem, Buber was not just throwing sand in Eliasberg's eyes. Though clearly not averse to letting his young friend glimpse his knowledge in order to impress him, his knowledge of Nietzsche was more than superficial. Indeed, before his Nietzsche period, Buber had been deeply influenced by Immanuel Kant, the rationalist philosopher of the Enlightenment, and that when he was only fourteen! Nor was this influence merely an intellectual one; it was deeply involved in the boy's personal existence. Whatever the link may have been between the three-year-old's loss of his mother, and the fourteen-year-old's terror before the infinity of the universe, we have no reason to doubt the authenticity of the crisis through which the boy Buber passed at fourteen, nor the serious-ness of his relationship to the philosophy that saved him from it. The inner Buber knew none of that easy success and mastery that the admiring Eliasberg reported of the outer.

In his "Autobiographical Fragments," Buber linked this crisis over the infinity of space and time, in which Kant helped him, to his seduction by Nietzsche when he was seventeen. In both cases, philosophy encroached directly upon his existence in a way that had nothing to do with his philo-sophical education. This education in philosophy was grounded in particular in a thorough reading of Plato, and was a gradual process. Buber's encoun-ters with Kant and Nietzsche, in contrast, "were catastrophic events which broke through the continuity—the presupposition of all genuine educational work."

When Buber related the first of these two events in "What Is Man?," he set it in the context of Pascal's recognition of the uncanniness of man's exis-tence beneath the infinite spaces between the stars. This confrontation with infinity makes man's very existence a casual and questionable one, for it makes of man the essentially vulnerable creature whose knowledge that he is exposed robs him of the sense of being at home in his world. As a result, any concept of space and time, a finite no less than an infinite one, becomes terrifying to man, for both make man conscious that he is no match for the world. The fourteen-year-old Buber—even more precocious in this respect than the young mathematical genius Pascal—experienced this in a way that deeply influenced his whole life:

> A necessity I could not understand swept over me: I had to try again and again to imagine the edge of space, or its edgelessness, time with a beginning and an end or a time without beginning or end, and both were equally impossible, equally hopeless—yet there seemed to be only the choice between the one or the other absurdity. Under an irresistible compulsion I reeled from one to the other, at times so closely threatened with the danger of mad-ness that I seriously thought of avoiding it by suicide.

In his "Autobiographical Fragments," written twenty years after "What Is Man?," Buber told us that the question about time had tormented him far more than that about space. He was irresistibly driven to want to grasp the total world process as actual, and that meant to understand time either as beginning and ending or as without beginning and end, each of which proved equally absurd:

If I wanted to take the matter seriously (and I was ever again compelled to want just this), I had to transpose myself either to the beginning of time or to the end of time. Thus I came to feel the former like a blow in the neck or the latter like a rap against the forehead—no, there is no beginning and no end! Or I had to let myself be thrown into this or that bottomless abyss, into infinity, and now everything whirled. It happened thus time after time. Mathematical or physical formulae could not help me; what was at stake was the reality of the world in which one had to live and which had taken on the face of the absurd and the uncanny.

Salvation came to the fourteen-year-old through a source that, however philosophically appropriate, can only seem amazing to anyone who is familiar with the text. Although the first sentence of Kant's *Prolegomena to All Future Metaphysics* warns that it is intended not for pupils but for future teachers, the young Buber dared to read it and found in it a philosophical freedom that produced a profoundly quieting effect on him. Through it, he came to the view that space and time are not real properties that adhere to things in themselves but mere forms of our sensory perception, the formal conditions by which we grasp the world of phenomena. The text further disclosed to him that the concept of the infinity of space and time is as impossible as that of their finiteness. Neither is inherent in our experience. They represent, rather, an irresoluble antinomy of ideas that do not necessarily correspond to any reality of being. A philosophy that produced in Buber's older contemporaries philosophical skepticism, along the lines of Vaihinger's "As If" philosophy, gave the boy philosophical peace.

As a result, the youth for whom philosophical questions had become matters of life and death no longer needed to torment himself by inquiring about an end to time. Time was no longer a sentence hanging over him, for it was his, it was "ours." The question was explained as unanswerable by nature, but, at the same time, he was liberated from having to ask it. This philosophical peace took on a mystical quality very foreign to the rationalist Kant, who spoke of man as a citizen of two worlds, the noumenal and the phenomenal, but claimed no direct contact with or knowledge of the former. At this moment, there appeared to Buber the intuition of eternity, an intuition that even at the end of his life he held to be the most remarkable intellectual achievement of man. Eternity is not endless time. It is rather Being as such, Being that is beyond the reach alike of the finitude and infinity of space and time since it appears only in space and time but does not enter into this appearance. Buber not only gained an inkling of the reality of eternity as quite different from either the infinite or the finite, he also glimpsed the possibility of a connection between himself—a man—and the eternal. Thus, in his uncharacteristic response to Kant, Buber got an inkling not only of the "I-It," or subject-object relation, but also of the "I-Thou."

This insight was dimmed for a period of years by the appearance on his horizon of the star of Nietzsche and in particular of Nietzsche's most impassioned and least philosophical book, *Thus Spake Zarathustra*. This book, characterized by Nietzsche himself as the greatest present that had ever been made to mankind, did not calmly confront the young Buber and liberate him as did Kant's *Prolegomena*. Rather, its grandly willed and splendidly expressed philosophy stormed over him and took possession of him, robbing him of his freedom for a long time to come. That this invasion and seduction could take place can be explained only by the fact that the glimpse of the eternity that Kant had afforded him had not become real enough to still within his turbulent soul the problem of time that tormented him. Almost seventy years later, a schoolmate of Buber's from the Polish gymnasium wrote him, after reading his *Meetings,* that he remembered Buber's great enthusiasm for Nietzsche's *Zarathustra* and how he always brought it with him to school!

In utmost contrast to the rationalistic Kant, Nietzsche offered a dynamism and a creative flow of life force that held the young Buber in thrall throughout the period of his earliest writings. Nietzsche himself saw the basic conception of *Thus Spake Zarathustra* as an interpretation of *time,* and he added to the Heraclitean emphasis on the flow of time an almost equally Heraclitean emphasis on the "eternal return of the same." Time, for Nietzsche, was not an endless line stretched out into the infinite, such as had tormented Buber when he was two years younger. It was an infinite and essentially circular sequence of finite periods of time, which are like one another in all things, so that the end phase of the period goes over into its own beginning. This conception, characterized by Nietzsche as "the most abysmal teaching," was dismissed by the mature Buber as "no teaching at all but the utterance of an ecstatically lived through possibility of thought played over with ever new variations." It is an untransformed Dionysian pathos, produced by the enthusiasm of the modern Dionysian over his own heights and depths. Even the seventeen-year-old could not accept this conception as such, but it produced in his spirit "a negative seduction."

The primal mystery of time—the manifest mystery of the uniqueness of all happening, namely, that each event takes place once and never recurs— was obscured by Nietzsche's pseudomystery of the "eternal return of the same." The fascination of *Zarathustra* eclipsed the youth's earlier intuition of that genuine eternity that sends forth time out of itself and sets us in that relationship to it that we call existence. "To him who recognizes this," the mature Buber was to say, "the reality of the world no longer shows an absurd and uncanny face: because eternity is."

If the influence of Kant thus foreshadowed Buber's later dialogue with the "eternal Thou," the influence of Nietzsche set him on the long road that led up to it. That he had not, in fact, moved beyond Nietzsche in the way that his statement to Eliasberg might suggest was made abundantly evident in the earliest of his German essays (he had written several essays in Polish before this)—"Nietzsche and Life-Values" (1900). What he said there of Nietzsche is so like what he himself became that it brings to mind Hawthorne's story "The Great Stone Face," in which the hero gradually takes on the image of the man whom for years he had admired and looked up to.

Buber was so taken with *Thus Spake Zarathustra* at the time that he decided to translate it into Polish. He had finished the first part and just started the second, when he received a letter from a well-known Polish author who had likewise translated several sections of the book and who proposed that they do the work in common. Buber preferred to leave the task to him. But the fascination of the book itself he could not renounce. He had to work his way through many stages of thought before he arrived at his criticism of Nietzsche's "will to power" as a "sickness," and of his teaching of the "overman" and of the value scale of strong and weak as "no teaching at all."

For years, a distinctly Nietzschean note sounded forth even in Buber's essays on Judaism, Zionism, and the Jewish Renaissance. The very emphasis in his early essays on the active and productive as opposed to the static and unproductive confronted Buber with the same problem with which Nietzsche wrestled, namely, the relationship between dynamism and form—between a "Dionysian" energy that may prove destructive of all form and an "Apollonian" limitation that may destroy all dynamism. Buber was equally opposed to the Dionysian principle when it becomes demonic and destroys form and to the Apollonian principle when it hardens, changing from a living creation to a decaying form that the Buber of this period identified as the unfruitful, life-denying intellectuality of the ghetto and the overemphasis of official rabbinic Judaism on a rigid ceremonial law. Correspondingly, Buber described Hasidism as the true bearer of the Jewish formative principle—the unifier of life and the spirit, the consecrator of actions through the intention of inwardness, the creator of a community of love and righteousness.

In "Twofold Future" (1912), Buber spoke in true Nietzschean fashion of an alternation between the forms of culture and the "fruitful chaos" of religion. When a culture disintegrates and loses the strength of its cohesion, there arises that fruitful chaos in which alone the seed of a growing religiousness can develop. Thus, Buber identified religiousness with the revolutionary principle that destroys old forms and releases suppressed power. This concern for time and for the dynamic remained with Buber in his later thought.

For Nietzsche, it was the "death of God" that enabled man to recover his alienated freedom, projected into the "celestial naught," and to express his will to power in the creativity that led upward to "the overman." For the young Buber, Nietzsche's celebration of creativity soon proved inadequate without those roots that would allow him to feel part of a larger community. "Today," Buber wrote in 1902, "faith lies to life and does violence to its surging meanings." But the "surging meanings" are not enough in themselves. Today, the tempter does not lead the creative man to a high mountain to show him all the kingdoms and splendor of the world, as Satan did to Jesus.

Instead, he tempts him through infinity—to lose himself in the unessential, to roam about in the great confusion in which all human clarity and definiteness has ceased. Thus, the threat of infinity that Buber experienced as a fourteen-year-old now takes on new form—the form of formlessness, of the whirl of unmastered possibilities that every young person who goes out into the world experiences, but that Buber himself experienced to an overwhelming degree.

As long as Buber lived with his grandfather, his roots were firm, although many questions and doubts perplexed him. Soon after he left his grandfather's house, and until his twentieth year and even later, his "spirit was in steady and multiple movement, in an alternation of tension and release,... taking ever new shape, but without center and without growing substance." He lived, in short, in the "World of Confusion," the modern equivalent of that abode to which Hasidic myth assigns the lost and wandering souls. "Here I lived," wrote Buber in 1918, "in variegated richness of spirit, but without Judaism, without humanity, and without the presence of the divine."

In an age which still values "creativity" and "self-expression" as the highest of intrinsic values, it may be hard to understand why young Buber should not have been happy and fulfilled during this period in which he began to discover and to realize his multiple gifts. But "creativity" can also be an expression of fragmentation rather than of the wholeness of the person. The need to direct that neutral but unchanneled passion that the Talmud calls the "evil urge," which Buber stressed in his Hasidic teaching; the need for "direction," which he intoned in *Daniel*; and the need for decision, which he put at the center of *I and Thou* — all became evident to him for the first time during this painful period of outer dispersion and inner turmoil. The implicit comparison of the creative person with Jesus — the essential, and, to Buber at this period, the creative, man of his age — is appropriate because Buber, too, was tempted. But his temptation was not the Yes or No that confronted Jesus. In the language of *I and Thou*, it was "the centreless Many" that "plays in the iridescent sameness of its pretensions."

> The fiery stuff of all my ability to will seethes tremendously, all that I might do circles around me, still without actuality in the world, flung together and seemingly inseparable, alluring glimpses of powers flicker from all the uttermost bounds: the universe is my temptation.

CHAPTER

♦ 2 ♦

Zionism

(1898-1904)

"**F**or him who has lost his God the people can be a first station on his new way," wrote Buber in the same essay as that in which he spoke of the temptation of the creative man. This was exactly Buber's own experience. The first impetus toward his liberation from "the whirl of the age" came from the young movement of Zionism, through which he took root anew in the community.

> No one needs the saving connection with a people so much as the youth who is seized by spiritual seeking, carried off into the upper atmosphere by the intellect; but among the youths of this kind and this destiny none so much as the Jewish.... The most sparkling wealth of intellectuality, the most luxuriant seeming productivity (only he who is bound can be genuinely productive) cannot compensate the detached man for the holy insignia of humanity—rootedness, binding, wholeness.

What delivered Buber from his youthful narcissism was the new Zionist movement of Theodor Herzl. When the young Eliasberg first made the acquaintance of Buber, the latter was anything but a Zionist. Except for the positive influence of his grandfather, he grew up, says Eliasberg, in the milieu of a superficial salon culture of bourgeoisie who despised everything Jewish from the bottom of their hearts. When Eliasberg got to know Buber, he would often hear from his lips the expression "really Jewish" used as a form of disparagement. Buber also remained close to Polish socialist circles and gave a much-applauded lecture at a secret conference of Polish students in which delegates from the three realms of the empire took part. But he was no Polish assimilationist. He read Herzl's journal *Die Welt,* to which Eliasberg was the sole subscriber in Leipzig, and often discussed Zionist questions. He even coined a striking personal formula for his unsureness in Jewish matters: "I will take on myself all the duties of Zionism, yet will enjoy none of its rights." But as important for him as Zionism at this time were the simple Jewish men whom he discovered in Hasidic synagogues.

Buber spent the summer holidays of 1898 on his father's estate in Galicia. From there, he wrote to Eliasberg that he had discovered a work that had finally converted him to nationalism and to Zionism. It was Mathias Acher's (Nathan Birnbaum's) *Modern Judaism.* According to Buber in *Israel and Palestine* (1945), this book completed what Moses Hess had begun—the synthesis of the national and the social idea in Judaism. Buber wanted to return to Leipzig in the winter and become politically active for Zionism, and Eliasberg was only too happy to have his friend join him in his cause. Buber carried on his activities with all the zeal of a neophyte. Although completely unschooled in political action, Buber and Eliasberg succeeded in creating a foothold for Zionism in Leipzig and ended by founding a local chapter and a union of Jewish students. Buber, of course, was elected its first president. In the ornaments of his insignia, though still without a beard, "Buber cut the figure of a young Samson."

In March, the Leipzig chapter sent Buber as their representative to the Zionist convention in Cologne, at that time the seat of the organization. Buber, who now longed for further study, did not return. As a parting present, Eliasberg sent him Jacob Burckhardt's *History of Greek Culture,* which had appeared shortly before. From Cologne, Buber wrote Eliasberg: "I have the book before me and ask myself when *we* shall have such a work, a 'History of Jewish Culture." Only after many years did Eliasberg understand the full import of these words.

If Buber's Jewish education had really been so superficial and his antipathy to things Jewish so basic as Eliasberg suggests, he could never have found his way to Zionism. His university years were, to be sure, a period in which he had largely lost his moorings from the thoroughgoing Judaism that dwelt in his grandfather, "without his troubling himself about it." But no "salon culture" could remove the lasting effects of those years between four and fourteen that he spent in his grandfather's home, surrounded by the world of the Midrash in which his grandfather lived "with a wonderful concentration of soul, with a wonderful intensity of work." Of his grandfather, Buber wrote:

> Without having ever appropriated the philological methods of the West, he revised the manuscripts with the reliability of the modern

scholar and at the same time with the presence of knowledge of the Talmudic master who has directly at hand for each sentence and each word whatever relates to it in the entire literature—not as material of memory alone, but as an organic possession of the whole person.

The extent to which Solomon Buber continued to be present for Martin as an image of authentic humaneness and authentic Jewishness even in the midst of cultural Zionism is shown by a letter Martin wrote his grandparents in January 1900 on the occasion of his grandfather's birthday:

> Since I have been away from home, I have made the acquaintance of many persons of culture: artists, poets, and men of science. But I have never seen the childlike magical force of the spirit, the might of a strong and simple striving so purely and beautifully embodied as in grandpapa, never has a scholar and worker with ideas seemed to me so worthy of love (I mean: so worthy of the greatest love). I can seldom hold back my tears— tears of the innermost veneration—when I think of his beloved face.... I cannot show my thankfulness and my love to you better than when I—in my spheres—emulate your manner and place my life, like yours, in the service of the Jewish people.

On the other hand, Buber's conversion to Zionism did not mean unqualified affirmation of everything Jewish and a complete reversal of his earlier critical attitude. On the contrary, his call for a "Jewish Renaissance" meant precisely the purifying and cutting away of the elements in Galut (exile) Judaism that he considered to be unhealthy degenerations—shallow adaptations to the surrounding culture or fossilized emphasis on hair splitting commentary and rules of ritual law. In one way, this call is a clearly Nietzschean celebration of the noble, the strong, the creative, the pure. But, in another, it is obviously a continued identification with the Jews and Judaism that prevented Buber, even when most alienated, from becoming an assimilationist like so many other Jews of that period. Zionism was the first political, secular movement in which Jews of "the better class" dared in polite society to speak the name "Jew" aloud. It is unthinkable that it would have attracted Buber had he really been a "Jewish anti-Semite," as Eliasberg imagined, and still less likely that Buber would have from the first seen Zionism as a Jewish Renaissance movement rather than as a purely political antidote to anti-Semitism.

The Zionism of Theodor Herzl, to be sure, was started as a direct reaction to the anti-Semitism that the Dreyfus trial laid bare in France. The French army, state, and church conspired to keep an innocent man—Alfred Dreyfus, a captain in the French army and a Jew—imprisoned for years on Devil's Island, until the great French writer Émile Zola won Dreyfus's freedom in a controversial action that shook France to its foundations. Chaim Weizmann also came to Zionism in part through the far more terrible anti-Semitism in Russia, culminating in the pogroms that led thousands upon thousands of Jews to flee to Western Europe and to America. But even this Zionism was by no means simply a negative or defensive movement. It was characterized in its early years by the heroic spirit lent it by Theodor Herzl, who incarnated the Nietzschean vitalism in a Jewish form that did much to assuage Buber's sensitivity to the negative effects of both ghetto Judaism and the Enlightenment.

Although in Germany a pseudoscientific racial theory had arisen aimed at justifying attacks on the Jews, most Western Jews, as Robert Weltsch has pointed out, ignored or expressly denied the existence of a "Jewish problem." It was considered tactless at that time to identify anyone as a Jew, nor did most Jews know any longer what such identification meant. The word "Jew" had lost all positive meaning, whether of religion or a people, and had become a mere term of abuse. Jewish learning was given up in favor of secular culture, and the difference between the image of the Jew held by the larger public and that which the new classes of assimilated Jews held of themselves was simply overlooked.

The Zionist movement, which arose in its Western political form with the First Zionist Congress in Basel, Switzerland, in 1897, represented for the first time a Jewish group that did not deny the existence of a "Jewish problem" but rather recognized it as a basic problem not only of the Jews but of the European world. For the Western Zionist, politics gradually came to replace religion as the focus of Jewish life. Herzl's thesis that the Jews were a single people with national rights like any other exploded on the European stage as an unprecedented political demand. The Emancipation ushered in by the Enlightenment and by Napoleon had liberated the individual Jew but not the Jewish people. The assimilated Jews feared that the Zionist claim would lead to the loss of even these individual rights. (The Nazis later made devastating political capital out of Zionism to precisely this effect.) The Zionists, in contrast, believed that the assimilated Jews would welcome the Jewish national movement as moral reparation for their wounded sensibilities, caused by increasing anti-Semitism, and for the shrinking of their possibilities for development.

Was anti-Semitism a direct or indirect cause of Buber's conversion to Zionism? We have no evidence other than his clear identification with the sufferings of his people and his enthusiastic adherence to the cause. Three years before the 1903 pogroms in Russia, Buber wrote to his fiancée, Paula Winkler expressing keen sympathy regarding his encounter with a group of leaderless and lost Russian Jews on their way to America and of his efforts to help them find food and shelter at the railway station in Berlin, where the officials "treated them like animals." Though Buber joined the movement in 1898, a year after the first congress, and admired its leader as a Jewish hero, his relationship to the movement from the start was very different from that of Herzl. He was, to begin with, one of that group of young men whom Herzl, with his talent for leadership, succeeded in winning to his cause— young men full of enthusiasm and the joy of discovery. What is more, Zionism meant for Buber a return to Jewish roots, which Herzl never had, and an escape from the very assimilation that, except for his political activity, marked Herzl to the end. If it had not been for Zionism, says Hans Kohn, Buber might have become one of the lonely and tragic literati, fascinated by all the cultures of the world yet without roots in any.

In embracing Zionism, Buber found for the first time a channel into which he could concentrate his energies, like his grandfather, and give himself to fruitful and unremitting work. The "Jewish Renaissance" that Buber anticipated in his essays of this period first took place in his own soul. Although Buber in his old age deemed only four of the poems of this period worthy of preservation in his "Gleanings," his other, specifically Zionist, poems give us an insight into his inner devotion to the movement that even his flaming and youthful prose does not afford us. The first of these, "Our People's Awakening," was published without Buber's knowledge by the much older Reverend William Hechler, whom Buber had met in a railway carriage in the autumn of 1899. In conversation, the two men discovered that, on entirely different bases, they shared a common interest in Zionism. Reverend Hechler held a firm eschatological belief in the living Christ, and he saw the return of the Jewish people to their homeland as the promised precursor for Christ's second coming. He was journeying at that time to the grand duke of Baden, whom he had a short time before introduced to Herzl. When Buber showed Hechler his "hymn," the latter was filled with such enthusiasm—"entirely without basis," Buber commented half a century later—that he declared he must read it to the grand duke. Not only did he do this, but he shortly afterward published "the questionable little opus" without Buber's knowledge, "after he had furnished it with some, if possible, still more pathetic titles for each of the stanzas."

The connection of this Zionist enthusiasm with the vitalism and creativity of Buber's Nietzschean period is evident, only now it is focused in a movement. Buber went so far as to claim that everything good and fruitful that took place within Judaism in the last two millennia was in a deeper sense Zionist because it led to life. In his essays on the Jewish Renaissance written in this same period, Buber called for a fight against the enemies within their ranks who divide and weaken the Jewish people, for the release of latent energies, and above all for the restoration of the unified, unbroken feeling for life of the Jews so that it might again find natural expression in reality and in art.

Renaissance does not mean return but rebirth: a renewal of the whole person. It will be more difficult for the Jews than for any other people to enter into this renaissance because of the inner *ghetto* and *Golus* (Exile) which fetter them: the *ghetto* of unfree spirituality and the compulsion of tradition divorced from the life of the senses; and *golus*—the slavery of an uncreative making of money and the hollow-eyed homelessness that destroys all unified will. Deliverance from these fetters can come not through the program of a *party* but through the unwritten program of a *movement*. Zion must be reborn in the soul before it can be created as a tangible reality. When such a Zion of the souls exists, then the other, the Palestinian Zion, will not be long in following.

The Jewish Renaissance is the goal and meaning of the Jewish movement; the Zionist movement is the consciousness and will that lead to the Renaissance. This consciousness and will are all the more necessary because neither Hasidism nor the Haskalah—the two great movements that arose in the mid–eighteenth century and prepared the way for the Jewish Renaissance—was able to issue into it by itself. Hasidism replaced the old compulsion of the law by the new Jewish mysticism, which liberated feeling, purified intention, and set as the goal of the law that man himself should become a law, should freely embody what was formerly an external command. Haskalah, the Jewish Enlightenment, stepping forth in the name of European civilization, liberated thought and led the individual Jew to independence. But neither one alone accomplished the full liberation and activation of the newly awakened forces of the people. The wonder was that these two movements produced what they did and not that the one degenerated and the other left no legacy of immortal works, for the inner liberation in Hasidism and the Haskalah was experienced only by the Jews of the East— the Jews of community—whereas the outer liberation, the emancipation, was enjoyed only by the Jews of the West—the Jews of the dispersion. This essay foreshadows Buber's own great accomplishment of combining and integrating Hasidism and the Haskalah.

In Zurich in the summer semester of 1899, in the Germanics seminar, Buber met Paula Winkler, whom he later married. At that time, a woman studying in a university was still a rarity. Paula Winkler combined great intellectual gifts with a personality marked by a strong drive toward freedom. Already, before her studies in the university, she had lived outside her parents' house in an artists' colony in Southern Tyrol. She was one of the first women to traverse the Alps on a bicycle. Her teacher at that time described her as a "wild elfin being, tough, gifted, unhesitating, uncannily intelligent, and of a commanding will." Her combination of realistic traits with a breath of the romantic anticipated the way in which her literary work wove precise portrayals of reality with myth and mystery. Theodor Herzl called her "a great talent" and was ready to print contributions of hers in the *Neue Freie Presse,* the newspaper in which all the young and unpublished writers of Vienna dreamed of being published. Her first book of stories, *Die unechten Kinder Adams (The Illegitimate Children of Adam),* appeared in 1912.

Paula was almost a year older than the twenty-one-year-old Martin, and she undoubtedly possessed the stronger and more mature personality of the two. "It is impossible," writes Grete Schaeder, "to overestimate the significance of the fact that in his youthful years Buber met a woman who was equal to, indeed superior to, him in poetic gifts and power of expression and understood and spurred on his productivity to the highest degree." Something of the quality of this relationship is conveyed to us by their letters of August 1899. "Sweet one, dear one, you must not be so alarmed when a letter does not reach you," Paula wrote to Martin. "But truly, you will not drive yourself too much? Above all, do not work nights! Dear one, Thou, promise me that!... I love your great work—I would never want to injure it. But I would like to slip myself like a sheltering cloud between you and your little daily cares." Buber replied, telling her of his Zionist activities: "I work mostly in silent, brief relationships, awakening slumbering thoughts.... For that which *I* have to say the time is not yet present. I do not know whether this Congress will bring it to me. But what I do is fruitful. Perhaps now will come the lightning which will draw forth my innermost powers." The one committee in which he took part, Martin informed Paula, was the Action Committee, "because I like that: to participate in movement." Paula replied with a long letter in which she castigated a friend who wanted to give up the categories Jew and Christian, French and German, man and woman, in favor of "cosmopolitanism." In ridiculing this position, Paula sounded quite a few Nietzschean notes of her own: "Why not intensify the man in man, the woman in woman to high perfection, to a wonderful flowering—in order that they can then stand as human being to human being?"

In July 1901, Martin wrote to Paula, unburdening all the pathos of his longing for creativity:

> Above all it has become irresistibly clear to me that I must with all my power collect myself in the next months, or rather weeks, must produce something, otherwise I shall lose all that remains of my artistic initiative, and without that all ability is like a bird without the strength to soar; of what use is it that one "can fly"? You know that I have no extensive talent, therefore the hand must be taut.... You must understand, dearest, that this is a question of life and death. It concerns simply my art: If I let myself go, I shall go to ruin—that is certain. Then I can further develop myself as a *Privatdozent* [unsalaried lecturer who receives only students' fees] and in general as a competent person; but that will be the end of creating living things.

At the very time when Buber was immersing himself completely in Zionism and the Jewish Renaissance, he married a woman who was a Munich Catholic by upbringing. This action of Buber's led his old friend Chaim Bloch to break off all connection with him until after the war, since in the circles in which Bloch moved, mixed marriages were seen as a form of apostasy. In

Buber's case, intermarriage was in no sense tantamount to assimilation. If anything, it was his wife who assimilated to the Jews. At the cost of a complete and permanent break with her family, Paula Buber formally converted to Judaism before her marriage; the process included the traditional *mikva,* or ritual bath. (Since Austria had no civil marriages, they lived together for several years and had their two children, Rafael and Eva, before Paula converted and they formally married.) For some time, Martin studied in Berlin while Paula and the children remained in Austria. Paula, to use her own phrase, was an ardent "philozionist." Buber's Zionism made a deep impression upon her, and she offered him in turn both understanding and a creative resonance of her own.

In October 1901, Paula announced to Martin that she wanted to be active with him on behalf of Zionism: "I have the feeling that I can, I must do something for it." The next day, she wrote "Dear Maugli," the pet name they called each other from Rudyard Kipling's *Jungle Book,* that, of all the plans for a unified Jewish artistic life, that of a Jewish stage, which he proposed, was probably the most difficult: "Are there plays there? And would it not be difficult to write plays for the stage? The idea demands time. You should not pluck any unripe fruit, dear one." "I grow in your cause," she added. "It will be mine and that of our children."

Martin's response to Paula powerfully confirmed the connection between Paula's greater maturity and the need for a mother that had marked his life ever since his own mother left him:

> [Y]our letters are the only thing that give me strength. Everything
> else is too interwoven with care and unrest.... Aside from them
> perhaps the thought that a mother is in you, the belief in that.
> Now I know: I have always, always sought my mother.

Paula Winkler's "Confessions of a Philozionist," published in *Die Welt* (the official organ of the Zionist party) is part and parcel of the same Zionist enthusiasm that fires Buber's early poetry and prose. It gives concrete details of her own background that are of help in understanding how this brilliant and proud young Catholic could respond with such generous enthusiasm to the movement of a people not her own and could join her life to that of one of its leaders. Her attitude toward the Jews was not the ordinary one, she averred, because her mother had lived as a young girl in the neighborhood of a small Jewish settlement and received from its life strong and lasting impressions. Her mother spoke often and with rare warmth of this little place, and this image remained with the child. But beyond all the charm of difference, strange and wonderful words and customs, there lay the dark background of a painfully moving past, a story of cruel suspicion and comfortless flight, a story of heroism and endless sufferings.

Among the people with whom Paula Winkler grew up, Jews were not singled out, and she hardly knew what a Jew was. But when she was twenty-three, she encountered anti-Semitism with frightening clarity while witnessing a gang of children turn on a brown-eyed little boy and torment him with cries of "Jew-child," until his slightly older sister came up with swinging fists and rescued him from his oppressors. Zionism itself was a word that she had hardly heard and whose meaning she did not know, she wrote, until the Third Zionist Congress in Basel in 1899, where Buber's speech evoked in her a lifelong response.

> A human mouth spoke to me with wonderful force.... And my heart stood still.... And then it was again as if he spoke with iron tongues, and all the bells in the world rang out over men. It was no longer an individual man... the uncanny longing, wish, and will of a whole people came pouring forth.... It came over me like everything great in life and like life itself—came and carried me with it.

It was as if she saw hovering over every Jewish head a crown of thorns, the very image of the crucifixion that Buber himself used in his poetry of this period. The ancient longing for the old earth will be fulfilled, she prophesied, and the primally deep wounds of this old, sick, noble people healed! "How I love you, people of affliction!... In being different lies all your beauty, all happiness and joy of earth. Remain your own!"

In October 1902, Martin wrote Paula from Lemberg, where he had gone to visit his family: "Here everything is as confined as in a dungeon. I regard you more than ever as my freedom. One must take the whole world-riddle into one's relationship to one person, otherwise one is badly off." In contrast to the Talmudic warning, Buber asserted that one may look at all the mysteries: "See them in one human being who is yours, and you lie at the heart of the world." Schaeder quotes a "monstrous document" of 1902 superscribed "For You," in which, as she comments, "a very young man could not distinguish between life and poetry": "Before you came, I was dream and Golem. But when I found you, I found my soul. You came and gave me my soul. Is not my soul, therefore, your child? So you must love it...."

Through Paula Winkler, Buber became more courageous and self-confident, stronger and firmer. This was the decisive relationship of his life.

Together with some older friends, above all Berthold Feiwel and E.M. Lilien, Buber took a leading part in the cultural unfolding of the Jewish Renaissance. This group enriched the movement not only with poems and stories but also with translations out of Hebrew and Yiddish. As Hans Kohn points out, the activity of Buber and his circle was not simply an artistic one. It converted the Zionism of the West into a broader and deeper stream and thus brought it closer to the older Jewish movement of the East.

> The Zionism of these young men produced... tangible reality,presence, fullness. All later cultural strivings of Zionism are

grounded in the activity of this circle of 1900 to 1904, in its tireless devotion and its youthful enthusiasm.

Buber was spokesman for the Agitation Committee at the Third Zionist Congress at Basel in 1899, and his speech was the watchword of the new cultural movement, as opposed to the narrower, purely political conception of Zionism. Zionism is no party matter, Buber said, but a *Weltanschauung*— a worldview. "We must win the *whole* people for our cause," he said, and win them not merely by external agitation but through inner transformation. They must not be Zionists as one is a conservative or a liberal, but as one is a man or an artist. This can be accomplished through "inner agitation, through nourishing Jewish culture,... the spirit of the people, its national history, and its national literature, through education of the people."

"Herzl had a countenance lit with the glance of the Messiah," Buber recalled in later years. Buber looked to Herzl as the charismatic leader by whose mere presence an irresolute group could be transformed into a great movement. Therefore, Buber was overjoyed when in 1901 he succeeded his friend Berthold Feiwel to the editorship of *Die Welt*. Writing Buber that Feiwel had to resign for reasons of health, Herzl invited him to take over the editorship and offered him a free hand in one-third of the paper, to fill it with whatever he wished, including his own editorials and even two pages of stories. Buber answered this call with the warmth and definiteness that already at this early age marked his character. "Your invitation has brought joy to my heart," he wrote, "because it is an indication of trust and because it offers a splendid possibility of work."

The enormous activity that the editorship of *Die Welt* released in Buber can be seen from his many contributions to the 1901 volume of the weekly, as well as from his other Zionist writings of 1901 and the years immediately following. This came about in part through his successful insistence that the editor of the paper must represent an independent power in the movement and not be entirely subservient to the Action Committee.

In 1901, at the Fifth Zionist Congress in Basel, it was Martin Buber who played the central role in the successful fight that the "Democratic Fraction" waged against Theodor Herzl for official recognition of the decisive importance of cultural Zionism. The one-sided spirituality of the ghetto, which regarded nature, the human body, and art as inimical, had been replaced in recent times, Buber stated in his speech on Jewish art, by a rebirth of creativity, the activity of the whole organism, and the renewal of seeing.

After nearly forty delegates (without preconcerted agreement) rose from their seats, left the hall, and decided to protest against Herzl's using his influence to secure the rejection of the proposals of the Culture Committee, Herzl supported and brought to the vote all the resolutions of the Culture Committee. Only one was voted down, the subsidy of Buber's and Feiwel's Jüdischer Verlag. The rest, including the first official resolution for the establishment of what later became the Hebrew University in Jerusalem, were approved, and the forty victorious delegates returned to their seats. Max Nordau later stated in an interview that in the Democratic Fraction lay the Golus, the exile. This view Buber vigorously rejected and with it the conception of a unity that would sacrifice differences of views for the sake of party discipline. Such forced unity was precisely what characterized the Golus, Buber asserted, and necessarily so because of the enmity of the outer world: "But now, in the new land of the spirits that we have created for ourselves, we need no such dearly bought conformity.... We too want a unity, but one which builds itself upon the harmony of free, full voices." The issue that Buber raised here was decisive both for the origin and continuation of Zionism and for the future State of Israel.

The Democratic Fraction did not arise out of the Fifth Congress as a spontaneous protest. On the contrary, it emerged as an organized group from a Young Zionist conference held in preparation for the congress. This gave Buber the assurance that he spoke for the Young Zionists and made possible the spontaneous and unplanned walkout on the part of so many when their aims were brushed aside. Buber formulated the slogan for the Democratic Fraction: *"Gegenwartsarbeit"*—work in the present for building agriculture in Palestine and for cultural and educational preparation in the exile rather than postponing these until that supposedly near hour when Zionist diplomacy would obtain from the Turkish sultan the charter giving official permission for settlement in Palestine.

One of the most important practical activities of the Democratic Fraction was the founding in 1902 of the Jüdischer Verlag, under the editorship of Buber and Feiwel. This press produced a Jewish almanac, books on Jewish art, and collections of Jewish poetry, to all of which Buber contributed as well as helped to edit. "You are the only really creative person in our small circle," Berthold Feiwel told Buber in 1902, "and you must reserve and prepare yourself for a place among the greatest of our movement." If this work was seen by Buber as an active contribution to cultural Zionism, it was also regarded by him as an attack on purely political Zionism.

A second important outgrowth of the Democratic Fraction was the pamphlet on a Jewish university that Buber, Feiwel, and Weizmann brought out in 1903. The Buber-Weizmann-Feiwel pamphlet was the first serious proposal in print for a Jewish university, and it received a warm and widespread welcome from Jews of many lands. Published in Hebrew, German, English, Russian, and Yiddish, it represented the second decisive step toward a goal that was realized only twenty years later, the resolution approved by the Fifth Congress being the first.

Another issue on which the Democratic Fraction cooperated under the leadership of Weizmann, Buber, and Feiwel was the opposition to Herzl's plan to establish the Jewish homeland in East Kenya (mistakenly called Uganda), a territory of the British Empire, rather than in Palestine. Although much of Herzl's support came from the *Hovevei Zion,* the Eastern Jews who were drawn to Zionism by their real love of Zion, he himself was not averse to finding a shelter in some other land for the Jews fleeing from Russian pogroms. Herzl saw himself as the founder of "the Jewish state," but he was not really a "lover of Zion" in any deep sense of the term. For the Young Zionists, in contrast, Herzl's proposal of Uganda was nothing less than a betrayal of the cause. The climax of this conflict came in the Sixth Congress. Herzl succeeded in winning the support of a majority of the congress for an expedition to investigate "Uganda." But almost half the delegates, among them the members of the Democratic Fraction, walked out in a mood of profound melancholy, weeping and declaring the Basel program betrayed.

Despite the apparent reestablishment of unity at the end of the Fifth Congress, this congress meant, in fact, the separation of Buber and his friends from Herzl. Herzl was not the man to tolerate such an open challenge to his authority, nor did his last-minute support mean a real understanding of the democratic-cultural Zionism for which Buber, Weizmann, Lilien, Feiwel, Trietsch, and others were fighting. According to Hans Kohn, it was only thanks to the circle surrounding the Jüdischer Verlag, particularly Buber and Feiwel, that Zionism in German-speaking Europe not only did not disintegrate with the death of Herzl and the disappointment over the futility of his diplomatic actions, but after 1910 was able to take an upward swing that made it for a time the most active and leading part of the Jewish Renaissance movement.

In 1944, Buber recorded a memory of Herzl from 1901 that throws great light on the difference in approach between the leader of the Zionist movement and his younger followers. "We venerated him, loved him," wrote Buber, "but a great part of his being was alien to our souls. In a word, Herzl the liberal was alien to us." To Herzl, cultural work was a mere accessory that added interesting, if slightly exotic, nuances to the Zionist movement but could never form a great and decisive reality in the life of the people. Buber was closest to Herzl in the year 1901. Before that, he had not been personally near to him, and after that his activity in the opposition led to an alienation of Herzl that the latter overcame only in the last days of his life. In May or June 1901, Buber and Herzl met in the Zionist Central Bureau in Vienna to discuss the editorship of *Die Welt.* On the wall of the room where they met hung the new Palestine relief map, which had just reached the bureau. After a brief greeting, Herzl led Buber at once to the map and began to point out to him the economic and technical future of the land. His finger glided over an empty plain, and there arose in powerful rows the factories of a hundred industries; it led over the Bay of Haifa and, through the force of his words, Buber beheld the "future port of Asia." Finally, Herzl's finger returned to the Jordan River, and he recited to Buber the plan to erect a mighty dam that with its energy would supply the total economic life of the land. And now his finger tapped on a point of the map, and he cried: "How much horsepower has Niagara? Eight million? We shall have ten million!" Buber stood entranced before this magic work. He seemed to feel the Jordan-Niagara Falls spraying over him, and at the same time he had to smile—how remote that was, how unreal! No, it was not for that, thought the young man, that we served; it was not to take part in the Americanization of Asia that we inscribed Zion's name on our banner. God be thanked that this was only a dream!

Only long afterward, many years after Herzl's death, did it become clear to Buber that at that time it was Herzl—and not he—who had meant the real Palestine. For Buber at that time it was "das geliebte und Gelobte"— the beloved and the Promised Land—that had to be won anew, the land of the soul and of the message, the land in which the miracle of redemption- would reach fulfillment. For Herzl, in contrast, it was a wholly particular land with wholly particular geographical and geological characteristics, and there- fore also with clearly determinable technical possibilities, which he not only knew but also beheld in his mind's eye.

The rift between Buber and Herzl that had begun with the Third Congress in 1901 became a decisive break in 1903. This time, however, the controversy was focused on personalities and seemed, to the young Buber, to demand a choice of loyalties between the two men who had been most important to him in his Zionism—Theodor Herzl and Ahad Ha'am. The year before, Herzl had published the novel *Altneuland,* his somewhat utopian picture of how life in the new Jewish state might be. Ahad Ha'am subjected this book to a penetrating criticism of Herzl's Zionism, which was to him nothing short of a new and more effective type of assimilation in which the author went out of his way to credit non-Jews for everything original in the new state and made no mention of Hebrew instruction or Hebrew culture either in its projected education or in its learned academy. At Herzl's request, his henchman Max Nordau directed a sharp and insulting personal attack against Ahad Ha'am himself, maligning Ahad Ha'am's person, his spiritual and cultural leadership, his very real devotion to a Jewish homeland in Palestine, and that cultural Zionism for which he and his followers in the Democratic Fraction stood.

Herzl mistakenly believed that Buber himself had inspired an article replying to Nordau, and his bitterness, as a result, was particularly directed against Buber. Herzl wrote Buber a letter that decisively alienated Buber and his friends and made any real reconciliation impossible. Herzl accused Buber, in effect, of having left the movement, and this Buber could not for- give. "Without going further into details," Herzl wrote Buber, "I shall not con- ceal from you my view that the so-called 'Fraction' for reasons unknown to me, has fallen into error. My advice is: Try to find your way back to the movement, which certainly—like everything human—has its errors, but.... consists for the most part of men of goodwill...." Reminding Buber of how he made both Feiwel and him editors of the party organ *Die Welt* and of

how few restrictions he placed on them, Herzl closed with the wish that their
minds would again become clear and that they would realize and actively
repent the serious errors that they had committed against Nordau. Buber
replied that he and his friends did not need to find their way back to the
movement, that they stood as firmly within it as anyone, "and, with all due
respects I cannot allow you to pronounce a negative judgement on this question."

In this decisive and tragic encounter of two men, "each of whom was
as he was," there was a remarkable foreshadowing of the conflict between
the Seer and his loyal but independent disciple the Yehudi in Buber's
Hasidic chronicle-novel *For the Sake of Heaven*. Here, too, there are not
enough resources in the relationship to prevent the differences from crystallizing into a fixed opposition. It was many years before Buber could overcome the anger that this "advice" of Herzl's aroused in him.

Buber inserted this incident in the midst of an objective analysis of
"Herzl and History" written in 1904, the year of Herzl's death. In this analysis,
he recognized Herzl's greatness but not his Jewishness. Herzl gave form to
Zionism, which, before him, was an inchoate mass: "Herzl laid his hand on it
with a firm, shaping pressure. A sure, but unheeding hand. How many noble
possibilities were killed!" Herzl was the first man to pursue Jewish politics in
the Exile, and that will never be forgotten. In the name of the Jewish people,
he negotiated with the great powers of Europe. Although involved in public
affairs and political conflicts, he was, said Buber, a thoroughly unpublic man
who bore within his soul deep, inescapable inner conflict. Both dreamer and
practical man at once, he was the hero of a time of transition, the lord of a
sick people. His greatest deed was that he gave his people an image—not
the image of a real man, but an ideal image, a heartening, uplifting proto-
type.

For all this, Buber emphasized, it is fundamentally false to celebrate
him as a *Jewish* personality, as one could celebrate Spinoza, Israel Baal-Shem
(the founder of Hasidism), Heinrich Heine, or Ferdinand Lassalle. He was
also incomplete as a Zionist, as Buber understood the term. He never
grasped the movement in its wholeness. He never saw the Zionist party as
only the conscious limb of a greater organism. He was never truthfully aware
of the Jewish Renaissance. Those intellectuals of independent thought who
left the party were in Herzl's eyes renegades, and Ahad Ha'am he saw as an
obscure, spiteful journalist. At this point, in logical, if hidden, association
with Ahad Ha'am—the cause of his break with Herzl—Buber told his own
experience—in the third person: "'Try to find your way back to the movement,' he wrote once to a representative of the radical-national wing of the
party. To the movement!"

What piqued Buber particularly about this was that Herzl identified the
movement with himself. This was, in fact, in Buber's eyes, Herzl's greatest
weakness and his greatest strength. Affirmatively, it gave him his upright,

unshakable optimism and his inexhaustible energy and made him into the most influential man of action of the new Jewish era: "He believed in himself not as in a person but as in a cause." But it is to the negative side of Herzl's identification of cause and person that Buber devoted his most illuminating reminiscence of Herzl and of Herzl's impact on his own development as a person and a thinker. The occasion was the Sixth Zionist Congress in 1903, and though the conflict was still between Herzl and the Democratic Fraction, the specific form of his "fulminating speech against the opposition" was an attack on Buber's friend and coworker Davis Trietsch, with no direct personal clash between Buber and Herzl.

Herzl countered Trietsch's criticism of his policy with a personal attack on Trietsch's own colonizing activities. After the speech, Herzl retired to the presidential room, and soon afterward Feiwel and Buber followed him in order to point out the untenability of his accusations and to demand an investigating commission. On the way to the presidential room, Buber was deeply disturbed. He had indeed stood in decisive opposition to Herzl since the previous congress, but that had always been entirely a matter of a difference of position. He had never for a moment ceased to believe in the man himself. But now for the first time his soul revolted—so powerfully that writing about it a quarter of a century later he could still remember it physically. Yet when he entered the room, the sight that met him transformed his excitement in an instant, and the heart that had a moment before been pounding now froze.

In the room were only Herzl and his mother. Madame Jeannette sat on a chair, unmoving, silent, but with eyes from which the most lively sympathy streamed. Herzl paced up and down through the room in great strides; his vest was unbuttoned, his breast heaving and sinking. This "caged lion," whose gestures had always been so mastered and masterly, now breathed wildly. Herzl's pallor struck Buber only later, so burning was his glance.

It had suddenly become compellingly clear to Buber that here it was impossible to remain inwardly the representative of *one* side. Outside was an injured man, his friend and fellow fighter, to whom a public injustice had been done, and here was the man who had done the injustice, who had inflicted the wound, yet a man who, even though misled, was still his leader, sick with zeal, consuming himself for his belief. "There were great and dreadful moments," Martin wrote Paula. "The shattering that I experienced is perhaps the greatest of my life." For the twenty-five-year-old Buber, this was one of the first times in which he set foot on the soil of tragedy, where all question of being in the right disappeared.

This was the last time Buber saw Herzl at such close quarters. Later, after Herzl's death, Buber found himself forced again and again to ponder the relation of "cause" and "person." He recognized that most men of action see no sense in discussing principles and methods when what counts in the last instance is the man who is entrusted with carrying them out. As long as a leader like Herzl has "charisma," then one who does not is in no position to judge him. Only a standpoint that Buber reached many years later—that which demands a real dialogical relationship between leader and led—could call this concept into question. Buber's later view of tragedy—where each is as he is and the resources to bridge the gap are lacking—is anticipated here even more powerfully than in his own earlier break with Herzl. With it is anticipated the fundamental principle of the life of dialogue that confirms the opponent even in his opposition because it does not see two *points of view* as opposing each other but two *persons*. It realizes that neither the truth nor the right is an affair of "monologue" that can reside simply in one side to the exclusion of the other.

Buber had to work through his relation to his two chief images of the human during this period—Herzl and Ahad Ha'am. In doing so, he made a decisive choice for the rest of his life—that between the leader and the true teacher. Ahad Ha'am dared what Herzl, with his devotion to the abstractions of political movement, did not—to bring idea and reality into faithful relationship. It was to him, at that time, despite all differences, that Buber gave his allegiance. Ahad Ha'am's Zionism was not "smaller" than political Zionism, but greater. He, too, strove for a Jewish communal life in Palestine, not even shying away from the designation of a "Jewish State," and he, too, saw a great mass settlement as the precondition for this community. But he viewed this mass settlement as the organic center of a great living world Judaism, whose existence depended on this organic center. What divided Herzl and Ahad Ha'am, wrote Buber, was "the difference between a transformation of the attitude and a transformation of the whole man,... between a slogan and a direction; more clearly still: it is the difference between a teacher and a leader."

> Leading without a teaching attains success: Only what one attains
> is at times a downright caricature of what, in the ground of one's
> soul,... one wanted to attain.... Unhappy, certainly, is the people
> that has no leader, but three times as unhappy is the people
> whose leader has no teaching.

If Buber could not in the end become both leader and teacher, he did become in the deepest sense the true teacher for the Jewish people, for modern Zion, and for the world.

✦ 3 ✦

Mysticism: The Discovery of Hasidism

(1904-1914)

As important as was Buber's contribution to early Zionism and the Jewish Renaissance movement, it represented in his own life and thought only the first step in his liberation from the aimlessness of the times. Later, Buber recognized what his early essays on the Jewish Renaissance show no inkling of—that becoming part of the Jewish nation does not by itself transform the Jewish man. It gives him roots, to be sure, but he can be just as poor in soul with it as without it. This does not mean that Buber later saw his early nationalistic fervor as entirely invalid. On the contrary, it was an important and essential stage that led to a further transformation. Yet it did so only because it was to him "not a satiating but a soaring, not an entering into the harbor but a setting out on the open sea." But there is a judgment here for all that. If it was a beginning rather than an ending, nonetheless it was "too easy," revealing more enthusiasm than substance: "I professed Judaism before I really knew it." Only after blind groping did Buber reach his second step, wanting to know Judaism, and by knowing he did not mean the storing up of knowledge, but the biblical knowing of involvement and mutual contact: the immediate, "eye-to-eye knowing of the people in its creative primal hours." Through such knowing, Buber came to the second important stage on his way, namely, the discovery of Hasidism.

Hasidism is the popular mystical movement of East European Jewry, Jewry founded by the Baal-Shem Tov (Good Master of the name of God), Israel ben Eliezer (1700–1760). The Hasidic movement arose in Poland in the eighteenth century, and, despite bitter persecution at the hands of traditional rabbinism, spread rapidly among the Jews of Eastern Europe, until it included almost half of them in its ranks. The Hasidim founded real communities, each with its own *rebbe.* The *rebbe,* the leader of the community, was also called the righteous or justified man. Each one of these *zaddikim* had his own unique teaching, which he gave to his community and which helped bring the people into direct relationship to God. Later, hereditary dynasties of Hasidim arose: The *rebbes* lived in great palaces, surrounded by awe and superstition, and the *zaddik* became more of a mediator between the people and God.

Buber first encountered Hasidism when his grandfather took him to Sadagora, the seat of a dynasty of *zaddikim.* There, Buber encountered the Hasidic movement, not in its flowering, to be sure—that had passed with the founders—but still in a living organic tradition. The descendant of the great founders could still evoke a shudder of profoundest reverence when he stood in silent prayer or interpreted the mystery of the Torah in hesitant speech at the third Sabbath meal. Even though the later Hasidim for the most part sought out the *rebbe* as a magic mediator, in their souls still glowed the old saying that the world was created for the sake of the completed man (the *zaddik).* "Here was, debased yet essentially intact, the living double kernel of humanity: genuine *community* and genuine *leadership.* " Buber wrote:

> The palace of the rebbe, in its showy splendor, repelled me. The prayer house of the Hasidim with its enraptured worshippers seemed strange to me. But when I saw the rebbe striding through the rows of the waiting, I felt, "leader," and when I saw the hasidim dance with the Torah, I felt, "community."

Although Solomon Buber was an "enlightened" Jew, a *Maskil,* he liked to pray among the Hasidim and used a prayer book full of mystical directions. He liked to take his grandson Martin to a small Hasidic *Klaus,* or synagogue, to pray. Buber's father, in contrast, occasionally lured him away from his grandfather to worship in the Temple of Lemberg, a liberal synagogue. This contact with "liberal" religion had so little influence on Buber that once on Yom Kippur (the Day of Atonement), young Martin caused annoyance in the Lemberg Temple by following the Orthodox tradition of bending his knee and prostrating himself.

When he was fourteen and currently living with his father all year-round on the estate in Bukovina, Martin ceased to put on *teffillin* (phylacteries). Until that age, he was a very observant and fervent Jew, and the high point of his religious experience came only a short while before his full observance ceased. Between his thirteenth and his fourteenth year, he experienced Yom Kippur with a force by his own account unequaled by any other experience since then. Nor could this experience be dismissed as merely that of a child, for this was near the very age when Martin almost committed suicide over the infinity of time and space. Perhaps, Buber suggested to Franz Rosenzweig when he was already forty-four, he was even less a child at thirteen than he was more than thirty years later, "and this in a poignant sense."

> At that time I took Space and Time seriously; I did not hold back as I do now. And then, when the sleepless night was heavy upon me and very real, my body, already reacting to the fast, became as important to me as an animal marked for sacrifice. This is what formed me: the night, and the following morning, and the Day itself, with all its hours, not omitting a single moment.

Buber's encounter with Hasidism can be described only as a breakthrough or a conversion, if one uses this latter term in the biblical sense of a total turning of one's existence rather than a leap of faith. After coming back to Judaism through Zionism and then realizing that he did not really know Judaism, Buber began around 1904 to return to the Hebrew of his childhood. Although at first repelled by the "brittle, ungainly, unshapely material," so foreign to any of the Western languages that he loved, he gradually overcame the strangeness and beheld with growing devotion what was essential in it. At this point, he came upon a little book entitled *The Testament of Rabbi Israel Baal-Shem,* a collection of sayings said to have been uttered by Israel ben Eliezer. Something of the combination of fire and spirit that Buber much later pointed to as the uniqueness of the "Besht" (as he was called after his initials) must have communicated itself to the soul of the young man in whom spirit and fire, intellect and passion, yearning and will, were also so strong.

It was the Baal-Shem's words about fervor that forever won the young man's soul: "He takes unto himself the quality of fervor. He arises from sleep with fervor, for he is hallowed and become another man and is worthy to create and is become like the Holy One, blessed be He, when He created His world." It is not that fervor had in any sense been lacking in Buber before. But this was fervor with direction, all the awesome power of the "evil urge" taken up into the service of God, Boehme's "ternary of fire" spiraling upward into the "ternary of light" without losing any of its power thereby. A theophany, an epiphany, a revelation, a breakthrough—call it what we will, this was one of the truly decisive moments in Buber's life:

> It was then that, overpowered in an instant, I experienced the Hasidic soul.The primally Jewish opened to me, flowering to newly conscious expression in the darkness of exile: man's being created in the image of God I grasped as deed, as becoming, as task. And this primally Jewish reality was a primal human reality, the content of human religiousness.... The image out of my childhood, the memory of the zaddik and his community, rose upward and illuminated me: I recognized the idea of the perfected man.

At the same time I became aware of the summons to proclaim it
to the world.

The combination of summons and sending, of revelation and mission, to
which Buber later pointed in *I and Thou,* came for Buber as a single moment
of meeting.

If it had been simply disillusionment with political Zionism that had
produced this meeting, one might have expected the already diversely occupied young man to fling himself into still other activities to substitute for
those from which he had withdrawn. Instead, at twenty-six, he withdrew
himself for five years from action in the Zionist party *and* from writing articles and giving speeches. In order to go forward, he had first to retire into
the stillness. "I gathered, not without difficulty, the scattered, partly missing,
literature," he wrote, "and I immersed myself in it, discovering mysterious
land after mysterious land." The breadth of his early activities was exchanged
for a work in depth; his public activity came to a total standstill; and he
labored with unremitting energy, exploring the new region, making it his
own, and giving it new form. Buber emerged from this retirement with a
new wholeness that kept in check his tendency toward dispersion. It also
gave him a unique personal direction from which, even in the most terrible
crises, he was never again deflected.

Buber produced his first two Hasidic books in Florence, Italy, where he
lived during much of the years 1905 and 1906. It might appear that Florence
represented still another temptation to the young Buber to fragment himself,
especially since he not only explored it and wrote about it but took part in
its cultural life and wrote essays on the theater there. The evidence is all to
the contrary. At Christmas 1905, he wrote in a letter from Florence:

> We must give up all that which is only seemingly ours, which
> does not really nourish and warm us, which does not stir us up
> and satisfy us, if we are to come to ourselves. I have experienced
> it.... How do I live? As at the beginning of a good path that I do
> not yet wholly know but that I know is right. I am glad that I
> have been set free from a false sphere of work; for it is only now
> that I can again work whole and free.... Even my connection with
> Judaism has deepened; if I enter party activities once again, again
> say something about this problem of problems, it will certainly be
> something purer and greater than I once said when I was impris-
> oned by catchwords.

It is remarkable how many motifs of Buber's later philosophy are contained
in this description of his experience: the contrast between "being" and
"seeming"; good is what one does with one's whole being, evil is what one
does with only a part of one's being; the "heart-searching" that brings one to
one's own unique way; and, above all, one's work not as a separate com-

partment of one's existence but as one's *direction* in response to the claim of the situation.

It was in Florence that Buber laid the groundwork for the two books that brought him his first period of fame—*The Tales of Rabbi Nachman* and *The Legend of the Baal-Shem*. It was also in Florence that he "fell in love" with Italian theater and the great Italian actress Eleonora Duse. And it was the love of Florence and Italy that set the pattern for the life of the Buber family during the years when Rafael, or Raffi, born in 1900, and Eva, born in 1901, were growing up. Every summer, the family went to Italy, and in 1906 they brought back with them from Florence to Germany Santina Santelli, an Italian maid who lived with the family for twenty years. Her favorite saying, "What can one do; that is life," became a household word and joke in the Buber family. Because of the summers in Italy and Eva's supposed sensitivity, Eva was not sent to school but taught at home by private tutors, something that she herself judged to be a mistake when she reflected on it in later years.

Unbeknownst to anyone other than Martin, Paula wrote some of the legends of the Baal-Shem herself. Indeed, Martin received untold help in retelling the legends of the Baal-Shem from his "heart's Maugli," Paula, with whom he divided the task of reworking the crude raw material of the originals into artistically fashioned stories. This fact remained a well guarded secret for over six decades, until after Buber's death, although in retrospect it is clear that Martin referred to it in the poem "Do You Still Know It?" with which he dedicated the collection of his mature *Tales of the Hasidim*, which he presented to Paula in 1949!

In Florence, Buber was in "the first real work period" of his life. When he began to translate the allegorical and even fairytale-like stories in which Rabbi Nachman of Bratzlav, the great grandson of the Baal-Shem, clothed his teaching, he discovered that mere translation left them even more paltry and impure than the distortions of form and the insertions of vulgar rationalistic and utilitarian motifs by Nachman's disciples. Rejecting his first attempts, Buber proceeded to the far harder task of real artistic creation: "I had to tell the stories that I had taken into myself from out of myself, as a true painter takes into himself the lines of the models and achieves the genuine images out of the memory formed of them." *In The Legend of the Baal-Shem*, too, he came to his own narration in growing independence, and the greater the independence became, the more deeply he experienced the faithfulness. What Buber wrote in the Introduction in 1907 was an honest report of his experience of the legend: "I bear in me the blood and the spirit of those who created it, and out of my blood and spirit it has become new."

The Hasidic legend that Buber strove to tell did not possess the austere power of the Buddha legend or the intimacy of the Franciscan. It was received and passed on haltingly: "It came to life in narrow streets and small, musty rooms, passing from awkward lips to the ears of anxious listeners. A stammer gave birth to it and a stammer bore it onward—from generation to generation." It was this stammer, too, that Buber heard and sought to repeat:

> I have received it from folk-books, from note-books and pamphlets, at times also from a living mouth, from the mouths of people still living who even in their lifetime heard this stammer.... I tell once again the old stories, and if they sound new, it is because the new already lay dormant in them when they were told for the first time.

What was missing in Buber's retelling, however, was precisely the stammer. What he received from the *spoken* word, stammered by "awkward lips," he transformed into artistic and urbane literature not destined for "the ears of anxious listeners" but for the sophisticated appraisal of readers attuned to the highest in German culture at the time. Buber never simply used Hasidism for the sake of his personal work or as a mere literary project. Rather, he saw himself from the first as an instrument—an honest artisan carrying out a commission to the best of his ability. He saw what commissioned him, moreover, as something hidden in Hasidism, which he could and should bring to the world, even against the wishes of Hasidism itself, which "wishes to work exclusively within the boundaries of Jewish tradition." Yet fifty years later, he recognized that he was then, for all that, an immature man, still subject to the power of the *Zeitgeist*—the spirit of the age—which led him to mix genuine testimony to a great reality of faith with an inauthentic desire to display the contents of exotic religions to readers motivated mostly by curiosity and a wish to acquire "culture." His *representation* of the Hasidic teaching was essentially faithful, but his *retelling* of the legendary tradition was not, for the form he gave to it was just that of the Western author that he was.

> I did not yet know how to hold in check my inner inclination to transform the narrative material poetically. I did not, to be sure, bring in any alien motifs; still I did not listen attentively enough to the crude and ungainly but living folk-tone which could be heard from this material.... The need, in the face of... misunderstanding, to point out the purity and loftiness of Hasidism led me to pay all too little attention to its popular vitality.

Buber opened *The Tales of Rabbi Nachman* with an essay, "Jewish Mysticism," in which he set forth many motifs that were later to become central both to his interpretation of Hasidism and to his own philosophy: the essential importance of *kavana*—the strength of inner intention, the possibility of apprehending God in each thing if every action, no matter how lowly, is a dedicated one, the notion that one's urges, far from being evil, are the very things that make greatness possible.

In his picture of the life of Rabbi Nachman, Buber spoke of him—as the year before he had spoken of Herzl—as "a great and tragic man." Nachman's dream for the *zaddik,* the leader of the Hasidic community, was to be "the soul of the people." Nachman did not find the yoke of service easy, "for he had a joyous strong disposition and a fresh sense for the beauty of the world"; yet he finally succeeded in basing his devotion on just this disposition and serving God in joy. He broke out of the centuries of ghetto existence into direct contact with the power of growing things and heard the voice of God in the reeds of the stream, in the horse that bore him into the forest, in the trees and plants, the mountain slopes, and the hidden valleys. Above all, he represented for Buber a new and more meaningful way of turning to the Jewish people—of living with them and bearing their pain and finding in them his consecration. For Nachman, as later for Buber himself, this living with others meant an insistence on the mystery of communication and on the mutuality of dialogue. The true word awakens the hearer so that he himself becomes a speaker and speaks the final word. The world was created only for the sake of the choice and the choosing one, for man is the master of choice. No limits are set to the ascent of man, and to each the highest stands open. "Here your choice alone decides." On the other hand, "[i]f a man does not judge himself, all things judge him, and all things become messengers of God."

The intensity of Nachman's messianic longing corresponded to Buber's own passionate quest for redemption. One must walk in loneliness, said Nachman, so as to be tranquil and composed when the Messiah comes. Perhaps the most moving of the six stories of Rabbi Nachman that Buber retold is that of "The Rabbi and His Son," in which the pathos of just this messianic longing is portrayed. An even more intense story of messianic longing was included in the original editions of *The Legend of the Baal-Shem* but was later renounced by Buber as not being carried through with sufficient effectiveness. For this very reason, it is significant for understanding the "immature" Buber. What is more, it is in *this* story that Buber first uses in written form his image of "the narrow ridge."

> Our year is a circle. We walk on a narrow, round ridge between two abysses and do not see the abysses. But when we have come to the end of the ridge which is its beginning, then fear and trembling descend upon us like the storm of the Lord, and the lightning of the Lord flashes across the abysses, and we see them, and we falter.... And the world shofar sounds and bears on its wings the soul that has been born from our souls and that is the soul of the Messiah, and it swings upward to the kingdom of the mystery and beats with its wings at the gate, and the gate opens wide and behold there is no longer gate nor wall but the city of the Lord lies there, open in all directions.

Even in this early usage, the "narrow ridge" is a metaphor for human exis-

tence itself: an existence in which one must walk with faltering step, threatened at every moment by the danger of falling into the abysses to the left
and to the right. Here we can glimpse Kierkegaard's "knight of faith," who
comes slowly creeping forward in "fear and trembling," in a tension that can
never be relaxed. Yet in "The New Year's Sermon," the awareness of the
abyss comes only at the end of the circle, which is its beginning, that is, at
the Jewish New Year, which is the commencement of the "Days of Awe." As
such, it presents a caesura in time, which otherwise seems to carry us
smoothly along in the regularity of the seasons and the round of the years.
When the awareness comes and the man's foot stumbles, he is upheld by
arms that arise from the abysses to the right and the left. The abysses are
threatening but they are not pure evil. But the man finds deliverance only
when both the abysses and the narrow ridge disappear in favor of the fullness of redemption in which everything earthly is transfigured. This exalted
tone is very different from the "hallowing of the everyday," the "obedient listening," the moment-by-moment response to the "lived concrete" that
marked Buber's later use of the "narrow ridge." Even Hasidism itself Buber
later defined as persevering in an *unexalted* life. Messianism later became for
him a "messianism of the everyday" rather than an apocalyptic longing for
redemption now. This is, in fact, the central conflict in his great Hasidic
novel, *For the Sake of Heaven.*

In later years, the abysses on either side of the narrow ridge tended to
become symbolic for Buber: the evasion of the concrete situation through
one or another type of abstraction—psychologism, historicism, technicism,
philosophizing, magic, gnosis, or the false either/ors of individualism versus
collectivism, freedom versus discipline, action versus grace. In "The New
Year's Sermon" and in many of the other stories in *The Legend of the Baal-
Shem,* the abysses seem all too real. When in "The Werewolf" the old Rabbi
Eliezer speaks to his son Israel on his deathbed, he describes the "Adversary"
as "the abyss over which you must fly." In the "Revelation," the abyss confronts Rabbi Naftali each day that he sets out to leave the innkeeper in the
Carpathians who has invited him to stay for the Sabbath and whom no one
yet knows to be the Baal-Shem.

> The world lay before him like an abyss. Out of the abyss emerged
> the solar disk in silent torment. In agonized birth pangs the earth
> brought forth trees and plants without number.... Each creature
> suffered because it must do what it did.... All things were
> enveloped by the abyss, and yet the whole abyss was between
> each thing and the other. None could cross over to the other,
> indeed none could see the other, for the abyss was between
> them.

This is the strongest expression Buber had yet made of the abyss *between*
each thing and the other, the abyss that must have opened for him personal-

ly when his mother left him and that each of his different ways of striving for unity sought to bridge. Redemption here, however, is not pictured as unity or joy, but as contact, touching, the restoration of "betweenness" through the very presence of the Baal-Shem.

> The man was here and everywhere, possessed of manifold being and overspanning presence. Now his arm clasped round the body of the trees, the animals clung to his knees and the birds to his shoulders. Then lo, comfort had come into the world. For through the helper, things were joined and saw and knew and grasped one another. They saw one another through his eyes and touched one another through his hand. And since the things came to one another, there was no longer an abyss, but a light space of seeing and touching, and of all that was therein.

It is no accident that this second image of redemption is not the establishment of unity but the establishment of contact—what Buber was later to call the realm of the "between." For in the Introduction to *The Legend of the Baal-Shem* Buber first speaks in a fully developed sense of the mutual relationship of I and Thou that later became the center of his life and thought. Here Buber distinguished between "pure myth," in which there is no "Thou" over against an "I," and "legend," in which there is "caller and called," "I and Thou."

> The legend is the myth of the calling. In it the original personality of myth is divided. In myth there is no division of essential being. It knows multiplicity but not duality. Even the hero only stands on another rung than that of the god, not over against him: they are not the I and Thou. The hero has a mission but not a call. He ascends but he does not become transformed. The god of pure myth does not call, he begets; he sends forth the one whom he begets, the hero. The god of the legend calls forth the son of man— the prophet, the holy man.
>
> The legend is the myth of I and Thou, of the caller and the called, the finite which enters into the infinite and the infinite which has need of the finite.

This passage contains in seed the dialogue between the "I" and "the eternal Thou" that Buber later set forth in the third part of *I and Thou*. And it is not Feuerbach or Kierkegaard that inspired it, but the Baal-Shem, who is seen, like Buber himself in his relation to Hasidism, as the man of summons and sending. "The legend of the Baal-Shem is not the history of a man but the history of a calling. It does not tell of a destiny but of a vocation."

Commenting on this passage in the short section devoted to himself in "The History of the Dialogical Principle," Buber wrote:

Here the dialogical relationship is thus exemplified in its highest peak: because even on this height the essential difference between the partners persists unweakened, while even in such nearness the independence of man continues to be preserved.

But he followed by pointing out how far this insight into legend was from the full reality of the life of dialogue: "From this event of the exception, of the extraction, however, my thought now led me, ever more earnestly, to the common that can be experienced by all."

Hasidism was not the only form of mysticism that occupied Buber during his early years. One of Buber's earliest encounters with mysticism was within an explicitly social context: the New Community, founded by the brothers Heinrich and Julius Hart in or near Berlin. The New Community was led and taught by the socialist Gustav Landauer. Next to his marriage, Buber's friendship with Landauer, who was eight years older, was probably the decisive relationship of his adult life. Buber met Landauer in 1899, when the latter was almost twenty-nine. Landauer undoubtedly encouraged the switch in Buber's university studies from science and the history of art to Christian mysticism. In 1906, Landauer published the first modern edition of the great German mystic Meister Eckhart, a translation that bore many resemblances to the basic principles that guided Buber's first attempts to translate Hasidic writings.

During the years 1899 and 1900, Buber was close to the New Community and gave lectures there on the great Lutheran mystic Jacob Boehme and on "Old and New Community." The lecture on Boehme undoubtedly formed the basis for the essay on Boehme that he published in 1901—the most original and impressive of his earliest writings. What Buber said of Boehme was certainly true of his own experience at this period: For all its effect on one, the world still remained eternally distant and strange. "The individual consumes himself in dumb, hopeless solitude." Nonetheless, we have a relation to the world, which is no completed whole compelling us, but is a continual process of becoming. We do not see the things-in-themselves, but our sense impressions—thus far, Buber looked back to Kant. But we enter into a creating and loving relationship with these very sense impressions through which we have an impact on them and they on us.

In this essay, Buber quoted Ludwig Feuerbach's thesis that "man with man —the unity of I and Thou—is God"—only to reject it. "We stand nearer today," wrote Buber, "to the teaching of Boehme than to that of Feuerbach, to the feeling of Saint Francis of Assisi, who called the trees, the birds, and the stars his brothers." But the prime fact of his experience was the division between the "I" and the world, and the rest of the essay focuses on conflict and love precisely as bridges between *separated* individuals. Things neither exist in rigid separation nor melt into one another, but reciprocally condition one another. It is significant that Buber did *not* turn to mysticism, as so many modern thinkers after him have done, as the negation of the self and of personality. What drew Buber to mysticism was, first of all, his own personal awareness of the threat of infinity and the sense of aloneness in the face of outer separateness and inner contradiction. But it was also clearly the mechanization and mass culture that Kierkegaard, Nietzsche, and Dostoevsky had protested against in the century that had just concluded.

For the medieval mystic, the individual was only the bearer of a life experience encompassing the transcendent. Individuation was given only to be renounced and overcome. The fifteenth-century mystic Nicholas of Cusa resumed in modern form, said Buber, the perseverance and the absolute value of the individual in his particularity. But individualism for Buber at this juncture, as for Cusanus, did not mean mere difference. It meant uniqueness—that which makes a person or thing of value in itself, that which is unrepeatable and for which no other value can be substituted, that which is not a matter of usefulness or function but, however much it may exist in relation to the others, is an absolute center in itself. This concept of uniqueness—the uniqueness of the person, but also the uniqueness of everything—is the first necessary step on Buber's way to the philosophy of dialogue, the "I-Thou" relationship. It is not a sufficient step, however, and for years it was for Buber himself a block to dialogue. Yet the true meaning of the unique relation of the unique person to the unique reality that he encounters can be neither understood nor approached except by way of this concept. This and the idea of the *coincidentia oppositorum*—the coincidence of opposites that unites them without diminishing their oppositeness—are two of the essential ingredients of the "life of dialogue" that Buber took from Nicholas of Cusa and Renaissance mysticism at the beginning of his way. The universe is included in each thing, but in each in the form of this particular thing. Each creature has its line of realization, but God is the point in which all lines of perfection meet. God does not want to abolish the differences of the things in which he reveals himself but rather to perfect himself in them.

In Boehme, Buber found a more modern thinker than Cusanus and one whose influence on him was equally great and lasting. Boehme combined a really modern dynamic with a dialectic of good and evil taken from the Hebrew Kabbala, a dialectic that Buber later encountered anew in another child of the Kabbala—Hasidism. "Each thing longs for the other, for it is determined by the other." Its powers are lured out of it and made actual through its encounter with the other. This process leads again not to the overcoming but to the intensification and spread of individuation.

Only through the creation of the world does God become God, in Buber's interpretation of Boehme. Only in man does God come to that self-knowledge that completes consciousness, that is, in the evolution of creation, the evolution of God in the world. Rosenzweig rightly contrasts this statement with Buber's later (1923) condemnation of "the hopelessly perverted conception that God is not but rather becomes—in man or in mankind."

Buber himself pointed to it later as something that had been destroyed in him during the First World War:

> Since 1900 I had first been under the influence of German mysti-
> cism from Meister Eckhart to Angelus Silesius, according to which
> the primal ground (*Urgrund*) of being, the nameless, impersonal
> godhead, comes to "birth" in the human soul; then I had been
> under the influence of the later Kabbala and of Hasidism, accord-
> ing to which man has the power to unite the God who is over the
> world with his *shekinah* dwelling in the world. In this way there
> arose in me the thought of a realization of God through man; man
> appeared to me as the being through whose existence the
> Absolute, resting in its truth, can gain the character of reality.

By 1907, Buber had already integrated his mysticism with his Hasidism. The introductory section of *The Legend of the Baal-Shem,* "The Life of the Hasidim," is divided into four parts, each of which deals with a central Hasidic attitude—ecstasy, service, intention, and humility. Each part is illus- trated by quotations from the *zaddikim,* but it is given richness and fullness by Buber's own powerful imagery. *Hitlahavut* is the ardor of ecstasy that can appear at all places and at all times. Only the moment lives, and the moment is eternity. Ecstasy is the way without end, the simple unity and limitlessness in which man is beyond all law and above all evil urge. *Avoda* is service. All is God, and all serves God: This is the primeval duality. Through creation, God is separated from his glory, his *shekinah,* but man, through binding all action into one and carrying the everlasting life into each deed, can reunite God with his exiled glory. To perform true service, man must say "Enough!" to his inner dissensions and become at one with himself. This wholeness is not attained through God's grace or through man's power alone but through the mysterious meeting between them.

Kavana is intention, the mystery of a soul directed to a goal. It is the ability of man through the singleness and purity of his will to liberate the fallen sparks of divinity that are imprisoned in the people and objects around him and to take part in the redemption of the world. But it is like the Taoist *wu-wei* in that it has no special aim or concrete object but is dependent on quietness of mind and wholeness of being.

> No leap from the everyday into the miraculous is required. "With
> his every act man can work on the figure of the glory of God that
> it may step forth out of its concealment." It is not the matter of the
> action, but only its dedication that is decisive. Just that which you
> do in the uniformity of recurrence or in the disposition of events,
> just this answer of the acting person to the manifold demands of
> the hour... just this continuity of the living stream, when accom-
> plished in dedication, leads to redemption.

Shiflut is humility. Humility, for Hasidism, begins not with self-denial but with the affirmation of one's true self, one's created uniqueness that is given one to unfold and to complete. We have already seen this uniqueness in Buber's presentation of Nicholas of Cusa, but now it has taken on intensity and depth:

> That which exists is unique, and it happens but once. New and without a past, it emerges from the flood of returnings, takes place, and plunges back into it, unrepeatable.... It is because things happen but once that the individual partakes in eternity. For the individual with his inextinguishable uniqueness is engraved in the heart of the all and lies forever in the lap of the timeless as he who has been created thus and not otherwise.

Here is the link that makes explicit why the understanding of uniqueness is the necessary prerequisite for the understanding of dialogue, for one can be truly open and ready to meet others only if one stands on the ground of one's uniqueness and deepens that ground through each new meeting. But here the corollary of the "between" is present and explicit, as it was not earlier. Humility is the love of a being who lives in a kingdom greater than the kingdom of the individual and speaks out of a knowing deeper than the knowing of the individual. This greater kingdom and this greater knowing is the realm of "the between," which Buber equated even at this early date with God: "It exists in reality *between* the creatures, that is, it exists in God. Life covered and guaranteed by life.... What the one is wanting, the other makes up for. If one loves too little, the other will love more."

In *Ecstatic Confessions* (1909), Buber brought together a large number of personal descriptions of mystic ecstasy from a wide range of times, religions, and cultures, which he had spent many years in assembling. In the introductory essay, "Ecstasy and Confession," Buber presented what he believed to be the essence of those experiences. The ecstatic at the time of ecstasy has achieved true and perfect unity, Buber claimed, in which the world and the "I" are one and all multiplicity has disappeared. The mystic desires to create a lasting memorial of his ineffable experience of ecstasy, and, in so doing, he brings the timeless into time and changes the unity without multiplicity into the unity of all multiplicity. The ecstatic experience is only one pole of the movement of the world spirit from the many to the one and the one to the many: "We turn inward and listen—and we do not know which sea's roar it is that we hear."

In "The Teaching of the Tao," written in 1910, Buber took a decisive step forward in integrating his encounter with mysticism into his personal philosophy. This essay focuses not upon mystical experience but upon a central teaching and a central person. The teaching is a simple whole that includes all of one's life. Genuine life is united life. Each thing reveals the Tao through the way of existence, through its life. But the oneness of the world is only the product and reflection of the oneness of the completed human being. The teaching is realized in genuine life, wrote Buber, the life of the "central man." The central man adds no new element to teaching. Rather, he fulfills it in authentic, unified life, raising the conditioned into the unconditioned.

The emphasis on realization of unity of life as more important than any philosophical knowledge or religious belief, and the doctrine of the action that is performed with the whole being, play an increasingly significant role in Buber's philosophy from this time forth and enter into his interpretation of Hasidism and Judaism. Yet the teaching of the unity of the central person and the world is still "mystical" in a sense that Buber's mature thought is not.

At this period and immediately after it, Buber was working on his first attempt at a comprehensive and original philosophical statement—*Daniel: Dialogues of Realization.* In *Daniel,* the mystic's demand for a life lived in terms of the highest reality, and the existentialist's demand for self-realization and genuine existence, meet in spirit. Thus, it forms an important transition between Buber's early mysticism and his later existentialism of dialogue. It also shows explicitly why Buber had to pass through mysticism in order to reach his own independent relation to being and why he could not simply reject mysticism after he arrived at dialogue, as so many of the Protestant theologians who have adopted the "I-Thou" philosophy do. The reason Buber had to turn his back on his earlier mystical philosophy is an existential one. He recognized that through this philosophy he had tried to attain unity at the cost of denying his life experience. Yet mysticism bequeathed to Buber a glimpse of an essential reality that had to be realized in the fragmentariness of existence. As Buber wrote in "The Altar" (1914), "We cannot penetrate behind the manifold to find living unity. But we can create living unity out of the manifold." This is clearly *panentheism,* in which existence is only potentially holy and needs to be hallowed, and not *pantheism,* in which the world is seen as already holy. It is life and world affirming rather than life denying. It is the qualified nondualism of the One becoming the many and the many returning to the One rather than a simple proclamation of the identity of the Self with Being as such.

Mysticism gave Buber a new approach to reality in which his heart could break through from the mechanization, superficiality, and indirectness of that period to the immediacy of spiritual life. But it also served to remove Buber into an ecstasy in which he no longer heard the call of the immediate hour. What was problematic was not the mystical experience itself but the interpretation of it and the effect of this interpretation on his life.

> Now from my own unforgettable experience I know well that there is a state in which the bonds of the personal nature of life seem to have fallen away from us and we experience undivided unity. But I do not know—what the soul willingly imagines and indeed is bound to imagine (mine too once did)—that in this I

had attained to a union with the primal being or the godhead. That is an exaggeration no longer permitted to the responsible understanding.

What *is* permitted to the responsible understanding, Buber asserted, is the recognition of an undifferentiated prepersonal unity hidden beneath all personal change, though even this is not *above* the creaturely situation but *beneath* it. In experiencing this unity of one's own basic self, one naturally tends to see it as unity in general for one is no longer aware of any reality other than oneself. The consequence of this compelling but "irresponsible" interpretation is the duality that rips life asunder into the everyday creaturely life and the "deified" exalted hours. The experience of ecstasy leads the mystic to regard everyday life from then on as an obstacle or at best a mere means for recapturing the moment of ecstasy. It is precisely this "exalted form of being untrue," as Buber later called it, that characterized Buber's own ecstasy and the divided life it produced:

> In my earlier years the "religious" was for me the exception. There were hours that were taken out of the course of things. From somewhere or other the firm crust of everyday was pierced. Then the reliable permanence of appearances broke down; the attack which took place burst its law asunder. "Religious experience" was the experience of an otherness which did not fit into the context of life. It could begin with something customary, with consideration of some familiar object, but which then became unexpectedly mysterious and uncanny, finally lighting a way into the lightning-pierced darkness of the mystery itself. But also, without any intermediate state, time could be torn apart—first the world's firm structure, then the still firmer self-assurance flew apart and you were delivered to fullness. The "religious" lifted you out. Over there now lay the accustomed existence with its affairs, but here illumination and ecstasy and rapture held, without time or sequence. Thus your own being encompassed a life here and a life beyond, and there was no bond but the actual moment of the transition.

Buber did not attain his ecstasies through the regular practice of "meditation"—quiet sitting and concentration of mind and spirit on some word or image. "I never had anything to do with willed, 'pre-meditated' meditations," Buber wrote me. "As to meditations coming spontaneously, I knew them in earlier days, but never since my thought reached its maturity." Buber reached his mature understanding after he not only gave up the *hours* of mystical exaltation but also the *belief* that accompanied it, namely the belief "in a 'mystical' unification of the Self, identifying the depth of the individual self with the Self itself." "Perhaps the main point in my personal evolution was the rejecting of *this* mysticism too."

How resolutely Buber turned away from such an illegitimate division of life we can only understand in the context of his encounter with the First World War. But Buber's "conversion" did not mean, as some have thought, a rejection of mysticism *in toto*. On the contrary, much of mysticism remained with him and informed his lifetime of work on Hasidism and his own philosophy. Presence, presentness, immediacy, ineffability, a meaning that can be lived and confirmed but cannot be defined, the action that appears like nonaction because it is whole and does not interfere—all these accompanied Buber on the long road ahead.

For Buber at this time, mysticism and myth were connected. In a 1913 speech on "Myth and Judaism," Buber defined "myth" as a narrative of a corporeally real event perceived and presented as a divine, an absolute, event. Primitive man had a heightened awareness of the uniqueness of each event, and even modern man, in times of high tension and intense experience, feels the shackles of causal awareness fall off him and finds within himself that mythmaking faculty through which the world's processes are perceived as meaningful beyond causality, as the manifestation of a central purpose that can be grasped only by the ardent power of one's whole being. In the *zaddik*, the mythical hero becomes, for Buber, a modern image of the human. "He is... the man in whom transcendental responsibility has grown from an event of consciousness into organic existence. He is the true human being, the rightful subject of the act in which God wants to be known, loved, wanted." Basic to this mythical and modern image of man is the personal wholeness that leads to the spontaneous response rather than to conscious imitation. It is the spontaneity of the *zaddik's* existence that exercises above all the purifying and renewing influence, to which the conscious expression in words is only the accompaniment. The stories of the many *zaddikim* that Buber recounted were attempts on his part to make the mythical hero living today, to place before modern man an image of true human existence. For countless readers, Buber's legends and tales of the Hasidim have had just this effect.

Buber's understanding of the *zaddik* as the *true helper* was deepened through an experience that he had four or five years after he wrote *The Legend of the Baal-Shem*. He had emerged by that time from his self-imposed retirement to give his famous "Speeches on Judaism" to the Prague Bar Kochbans. At the end of the third of them, he went with some members of the Bar Kochba Association into a coffeehouse. "I like to follow the speech given before an audience, whose form allows no reply," remarked Buber when he related this incident, "with a conversation with a few in which person acts on person. In the latter I express my view in the dialogue with my partners through going into their objections and questions." They were discussing some theme of moral philosophy, when a well-built, middle-aged Jew of simple appearance came up to the table and greeted Buber. When Buber failed to recognize him, he introduced himself as M., the brother of a former steward of Buber's father. Buber invited him to sit with them, inquired about his life, and then turned back to the conversation with the young people. From time to time, Buber turned to him and urged him to say whether he had some particular wish.

His words punctuated by pauses, M. announced that he had a daughter, that he had a young man for his daughter, and that the man was a student of law who had passed the examinations with distinction. During the long pause that followed, Buber looked at him encouragingly, supposing that he would ask him to use his influence in some way on behalf of the presumptive son-in-law. Instead, to Buber's surprise, he asked, "Doctor, is he a steady man?" and then still further, "But, Doctor, does he also have a good head?" Feeling that he could not refuse to answer, Buber said that the young man must certainly be industrious and able and that he must also have something in his head, for he could not have succeeded by industry alone. But in reply to M.'s final question—" Doctor, should he now become a judge or a lawyer?"—Buber could give no advice at all. Then M. regarded him with a glance of almost melancholy renunciation and spoke in a tone composed partly of sorrow and partly of humility: "Doctor, you do not *want* to say—but I thank you for what you have said to me."

This humorous occurrence gave Buber a new and significant insight into the role of the *zaddik* that went beyond his own teaching of the perfected man who realizes God in the world. Now he understood more profoundly the image he had glimpsed in his childhood: the *zaddik's* function as a leader. Each person has an infinite sphere of responsibility, but there are persons who are hourly accosted by infinite responsibility in a special way. These are the leaders—not the rulers and statesmen who turn away from the individual, problematic, personal lives to deal with the external destiny of great communities but the true *zaddikim* who withstand the thousandfold-questioning glance of individual lives and give answer to the trembling mouth of the needy creature who time after time demands decision from them. The true *zaddik* is the man who constantly measures the depths of responsibility with the sounding lead of his words: "He is the helper in spirit, the teacher of meaning whom the world awaits evermore."

In relating this story, Buber did not in any way imply that he saw himself in the role of the *zaddik*. On the contrary, he explicitly contrasted himself with the *zaddik* even at the moment he attained a glimpse into his role:

> I, who am truly no zaddik, no one assured in God, rather a man endangered before God, a ·man wrestling ever anew for God's light, ever anew engulfed in God's abysses, nonetheless, when asked a trivial question and replying with a trivial answer, then experienced from within for the first time the true zaddik, questioned about revelations and replying in revelations. I experienced him in the fundamental relation of his soul to the world: in his responsibility.

"Endangered before God,... wrestling ever anew for God's light, ever anew engulfed in God's abysses," this portrait that Buber gave of himself when he was nearly forty probably continued to hold true of him for the almost half century that he had yet to live. It is, indeed, the very heart of the "narrow ridge" that he walked. Although his friend Franz Rosenzweig could refer to him jokingly as Reb. Martin of Heppenheim (his home in Germany for many years), Buber was never a *zaddik*. Yet the *zaddik* was without question for him an image of the human, and, in the years that he lived beyond this essay, he took on ever more powerfully the lines of the "true zaddik" he himself had described. He did not become a leader of a genuine community, but he withstood the thousandfold-questioning glance of countless sorely troubled persons and constantly measured the depths of responsibility with the "sounding lead" of his presence and his words.

◆ 4 ◆

Prewar Teachings of "Realization"

(1909-1913)

Buber took his first step toward full responsibility in his relationship to others precisely at the time of his encounter with M., in 1909 or shortly afterward, for it was then that he emerged from his five years of seclusion devoted to Hasidism to become the acknowledged leader of the young Jewish intellectuals and particularly the Young Zionists of central Europe. The occasion was the invitation to Buber to speak to the Zionist student association in Prague, which called itself the Bar Kochba Union, after the famous military leader of the Jewish rebellion against the Romans. The name was given to the group during the heroic era of Zionism that Herzl had ushered in, but the overture to Buber already signified the inadequacy of a merely external Zionism and heralded the entrance into a new period.

A truly momentous encounter took place here between this remarkable group of Young Zionists, many of whom later become influential figures in Zionist, Jewish, intellectual, or literary circles, and Martin Buber, who emerged from his self-imposed retirement with a stature and dignity that made men only ten years his junior look up to him as a leader and a sage. This return to activity on Buber's part in no way meant a turning away from Hasidism. On the contrary, it was precisely through his deep immersion in Hasidism that he was able to make true the words that he wrote in his letter of 1905—that if he *should* return to activity in the Zionist movement it would be with something more significant and profound to say than the catchwords he had been uttering during his early years in the movement. The Prague Bar

Kochbans, for their part, invited Buber not merely as the man who had been active in the movement five years before, but as the well-known author of *The Tales of Rabbi Nachman* and *The Legend of the Baal-Shem*—the man who asserted that no renaissance of Judaism could take place that did not bear in it some elements of Hasidism.

The heroic epoch of the Prague Bar Kochbans was characterized by the will to make the impossible possible, a new spirit that scorned all difficulties and that willed from the first to bring Jewishness to realization and to make one's personal and one's political life a single unity. Buber and Berthold Feiwel had already spoken before the Prague Bar Kochbans in 1903 on the "Jewish Renaissance," and it was then that Buber first came into contact with his lifelong friend Hugo Bergmann, later one of Israel's most eminent philosophers and moral leaders. The very striving for cultural Zionism that Buber had championed characterized the position of the Bar Kochbans within the total Zionist organization and led them to a bitter fight with the bourgeois Zionists and the liberals, who were closer to assimilation. Bar Kochba represented the democratic and progressive direction, and it was no accident that its delegate to the 1903 Zionist Congress was Martin Buber, one of the leaders of the Democratic Fraction.

After Herzl's death in 1904, the heroic Zionist activity subsided, but the "practical" as opposed to the "political" Zionists were also few, and the Prague Bar Kochbans suffered the stagnation that followed from espousing a Zionism without content. This situation led to the invitation to Buber. Buber's thought and personality ushered in a new era for the Prague Bar Kochbans and, radiating out from there, for central European Zionist youth in general. The Prague Bar Kochbans became Buber's community, and from it emerged some of Buber's most influential disciples and lasting friends, men such as Hugo Bergmann, Max Brod, Robert and Felix Weltsch, and Hans Kohn. The result was that the Bar Kochba in this era proved itself a much deeper and more revolutionary element in Zionism than in its heroic epoch.

In a letter of November 14, 1908, Leo Hermann had written to Buber telling him of the isolation in Prague between German and Czech, between German and Jew, and asking him how the Western Jew was to make his own that part of the Jewish being that he did not possess. Buber had replied warmly, and out of their exchange of letters both the title and the content of his talk developed. Buber arrived unexpectedly ahead of time the night before the festive evening. As a result, his first meeting with the Young Zionists took place in walks around the city and in informal talks. Writing more than half a century later, Robert Weltsch declared that of all the many times that they showed distinguished visitors through the streets of historic Prague, it was the walking tour with Martin and Paula Buber that remained foremost in his mind. No other visitors had showed so much genuine understanding and informed knowledge of the architectonic and artistic splendors of the city, or felt so deeply its magic and mystery. Buber discovered similarities between Florence and Prague, and from this time on remained closely tied to Prague until the old Jewish Prague disappeared.

The members of the Bar Kochba sat together with Buber in a small circle, and he spoke to them for the first time of his position regarding Jewishness and Zionism. "Then we knew," said Leo Hermann, "that he would help us further on our way." From that time on, they looked on Buber as a man of incontestable authority. Buber, too, found this meeting of great importance; here there existed young people, he realized, who could show once again that there is a new beginning and new hope.

At the end of March 1910, Buber was in Vienna and then returned to Prague with Paula. Again the Bar Kochbans walked with them in the old city of Prague, along the old city circle and the bridge over the famous Prague castle, the Hradshin, until, as they stood above, the lights sprang up on the dark city and along the Moldau. When they returned, the others were already waiting in a local union of the Bar Kochba. Buber opened the discussion with a continuation of the conversation that had been begun above the Hradshin. He spoke about the meaning of the concept "blood," about the specific Jewish characteristics, the resolution of one's personal "Jewish question," the relationship of the Western Jews to Palestine, the hope of a great religious upheaval that alone could bring renewal for the Western Jews, too. To the question of one woman as to whether he could instruct them in a method of self-liberation, he refused to reply, but to the question whether in the last analysis one really had to accept Palestine as the only way, he answered with a clear "Yes."

The next day in the Jewish council house, Buber delivered a public lecture on "Judaism and Mankind." He formulated clearly and strongly the answer to the questions on which the discussion of the evening before had centered: the demand for unity born out of one's own inner division and the redemption from it.

Buber's distinguished face above the lectern, with its impressive composure; his brown eyes, often prophetically flashing; and the clear words that he drew forth from a rich treasury of images, as if used for the first time—all these worked together to make of his speech an address to be listened and responded to, not only on an intellectual level but with one's whole being. The applause that broke out lasted until the last guests had left the hall. After the Bubers left, the Bar Kochbans spent the whole afternoon discussing Buber and his speech. "It was remarkable," says Hermann, "that almost every one of us remembered a large part of the speech almost word for word and that we felt as if it had penetrated our blood."

The revolutionary element in Buber's "Three Speeches" (the 1909–1911 first triad of Buber's *Speeches on Judaism,* originally delivered to the Prague Bar Kochbans) is one that today we might call "existentialist," for it turned the "Jewish question" from an abstract question about whether Jews are to be considered members of a race, nation, or common creed to that of the deepest personal meaning of Judaism to the Jew himself. The Western Jew is a divided person because his community of land, speech, and custom is different from his community of blood. We are, said Buber, in a more pregnant sense than any other civilized people, a mixture. But we want to be not the slaves but the masters of this mixture. The choice means a decision about which shall be the ruling element and which the ruled in us. When out of deep self-knowledge we shall have said "Yes" to our whole Jewish existence, then we shall no longer feel ourselves as individuals but as a people, for each will feel the people in himself. My soul is not with my people; rather, my people *is* my soul.

"When I was a child," Buber concluded, "I read an old Jewish saying that I could not understand...: 'Before the gates of Rome sits a leprous beggar and waits. He is the Messiah.' Then I went to an old man and asked him: 'For what does he wait?' And the old man answered me something that... only much later I learned to understand. He said: 'For you!'"

Of all the doctrines that Buber ever enunciated, this one of the "blood" is perhaps the most problematic and the most difficult to comprehend. Despite his clear statement that the Jewish people, more than any other, is a mixture, Buber's concept of "the community of the blood" has often been identified retrospectively with the type of racial mysticism prevalent in Germany at the time and later incorporated in cruder form into the myths of Nazism. To some, this judgment may seem to be confirmed by the fact that Alfred Rosenberg and his lawyer cited Buber at the Nuremburg trials as evidence that the Nazi philosophy was part of a *Zeitgeist* that had no necessary connection with anti-Semitism. There is, indeed, an element of biological vitalism and irrationalism in this concept of the "blood" that is bound to disquiet those who have lived through the Nazi era. But the differences, for all this, are more important than the similarities. Buber was not emphasizing the *superiority* of one people over another but the precious uniqueness of each. Buber wanted to know the unique potentialities and tasks of the Jewish people from within. The Nazis, and the racial theorists who preceded them, compared and contrasted from without. "Ignorance and distortion are... the pillars of the modern race psychology treatment of the Jewish people," Buber wrote in 1916.

What Buber really meant by "blood" was illustrated by a comment he made to his former teacher, the German Jewish philosopher Georg Simmel, around 1909. Simmel affirmed the perseverance of the Jewish *spirit* as highly worth striving for. Whereupon Buber remarked, "But how can you conceive of perseverance of a particular spirit without a biological foundation?" Simmel was thinking as a *Luftmensch,* the intellectual Jew of the Diaspora, who meant perhaps a certain quality of spirit but not a total existence. Buber was thinking, in contrast, of a full Jewish existence lived by Jews together in organic community. In a comment on this conversation half a century later, Buber added, "If this biological foundation is given and the spirit is now one that wants to be realized in the fullness of public life, then one must give it... the possibility of determining its own social and political life forms." Thus, as even Alfred Rosenberg recognized in however grotesque and distorted a form, there was an integral connection between Buber's concept of "blood" and his Zionism." By "blood," he meant nothing more nor less than the link of the generations, and by Zionism he meant not political action and diplomatic negotiations, but the task of building organic community on the land.

The process of concentrating himself that Buber went through in his period of retirement clearly had as its corollary a facing of his own inner duality in a way that he had not before. His call to his fellow Jews was a call that he himself had answered. "It does not become us," he wrote, "to evade the deep reality of our existence, and there will be no salvation for us before we have confronted it and stood our ground before it." What is in question here, Buber stated, is not basically an *ethnic,* but a *human,* question. The Jew may experience a specially heightened inner duality because of the disparity between the community of the generations and the community of his immediate environment, but all persons know the inner duality that Buber knew in his own soul and strove to overcome.

If in 1903 Buber proclaimed evolution as *the* modern idea, at the end of 1910—in the third of his three *Speeches on Judaism*—Buber attacked it unconditionally. The concept of evolution that dominates the typical man of this time, he said, is the concept of gradual change coming from the working together of many little causes. "When I speak of renewal," Buber said, "I am aware that I am leaving the ground of this age and am entering that of a new, coming one. For I mean by renewal nothing at all gradual... but something sudden and enormous, ... no continuation and betterment, but radical turning and transformation. Indeed, just as I believe that in the life of an individual man there can be a moment of elemental revolution, a crisis and shattering and a new becoming from the roots to all the branches of existence, just so I believe in it for the life of Judaism." Thus, the teaching of renewal that Buber realized in his own life when he turned from active Zionism to the re-creation of Hasidism, he now applied to the Jewish people as a whole.

If Buber was critical of the inadequacy of Nietzsche, Ahad Ha'am, and his own early teachings, he was still more critical of the claim of liberal and Reform Judaism to be a renewal of Judaism. Rationalization of the faith, simplification of the dogma, relaxing of the rituals—all this is negation, nothing but negation! This is not a renewal of Judaism but its continuation in an easier, more elegant, more European, salonlike form. The prophets certainly spoke of the insignificance of all ceremonies, but not in order to make the religious life easier. They sought rather to make it more difficult, to make it genuine and whole, to proclaim the holiness of the *deed*. Prophetic Judaism demanded that man live unconditionally, that he be whole at every hour and in all things, and that he *realize* his feelings of God at all times. This meant the realization of three interrelated tendencies—the striving for unity, for the deed, and for the future. These tendencies find their strongest expression in messianism—the deepest original idea of Judaism. In messianism, the relativity of a far time is transformed into the absolute of the fullness of time. Here, for the first time, the Absolute was proclaimed as the goal—the goal in mankind and to be realized through it. This unconditional demand Buber tried to renew in his time for every Jew who was willing to listen and respond as a Jew. "We stand," Buber proclaimed,

> in a moment of the greatest tension and of ultimate decision, in a moment with a double face—one looking toward death, the other toward life. The renewal of Judaism means to put aside the dualism between our absolute and our relative life in order that the fight for fulfillment may grasp the whole people, that the idea of reality may penetrate everyday, *that the spirit may enter into life!* Only then when Judaism extends itself like a hand and seizes every Jew by the hair of his head and bears him in the storm between heaven and earth toward Jerusalem will the Jewish people become ripe to build itself a new destiny.

What is at stake here is not the destiny of the Jewish people alone, Buber asserted, but a new world-feeling to be brought to mankind. The formation of this new world-feeling and the renewal of Judaism are two sides of *one* event. The basic tendencies of Judaism—the striving for unity, deed, and future—are the elements out of which a new world will be constructed. "And so our soul's deepest humanity and our soul's deepest Judaism mean and will the same thing."

In his 1910 semester report on the activities of the Prague Bar Kochbans, Oskar Epstein said of Buber's third speech, "Judaism and Mankind," that it was of "surpassing significance for the spiritual development of the Union."

> Buber illuminated the center of the question like a flash of lightning. He said to us simply what we wanted and longed for from our deepest hearts.... Not only new, valuable knowledge, but the holy seriousness and the deep yearning for truth in Buber's words has powerfully influenced the spirit of the Union and helped to mold it. We can also say rightly that the fact that the Union has become dear to a man like Martin Buber can fill us with satisfaction and justified pride.

One of the ways in which Buber himself tried to "prepare a highway for the Lord" in the desert of the Diaspora was the attempt to establish a College of Judaism in Germany. The interchange on this subject between Buber and his friend the Viennese poet and playwright Richard Beer-Hofmann was a significant event in itself. Early in April 1913, Beer-Hofmann wrote a letter to Buber expressing in all frankness his fear that the proposed college would expose

Jews still more cruelly than they already were to the anti-Semitism of the time. Buber's reply to Beer-Hofmann gives us a glimpse in rare depth not merely into the philosopher and Jewish thinker but into the man. It anticipates the Buber who twenty years later was to walk on the stage as leader of the spiritual battle of the German Jews against Nazism.

> You are right: all that we Jews do takes place on a stage. But what is fundamentally wrong is that for so long we have let this fact determine our doing and our not doing. The great man too is looked at by the world; if he pays any attention to it, his greatness is threatened in its heart. It is not possible for him to live at one and the same time from his power and from his image—no matter whether it is his image in the eyes of his friends or of his enemies. If God looks at me, I cannot show myself more gently to his glance than when I do not concern myself about it, and if Satan looks at me, I cannot put his glance more fully to shame than when I do not concern myself about it.

In his second series of talks, *Speeches on Judaism,* which he gave at the invitation of the Prague Bar Kochbans between 1913 and 1915, Buber spoke of the three stages of the realization of God that can be distinguished in Jewish religiousness. In the first, the biblical stage, realization of God was conceived as an *imitatio Dei.* In the second, the Talmudic stage, the realization of God was conceived as an enhancing of his reality. In the third, the Kabbalistic, stage, realization of God was raised to the working of man's action on the fate of God. All three stages, asserted Buber, are united in the conception of the absolute value of the human deed. The human community is an important work that awaits us; a chaos that we must order, a diaspora that we must gather, a conflict that we must resolve. But we can do this only if each one of us in his place, in the natural realm of his life together with men, does the right, the uniting, the shaping, because God does not want to be believed in, discussed, or defended by man—he wants to be *realized.* From this point onward, Buber uses the term *teshura,* turning to God with one's whole existence, for the renewing revolution in the course of existence.

A moving witness to the influence of Buber's *Speeches on Judaism* over that generation of Jews came thirty years later from Gershom Scholem, the distinguished founder of the science of Jewish mysticism and, at the end of Buber's life, the harshest critic of his interpretations of Hasidism. Around 1913, Buber had immense influence on Jewish youth circles in Germany and Austria, as Scholem testified in an appraisal written on Buber's seventy-fifth birthday.

> We secondary school and university students looked for a way....
> Our sources were few: we knew no Hebrew: the first-hand
> sources were thus closed to us and the way to them seemed very

long. We looked for an interpreter of the phenomenon of Judaism and its heritage... The voice speaking from his books was promising, demanding, fascinating, uncovering hidden life beneath the frozen official forms, uncovering hidden treasures, if only we knew how to get in... He demanded attachment to and identification with the core of the people as he understood it, demanded of the youth that they be an additional link in the chain of hidden life, that they be heirs to a sublime and hidden tradition of revolt and uprising.

Particularly attractive to the young Jews of that time, said Scholem, was the strong individualistic, personal, and even anarchic note that characterizes the "Three Speeches." More than any other spokesman of Zionism, Buber went to the heart of the problems of the Jew as an individual. The basic conviction of Buber's Zionism was that the decision of every single individual Jew, made in the depths of his heart, decides the fate of the Jewish nation, prior to all political and social facts and slogans. When the destiny of the Zionist movement depended upon its *moral* stance, Buber's words had widespread influence. Already in 1913, Gustav Landauer called Buber "the ambassador of Judaism to the nations."

"I know of no other book about Judaism during those years that even approaches the influence" of Buber's *Speeches on Judaism,* Scholem wrote after Buber's death, in a comprehensive essay on Buber's conception of Judaism. No one performed greater service than Buber in making visible again precisely those traits in Judaism that were most lacking, indeed, that were actively rejected in nineteenth-century Judaism—mysticism and myth. Buber's work on the Hasidic tradition moved between these poles of mysticism and myth. "Buber was a great listener. Many voices pressed toward him, among them ones which had become entirely incomprehensible to the generations before him, voices whose call moved him deeply." "Buber was the first Jewish thinker," wrote Scholem, "who saw in mysticism a basic trait and continuing strain of Judaism."

The tremendous appeal of *Speeches on Judaism* was not so much a mystical as an existential one—their personal appeal of the speeches to the Jew as an individual to decide to join his people—and it was precisely this existential appeal that spread from Bohemia to Galicia to Hungary. "Buber's real influence started with the *Speeches,*" writes Ernst Simon. Buber was a middleman addressing others who also stood between Eastern and Western Jewry, between the masses of traditional Jews and deteriorating Judaism, between a continuous heritage and the loss of all traditional values. Members of the Bar Kochba Union in Prague and the youth movement of Hashomer Hatzair in Galicia became Buber's ardent followers because he offered them direction at a time when they found themselves in the midst of three crises: the European crisis of the approaching world war, the crisis of the Jewish nation in the face of the pogroms of Eastern Europe and the intermarriage and assimilation of the West, and the crisis of the modern personality, which even then lacked guidance and a definite way of life. Only through the war, however, was the generation to which the "Three Speeches" were addressed confronted by reality.

As if in farewell to the Buber of *Speeches on Judaism,* in 1925 Buber wrote to the Zionist activist Sigmund Kaznelson:

> Are you more faithful to the Buber of the "Three Speeches" than I am? I am not even permitted to be faithful to "me," and I only know this one thing—that for the whole of my life I do not ever run the danger of being unfaithful—that is to change over from the "lonely beggars" to the secure and safe ones.

In the course of his evaluation of Buber's impact on the young men of that period, Gershom Scholem pointed out that Buber's book *Daniel* (1913) supplied the philosophical background for the emphasis on "realization" in *Speeches on Judaism. Daniel* is in no sense a Jewish work, much less a Zionist one. Yet the connection between this first work of general philosophy on Buber's part and his philosophy of Judaism is unmistakable. In 1911, Buber read parts of the unpublished manuscript of *Daniel* to the students of the Bar Kochba Union in Prague. The contrast between "orienting" and "realizing" that stands at the heart of *Daniel* almost had a more lasting effect on the worldview of the Bar Kochbans of that time than did Buber's Jewish writings. There is little in *Daniel* to make the reader feel that the author is a Jew. Yet Buber's devoted study of Hasidism and his writings on Judaism influenced *Daniel* just as *Daniel* influenced the later *Speeches on Judaism.* Both the *Speeches on Judaism* and *Daniel* deal with the problems of decision and of the unity which is man's task, as well as with the idea of the deed and the future.

Daniel was written in Buber's second period of fame, Ernst Simon points out, his first being the period of *The Tales of Rabbi Nachman* and *The Legend of the Baal-Shem.* From this point onward, Buber's influence developed in two separate streams, which had a common origin but were distinct along most of the way—that of his Jewish writings and that of his general philosophy. *Daniel* is the real fountainhead of the second stream, not only anticipating the later developments of Buber's philosophy of dialogue but also many developments in existentialism in general. *Daniel* was a hard-won and crucial step toward the philosophy of dialogue through which, in its many ramifications, Buber was to exercise his most profound, widespread, and lasting influence.

The significance of *Daniel* is best comprehended in the formula that Buber himself used so often in the book—"holy insecurity." Along with the "narrow ridge," "holy insecurity" remained the most important single motif in Buber's writings throughout his more than sixty years of productivity. Like Kierkegaard's *Angst,* what is significant about Buber's "holy insecurity" is not

the insecurity itself but the response to it: the willingness to meet it in openness and trust and to answer it with one's life, as opposed to all attempts to
guard oneself from it or to reduce it to manageable proportions.

One event that illuminates Buber's concern with insecurity was his
experience with two of his fellow pupils in the Polish gymnasium. When
Buber was twelve years old, one autumn was spoiled for the pupils by inces-
sant rain. Instead of rushing to the square outside to play during the recess-
es, they had to sit at their benches. At this time, two of the boys undertook
to entertain the other boys as mimics, with clownlike agility, trying their best
to remain straight-faced to avoid being seen by the master. After a while,
however, this game took on an unmistakably sexual character, and now the
faces of the two boys looked to Martin like the faces of the damned souls
being tormented in hell, which his Catholic schoolmates had described to
Buber as if they were experts on the subject. The other boys looked on but
said nothing to one another about these occurrences. About two weeks after
the game had taken on this character, the master called the young Buber to
his office.

"Tell me what you know of what those boys have been doing," he said
with the gentle friendliness that the pupils knew to be an essential part of his
nature.

"I know nothing!" Martin screamed.

The master spoke again, as gently as before. "We know you well," he
said. "You are a good child—you will help us."

"Help? Help whom?" the young Buber wanted to reply. But instead he
stared silently at the director. Finally, a great weeping overcame him such as
he had never experienced before, and he was led away almost unconscious.
Yet a few hours later, when he recalled at home the last look of the director,
it was not a gentle, but a frightened, one.

He was kept at home for a few days, and then he returned to school.
When he came into the classroom, he found that the bench where the two
boys had always sat was empty. It remained empty until the end of the
school year.

It was many years before Buber understood the full ethical implications
of this event and could formulate the lesson that it taught him: that the true
norm commands not our obedience but ourselves. But even at that time he
began to realize "the problematic relation between maxim and situation"—
the shattering of the security that the simple childhood norms of obedience
to authority had given him until then. When he wanted to shout, "Help? Help
whom?," he was aware, as the master was not, of the suffering of the two
boys and of the impossibility of his accepting the bribe of being "a good
child" who "will help us" in return for betraying them. He also must have
known the confusion and pain that he and the other boys experienced, looking on without speaking, vicariously taking part in something that they
would not have dared to do themselves. Most importantly of all, he began to

realize at that moment the choice that had to be made between finding security in the "once-and-for-all" of general moral norms—to be a good child, obeying authority—and living with the insecurity of being open and responding to the unique and irreducible situation to which no general categories could ever do justice. With this convulsion of his childhood, Buber began the long series of lessons that led him to understand what it meant to stand one's ground before the situation in openness and strength and to respond to it with trust. An important milestone on this road was *Daniel*.

Each of *Daniel's* five "Dialogues on Realization" has its jumping-off point in a particular setting in which Daniel and one of his friends (a different one in each dialogue) happen to be together. What develops from this conversation in every case is discussion revolving around one particular existential problem. Thus, the dialogue in the mountains deals with personal direction, the dialogue above the city with reality, the dialogue in the garden with meaning, the dialogue after the theater with polarity, and the dialogue by the sea with unity. If we are to retain our focus on the events and meetings that were the matrix of Buber's thought, however, we shall have to approach *Daniel* with a very different ordering: the progression from ecstasy and the isolated "I" through the experience of the abyss to holy insecurity and "inclusion." These are the headings under which we may group the personal experiences that Buber incorporated in *Daniel*.

The sea, the night, and the abyss are various symbols of the threat of the infinite that was so basic in Buber's experience and in his thought. Most often, it is the sea that enters these dialogues as a symbol of an incomprehensible infinity that threatens man's existence, or a motherly infinite with which man desires to become one. From day to day, the question mounts in Daniel: What sort of a sea is it on which we voyage, what sort of a sea is it that has given birth to us, what is the holy sea that bears life and death in its hands?

Reinold's experience of the abyss in the third dialogue is clearly a continuation of many motifs in Buber's earlier writings—the individual's hopeless solitude and eternal distance from the world, the schism between thought and action, life and spirit, the abysses of being that the creative man must face, and the universal inner duality of man. The collapse of the secure and harmonious world of childhood comes sooner or later to every person and the abyss at his feet suddenly becomes visible. "All religious reality," Buber was to state many years later, "... comes when our existence between birth and death becomes incomprehensible and uncanny, when all security is shattered through the mystery."

In the fifth dialogue of *Daniel*, the death of Elias leads Lukas to a realization that life and death do not alternate with each other but lie in an endless embrace. Lukas realizes that it is foolish to limit death to any particular moments of ceasing to be or of transformation. It is an ever-present force and the mother of being. Out of this realization is born for him the holy insecurity: "This certitude was not unholy; it was, indeed, no feeling of being secure in any certainty but the unarmed trust in the infinite." Now that he no longer sees life as handing him to death like a torch that the hand touches only to fling it onward, he is driven to penetrate behind life and death into the infinite that bears them both.

Daniel, in turn, tells Lukas, of an event out of his own youth. What he describes is the response that Buber himself had at the age of seventeen, when his uncle was killed by a fall from a horse while the horrified boy looked on. "Death laid itself about my neck like a lasso," wrote Buber/Daniel. He felt the presence of death in the world to be his own sin, for which he had to do penance. His overwhelming sense of isolation prevented him from sleeping, and his disgust with living prevented him from eating. His family did not understand him, and, supported by friends and physicians, they dismissed what he was going through as a problem of adolescence. Only his father met him with a calm, collected glance so strong that it reached his heart, sealed off from all other perceptions. His father then took matters into his hands and sent the boy off alone into a secluded mountain place. This action saved the young Buber and resulted in an experience so profound that he wrote at thirty-four that he believed that images of the time he lived through then would return to him in his dying hour. Stripped clean of his foolishness, he no longer lost himself in penance but won himself through despair. "For despair... is the highest of God's messengers; it trains us to be spirits that can create and decide." Here, in contrast to "The Revelation," it was the divided person himself who overcame the abyss between himself and the world, by overcoming the abyss within himself. When his body became united, the world became one for him. Yet the deep union that he now experienced from life to death, from the living to the dead, was a product of his inner unity rather than of any meeting with the world.

At that moment, Buber claimed, the teaching, the one thing needful, came to him and remained with him so that he sensed its presence in all his wanderings. Yet he was not really aware of it until a later time, when, as a result of one moment joining itself to another, he reached the final level of the teaching. Walking along the highway on a gloomy morning, he saw a piece of mica lying on the ground, lifted it up, and looked at it for a long time until the light caught in the stone dispelled the gloom of the day. When he raised his eyes from the mica, he realized that, while he was looking at the stone, it and his "I" had been one, beyond all consciousness of "subject" and "object." Closing his eyes, he gathered in his strength, bound himself with his object, and raised the mica into the kingdom of the existing. "There," Buber wrote, "I first felt: I; there I first was I." He regarded his earlier unity as the marble statue might perceive the block of stone out of which it was chiseled; it had been the undifferentiated, the amorphous, but his "I" was now unification. This unity cannot be found but only created—by him who realizes the unity of the world in the unity of his soul.

"Holy insecurity" was, for Buber, the decisive transition between his earlier responses to the threat of infinity—his attempts to find unity either apart from or with the world—and the existential thrust of his philosophy of dialogue, which does not demand either continuity or unity but accepts the "graciousness" of the coming of our meeting with the Thou (for it cannot be willed) and the "solemn sadness" of its going (for it cannot be held on to). Buber began, as we have seen, with a whirl of possibilities that threatened to overwhelm him. He did not succumb to the temptation to dissipate his energies by realizing them all, but neither did he simply reject them, for "in the world of mankind there is no other beginning than reality." Buber's greatness lay in his insistence on starting with the chaos as the reality given to him *and* on transforming this chaos through the discovery of direction. There are men, says Daniel in the fourth dialogue, "in whom the existence which has not been worked out longs so strongly for fulfillment that no illusion lasts for them. They shatter on their contradiction, *or* it becomes creative in them."

Although the "between" is not reached in *Daniel* as a whole, any more than in the specific experience with the fragment of mica, it is so far anticipated that in the fourth dialogue, "On Polarity," Buber first uses the term "inclusion" (*Umfassung*) in the sense that later became central to his philosophy. Nor is "inclusion" present only as an idea but, rather, as a series of events and meeting—Buber's relation to nature, to people, to drama, and to love.

Buber's experience of inclusion in relation to nature is perhaps the most consistent thread in his entire philosophy. The complete intertwining of sensory and spiritual spontaneity out of the undivided depth of the soul was characteristic of Buber's personality. Already as a child left to himself, his intensive life experience and an elemental openness to the world supplemented and contended with each other. In the first dialogue, Buber has Daniel distinguish between trying to know a stone pine through comparison and contrast, categories and classifications, and knowing the truth of its being "with all your directed power" so that you "receive the tree, surrender yourself to it."

> Until you feel its bark as your skin and the springing forth of a branch from the trunk like the striving in your muscles; until your feet cleave and grope like roots and your skull arches itself like a light-heavy crown; until you recognize your children in the soft blue cones...

Yet Daniel remains enraptured by the *inner* and does not really reach the between: the tree "is transplanted out of the earth of space into the earth of the soul." From being just a tree among trees, it had become for him "the tree of life."

A fuller understanding of inclusion is found in the original Preface to *Daniel,* which Buber omitted from later editions yet included in his

"Autobiographical Fragments." In this preface, Buber first used the word "dialogue" not in the literary and dramatic sense of *Daniel,* most of the "dialogues" of which are really monologues, but in his later sense of a meeting with the other in which one retains one's uniqueness yet experiences the relationship from the side of the other as well as one's own.

He writes there of a descent during which he had to utilize, without stopping, the late light of a dying day; he stood on the edge of a meadow, now sure of the safe path, and let the twilight settle upon him. Not needing a support, yet wishing to find a fixed point for his lingering, he pressed his stick against the trunk of an oak tree. Then he felt his contact with the tree both from his own side, where he held the stick, and from the other, where the stick touched the bark. "At that time, dialogue appeared to me; for the speech of man is like that stick," Buber concluded his original preface to *Daniel.*

Daniel represents a clear continuation of Buber's early interpretation of Hasidism in its emphasis on the immanence of God not as an accomplished fact but as a task. The presence of God must be actualized through our every action. The image of the realizing man in *Daniel,* who "wants only to live this here... so completely that it becomes for him reality and message," can be identified with Buber's 1908 image of the Hasid, for whom the character of the action is determined by its dedication, the man who is at home in the world without any special protection and greets God's messengers as trusted friends. The realizing man, too, knows "summons and sending,"receiving what befalls him as a message and doing what is necessary for him as a commission and a demonstration. But he can also be identified with the perfected man of "The Teaching of the Tao," who purifies the world through purifying himself, who is helpful to others through unifying himself, and who renews creation through true action, or "nonaction," the working of the whole being. In "The Teaching of the Tao," as in *Daniel,* the teaching means the realization of unity in genuine fulfilled life, lifting the conditioned into the unconditioned by allowing all that is scattered, fleeting, and fragmentary to grow together to a unity. *Daniel* attempts to move away from the unity of ecstasy, above the world, toward the unity of existence that is brought about through the inclusion of one's day-by-day life. Yet far from completely rejecting mysticism, Buber explicitly fused it with his existentialism. The motto that Buber set above *Daniel* in the first edition, and later left off, was a sentence from the medieval theologian Scotus Eriugena: "Deus in creature mirabili et ineffabili modo creatur." In a wonderful and inexpressible way, God is created in his creatures.

The fourth dialogue of *Daniel,* "On Polarity, Dialogue after the Theater," leaves us with the question of how the word becomes speech and speech becomes event, of how drama relates to the theater. Buber did not attain full clarity on this subject until after he had broken through to his "I-Thou" philosophy. But an important element in Buber's developing understanding of the relation between drama and theater was the work that he did in advising and directing experimental theater productions, first in Hellerau and later in Düsseldorf. This work extended from 1912 or earlier, through 1920 or later.

In 1913, Emil Strauss and Martin Buber of the "Thursday Society," Jakob Hegner (later famous as the publisher of Jakob Hegner Verlag), and the great French dramatist Paul Claudel founded a Hellerau Dramatic Union for the production of epic dramatic works. Buber took an active part in the preparation of the festival of plays that celebrated the opening of the Hellerau Playhouse. This festival began in 1913 with a production of Claudel's mystery play *Verkündigung* (The Annunciation), translated by Jakob Hegner from the original *L'Announce faite à Marie*. "The Space Problem of the Stage," the essay that Buber wrote in 1913 for the "Claudel Program Book," is even today a radical approach to the theater and one that anticipates Buber's philosophy of dialogue and still more his later philosophical anthropology, with its emphasis on the two primal movements of "distancing" and "relating."

Under the direction of Louise Dumont, the Düsseldorf Playhouse worked in the 1910s and 1920s toward becoming a German "theater of culture." It edited the periodical *Masken* and worked closely with Gustav Landauer and other creative figures in Germany. Buber took part in the development of the Düsseldorf Playhouse, as he had in the Hellerau experimental theater, and it was in *Masken* in 1925 that Buber published his mature statement "Drama and the Theater." The road to *I and Thou* is in part identical with Buber's deepening understanding of the relation between drama and theater.

Buber's preoccupation with drama, "inclusion," and distance and relation at this period was not the only thing that led into his philosophy of dialogue. His concern with direction in the first dialogue of *Daniel* both continued and presaged his lifelong emphasis upon combining passion and direction, turning to God with all the strength of the "evil" urge. It also presaged Buber's important later doctrine of personal direction as one's unique path to God, through which one fulfills the task to which one is called in one's creation. Direction is neither destiny nor predestination. It is discovered through openness to the seemingly chance, ever-new, present situation. Here is its relation to holy insecurity and to inclusion. For direction is not some fixed goal that excludes the other, but a pointing: "It does not know where north is; rather its north is there where it points."

Only the combination of direction with polarity led Buber to Daniel's full teaching of realized unity. This is not the polarity of good and evil or of any external valuation, but of being and counterbeing—"the free polarity of the human spirit." In human life, as in drama, all high excitement has its origin in a polarity which is to be lived, realized. Polarity as task and realization is the positive content of the holy insecurity, which is attained after the discovery of the abyss. Therefore, one must love danger, or one has no security in the world, but one has direction and meaning and with them God, the risking God, who is near at all times.

The statement at the end of the third dialogue—"You must descend ever anew into the transforming abyss, risk your soul ever anew, ever anew dedicated to the holy insecurity"—would hold good for all of Buber's thought from this time on. But the earlier statement in this same dialogue— that "God cannot realize himself in man otherwise than as the innermost presence of a life-experience, and... therefore it is not the same, but ever the new, the uttermost, the god of this life-experience"—would not. "This is the kingdom of God," Daniel says to Reinold, "the kingdom of danger and of risk, of eternal beginning and of eternal becoming, of opened spirit and of deep realization, the kingdom of holy insecurity." Buber later rejected this teaching as still belonging to the "easy word." Yet much in *Daniel* was seminal for Buber's later thought.

The essay that more than any other stands as the transitional stage between *Daniel* and *I and Thou* is "With a Monist" (1914). In "With a Monist," we again find the realizing of *Daniel,* the person who sees reality not as a fixed condition but as a greatness that can be enhanced, the person who does not want to remove the world of the senses but wants to intensify it, the person who establishes unity in the world of experienced unity, for "unity is not a property of the world but its task." Now, however, the orienting and realizing aspects of life no longer apply merely to the person himself but to that person's relation to what meets him. The "I" that exists through the "shoreless becoming of the deed" is no isolated self. On the contrary, it is the self that comes into being in its mutual contact with the unique reality that it meets. The world is no longer displaced into the soul, as Daniel did with the stone pine and the piece of mica. It is *met* in its incomprehensible, but nonetheless encounterable, otherness. I give reality to my world "by bending over the experienced thing with fervor and with power and by melting the shell of passivity with the fire of my being until the confronting, the shaping, the bestowing side of things springs up to meet me and embraces me."

If Daniel's task of creating unity out of duality was one stepping-stone for Buber to the life of dialogue, the immediacy between person and person was another. Only the two together could reveal the full meaning of the insight that Buber attained at the end of *Daniel*: "Human life cannot escape the conditioned. But the unconditioned stands ineffaceably inscribed in the heart of the world." Love, as much as drama, was the origin of Buber's understanding of "inclusion":

> [T]he love in which a genuinely present man embraces the crea-
> tures, so that he may live, remaining with himself in perfect
> power, the whistle of the tramp on his lips and the look of the
> fool in his eyes and, before he takes the poisoned drink, lament

like Socrates the beautiful hair that the young Phaedo will sacrifice in mourning for him.

But it is the love between a man and a woman that Buber had in mind when he justified his use of the word "inclusion" by referring to "the loving man... who has a living experience not only of his struggling desire but also of the blossoming beloved and includes what is opposite him as primally his own." In a letter to Landauer, Buber wrote:

> The duality of the masculine and the feminine belong, I feel, to the tensions which are spoken of in the last dialogue of *Daniel*. In spirit this tension is formed together. The genuinely thinking man must live through the feminine, the genuinely thinking woman the masculine; each must find therein the counterpole to his own in order to allow the unity of the spiritual life to develop from both. That I mean by that no blurring of opposites and no neutralization, you know. But most forms of manifestation of sexual thought are only forestages and presuppositions of the spirit.

When in 1905 Buber began to edit his series *Die Gesellschaft* (Society), he planned to write one himself on sex. In a letter to Hugo von Hofmannsthal, he described his intention as "a deduction of the interhuman," at whose center would be the sexual problem. The announcement of this projected volume appears in the earlier volumes of the series and then drops out in favor of *The Erotic* by Lou Andreas-Salomé, whose close friendship with Nietzsche, Rilke, Freud, and many other men made her much better qualified for this task. Buber had come to know Lou Salomé through her essay "Der Mensch als Weib" (The Human Being as Woman).

In 1910, Lou timed a trip to Berlin so as to meet Buber, with whom she struck up a friendship based on mutual esteem. "How alike we think about 'experience,' about idealization as realization, about polarity as the point of departure for experiencing unity!" she once exclaimed, obviously in response to Buber's sharing with her his thoughts or his unpublished chapters of *Daniel*. When Buber proposed to write a critical book on Freud, Lou wisely dissuaded him on the grounds that the young movement of psychoanalysis was just establishing itself. Nearly forty years later, Buber would write such a work (*Moses*), but it would be on Buber's ground and not on Freud's.

Buber and Lou Salomé knew each other well. From 1906 to 1925, they exchanged some fifty postcards and letters. She visited Paula and him in Berlin and in Heppenheim, and he visited her in Goettingen. Buber seemed to Lou to embody the uttermost élite of that which Judaism could become. In Buber, she found the feminine and the masculine united.

Though *Daniel* is still of genuine value both as literature and as philosophy, some of it is definitely dated—in thought, spirit, and style. There is much in *Daniel* that is beclouded with aesthetic language and a very special and subjective mystical emotion. We can see this particularly clearly by comparing *Daniel* with *I and Thou,* in which many similar concepts are expressed in much clearer form and illustrated in terms of much more universal experience, while the language has gained in beauty and force. For many years Buber refused to permit the publication of an English translation of *Daniel* on the grounds that it did not represent his mature thought and thus might mislead his reader. Finally, he consented under the express condition that I should

> write an introduction explaining, even at some length, that this is an early book in which there is already expressed the great duality of human life, but only in its cognitive and not yet in its communicative and existential character. *Daniel* is obviously a book of transition to a new kind of thinking and must be characterized as such.

◆ 5 ◆

The First World War and the Breakthrough to Dialogue

(1914-1918)

The First World War made real for people all over the world the abyss that Buber had pointed to in *Daniel*. It shattered every comfortable view of individual life and society, every assumption of progress and enlightenment, every once-for-all meaning and worldview. This was especially so for the most sensitive and prescient persons of the age, many of whom, like Buber himself, had anticipated the crisis before it came. But anticipation did not mean that they were prepared to withstand the onslaught of chaos or that they could emerge from the slaughter as they were when they entered it.

Although by no means the most dreadful crisis Buber had to confront (the Nazi Holocaust was still to come), the First World War was the turning point in Buber's life. What happened in those years can only be described as a breakthrough, as Hans Kohn puts it—a breakthrough to dialogue. This breakthrough was so decisive that, in his will, Buber directed his literary executor not to allow the publication of anything written before 1916 if it had not already been published before his death.

What led up to this breakthrough was a process, beginning shortly before the First World War, in which Buber's experience decisively matured him. This process lasted over eight years and was completed only after the war. All the experiences of being that Buber had during the years 1912–1919 became present to him in growing measure as *one* great experience of faith. By "experience of faith," Buber did not mean a conversion in any ordinary sense or any specific religious experience or religious ecstasy. On the contrary, he meant something that transcended all experience and seized him as a whole, transporting him in *all* his being, his capacity for thought and reason included. The very validity of this religious totality is witnessed by the fact that nothing separate was given to Buber, that he received no message that he might transmit: "As we reach the meeting with the simple *Thou* on our lips, so with the *Thou* on our lips we leave it and return to the world." As he was to say in *I and Thou,* what he received was not a specific "content" but a Presence, a Presence as power. Of this Presence, he could only say that it included the whole fullness of real mutual action, the inexpressible confirmation of meaning, and meaning not in any world "yonder," but here and now, demanding confirmation in this life and in relation with this world. Buber could only describe these experiences of being that converged into a single great experience of faith as just a pointing to this ineffable wholeness that transported him in such a way that, all the doors springing open, the storm blew through all the chambers of his being.

As in *Daniel,* this meaning was clearly linked up with holy insecurity, the trusting response in confrontation with the abyss. The approach of the first stage of the catastrophe in the exact sense of the term became evident to Buber in the year before the First World War, though again it was only after the end of the war that this gradual realization suddenly exploded into certainty within him. The certainty that he attained was no philosophical conviction or existentialist thesis. It was a question, rather, of the claim of existence itself, a claim that had grown irresistible. The philosophy of dialogue that developed at that time was only the intellectual expression of this claim. Buber realized, of course, that the crisis of Western man did not begin with the First World War. It had already been recognized by Kierkegaard over a century earlier as an unprecedented shaking of the foundations of man as man: "But it is only in our generation that we have seriously begun to occupy ourselves with the fact that in this crisis something begins to be decided that is bound up in the closest manner with a decision about ourselves." Partial explanations, such as Marx's concept of the radical alienation of man through economic and technical revolutions, and Freud's concept of individual neuroses, do not yield an adequate understanding, any more than existentialist analyses. "We must take the injured wholeness of man upon us as a life burden in order to press beyond all that is merely symptomatic, and grasp the true sickness." The true sickness Buber described as "massive decisionlessness," dualism, the radical separation between ideas, ideals, and values and personal existence, on which the spirit no longer has any binding claim.

The specific form in which the approaching catastrophe made itself known, of course, was the threat of war. That Buber had some premonition of the crisis is suggested by his statement to Arnold Zweig, in connection with the publication of "With a Monist" in 1914: "I have now a strong need to contend with the things of the time." At that time, under the initiative of the amazing Dutchman Frederik Van Eeden, a remarkable group came into being that had as its purpose some common front across the nations that might serve in some way to avert the catastrophe. Although the ultimate goal of this group, drawn together by some undefined presentiment of catastrophe, was to make preparations for the establishment of a supranational authority, the original number was only eight—five Germans, two Dutchmen, and one Swede. The great French writer and peacemaker Romain Rolland had originally planned to attend but was unable to do so. But he stood in close relation to the spirit of the group and to Van Eeden in particular. Van Eeden himself, a doctor whose writings were respected and cited by Freud, was a rebel against urban life who built himself a cottage in the country and called it "Walden" after Thoreau, a social reformer and utopian who kept up a vigorous interchange with Upton Sinclair, Gandhi, and Rabindranath Tagore, and at the same time a man of such great personal warmth and understanding that he was able to knit together into one spirit eight remarkable persons, each one of whom was a prominent intellectual and author in his own right. Buber had had contact with Van Eeden as early as 1910, when he had corresponded with him about contributing to *Die Gesellschaft,* and there was a remarkable convergence of their ideas, as Van Eeden pointed out after receiving a copy of *Daniel.* Direction, holy insecurity, and polarity were all anticipated by Van Eeden in his own poetry and thought.

The men who met at Potsdam in Germany were Van Eeden; Buber; Gustav Landauer; Eric Gutkind, the German-Jewish philosopher of religion and of science; the German Protestant pastor and lawyer Florens Christian Rang; the Swedish psychoanalyst and author Poul Bjerre; the Dutch author and expert Henri Borel; and the Swedish author Theodor Gustav Norlind. Although "I and Thou" suggests at first glance a relationship of only two people, it was not the one-to-one meetings described in *Daniel* that led Buber to a mature understanding of the life of dialogue but *this group of eight.* The conversations of the group, Buber testified, were marked by an unreserve whose substance and fruitfulness he had scarcely ever experienced so strongly. This reality of group presence and presentness had such an effect on all who took part that the fictitious fell away and every word was an actuality.

It was not like-mindedness but mutual presence that Buber remembered when he looked back on those days sixteen years later. The circle failed to accomplish its goal of bringing the unity of mankind to authoritative expression at that decisive hour. Yet this did nothing to dim the memory of those three days of strenuous and inward being with one another, without reservation, on the part of eight such different men. The more powerfully divided they were in their opinions, the more truly close they became! Forty years later, in his important anthropological essay "Elements of the Interhuman," Buber again alluded to this meeting as an example of the experience of the interhuman in a dialogue in which several have taken part:

> Without our having agreed beforehand on any sort of modalities
> for our talk, all the presuppositions of genuine dialogue were ful-

filled. From the first hour immediacy reigned between all of us, some of whom had just got to know one another; everyone spoke with an unheard-of unreserve, and clearly not a single one of the participants was in bondage to semblance. In respect of its purpose the meeting must be described as a failure (though even now in my heart it is still not a certainty that it had to be a failure).... Nevertheless, in the time that followed, not one of the participants doubted that he shared in a triumph of the interhuman.

In this interhuman reality, Van Eeden played a special role. "You did not take an active part in any of the questions at issue," Buber wrote to him,

> and yet you were present in each of them by virtue of the trusting kindness of the look with which you regarded each of us. You beheld us with your whole soul.... You saw with loving clarity the to-each-other in the against-each-other, saw the mysterious growth of the union, saw the new shape of the true rise naked and splendid out of the fervor.... And when we met in battle and in the mutual redemption of each other, we met at the same time in the life of your glance. And that helped us.

After the Potsdam meeting, Van Eeden recorded his impression of Buber in his diary, giving us an invaluable glimpse of Buber as a person when he was in his late thirties: "The slender, fragile, subtle but strong Buber, with his straight look and soft eyes, weak and velvety, yet deep and sharp. The Rabbi, but without the narrow mind, the philosopher, but without the aridity, the scholar but without the self-conceit." It is significant to compare this portrait of softness combined with strength with Landauer's article of a little over a year before with its hint of a determined and uncompromising will making its way through the layers of poetic richness and subjective emotion until it became manifest in the person and in his writings. Still more significant is the comparison of this emerging openness and strength with the picture that Landauer's and Buber's mutual friend Margarete Susman has left us of her first meeting with Buber ten or more years before the Potsdam conference. "I came to know Buber in a private seminar of his teacher Georg Simmel the great German sociologist and philosopher," she related, "at a time when he was not yet famous. He was "a young man of the utmost sensitivity. My first impression on looking at this delicately built man was: that is no man, that is pure spirit."

Buber certainly was not "pure spirit" in the dialogues at Potsdam. He was very much present as the body-and-soul person that he was, and he stood his ground in the give-and-take with as much force as any of the other disputants. But here, more than in any dialogue recorded in *Daniel*, more even than in the dialogue with the monist, Buber discovered the spirit that is in the "between," in the stern "over-againstness" of two or more truly distinct persons who really meet each other without lessening anything of the distance from which they start out. These days taught Buber not the harmony of Plato's chord but that of Heraclitus' bow, and with it the possibility of confirming the other even in opposing him.

At Potsdam, Buber met for the first time the lawyer and former minister Florens Christian Rang, a man whose impact upon Buber was perhaps next in importance only to that of Paula, Gustav Landauer, and Franz Rosenzweig. Yet this friendship began in purest opposition. When the members of the circle came to discuss the composition of the larger group from which public initiative should proceed when they met again, as they planned, in August, Florens Christian Rang, "a man of passionate concentration and powerful love," suggested that too many Jews had been nominated, so that several countries would be represented in an unbalanced fashion by their Jews. Buber's position, of course, was that of a Zionist who wanted the Jews to gather into a community of their own, and he saw this as the most effective way in which his people could share in the building of a stable world peace. From this standpoint, he did not actually disagree with Rang. Yet he felt that the way in which Rang had expressed his objection was unjust. "Obstinate Jew that I am," Buber later wrote, "I protested against the protest." At this point, from being a political discussion, it became a Jewish-Christian dialogue—one of the most remarkable ones, surely, that has ever taken place. Buber came somehow to speak of Jesus and to say that the Jews knew him from within, in the impulses and stirrings of his Jewish being, in a way that remains inaccessible to those who worship him: "In a way that remains inaccessible to you"—thus he directly addressed the former clergyman. Rang stood up, Buber stood up, and each looked into the heart of the other's eyes. "It is gone," Rang said, and before everyone Buber and Rang gave each other the kiss of brotherhood. "The discussion of the situation between Jews and Christians had been transformed into a bond between the Christian and the Jew," Buber later commented. This was a bond that was to last and to grow ever deeper until Rang's death in 1926.

Within a month after the Potsdam meeting, Buber took part in another dialogue with a Christian, though in this case one that was as much mismeeting as it was meeting. This dialogue was as decisive for Buber as the one with Rang in leading him to the life of dialogue. The content of the interchange was the relationship between man and God, but the context was the imminent catastrophe—the disintegration of the relationship between person and person.

In May 1914, Herzl's friend and supporter the Reverend William Hechler came to visit Buber in Zehlendorf, the suburb of Berlin where he lived. He apparently had not seen Buber at close range since the time they rode together on the train in 1898, for he brought with him the manuscript and proofs of Buber's youthful Zionist poem that he had taken with him to the grand duke of Baden and then published, without Buber's knowledge, in

Die Welt. When Buber opened the door to Hechler, he was struck by how aged he was, but also by how straight he stood. After the warm mutual greeting, Hechler drew forth from one of the gigantic pockets of his havelock a bundle of papers wrapped in a blue-white cloth. Out of it, first of all, he took Buber's youthful poem, but then a large sheet, which he slowly unfolded. It was a graphic representation of the prophecy of Daniel, on which he indicated to Buber, as if on a "histomap," the exact point in which they now found themselves. Then he said to Buber: "Dear friend! I come from Athens. I have stood on the spot where Paul spoke to the Athenians of the unknown God. And now I come to say to you that in this year the world war will break out."

What struck Buber most forcibly in Hechler's statement was not so much his prediction itself as the term "world war," which he had never heard before. What kind of a war was it, he asked himself, that embraced the world? He imagined it to himself as something terrible, utterly unlike any previous war that mankind had known. From that hour, the presentiment grew in Buber that something ever more monstrous was getting ready to consume history, and with it men, a premonition that has proved as true of the generations that followed as Hechler's prophecy of the immediate future.

Hechler stayed a few hours with Martin and Paula Buber. Then Buber accompanied him to the railway station. In order to get there, they first had to go to the end of the small street of the "colony" in which Buber lived and then on a narrow path covered with coal dust, the so-called black path along the railroad tracks. When they had reached the corner where the colony street met this path, Hechler stood still, placed his hand on Buber's shoulder, and said: "Dear friend! We live in a great time. Tell me: Do you believe in God?" It was a while before Buber answered. Then he reassured the old man as best he could that there was no reason to worry about him on that score, and they walked on to the railway station.

When Buber, returning home, again came to that corner where the black path issued into his street, he stood still, forced to ponder deeply the event that had just taken place there. He asked himself now whether he had told the truth, whether he really did "believe" in the God whom Hechler meant. He stood a long time on the corner, determined not to go farther before he had found the right answer.

Suddenly, in his spirit, there where speech again and again forms itself, there arose, word for word, distinct, without having been formulated by him, this answer: "If to believe in God means to be able to talk *about* him in the third person, then I do *not* believe in God. But if to believe in him means to be able to talk *to* him, then I do believe in God." After a while, new words came:

> The God who gives Daniel such foreknowledge of this hour of
> human history, this hour before the "world war," that its fixed

place in the march of the ages can be predetermined, is not my God and not God. But the God to whom Daniel prays in his suffering is my God and the God of all.

Buber remained standing for a long while on the corner of the black path and gave himself up to the clarity—now beyond speech—that had begun.

Hechler, of course, was proved right, probably sooner and certainly more terribly than he himself could have imagined. But Buber's rejection of Hechler's God had nothing whatever to do with whether his prediction was right or wrong and would not have even if Buber had not realized later that Hechler's certainty stemmed from a peculiar fusion of the Book of Daniel with the indications of imminent crisis that he had unconsciously picked up in the courts of Europe, where he was tutor to many royal families. What Buber rejected was the very form of the apocalyptic itself, which forfeited the "holy insecurity" of Buber's *Daniel* for the certain future of the biblical book of the same name. Here we can see in a single event one of the most important origins of three of Buber's central and related contrasts—between prophetic openness and choice and apocalyptic closedness and certainty, between unconditional trust in relationship *(emunah)* and faith that begins with a proposition in which one believes *(pistis)*, and between the attempt to comprehend the whole of reality and schematize the mystery *(gnosis)* and the willingness to meet what comes and to go forth from that meeting as one summoned and sent *(devotio)*.

We can also see here, as in Buber's childhood experience with the two boys in his gymnasium, the first dawning of a realization that only later became conscious and articulated. For just as Buber did not, when he was twelve, know of "the problematic relation between maxim and situation" but only of an overwhelming stalemate, so here, too, in fact, he was unable to find any really meaningful response that would satisfy him. As Rivka Horwitz has shown, only in an event that took place six months before his Lehrhaus lectures in early 1922, and which he recounted in those lectures, did he arrive at the radical assertion of the "eternal Thou," the God who is always met as Thou and cannot be known as an object, the God whom we can speak *to* but not *about*. The above story is related as Buber himself told it to me, because his memory had the faithfulness of the Hasidic "legendary anecdote": It telescoped into one event what actually took place in two events seven years apart, both curiously enough connected with a train (for he found the "answer" in 1921, when riding on a train). Though he did not yet have the language to describe what he was groping for, his discovery, nonetheless, *began* in that *event* of 1914.

As decisive as was the content of this revelation, equally decisive was its context. The sense of impending catastrophe gave a new depth of meaning to Hechler's question: In the face of the abyss, one can say only what one really knows, only that truth with which one is ready to descend into the abyss itself. Buber did not understand the demand that this question placed upon him when he first answered it. Only later, after Hechler left, did he know it as a question addressed to his life itself, a question that could be answered only with his life. This wholehearted turning and decision came two months later, in July 1914, in the event that Buber called a "conversion."

About this time, as we have seen, Buber was given to hours of mystic ecstasy. The illegitimacy of this division of his life into the everyday and a "beyond," where illumination and rapture held without time or sequence, was brought home to Buber by "an event of judgment" in which closed lips and an unmoved glance pronounced the sentence. One forenoon after a morning of mystic rapture, Buber had a visit from an unknown young man named Mehé. Buber was friendly toward the young man but, inwardly absorbed by the mystical experience that he had just emerged from, he was not present in spirit. It is not that Buber was indifferent or abstracted in the usual sense. Wherein then was Buber remiss? He conversed attentively and openly with Mehé and answered the questions he asked. But he failed to guess the question that the young man did not put. Two months later, one of Mehé's friends came to see Buber and told him of Mehé's death *and* of what his talk with Buber had meant to him. He had come to Buber not casually, but as if borne by destiny, not for a chat but for a decision.

The decision was one of life or death, but not in the sense that many assumed. Mehé did not commit suicide, as some commentators have asserted. Rather, he died at the front in the First World War, as Buber himself wrote me, "out of that kind of despair that may be defined partially as 'no longer opposing one's own death.'" Even in a psychologizing age such as ours, the difference between actual suicide and such despair should be evident. The something monstrous that was getting ready to consume history and mankind is the qualitatively different era that began with the First World War, continued with the Second, and outstripped imagination in the Nazi extermination camps, Hiroshima and Nagasaki, and the "Gulag Archipelago." In such situations, those who do not fight wholeheartedly against their death will certainly be killed, whereas those who do *might* remain alive. The despair that prevents such wholehearted contending may indeed contribute to one's death, but to equate it with suicide is to reduce the dialogue between person and situation in our time to an intrapsychic monologue, and thereby obscure its terrifying reality.

Buber experienced this event as a judgment and responded to it with a "conversion" that changed his whole life. Buber's feeling of guilt was not based on any illusion of omnipotence, as if he *should* have been able to remove Mehé's despair regardless of the circumstances. Buber told me that Franz Kafka came to see him several times in Berlin in 1910 and 1911. "He was a really unhappy man," Buber added, but without the slightest look or intonation that might suggest that he felt himself guilty for not being able to lighten Kafka's load of despair. In Mehé's case, Buber was personally guilty in the exact sense in which he himself later defined existential guilt because he withheld himself; he did not respond as a whole person to the claim of the situation, and through this withholding he injured the common order of existence, which he knew to be the foundation of his own and all existence. This withholding of himself did not arise through any conscious decision or willful detachment, but through a habitual way of life that removed him from the everyday to a "spiritual" sphere that had no connection with the everyday. With the best intention in the world and with all the resources that he could muster at that moment. Buber still was not "there" for Mehé, who had come to him in that hour. It is not that he did not *say* the right thing, but that he failed to make real, insofar as it was up to him, the possibility of genuine dialogue that that hour offered. The question that Mehé did not ask was not a philosophical or theological question, but one much more basic, the question of trust in existence. And Buber did not hear and answer this question in the only way in which it could be answered—through his full presence. "What do we expect when we are in despair and yet go to a man?" Buber asked of himself later when the lips of the questioner were forever sealed. "Surely," Buber answered himself, "a presence by means of which we are told that nevertheless there is meaning." More than forty years later, Buber could speak of himself as one who dealt with problematic persons who had lost the ground under their feet, who had lost their trust—not in this or that person but in existence itself. If that became so, it was only because at this crucial point, Mehé's death came home to Buber as a demand that he change his life, that he practice that asceticism that means giving up mystical rapture rather than the things of this world. He answered this demand with the turning of his whole existence to the meeting with reality *in* the world and not apart from it: "Since then I have given up the 'religious' which is nothing but the exception, extraction, exaltation, ecstasy; or it has given me up. I possess nothing but the everyday out of which I am never taken....I know no fulness but each mortal hour's fulness of claim and responsibility."

Thus, Buber gave up the much more perfect and satisfying fullness of mystic rapture, in which the self experiences no division within or limit without, for the always imperfect fullness of the common world of speech-with-meaning built up through ever-demanding, ever-painful meetings with others. Not expansion of consciousness to the All but awareness of otherness, not universality but uniqueness, not perfection but the unreduced immediacy of the "lived concrete," became Buber's way from this time on.

"Let us believe in man!" These words, with which Buber concluded "With a Monist" just a few months before, were destined to undergo trial by fire during the months and years to come. In contrast to the years before 1914, war and crisis were the "normal" situation for the rest of Buber's long life, and the challenge of this crisis, more than any other, was whether in the midst of it these words could be authenticated and confirmed. If the fruitless attempts at finding a meeting of minds in the face of the crisis did not shatter

Buber's trust in men, at the very least they sobered it. On the other hand, the monstrous inhumanity of the war itself turned him more and more to direct meeting with persons and completed that breakthrough from inner realization to the meeting with otherness that began in the "conversion." What this extension of "inclusion" meant for Buber during wartime is shown most clearly in the hymn "To the Contemporary," which he put at the end of his book *Events and Meetings*. "To the Contemporary" is the one essay in the book written after the beginning of the war, and, like Buber's "conversion," it represents a turning *away* from the spiritual life that had formerly absorbed him as well as *toward* the irreducible and far less agreeable concreteness of the reality of the present. Written in the autumn of 1914, even today this "hymn" needs no footnote to identify the "invading power of the contemporary!" to which Buber referred. Beautiful as the language remains, there is something about this hymn that breaks out of any "wonderful world feeling" and ushers in a new soberness and concreteness that finally led Buber to recognize that his early meetings with nature took place *within* himself and not *between* himself and the tree or the fragment of mica.

The "event" behind this essay is sublimely simple, as Buber described it. He sat once in the steel blue solitude of the evening, opened his window, and suddenly felt the full reality of the *moment* as if it were a moon-colored bird that had flown into his window laden with the fearful and the sweet. Mixing his metaphors, Buber pictured the bird as laying "the earth-space of this moment" upon his breast like "a skein of wool." With the moment came the inrush of otherness—he breathed the dreams of far-distant beings, impulses of unknown creatures gathered in his throat, and the elements of many souls mixed in his blood. The present entered into him like a music composed of tension, impulse, and rapture of the living. He withstood the infinity of the moment, but he did not know whether it ruled him or he it; he knew only that it was bound into bodily music. He did not yet know that the call of the contemporary meant the renunciation of a life absorbed in the philosophy and wisdom of the ages. He was still able to close his window and feel himself at one with all time. Now they were again with him, Lao-tzu the Old and the golden Plato, and with them, kindred to them, the whole present. Here is still the all-colored mysticism of "The Altar," in which the ages unite and the timeless is near.

But now the invading power of the contemporary broke in upon Buber with a force that could not be denied: the dreadful and inhuman happenings of a war such as mankind had never known before—shrapnel wounds and tetanus, screams and death rattle, and the smile of the mouth above the crushed body. Now Buber could no longer see this present as bound into music or imagine in what heritage of aeons it might find its song. Yet, along with the claim of each hour, which he took upon himself in his "conversion," he accepted once and for all the terrible, absurd concreteness of the historical hour in which he lived, and renounced forever the refuge that companionship with the great spirits of the ages had afforded him. As Boehme's ternary of fire is transmuted into the ternary of light, as the rabbi in "The Revelation" sees the fire rising over the body of the praying Baal-Shem and being turned into light, so here Buber sees himself as the sacrificial offering in which fire suffers transformation into light:

> But never again, O moment, O instorming power of the contemporary, never will I bid you go…. Rather shall I be prey and fuel to your fire all the moments of my life. Out of your fire light is born, and nowhere does it flash except out of your fire. I am consumed in you, but I am consumed into light.

Far from setting fire and light into an irreconcilable dualism, Buber came to the realization that only out of fire—the fire of horror and despair, of absurdity and death—could come the "hidden light" of meaning, the meaning of the "lived concrete" which derives not from the exclusion of otherness but from the meeting with it. The war added the real world tension to the inner, freely chosen one, Schaeder rightly observes. It taught Buber the weakness of the creature and the fear of God's judgment. It deepened "cosmic unification" into suffering with one's fellow creatures, the "courage to create" into the power to withstand. Out of all this, it transformed the "realization" of *Daniel* into the "over-againstness" of *I and Thou*.

This was not a process that took place all at once, however, but, as Buber himself indicated, over a period of a dozen years. Buber was never a German superpatriot, like Hermann Cohen, the great neo-Kantian philosopher and leader of German Liberal Jewry, nor is there any evidence that he ever signed any document supporting the kaiser, as some German intellectuals of that time did. On the other hand, he was neither a pacifist nor an anarchist like Gustav Landauer, and, during the first year of the war, he was not able to maintain Landauer's almost fanatic clarity of opposition. Instead, he succumbed at times to seeing the war, despite and even because of its frightfulness, as a chaos from which a new cosmos would emerge. In the first instance, he saw this as a "movement" that would transform Germany and Europe into a real community and, in the second, as we shall see, he saw it as an upheaval that might decisively improve the situation of the German, and still more the Eastern European, Jews.

"I am shaken by what has happened as never before in my life," Buber told Rappeport in August 1914, and in September he wrote him: "The time is exceedingly beautiful with the might of its reality and with its demand on each of us." To Ludwig Strauss, Buber declared in the same month: "For the first time the nations have become wholly real for me." Buber's friend Margarete Susman was far more realistic. Although she granted that some illumination might come out of the darkest and heaviest fate, all that she could experience, she wrote Buber, was "the monstrous compulsion over the human of objective powers that are themselves only human." The letters that

Buber received from his Bar Kochba friends, who were now scattered over various fronts of the war, were still less enthusiastic, and Buber was disappointed by their mood. "Here it is entirely otherwise," he informed Hans Kohn. "Never has the concept *'Volk'* become so real for me as during these weeks." The Jews in general shared this feeling, Buber claimed, which led many, including the German-Jewish poets Karl Wolfskehl and Friedrich Gundolf of the Stefan Georg school, to volunteer. Buber expressed his own disappointment in not being found suitable to enter the army. He also told Kohn of joining the Jewish Socialists of Germany to organize a committee for the Eastern Jews in Poland and Russia, whom they hoped to "liberate." (In October 1914, Buber cosigned a three-page letter describing the plight of the Eastern European Jews—an act that seemed half based on genuine concern for these refugees and half an unconscious extension of German propaganda concerning the Russians.) The last sentences of Buber's letter to Kohn unfolded for full view what Landauer later called the *"Kriegsbuber"* (War-Buber):

> For each who wants to spare himself in this time the statement of the Gospel of John is valid: "He who loves his life will lose it." …When we Jews then feel, wholly feel to its core what this means: then we shall no longer need our old motto, *Not by might but by spirit*, since force and spirit shall now become one for us. Incipit vita nova!

Thirty-five years later, Buber was to say that those Jews who wanted to effect by might rather than spirit were aping Hitler! But less than two years later, Buber returned to the "old motto," "Not by might but by spirit."

"Tonight cannon shots from the sea awoke me," Buber wrote in a collection of war diaries of artists.

> I stood at the window above the primevally silent strand and heard the rolling out of the uncertain distance. I did not know "what" it was—a battle between German and English ships?—only that it was destruction, far-reaching destruction from all sides, and—purification of the spirit. It tore me out of my limits, bore me into the midst of the conflict, I lived for a moment shattered and *liberated*. And now I feel one thing: that the spirit does not submit to all this patiently, that it means and wills all this as the way to it.

"When I go through the streets [of Berlin]," Buber wrote in a second war diary,

> I recognize, probably more strongly than I should be able to on the battlefield itself, the threefold present reality: the plowshare, the turned-up-earth, and the coming seeds. I see, deep beneath

all intentions and actions and infinitely more real than they, the preparation.

Kinesis, movement: thus the Greeks named the transition from the quiescent to the acting force, from being able to be to being. The age of kinesis into which we have entered did not begin with this war; it only became manifest in it. This is the age in which the soul of man no longer stands and stares but rises upward to the highest deed; the age in which the deed of man is no longer confined by many petty aims but wins its freedom and its completion in sacrifice. It is not the name of the value for which the sacrifice is made that is the inner truth of the event but the fact that men are willing to die for it. The divine is made manifest not in their creed but in their devotion.

In these words, we find an echo of Buber's formulation of *kavana* in *The Legend of the Baal-Shem*: "It is not the nature of the action that is decisive but its dedication." But now, somehow, a new dualism has entered in, where the action itself becomes almost indifferent, the inner attitude all. And in this context, such a dualism has sinister implications that Buber himself later became aware of. The same holds for the sentences that immediately follow:

They cast aside the familiar, the safe, the conditioned in order to hurl themselves into the abyss of the unconditioned, and just this, that they do it, is the revelation of the unconditioned in a time that appears to be abandoned by it. For this reason we have to rejoice in the terror and bitter suffering of these days. It is a fearful grace; it is the grace of a new birth. Even he who condemns the war cannot close his ear to the roar of kinesis. Our cause is that it should swell beyond itself and become the power of new aeons—realization.

Here the language of *Daniel* and the "Speeches on Judaism" are used to celebrate movement and change as almost a good in itself, something that must inevitably do the work of the spirit!

This was the trial by fire of Buber's early philosophy, and in this trial it was found wanting. The emphasis on realization and unconditionality without the check of the faithful meeting with otherness can lead straight into the hell of the most terrible demonism and celebrate it as if it were a path to the divine. "Tomorrow," Buber added, "we shall have to point to the direction, for direction without kinesis is lame, but kinesis without direction is blind. *After* the war the great task begins. Now the plowshare does its work, but then the upturned earth will receive the seeds that fall into it." Buber's acceptance of movement now and direction later made it impossible that the *kinesis* he celebrated would ever take on the meaning and decision that he desired. Buber was neither a chauvinist nor a militant German nationalist, but his own philosophy helped to seduce him into an enthusiasm in which even his faithfulness to that philosophy became questionable. The bitter disappointments that followed contributed to Buber's breakthrough to the philosophy of dialogue.

Twenty years later, another German existentialist philosopher—Martin Heidegger—tied his philosophy to a German nationalist movement in a remarkably similar way. But in marked contrast to Heidegger, Buber learned one of the deepest lessons of his life from this wedding of his thought with the demonic—a lesson that resulted in a decisive change in Buber's philosophy such as is nowhere evident in Heidegger.

During this period, Buber remained in close personal contact with Landauer, who did not share his enthusiasm, as well as in correspondence with the members of the Forte Kreis, the circle of those who met in Potsdam and who had planned, before the war broke out, to reassemble at Forte in Italy. Not only the war prevented the group from meeting again, but also the effect of the war on the members of the group. The national feelings that arose were too strong to enable even as deep a unity as was experienced in Potsdam to prevail. Some members of the group, like Landauer, Frederik Van Eeden, Poul Bjerre, and Romain Rolland (who was unable to come to the first meeting but was planning to come to the subsequent ones), remained quite clear in their opposition to the war. Others, like Eric Gutkind and Florens Christian Rang, became strong German nationalists, a position that Rang wholeheartedly and actively rejected after the war. Buber remained in between the pacifists and the militants, but with enough faith in the war as "movement" to resent bitterly the characterization of that movement as "mass suggestion" not only by the pacifists but also by the neutrals, such as the Dutch still were at that time. In particular, Buber resented an "Open Letter to Our German Friends," which Van Eeden published in September 1914, castigating German intellectuals for abetting the current war psychosis, and two circular letters to members of the Forte Kreis.

Buber's breakthrough to dialogue in these years also meant a breakthrough to a new relationship with Zionism, Judaism, and Jewish education. None of these were new concerns for him, yet all of them had to pass through the refining fire, out of which they came transformed and tempered. The final results of that tempering are not evident until Buber's Foreword to the collected edition of his *Speeches on Judaism* (1923). But there are many tokens in Buber's life and thought during this period of the ever-renewed process of plunging into the fire.

What Buber hoped for from the war is explicitly indicated by a note of September 14, 1914, which he later cited: "The frightful thing that is taking place has for me a three-fold promise: the liberation of the Central European man for public life, the awakening of the Russian man to constructive life, the rescue of the Near East for a Semitic regeneration." Only later did he come to the painful recognition of what he did not suspect at the time: that, in conformity with the nature of our time and the situation in which it took place, each of these events had of necessity to bring forth a new, difficult problem. It was, indeed, the *problematic* aspect of the war that, despite Buber's deep concern about preventing it, seemed to have dropped out of sight for Buber during the first months of the conflict, when the stirring and rising of the nation was more evident than the abyss into which it marched.

In this respect, Buber differed from Landauer, whose pacifist-anarchist opposition to the war remained unchanged throughout. But the friendship between Landauer and Buber continued in undiminished intensity during this same period, and this meant that Buber's enthusiasm necessarily had to accept the polar tension of Landauer's rejection of the war and the perspective that it afforded. Two days after he wrote his long letter to Van Eeden, Buber wrote to Landauer that he believed their relationship to be anchored so deeply that it could not be shattered and that he hoped he felt the same. He did not want to write to Landauer concerning their differences, as he had to Van Eeden, but preferred meeting with him either in his house or in Buber's own. "There are many things that I could not write to him that I can say to you.... Gutkind reports that you reproach me—like him—with aestheticism. Shall you really misunderstand and confuse me with others? I cannot believe it."

Later in 1914, Landauer went to visit Buber to discuss with him his correspondence with Bjerre, as well as to discuss a plan for communal-educational activity. An illuminating picture of Buber's relation to the war at this time and of Landauer's relation to Buber emerges from Landauer's report of this conversation to his second wife, the poet Hedwig Lachmann. "My answer to Bjerre cannot be entirely agreeable to him [Buber]," Landauer wrote,

> because he feels many of the passages to be aimed at himself too. As well he should. Despite this, I feel toward no one as forbearing and as trustfully expectant as toward him. To me it is really touching how, before, I had to defend Germanness, which he regarded as something not at all essential to the Jews, and how, today, Germanness stirs so sensitively in him against his will that he would rule out every distinction between the deeds and sins of individual regimes. He loves everything and acknowledges fully and without reservation my complete rejection of the war; but he also finds such an unconditional [willingness] in the unanimity of the German people, the readiness for death of the young generation, and he brings to it no analysis of any sort and is especially embittered if one speaks of mass suggestion.

Two days later, Landauer wrote his wife that in contrast to Kurt Hiller, with whom he had politely conversed for some time but who was at the antipodes from him in essential things, it was wholly otherwise with Buber. "I understand and love his ardent passion for the heroic and what still separates us in our judgments of things and men (it is no longer much) is wholly inessential." This depth of understanding and sympathy grew during the war years. Buber joined Landauer in withdrawing from the Forte Kreis, expressing his renunciation "in a manner very dear to me," Landauer wrote to Walter Rathenau, and Landauer joined Buber in the attempt to establish an independent circle in Germany and Austria.

If Buber's general expectations of the "movement" set in motion by the war were soon disappointed, his specific expectations of its effect on the situation of the Jewish people were still more bitterly so. Yet it was precisely this situation that prompted Buber to renewed Jewish activity in ways destined to have a lasting effect on the German Jews and the Zionist movement. When the war broke out, Herman recorded, Buber felt like all of them that the destiny of the Jewish people was bound to be set in "movement" by it. "One must do something—I heard this from him often at that time," wrote Hermann, "almost every day." On the one hand, the fate and danger of each individual who was in the field moved him. On the other, he was open to every initiation that sprang from the concern for the future of the Jewish people and above all for that part of it that was Jewishly alive. Buber belonged to the founders of the Jewish National Committee, which was already established in October 1914. "The Jewish National Committee wants to help prepare for a national freedom movement," concluded the sketch of a short program that Buber himself wrote.

The Jewish National Committee interested important forces in the Socialist party of Germany in the Jewish national cause, secured valuable support in the fight against the persecution of the Jews in the East by the occupational authorities, and prepared an atmosphere out of which grew, even during the war, a pro-Palestine Committee. It was out of the considerations of this Jewish National Committee, too, that a decision was born to take seriously the founding of a monthly. Buber would become the editor only when he was convinced that a strong group of leading intellectuals would really go along. In naming the journal, Buber consciously reached back to the earlier journal that Weizmann, Feiwel, and he had attempted unsuccessfully to launch in 1903—*Der Jude,* "The Jew." The new attempt succeeded beyond all expectation and lasted through 1924 as the leading organ of German-speaking Jewry, for the most part under Buber's direct, personal supervision.

In May 1916, Landauer came for a visit of several days. "I had not been in the company of the 'War-Buber' and had almost forgotten him," Landauer wrote later. In Buber's opening editorial for *Der Jude*—"The Watchword"— and "The Spirit of Judaism" in the second of three of Buber's *Speeches on Judaism,* Landauer found passages that offended him so deeply that he denied Buber the right to speak publicly of the events of the war and "to incorporate these confusions into your beautiful and wise generalities. I confess that it makes my blood boil when you single out Germany without qualification as the only redeemer nation without reference to how Germany in the last decades had pursued colonization through conquest. That is War Politics!" Landauer exclaimed. "Virility, manliness, sacrificial courage, devotion" are not implicit in the content and meaning of this atrocity. "The community that we need is far from all that war means today. Dear Buber, you must at the very least recognize that among the hundred thousand Jews there were, say, 23 or 37 who... did not enter this war with a passionate longing. And if you cannot, then in my opinion you ought not speak."

Landauer declared himself unwilling to contribute to Buber's new journal *Der Jude*. "A journal that says what the Hapsburgs, Hohenzollern, and the interest groups bound up with them would gladly hear and does not say what is opposed to that, cannot be my journal." To speak of the Jewish stake in German victory was to ignore all the Jewish blood spilled by the murder of Germans, Slavs, Rumanians, Italians, Austrians, and Russians. "A pity for the Jewish blood, indeed a pity for every drop of blood that is spilt in this war;... a pity for the men; a pity also that you have gone astray in this war!"

No answer to this bitter condemnation is extant; Buber may have taken a train to Berlin and replied to Landauer in person. In any case, after they met for several days in Berlin in July 1916, Landauer sent Buber a note expressing his satisfaction with *Der Jude* and his readiness to contribute to it: "The level of your periodical is so high and the whole attitude of the recent issues pleases me so much and, above all, my desire to work up the essay on Judaism and Socialism is so great that I consider it best to write a formal assent." It is unthinkable that Landauer could have thus reversed himself unless Buber satisfied him not only by explanation but by a change of attitude.

The best of Jewish writers and thinkers and a number of non-Jews, testifies Simon, saw it as a great honor to participate in Buber's monthly. This applied to both Zionists and non-Zionists, writers in German, Yiddish, and Hebrew. The journal combined a wide spiritual scope with high quality, and it overcame the artificial frontiers that cut the Jewish world in half at that time. In its translations, notes, and summaries—political, economic, and literary—*Der Jude* reminded the Jewish world of the unity it had once possessed and prepared it for that which it might possess again. It thus fulfilled on the highest level, states Simon, a national Jewish task encompassing many countries. Its scope was broad yet centered in a clear and special principle— Zionism according to the national concept of its editor.

The influence of *Der Jude* was very great almost from the first moment, Simon reports. Even an anti-Zionist like Franz Rosenzweig wrote to his parents that it was becoming the only organ of German Jewry that could be taken seriously and that deserved support. For seven years, Buber tried to influence the Zionist movement through *Der Jude*, fighting for its organic tie with the Jewish nation living and creating all over the Diaspora, for its progressive social and political character. Despite all the freedom of speech and discussion accorded to the many and various participants, this was a consistent tendency of the editorial board.

As a successful editor, Buber understood and practiced what was to become a central concern in his philosophical anthropology—inclusion. Franz Kafka wrote Felice that Buber had rejected his prose piece "A Dream," taken from his work on *The Trial,* with a letter that was more respectful than any ordinary acceptance could have been. (Later it was printed in *Das Jüdische Prag,* a collection that Buber coedited.) Ernst Simon reported that his first meeting with Buber came when Buber invited him to his home to tell him in person that an article he had submitted was a fine one, which he would be happy to publish in *Der Jude,* but also that he was uncomfortable with a parallel Simon had drawn between the biblical Balaam and the Jewish historian Simon Dubnow. Dubnow was an important Jewish scholar, Buber pointed out, while Balaam was a Mesopotamian diviner who served Israel's enemy. Simon agreed to change the text, but what impressed him was that Buber had chosen to discuss the change in a face-to-face meeting.

Buber's growing alienation from the war is strongly hinted at in one of his most moving utterances of this period, a letter he wrote to his Prague friends, his disciples among the Bar Kochbans, in September 1916. Looking back, Buber now saw with different eyes the charismatic figure that he had been for them at that time: "I spoke and you heard too much pride; you spoke, and I heard too much humility." Buber related a legend from the lore associated with the Golem, the Frankenstein monster that the great Rabbi Lowe of Prague was said to have created to protect the Jews of the seventeenth-century Prague from their persecutors. Every Friday evening before it was Sabbath, Rabbi Lowe drew forth the name of God from under the tongue of the Golem and he became again a lump of clay. But once, Rabbi Lowe forgot to do this and went into the Old-New Synagogue to pray with the community. They had already begun to recite the Sabbath song when Rabbi Lowe recollected that he had left the Golem living. Immediately he called out, "It is not yet Sabbath! It is not yet Sabbath! It is not yet Sabbath!" And because, went the legend, the Old-New Synagogue was built out of the stones of the original Temple in Palestine, his wish was granted and it was not yet Sabbath in heaven or on earth. "Friends," Buber concluded, "it is not yet Sabbath! First we must draw forth the name from under the tongue of the Golem!" The redemption of the Jewish people and of mankind, to which Buber and the Bar Kochbans had looked in the days of Buber's *Speeches on Judaism,* was obstructed by the Golem, the Frankenstein monster of war that the nations had created but could not control. To draw the name of God forth from under the tongue of this Golem meant to put an end to it by putting an end to the pretense of divine sanction and divine meaning with which it had been endowed.

In December 1916, Buber wrote "A Hero Book," in which he celebrated those who had rejected the false values of Europe and America for the building of values that no success or power guaranteed. The true heroes are those who fell voluntarily guarding the collective settlements in Palestine, rather than the soldiers in the war in Europe who did not fight or die of their own free choice. Thus, Buber had reached the very standpoint from which Landauer had once criticized him. This same contrast between the German and the Jewish hero entered into a talk on Jewish education that Buber gave at a Zionist conference in January 1917.

Buber shared with the other German Jews the expectation that the cessation of party strife proclaimed by the kaiser would give the Jews for the first time full protection and genuinely equal rights. But this proved to be anything but the case. The anti-Semites soon complained that few if any Jews were to be found in the front line, and the German army itself conducted a fake census to "prove" this contention true. These experiences within Germany, plus the disillusionment with the war itself, led to a gradual change of emphasis which, without weakening his deep ties to the German language and folk spirit, nonetheless led Buber to insist ever more unambiguously that the German Jews' primary identification had to be with the Jewish people, where their roots lay, rather than with the German, even though their language and culture were formed by the latter. The rising tide of German anti-Semitism made *Der Jude,* precisely in its character of an independent cultural organ of great breadth and high quality, a first-class, great political force.

The frequent correspondence among Buber, Hermann, Viktor Jacobson, Julius Berger, and other prominent Zionists over the content of the articles for *Der Jude* suggests that unofficially *Der Jude* was regarded as the spokesman for Zionism, even though it was independent of any political party. Without censorship by any organization, there was a remarkable amount of collaborative control in the production of *Der Jude.* Jacobson took exception to a central theme in one of Buber's own essays, the one that contained the first reply to Hermann Cohen in the famous debate between them over Zionism. Hermann Cohen was the great neo-Kantian philosopher of Marburg and the recognized spiritual leader of German Jewry. Cohen identified himself with the Liberal Jews and the anti-Zionists, although, unlike many of them, he had vivid sympathy for and understanding of the Polish Jews and contributed an article to *Der Jude* on this subject. Buber was an atypical Zionist and Cohen an atypical anti-Zionist, as Ernst Simon has pointed ed out in a historical reevaluation of their debate. The point at issue, nonetheless, was that between a man who, for all his universalism, gave the primacy to the German state, and a man who, for all his allegiance to the community in which he lived, pointed to the Jewish people as a more basic reality for the German Jew than was the German state. Buber looked up to the older man as a great thinker and even a great Jew, but he found himself compelled to reply to Cohen's fiery and unjustified attacks against the whole of Zionism. There was, in fact, as Ernst Simon has said, no one except Buber who could answer Cohen on behalf of the Zionists. This was because only Buber had the intellectual and spiritual stature in the German-Jewish community to make him a worthy opponent of Cohen's. But it was also because Buber was at this point the most representative spokesman, even if not the real political leader, of the German Zionists.

The occasion and implicit central topic of the interchange between Cohen and Buber was the war itself. Buber pointed out at the beginning of his open letter to Cohen that Cohen justified his position by citing his fear that the danger that he saw in Zionism would become ever greater and more real as a result of the heightened international tension. The thrust of Buber's further reply was a distinction between people and state that Cohen was not ready or able to make, a distinction that guarded Buber against *both* German nationalism and Jewish nationalism being made ends in themselves. This position contains in germ Buber's much later central distinction between "the social principle" and "the political principle." But its first application and its first occasion here was a radical and permanent change in his relationship both to the First World War and to the Zionist movement.

Buber sharply rejected Cohen's definition of nationality as a purely natural fact, in favor of the understanding of nationality as a reality of the spirit and of the ethos that demands to be realized in our own lives. But at the same time and for the same reason, Buber attacked Cohen's definition of "nation" as being identical with a community established and founded by the state. There were levels of German Jewry that Buber confessed he could not regard as a nationality: "But I need only read a verse from Bialik [the great Hebrew poet of the twentieth century] or a letter from Eretz Israel [the Land of Israel] and I feel: here is nation, no, here is more than nation—here is a people." "Nation" could be understood after the pattern of modern nationalism; "people" established the link not only with the history of the Jewish people in the Diaspora but with the very covenant that made them a people in the first place and preserved them as a people down through the ages. This simple distinction represents the decisive transition from Buber's Zionism of the Jewish Renaissance, with its celebration of the dynamism and creativity of the awakening people, to his later biblical Zionism, with its understanding of the inseparable connection of the land, the people, and the task of making real the kingship of God.

The war clearly was no longer, for Buber, a movement of the German community but an activity of the German state. His unconditional denial of Cohen's religion, controlled by an ethics that is, in turn, controlled and consummated by the state, was equally an expression of his growing alienation from the war with which formerly, at least in its aspect of a new awakening, he was able to identify himself. This same experience also protected Buber against any narrow Jewish nationalism in which the "Jewish State" should become an end in itself.

In 1918, Landauer's friend Fritz Mauthner, the distinguished philosopher of speech, stated, on the basis of his belief that the German Jews should be assimilated into the German population, that the border of Germany should be barred to the Jews from Eastern Europe. Buber was pained by this statement and, precisely because he cherished his own relationship with Mauthner, felt he could not remain silent concerning it: "In my experience the atmosphere between real persons is only troubled when it remains unspoken." To this he added that even the most German of Jews should—despite all aesthetic considerations—know and recognize that the *Ostjuden* represent "an enormous reservoir of spiritual, moral, and social energy." In an article of October 1917, Buber singled out for special attack those German Jews who rejected the Jews of the East. The East is the great basin from which the Western Jews, including these self-styled German patriots, have always renewed themselves, Buber declared.

When Buber learned that his friend the Jewish novelist Jakob Wasserman* had made a disparaging statement about the Eastern Jews, Buber called him to account at their next meeting, and the two men never spoke again.

By October 1917, Buber's critical attitude toward warring Germany, the antithesis of everything he stood for, had become so sharp that he published a bitter attack on the growing German anti-Semitism and the German nationalism that had bred it. Equal rights cannot be made dependent upon belonging to the nation dominating in the state, Buber declared. Like Landauer, Buber now stood in unequivocal opposition to the war, but his ground was not only humanity but also Judaism. In explicit opposition to his friend Walther Rathenau and all the other apologists who tried to make Judaism respectable by presenting it as a minimal religion, Buber declared that Judaism was founded on the memory of a great and meaningful destiny and the hope of the fulfillment of its meaning in a messianic future. One can no more tear out of Judaism this connection of the generations without shattering its structure, than one could tear the person of Christ out of Christianity: "He who does not *remember* that God has led him out of Egypt, he who does not *await* the Messiah is no longer a true Jew." Not "blood" but history now gave Buber a solid ground from which he could publish a clear and unprecedented denunciation of the perverted attitude that had become common in wartime Germany. Only a country that nourishes mistrust would lay the ground for new mistrust, he wrote. Only a country that refused to share civilian rights and freedom until they can no longer be withheld lives in fear of their consequences.

The First World War was Buber's breakthrough to dialogue, and this breakthrough was not a single event, "conversion," or experience of faith but an ever-repeated alternation of darkness and illumination, of finding a way forward and of knocking his head against a wall, of repeated efforts to recap-

---

*(1873–1934). Famous German author of novels and stories, essays, biographies, and autobiographical pieces.

ture the open immediacy of the Potsdam meeting and of repeated recognition of the limitation of actual community. "During the First World War," declared Buber in 1952,

> it became clear to me that a process was going on which before then I had only surmised. This was the growing difficulty of genuine dialogue, and most especially of genuine dialogue between persons of different kinds and convictions.... I began to understand at that time, more than thirty years ago, that this is the central question for the fate of mankind.

It is no accident that out of this experience of the growing difficulty of genuine dialogue Buber came to his first formulation of his classic statement of the philosophy of dialogue. It was at the very height of the war, in 1916, that Buber wrote his first draft of *I and Thou*. What he said of this draft in his 1957 postscript does not suggest a catastrophic breakthrough that rejected all his prior thought and experience. Nonetheless, only the encounter with the terrible realities of the war had enabled Buber to achieve a clearer vision:

> When I drafted the first sketch of this book (more than forty years ago), I was impelled by an inward necessity. A vision which had come to me again, had now reached a firm clarity. This clarity was so manifestly suprapersonal in its nature that I at once knew I had to bear witness to it.

Only after the war, in 1919, was Buber able to write a new draft of *I and Thou*, and only in the years between 1919 and 1923 was he able to find the right words as well and rewrite the book in its final form. Before this was to take place, Buber had to live through some of the most active and terrible years of his life—the years of his call for religious socialism and true community, the years of postwar disintegration and the murder of his friends Landauer and Walther Rathenau. But his "conversion" was irreversible. The First World War was the real turning point in Buber's life, one that led to ever-greater soberness and concreteness in walking the "narrow ridge."

A visible symbol of the change that the First World War wrought in Buber was the inner necessity to move from Zehlendorf, the suburb of Berlin in which he had lived since his return from Florence, to Heppenheim an der Bergstrasse. Before we tell this story, it will be helpful if we fill in some details concerning the Buber family life in Zehlendorf not yet touched on in earlier chapters.

Paula and Martin were inseparable for sixty years and lived in strong mutual dependence. Martin came from a well-to-do family that brought in the money, while Paula had no connection with her family from the time she married. Paula dominated the household and set the tone for the family. Like Martin's grandmother, Adele, she protected Martin from the interference of the little things that arose in the household, distanced him from everyday events, and made sure that the children did not bother him or make too much noise when he worked. The family took its meals together, with Martin presiding. Raffi also did not go to school at first, though later he went to high school, as Eva did not. As citizens of Austria living in Germany, the Buber's were not required to send their children to school as they would have had they been German citizens. Eva went to school for a short period when she was six or seven, but her parents withdrew her. Her mother taught her reading and writing, and, in the beginning, she also taught her mathematics.

When Eva grew older, she studied history with her father, and also had a private tutor who taught her French. Once a week she went to the progressive Odenwaldschule near Heppenheim to receive a French lesson from a teacher there whom she liked very much. When she was fifteen years old, one of her parents' uncles, who was a math professor, came to Heppenheim at times to teach her mathematics.

Raffi was stronger than Eva, but they played together and slept in the same room when they were children. They shared a whole world of the imagination that they never told anyone about. Thus was set a foundation of good and close relations that lasted them all their lives. Yet their ways of adjusting to living with two such strong and gifted parents were almost opposite. Raffi again and again showed himself the rebel who broke away from the family, while Eva was the obedient child who remained close to the family even after she married an older poet who was a friend of her father's. Eva remained close to Martin; Raffi distanced himself from him but not really from Paula, to whom he bore a striking resemblance as he aged.

A glimpse into the Bubers' family life of the time is provided by Eva, who recalled many years later that, when she and Raffi were young children, most of the education was in Paula's hands while there was little relationship with Martin. Paula took care of them, washed them, combed their hair, and even taught them. The atmosphere of the family was a patriarchal one. The servants were treated as part of the family, and at times the children played with them. One touching story Eva told was of the time (1911) that she told an intimate secret to her mother, which her mother, to her horror, proceeded to tell others.

> I got so angry that I grabbed her and started yelling at her. Then Father came out of his study and beat me very hard. Strong smacks. I was about ten years old then. After I quieted down I thought about it and entered his study and told him that he had made a mistake in hitting me before hearing my side. He told me that he was sorry and that the beating would stand to my credit, so the next time I was wrong he wouldn't beat me. But I was a good girl and never had the chance to use my credit. Still I enjoyed hearing him say that he was sorry.

In September 1915, Buber announced to Landauer that Paula and he had decided to buy a house in Heppenheim, which they were going to move into in April. The first enthusiasm of the war that had led Buber to celebrate Berlin, even in all its ugliness, now gave way to a raw sensitivity that made this center of bustling war activity impossible for him. But the strongest ground for the Bubers' change of place was "the need for a life with nature in landscape adequate to our feelings." Almost half a century later, when he was awarded an honorary doctorate at Heidelberg University, Buber testified: "Shortly after the beginning of the First World War—which I already at that time experienced as the beginning of the crisis of mankind—I found living in Berlin all too painful." The income from his father's estate enabled Buber to live independently, and it was not for another eight years that he was to enter academic life as an instructor of Jewish religion and ethics at Frankfurt University. Yet even now, university life must have attracted Buber, for when he looked around for a quieter dwelling place, his choice fell on the neighborhood of Heidelberg. Buber had not studied at Heidelberg and had no official connection with the university until 1964, when he received the honorary degree. Yet in the world of imagination of young men of that time, Heidelberg was "the exemplary abode of great teaching."

Thus, when Martin was thirty-eight years old and Paula thirty-nine, they moved from Berlin to Heppenheim, a charming, flower-mantled village in the Bergstrasse wine-growing region south of Darmstadt. There they lived for twenty years in a three-story gray house at Werlestrasse 2, a quiet corner in a residential neighborhood. During those years, Buber appeared to his neighbors to be an unusually shy man who seldom spoke, someone out of whose way even children stayed, as though they were afraid of him. He always wore a long black beard and a black hat that sat on his head "like a duckpond." Buber could be seen nightly through a big window of his house, sitting up very late, his head framed by both hands, deeply engrossed in his books. Paula Buber described him in those days as someone who was so absorbed in his work that people mistakenly thought him unaware of what was going on around him. But those who really knew him, as she did, knew that he was always fully aware of, and very much concerned with, the events of the household, the city, the country, and the world. What appeared to strangers as absentmindedness was really an extraordinary capacity for the most intense concentration.

In August 1917, Buber wrote Ludwig Strauss, thanking him for the cycle of poems he had sent and dedicated to him and Paula, "Visit to H."—a wonderful poetic evocation of the garden behind the Bubers' new home in Heppenheim and the river that adjoined it. "It was and is a very great joy to both of us. It is at once heartmoving and heartstilling, to see our moments in common so tied in with the timeless memory of the poem. And when, after I had read it, we walked through the garden, it too seemed to express a thankful agreement." In December 1917, Strauss, though the younger man, showed his personal and literary independence by writing Buber a critical letter concerning the way he had put together pieces of various kinds and various times in his book *Ereignisse und Begenungen* (Events and Meetings). Buber, in no wise put out, thanked him, even though he was not able, for the most part, to agree with him.

From the time that she was fifteen years old, from 1916 on, Eva had conversations with her father on spiritual topics. Martin would clarify concepts and define them in such a way that it was a regular exercise in philosophy for her. When she was sixteen, Martin read her the first draft of *I and Thou,* an event that sixty years later she said had influenced her entire life, including her relationship to religion: "I always tried to live in the light of the book's message." She had private teachers for English and French, read Shakespeare in English, understood Italian, and learned geography, physics, and chemistry from her parents. Her friends in Berlin included Gustav Landauer's daughter Lotte, to whom she was especially close. When the family moved from Berlin to Heppenheim, she joined the *Blau-Weiss* Jewish youth movement, which had a meeting place close to Heppenheim. They discussed topics brought up by the counselor, to whom she felt close, and went hiking and visited places like Mannheim. At times, all the members of her *Blau-Weiss* group came to visit her and stayed at her house. The members of the movement had good relations with her father and mother. Martin, in fact, was one of the acknowledged spiritual leaders of the movement. Once, when Rafael and Eva went to a party supporting the war, Martin and Paula told them they were not happy about their being with all those German chauvinists. This, of course, was after Martin had changed from being a patriot to a critic of the war.

Raffi suffered from being the son of someone who at the age of thirty was already a famous Jewish leader and a well-known philosopher. When Raffi was a teenager, the name of Martin Buber was surrounded by glory, which made life very difficult for him. Once when he went to a summer camp, so many people asked him if he was Martin Buber's son that he wrote a big sign with the word "Yes" on it and paraded around in it! He, too, suffered, like Eva, because his parents did not send him to school but had him tutored privately, a convenience for Martin and Paula but a deprivation for their children.

At the age of twelve, Rafael, unlike Eva, was sent to high school. Martin demanded that he bring home high grades, but private tutors did not prepare Rafael adequately for school. Raffi was an adventurous boy who would disappear from home suddenly. Once he ran away from home and joined a circus. Paula even wrote a story about a boy called Raffi who would do all sorts of things that were nice but that made his parents worry. At the age of fourteen, he had a steady girlfriend, something that his parents could not have been happy with. During the war, a plane fell near Heppenheim. Raffi went to guard the plane and caught pneumonia.

Raffi was bright and promising but, in later life, Paula was disappointed in his development. In short, both his parents, by what they were as much as what they said, placed demands on him that he found impossible to meet. Later, Raffi became an anti-intellectual and wanted to show off how well he dealt with worldly matters. Martin and Paula did not want him to go into business, so they sent him to a technical school in Vienna to learn mechanical engineering, especially of agricultural machines. When Raffi was seventeen, he left high school and enlisted in the Austrian army. All the young teachers in his high school had gone into the army, so that only the old and sick ones remained. As Haim Gordon reports in his interviews of the family, there was one old teacher who kept cursing his students, saying, "Our boys are at the front and you are sitting here spending your time on foolish endeavors. Go join the army." Sick of hearing all that preaching, Raffi did just that. At first, both Martin and Paula were very upset, but they ordered a uniform for him and, in the end were proud of him. However, when Paula got angry, she would speak of the tension between Rafael and herself.

Both parents were very domineering with their children, but, many years later, Paula said to her granddaughters, "Now I understand many things that I didn't understand when your father was young—for instance, that it is natural for a boy to be mischievous." Martin placed demands on Raffi and told him off when he was out of order, at times hitting him and slapping him in the face as well.

When Buber wrote Rappeport in January 1918, telling him of the mustering of his seventeen-year-old son, he commented that for some years they had not been in the age of war but of something else, something nameless. He asked Rappeport to keep an eye on Raffi and suggested that he could have an important influence on his life that Buber as his father could not exercise: "I have a deep concern about this still unfinished, still wholly unformed youth whom I must allow to wander forth into the world of confusion." In March 1918, Buber wrote Ludwig Strauss that he felt close enough to Strauss to confide in him that Paula had taken Raffi's enlistment to heart far more than he had foreseen. Buber asked Strauss to write and postpone his visit without indicating that Buber had written him.

Several long letters that Martin and Paula wrote to their young friend Rappeport in April 1918 reveal their great concern about Raffi and his situation, which seemed uncertain to them, and they enlisted Rappeport's help as far as they could. Paula also wrote Rappeport about her garden, including the vegetables, which were Martin's responsibility. In a long, loving, impassioned letter that Martin wrote Paula in October 1918, he told her, among other things, not to be concerned about Raffi or about their house or about what other people said: "Your truth will win out." This letter is a powerful testimony to the unique and enduring quality of the love between Martin and Paula.

♦ 6 ♦

Communal Socialism and Revolution: The Murder of Landauer

(1906-1919)

Without question, the single most important influence on Buber's teaching of community was his friend Gustav Landauer's socialism. The chapter that Buber devoted to Landauer in *Paths in Utopia* (1949) clearly coincides with Buber's own views and is, indeed, a memorial to his friend, whose own writing was tragically cut off along with his life. Landauer's opposition to the war was based not only on pacifism but also on an inherent antagonism to the state, which made him as clearly an anarchist as a socialist, or, putting it differently, a socialist of community and of communities of communities as opposed to a socialist of the state. "In our souls we take no part in the compulsory unity of the state," Landauer proclaimed, "since we wish to create a genuine human bond, a society proceeding from the spirit and therefore from freedom."

In his funeral speech for Landauer's daughter Charlotte in 1927, Buber summarized Landauer's socialism in a single sentence:

> Gustav Landauer had recognized that the new community of mankind for which we hope cannot coalesce out of individuals, that it cannot arise out of the chaos in which we live, out of this atomizing of individuals, so that individuals would come to individuals and join with them, but that there must exist cells, small community cells out of which alone the great human community can be built.

Elsewhere, Buber characterized the building of socialism, as Landauer in his

mature spirit understood it, not as political action but as immediate beginning, as an elemental commitment to living and realizing. "No one has
preached socialism in this epoch so fervently and powerfully as he, and no
one has so led the great attacks on the party programs and party tactics
which are almost universally identified with socialism."

According to Eugene Lunn, "Landauer was a gentle, thoughtful,
humane man who was not given either to violent behavior or to doctrinal
fanaticism, a man with a voice so peaceful and soft that it at once won trust
and affection and with words, every one of which came from the soul and
bore the stamp of absolute integrity." The intense ethical fervor that Landauer
experienced during World War I and the 1918–1919 Revolution led him to
make heavy demands upon himself and others and to display impatience,
restlessness, and irritability. It also led many to compare him with the
prophets of the Hebrew Bible or with Jesus, impressions heightened by his
physical appearance:

> He was thin, narrow-chested, and more than six feet tall; his deep
> black hair hung down to his shoulders, while his full dark beard
> framed a long, pale, and even gaunt face. He walked with giant
> steps along the street, often wearing a long cape and an unfash-
> ionable old hat.

Because of the closeness of their friendship, the impact of Landauer on
Buber was not merely one of ideas and doctrines but also of personality.
Indeed, the former were inseparable from the latter. The glimpses that we
have had of that personality in its relationship to Buber are supplemented by
the testimony of another close friend of Landauer's, Julius Bab:

> ...In the midst of this ever-new interest in works, men, and
> groups, Landauer was still solitary, had very few friends in the full
> sense of this difficult word and also not many lasting comrades....
> The demon in Landauer that sacrificed all the forces of his inner
> life to a passionate goal, also sacrificed friendships and comrade-
> ships in great number. In the midst of his tireless strivings he
> could have no patience with men; he was not patient, he was not
> tolerant—as the wholly unavoidable reverse side of his truly great
> courage a frightfully rigid pride at times became visible....
> Landauer recognized himself to be a "man-eater," a restless con-
> sumer of men.... Thus this prophet of the commune was in his
> personal life almost a solitary man, and he was, remained and had
> to remain a *poor* man.

From his earliest beginnings in the anarchist movement, Landauer was pursued by the Prussian authorities, and for years he was continually trailed by
police spies. He was one of the most-watched men in Germany. He passed
eleven months of his youth in prison because of his statements on freedom,
and later another six months because he wanted to save an innocent

man who was imprisoned as a murderer and to this end advanced weighty, solidly grounded, but not fully provable, complaints against the police prosecutors.

Even within the sphere of the anarchist and revolutionary movements, Landauer's enormously creative writings remained almost unnoticed. For his whole life, he was without means, without security, and without regular occupation, not only in terms of his practical needs but, above all, with regard to the possibility of expressing and furthering his cause to the full extent that he longed to. Gustav Landauer's downfall came, according to his friend the noted language scholar Fritz Mauthner, because he was no politician and yet was driven, by intense sympathy with the people, to declare himself politically. Too proud to join a party, not narrow enough to form a party in his own name, he was thrown back on himself, a leader without an army. Once, before the turn of the century at an international party meeting in Switzerland, he was publicly abused by August Bebel, the German Social Democratic leader, as an *agent provocateur* of the German government, and in consequence was beaten by some of the comrades. He did not get angry, but instead said to Mauthner: "And this Bebel is one of the best, an exemplary man; he is so stupid only because he is a politician."

Landauer possessed an extraordinary spiritual power over the people to whom he spoke, according to Mauthner: "He could have been a demagogue of the first rank, like Ferdinand Lassalle." Perhaps it is because Landauer did not fall into the temptation of becoming a demagogue that his image remained intact for Buber, as that of Lassalle, the hero of Buber's early youth, did not.

In 1906, Buber wrote to Landauer a long letter, urging him to write the pamphlet entitled "Revolution" for the forty social-psychological monographs that Buber edited from 1905 to 1919 under the title *Die Gesellschaft.* Buber thought rightly that Landauer was qualified as no one else to set forth what revolution means as a psychological and spiritual process. Landauer wrote the monograph—a meaningful, yet, as it turned out, sinister foreshadowing of the revolution in which he lost his own life.

Buber held that Landauer's monthly, *Der Sozialist,* was the best journal of its kind in Germany. Others, Eugene Lunn notes, have esteemed it the best anarchist journal in the world at that time:

> The paper was an ideal vehicle for Landauer's myriad interests in world literature, philosophy, and current social and political problems. Its wide range and its theoretical focus, however, created a handicap for the development of the movement whose organ it was: the Socialist Bund tended to attract largely middle-class intellectuals, instead of elements from all sections of society as Landauer had hoped.

Landauer anticipated by half a century the women's liberation movement. He refused to take part with Buber in the founding of a college unless women were included in the student body, and Buber went along with this radical stance. Yet Landauer's views on feminist thought boomeranged ironically in his relationship with the Bubers. Landauer had urged Buber to encourage Paula to do writing of her own, and shortly after this last interchange, Paula did, in fact, publish her first book of stories, *The Illegitimate Children of Adam*—under a masculine pseudonym, Georg Munk. Buber confided to Landauer who the author of the stories really was, and Landauer made the mistake of mentioning this at a party at the Bubers', an indiscretion for which Paula Buber never forgave him. No doubt his pleasure in Paula's creativity and his desire to communicate it were entirely in accord with his theories about feminist thought, but not with Paula's personal preferences. "My wife has the uncommon, intensive, and steady wish," Buber wrote him, "not to see her relationships to persons and to human society in general influenced by literary activities." This breach Landauer tried to heal through a letter to Buber. "I believe that I have discretion in my blood," wrote Landauer, "but I also have something else: ...wrestling for wholeness in friendship." He pointed out that Buber had freely revealed to him Georg Munk's identity and with the consent of his wife. "The question is," he continued, using Buber's own concept of inclusion, "whether I also must be discreet in relation to your wife, or whether she will give me permission to include this part of her being when I speak with her." It is not that Landauer wanted to speak with her about her authorship but that he wanted in talking with her to feel that he could really speak to her as whole person to whole person. "Dear, honored Mrs. Buber," Landauer concluded in a touching plea, "please receive in a friendly way these words which particularly and again seek to attain your friendship. The world is very lonely, and breaking through the crusts is a calling that was once given to me and to which I will not become untrue." Martin replied that naturally Landauer did not have to be "discreet" with Paula, but he suggested that Landauer erred when he represented to himself the genuine being of women as existing, incomparably more than that of men, in the way of living and not in *what* they did, for this was true of men and women alike.

In a pencil sketch of a letter to Landauer in his notebooks on *Daniel*, Buber wrote, "You are the only one among my friends for whom Daniel was there from the beginning. So it is as more than an expression of a feeling that I dedicate this first proclamation of his life." In July 1912, Buber sent to Landauer the first dialogue of *Daniel*, "On Direction," and Landauer responded with enthusiasm and the highest praise.

Landauer's reaction to the second dialogue, "On Reality," was more critical. You must give us more concreteness, visibility, vitality." A still more significant criticism was evoked by Landauer's reading of the fourth dialogue, "On Polarity":

Here now in this dialogue there is the peculiar fact that Daniel does nothing else at all than to tell of the way that he has gone (in a wonderfully beautiful, ever more intense structure); yet in the description of the way, there is, for my understanding, too little chaos, too little passion of struggling, questioning, forming, too much terminology, finish, and compactness. You must not content yourself with beholding the results within yourself, artistically yet composedly, and transcribing them from your soul. You must compel us in a stronger and more living fashion.

Without any question, the criticism of this older man whom Buber looked up to, and who spoke his opinions with honesty and love, must have had a great salutary influence on Buber in weaning him away from abstraction, vague emotion, and the "easy word," to ever-greater concreteness and solidity. However much Buber saw *Daniel* as the "final teaching," Landauer did not. "When despair is talked about in the last and most significant dialogue of *Daniel,* we long for more agitation, more volcanic and even common expression. Martin Buber is an uncompromising and not easily satisfied man," Landauer concluded. "We ought not to bestow any applause on him of which he would be ashamed."

"There was in Germany in the time of its greatest distance from God," wrote Buber after Landauer's death, "a man who, as no other, summoned this country and this hour to the turning. For the sake of coming humanity that his soul beheld and longed for, he strove against the inhumanity in which he had to live." Landauer rejected the centralistic, mechanistic pseudosocialism because he bore in his heart a federalistic, organic, community socialism. Thus, in a society in which all public life was narrowed to politics, and creativity frozen to party activity, he had to remain without allies and to propagate his truth with great difficulty. As powerful and impassioned as his speech was, it always moved only individuals: the few who were inwardly open and ready. For Landauer demanded something unheard of: that one not be content with acknowledging an idea and espousing it but that one must take it seriously and begin to act upon it; that socialism is not an affair of then and there but of here and now. Proletariat and intellectuals alike were impervious to such a demand: the proletariat because they had grown up with the doctrine that socialism is an inevitable end product of an unalterable, scientifically accountable development, and because this teaching had stifled in them the courage to dare that is the primal principle of all real beginning; the intellectuals either because they were fully estranged from social events or because they imagined they could master them with political slogans.

The motif of community had entered permanently into Buber's Zionism at the time of the First World War. In its name, he even shoved aside what until now had occupied the central place in his teaching of the Jewish Renaissance and his renewed Zionist activity—cultural work. We do not want "culture" but life, Buber declared to the delegates at a meeting of German and Dutch Zionists in February 1917. A *Jewish* life can only be the life of a *community*. Those who try to secure a homeland in Palestine will not have it unless in all their actions they guard the responsibility to found a pure and just human life together. Social education without national education would mean working in a dream, but national education without social education would mean waking in madness.

In February 1918, in reply to a long anti-Zionist letter from Stefan Zweig,* Buber declared that he knew nothing of a "Jewish state with cannon, flags, and medals" even in the form of a dream. His concern was to build community. He saw a Jewish Palestine only as the beginning of a movement in which the spirit would be realized. To Trotsky, at that time one of the leaders of the Russian Revolution, realization would be denied because the ideal lived only in the doctrine but not in the method. Buber invited a number of persons to contribute to a collection of essays against the penetration of imperialism and mercantilism into Palestine, essays that would not be polemical in character but would point to the threatening danger and offer an image of community. Gustav Landauer rejected this invitation out of hand, which reflected not only his non-Zionism but also his reaction to the events of the time, including the Russian Revolution: "The real event that is significant and perhaps decisive for us Jews is only the liberation of Russia." Landauer's response foreshadowed his own tragic participation in the Munich Revolution.

One of the most effective forms in which Buber himself carried on Jewish politics during those years was in his relation to the Jewish youth and in particular the Jewish youth movement. During the war and during the 1920s, Buber also had a considerable influence on the German youth movement in general, earlier through his presentation of the parables of Chuang-tzu and the teaching of the Tao, later through his emphasis on community. But he also had a quite specific and much greater impact on the Jewish youth movements of Germany and Austria, including the famous Blau-Weiss group, which had established itself when Aryan clauses excluded Jews from the Wandervogel and other general youth groups during and after the First World War.

In March 1917, Buber wrote Franz Werfel that, in his view, youth is indeed the true bearer of *every* great movement, but it cannot be the *object* of a true movement; it is the immortal shaper of the program of humanity, but it may not itself become that program. This criticism of the youth movement in no way meant a withdrawal from it on Buber's part. Siegfried Bernfeld, a psychoanalyst in Freud's second circle, leader of the Jewish youth movement in Austria, and later Buber's own secretary, wrote Buber in September 1917, telling him how central his participation in a youth day for the Vienna Jewish youth groups would be: "In our feeling the conference is

*(1881–1942). Lyricist, dramatist, storyteller, author of biographies and essays.

senseless if it is not you who form its center." In May 1918, Buber published in *Der Jude* a classic address entitled "Zion and Youth," which was destined to have a far-reaching effect upon the development of the Jewish youth movement in the years to come. "Youth," said Buber, "is the eternal chance for happiness of mankind, the chance for happiness that is offered it ever anew and injured by it ever anew." Now, for the first time, Buber saw the call to youth as made up of three inextricable elements—the national, the social, the religious—and its task as the fight for freedom, revolution, and apostleship. A true Jewish community cannot be any other than that in which the commands of Moses for the equalization of property and the call of the prophets for social justice become a reality in a form including and mastering the economic relations of our time. To build Zion means to found a living immediacy between men. Buber's hope and faith now rested on the new tillers of the soil in Israel, the pioneers *(Halutzim)*.

The distinction that Buber made between the surface success of Herzl and the underground "dark charisma" of his defeated opponents within Zionism, Buber now applied to the contrast between "this world's madness for success, which today presumes to be the real world and is in reality only a power-swollen puppet," and the very different world history of Amos, Jeremiah, Jesus, and Spinoza, the earthshakers who died without "success." He called on the Jewish youth to reject the former for the latter, rejecting thereby the world of lies and godforsaken dualism, in which men substitute the rhetoric of ideals for personal commitment.

On receiving Buber's book *My Way to Hasidism* (1917), Landauer wrote Buber that this progress from report to confession to teaching had done Landauer's heart much good. Strikingly, precisely in *My Way to Hasidism*, which Buber wrote in 1918 and dedicated, when it was published in 1919, to Landauer's memory, Buber pointed in particular to Hasidism "as a bold endeavor to establish," in the midst of the confusion of the Diaspora, "a true community, and to create a brotherly union out of all the people bent under the yoke of an alien environment and threatened by degeneration."

The religious socialism that Buber developed in 1918 and 1919 was a *social* and *decentralistic* socialism in the strongest possible contrast to the *political* and highly centralized socialism that was developing in Russia in the aftermath of the Bolsheviks' taking power. Even in 1919, Buber saw the true nature of the socialist power-state which, in the name of compulsory justice and equality, makes impossible spontaneous community and genuine relationship between man and man. True to the "narrow ridge," he refused the clamoring either/or of the modern world—the demand that one accept a centralized socialist state because of the defects of capitalism or a capitalist society because of the defects of socialism. If Buber rejected Marx's economic determinism and the centralism of the Soviet state, he did not fail to recognize the part that the profit motive at the heart of the capitalist system played in causing and prolonging the war.

In a series entitled *Words to the Age,* planned in 1919 for the Three Country Publishers of Munich, Vienna, and Zurich, Buber published two pamphlets, "Basic Principles" and "Community." It is in "Community," the second of Buber's *Words to the Age,* that he set forth most clearly his criticism of Marxism as the completion of that very process of development from community to association that capitalism has begun. The state of universal paradox in which we have lived until now is that of a fever-ridden tyrant whose spasms mean the suffering and ruin of millions, yet in whose kingdom the holy child of community lies concealed in the trappings of unions and comradeships. The state of the socialist order, if it ever attains undisputed sovereignty, will be a blank-eyed, indifferent ruler who will prevent all exploitation of men by men yet in whose realm there will be no room for community. "Community" *(Gemeinschaft),* of all Buber's early works, most clearly looks forward to *I and Thou* both in language and in thought. It was during this very year, 1919, indeed, that Buber completed his first draft of *Ich und Du.* Yet we cannot understand the road to *I and Thou* adequately without considering the murder of Gustav Landauer.

Landauer's second wife was the noted German poet Hedwig Lachmann, who composed the libretto for Richard Strauss's opera *Salomé.* When she succumbed to a fatal illness in February 1918, at the age of thirty-five, it was for Landauer a fearful blow. "One could since then observe something unsteady in him," testified a friend,

> an unrest that drove him to expend his life. I believe that since then an impatience came over him for some definitive self-involvement and action from which a contemplative aspect of his personality had formerly held him back. The calm warming light of his being was caught upward into a self-destroying flame. This was his state of mind when he was taken hold of by the revolution that demanded and needed him.

The so-called German Revolution was really a series of revolts in a number of major cities occasioned far more by the defeat in the war than by the example of the Russian Revolution, itself a product of the war and the virtual breakdown of the Russian army. On November 11, 1918, the Allies signed an armistice with Germany and the Austro-Hungarian Empire, and it was in that same month that the "Revolution" began in Munich, Berlin, and other parts of Germany, lasting sporadically until the following May. Fritz Mauthner reported that Landauer came to him in the fall of 1918 in feverish expectation of the "world revolution" that he had helped prepare and for which he had for thirty years suffered privation. When the revolution broke out soon after, Gustav Landauer was ready—ready for death.

The German Revolution meant for Landauer no lessening of the isolation in which he had always lived and no real illusion that this revolution would differ from the others about which he had written. In April 1918, he wrote: "Ah, how I am needed! And how I have no more desire to give advice that will not be taken and to criticize what is not done." In fact, his advice was not taken, and the great hope that he had cherished for so many years was lost.

When the German Revolution broke out, Landauer was fully aware of the tragic failure of all previous revolutions and of the fact that socialism had never once existed as a reality. The feeling with which he entered the revolution was not hope but grim decision to do in this crisis what he was obliged to do, not as a spiritual leader and pathbreaker, but as one of the small band of constructive German revolutionaries: to effect what he could of the blessings of revolution and avert what he could of its curse.

On November 15, 1918, Landauer announced to Buber that he was bitterly opposed to the coming summons to a so-called national assembly: "Behind it is hidden only the long-dead party." Nonetheless, he did want to take part in the preparation for the new democracy. "I should like to go to Berlin as representative of Bavaria," he wrote Buber, "and that you should work in Vienna in the same capacity." This dream of his was not to be realized. In its place came the revolution in Munich. On November 22, exactly one week after the earlier letter, Landauer told Buber that he wanted to return to Munich, where he found himself in the closest agreement with Kurt Eisner, German journalist and socialist leader in Bavaria. "The situation is very serious: if the Revolution emerges intact from *this* liquidation of *this* war, it will be almost a miracle.... Despite all, this I can promise you, Bavaria will not give up its autonomy." Landauer then asked Buber to sketch for him his thoughts on the education of the people, the nature of publication, and so forth, or, better still, to come soon to Munich. There Buber would find Landauer working splendidly, together with Kurt Eisner, whose democracy was as anarchistic as Landauer's own. On December 13, Landauer wrote Buber, urgently asking for information on the fight of the Bolsheviks against the Left Social Revolutionaries. Yet Buber did not take part in the preparation for the Munich Räterepublik in which Landauer briefly held power.

Buber could not go along with Landauer's revolutionary activities and remain faithful to his own insights. Landauer entered the revolution ready for sacrifice not only of his person, but of his cause; so Buber wrote after his death. While bitterly resenting the calumnies against Landauer in the press, Buber confessed in his memorial speech that, in his opinion, Landauer made the wrong choice.

> According to my insight, there existed on November 7th, 1918, a higher duty and a greater responsibility for Gustav Landauer: namely toward his cause and thereby toward the cause of a true transformation.... He did not decide on the 7th of November to detach himself and concentrate on his work, or even, if that were possible at the same time, to speak his word and to await the reverberations from it, or even to unite the true socialists and out

of them then build the kernel of the new community. Rather he decided to throw himself into the breach, which needed a human body to fill it up. Stronger than his responsibility to the future, the dreadful need and problematic of the moment pressed down upon him, and he succumbed. I believe that he erred; but I also believe that no man has ever erred out of purer motives.

Those days of postwar chaos and revolution paved the way for the coming to Germany of the blackest reaction. The milestones on this path were a series of fateful murders and assassinations of revolutionaries and later even of liberal statesmen who, despite all the differences between them, had in common their dedication to the task of building a new social order in Germany *and* the fact that they were Jews—a fact that probably played no small part in the assassinations and certainly in the justifications of them after the fact. The first of these were the brutal murders in Berlin of the famous socialist leaders Rosa Luxemburg and Karl Liebknecht, killed in their cells after long imprisonment. These murders, still remembered among socialists and communists everywhere, troubled all German liberals exceedingly, testified Margarete Susman, "and gave us a foreglimpse of a frightful German future that was near at hand." In June 1919, Arnold Zweig told Buber that he encountered in Tubingen "an unimaginable mood of counterrevolution, which is identical with anti-Semitism." In August, the actress Louise Dumont asked Buber if he knew of the anti-Semitic agitation in German countries. "It assumes forms that seem to mean a final battle—if it is decided that this is what it means to be German, then one can no longer remain in the country; then the die will finally be cast against Germany." Buber, with less prescience of the future than Louise Dumont, responded that the persecution of Jews, like all the troubled waves of the moment, did not concern him very much: "I am used to excesses, they belong to the present turmoil, but I do not see a final battle."

Although Landauer represented a very different type of socialism from Liebknecht and Luxemburg, he delivered a memorial address for them in Munich on February 6, 1919.

About two weeks after Landauer's memorial address on Karl Liebknecht and Rosa Luxemburg, Buber was with him and several other revolutionary leaders in a hall of the Diet building in Munich. Landauer had proposed the subject of discussion—the terror. But he himself hardly joined in. To Buber, he appeared dispirited and nearly exhausted. His wife had succumbed to illness the year before, and now he was clearly reliving her death. The discussion was conducted for the most part between Buber and a leader of Spartacus (Liebknecht and Luxemburg's subversive organization, which disseminated illegal propaganda against the war) who later became well known in the second communist revolutionary government in Munich, which replaced the first socialist government of Landauer and his comrades. The

Spartacus leader, who had been a German officer in the war, walked with clanking spurs through the room. Buber declined to do what many apparently had expected of him—to talk of the moral problems. But he set forth what he thought about the relation between ends and means. He documented his view from historical and contemporary experience. The Spartacus leader, too, sought to document his apology for the terror by examples. "Dzerzhinsky," he said, "the head of the Checka, could sign a hundred death sentences a day, but with an entirely clean soul."

"That is, in fact, just the worst of all," Buber answered. "This 'clean' soul you do not allow any splashes of blood to fall on! It is not a question of 'souls' but of responsibility." Buber's opponent regarded him with unperturbed superiority. Landauer, who sat next to Buber, laid his hand on Buber's. Landauer's whole arm trembled. "I shall never forget that night," wrote Buber. When he had returned to Heppenheim from Munich, Buber reported to Ludwig Strauss that he had "spent a deeply moving week in steady interaction with the revolutionary leaders."

> The innermost human problems of the revolution were discussed without holding back. I entered into the happenings, questioning and answering, and we experienced night hours of an apocalyptic heaviness in which silence spoke with eloquence and the future became clearer than the present.... At times I was expected to play the role of Cassandra before them. I beheld Eisner in the demonry of his divided Jewish soul.... Landauer persevered in his faith in Eisner, with the utmost exertion of his soul and protected him by virtue of a shocking self-deception. The whole a nameless Jewish tragedy.

More terrible and fateful for Landauer than the murders of Luxemburg and Liebknecht was the murder of his close friend and coworker Kurt Eisner, which took place on February 21, 1919, the anniversary of Hedwig Lachmann's death one year before, and, as it chanced, on a day when both Landauer and Buber were away from Munich. Landauer had been called away on that day to where his children (Lotte and her two younger sisters) were living, outside of Munich. When, at midday on the anniversary of his wife's death, his mind full of thoughts of that occasion, he descended from the train, he received the message that Eisner was dead. "In the weeks that followed," Landauer wrote to Buber, who had sent him words that comforted him, "I was so racked that I now know how suffering can become strength. When the heroic epoch was at an end and the scandalous episode of party intrigue took over, I came here [Krumbach in Swabia] for a rest. But my rest takes place, as I should have expected, under an extraordinary tension."

Instead of withdrawing from further activity, as might have been expected after this trauma, Landauer returned to Munich and attempted to accomplish alone what he and Eisner had not been able to do together. He sought to carry on Eisner's task with inadequate means and to make the seething Munich proletariat into the socialist community of which he had so long dreamed. In the beginning of April 1919, the independent socialists overthrew the majority socialist government, and the Räterepublik was proclaimed. In the governing central council sat Landauer. "Landauer is now the most important man in Munich," wrote the German writer Stefan Grossmann to the novelist Auguste Hauschner on April 13, 1919, "because he is the only one in the ministry with a feeling of responsibility, also with insight." Buber's judgment was not so sanguine. Landauer's "entrance into the revolution seemed to be a failure in his task," wrote Buber later.

> His entrance into the government was certainly a failure in his reasoning. He joined himself with men of whom in earlier days— in the time of the full integrity of his spirit—he would have recognized at first glance that in cooperation with them no work, and least of all this most difficult, sheerly hopeless work, could succeed. But his anguish over the crumbling away of the revolution had clearly impaired Landauer's superior powers.

Landauer was actually in power only a few days. The communists very soon came to the helm, and the Spartacist second Räterepublik succeeded the first. From that time on, Landauer no longer had an active part in all that happened in Munich. He remained close to the government only in a restraining, advisory capacity. In continual conflict with the Spartacists, Landauer sought to hinder the shedding of blood. The days that now followed were, according to all reports, the hardest in Landauer's extremely hard life. All around him were destruction and dissolution, contradiction and absurdity: in the masses, among the leaders, in his closest surroundings. He bore his head high through it all and did what was his to do. That was, above all—as much while he took part in the government as afterward, until the end—the fight against acts of violence. A young student who experienced all the wild upheavals of those weeks in Munich declared that nothing had moved him nearly as much as the kindness, the humaneness, with which Landauer spoke in all the squares, street corners, and halls—not only to large crowds, but also to small groups and individuals. He was always ready to help, to encourage, to revive, to instruct, to comfort. Concerning these activities of Landauer, so-called reporters issued such a flood of lies that Buber and his friends were overcome with horror.

Despite Buber's criticism of Landauer's entry into the first Räterepublik, Buber insisted that Landauer remained faithful to the cause of nonviolence from the time he first espoused it until his death. In 1901, Landauer had written: "A goal can only be reached if the means are in consonance with its essential nature. One will never attain non-violence through violence." In 1914, he said: "Now it can become clear to man that freedom and peace of the nations can only come when as Jesus and his followers, and in our time above all Tolstoi, advised, they choose to fully abstain from any violence." "This truth Landauer served until his death," asserted Buber. "When I think of the passionate glance and words of my dead friend, I know with what force of soul he fought to protect the Revolution from itself, from violence."

The precariousness of Landauer's political position and even of his personal safety was fully evident to Buber during the very days when Landauer was in power. Two days after Grossmann wrote to Auguste Hauschner about Landauer's key position in the ministry, Buber wrote to her from Heppenheim, concerning what Buber and Landauer's other friends wanted to undertake on his behalf. "An action is... not possible at this time," Buber stated, "because the situation has not yet been clarified, and we cannot therefore formulate clearly what we demand." What is more, so long as the fighting continued in any form, they had to remain altogether inactive, Buber declared.

> On the other hand, we must already now prepare for the moment when a public appeal shall perhaps be necessary. To this end a committee should be immediately formed from his circle of friends who will turn to the personalities we shall consider in Germany and German-Austria with the request that they allow their names to be set down on a possibly necessary appeal. To this committee should perhaps belong: you, me, Dehmel, Einstein, Dumont, Mauthner, Mombert, Susman—Who else? Of these I am not certain only in the case of Professor Einstein whether he stands close enough to Gustav; will you speak with him?...

On April 15, Buber wrote to Fritz Mauthner about the formation of a committee that might publicly intercede for Landauer. Mauthner replied that they must indeed attempt to rescue Landauer, without approving his politics. He placed his name at Buber's disposal, but left the leadership of the undertaking to him. "We cannot protect him from himself," he added, "he would reject that." "It is very sad," he concluded, "that it is precisely the idealism of his circle [that]... will let loose a new wave of anti-Semitism over Germany." On April 19, Mauthner reported to Auguste Hauschner that he had heard that Gustav was apparently not hindered in his movements at all, but lived unmolested in Munich. A manifesto had just appeared, in fact, in which Landauer declared himself in agreement with the most radical movement. On April 25, he wrote again that the children of Gustav Landauer (with the children of Kurt Eisner) were in Meersburg living with Landauer's cousin, and that Landauer was quite certainly not arrested, but was still in Munich. On April 30, Landauer's friend, Louise Dumont, wrote to Auguste Hauschner from Dusseldorf, conveying the latest report on Landauer, from a nephew of hers studying in Munich. Although he had little good to say of Landauer's health, he spoke of "his astonishing activity in work which occupied him day and night" and of his remarkable inexhaustible patience. On April 28, Buber informed Siegmund Kaznelson that Landauer had been only a few days in the first revolutionary government and not at all in the present one. "That he entered the first was a serious error but not at all the offence that you suppose; he had no part in the bloodbath." Buber also pointed out that Landauer stood firmly on his side when Buber expressed to the Munich leaders the inadmissibility of all forms of terror and the ruinous influence of the use of violence.

While these rumors and alarms were circulating among Landauer's friends, Landauer was, in fact, staying outside Munich in the house of the widow of Kurt Eisner, his murdered friend, not secretly but having notified the police. He came several times to Munich for consultations with those close to his views and planned an exodus of women and children in order to avoid a possible bloodbath. Meanwhile, the Munich assembly entered a vote of no confidence in the communist regime of the Spartacists. On April 30, the dictatorship of the Red Army was proclaimed in Munich. On the morning of May 1, the troops of the German Reich marched into that city. On May 1 and May 2, a fearful battle raged in the streets there, claiming hundreds of lives. In the course of it, the Red Army succumbed to the superior might of the Reichswehrtruppen. During all this time, and especially when the situation became critical because of the approach of the government troops, and threats and warnings became vociferous, Landauer's friends offered to help him escape and implored him to do so. At first, he refused, but then let himself be talked into it and preparations were made to flee across the Lake Constance to Switzerland. But on the next day, he declared himself unwilling to go, and thereafter no argument of any kind could change his mind.

On the afternoon of May 1, Landauer was arrested in the house of Mrs. Eisner, on the basis of a denunciation, and at first taken in a truck to the cemetery, a quarter of an hour distant, to be shot there. A member of the colony intervened, pointing out that Landauer had not belonged to the communist Räterepublik. He persuaded the lieutenant that Landauer should not be shot merely because of a denunciation but should be brought first to a hearing. Thus, Landauer was taken to Starnberg and put in the prison of the lower court, where he underwent a hearing. There, according to the report of an eyewitness who photographed Landauer escorted by the White Guards on his way to prison, Landauer defended himself splendidly.

On the morning of May 2, Landauer was transported with three other prisoners to Stadelheim. From the moment of his delivery there, Landauer was turned over, defenseless, to the soldiers, who, far from being restrained from their bloody act by their officers, were incited to it by them. It was an officer who called to the group of soldiers in whose midst Landauer was walking, "Halt! Landauer is to be shot at once." Another officer, Freiherr von Gagern, beat him over the head with the handle of his horsewhip. This was the signal for the soldiers, who now fell on him like a pack of hounds. Landauer was shot and beaten and kicked to death. According to one account, Landauer's last words were: "Now comes death, now one must hold one's head high." According to the report of another witness, Landauer cried to the soldiers: "Kill me then! Since you are men!" (*Dass Ihr Menschen seid!*).

Meanwhile, none of Landauer's friends could find out exactly what had happened. Lotte had telegraphed Buber that her father was not in danger, others did not respond to Buber's telegrams, and from Auguste Hauschner, Buber received a telegram on May 5 saying, "Just the awful certainty." "I have no more hope," Buber wrote Mauthner on May 7, but he could not dismiss the possibility that Lotte's information meant something. "In these days and nights I have myself wandered through Sheol," Buber concluded. It was only later that his worst fears were confirmed.

"Gustav Landauer died the death that matched his life," wrote his friend Margarete Susman, "— not a gentle, not a gradual, not a passive death, but the bitter, sudden, ugly death of the revolutionary, which is at the same time a radiant sacrificial death." "Beaten to death like a dog," exclaimed Fritz Mauthner, "interred like a dog in a mass grave, treated like a dog by the German nationalist and Catholic papers!" The most atrocious calumnies, in fact, continued to spread after Landauer's death: Landauer had incited men to attack the honor of women; Landauer had directed hordes to break their way into the fenced-in yards of dwelling places to plunder; Landauer had instigated violence and murder.

In April 1922, Buber informed Mauthner that Lotte had told him that her father's ashes were preserved in a cellar; he saw this as an indignity. "Transporting them to a more worthy place should be a cause for those in whom his memory is alive, I feel." Buber saw a summons to his closest friends as the best way to achieve removal of the ashes, and he invited Mauthner to join Louise Dumont, Margarete Susman, and himself in signing a letter proposing this, "without any party matter mixing in." In 1923, the year of Hitler's unsuccessful beer-hall putsch and the year in which Buber published *I and Thou,* a simple but imposing obelisk was erected in the woods of Munich, bearing the inscription "1870 Gustav Landauer 1919" and over it the words from his "Summons to Socialism": "What is needed now is to bring a sacrifice of another kind, not a heroic one, but a silent, unpretentious sacrifice in order to give an example of a true life." Ten years later, when Hitler came to power, the obelisk was torn down.

Buber concluded his own essay, "Landauer and the Revolution," with a comparison of Landauer and Jesus:

> In a church in Brescia I saw a mural whose whole surface was covered with crucified men. The field of crosses stretched to the horizon, and on all of them hung men of all different shapes and faces. There it seemed to me was the true form of Jesus Christ. On one of those crosses I see Gustav Landauer hanging.

To the personal responsibility of the revolutionary, which, despite all, Buber saw as embodied in Landauer, Buber ascribed the central point in his own developing social thought: the teaching of the "line of demarcation" that is drawn anew at all times and in every situation. The watchword of the revolutionary's spirit is "Up to here," and for that "Up to here," for that drawing of the line, there is no fast rule. The revolutionary lives on the knife's edge, not of "selling his soul to the devil" in order to bring the revolution to victory, but of the practical tension between ends and means. "I cannot conceive anything real corresponding to the saying that the end 'sanctifies' the means," wrote Buber. "But I mean something which is real in the highest sense of the term when I say that the means may profane, actually make meaningless, the end, that is, its realization!" The farther the means are from the goal, the farther, too, is what is achieved. It is in this connection that Buber developed his all-important teaching of the "crossfront," the true front that runs through each party or group and through each adherent of a party or group. On the true front, each fights against his fellows and himself for the sake of the genuine realization of the cause. The "democratic centralists" say of these men that they have weakened the fight but, in fact, it is they who keep alive the truth of the battle. Such a man was Gustav Landauer.

When Buber spoke at the funeral of Charlotte Landauer in 1927, he spoke of the life of this faithful daughter in the context of the uncanny, "to us barely graspable meaning of Gustav Landauer's death... a death in which the monstrous, sheerly apocalyptic horror, the inhumanity of our time has been delineated and portrayed."

Landauer became for Buber the image of the authentic social and political person, the image of the person who has to stand and withstand in the "lived concrete," the situation in which he finds himself, "whether in the field of work or the field of battle." Buber had Landauer in mind when, in a public discussion in 1929, he spoke of the religious tragedy of the revolution—namely, that its means are untrue to its end. This is the real unfaithfulness of the revolutionary that perhaps even the religious person may not escape. But when the latter does enter into the revolution, then he has the special responsibility of fighting step by step for the purity of the image. His function in the revolution is to be *defeated* in an exemplary fashion, as one who bears the organic substance *through* the abyss into a new world. Thus, in a remarkable fashion, the religious revolutionary fused for Buber with the man of the "dark charisma," who knows no historical success, the "suffering servant" who works in the depths of history. As the suffering servant is an arrow that remains hidden in the quiver, so the true religious revolutionary is a person the effect of whose work is ultimately shrouded in mystery.

Buber's response to the news of Landauer's death was probably, next to his "conversion" and the early separation from his mother, the most important single event in his life. Yet this is one "autobiographical fragment" that Buber could not write. When I urged him to do so in Jerusalem in 1960, he confessed that he had tried and found himself still too close to this event to be able to write about it beyond his reference to the "death of a friend" in the dialogue with the American psychologist Carl Rogers in 1957.

In his dialogue with Rogers, Buber spoke of "a certain inclination to meet people," to change something in the *other*, but also to let *himself* be changed by *him*. This inclination was enormously strengthened by the First World War, at the end of which he realized for the first time how "terribly influenced" he had been by the necessity of expanding "inclusion" to "imagining the real," in the most concrete sense of what was happening in the world at just that moment. The climax and the most important event of *imagining the real* came when he received the news of Landauer's barbaric murder: "Now once more—for the last time—I was compelled to imagine this killing, not only visually, but with my *body*." By this, Buber meant that he had to feel in his own body every blow that Landauer suffered in that courtyard where he was beaten to death. Not, as in the example Buber gives in "Education" (1926), suddenly experiencing from the other side the blows that one is inflicting oneself, but experiencing at a distance the blows that others, strangers, had inflicted on his friend. "This," said Buber, "was the decisive moment, after which, after some days and nights in this state, I felt, 'Oh, something has been done to me.'" From then on, his meetings with people, and particularly with young people, took on a different form. Now he had to give them something more than his inclination to exchange thoughts and feelings. He had to offer the fruit of a profound experience, that of the four years of the war and, capping it all, the trauma of Landauer's murder.

♦ 7 ♦

Postwar Zionism, Education, and Politics

(1918-1922)

An incomparable picture of Buber's family life in 1921 is given us by a letter from Paula to E.E. Rappeport. Their daughter, Eva, was at home for the winter and was receiving lessons in Hebrew and English. Raffi was in Berlin at the school for agricultural economy. He was still an "unbaked piece of bread," Paula wrote, and she regretted not having Rappeport nearby to help prepare Raffi's parents for his various transformations! In the fall, Paula had planted her garden almost anew, "also with beautiful and rare shrubs which I have never yet seen bloom, and I await it in my full garden-joy." Paula did not fail to tell Rappeport about the cats:

> Do you still remember the little cat whose matted hair you cut off? He is still with us and I hope to have him for a long time. He has become my favorite. At every meal he sits on my knees and lays his forepaws on the table. He lives among us like an imp. He loves Martin most respectfully, me most tenderly, Eva he trusts boundlessly, but with Raffi he has, with reason, some anxiety.

In the midst of all this, Paula was actively writing, and, in 1921, published her second book of stories, *Sankt Getrauden Minne.*

Another glimpse of the Buber family life comes to us through Eva. If Buber did not *impose* education on his daughter Eva like a propagandist, neither did he help her to *unfold,* as one might expect from his philosophy of education. In this, Paula and her domination of the family, including Martin, was certainly equally responsible. Eva finally went to a school when she was

eighteen years old—a gardening school that attracted her as a possible training ground for a profession. Later, she wanted to continue her studies in this
field in Stuttgart, but her parents were against it. As usual, in contrast to her
rebellious brother, she gave in. Her father influenced her to give up the idea.

> He said that a person has to be in a certain place and to have
> influence in that place. He added that Mother needed me then
> and that was the place where I should be and strive to have an
> impact. I believe that Father was right when he said that each per-
> son must try and be in the right place to make a mark, and this
> statement has accompanied me my entire life. I felt that many
> times I lived according to this statement. But in that specific
> instance my father was wrong. A young woman should leave her
> home and learn outside of home. It was Father's mistake; Mother
> influenced Father and it was his mistake. A young person should
> learn to live outside of home, and then do what Father said.

Eva continued her studies by auditing courses, traveling to Heidelberg for
lectures, mainly on literature. Later, she wanted to learn to work with abandoned children at an institute in Freiburg, but again her parents were against
it and for the same reason: They wanted her to stay at home. She stayed at
home and did some gardening in their great garden in Heppeneheim, where,
as we have seen, even her father worked at times. It was not until a great
many years later, after she was married and living in Israel, that she entered
her true vocation. She audited some courses in psychology at the Hebrew
University of Jerusalem and, under the guidance of her psychology professor,
began working with problem children.

   Looking back on her life, Eva recognized that she had an inferiority
complex when she compared herself to her mother or father. They were
great personalities, and she did not feel that she was one. Once her father
told her that every person should be satisfied with what she received, and
after that she felt better. When Eva was young, she received warmth and
motherly love from Paula. But the major influence on her life came from
Martin. Yet she did not overcome the feeling of inferiority and become more
secure as a person until after she married a husband who confirmed her
identity as a person and not just as her parents' child, and who gave her a
feeling of security. The man she married (in 1925, three years after his first
wife left him) was Ludwig Strauss, a distinguished poet, some years older
than she, who was an old friend of her father's. We may infer that Eva did
not entirely escape from the dominance of her father and mother even in her
marriage, and the facts, as we shall see later, bear this out.

   The political realism that Buber brought to the Russian and German
revolutions he also brought to the British Balfour Declaration in 1917, officially committing Britain to the support of the creation of a Jewish Homeland
in Palestine. Buber did not look to any such purely political document, tied

as it was to the shifting political interests of the British Empire, as a secure hope for the Jewish settlement in Palestine. In January 1918, after Lord Allenby conquered Palestine against the Turks, Buber wrote an article insisting that Palestine, could only be "conquered" by the people who could make it their own. England, with all its freedom and force, could no more awaken Palestine than could the Turks. One cannot truly pay for this earth in any other coin than lifelong work and the involvement of one's whole person. England will apply in Palestine the tactics that were successful so many years in India—divide and conquer—Buber wrote Leo Hermann in 1922. What is needed, Buber told Moritz Spitzer in January 1919, is the foundation of groups and unions of groups dedicated to the creation of a genuine community in Palestine and the willingness to work there themselves on this task.

In the middle of March 1919, Buber saw the Zionist movement as facing a critical decision due to the treaty deliberations in Paris, where the representatives of the great powers considered the new order of European and Near Eastern territorial relations. True to the teaching of nonviolence and genuine social constructiveness that Landauer had espoused, Buber rejected the notion that the Jewish people could be liberated by any actions that did violence to the immanent demand of Judaism that there *be justice and truth between the peoples*. What was being prepared in Paris, Buber prophetically asserted, was a league of state structures, not of peoples, even though the peoples, through every type of propaganda, were being persuaded to identify themselves with the states. If we let Palestine be included in the dominant politics, economy, and culture, declared Buber, it will never really be ours. In the place of assimilation of the individual, we shall have simply brought about assimilation of the people. A truly Jewish Palestine might play a mediating function between West and East. But if an agent of economic and political imperialism—of "English-American capitalism, swollen with power yet soon ready to collapse"—is erected on Zion, then all our efforts will be in vain. The bridge, which the unholy spirit of Versailles will never bring about, the Jewish people can build—out of its own socialist truth.

The decade between 1919 and 1930 in Buber's life, writes Ernst Simon, can be compared to the days of his youth between 1898 and 1904. Both were periods in which Buber made a devoted and desperate attempt to influence Zionist policy directly through its institutions and central figures, as well as indirectly through articles, speeches, and intermittent activities with small sectarian circles that intentionally deviated from the *via regia* of the movement. The preparation for this decade of activity was Buber's indefatigable work as editor of *Der Jude,* the teaching of Zionist communal socialism in *The Holy Way,* and his implacable hostility to all forms of narrow, self-serving nationalism. The lesson of the First World War had not been lost on Buber, and once learned it was never forgotten, nor was there ever, from this time until his death, any relaxation in his warnings against the *Yishuv's* (the Jewish settlement in Palestine) becoming "a nation like all the nations."

Modern nationalism, to Buber, meant idolatry, and it was not any less so if the idol bore a Jewish name. The "dominant dogma of the century" is "the unholy dogma of the sovereignty of nations," which makes every nation its own master and judge, "obligated only to itself and answerable only to itself." A genuine renaissance has never emerged from exclusively national tendencies, but from a passionate reaching out for renewed human content. "Not Hebraism but Hebrew humanism... will have to be at the core of a Jewish movement for regeneration." To accomplish this liberation and redemption, a land of one's own and true community are necessary. "True community is the Sinai of the future."

At this point, Buber's teaching coincided with the new form of collective settlement that was already being built in Palestine, the kibbutz. Buber called for a "revolutionary colonization" that would reject already existing structures in favor of a transformation and reshaping within and through the Jewish settlement, conducive to its growing into a truly communal structure. Many of the Jews who went to Palestine at this time were motivated by the desire to build a new community, a large number of them, including Buber's friend Hugo Bergmann, because of Buber's influence. In 1922, Buber informed Ernst Elijahu Rappeport, who had made "Aliyah" ("going up to the land") to Palestine under Buber's influence, that he was beginning hours of conversation in Hebrew.

Buber's idea of the realization of community contributed to the rise of the Halutz, or pioneer, movement during and after the First World War, and to the beginnings of so-called Labor Zionism. In his conception of Zionist socialism and "revolutionary colonization," Buber's thought converged at many points with the community of workers of the land that had arisen in Palestine, who were known as the Young Workers, or Hapoel Hazair. Until 1920, Hapoel Hazair was not a party, but a living community of closely bound men. Its emphasis, like Buber's own and that of Landauer, was not on politics or the state, but on personal realization, the involvement of one's whole humanity as the bearer of the Jewish rebirth. At the center of Hapoel Hazair stood the labor philosopher and pioneer A. D. Gordon, who came to Palestine from Russia at the age of fifty and lived on a kibbutz until his death sixteen years later. A. D. Gordon was the last figure that Buber dealt with in his book *Israel and Palestine: The History of an Idea,* the man who took on more significance for Buber than any other modern exponent of Zion, from Moses Hess, Pinsker, and Herzl to Ahad Ha'am and Rav Kook. Buber had chosen Ahad Ha'am the teacher over Herzl the leader, but he found in A. D. Gordon, even more than in Ahad Ha'am, "the true teacher" whose teaching was that of the human image, the teaching of Gordon's life itself, self-evident, casual, where silence is more important than words. Buber saw in Gordon the man who, in fact, *realized* the idea of Zion, the idea of *realization* that Buber himself *taught* but was not able to embody. In *Israel and Palestine,* Buber wrote: "[He] was better able than anyone else in the modern

Jewish national movement to renew the insight into the unique relationship between the people and the land of Israel."

"The 'main thing,' Gordon says, is to establish for ourselves a new relationship 'to the mystery of existence and life.'" Just as Israel can participate in the cosmos only in the land of Palestine, "so too it is only there it can regain a religious relationship to the mystery of existence." Gordon became for Buber the image of the true pioneer, who called to his comrades on the kibbutz not to lose themselves in the moment and to his fellow Jews in the Diaspora not to lose themselves in history, but to bind the present work to the eternal, the truth of the millennia to authentication in the everyday.

Out of the similarities of their thinking concerning "revolutionary colonization," Buber and his followers and Gordon's Hapoel Hazair merged forces during the years 1919 to 1921, producing a fresh spurt in the Halutzim movement. These were the years, according to Hans Kohn, in which the best of the Jewish youth prepared themselves in many ways to leave Europe and go to Palestine, in order to take up there a life of work and community for the building of a new Jewish and human society. As Kohn explains:

> Sons and daughters of the middle class, educated for middle-class and academic callings, forsook their middle-class existence: not as in war for a short time only to return later to their secure existence, but in earnest and forever because they felt that this bourgeois existence could not be the clothes of their souls.... They wanted to reverse the development of the bourgeois age...; from the great city back to the land, from industry to agriculture, from abstract learning to concrete, close-to-earth forms of life in accord with nature's rhythm.

At the end of March 1920, a conference took place in Prague in which the representatives of Hapoel Hazair from Palestine, under the leadership of A.D. Gordon, and the representatives of the Zionist youth of Central and Eastern Europe, under the leadership of Buber, came together to establish a world union of socialist, but not Marxist, Labor Zionists, the first principle of which was that the national and the social problems of the Jewish people form an indivisible unity. "Not power but power hysteria is evil," stated Buber, and the chief mark of this hysteria is surrendering the responsibility of the "demarcation line," the task of constantly demarcating anew one's own rights, as an individual and as a nation, from the rights of others. The values of a true nation are *unique*; they need not be compared with the values of any other. But the nationalist declares his people *the best* while at the same time considering his nation responsible only to itself. Such a nation becomes "a Moloch which consumes the best of the people's youth."

This distinction between legitimate and arbitrary nationalism is, for Israel more than for any other people, the distinction between life and death,

Buber asserted in 1921 at the Twelfth Zionist Congress in Karlsbad. "Israel cannot be healed, and its welfare cannot be achieved by severing the concepts of people and community of faith," but to include both as organic parts of a new order is to recognize the supernational responsibility and obligation at the base of Israel's unique history and situation.

The most remarkable outcome of the Prague Conference at the Karlsbad Zionist Congress was not the Zionist socialism that Buber put forward, but its practical corollary, which only he and a few of his friends saw at that time—namely, the necessity for cooperation with the Arab peoples living in and around Palestine, to go hand in hand with the task of building up communal settlements and making Palestine a center and example of social regeneration in the Mideast.

Ernst Simon, who was present at the Political Committee of the Twelfth Zionist Congress, testifies to the many things that Buber said about the Arab problem there. Most importantly, he enunciated a universal historical law: The advance and progress of one people will lead to the advance and progress of neighboring peoples; the Zionist movement will hasten the acceleration of the unity of the Arab nations. The Jews in Palestine are to help their Arab neighbors progress rather than to turn them into sworn enemies with whom reconciliation would be very difficult. This argument, which turned out to be a prophecy, found no listeners, says Simon, and instead of increasing Buber's influence, it detracted from it.

Simon tells of one exception to those who paid no attention to Buber's prediction, namely, "one young usher who was removed from his voluntary service because he manifested his agreement with this attitude, which in view of his job he should have treated with utter indifference." His "unseemly" demonstration took the form of applause, and the twenty-two-year-old usher was Simon himself! The impression that Buber's two great speeches made on Simon remained with him decades later, as he testified in 1966, but it was in the Political Committee that he was able to recognize and observe Buber as the far-seeing realistic politician (*Realpolitiker*) that he was, even if not as an unusually clever tactician. "Since that time Buber's words did not leave my heart and were one of the factors determining my way of Zionism at the side of Buber these forty years," added Simon. Anyone who knows the part that Simon played in Israel's politics, and above all in the attempts of B'rith Shalom and Ihud to bring about rapprochement with Arabs, will not think this an inconsequential effect of Buber's words.

On September 2, 1921, three days before he gave his address entitled "Nationalism," Buber gave another address to the Twelfth Zionist Congress, this one specifically concerned with the Arab problem. Recognizing the enormous difficulties in establishing relationships with a people not yet constituted and without legitimate representatives, he insisted nonetheless that such relationships must be established—and not merely with one or two Arab notables. The grounds for this step would be a planned beginning of a great real effort of colonization and a concrete political and economic program, both of which were lacking.

> In a just union with the Arab people we want to make the common dwelling place into an economically and culturally flourishing commonwealth whose extension will guarantee each of its member nations an undisturbed autonomous development.... In this social character of our national ideal lies the powerful warranty for our confidence that between us and the workers among the Arab people a deep and lasting solidarity of real interests will manifest itself which must overcome all the antagonisms produced by the confusions of the moment.

This resolution clarifies why the Zionist Socialism that Buber represented for Hapoel Hazair was inextricably connected with the concern for the Arab workers and the Arab peoples and with the refusal to transplant European methods of imperialistic colonization to Palestine. In this resolution lay the great advance of the second Aliyah over the *bilui,* who hired Arabs to do their work for them. But the Zionist movement at large had not yet caught up to the communal socialist realities that were being built in Palestine *nor* to the absolute top priority of working toward cooperation with the Arab inhabitants of the land. Here and there a brave voice, such as that of Ahad Ha'am, spoke up clear and true at this time, but otherwise the problem was largely ignored. Yet at that time there still *was* the possibility of which Buber spoke, for the situation had not yet polarized, in political slogans or in tragic reality, into Zionism versus anti-Zionism, the Jews inhabiting Palestine at the expense of the Arabs or the Arabs running the Jews into the sea. In 1921 and every year of his life thereafter, Buber pointed to the "narrow ridge" between the disastrous extremes, with all the realism, earnestness, fervor, and responsibility at his disposal. What was at issue was not merely an "Arab problem," important as this was, but the whole question of Jewish nationalism. Buber and his friends recognized the central significance of the Arab question for Jewish nationalism precisely because they recognized that the uniqueness of the Jewish people could not be preserved if they became a "modern" nation that put its own interests above all others.

On the face of it, Buber was successful, for he was able to get through the congress a resolution in this sense. With the exception of the 1901 Congress, it was, indeed, Buber's only success in practical Zionist party politics. But it was a success in appearance only. By the time Buber got it through the Editorial Committee, it had lost most of its effectiveness. Nor was any serious attempt ever made to carry it out in practice. The congress would not have dared to reject such a proposal, Robert Weltsch points out, because that would have given substance to the Arab and the English anti-Zionist claim that the Zionists wanted to oppress or suppress the Arabs. But the

Editorial Committee sought to water down Buber's original text as far as possible, as Buber himself revealed twenty-six years later on the occasion of Judah Magnes's seventieth birthday. Buber experienced the committee's action as a deep personal shock that led him to withdraw once again from active Zionist politics:

> Many years ago when I fought in the Zionist Congress for the concept of a Jewish-Arab unity, I had an experience that was like a nightmare to me and that determined my future life. I had put forward a draft resolution emphasizing the community of interests of both peoples and pointing the way to a cooperation between them—the only way that can lead to the salvation of Palestine and its two peoples.... Then something happened which is entirely usual and self-evident to a professional politician, but which so horrified me that to the present day I have not been able to free myself from it. In the Editorial Committee, which was composed for the most part of old friends of mine, one little amendment was proposed and still another little amendment and so on....
>
> ...I fought each time in defense of the text that I had proposed but gave in time and again when the fate of my resolution depended upon this giving in. When the Editorial Committee had finished its labors and the agreed upon version was brought to my hotel in a clean copy, I saw, to be sure, a series of beautiful and convincing statements, but the marrow and the blood of my original demand were no longer in them.

If we compare the resolution that was passed with the original one that Buber proposed, we can see that what was left out was the very thing that gave Buber and the Zionist youth for whom he spoke the assurance that these were not just empty phrases—namely, the necessity of a communal socialist building of the land that would *not* entail the evils of exploitation and suppression that every capitalist expansion of Europe had always brought with it. "Our claim has been so mixed up with furthering the cause of *England's* Mandate over Palestine," wrote Buber, "that we pass in Europe and Asia as the handy man of British imperialism—a false slogan, but one that it is very difficult to correct."

Buber accused the majority of Zionists of forgetting that Israel's sovereigny is also the sovereigny of its rivals and of its enemies, that the Lord who led the children of Israel out of the land of Egypt also led the Philistines out of Caphtor and the Syrians out of Kir (Amos 9:7). In the spirit of this internationalism, on the occasion of the congress, Buber and some friends made an attempt to found a "Jewish Society for International Understanding," a union of genuine human communes that would replace the present all-powerful method of politics—as the open or secret attempt at *exploitation* of the human soul—by the method of *education*—as the great attempt at an *unfolding* of the human soul. This proposal contained the seed of one of

Buber's most important later contributions to the philosophy of education: The distinction between the propagandist, who imposes his "truth" on those he manipulates, and the true educator, who is concerned with the unfolding of others and trusts that each will find his own unique relationship to the truth for which the educator witnesses: "All true education is help toward self-discovery and toward self-unfolding."

The primal evil of modern man, wrote Buber in "The Task" (1922), is that "politicization" of all of life, "which is already preparing to annihilate him and his world." The educative attitude that opposes this domination of the political is a *response* "in this hour of pain, of question, of rebellion." What we are educating toward depends upon our willing without willfulness, without arbitrariness, facing and responding to others rather than experiencing and using them, truly present to them, "saying Thou to them awakening the Thou in them."

♦ 8 ♦

Ascent to *I and Thou*

(1916-1923)

When reading the manuscript of my book *Martin Buber: The Life of Dialogue,* Buber came across a quotation from his book *Daniel* describing God's kingdom as "the kingdom of danger and of risk, of eternal beginning and of eternal becoming, of opened spirit and of deep realization, the kingdom of holy insecurity." "Today," Buber declared, "I would no longer describe the kingdom so extravagantly! (*Daniel* is still too much a book of the 'easy word')." The corollary of the breakthrough to dialogue that came to Buber through the war years and the murder of Landauer was his painful progress from the "easy word" to the hard one: "[I]n the storm of the World War, which made manifest the innermost threat to man, I struggled through to the strict service of the word and earned the heritage with as much difficulty as if I had never supposed that I possessed it."

In *I and Thou,* the poetic quality and beauty of *Daniel* were now mastered by an all-encompassing purpose; poetic and conceptual language are perfectly fused into one. An occasional exclamation in the form of a purely lyrical line does not come as an ornament, but as a culmination, as in Buber's description of the persons who close themselves off in the world of It and protect themselves from the openess of the Thou: "O lonely Face like a star in the night, O living Finger laid on an unheeding brow, O footstep whose echo is fading away."

Like the *zaddik* who exclaimed, "Before I speak beautifully, may I become dumb!," Buber's road from the "easy word" to the hard one was a road from "speaking beautifully" to rejecting any expression not fully mas-

125

tered by intention and devotion to the word. On this road from the "easy word" to the difficult one, Buber developed his philosophy of the "word," of the word that is spoken, of speech as event and event as speech, of the world as word and human existence as address and response. Spoken as opposed to written speech is the great discovery, the great rediscovery, of the life of dialogue. The genuine spoken word is spoken in the context of relationship, of mutuality, and takes its very meaning from the fact that it is said by one person and heard by another who relates to it from an entirely different ground. Speech is the high road on which the Thou attains its full reality in knowing and being known, loving and being loved, and, as such, it is the real simile of the relation with God. "In it true address receives true response; except that in God's response everything, the universe, is made manifest as language." Real speaking takes place out of tension, Buber said in 1923. Speech is not community, but multiplicity. It is born of a living dynamic. This fruitful essential tension expressed through speech acts as a stimulus for us to come toward each other: "The Shekinah is between the beings."

In his Afterword entitled "The History of the Dialogical Principle" (*Between Man and Man*), Buber recounted that he was able to begin the final writing of *I and Thou* "after he had set forth his train of thought in a course that he gave at the Freie Juedische Lehrhaus in Frankfurt founded and directed by Rosenzweig." Rivka Horwitz has set these lectures entitled "Religion as Presence" at the center of her book *Martin Buber's Way to I and Thou*, because the fourth, fifth, sixth, and eighth of them form an early version of segments of the first and third parts of *I and Thou*. This is a remarkable example of an oral and dialogical origin of a classic piece of writing. If the poetic quality and the mastered whole came only later, nonetheless, passage after passage was taken over almost word by word.

When *I and Thou* was being prepared for its second, American, edition in 1958, Buber said to me that he would not now change the original text, since the whole was written in a type of creative ecstasy that even the author himself had no right to tamper with retrospectively. "At that time I wrote what I wrote in an overpowering inspiration," Buber said elsewhere. "And what such inspiration delivers to one, one may no longer change, not even for the sake of exactness. For one can only measure what one might acquire, not what is lost."

"Now happily I did not need to choose my language," Buber said of *I and Thou*; "that which was to be said formed it as the tree its bark." There are poetic remnants in *I and Thou* of the style of earlier works: "So long as the heaven of Thou is spread out over me, the winds of causality cower at my heels, and the whirlpool of fate stays its course." And poetical motifs reappear. The celebration of danger in *Daniel* as the "holy insecurity" of the realizing man now reemerges in the spiral descent of cultures through the spiritual underworld, which is also an ascent to the turning, the break-

through, the "trial of the final darkness." This passage ends with an unac-
knowledged quotation from Hölderlin, whose spirit also informed Daniel:
"Where danger is, the delivering power grows too."

Because the absolute is experienced by the person as the Thou, Buber
asserted in 1919 (in contrast to his earlier teaching) that it is not God who
changes but only the theophany, the manifestation of the divine in man's
symbol-creating mind, until no symbol is adequate any longer and the life
between person and person itself becomes a symbol, "until God is truly present when one person clasps the hand of another." The person who lets his
whole being be affected by contact with the unconditional must guard
against psychologizing it into an "experience" *(Erlebnis)*, Buber added, turning his back on one of his own key terms, which he now associated with
mood and superficial emotionalism rather than real response. "I am accustomed to the hell that the misuses of this word *(Erleben)* means," said Buber
in his lectures entitled "Religion as Presence." Correcting Walter Kaufmann,
who asserted that his concept of meeting originated in *Erlebnis*, Buber later
testified:

> In reality it arose, on the road of my thinking, out of the criticism
> of the concept of *Erlebnis*, to which I adhered in my youth,
> hence, out of a radical self-correction. *"Erlebnis"* belongs to the
> exclusive, individualized psychic sphere; "meeting"... transcends
> this sphere from its origins on. The psychological reduction of
> being, its psychologizing, had a destructive effect on me in my
> youth because it removed from me the foundation of human reali-
> ty, the "to-one-another." Only much later, in the revolution of my
> thinking that taught me to fight and to gain ground, did I win
> reality that cannot be lost.

What is today called *Erlebnis* transforms life into a fetching forth of things for
the use of our subjectivity so that nothing remains but unsteady moments,
experiences *(Erlebnisse)*, precious moments of the soul. What is common to
all these attempts is that they see the religious as happening *in* the person, in
that encapsulated sphere that this psychology calls soul. What is understood
by the "religious" today is mostly inwardness, religious "feeling." What really
matters is not the "experiencing" of life but life itself, not the "religious experience" but the religious life. What "emerges" in the religious life is not God
himself but man's going forth to meet God, and what is "realized" in this life
is not God but rather preparing the world for God, as a place for his reality—making God and his world one.

Thus, Buber coupled his attack on *Erlebnis* with an attack on "the great
foolishness of our time"—that of a becoming God who needs to be realized
and brought forth by the human spirit. Against the "hopelessly perverted
conception that God is not, but that He becomes," Buber now counterposed
the primal certainty of divine *being* that enables us to sense the awesome

meaning of divine becoming, in which God imparts himself to his creation and participates in the destiny of its freedom. What was essential here was not the rejection of "becoming" for "being," but the rejection of the elaboration of subjectivity for the wholehearted meeting with *otherness*.

When Buber was writing the final version of *I and Thou*, he was fully immersed in Jewish education and Jewish spiritual concerns. For all this and for all the fact that *I and Thou* is unthinkable without the wisdom of Hasidism and of the Hebrew Bible, in its form and its intent it is a universal book, concerned not with the Jews but with modern Western man. It was necessary for Buber to attain the major breakthrough to this classic universal statement before he could go forward (not back) to the particular work on Hasidism and the translation and interpretation of the Hebrew Bible that occupied so much of the rest of his life.

> If I myself should designate something as the "central portion of my life work," then it could not be anything individual, but only the one basic insight that has led me not only to the study of the Bible, as to the study of Hasidism, but also to an independent philosophical presentation: that the I-Thou relation to God and the I-Thou relation to one's fellow man are at bottom related to each other.

When Buber began to grasp and to express in writing his philosophy of dialogue, he knew of no related teaching from his own time. Within a few years thereafter, he encountered Ferdinand Ebner, Rosenzweig, and others, and realized that in the stillness a small band had arisen to reveal, out of the fullness of suffering from the great aberration, a new foundation for human possibilities of life, a new meaningful and preserving worldview. After the first, still unwieldy, draft of *I and Thou* in the autumn of 1919, Buber underwent two years of "a spiritual *ascesis*" in which he could do almost no work except on Hasidic material and read no *philosophica* with the exception of Descartes's *Discours de la Methode*. He read Ebner's *The Word and the Spiritual Realities* (1921), Hermann Cohen's *Religion of Reason out of the Sources of Judaism* (1919), and Rosenzweig's *Star of Redemption* (1921) "only later, too late to affect my own thought." Ebner's book showed Buber, "as no other since then, here and there in an almost uncanny nearness, that in this our time men of different kinds and traditions had devoted themselves to the search for the buried treasure." The nearness that Buber experienced was Ebner's insistence that God is a Thou who cannot become an It. But there was also a farness, not only of Ebner's Christology but his turning away from the I-Thou relationship between person and person. In both these senses, Ebner was a true disciple of Kierkegaard, as Buber was a rebellious one. Ebner

acknowledges himself, in a more direct fashion than Kierkegaard, as one who is not able to find the Thou in man.... To be sure, he also postulates, as does Kierkegaard: "Man shall love not only God but also men." But where it is a question of the authenticity of existence, every other Thou disappears for him before that of God.

The steady clarity of vision and the inward necessity of writing *I and Thou* came to Buber some years before he received the right word as well and was able to write the book in its final form. From 1916 to 1919, Buber envisaged it as the first volume of a five-volume systematic and comprehensive work. The very systematic character of this projected work increasingly alienated Buber from it, and the "right word" came to him only when he condensed what he had to say into a small, unsystematic volume.

To insert his experiences into the human heritage of thought, Buber had to relate the unique and particular to the general, to express what is by its nature incomprehensible in concepts that could be used and communicated, to make an It out of what he had experienced in and as I-Thou. He had to make manifest the duality of primal words that "is the basic relationship in the life of each person with all existing being," yet which was, until then, barely paid attention to: "A neglected, obscured primal reality was to be made visible." But this did not entitle him to treat being as such, but only the human twofold relationship to it. Therefore, his philosophizing had to be essentially an anthropological one, with the question of how man is possible as its central theme. His task was not to expound a doctrine but to point to a reality—to take his partner by the hand, lead him to the window, and point to what is outside. "I have no teaching, but I carry on a conversation," Buber testified. Such a conversation can never be a system, for a system is always monological.

> No system was suitable for what I had to say. Structure was suitable for it, a compact structure but not one that joined everything together. I was not permitted to reach out beyond my experience, and I never wished to do so. I witnessed for experience and appealed to experience. The experience for which I witnessed is, naturally, a limited one. But it is not to be understood as a "subjective" one. I have tested it through my appeal and test it ever anew. I say to him who listens to me: "It is your experience. Recollect it, and what you cannot recollect, dare to attain it as experience."

In "Ecstasy and Confession" (1909), Buber spoke of the grace of unity that may be kindled through looking at a heap of stones. One is no longer aware of looking at a rock, he wrote; one experiences only unity, the world: oneself. All forces are united and felt as unity, and in the middle of them lives and shines the stone that is contemplated. The soul experiences the unity of the "I" and in it the unity of "I" and the world, no longer a content but that which is infinitely more than all content. This is the unity realized apart from the world, the unity of the nondualist mystic that Daniel later was to describe as one of the wrong ways from which the faithful man turned. Commenting on a similar experience of looking at stone, that of the fragment of mica, Buber said three years later that the only real "I" is the "I" that is produced by the awakening of tension: "Only polarity, only stream, only unification can become 'I'." Accordingly, in the Introduction to *Die Rede, die Lehre, und das Lied* (1917), Buber explicitly rejected his treatment of unity in "Ecstasy and Confession" for that of the fifth dialogue of *Daniel*.

Buber's reinterpretation of his earlier mystical experience in the light of later experience and thought shows the limitations of any one experience, even a mystical one, in providing a permanently valid knowledge. But it also shows how all previous experience may enter into and remain the material for a growth in wisdom that rejects no earlier stage yet does not remain fixed in any one formulation. It is not, as Buber puts it in this dialogue, that one experience simply joins itself to another and thereby reveals the truth of the first. On the contrary, our interpretation of each successive experience is itself a dialogue with that experience. The truth we receive is the product of this active dialogue rather than the passive imprint of the experience itself. Thus, in *I and Thou* (1923), Buber took up the experience of looking at the mica again, only to recognize that the knowledge gained from the experience was limited:

> O fragment of mica, looking on which I once learned, for the first time, that I is not something "in me"—with you I was nevertheless only bound up in myself; at that time the event took place only in me, not between me and you.

Thus, the event itself stayed with Buber as a hidden store of potential knowledge, not simply reinterpreted but ever more deeply understood in the light of new events.

In 1958, Buber told me that were he to write *I and Thou* again, he would not deny the I-Thou relationship with nature but neither would he use the same terminology for the relationship between person and person and that between man and nature. In *I and Thou,* the sense of relatedness to nature—to trees and animals and stars—which marked Buber's writings from his early essay on Boehme, is fully present but now not in any way that implies empathy or identification or minimizes the otherness and the distance of that nonhuman reality to which one responds. The tree, transcending any play of imagining or mood, "is bodied over against me and has to do with me, as I with it—only in a different way." Now it is not merely the horse on his father's farm that is uncanny but the household cat (Martin and Paula were great lovers of cats and always had a number in the house).

What Buber's childhood experience of "mismeeting" taught him—which, he realized ten years later, concerned everyone—he now grasped as basic to every child's becoming a person. Now Bachofen's "Great Mother" becomes the cosmic connection that the child loses—not in exchange for the terror of the infinite, but for the ever-renewed distancing and relating of I-Thou.

> This separation does not occur suddenly and catastrophically like the separation from the bodily mother; time is granted to the child to exchange a *spiritual* connexion, that is, relation, for the natural connexion with the world that he loses. He has stepped out of the glowing darkness of chaos into the cool light of creation.

The "cool light of creation" is not something that is given a child to possess. Rather he must draw it out and make it into a reality for himself. There are, in fact, no "things" for the child until this groping and reaching out has taken place, as "the correspondence of the child... with what is alive and effective over against him." This implies a theory of knowledge, but underlying this, in turn, is an anthropology—an understanding of what man is *as man*—and an ontology—a judgment as to what is "really real." At the deepest level of all is the existential trust that was already implicit in the link between Buber's accepting the separation from his mother and his willingness to go out again to meet what came to meet him. Only through the I-Thou relationship, through going out to meet *and* through being met, does the infant, the individual, become a person at all: "We live our lives inscrutably included within the streaming mutual life of the universe."

The meeting with the Thou is like Daniel's "kingdom of holy insecurity" "Strange lyric and dramatic episodes, seductive and magical, but tearing us away to dangerous extremes, loosening the well-tried context, leaving more questions than satisfaction behind them, shattering security", but it is the insecurity not only of danger and openness but of personal involvement and mutual giving, of the trust that accepts "the exalted melancholy of our fate, that every *Thou* in our world must become an *It*," no matter how exclusively present the Thou was in the direct relation. You cannot make yourself understood with others concerning it.

> But it teaches you to meet others, and to hold your ground when you meet them. Through the graciousness of its comings and the solemn sadness of its goings it leads you away to the *Thou* in which the parallel lines of relations meet. It does not help to sustain you in life, it only helps you to glimpse eternity.

The comings of the Thou are gracious not because we are entirely dependent upon grace, but because we cannot will both sides of the dialogue. Its goings are solemnly sad because we must return to the world of It: "Without

It man cannot live." Yet the person who lives with It alone has so fully missed authentic human existence that he is not human. The individual finds the meaning of his existence in the "between," in the reality of the spirit, which in its human manifestation is a response of man to his Thou. The "delusion" in which God and the world are "psychologized"—drawn into man—the colossal illusion of the human spirit that is bent back on itself, is that spirit exists in man. Actually, it is man who lives in the spirit, if he is able to enter into relation with his whole being and respond to his Thou: "All real living is meeting."

Again and again, natural "objects" "blaze up into presentness" and are "lived in the present by men." Before we grasp what is over against us as an object, compare it with other objects, classify and analyze it, and register it in the structure of knowledge, we see it with the force of presence and thereby grasp it in its incomparable uniqueness. We know this uniqueness as we meet it and as it, in a sense, comes to meet us. Along with all the perception of the senses and the categories of the mind, we feel the impact of real otherness. Buber recounted that several times in his youth he wanted to fix an object, to compel it, as it were, in order to find through so doing that it was "only" his conception. Every time he tried to do this, the object refuted him through the dumb force of its being! The person who frees the event from the *It* of established ideas "and looks on it again in the present moment, fulfills the nature of the act of knowledge to be real and effective *between* men."

Buber's relationship to his wife Paula was probably more decisive for the development of his I-Thou philosophy as a whole than any of the events and meetings with which we have dealt. Buber's dialogical thinking could have grown only out of his marriage to this strong and really "other" woman, this modern Ruth who left her family, home, and religion, and finally even her country and people, for him. The fundamental reality of the life of dialogue—that it is a confirmation and inclusion of otherness—was understood and authenticated in the love and the marriage, the tension and the companionship, of his relationship to Paula.

If the failure of Buber's mother to return when he was four years old was the crucial "mismeeting" of his life, Martin's marriage to Paula was the crucial *meeting*—one that could be so only because of the remarkable personal strength that each of them possessed, their very real otherness, and the greatness of their love. If this meeting did not entirely remove the inner division that his mother's disappearance had brought about, it nonetheless made possible a life of trust in which Buber found again the strength to go forth to meet the unique and unforeseeable person or situation as his Thou. The threatening insecurity of Buber's being, Grete Schaeder perceptively comments, receded when he met and married Paula Winkler. One can go further and say that the existential trust that underlies *I and Thou* and all of Buber's mature works would have been unthinkable without his relationship to Paula. This is perhaps the unique case of a philosopher whose thinking did not emerge from his individual being but from the "between," which he knew first and foremost in his marriage.

The precise effect of Paula's strength—her integrity, her honesty, and her responsibility—is movingly depicted in a poem that Buber wrote for her on his fiftieth birthday in 1928:

◆ **On the day of Looking Back**

> The roaming one spoke to me: I am the spirit.
> The iridescent one spoke to me: I am the world.
> He had hovered round me with wings.
> She had encompassed me with her play of flames.
> Already I wanted to pander to them,
> Already my heart was duped,
> When there stepped before the demons
> A presence.
>
> To the roaming one it said: You are madness.
> To the iridescent one it said: You are deception.
> Then both spirit and world became open to me,
> The lies burst, and what was, was enough.
> You brought it about that I behold,—
> Brought about? you only lived.
> You element and woman,
> Soul and nature!

"On the Day of Looking Back" describes how Paula helped Buber to escape from the danger presented by the very multiplicity of his gifts, to find serious and responsible direction amid his wealth of talent.

A similar acknowledgment came from Martin to Paula a year later in the dedicatory stanza to his book *Dialogue:*

◆ **To P.**

> The abyss and the light of the worlds,
> Time's need and eternity's desire,
> Vision, event and poem:
> They were and are dialogue with you.

Even Goethe's epigraph, with which Buber opens *I and Thou,* is understood by Grete Schaeder as a concealed dedication to Paula Buber:

> So waiting I have won from thee the end
> God's presence in each element.

In *I and Thou,* Buber echoed Paula's watchword—" Responsibility is the umbilical cord of creation."

> Love is responsibility of an *I* for a *You.* In this consists what cannot consist in any feeling—the quality of all lovers, from the smallest to the greatest and from the blissfully secure whose life is circumscribed by the life of one beloved human being, to him that is nailed his life long to the cross of the world, capable of what is immense and bold enough to risk it: to love *man.*

Feelings are within the person, but the person stands within love; for love is between I and Thou.

Buber's attitude in *I and Thou* toward the relations among politics, economics, and the state, on the one hand, and genuine community, on the other, is identical with his attitude toward love and, by implication, to the relation between sex and love. Politics, economics, and the state are not evil in themselves, as they were for Gustav Landauer, but only when they became independent of the aim of building genuine community to which they are legitimate means. Economics (the abode of the will to profit) and the state (the abode of the will to be powerful) share in life only as long as they share in the spirit—as long as the structures of man's communal life draw their living quality from the power to enter into relationship. The dualism that would keep "spirit" in one compartment and economics and the state in the other would mean yielding up to tyranny once and for all the provinces that are steeped in the world of It *and* thus robbing the spirit completely of reality. "For the spirit is never independently effective in life by itself alone, but in relation to the world: possessing power that permeates the world of *It,* transforming it."

I and Thou is not a teaching of compromise but of spiritual realism. The question is not what one ought to do in general, but what is possible and desirable for us at this moment and in this situation. Those who instead profess the ideal of total love and renunciation of power rob power of its direction, love of its force, and life of its reality. This is what Buber clearly stated in the poem "Power and Love" (1926):

> Our hope is too new and too old—
> I do not know what would remain to us
> Were love not transfigured power
> And power not straying love.

> Do not protest: "Let love alone rule!"
> Can you prove it true?
> But resolve: Every morning
> I shall concern myself anew about the boundary
> Between the love-deed-Yes and the power-deed-No
> And pressing forward honor reality.

> We cannot avoid
> Using power,
> Cannot escape the compulsion
> To afflict the world,
> So let us, cautious in diction
> And mighty in contradiction,
> Love powerfully.

The Taoist teaching of the noninterfering action of the whole being remained central in Buber's mature thought when other aspects of his mysticism fell away and issued into his contrast between "person" and "individual," "free man" and "willful man." "The free man... no longer interferes, nor does he merely allow things to happen. He listens to that which grows, to the way of Being in the world... in order to actualize it in the manner in which it, needing him, wants to be actualized by him." The willful person, in contrast, knows neither meeting nor presentness, but only a feverish, cluttered world of purposes and a feverish desire to use it.

Modern man's wish to be all or nothing is born of his dread of the infinite universe that confronts him and still more of his mistrust in the possibility of living vis-à-vis either nature or his fellow man. People try to escape from the impersonal golem of institutions to the "personal" world of feelings, but feelings per se are no more personal than institutions. They are personal only when they are brought as by-product and accompaniment into the response of the whole person to what meets him, not when they are themselves assumed to be the touchstone of reality. Institutions equal "otherness" without involvement: feelings equal "involvement" without otherness.

"Whoever goes in truth to meet the world, goes forth to God." To love the world means to be ready to meet the real world with all its uncanniness, horror, and evil. Those who are afraid to do this escape the meeting through *psychologizing* the world, through removing it into the sphere of one's feelings, one's thoughts, or one's analyses. Buber's opposition to psychologism was in no sense a disparagement of psychology or psychotherapy per se, but only of the attempt to subsume all reality under psychological or psychoanalytic categories. By the psychologizing of the world, Buber meant an inclusion of the world in the soul that goes so far that the essential basic relation from which our life receives its meaning is damaged: the facing of I and world in which the real happens. Insofar as the soul is comprehended exclusively as I, it is comprehended in amputation, in abstraction, not in its *whole* existence. "Psychologizing of the world" thus means an attempt of the soul to detach itself completely from its basic character of relationship. How important this fall of man into psychologism and the bending back of the spirit on itself were for Buber can be seen from the fact that the major categories of "Dialogue," Buber's first major application of the I-Thou relationship to the interhuman as such, are defined in terms of it.

Buber was a leading influence at this very time in the German Youth

Movement, that powerful stream of political, philosophical, and social ideals that succeeded the *Wandervogel.* But he saw quite clearly how the relation between oneself and another was referred by each member to his own person: "*My* kind... *My* blood... *My* destiny." This clear insight also carried over to the erotic. The erotic is almost exclusively differentiated self-enjoyment, Buber declared, and what is elementally perceived is what takes place in one's own soul. Even the attempts at the spiritual and religious life are soaked through with the same poison—the poison of the human spirit bent back upon itself and deluding itself that spirit occurs in man.

Going beyond legitimate self-experience, the natural growth of consciousness, one falls into *self-observation,* Buber said, an interference that wills to further the growth of the self and, in so doing, thwarts it. The deeper self-experience that one seeks and seemingly finds is actually a distortion and a belaboring that produces the disintegration of the self. One can only legitimately experience without willfulness.

The therapist deals with the patient as an individual, yet the sickness is a sickness of the "between." "The sicknesses of the soul are sicknesses of relationship. They can only be treated completely if I transcend the realm of the patient and add to it the world as well. If the doctor possessed superhuman power, he would have to try to heal the relationship itself, to heal in the 'between.'" Thus, in psychotherapy itself, Buber was aware of the need to burst the bounds of psychologism, which refers all events and meaning back to the psyche, and to reach the ground of "healing through meeting"—a healing *in* and *of* the "between."

Psychopathology had exercised an active fascination upon Buber since his student days, when he studied psychiatry, attended clinics of Flechsig, Mendel, and Bleuler, and tried to discover whether it is possible to meet, to establish a real relation between a "sane" person and a "pathological" one. "The relation of the soul to its organic life," wrote Buber in 1921, "depends on the degree of its wholeness and unity. The more dissociated the soul, the more it is at the mercy of its sicknesses and attacks; the more concentrated it is, the more it is able to master them." The soul saves and protects the unity of the body. When a whole, united soul (such as that of the *zaddik)* lays hold of the dispersed soul, agitating it on all sides, and demanding the event of crystallization, "there takes place rapidly and visibly there what otherwise only grows in vegetative darkness, the 'healing.'" "The more fully and genuinely the healer fashions a ground and center in the fellow-soul, the less does the appealing soul remain dependent upon the helper." But the less, too, does it fall back into psychologism.

Psychologism develops into self-contradiction when it becomes so intensified that one can no longer bring one's inborn Thou into the meeting with others, with the world. Here, at the farthest point of emptiness, is also the point of the turning, a turning that cannot be accomplished by the individual alone, but only by community. But community itself, in a time like ours, can happen only out of breakthrough, out of turning, when the need aroused by the uttermost sundering of self and world provides the motive force for it. Genuine community begins with the discovery that reality is more than psychological.

> If one knows this, then one also knows that community in our time must ever again miscarry. The monstrous, the dreadful phenomenon of psychologism so prevails that one cannot simply bring about healing, rescue with a single blow. But the disappointments belong to the way. There is no other way than that of this miscarrying. That is the way of faithful faith.

As despair in *Daniel* is the gateway to reality, so despair in *I and Thou* is the soil out of which the turning grows. The self-willed person, who is wholly and inextricably tangled in the unreal, directs the best part of his spirituality to averting or veiling his thoughts about his real self. But it is only these thoughts about the I emptied of reality and about the real I that enable one to sink and take root in the soil of despair, so that, out of self-destruction and rebirth, the beginning of the turning might arise. Through that turning alone can one meet the "eternal Thou."

Every real relation with a being or life in the world is exclusive in the sense that, while it lasts, the Thou steps forth free and single and confronts one, and all else lives in *its* light. Only the relationship with the eternal Thou is both exclusive and inclusive. The eternal Thou is met in each particular Thou, yet it cannot be fixed in any of them. The eternal Thou does not become "It" when the others do—not because it is some universal essence of Thou, but because it is the present reality, the ever-renewed presentness of meeting, *eternally* Thou. It is the bond of the absolute with the concrete and particular, not with the universal. "If you explore the life of things and of conditioned being you come to the unfathomable, if you deny the life of things and of conditioned being you stand before nothingness, if you hallow this life you meet the living God." God is the "wholly Other" of Karl Barth, but he is also the wholly Same, the wholly Present. He is Rudolf Otto's *Mysterium Tremendum* that appears and overthrows, but he is also the mystery of the self-evident, nearer to me than my I. This is the one, all-embracing relation in which potential is still actual being, the only Thou that by its nature never ceases to be Thou for us.

The person who meets the eternal Thou is the free person of dialogical will. Ready, "not seeking he goes his way; hence he is composed before all things, and makes contact with them that helps them. But when he has *found,* his heart is not turned from them, though everything now meets him in the one event." All revelation is summons and sending. "Meeting with God does not come to man in order that he may concern himself with God, but in order that he may confirm that there is meaning in the world." Thus, for Buber, in contrast to Kierkegaard, there is no such thing as an I-Thou relationship with God that comes when one turns away from one's fellow men and the world: "We can dedicate to God not merely our persons but also our relations to one another. The person who turns to him therefore need not turn away from any other *I-Thou* relation; but he properly brings them to him, and lets them be fulfilled 'in the face of God.'" By virtue of the privilege of pure relation, where exists the unbroken world of *Thou,* the isolated moments of relations are bound up in a life of world solidarity. As a result, spirit can penetrate and transform the world of It. In the turning—the recognition of the Center and the act of turning again to it—the buried relational power of man rises. "The man who says Thou ultimately means his eternal Thou." In the eternal Thou—not as separate from the interhuman, the communal, and the social, but as the radial center of all of them—Buber found at last that home wherein modern man could live in spite of the threat of infinity that had tormented Buber from his childhood, "a world that is house and home, a dwelling for man in the universe."

Sometime in 1920 or 1921, Buber spoke on three successive evenings at the adult folk school of a German industrial city on the subject "Religion as Reality." What he meant by this, as he had in his attack on psychologism, was that "faith" is not a feeling in the soul, but an entrance into the *whole* reality. Concerned because none of the workers in the audience spoke up, Buber readily agreed to meet with them alone the next day, all the more so because real listening, he believed, is found most often among workers, who are not concerned about the reputation of the person speaking, but about what he has to say. When an older worker, whose intentness had particularly struck Buber, said, "I do not need this hypothesis 'God' in order to be quite at home in the world," Buber decided that he must shatter the security of the man's *Weltanschauung*. Drawing on a knowledge of twentieth-century physics to which the man had no access, Buber asked:

> Is there some larger reality that can encompass both the I and the world and that meeting between them in which each is included in the other without either losing its own independence and otherness? The unknown "objects" there, the apparently so well-known and yet not graspable "subjects" here, and the actual and still so evanescent meeting of both, the "phenomena"—was that not already three worlds which could no longer be comprehended from one alone?

When Buber was through, the worker, whose eyes had been lowered the whole time, lifted his head and said slowly and impressively, "You are right." Buber than realized with horror that he had led the man to the threshold beyond which there sat enthroned the majestic image that Pascal had called the God of the Philosophers, rather than him whom Pascal called the God of Abraham, Isaac, and Jacob, the living God to whom one can say Thou. He could not accompany this man into the factory where he worked, become his comrade, live with him, and win his trust through real life relationship.

Buber had tried to point to the reality of the life of dialogue by making use of philosophical dialectic. But the worker heard only the dialectic and not the dialogical voice speaking through it. As a result, his acceptance of Buber's statement as "right" was nothing more than the substitution of a new *Weltanschauung* for the old one, a new security of It that would make unnecessary the going forth to meet the Thou. But Buber himself had pointed to "the being that gave this 'world,' which had become so questionable, its foundation," and in so doing had pointed to an It, and not a Thou. He had not pointed to the life of dialogue itself but to an objective, third-person concept that was supposed to stand for it. This is why Buber described this talk as one that apparently came to a conclusion, as only occasionally a talk can come, and yet in reality remained unconcluded.

There was a sequel, however, of which Buber said just the opposite: Though it was apparently broken off, it found a completion such as rarely falls to the lot of discussions. Some time later, in 1922, Buber was the guest of the German philosopher and educator Paul Natorp, whose acquaintance Buber had originally made at a conference where Natorp gave a lecture on elementary folk schools and Buber gave one on adult folk schools. Natorp asked Buber to read aloud the galley proofs of his Foreword to the collected *Speeches on Judaism*. Natorp listened courteously but with growing amazement, which ended with an intensely passionate protest: "How can you bring yourself to say 'God' when what you mean is something above all human grasp and comprehension? The word 'God' has been defiled and desecrated by all the innocent blood that has been shed for it and all the injustice that it has been used to cover up!"

"Yes, it is the most heavy-laden of all human words," Buber replied. "None has become so soiled, so mutilated. It is for just this reason that I may not abandon it."

Generations of men have laid the burden of their anxious lives upon this word.... Certainly, they draw caricatures and write "God" underneath; they murder one another and say "In God's name." But when all madness and delusion fall to dust, when they stand over against Him in the loneliest darkness and no longer say "He, He" but rather sigh "Thou," shout "Thou," all of them the one word, and when they then add "God," is it not the real God whom they all implore, the One Living God, the God of the children of man? Is it not the word of appeal, the word which has become a *name* consecrated in all human tongues for all times?

Natorp came over to Buber, laid his hand on his shoulder, and said, "Let us say Thou to each other."

Jesus said, "When two or three are gathered in my name, I shall be there." Buber, at the end of this account, turned the saying around. Instead of the name coming first and then the presence, the presence of God came first and then the name: "For where two or three are truly together, they are together in the name of God." The word "God" is indispensable, not because the name itself is sacred, but because in every language it is the first of all the word of appeal and only later a name. "All God's names are hallowed," said Buber in *I and Thou,* "for in them He is not merely spoken about, but also spoken to."

The name of Christ, too, was hallowed for Buber *as a word of address,* but not as a theological proposition which says that in this form only can one meet God. To Buber, Jesus the man, Jesus the Jew, who stood in unique and unmediated relationship with God, was not identical with the Christ of Christian faith whom men worshiped as the Savior. If Buber used Goethe in the second part of *I and Thou* as the example of the person who spoke the legitimate I of pure intercourse with nature and Socrates as the one who spoke the I of endless dialogue, it is Jesus whom he chose as his illustration for man's relation to the eternal Thou:

> How powerful, even to being overpowering, and how legitimate, even to being self-evident, is the saying of *I* by Jesus! For it is the *I* of unconditional relation in which the man calls his *Thou* Father in such a way that he himself is simply Son, and nothing else but Son.

Buber saw Jesus as man, not God, and as standing on man's side of the dialogue. Jesus's uniqueness does not lie in his being inseparable from God, but in the immediacy that uses even separation for greater solidarity of relation. Buber did not see Jesus's uniqueness as consisting of something *in* him—a power in itself—for this would mean to empty the real, the present relation, of reality. Rather, Jesus's uniqueness lay in the strength, the immediacy, the unconditionality, of the "between."

But even here Buber set up no qualitative difference. He did not hold, as Karl Barth was later to do, that Jesus as the "one man sinless" was the only one who could really relate to God as Thou. "Every man can say *Thou* and is then *I,*" Buber wrote at the end of this passage about Jesus; "every man can say Father and is then Son." Jesus is not the exception but the illustration, not the image of God but the image of the human. Buber's confidence in his understanding of Jesus's I-Thou relationship with the father was so great that, in the third part of *I and Thou,* he dared to interpret the Gospel according to John, generally taken as the most mystical of the four Gospels—"I and the Father are one"—as "the Gospel of pure relation." What is more, the relation, to Buber, was not just that of the Father and the Son, in the Christian sense of Jesus alone, but of God and man:

> The Father and the Son, like in being—we may even say God and Man, like in being—are the indissolubly real pair, the two bearers of primal relation, which from God to man is termed mission and

command, from man to God looking and hearing, and between both is termed knowledge and love.

For Buber, Jesus was and remained a Jew. To Buber, organized Christianity was a distortion of the essentially Jewish teachings of Jesus and of the communal immediacy of the life of the early Christians.

> Whatever in Christianity is creative is not Christianity but Judaism;... we carry it within us, never to be lost. But whatever in Christianity is not Judaism is uncreative, a mixture of a thousand rites and dogmas; with this—and we say it both as Jews and as human beings—we do not want to establish a rapprochement. (1910)

Although Buber's position was opposed to the Paulinian attitude that favored faith over deed, it came quite close to the synoptic Gospels in its attitude toward what it held to be the rigidity of the law and its alienation from life. The aim of early Christianity and Hasidism, Buber maintained, was not to abolish the law but to fulfill it: "to raise it from the conditioned to the unconditioned, and at the same time to transform it from the rigidity of a formula into the fluidity of the immediate." But early Christianity was lost as a source of renewal for Judaism when it became untrue to itself and narrowed the idea of the "turning" to a communion with Christ by grace. Even though Christianity rose to dominion over the nations, and Judaism sank into rigidity, humiliation, and degradation, the core of Judaism "unshakably maintained its claim to be the true ecclesia, the ever-faithful community of divine immediacy" (1913).

> It is up to us whether we want to live the true life in order to perfect in it our uniqueness. But according to the Christian teaching, which has perverted the meaning and ground of Jesus, it is not up to us but depends on whether we are chosen.... In so far as it refers to grace, that teaching which calls itself Christian hinders the person from decision, the *metanoia* proclaimed by Jesus.... Therefore, I will and shall fight for Jesus and against Christianity. (1917)

Into Buber's attitude toward Christianity at this time, there also entered the war-born emphasis upon the unredeemedness of the world, which was central to the Jewish understanding of messianism and which Buber was to unfold in his translation and interpretation of the Hebrew Bible during the last forty years of his life:

> Redemption—that is a transformation of the whole of life from the ground up, the life of all individuals and all communities. The world is unredeemed—do you not feel that as I do in every drop

of blood? Do you not feel as I do that the messianic only happens... as that on whose realization we can work at every hour?
(1917)

I believe in the fulfillment at the end of days that nothing past can
anticipate but everything past may and shall prepare for.... But
just from this it follows that the fulfillment cannot be anything that
has happened, that can be localized in a conscious stretch of the
historical past. (1917)

Thus, Buber fought *for* Jesus and against Christianity, *for* the decision and
turning that Jesus called for and *against* faith in Christ as the prerequisite to
man's moving to meet and respond to God. The original Jewish spirit of true
community was concentrated in Jesus, Buber asserted:

What he calls the kingdom of God—no matter how tinged with a
sense of the world's end and of miraculous transformation it may
be—is no other-worldly consolation, no vague heavenly bliss. Nor
is it an ecclesiastical or cultic association, a church. It is the perfect life of man with man, true community, and as such, God's
immediate realm, His *basiliea*, His earthly kingdom. (1918)

Jesus wished to build the temple of true community out of Judaism. But two
millenia of Western history are filled with such massive misinterpretations of
his teaching that the Jewish consciousness of a world that man can help
reunite with God is replaced by an unbridgeable dualism between human
will and divine grace. True community is no longer to be realized in the
totality of human life together—in the hallowing of the everyday—but in the
Church, a community of the spirit separated from the community of the
world. In this atmosphere, said Buber, Christianity gave so much to Caesar
that there was nothing left to give to God. Paul transformed Jesus's teachings
into the dualism between faith and works, spirit and action. Thus, he handed
to the peoples "the sweet poison of faith, a faith that was to disdain works,
exempt the faithful from realization, and establish dualism in the world. It is
the Pauline era whose death agonies we today are watching with transfixed
eyes."

"Jesus's last words contain sacrifice, but they also contain the humanity
of *not* sacrificing oneself," said Buber in 1923. This insistence on the biblical
"over-againstness" of God and man in dialogue, through which Buber recap-
tured the Jewish Jesus, is repeated in *I and Thou*. "God needs you—for that
which is the meaning of your life," Buber said in Part III. In the same subsec-
tion, using a sentence from the Lord's Prayer as his springboard, Buber
added that he "who offers his little will to God and encounters him in a great
will" says only, "Let your will be done." "But truth goes on to say for him:
'through me whom you need.'"

The only gate that leads to the Bible as a reality, wrote Buber in 1930, is the faithful distinction between creation, revelation, and redemption, not as "manifestations of God, but as stages, actions, and events in the course of His intercourse with the world." These "stages, actions, and events" were already fully present and explicit in *I and Thou*. Nothing is more central to *I and Thou* than Buber's understanding of creation. Creation in the biblical sense underlies Buber's assertion that man is given a ground on which to stand and that he is able to go out to meet God, man, and world from that ground. Creation informs Buber's belief in man's spontaneity and freedom, which cannot be modified by any original sin, and in man's responsibility, which cannot be abridged by any fate. This approach to creation is also inherent in Buber's understanding of God as the "absolute Person," who *is* not a person but becomes one, so to speak, to love and be loved, to know and be known by us. "There is divine meaning in the life of the world, of man, of human persons, of you and of me.... *We take part in creation, meet the Creator, reach out to Him, helpers and companions.*" With these words, Buber reached decisively and forever beyond the God realized in man to the God met in present being, and he reached it without exchanging process and becoming for the absolute, unmovable Being of the metaphysicians. The paradox of the "becoming of the God that is" sets Buber against traditional metaphysics, which demands the choice between an absolute that is not in relation to the world and a God who is in relation and therefore less than absolute.

In *I and Thou*, Buber criticized Kierkegaard unmistakably, though not by name, because of his depreciation of man's relation to creation. Speaking of the assertion that the "religious" person stands as a single, isolated being before God and has therefore gone beyond the responsibility and the ought of the "moral man," Buber passionately protested:

> But that is to suppose that God has created His world as an illusion and man for frenzied being.... The world, lit by eternity, becomes fully present to him who approaches the Face, and to the Being of beings he can in a single response say *Thou....* he *will have to practice, till death itself, decision in the depths of spontaneity, unruffled decision, made ever anew, to right action.* Then action is not empty, but purposive, enjoined, *needed, part of creation.*

The paradox of creation is that God sets the world and man at a distance and yet remains in relationship with them, that he gives man ground on which to stand and yet that the very meaning of man's free standing on this ground is that he can go forth to meet the Creator who addresses him in every aspect of his creation. This paradox carried over for Buber into that of revelation, for revelation, to Buber, was neither fixed objective truth nor free subjective inspiration but hearing and responding to the voice that speaks to man out of creation and history. Hence, "all revelation is summons and sending."

Knowledge, from this point of view, means mutual contact and communication rather than a detached observation of an object. Thus, the knowing within the ordinary I-Thou relationship and the knowing of revelation are not different in nature, however different they may be in intensity or historical impact. "The mighty revelations at the base of the great religions are the same as the quiet ones that happen at all times." The only authentic assurance of continuity is if man realizes God anew in the world according to his strength and to the measure of each day. "In belief and in a cult form can harden into an object; but in virtue of the essential quality of relation that lives on in it, it continually becomes present again," as long as the power to enter into relation is not so buried under increasing objectification that the movement of turning is suppressed.

Redemption, too, is an event of the "between" and cannot be relegated simply to God's side or to man's, to divine grace or to human will, to apocalypse or historical process.

> According to the logical conception of truth only one of two contraries can be true, but in the reality of life as one lives it they are inseparable. The person who makes a decision knows that his decision is no self-delusion; the person who has acted knows that he was and is in the hand of God. The unity of the contraries is the mystery at the innermost core of the dialogue.

The completion of creation and the response to revelation are the beginning of redemption. Redemption means bringing ever-new layers of the world of It into the immediacy of the Thou. The partnership of man and God in creation, the rising of a human cosmos built out of genuine community and a redemptive life of relationship, the shining, streaming constancy that the Thou may win in the It, are all hints of redemption. The true beginning, if not the completion of redemption, again and again comes from man's side as the event of turning, turning back to God—in joy, in thanksgiving, in wonder, but also in despair, in crisis, in insecurity. The collapse of the spiritually apprehended cosmos and the destruction of the *form* of spiritual life may nonetheless be the breakthrough to a renewal of genuine relationship. At the end of *I and Thou*, Buber affirmed an existential trust in history in which the very turning away from reality prepares the ground for a fuller and deeper redemption. In this redemption, the alien, the exiled, the problematic, the "evil" are brought—unreduced and undenied, yet transformed and transmuted—into the renewed reality of relationship. Here creation, revelation, and redemption show themselves as three aspects of a single event.

◆ *Adele Buber,*
Martin's paternal
grandmother.

◆ *Solomon Buber,*
Martin's paternal
grandfather.

◆ *Elise Buber,
née Wurgast,
Martin's mother.*

◆ *Carl Buber,
Martin's father.*

◆ *Martin at about age four.*

◆ *Martin at about age seven.*

◆ *The student Martin Buber, in Leipzig in 1897.*

◆ *Martin's special friends, leaders of the Democratic Faction of the Zionist Party (facing page, clockwise from lower left), Berthold Feiwel, E.M. Lilien, Chaim Weizmann, Davis Trietsch, Buber.*

◆ *Among his fellow students at the University of Vienna, Martin is standing behind the table holding a sword.*

◆ *Paula Buber as a young woman.*

◆ *Paula (right) with children Eva and Rafael.*

◆ *The Buber House in Heppenheim an der Bergstrasse, Germany (1916-1938).*

◆ *Gustav Landauer.*

The Weimar Republic and Nazi Germany

(1923-1938)

❖

PART

✦ II ✦

The Weimar Republic and Nazi Germany

(1923-1938)

✦

♦ 9 ♦

Franz Rosenzweig and the Buber-Rosenzweig Bible

(1921-1929)

Buber's interest in general folk education stood in fruitful interaction over the years with his concern for Jewish adult education. The great impetus to his participation in the latter during the post-World War I years came through the "free Jewish House of Learning" founded at Frankfurt by Franz Rosenzweig. Buber's most significant personal encounter, next to Paula Buber and Gustav Landauer, was his friendship with this profound existentialist philosopher and interpreter of Judaism. In July 1913, a year before Rosenzweig's first visit to Buber, Rosenzweig had decided to convert to Christianity. He wished to enter Christianity as a Jew and not a pagan, and for that reason he waited until Yom Kippur, the Jewish Day of Atonement, and went to the service so completely open that he emerged converted not to Christianity but to Judaism! From that time on, his path and the path he showed to others was that of the Baal Teshuvah, the "master of the turning," who has turned away from Judaism but is now turning back. As he swung away from Judaism to a degree unthinkable to Buber, so in his swing back he went beyond Buber in both observance and belief. Yet the kinship between the two leading Jewish religious philosophers and existentialists of the twentieth century was recognized by both men in a fruitful personal and intellectual interchange that made their friendship one of the most memorable episodes in recent Jewish history.

Martin Buber was already famous in Germany as a Zionist, the re-creator of Hasidic legends, and the author of the widely influential *Speeches on Judaism* before Rosenzweig, younger by eight years, met him. Rosenzweig, on his part, stood in the stream of late German Idealism, as Buber never did, and produced a two-volume work, *Hegel and the State*, before turning away from Hegel in his *Star of Redemption*. The distrust that this rationalistic non-Zionist young philosopher felt for Buber's mystical thought and poetic writing was reinforced by Buber's famous controversy with Rosenzweig's teacher and friend Hermann Cohen.

Although Buber and Rosenzweig had met once in 1914, it was not until their second meeting in 1921 that they really came to know each other. The war years, which had had a decisive effect on the thought of both men, had brought them closer together without their realizing it. In 1919, Rosenzweig wrote Buber, asking that he read the manuscript of *The Star of Redemption* and put in a good word with the Jüdische Verlag or with Löwit Verlag. Rosenzweig justified his bold request on the ground that the book would eventually find its circle of readers, Buber among them (a true prophecy!). "I have the unshakable feeling that I have attained here the summit of my intellectual existence and that all that follows will be merely appendices." At the same time, Rosenzweig wrote that he was not at all sure of receiving a favorable verdict from Buber: "For so far as I can see, the whole manner and direction of my work lies rather far from yours—perhaps not so far as the various schools of "Idealist' philosophy but for all that still far." Rosenzweig counted, nonetheless, on the breadth and openness that Buber had time and again shown as editor of *Der Jude* and asked him to judge "whether you see an objective necessity for the view that I here put forward being published as a Jewish view, whether or not this view pleases you yourself."

Rosenzweig's *Star of Redemption* was the product of the war in an even more literal sense than Buber's *I and Thou,* since the first part of it, in Rosenzweig's own words, "was written down on army postcards, in the midst of conversation with comrades and superiors."

Existential thinking, to both Buber and Rosenzweig, meant that truth must be discovered and confirmed by the whole human being. Such an approach set them in unalterable opposition to all philosophy that seeks for the "essence" of things in abstraction from the concrete reality of personal existence. This reality includes time, change, the limitations of each person's perspective, and the necessary acceptance of the fact of death. The sickness of reason, wrote Rosenzweig in *Understanding the Sick and the Healthy*—an attack on Idealist philosophy—is an attempt to elude death by stepping out of life into the paralysis of an artificial life above time and change and reality. The cure for this sickness, conversely, must be the realization that to live means to move forward to death, that death is the ultimate verification of life.

The fundamental concept of the new theory of knowledge, wrote Rosenzweig in "The New Thinking," is that truth ceases to be what "is" true and becomes a verity that must be verified in active life. From the unimportant truths, such as "two times two are four," on which people agree with a minimum use of their brains, "the way leads over those truths for which man is willing to pay, on to those that he cannot verify save at the cost of his life, and finally to those that cannot be verified until generations upon generations have given up their lives to that end." Real dialogue is the way to existential truth. The New Thinking "needs another person and takes time seriously—actually, these two things are identical." "To require time means that we cannot anticipate, that we must wait for everything, that what is ours depends on what is another's." "Whatever *The Star of Redemption* can do to renew our ways of thinking is concentrated in this method."

In the years to come, Buber recognized that Rosenzweig's *Star* had explicitly shown the gateway to the Bible as a reality in a way that he himself had done implicitly in *I and Thou*—through the faithful distinction between creation, revelation, and redemption as stages, actions, and events in the course of God's intercourse with the world. "The catastrophes of historical realities are often at the same time *crises in the human relation to reality,*" wrote Buber in 1930, a year after Rosenzweig's death. "Of the special way in which our time has experienced this crisis, I know of no greater and clearer example than that of Franz Rosenzweig."

But the remarkable parallels between Rosenzweig's and Buber's thought ought not obscure the highly significant differences. Buber's concern with Hasidic tales and Jewish mysticism was as foreign to the more rationalistic Rosenzweig as Rosenzweig's tremendous philosophical-theological system was to the intuitive, largely unsystematic, and only reluctantly theological Buber. Despite his great respect for Buber's position, moreover, Rosenzweig never came to see Zionism as other than a final aspect of redemption rather than as an immediately attainable goal. Rosenzweig's understanding of language as the bridge between God, world, and man can be contrasted with Buber's understanding of language as I-It as well as I-Thou and of genuine dialogue being silent as well as spoken. Rosenzweig saw Judaism as already in eternity, whereas Buber saw Judaism as bound to the concrete historic situation—tempted, but less strongly than Christianity, to move away from this situation through apocalyptic emphasis on a fixed future or through faith with a knowledge content that fixes God in a certain image.

The two philosophers of speech came together as persons and as coworkers in Rosenzweig's Freies Jüdisches Lehrhaus. It was Buber's first experience with the give-and-take of real discussion during a presentation. Until then, he had always lectured. The uniqueness of the Lehrhaus attracted him, the interruption of a presentation to answer a question, teaching instead of speech making. From that time, Buber was one of the pillars of the Lehrhaus, and, what was most beautiful to Rosenzweig, not the finished and past Buber but the becoming and future one. In January and February 1922, Buber spoke before writing down what was to have been the first volume of his five-volume systematic presentation of *I and Thou* and, the following winter, he spoke before writing the second, with it being understood that he would accompany the other volumes with lectures at the Lehrhaus. Buber found that these lectures took some pains because it was in the course of them that he first learned with what difficulty an audience hears, and in particular how unwilling they were to hear his new words because of their familiarity with his old ones.

Nahum Glatzer described Buber's lectures entitled "Religion as Presence" to the Jewish and Gentile public at the Lehrhaus as "a present-day event of startling immediacy." Buber himself made plain the personal connection between this event and his friendship with Rosenzweig. "Already with the second sentence of your letter my answer was assured," he told him. "Of course, I shall undertake the lectures if I can thereby fulfill a personal wish of yours."

To a friend, Rosenzweig wrote a few months earlier that not only was Buber's *Der Jude* one of the best if not the best German periodical and the representative organ of German Jewry, but that Martin Buber himself, without wishing it, had become recognized by intellectual and spiritual Germany as *the German* Jew. To another friend, Rosenzweig wrote that, from his meeting with Buber, he had taken away with him the certainty of Buber's absolute genuineness, or rather of his having become genuine. "He is in intellectual matters the most honest, in human matters the most genuine person I know," witnessed Rosenzweig, and added, "I do not speak easily in superlatives." Before Buber's general knowledge, Rosenzweig declared himself a dwarf, and he was equally impressed by Buber's knowledge of Jewish sources, from the Talmud to eighteenth-century Mussar literature. Rosenzweig also gave an impressive testimony of Buber's confirming his partner in dialogue thirty years before Buber singled out "confirmation" as a central concept in his philosophical anthropology. Speaking of his work translating the medieval Jewish philosopher and poet Yehuda Halevi, Rosenzweig wrote a friend: "With each new poem the technical problem during the work itself is so oppressive that I lose all perspective so that I must first hear through another that something will still come of it. In decisive moments Buber has been that other. Without him the book would not have come into being."

During this period, the real friendship and closeness between Buber and Rosenzweig began. "Buber has meant a great deal to me personally," Rosenzweig wrote to a friend. "My acquaintance with him would have been epochal in my life if there had been opportunity. Even the similarity of thought is very great in his lectures; have you not noticed it? But of greater importance to me is the awesome (indeed almost unhealthy because more than personal) genuineness of his being." A few months later, he declared to Buber himself that he could understand it when someone else's thought differed sharply from his own, as with Georg Simmel, for example, or when two who had been on a common course thought the same. But when neither was the case, as with the two of them, when "our thoughts *themselves* met and would have met even if you and I had not," then the question of how to understand this grows enormous. "I have always been reluctant to accept books as realities," Rosenzweig added, "but I feel compelled to here."

The Israeli theater director Benno Frank tells how as a young man he was close to suicide because of his isolation from his Orthodox Jewish background and from his father. He attended the lectures at the Frankfurt Lehrhaus and finally spoke of his situation to Franz Rosenzweig. Rosenzweig, though already ill, alerted Buber, who took Frank aside, helped him to unburden himself, and then uttered the sentence that became a direction for Frank's life: "Become an actor: On the stage you will be able to live many lives and to die many deaths." Frank gave up thoughts of suicide and became an actor and director, just as Buber had advised.

In November 1921, not long after he had written metaphorically of the paralysis of Idealist philosophy, Franz Rosenzweig noticed symptoms of a disturbance of his motor system, which his friend Dr. Viktor von Weizsäcker diagnosed as the beginning of a literal paralysis. This diagnosis was confirmed by Rosenzweig's friend Professor Richard Koch the following February. In a few months, this paralysis, as Nahum Glatzer has expressed it, "turned the young, vigorous man into an invalid deprived of movement and speech," though he lived on for almost eight more years and not just for a year as Koch expected. At an early stage of his paralysis, Rosenzweig forewarned Buber that, when Buber came to see him, he would not find him much different in appearance but that, aside from his being unable to walk, his speech was disturbed.

> I can still be understood—more than it will appear to you in the first moment. One can get used to that. But my speech sounds like that of a very old man and comes out in a dreadfully tiresome way, still more tiresome for others than for myself. All nuances are impossible for me. In appearance, if I do not speak right away, I appear pretty much unchanged. I am wearing pyjamas. So—after this tragicomic rendez-vous signal, you will easily overcome your first shock.

Throughout the years of Rosenzweig's paralysis, Buber continued to share deeply with him. One such sharing concerned the mythological theme of Gog from the Land of Magog, who, according to biblical and later Jewish tradition, would challenge God to battle and force him to send the Messiah. Much later, this theme became the kernel of Buber's Hasidic chronicle-novel, which he entitled "Gog and Magog" in the German and Hebrew editions and *For the Sake of Heaven* in the English. "The 'Gog' oppresses me very much," Buber wrote Rosenzweig, "but not just as subject for a novel. Rather I fight with full clarity of mind, entirely different from all fantasy, to track down how 'evil' belongs to the coming of the kingdom." In another letter to Rosenzweig, Buber wrote:

> As far as Gog is concerned, it is good that today I am forty-five years old. Otherwise the fellow would gobble me up. Try to imagine, yesterday I suddenly awoke from an apparently dream-less sleep and saw bodily before me the Phoenician devil with pinched lips staring at me with a superior air like that of the Roman Imperator of the old Rembrandt in the Carstanjousel self-portrait ("Oh, Rembrandt was not a fantasist," said the curator to me, when I tried to draw his attention to the fact that the "bust" when well lit becomes a face).

At the end of 1923, Buber notified Rosenzweig that he had not dared to work on the Gog for a long while: "He has caused me too much pain."

In 1924, in an effort to make the best possible adjustment to his grow-ing paralysis, Franz Rosenzweig himself prescribed in detail methods for nursing, for his communicating with those around him, and for his study and writing. Several nurses broke down under the strain of serving him, which included lifting, bathing, feeding, and helping him to walk a few yards, two and a half hours in just getting him out of bed and dressed (because the stretching of the legs brought on cramps, slipping, pain, and the repeated necessity of bending his legs for him), an hour for breakfast and even longer for other meals. Yet Rosenzweig wrote—from about eleven o'clock in the morning until about one in the afternoon; from half past four until eight; and after dinner until midnight or longer. When he could no longer turn the pages of his books, the nurses were summoned by a turning of the head as he read difficult Talmudic passages. When oral diction became impossible, as the paralysis of his organs of speech intensified, a specially constructed type-writer enabled him to indicate words, one letter at a time, though soon only his wife Edith was able to guess which letters he meant, as Nahum Glatzer relates:

> Through years of close association Mrs. Rosenzweig had acquired an instinctive understanding which seemed miraculous to out-siders. Mrs. Rosenzweig also managed every conversation with visitors, by guessing often recurring words after the first or second letter. The patient's extraordinary memory enabled him to dictate and have typed in this fashion, during three or four hours of work, the final draft of what he had worked out, down to the smallest detail, during a sleepless night. This method was fol-lowed up to the time of his death.

In 1925, after he had been invited to write the article on Buber for *Jüdisches Lexicon,* Rosenzweig confessed to Buber:

To parody, and exclaim: Here you may view the holy beast of the Jews, and no mystic! is something I can and will do. It is a cry that must be raised for the sake of the good cause, and in such cases I don't take cover behind my soul. But to portray you, to write "about" you, is something I can't do. My illness has removed me to such an extent from my older friends that I could, today, write about them, just because I can no longer, or only to a lesser degree, write to them. But you, who entered on the "seventh day of the feast" are still much too "new (and ever again new) a face" for me to be able to portray you before the public. I must leave it at the fleeting image on my retina, and I hope it will not change while I live.

On Rosenzweig's fortieth birthday, on December 25, 1926, Buber presented him with a map containing handwritten contributions by Rosenzweig's friends. In his letter of thanks, Rosenzweig particularly noted the presence of a letter from Buber's wife, which he had not expected ("Her letter was the great surprise of the day,") and added by way of comment that, when a man is in his thirties, he is still always something of a baby: One is allowed occasional stupidities. But when he enters his forties, then he is finally and irrevocably grown up.

During the 1920s and continuing into the 1930s, the underlying thought and program of the Frankfurt Lehrhaus served as a model for the establishment of similar institutions in Stuttgart, Cologne, Mannheim, Wiesbaden, Karlsruhe, Munich, Breslau, and Berlin. In many of them, Buber was just as active as he was to be in the reopening of the Frankfurt Lehrhaus in Nazi Germany. Meanwhile, Rosenzweig drew Buber further into teaching by persuading him to accept the lectureship in "Jewish Religious Philosophy and Ethics" at the University of Frankfurt. In urging Buber to take over this position, which had originally been intended for himself, Rosenzweig pointed to the elasticity of the university framework, the danger that it might become just one more institution for the training of rabbis, and the effect that Buber's presence and his "guaranteed *apikoros* personality" would have on the character and direction of the Jewish faculty that might later be appointed. "This can be done only by someone who is wholly free of any undue deference for the existing university, and who, at the same time, brings to the job the kind of personal reputation which will forbid the university's interfering with him."

It was not at all easy for Buber to make up his mind to accept the academic chair created for Rosenzweig but vacated due to his illness. Although Buber finally accepted the position, a comment that he made to his friend Hugo Bergmann in a letter of 1936 when the Nazis forced Buber to leave the position, casts light on the spirit in which he did it:

That I—after giving up a university lectureship as a young man and rejecting a prestigious academic position [at the University of Giessen] as a forty-year-old—accepted the call to the Frankfurt chair, is bound up with my relationship to Franz Rosenzweig in a manner that I must perceive as tragic. It had the character of a sacrifice.

The first person to whom the chair had been offered was Rosenzweig's mentor and friend Rabbi Nehemiah Nobel of Frankfurt, who died before he could take it. In the volume published in celebration of Rabbi Nobel's fiftieth birthday, Ernst Simon related how Buber went to visit Rabbi Nobel and his wife. When it came time to have a bite to eat, Rabbi Nobel asked Buber delicately whether he would perhaps like to wear a very small yarmulke (skullcap) for the occasion. Observing the look on Buber's face, he added, "Or would even the smallest one be too large for you?" "In a traditional Jewish home," Buber replied, "I would not be averse to wearing one. But with you, Rabbi Nobel, I will not grab hold of the small end of the Halachot [the Jewish laws] in this way." Then Rabbi Nobel recited the benediction silently, as if there were only two present, for only when at least three are present may it be said aloud. (Nobel was what we would call a Conservative Jew rather than an Orthodox one.)

It was in 1923, when the collected *Speeches on Judaism* appeared, that Rosenzweig was able to get the overview of Buber's developing thought on revelation and law in Judaism that prompted Rosenzweig to write his famous letter "The Builders." "You have been," Rosenzweig told Buber, "the leader of my generation and the one that came after it in freeing the teaching from the fetters which the nineteenth century put upon it. But you have not made the same step in your understanding of the Law. Here you still distinguish between what part of the Law is 'essential' and what is not." As with the teachings, the content of the Law must be transformed into the inner power of our actions: general law must become personal command.

> Law *(Gesetz)* must again become commandment *(Gebot)* which seeks to be transformed into deed at the very moment it is heard. It must regain that living reality *(Heutigkeit)* in which all great Jewish periods have sensed the guarantee for its eternity. Like *teaching*, it must consciously start where its content stops being content and becomes inner power, our own inner power. Inner power which in turn is added to the substance of the law.

The selection of the part of the Law that the individual shall perform is an entirely personal one, claimed Rosenzweig, since it depends not upon our will but upon what we are able to do. Hence, in contrast to the Paulinian all-or-nothing, Rosenzweig envisaged a gradual growth of the Law in consonance with the personal existence of the doer. This means that no one can or should even wish to anticipate the boundary of the Law or what belongs to its sphere. "We do not know how far the pegs of the tent of the Torah may be extended, nor which one of our deeds is destined to accomplish such widening."

"Your 'Builders' has moved my inmost soul," Buber responded, "and appears to have broken through a secret door. If I answer you (which hopefully will be granted me after my return from Karlsbad), I must now really express what has long been withheld. In terms of ideas, yes, but at the same time autobiographically—much more intimately so than in the Foreword [to the collected edition of his *Speeches on Judaism*]; for what I really have to say to you can only be taken from the secret archives of the person." Actually, the only reply that Buber ever made was in the form of letters. In a rare personal confession of belief, Buber said that it was his faith that prevented him from accepting Rosenzweig's premises. It was an integral part of Buber's personal being that he could not identify the Law and the word of God, nor could he imagine that this position would ever change for him. He experienced this fact so keenly during the week preceding his letter, he said, that it even penetrated his dreams. Thus, Buber made a distinction between revelation and the giving of the Law that Rosenzweig had failed to make:

> I do not believe that *revelation* is ever lawgiving. It is only through man in his self-contradiction that revelation becomes legislation. This is the fact of man. *I cannot will to obey the law transformed by man if I am to hold myself ready for the unmediated word of God directed to a specific hour of life.* [Italics added]

Thus, the immediacy of the dialogue with God made it impossible for Buber to follow Rosenzweig in affirming the whole of the Law to be divine prior to one's personal appropriation of it. It was not, as Nahum Glatzer has suggested, the fact that Buber was the "spokesman of a new, universal, religious and philosophical orientation" in contrast to "Rosenzweig, who found his peace in the practice of Halakhah where the... longing for salvation is resolved in the sober conformation to the Mitzvoth." We do not know in advance that any particular part of the Law can always be changed back into a commandment in any particular situation. Rosenzweig failed to consider "that it is the fact of man that brings about transformation from revelation to what you call commandment (*Gebot*)." Rosenzweig accepted the command as from God and left open only the question of whether the individual could fulfill it, whereas Buber remained closer to the immediacy of dialogue and made the real question whether it actually is a command of God to oneself.

> I cannot accept the laws and the statutes blindly, but I must ask myself again and again: Is this particular law addressed to me and rightly so? So that at one time I may include myself in this Israel

which is addressed, but at times, many times, I cannot. And if there is anything that I can call without reservation a *Mitzvah* within my own sphere, it is just this that I act as I do.

As the correspondence continued, Buber found it necessary to make clear to Rosenzweig that while man was for him a law receiver, God was not a lawgiver. This led Buber to the decisive statement of his difference from Rosenzweig and from most observant Jews, including many of his own followers, such as Ernst Simon: "Therefore the Law has no universal validity for me, but only a personal one." This position did not mean either individualism or anarchism, but dialogue: "I accept only what I think is spoken to me." As an illustration, Buber cited what was for him a developing relationship to the Sabbath: "The older I become, and the more I realize the restlessness of my soul, the more I accept for myself the Day of Rest."

"I am responsible for what I do or leave undone in a different way than for what I learn or leave unlearned," Buber asserted to Rosenzweig. "For me, too, God is Not a Lawgiver," declared Rosenzweig and acknowledged Buber's response to the question of the command to be as legitimate as his own. In another letter of this time, Rosenzweig wrote, "Buber's No is perhaps more important for the 'Building' than Ernst Simon's and my and your Yes." In every case, it was not Rosenzweig but Buber who restricted himself to personal testimony and refused to make any statements of a general nature either for or against the Law, much less any attempt to persuade Rosenzweig that he should or would in the future come closer to Buber's own witness. This was eminently the case with Buber's final letter of June 1925:

> Whether the "law" is God's law is and remains for me the only question that is really sounded in my soul from abyss to abyss. The other abyss really does not answer this question with silence. But if it should answer it with Yes, I would not ponder whether the law is a force making for the wholeness of life—that would then be irrelevant. On the other hand, no ever so certain affirmation of this or any similar question could take the place for me of that missing—not quietly but thunderously missing—Yes.
>
> Revelation is not lawgiving. For this statement I would hopefully be ready to die in a Jewish world-church with Inquisitorial powers.

Despite their basic divergence on the relation of revelation to law, Buber and Rosenzweig were able to work together on what became for each of them his most profound and serious life task: the translation of the "Old Testament" from Hebrew into German. The impetus for the translation did not come from Buber, but from the young Christian publisher Dr. Lambert Schneider. As a university student, Lambert Schneider had first discovered the Bible for himself—in particular the Old Testament—"and this splendid and fascinating book, often understandable only with difficulty, often vexatious, never again loosed its hold on me." Schneider wanted a new translation by a Jew, by a man who was familiar with the original text and for whom at the same time the German language was a powerful instrument of expression. This led him to think of Martin Buber, who was already at that time the one German Jew recognized by German intellectuals as both an important contributor to German culture and a representative of Judaism.

Schneider wrote a letter to Buber in which he stated his proposal for a new translation, and Buber invited Schneider to visit him at his home in Heppenheim an der Bergstrasse. A few days later, Schneider sat facing Buber in his study. While he explained his wish to Buber, the latter's brown, kind eyes rested on him, "and he listened to me attentively, so attentively and openly as no one had listened to me for a very long time."

> Then he took from a shelf Luther's translation of the Bible, opened it to a passage, read it aloud to me and translated the same passage freely from the Hebrew text to show me that my view had its justification. But at the same time he made clear to me what inconceivable work, what responsibility lay in such an undertaking—all this without grandiloquence—and let me know that he did not believe he could accept such a task which would claim his time for years. All this was put forward so simply and plainly that I made no attempt at all to press him further and stood up to take my leave.
>
> Outside the sun played in the first green leaves of the trees. It was very silent in the street and in the house as Buber, standing by his desk, began once again to speak. He did not want to refuse me definitely but wished to talk the matter over with his friend Franz Rosenzweig. Because such a request from a young man who was a Christian, seemed to him a sign that he could not dismiss without further ado. He would give me a response soon, he said, and then gave me his hand in parting.
>
> On the way to the train station in Heppenheim, I regarded my plan as having fallen through; for his last words seemed to me to be only a little consolatory speech for my return journey to Berlin. Yet eight days later the publisher's contract for the translation was already drawn up. It was no little speech for my way back; it was an answer of Martin Buber's in the deepest sincerity.
>
> What it is to listen and to answer I know since that first meeting with Martin Buber.

The translation that Schneider initiated and that Buber and Rosenzweig carried out not only gave Schneider the direction for his publishing work but also inculcated in him, according to his own later testimony, the freedom from prejudice that enabled him to withstand all the political confusions of Nazi Germany. Buber received from Schneider a monthly honorarium for the work of translating the Bible, independently of the publication of the individual volumes.

Buber's remarkable assent to Schneider's proposition can be understood on many levels. Everything that had gone into Buber's understanding of the world as Word had prepared him for this decision: his concern for translation of many languages into German; his concern for myths, sagas, and legends; his only recently matured philosophy of dialogue with its emphasis upon lived speech and the back and forth of address and response; even his concern for drama and for poetry. The idea of the task itself was not a new one to Buber. Even before the First World War, Buber had made plans for a translation of the Hebrew Bible into modern German. At that time, he maintained that only a community could undertake this—a community, what is more, that was also personally bound to one another, and that, in this way, they could help one another in their work at a deeper level than is ordinarily possible.

Buber visited Rosenzweig and read him Schneider's letter proposing the translation of the Bible, to which he added that he was inclined to accept the proposal but only if Rosenzweig would join him in the task. Buber noted that this statement at once gladdened and disturbed Rosenzweig. Later, Buber understood: Rosenzweig no longer, to be sure, expected to die in the next weeks or months, as he had in the early period of his illness, but he had given up believing that he had much time at his disposal. By offering Rosenzweig a share in this task, Buber implied that he was capable of years of the most intensive work. It meant entering into another reckoning of the future. From this stemmed the expression used on the title page, "zu verdeutschen *unternommen* von Rosenzweig" (literally, "undertaken to translate by Rosenzweig").

Buber, in contrast to Rosenzweig, did not believe that they should start with any restriction, not even the relatively flexible one set by undertaking a radical revision of Luther's translation. Only an experiment, demanding and using the whole person, hence a bold plunging ahead that knew and made use of all earlier translators but bound itself to none of them, could yield an acceptable answer to their question of whether the Bible could and should be translated anew. This is the path that they finally took. Rosenzweig saw his role in this common work as that of the founding muse (Diotima and Xantippe in one person), the role Buber had in Rosenzweig's translation of Yehuda Halevi. But that, added Rosenzweig, is no small thing, even though he felt that he knew much less Hebrew than did Buber.

The form of the cooperation between Buber and Rosenzweig remained the same until the latter's death. Buber from time to time translated and sent to Rosenzweig pages of his first translation of the text, mostly by chapters. Rosenzweig answered with his comments: rejections, hints, proposals for changes. Buber made use of these at once in the form of changes insofar as they made immediate sense to him; and about the rest they corresponded.

What they could not agree on, they discussed during Buber's Wednesday visits (Buber lectured every Wednesday at Frankfurt University and spent the rest of the day at the Rosenzweigs'). The same process was repeated with the second version of the translation, through three sets of proofs. With the pages of the first version, Buber gave Rosenzweig the reasons for having translated it thus and not otherwise, in order to make an overview easier for him. In order to spare him from looking through books, Buber described for him the controversial opinions concerning each of the difficult passages, from the earliest exegetes to the most recent essays in scientific journals. Nonetheless, the correspondence concerning a single word often had to go on for weeks. Thus, in the framework of an exchange of letters, the Bible became illuminated in the most living commentary possible. Rosenzweig wrote to a rabbi that he had, during the Bible translation, learned a great deal that he did not know when he had written the postscript to his translation of Yehuda Halevi—not only because each new task demanded a new method but because Buber had opened to him new insights into method.

In a celebration at Buber's house in Jerusalem in 1961, marking Buber's completion of the translation of the Bible more than thirty years after Rosenzweig's death, Rosenzweig's friend Eugen Mayer spoke of how Buber had devoted most of his time to the indescribably difficult and time-consuming task of working with Rosenzweig and thus filled the latter's final years with satisfaction and meaning. "For him who does a gracious deed for a great one of Israel," Mayer cited from the Midrash, "it is as if he had done it for all Israel." Rosenzweig himself fully appreciated what working with Buber on the Bible meant to him. When Buber sent him the last section of the book "In the Beginning" (Genesis), Rosenzweig responded with a poem thanking him for making it possible for him to live through this work.

Buber responded to Rosenzweig's poem by asking Rosenzweig to address him by the German *Du,* or "thou," the symbol of intimate friendship. "With Florens Christian Rang," Buber confessed, [using "thou"] was not easy for me in the beginning," and with Paul Natorp the difference in age prevented it and the formal usage remained. "But between us, thank God, the difference in age is not so great." Rosenzweig replied that it was not at all difficult for him to address Buber as "thou," for he had done so all too often in silence. The difference in age did not so much account for the distance between them. "Although a nearly ten-year span of human world-experience increased it—for you were already a public figure at twenty while I still danced to the Rumpelstiltskin riddle at thirty—but a feeling of respect that till now I could express by my usual signature to my letters. I almost regret giving up that [signature]; but it will remain as my silent undertone, as formerly my silent thou."

One of the most charming chapters in the Buber–Rosenzweig Bible translation included the reactions of Rosenzweig's young son Rafael, whom Buber's wife declared looked so much like his father and whom, like him, was so distinct a personality. As Buber and Rosenzweig worked at the translation, Edith Rosenzweig read passages of it to their little son Rafael, and they delighted in his response. "Rafael needs no selection; he treasures it all," Rosenzweig wrote. "And he has besides a nose for what can be criticized in our Genesis. Recently he declared: 'I like Adam and I like Eve and Abraham and Sara and Lot and (before) the serpent, but the dear God is wicked and water is wicked.'" When little Rafael was five, he still insisted, despite all assurances to the contrary, that his papa and Uncle Buber were the authors of the Bible! When Rafael was seven, Buber told the Rosenzweigs that Hans Kohn was writing his biography, and said that, along with the astonishing amount of material, much of it unknown to Buber himself, that Kohn had dug up, there was also, God be thanked, much more that still remained unknown. Rosenzweig said: "Rumpelstiltskin." At that, Rafael, who had been painting at the table, shouted out jubilantly, "Ah, how good that no one knows" and continued ingenuously with "that I have translated the Bible!" instead of with the words of the fairy tale (that my name is Rumpelstiltskin!), which Rosenzweig had been sure he would say. Buber, never put out of countenance, responded, "Now just not that; one knows that I am translating the Bible." Whereupon Rafael, without reflecting, said, "that I have made so many beautiful things."

When the great Enlightenment Jew Moses Mendelssohn translated the Hebrew Bible into German in the eighteenth century, his goal was to teach the German Jews German, and for that purpose, even though, as in Yiddish, he used Hebrew letters, he made his translation as German as possible. The goal of Buber and Rosenzweig was the exact reverse, as Rosenzweig himself recognized: to make the Bible, even in German, as Hebrew as possible and thereby bring the German Jews back to the original text. For this reason, even today, the Buber-Rosenzweig Bible serves many Israelis as a commentary on the Hebrew original. This does not mean that Buber and Rosenzweig made the task of the reader any easier than the original did. On the contrary, as Gershom Scholem pointed out in the 1961 celebratory volume marking the completion of the task, Buber's and Rosenzweig's chief intention was to exhort the reader to go and learn Hebrew and therefore they left the clear clear, the difficult difficult, and the incomprehensible incomprehensible. Rather than smoothing out and making pleasant, they left the text purposely rough and crude, never providing a transition or a completion where the Hebrew does not do so. "In contrast to the Luther and all other former translations," Buber wrote, "we are ready in order to save a treasure such as this, to go the limits of the German language—without overstepping them."

Ernst Simon singled out three interconnected characteristics that distinguish this Bible translation from all others: the oral element, the sensual element, and the maximum preservation of the Hebrew form of speech in a foreign idiom through which, in Buber's own words, the Bible was liberated from the "plague of familiarity." "We wish to break through to the spokenness of the Word, to its having been spoken. The Bible is to be read *in living Presence."*

From the Septuagint on, all translators had endeavored to transport the Hebrew Bible into their *own* spiritual world. Even Jewish translators and exegetes could not escape these tendencies to modify the Bible to fit Western theological and cultural ways of thinking and speaking. The fundamental direction of the Buber-Rosenzweig Bible was the opposite.

Perhaps the most significant of these changes from written to spoken and from static to dynamic is the Buber-Rosenzweig translation of the Hebrew *kadosh* not as "holy" but as "hallowing." *Kadosh* does not mean a state of being but a process: that of hallowing and of becoming hallowed. Moses stands before the thornbush not on holy ground but on the ground of hallowing. When Aaron is consecrated as a priest, he is clothed in the garments of hallowing and anointed with the oil of hallowing. The Sabbath is a festival of hallowing, and the sons of Israel are called by God to become people of hallowing (not a holy people).

This rendition at one stroke changes the whole meaning of the relationship of God to the world and of the sacred to the profane and lays the groundwork for Buber's later characterization of Hasidism as regarding the profane not as an antagonist of the holy but as the not-yet-hallowed, the not-yet-sanctified. No separate spheres of sacred and profane insulated from one another by taboo can endure before the onrushing *Geistbraus* of the God of spirit *and* nature. If we apply this change to the translation of a familiar Hasidic tale, the power of this understanding of hallowing the everyday or sanctifying the profane becomes unmistakable:

> The rabbi of Kobryn taught: God says to man, as he said to Moses: "Put off thy shoes from thy feet"—put off the habitual which encloses your foot, and you will know that the place on which you are now standing is ground of hallowing. For there is no rung of human life on which we cannot find the hallowing of God everywhere and at all times.

Holiness is not a simple state accessible to the enlightened who can see through the illusion of existence. It is a *task* in which man's hallowing and God's hallowing meet. When Rabbi Mendel, of Kotzk's question regarding where God dwells, was answered by the verses "The whole earth is full of His glory," he retorted, "No, God dwells where man lets Him in!"

What had been previously translated as the Lord was now rendered as I, THOU, HE—that is, extrapolates Everett Fox, as "I who am–there with you, You who are–there with me, He who is–there with me." This means, as Rosenzweig explained, recognizing all Platonizing tendencies and guarding against their indirect philosophical consequences, that God does not name himself at the thornbush as Being but as Existing, as being-there, as being present, being with, coming to, and helping those whom He addresses.

Thus, the absoluteness and eternality of God is really the capacity of this present moment and any future moment to be one in which I find myself addressed in my present existence. The eternality of God's presence is here, as in *I and Thou,* not the *"eternal"* Thou but the *eternally* Thou, the ever-renewed concreteness and uniqueness of the meeting with the Thou. Starting from Moses's relationship to God, Buber comments: "Man cannot 'see' God's face (in our terminology: he cannot make God into an object), but he can let himself be addressed by him in his inmost self and stand in dialogue with him (in our terminology: he can become a partner to God)." God says to his creature what he needs to know—that he is there with him, is present to him, but in always new, never-to-be-anticipated forms, in the forms of this, his creature's, own life situations, and that what matters thus is nothing else than recognizing him again and again in them.

The Hebrew Bible wants to be read as one book, wrote Buber, so that none of its parts remain shut within themselves; rather, each remains open to the other. It wants to be present to its reader in such intensity as one book that, in reading or reciting a certain passage, it brings to mind those passages connected with it, especially those identical, close, or related to it in speech, and that they all illuminate one another in such a manner that they come together into a theologoumenon—a conception that is not expressly taught but immanent in the words, emerging from their relations and correspondences. The repetition of the same or similar-sounding words, or words and phrases the same or similar in root within a passage, within a book, within a group of books, shows the linguistic relationship between the prophets and the Pentateuch, between the psalms and the Pentateuch, between the psalms and the prophets.

One striking example of this linking of words through sounds or roots is from the story of Jacob and Esau. Jacob, who has obtained by trickery his father's blessing of the firstborn, must, after he returns from fourteen years of service with his Uncle Laban, face the wrath of his brother Esau and the possibility that Esau will kill him. The night before he is to meet Esau, he goes apart alone and encounters a strange man with whom he wrestles until dawn and whom he will not let go until he has received his blessing. After this trial, Jacob is now ready to go to Esau to seek forgiveness, to repair the injured order of existence, and, if necessary, to give his life in the process. Thus, what was won by deviousness could be retained only by openhearted directness and great personal and spiritual courage.

These meanings are not read into the text. They are already present as hidden connections that need be brought to light only by paying attention to the significant repetition of leading words or motifs.

The integral connection between the story of Jacob wrestling with the "angel," which is so often dealt with out of context, and his flight from the wrath of Esau and his return to face it, is given in the text through the repetition of the motifs of covering the face and seeing one's face, the parallel between seeing the face of God and seeing the face of Esau, and the parallel between the blessing, or gift, that God gives to Jacob and the gift that Jacob gives to Esau.

Esau links Jacob's name, "heel-sneak," with the way in which Jacob has twice sneaked what was Esau's: first his birthright, then his father's blessing (Genesis 27:35-36). This mean way of of fighting is atoned through the good, the name that has become shameful replaced by one that is hallowed. Soon, God himself expressed the renewal of the man Jacob-Israel, and completes the blessing, but only after he is reconciled with his brother Esau. The blessing between man and man is followed by that between God and man.

"The strongest, most stiff-necked and demanding of the critics of your work," Scholem said to Buber, "was yourself, the artist, the master of speech, the *homo religiosus* who tirelessly wrestled for the exactness and fullness of expression which alone could correspond to your intentions." And many years later, Scholem added his own testimony to that of the many others who have found in the Buber-Rosenzweig translation an invaluable commentary on the text itself: "Many of us have again and again, when we read difficult passages of the Bible, asked ourselves, what would 'the Buber' say—not otherwise than we ask, what does Rashi [the great medieval Jewish commentator on the Bible] have to say?"

The great German-Swiss novelist and poet Hermann Hesse wrote in three separate places, "I must also name the Bible translation of Martin Buber, with the sincerity and strictness of its struggling for the word, one of the noblest strivings of the German spirit in our time." When Hesse nominated Buber for the Nobel Prize in literature in 1949 and again in 1958, he gave as the basis for his proposal, along with other things, the translation of the Bible. Buber's son Rafael, who, as a communist, was by no means close to his father at this time, wrote in 1926:

> Genesis is very beautiful in your translation. I gladly read in it and often in so doing have the feeling that I am reading Hebrew.... It is not only the faithful rendering in the rhythm of the Bible but also the primordial text in the beautiful German language. At any rate I read it in German and understand it in Hebrew.

The Buber-Rosenzweig Bible came as both the supreme cultural achievement and the termination of what Buber himself called the German-Jewish symbiosis. Ernest M. Wolf, like Scholem and Simon, testified to its great importance for Jewish youth both as a substitute for the original and as a favorite commentary, or *targum,* on it. It gave a solid foundation to the renaissance of Jewish learning that had been stirring from the early years of the century, even before the impact of Hitler's anti-Semitism, and "regular and systematic courses in Bible study became one of the major forms of educational endeavor in the Jewish community."

There was hardly a meeting, a seminar, a conference, or a camp of Jewish youth organizations where Bible study was not part of the program, and usually a major and central part of it.... Had the generation of young Jews that went through the Buber-Rosenzweig school of Bible reading and Bible interpreting been permitted to grow up and to remain together, they would probably have become the most Bible-conscious Jews since the days before the ghetto-walls had fallen in Europe.

Writing to a friend after the completion of the Book of Samuel, Rosenzweig said of the translation: "It was a heavy task, Buber says the heaviest of his life." What his heavy task meant to Buber personally as a progress from the "easy word" to the hard one is vividly portrayed by the poem "Confession of the Author," which Buber wrote in 1945 and dedicated to Ernst Simon:

> Once with a light keel
> I shipped out to the land of legends
> Through the storm of deeds and play,
> With my gaze fixed on the goal
> And in my blood the beguiling poison—
> Then one descended to me
> Who seized me by the hair
> And spoke: Now render the Scriptures!

Who or what was it that descended to Buber, seized him by the hair, and commanded him to "render the Scriptures"? Not a voice from heaven, but the address heard in the situation itself. Buber's Bible translation, too, is a "Word to the Times"—a faithful listening and response to the demand of the hour, which in this case meant bringing the biblical word to an age probably more alienated from and hostile to it than any earlier one within the history of Judaism and Christianity.

Nowhere is this prophetic voice in an alien world expressed with more force and clarity than in Buber's essay "The Man of Today and the Jewish Bible." "Nowadays 'religion' itself is part of the detached spirit," one of its subdivisions that only serves to reinforce the dualism between "spirit" and "life." This is why Buber later sardonically described religion as "the great enemy of mankind." The so-called Old Testament, in contrast, is the greatest document of a reality in which the spirit is made incarnate and everyday life hallowed, in which the Torah is designed to cover the natural course of man's life and the covenant is a demand not for religiosity but for real community. The man of today, who "has no access to a sure and solid faith," can, nonetheless, "open up this book and let its rays strike him where they will, without prejudgment or precommitment." Revelation takes place ever anew in the present *if I am there*. This implies living in genuine responsibility, which is just what the man of today does not want. "Man of today resists the Scriptures because he cannot endure revelation. To endure revelation is to endure this moment full of possible decisions, to respond to and to be responsible for every moment." Here is the link between *I and Thou* and

Buber's 1928 essay "Dialogue," in which every event is seen as a "sign of address." "Do we mean a book? We mean the voice. Do we mean that one should learn to read? We mean that one should learn to hear." The spoken quality of the Bible is inseparable from the demand upon our existence for *teshuvah,* for the turning of our whole being so that we find ourselves, not back on some earlier stretch of our way, but there where the voice is to be heard!

Because of the central importance of Buber's work on the translation of the Hebrew Bible, it is not surprising that it penetrated his home life. Buber worked on translating the Bible in the bedroom. According to his grand-daughter Judith (Rafael's daughter), who lived with him at the time, there were two large tables in the bedroom with all the books and materials that he needed and an adjoining room full of books that had to do with the trans-lation. After breakfast, Buber would always work on his Bible translation until a set hour and then come down from the bedroom to his study to work on other topics. Even when the family went walking in the Alps, during the breaks Buber would take out the proofs of his Bible translation from one pocket and a Hebrew-German dictionary from the other. Then, in the midst of the beauty of the Dolomites, he would conduct a long discussion with Paula as to which word was appropriate for translating a specific verse.

During the mealtimes at home, many of the arguments between Martin and Paula were about his choice of words and linguistic formulations. Paula took Martin's work very seriously and greatly honored it, requesting Judith and her older sister Barbara to be quiet so as not to interfere with his work. Occasionally, though, Paula would burst out bitterly and angrily, for at times it peeved her always to give up her own time and energy and dedicate them to Martin's development. To an extent, both grandchildren were educated through Buber's translation of the Bible. He taught Barbara and Judith the Bible, and in that way they learned Hebrew.

In "Biblical Leadership," a lecture Buber delivered in Munich in 1928, his understanding of biblical dialogue deepened to include the paradox of historical success and failure and with it an understanding of redemption and messianism as inseparable from the suffering of the "servant" depicted in the famous passages about the suffering servant in Deutero-Isaiah:

> The way, the real way, from the Creation to the Kingdom is trod not on the surface of success, but in the deep of failure. The real work, from the biblical point of view, is the late-recorded, the unrecorded, the anonymous work. The real work is done in the shadow, in the quiver.

How thoroughly this understanding of the connection between genuine dia-logue and historical failure permeated Buber's consciousness at this time is shown by two other "Words to the Time," which he wrote at this juncture, both of which are far removed from the context of the Bible. In the fall of

1928, Buber gave an address on "China and Us" for a conference of the China Institute at Frankfurt-am-Main. Our age has begun to learn "in the bitterest manner, indeed, in a downright foolish manner," that historical success is of no consequence. We have begun to doubt the typical modern Western man "who sets an end for himself, carries this end into effect, accumulates the necessary means of power and succeeds with these means of power." The Taoist teaching (*wu-wei*), that genuine effecting is not interfering, not giving vent to power, but remaining within oneself, points us to that powerful existence that at first appears insignificant or even invisible, yet endures across the generations to become perceptible in another form. "There where we stand or there where we shall soon stand," Buber prophetically concluded, less than five years before Hitler came to power, "we shall directly touch upon the reality for which Lao-tzu spoke."

In 1929, Buber took up this theme of the hidden leadership in still a different context—that of Zionism, modern politics, and Max Weber's famous sociopolitical concept of charisma. At this time, Buber recounted, as a contribution to a number of recollections of Theodor Herzl by his contemporaries, the conflict between Herzl and Davis Trietsch that we have already discussed in connection with Buber's early Zionist politics. At the end of this story of how he first set foot on the soil of tragedy, Buber inserted a reflection that came directly from his fiftieth year and not his twenty-fifth. It was Trietsch's fiancée who stood facing Herzl with flashing eyes, who impelled Herzl to answer as he did. If this incident showed a dreadful lack of objectivity on Herzl's part, the fact that his opponent had one human being who would take his part this way may have raised in Herzl's mind the possibility that there might be another reality, different from obvious world history—"a reality hidden and powerless because it has not come into power."

> ...whether there might not be, therefore, men with a mission who have not yet been called to power and yet are, in essence, men who have been summoned; whether success is the only criterion; whether the unsuccessful man is not destined at times to gain a belated, perhaps posthumous, perhaps even anonymous victory which even history refuses to record; whether, indeed, when even this does not happen, a blessing is not spoken, nonetheless, to these abandoned ones, a word that confirms them; whether there does not exist a "dark" charisma.

Buber did not suggest that the man who acts in history could allow himself to be overwhelmed by such questions, for, if he did so, he might have to despair and withdraw. "But the moments in which they touch him are the truly religious moments of his life." Here, religion is not just the meeting with the "eternal Thou," or even "dialogue," but the suffering of the servant in the depths.

Whether or not in writing about the "dark charisma" of Davis Trietsch,

Buber was also thinking of his own life experience of one political disappointment after another—an experience he was to go through again and again in the remaining thirty-six years of his life—it is certain that he associated his friend Franz Rosenzweig with the "suffering servant," an association that became clear and unmistakable in the last years of Rosenzweig's life.

On Friday evening, December 6, 1929, Rosenzweig was attacked by a feverish illness that developed into a severe bronchial pneumonia. After forty-eight hours of sleeplessness and gasping for breath, in which those around him tried in vain to find a comfortable position for his paralyzed limbs and to make out what he wished to say, on Monday, December 9, he fell into a refreshing sleep. On Monday afternoon, the doctor, who had given up the idea of using an oxygen tent in order that Rosenzweig might communicate with his family, consented to his request that he be brought to his chair in the study. It took two hours to transfer him from his bed to his chair, where he slept from 1:00 P.M. to 4:00 P.M. When he awoke, he took some food, the first in several days, and asked that his hand be brought into position for a dictation, to be transliterated into the copybook used for his correspondence with Buber. Pointing to the letter plate of his typewriter, letter by letter, he spelled out, slowly and laboriously, "... and now it comes, the point of all points, which the Lord has truly revealed to me in my sleep: the point of all points for which there...." He was referring, as Buber himself has said, to one of the passages on the suffering servant from Deutero-Isaiah. The writing was interrupted by the entrance of the doctor, whom Rosenzweig, with infinite trouble, managed to ask (through their spelling out the alphabet and his nodding) whether the B'nai B'rith Lodge, of which the great German-Jewish thinker and spiritual leader Rabbi Leo Baeck was president, had acceded to Baeck's extraordinary request, actually a decree, that the lodge buy seven thousand copies of the Buber-Rosenzweig translation of the Pentateuch. The doctor, an influential member of the lodge, was not at all sure what the outcome would be, but realizing this might be his last chance to talk with Rosenzweig, he said that the lodge would accept, an answer that seemed to please Rosenzweig, who decided not to finish the interrupted sentence, the last he ever wrote. Sometime after one o'clock in the morning of December 10, he died.

A week or so after Rosenzweig's death, Buber wrote an essay about him, which he titled "Für die Sache der Treue" (For the Cause of Being True). Buber spoke of how Rosenzweig set aside the writing of books after the completion of *The Star,* in favor of a life in which he wished to confirm the truth as husband, father, teacher, learning from the Torah and working in Israel. But then it was made clear to him that this was still "too little to become My servant." "An unspeakable load, unspeakable, was to be laid on and borne by him"—his illness. Instead of dying within a year, as he had expected, he had to suffer for eight years. "In those eight years Rosenzweig confirmed in the Face of God the truth that he had seen. Lamed in his whole body, he fought for the truth through being true." His doctors said of him that he was a "phenomenon of the spirit," but Buber insisted that he was a phenomenon of the spirit that willed to become wholly manifest in concrete existence.

Faith alone would not account for such great endurance and determination, Buber asserted. It needed the companionship of humor. Faith means taking a vow, but humor is necessary to fulfilling this vow in the midst of all the vexatiousness and contrariness of existence. He who believes accepts life as a whole, but to accept life in its individual events, moment by moment, a life of the utmost pain, requires a deep-seated humor.

> In all these years of suffering I have admired nothing in Rosenzweig so much as his smile... it arose out of the basic genuineness of the creature. It was not superior and not resigned, it was full of faith and presence. The jokes that stood on almost every page of [Rosenzweig's] comments on my translation manuscript were entirely natural jokes and yet like prayers of thankfulness.

In a 1956 essay in which he contrasted Rosenzweig with Heidegger and other existentialist thinkers as one who really let his truth transform his life and really lived it in his life, Buber again reverted to this theme of faith and humor. Rosenzweig's paralysis was so monstrously difficult for a thinker such as Rosenzweig because it crippled not his thoughts but his expression of them. Yet "I can testify," wrote Buber, out of our unique contact through six years of working together, how Rosenzweig, sinking ever deeper into the abyss of sickness, remained uninterruptedly faithful to his service. "The great lesson that I at that time received from my younger friend was the merging of faith and humor in such a test."... "It is thus that an existence that confirms the truth appears."

At the end of his "Gleanings," the collection of short fragments, poems, and essays that Buber selected to be preserved in book form just before his death, Buber placed the short answer to the question of what happens after death, which he wrote for a French journal in 1927 and which was printed in German in 1928 on his fiftieth birthday. That Buber took the trouble to write this statement out for Rosenzweig in the French in which it was originally printed suggests that he may have been thinking of Rosenzweig and his imminent death when he wrote it.

> We know nothing of death, nothing other than the one fact that we shall die—but what is that, dying? We do not know. So it behooves us to accept that it is the end of everything conceivable by us. To wish to extend our conception beyond death, to wish to anticipate in the soul what death alone can reveal to us in existence, seems to me to be a lack of faith clothed as faith. The gen-

uine faith speaks: I know nothing of death, but I know that God is eternity, and I know this, too, that he is my God. Whether what we call time remains to us beyond our death becomes quite unimportant to us next to this knowing, that we are God's—who is not immortal, but eternal. Instead of imagining ourselves living instead of dead, we shall prepare ourselves for a real death which is perhaps the final limit of time but which, if that is the case, is surely the threshold of eternity.

CHAPTER

♦ 10 ♦

The Weimar Republic

(1922-1932)

In 1925, Buber wrote to his father, conveying best wishes for his birthday and, as usual, sent him the latest books that he had published, in this case, his Bible translations. Carl Buber wrote of his surprise that his son had taken on a project of such magnitude and of his joy at receiving the books. He also predicted that Martin would have great success in the world as a result of it, the rays of which will warm "all of us." In 1930, Buber journeyed again to visit his father in Lemberg, and in 1931 his whole family went there for the funeral of his stepmother. On that occasion, Buber spoke of his eighty-three-year-old father as "a man of astounding strength and uprightness," proving that the admiration which he felt for his father as a boy had in no way diminished.

Martin Buber's son, Rafael, or, as his family nicknamed him, Raffi, remained in friendly communication with his parents during these years. After the war, he matriculated at the age of nineteen, got involved in politics, and dealt with refugees from the East. For a year, he studied practical subjects in Mannheim and finally decided to become a practical person who deals with worldly things. This decision distanced him from his father, who was anything but practical and worldly, and brought him closer to his grandfather, Carl. During that period, Raffi was active in the Communist youth organization, thus widening the generation gap—or rather giving expression to it since his generation was skeptical and cynical toward all the values of their parents. He became a communist for a time and married a communist— Margarete Thuring, who later became known for her book *Under Two*

Dictators, describing her experiences in the Nazi extermination and the Soviet slave-labor camps. In a letter of 1923, Buber wrote of how painful their relationship with Raffi was—for he had given them all kinds of worries. "Now," Buber wrote, "he is visiting us with his wife and a most darling child, named Barbara, who resembles my wife." But the following week, Raffi was going to Worpswede to join the settlement of Heinrich Vogeler, a painter and German communist who migrated in 1925 to the Soviet Union and spent the rest of his life there. Despite this growing gap, Raffi wrote his father a warm letter in August 1926, in which he not only laid plans for a trip to Frankfurt, including a visit with Franz Rosenzweig, but also said that, even though some things in his father's letter had disturbed him, he could see that Martin was really his friend.

Although Buber, as a federalistic, communitarian socialist, was certainly pained by his son's becoming a communist, there were far more practical concerns that upset Martin and Paula, in particular the schooling and upbringing of Barbara and later of her younger sister Judith. In 1928, these concerns came to a head in the difference between Martin and Paula, on the one hand, and Margarete, on the other, with regard to Barbara's education. Margarete came to visit in order that they might try to come to an agreement. This proved to be in vain, and Paula Buber took the unusual step of going to the courts and getting custody of both Barbara and Judith, presumably on the grounds that their parents' way of life prevented their raising the children as they should. Thus, ironically, family history repeated itself, even though for very different reasons, and Buber's grandchildren came to live with him as he had with his grandparents. This irony came full circle when Barbara lived with Buber in Jerusalem in his old age and helped to take care of him.

Paula discussed the situation with Barbara and Judith, but Buber himself shied away from it until thirty years later, after Paula had died. At that time, having become friendly with Margarete Buber-Neumann (as she called herself after her marriage to her second husband) who was living in Germany, he asked Judith what her own relations with her mother were. He was surprised to learn that not only were they good, but that Margarete was also playing very well the role of grandmother to Judith's daughter. When Buber suggested a parallel, since his own mother had never been a mother to him, Judith pointed out an even more significant difference. Margarete never gave up her children willingly, as Buber's mother had done, but, on the contrary, ran away with them for fear that they would be taken from her. She fought the lawsuit all along and only when she had lost did she give them up to Martin and Paula. After the divorce and the lawsuit, Martin and Paula accepted Margarete and encouraged Barbara and Judith to save money from their allowance so that they could buy presents for their mother. Margarete would come and stay in the Buber house for a few days when she visited her children and seemed to feel comfortable in doing so. After she fled from Germany to Switzerland in 1934, she wrote a letter under a false name, asking her children to come visit her. Buber and Paula identified the handwriting, and though it was in the middle of the school year, all four of them dropped everything and took off immediately for Switzerland to spend two days with Margarete. Eva, the younger child of Martin and Paula, married later than Rafael. Writing to a family friend living in Jerusalem in 1923, Buber said that Eva was exactly as he always knew her: "She does not change but remains always the child and the world creature that bears its certainty in itself." Two years later, Eva, with a more delicate build and a more sensitive and aesthetic nature than her older brother, Rafael, became engaged to, and then married, the poet Ludwig Strauss.

Eva's father and Ludwig Strauss had already been friends for years, as we have seen, with a rich association—in publishing, in intellectual, poetic, spiritual, and personal matters. From the letters of many decades between them, it is clear that Buber responded from the heart to the trust that the younger man brought him, recognized his poetic gifts, and took part in the development of the personality that he encountered in him. When Strauss became Buber's son-in-law, Buber concerned himself more and more with his economic circumstances and helped him find one piece of publishing or literary work after another.

Strauss was a participant in the seminar on Lao-tzu's *Tao Te Ching* that Buber gave in Amersfoort, the Netherlands, in August 1924, along with Hans Trüb, Emma Jung (the wife of C. G. Jung), and a number of other notable persons. Strauss wrote Buber in the following months, expressing his heartfelt thanks for all the spiritual and personal good, the gentleness and severity, and all that had passed between being and being in those three weeks.

Buber's reply to Strauss gives us a glimpse of what their summer vacations in the mountains meant to the Buber family. Writing Strauss from Tuscany, Buber spoke of a splendidly isolated beach and of a pine forest in the midst of which they lived. "And when one goes out on the water, one sees unbelievably near before one the blue chain of the Appenine Alps and there in between the white marble mountain of Carrara." It did them all good, but most of all Paula, for whom this relief after toil was especially important. Buber also reassured Strauss that Eva's difficulty in writing him was a deep matter arising from the separations that one must respect and that would go away of itself if something really concrete, say a matter of providing help, should arise. To this Buber added, concerning a mutual acquaintance, that his actions had taught Buber at how deep a level the true difficulties of our life are to be sought. In later letters, Buber informed Strauss that he had given the poems that Strauss sent him to Eva, as she was their true recipient and, later still, that Paula had accepted Eva's relation to Strauss more positively than Buber had anticipated.

In 1930, Buber wrote Hans Trüb that the feeling tone of their life had been deeply influenced by the court's assigning custody of their granddaughters Barbara and Judith to them. "In particular it does my wife much good by relieving her of her anxiety concerning the fate of the children." The whole period of the fight for custody had been much harder for Paula than for him, Buber wrote Elijahu Rappeport at the same time. Martin and Paula were very affluent at this time and had a large house with a garden, whereas Barbara and Judith's mother worked in an office and their father in a merchant's firm. Even though Rafael remarried shortly after the divorce, Martin and Paula clearly believed that Barbara and Judith would have better conditions in their home. Most of the money came from Poland, where Buber's father Carl lived and had large estates, property, and investments. Barbara lived with her grandparents even before the court decision, since both of her parents had agreed to it. Martin and Paula offered to send her to the Odenwaldschule, but the doctor suggested keeping her at home because of the scarlet fever that she had when she was four. She was tutored privately and did not go to school until the third grade, at which time Judith, who was now living with them, too, entered the first grade.

An incomparable glimpse of the life of the grandparents and grandchildren is afforded us by the testimony of Judith and Barbara nearly half a century later. Although Martin was their formal guardian, Paula was in charge of their physical cares and their day-do-day education, while Buber, "rather remote," spent many hours each day in his study. The family met during meals and went on vacation together. Otherwise, meetings with their grandfather occurred when a crisis arose. On the other hand, many young and not-so-young persons with problems would come to visit Martin. Though strict about his working hours, he would stop everything in order to meet with such persons.

> Frequently, some young people who would be hiking through Germany would stop at Heppenheim and come to visit Grandfather. At times, they would even sleep over at our home. It seemed to me that everyone wanted to speak with my grandfather. There were also many persons who came from far off, and wore all sorts of weird clothing. The story in Heppenheim was that when the railroad stationmaster saw a person with a turban or a fellaba or any other weird clothing get off the train at Heppenheim, he would immediately tell him to go to the right and then turn left at the first corner, and go straight until he reached Buber's house. He never waited for the person to ask how to get to Professor Buber's home.

Every Friday evening, Paula lit the Sabbath candles, and, after the meal, Martin would always read something to the family "He knew how to read beautifully"—most often a Hasidic tale. Paula converted to Judaism without intending to keep all the *mitzvot* (commands), but she was happy that the children received a Jewish and Zionist education. When Martin wanted to keep Jewish holidays, Paula helped him willingly, and she did everything with German correctness, including the Passover Seder, Hanukkah, Purim, and other holidays. From the age of eight, the children learned Hebrew, and they always had Hebrew teachers so that, when they came to Palestine as teenagers, they were already able to read the newspaper without difficulty. When Barbara and Judith grew older and Buber learned that they did not believe in God, it was difficult for him. He used to make a Kaddish blessing on Friday evening before the Sabbath meal, but, after a few years, he stopped because he did not want to impose Judaism on the children.

In addition to the moments of crisis, the children would approach their grandfather when they did not have something to read. "Well, have you finished all of Dickens?" he would ask them and then lead them into his library. But he would not permit them to read everything. He told Judith that Dostoevsky was not for her, as a result of which she sneaked into his library, took out a novel of Dostoevsky's, and read it secretly the entire night, hiding it under her pillow before returning it secretly to the shelf in the morning. Martin would also discuss with the children what they had read and compliment them on their evaluations so that they did not feel themselves to be "total ignoramuses."

Paula had what Judith described as a Swiss approach to receiving guests. The house in Heppenheim had eleven or more rooms, and there were many extra beds and mattresses. There was always enough for all the guests, and everything was always immaculately clean and aesthetic. In bringing up the children, Paula was very rigid. She knew what was good and bad, right and wrong. Martin knew in theory that imposing such rigidity was wrong, but in practice he went along with it. This was in part because he left the upbringing of the grandchildren, as of their parents before them, to Paula, partly because of the dominance of her personality, and partly, no doubt, because he found it difficult to put himself into the world of young people. He quarreled with Barbara and Judith when they wanted to go on hikes that he did not approve of when they were teenagers or when they did not work hard enough at their studies. At times, when he was exasperated, he threatened to get in touch with their father, saying "I can no longer be responsible." The children did not take these threats seriously, since they regarded their father as a sort of older brother. Buber's ideal of the family as a small society with many mutual goals also remained largely theoretical, since he hardly got involved with the family. However, according to Judith, one place where he was involved was in the garden.

> He had a very specific role in the upkeep of the large garden around our house in Heppenheim, although the responsibility for the garden was entirely in Grandmother's hands. He was in charge of sorting the dahlia bulbs, cataloguing them and labelling them in the fall, and helping sort them for planting in the spring. That was Papa Martin's job. He would be called from the study, and told that the time for work had come, and he would dedicate

himself for hours to arranging them, writing a note attached to each dahlia, specifying its type.

Paula was a sportswoman who swam well and rode a bike. Martin knew how to dance, as we have seen, but he seldom danced. One thing he did enjoy doing and did for many years was hiking in the mountains. He was very good at climbing, but going down was often a problem for him. Each summer when the family hiked in the Swiss Alps or the Dolomites in Austria and Italy or in the Italian Alps, Buber would study the maps, decide on where the family should take breaks, and lead the family all the way.

Buber did try to converse with simple people, such as the tax collector or the grocer, but despite the impression one gets from reading his works, he did not relate easily to children, to other persons, or to animals. He made a sincere effort, but he had difficulties. In contrast to his friend and disciple Ernst Simon, Buber was not a naturally sociable, outgoing person, though he was both affable and charming when he was with people. Buber would often fondly call Paula "Paulaschöne" and would at times kiss her hands. Buber offered only a few expressions of love toward Barbara and Judith. When they would meet their grandfather after being away for an extended period, he would kiss their heads or pat them and say, "A Jewish head." Barbara and Judith belonged to a sports club and were taught to ski by a private teacher, all these activities being handled by Paula, who was clearly to the grandchildren the stronger person in the household, the one who determined things. At times, Paula would organize an evening of games in which all persons in the household, and perhaps a guest or two, would participate. Then Barbara and Judith would sit together with the grown-ups and play games. The two house servants would participate and also Martin's secretary. At these planned evenings, Martin would be very entertaining. Paula told the children stories before they fell asleep. She once promised to tell them one thousand different stories, and she held that she had kept her promise. She took many of these stories from folk legends with which she was acquainted. She herself was the author of stories as well as novels. Paula would also put out the shirts Martin was to wear, just as his grandmother used to tie his shoelaces for him. The children showed their report cards to Paula, but Martin was in charge of preaching to them if something was not in order. Barbara and Judith would go and visit their father on vacation or he would come and take them on trips, but they continued to live with Martin and Paula.

Emmanuel Strauss, the son of Eva and Ludwig Strauss, recalled with great fondness childhood visits to his grandparents. Sometimes Martin would play with him, for example, staging a boxing match. "When I would tell him that I'd smear him to the wall, he would laugh. But grandmother did not like my saying that." In the large garden, he would often play with Barbara and Judith, and at times Martin would join the games, including hide-and-seek.

"We once visited them for Passover, and I remember them hiding colored eggs in the garden, and we all went out to look for them." Martin also presided at the family Seder. Emmanuel and his brother (named Martin, after his grandfather) looked forward eagerly to these trips to their grandparents:

> We liked the atmosphere, the feeling that the maids were there to wait upon you, the rich meals, the big garden, the bicycles, and also the entire area was enchanting. Even though grandmother was a tough person, we wanted to come. When we were young children, we'd get up early on Saturday and Sunday and steal into their beds. Grandfather and Grandmother liked it, but when we grew older—8 or 9 years old—we stopped doing it. When we were young, Barbara and Judith would join us in our grandparents' bed, and all of us would have a great time.

Emmanuel and his brother Martin went to Heppenheim only during school vacations. On Sundays, the whole family would go for hikes. There was a fortress above the town that they would walk to, talking along the way. There were joint meals with their parents and grandparents, Barbara and Judith and Martin and Emmanuel. Paula was a good cook, and she taught the maids to cook well. As a result, the meals were like celebrations.

A good atmosphere prevailed in the Buber household. There was tension at times, but it differed from what Emmanuel saw in other families. "I don't remember Buber raising his voice. He was always temperate. Paula could be sharp." Martin was very open. Whoever called and asked to speak to him was accepted, said Emmanuel: workers, students, intellectuals. At times, Paula would guard Martin's time and not let him sit too long with someone. Martin was not an intimate person, and he did not tell his grandchildren his own problems. But he was never against opposite views, and he never tried to impose his own views on anyone.

Paula once told Hermann Gerson that she could never leave the children in Martin's charge, and added jokingly that he would simply close them in a drawer of his desk and forget about them. Paula guarded Martin from his children and grandchildren, but in another sense, witnessed Gerson, she helped keep him from becoming a remote intellectual: "She often connected him to reality."

Another warm friendship of Buber's—one that was not so close as that with either Landauer or Rosenzweig but that lasted a great many years longer—was that with the German-Swiss poet and novelist Hermann Hesse. In 1927, Buber felt compelled to express to Hesse how very attached he was to his novel *Steppenwolf*. To Buber, it was as though the book were a through-and-through living being, a genuine person and not a "personality," and a friend—"in no way an always friendly friend, but a friend." In order to experience this, Buber added, one must have really read the book, in contrast to the critics who mention it without having opened themselves to it.

As a present to Buber in Christmas of 1927, Hesse sent him "a few poems." Buber was unable to write him his thanks for them until a few days before his fiftieth birthday because of an operation that Paula had to undergo. But he assured Hesse that his present was received from the depths of his heart. Around this same time, Buber sent Hesse a remarkable poem of his own, meditating on how the light and dark principles were born from the Zoroastrian deity Zervana, one out of knowing and word, which gave soul to heaven and earth, the other out of doubt and interruption: "Now, World, you jerk back and forth between them." In 1932, Buber wrote Hesse, thanking him for his novel *The Journey to the East,* which had been published that year in Berlin. It was, said Buber, "an astonishing and delightful book, pure and right. It does one good that such a book is still possible." Hesse replied that it made him glad to receive such an enthusiastic response to *The Journey to the East,* which was so little understood. "With the years," Hesse added, "it is as if I suffer my writings rather than create them. I cannot protect myself against what makes them understandable only with difficulty. One of them, *Steppenwolf,* has been wholly and totally misunderstood, and just because of this misunderstanding has become a popular success!"

Another close friend of Buber's, one at whose home Buber stayed and to whom Buber turned for financial advice and even for loans, was Hans Trüb, the Swiss therapist. Some months after a meeting with Buber in October 1925, Trüb wrote Buber how important it had been to him when Buber had asked, in response to an account of a case that Trüb gave him, whether his female patient was afraid of responsibility. "If one makes present to himself the whole depth of its meaning," wrote Trüb, "one comes of necessity to the question with which you ended your lectures in Holland: Are you ready, with your whole, collected person... to be responsible for your existence with nothing other than your 'I am there'?" Trüb had found himself instinctively moving in this direction for the past six years, to the place where he had himself in his practice replaced the emphasis on "analysis" with an emphasis on the event of meeting that cannot be reduced to the psychological, but lies *between* persons. This led him to share his own responses with the patient, a method that he himself called "analysis of relationship" in a lecture to the Zurich Analytical Club four years before: "The object of our consideration must not be the 'other' but the reality of our relationship." To this, Trüb was helped not just by Buber's writings but by his glance.

> I know your work as a true, honest report of what has again and again been seen by your good, true eyes, in which you have placed your trust at every moment—even the most shattering ones. Your glance is to me unforgettable. It is penetrating and yet in no way injuring; severe, unrelenting, and yet of unmistakable kindness!

Buber wrote to Trüb in 1928, strongly encouraging him to write down in a series of images his experience of the limits of psychology, to tell from within what he and his "patients" went through in common. "To such writing," Buber said, "grace will not be denied." And that is how it turned out for Trüb in the years to come. Trüb, even in his turning toward dialogical anthropology and away from analytical psychology, still remained in essential *Auseinandersetzung*—dialogue and contending—with his master and teacher Carl Jung.

One of Buber's lasting associations during his years in Germany was that with the progressive school Odenwaldschule, located in a forest not far from his home. Personally close to its leaders, Buber also came there as a visitor and, occasionally, as a speaker. "In the Odenwaldschule it was beautiful," Buber wrote his friend Franz Rosenzweig about one such visit. "One could see in the eyes of the fifteen- to eighteen-year-olds how they took in what I had to say about names and still more what I read—in a fresh way, almost as in the Lehrhaus."

Buber had an equal, though not so untroubled, impact on progressive educators. He was invited to give the keynote address at the Third International Pedagogical Conference of the International Work Circle for the Renewal of Education, which was held in Heidelberg August 2–5, 1925. The overall theme of the conference was "The Unfolding of Creative Forces in the Child," and it was in response to this theme that Buber produced his important essay on "Education," written three years before "Dialogue." Buber saw his task as in a large part a critical one—critical both in relationship to the theme of the conference and in the program—and he warned the leaders of this in advance.

Buber's stance provides us with a classic illustration of his life as an "encounter on the narrow ridge." In place of the easy opposites of conservative versus progressive, or discipline versus freedom, Buber offered a third, more concrete and realistic, alternative of education as dialogue: The teacher makes himself the living selection of the world, which comes in his person to meet, draw out, and form the pupil. In this meeting, the teacher puts aside the will to dominate and the will to enjoy the pupil that threaten "to stifle the growth of his blessings." The teacher is able to educate the pupils whom he finds before him only if he is able to build real mutuality between himself and them. This mutuality can come into existence only if the child trusts the teacher and knows that he is really there for him. "Trust, trust in the world, because *this* human being exists—that is the most inward achievement of the relation in education." But this means that the teacher must really be there facing the child, not merely there in spirit. "In order to be and to remain truly present to the child, he must have gathered the child's presence into his own existence as one of the bearers of his communion with the world, one of the focuses of his responsibilities for the world." This "inclusiveness" is of the essence of the dialogical relation, for the teacher sees the position of the other in that person's concrete actuality yet does not lose sight of his or her own. Unlike friendship, however, this inclusion must be largely one-sided: The pupil cannot be expected to be concerned about the teacher's becoming educated through their interchange without the teaching relationship being destroyed thereby. Inclusion must return again and again in the teaching situation. Through discovering the "otherness" of the pupil, the teacher discovers his or her own real limits; through this discovery, the teacher also recognizes the forces of the world that the child needs to grow and he draws those forces into himself. Thus, through his concern with the child, the teacher educates himself. The old educators picture education as the passive reception of tradition poured in from above—in Buber's image, "the funnel"; the new educators picture education as drawing forth the powers of the self that are already present—in Buber's image, "the pump." In education as dialogue, the pupil grows through his or her encounter with the person of the teacher and the Thou of the writer, composer, or artist. No real learning takes place unless the student participates, but it also means that the student must encounter something really "other" before he or she can learn.

It is not freedom and the release of instinct that are decisive for education, Buber declared, in direct opposition to the trend of "progressive education" shared by most of those participating in the Heidelberg Conference, but the educative forces that meet the released instinct. Proponents of the old, authoritarian theory of education do not understand the need for freedom and spontaneity. But proponents of the new, freedom-centered educational theory misunderstand the meaning of freedom, which is indispensable but not in itself sufficient for true education. The opposite of compulsion is not freedom but communion, Buber asserted, and this communion comes about through the child's first being free to venture on his own and then encountering the real values of the teacher. The teacher presents these values in the form of a lifted finger or subtle hint rather than as an imposition of what is "right," and the pupil learns from this encounter because he or she has first experimented.

We can detect an unmistakable autobiographical note in Buber's statement about freedom, growing out of his profound personal identification with Gustav Landauer during the Munich revolution *and* his simultaneous feeling that Landauer's entering the government of the first Räterepublik was a serious error on his part: "Freedom—I love its flashing face:... I give my left hand to the rebel and my right to the heretic: forward! But I do not trust them." We can also sense, in the paragraph that follows, Buber's contrast between those, like Landauer, who really involved and sacrificed themselves and those who use "freedom" and "rebellion" as political slogans and catchwords:

> ...To become free of a bond is destiny; one carries that like a cross, not like a cockade. Let us realize the true meaning of being free of a bond: it means that a quite personal responsibility takes

the place of one shared with many generations. Life lived in freedom is personal responsibility or it is pathetic farce.

When in his Heidelberg lecture Buber gave as his first illustration of inclusion a man who kicks another and then unexpectedly feels his kicks from the other side, he may also have been thinking of that week in 1919 when he had imaginatively to experience in his own body the blows with which Landauer was brutally kicked to death:

> A man belabours another, who remains quite still. Then let us assume that the striker suddenly receives in his soul the blow which he strikes: the same blow; that he receives it as the other who remains still. For the space of a moment he experiences the situation from the other side. Reality imposes itself on him. What will he do? Either he will overwhelm the voice of the soul, or his impulse will be reversed.

Another concrete example of inclusion that Buber gave is even more certainly autobiographical, for no one who has not had the experience that he describes could possibly have imagined it.

> A man caresses a woman, who lets herself be caressed. Then let us assume that he feels the contact from two sides—with the palm of his hand still, and also with the woman's skin. The two-fold nature of the gesture, as one that takes place between two persons, thrills through the depth of enjoyment in his heart and stirs it. If he does not deafen his heart he will have—not to renounce the enjoyment but—to love.
>
> I do not in the least mean that the man who has had such an experience would from then on have this two-sided sensation in every such meeting—that would perhaps destroy his instinct. But the one extreme experience makes the other person present to him for all time. A transfusion has taken place after which a mere elaboration of subjectivity is never again possible or tolerable to him.

Buber's address "Education" aroused a storm of controversy among the assembled educators and involved him in constant exchanges both in the plenary session and in the smaller workshops that made up the two-week international conference. Elisabeth Rotten, in reporting on the conference, described it as passionate wrestling and contending. What was most important to Buber, however, was that his speech brought the battle into the open, in the true space of decisions, thus foreshadowing a future dispute within the camps of the educators themselves.

Meanwhile, Buber was also continuing his work on specifically Jewish education, particularly the adult education at Rosenzweig's Frankfurt Lehraus. In 1922–1923, Buber gave a series of lectures entitled "Original Forms of

Religious Life" (Magic, Sacrifice, Mystery, Prayer), and gave a seminar in which he analyzed ancient Near Eastern, Greek, Jewish, and Christian writings. The lecture series included the material that Buber intended to publish as the second of his five projected volumes, under the title "The Basic Forms of Religious Life." His second lecture course that year was on "Prayer", with a seminar in the interpretation of Psalms.

On July 17, 1923, Rosenzweig wrote a joint letter to Eduard Strauss, Buber, Richard Koch, and Ernst Simon, asking them whether they could take over the leadership of the Lehrhaus without him. Simon responded in the negative, as a result of which the leadership from then on was shared among Rosenzweig, Buber, Strauss, and Koch. Buber at that time took Simon severely to task for his unwillingness to help out in this situation. "Your answer to Rosenzweig's letter has affected me painfully," Buber charged. "It is entirely lacking in human response. Have you then, you fine and proud young people with your preoccupation with literature and history, with directions and institutions so lost the natural human glance of love that you can no longer recognize the gestures of your brother who is in pain?"

Three months later, Simon wrote a long and impassioned letter to Buber, protesting against his way of conducting his seminar on Hasidism and, by implication, explaining his decision not to cooperate in the leadership of the Lehrhaus. "You have demanded of the people assembled there that they really 'express' themselves," Simon wrote, with the result that there developed

> an at times hysterical, at times shameless, kind of questioning, typically carried out almost exclusively by women, which deeply repelled not only myself but also a great number of the younger and older people and hurt them at the very core of their beings. Although you stood your ground heroically and said a great many things worth hearing, you did not take my hand which offered to rescue you from the assault of the hysterical and the less than honest.

After long pondering on why Buber himself seemed to be unaware of this situation, Simon came to the conclusion that it was connected with Buber's lack of any sense of his public and the spurious use that it made of his truth. This, moreover, Simon saw as closely connected with Buber's metaphysical position, which was expressed in *I and Thou* and which Simon protested against, namely, the lack of any sense of the *tragic*. "Our human existence is *constituted* by the fact that we have eaten of the tree of knowledge of good and evil.... We know shame and with it the tragedy of *sex*." To know men, we must see them neither as animals nor angels, but as creatures expelled from paradise and condemned to the tragedy of *work*, beings who represent a mixture of the dust of the earth and the divine soul and who, if they wish to bind themselves to God, must take on themselves the *tragedy of the law*.

Buber's error of paying too little attention to the "law" carried with it, Simon declared, the corresponding error of paying too much attention to the relationship to his fellow men. In contrast to Hermann Cohen, who was an Idealist, Buber would not be one at any price. Yet he fell into it ever again when he took "standing before the Face" for the *only* side of "reality" and acted accordingly. "The reality of our human life has a tragic double face.... You believed yourself to be standing 'naked before God' and, in fact, stood naked before Fraulein H.—a fearful sight! Everyone who loves you must inwardly grieve at this, and you do not notice it." This does not apply to you alone, Simon added. In shameless questions and still more shameful answers lie the central danger of the Lehrhaus, "the reason why I cannot take part in its direction."

Buber wrote Rosenzweig, commenting, "He is right, but only on the far side of love." Rosenzweig replied that Simon had shown this letter to him in advance and added,

> Naturally he is "right." As right as one can be who does not believe that a minyan can turn a group of tradesman into praying men. The translation of sensationalism into genuine need is not, of course, demonstrable. Yet one must believe in it, and even E. Simon will one day believe in it... when he comprehends the healing forces of freedom, which now he can only hold to be a poison flower (which it certainly *also* is).

This letter of Simon's stands in striking contrast to his letter to Buber of two months earlier, when, in connection with his editorship of *Der Jude,* he informed Buber that he considered it a great fortune to have experienced Buber's real faithfulness to the smallest detail, his responsibility to the word: "I have learned a great deal for myself from this." Grete Schaeder feels that Buber replied to Simon a half year later in his speech "Education," in which he made it clear that the relationship between teacher and student cannot be a fully mutual one, and she implies that this speech may reveal the impact of Simon's letter. Buber's greatness showed itself not only in his intellectual reply to Simon's criticism, Schaeder adds, but also in his human greatheartedness: He simply accepted the "disciple" Simon as a friend. In August 1923, Buber had written Simon that he was heartily sorry that their work together was of such short duration and thanked him from his heart for the lessening of his work load during a critical period of his life. A few days later, he added that, despite all the little issues that had arisen, his relationship to Simon had in no way changed and that he wished from his heart that their mutual relationship might endure uninjured.

The course in Hasidic teachings that Buber gave at the Frankfurt Lehrhaus he later published under the title *Das Verborgne Licht* (The Hidden Light)—the identical title that he was later to give to his new and enlarged collection of Hasidic tales in the Hebrew edition (*Or Hagganuz*). When he had read the booklet of Hasidic sources that, at Scholem's urging, Buber published along with his preceding Hasidic book, *Der Grosse Maggid,* Rosenzweig wrote Buber in 1923: "Should there not also be historical books?" This question, which was to be hurled at Buber many years later by Gershom Scholem as an accusation of "unscientific" interpretation, was answered by Buber in the following year through the plan of a many-volume complete edition of Hasidic sources, *including the formal books of Hasidic teachings,* that he and Agnon were undertaking together. (Nahum Glatzer testified that the *Corpus Hasidicum* was to include the formal teachings of the Hasidic *rebbes.* "I did the legwork for them," Glatzer said to me.) A fire in Agnon's house destroyed four thousand books, all his possessions, and a great deal of his unpublished writing, including a half-completed novel, many parts of which he had read to Buber. Among the other manuscripts, the almost completed volume of the *Corpus Hasidicum* was destroyed, which led Agnon to give up the plan "for years." Buber knew that probably meant forever. In any event, the possibility of close cooperation was removed by Agnon's emigrating to Palestine in the fall of 1924. When Buber came to Palestine many years later and proposed to Agnon a similar cooperation, Agnon declined.

In 1928, when Buber was fifty, he heard of a lecture by Edmund Husserl, the German philosopher who founded the school of phenomenology that influenced thinkers such as Maurice Merleau-Ponty, Martin Heidegger, and Jean-Paul Sartre. Anxious to hear Husserl, Buber went to the lecture hall, where someone from the Philosophical Society recognized him and asked him to sit at the head table. When Husserl appeared, he gave those at the head table a quick greeting before stepping up to the lectern. "My name is Buber," Buber said. Husserl was taken aback for a moment and asked, "The real Buber?" Buber hesitated to give any further explanation, whereupon Husserl exclaimed, "But there is no such person! Buber—why he's a legend!"

The first book on Buber was published two years before his fiftieth birthday by the German Protestant Wilhelm Michel: the slender, beautifully written *Martin Buber's Path into Reality.* Michel saw Buber as paradigmatic of the time because Buber had taken the scattered fragments into himself and made them whole, confronting the illusions of the age with an image of reality. Michel ranked Buber among the influential German speakers of his time, someone whose words led to decision and reality. With what in retrospect seems tragic irony, Michel asserted that Buber "belongs to us": "There lives in him the *German* world-hour, no matter how exclusively he may seem to concern himself with the particular question of Judaism.... One does not speak the German language as he does without deeply and seriously entering into the destiny of the people from whom this language stems." Commenting on this statement, Ernst Simon wrote, "No German intellectual had ever before expressed such recognition of a representative of Judaism," and added that Buber "is the first Jewish author to enter German cultural history on an absolutely equal footing of give and take both with regard to his general as well as his specifically Jewish contribution."

By 1922, two years before it ceased publication, Buber had already turned over the actual editorship of *Der Jude* to Ernst Simon. He felt the need of getting on with his own work, such as *I and Thou*, but he also felt the intra-Jewish dialogue too confining for the needs of the time. As a result, from 1922 to 1932, Buber gave ever more time and energy, both in speaking and writing, to Jewish-Christian dialogue, particularly within the post–World War I movement of religious socialism and, from 1926 to 1930, in coediting the journal *Die Kreatur.*

Buber found common cause with Christian socialism and religious socialism in general in the years of the Weimar Republic. Education of the people, politics out of faith, socialism derived from the Gospels or from the prophets, formed for Buber and his circle a social concern that stayed clear of the state and of party politics. Although Buber's major sympathies lay with Leonhard Ragaz's religious socialism, he also met with religious socialists of all types during the 1920s, including a conference held at his home village of Heppenheim in 1928 in which he was a central figure.

At one such meeting, Buber first met Paul Tillich, a younger man than Buber, well known in certain circles but not yet the world-famous Protestant theologian he later became. As a member of a committee of socialists, some religious and some not, Tillich reported to the larger conference the conclusion that a word should be found to replace "God" in order to unite in the common cause of socialism those who could use this name and those who could not. After he had given this report, Tillich himself has recounted, a short man with a black beard and fiery black eyes stood up in the back and said "Aber Gott ist ein Urwort!" You cannot do away with a primordial word like God, said Buber, even for the sake of attaining unity. "And he was right!" Tillich exclaimed.

"Being open to the world and withstanding concrete reality were always a measure," writes Schaeder, "of whether a Christian thinker could come close to Buber." Among these thinkers were such neo-Orthodox, or dialectical, theologians as Karl Barth, Emil Brunner, Eduard Thurneysen, and Friedrich Gogarten. Their conversion into Christology of Buber's I-Thou relationship between God and man, Buber could not, of course, follow (as is, demonstrated at length in the chapter entitled "Christianity" in my book *Martin Buber: The Life of Dialogue*). Unlike his friend Rosenzweig, Buber could not acknowledge the equal validity of Judaism and Christianity, one as being already in the eternity of God, the other as being the historical way to God. "We cannot simultaneously stand within and look with the objective eye that gives equal validity to two opposing *claims*. We know the Christian claim only from the outside and we cannot accept it." If each fights for the sake of heaven, that does not mean that either side possesses some Hegelian overview of the progress of spirit in history toward a perfection in which all differences will be abolished or suspended.

From July 20 to July 25, 1925, Buber gave a series of lectures entitled "The Belief in Rebirth" at an academy at Amersfoort, Holland. The response of the Jungian psychiatrist Hans Trüb to this event is a far better example than any public debate could be of genuine Jewish-Christian dialogue. "My thoughts return to Amersfoort day after day," Trüb wrote Buber in August. "This one short week illuminated our whole past and future lives," he added.

> We all seek for the same One that you revealed to us through your heartfelt speech. It *could* not be misunderstood. The absolute integrity with which you shared with us *what your eyes see* [italics added] is a present which we can only accept with the deepest gratitude. I know indeed that ever again in the present the "great" happens, that there where persons really meet the infinity of creation reveals itself to us. But that a man without holding back takes it upon himself to live this faith makes me happy.

To this Buber responded: "Your words have gladdened my heart. I too think warmly about Amersfoort, as about a young tree that one may trust."

In what Trüb wrote about Amersfoort, he best expressed the aspect of Buber's personality that I myself found central in my personal encounters with Buber more than a quarter of a century later. Although the great emphasis of Buber's philosophy, as of his interpretation of biblical and Hasidic Judaism, is on the word—hearing and responding—first of all Buber was a person who *beheld*—not with the analytical eye of the thinker or the aesthetic eye of the artist or the subjective eye of a person trying to select from his encounters with the world what would confirm the opinions and mind-sets he already had, but with the calm, open, genuinely interested but not personally biased eye of one who chooses reality just because it *is* reality. Only then did the next two stages that Trüb spoke about come into play—living without reservation what he knew and speaking about it to others from the heart.

In 1924, Buber allowed *Der Jude* to cease publication, except for occasional special issues, because he was moving in the direction of Jewish-Christian dialogues. This direction took on its fullest concrete and symbolic expression in his founding the first high-level periodical coedited by a Protestant, a Catholic, and a Jew. This journal, *Die Kreatur* (The Creature), was also highly successful and prestigious, and, during the four years that it lasted (1926—1929), Buber gave to it almost as great devotion as to *Der Jude*. Rang had suggested calling the journal *Greetings out of the Exiles,* but Buber preferred the more positive title *The Creature,* indicating the basis on which the three different religions could come into fruitful dialogue.

The impetus to found *Die Kreatur* (The Creature) had come to Buber through his close friendship with Florens Christian Rang, the former pastor turned lawyer with whom he had had the argument about Jewish representatives in Easter of 1914, at the first and only meeting of the Forte Kreis. The kiss of peace that the two men exchanged at the time proved to be more enduring than the superpatriotic and nationalist stance that Rang adopted during the war, which he himself deeply regretted and sought to atone for after the war. Buber opened *Die Kreatur* with an editorial acknowledging and adopting Rang's belief that every religion is an exile that only God can liberate, but that there is need for genuine dialogue between each of these houses of exile without presuming to abolish the separateness of the religions in favor of any universal "essence" of religion. In 1932, Buber dedicated *The Kingship of God,* his first scholarly work on the origin of messianism in the Bible, to his Jewish friend Rosenzweig and his Christian friend Rang. In the first issue of *Die Kreatur,* in the spring of 1926, Buber dedicated the journal to Rang: jurist, philosopher, and theologian — all in one.

In 1925, Buber wrote to Hans Trüb that *Die Kreatur* would be dedicated to a philosophical anthropology that had as its concern the wholeness of the human in its connection with the wholeness of being. "In this the crisis of psychologism and the necessity for a recognition of the boundaries of psychological observation that grows out of it shall have a special place."

The three editors of *Die Kreatur* belonged to no common circle. Rather, Buber with great care and thought chose a Protestant and a Catholic thinker, each of whom made "meeting" real in his own sphere. As strange as Buber's choice of the psychiatrist Viktor von Weizsäcker as the Protestant editor of *Die Kreatur* might seem, the choice of Joseph Wittig as the Catholic editor seemed even stranger. At first glance, Wittig would seem, of the three of them, the most representative of his religion, being both a priest and a professor of Catholic theology. But von Weizsäcker's later observation that "[t]he Catholic was no proper Catholic, the Protestant no proper Protestant, and the Jew no proper Jew" was true for Wittig to an even more startling degree than it was of his two coeditors. It was in the midst of a feud between Cardinal Bertram and Father Wittig that Buber invited Wittig to be the Catholic editor of *Die Kreatur.* "Cut off from the Church, I think I would be of no use to you," Wittig said to Buber.

Buber's reply to Wittig made it quite clear that Wittig represented Catholicism by what he was and did, what he wrote and said, and as a person, and not by his official position in the church. To Wittig's first question as to whether Buber would agree to his complying with the canonic law, Buber asserted categorically, "I have turned to you in truth as the unique person that you are. That means that I had lived through in my consciousness, as much as I was able to, your personal situation including, naturally, your office and your order and have accepted it insofar as I can from the standpoint of my task." This statement in turn touched on the second question of whether, cut loose from the church, Wittig would be of no value to

Buber. To this, Buber's response was equally categorical: "Because I have turned to you in truth as the person that you are, therefore—may I be allowed to say this in all respect and humility as one praying man to another—nothing on this earth could ever take away from you your representative character as a Catholic in my eyes." Even if it were a major excommunication from the community of the church and not just from its sacraments and offices, Wittig could never cease to be a Catholic.

Die Kreatur became a center for a group of kindred spirits concerned with education, psychotherapy, religious socialism, international understanding, religion, and poetry. Buber himself first published in it such important writings as "Education," "Dialogue," and "Gandhi, Politics, and Us." Rosenstock-Huessy wrote Buber that the third issue of *Die Kreatur* possessed an "unheard-of-beauty"—an "awesome symphony" that answered his own earlier criticism of a lack of specific direction.

The one thing that troubled von Weizsäcker was Buber's silence as editor. In contrast to his work for *Der Jude,* Buber never wrote any editorials for *Die Kreatur.* This was a deliberate, self-imposed limitation to avoid his possibly dominating this exchange of free and profound spirits. While honoring this silence, von Weizsäcker asked Buber whether it was not up to him, the most summoned man of the hour, to set a tone that would guide others in contributing to *Die Kreatur.* According to von Weizsäcker's own later testimony, however, *Die Kreatur* did not end because of any decline of quality, but simply went out of existence when it had served its function as a forum for the chorus of rich and creative voices that it had brought into polyphonic, and often antiphonal, harmony.

What Wittig's association with Buber meant to him is expressed in a touching letter that he wrote Buber after the appearance of the last issue. "I know that there will be a life for us after the completion of *Die Kreatur.* But it will always be for me an Easter day whenever we meet each other again, whether in work, a letter, or a visit." One such "Easter day" for Wittig came in 1932, when he received Buber's gem *Zwiesprache* (Dialogue), now published separately as a book. In a letter to Ernst Simon, Buber spoke of *Dialogue* as "the little book of my heart," and it is indeed a book that emerges from the heart, uttering words that with their simplicity and power have gradually found their way into the minds and hearts of countless people the world over. "I believe in general that I have given no 'answer,'" Buber wrote, "not merely no total answer, but also no piece of one, rather a pointing in the literal sense."

The essence of genuine dialogue lies in the fact that "each of the participants really has in mind the other or others in their present and particular being and turns to them with the intention of establishing a living mutual relation between himself and them." The basic movement of the life of "monologue," in contrast, is not turning away from the other but "reflexion" (*Rückbiegung*) in the physiological origin of the term—bending back on oneself. "Reflexion" is not egotism but the withdrawal from accepting the other person in his particularity in favor of letting him exist *only as one's own experience,* only as a part of oneself. Through this withdrawal, "the essence of all reality begins to disintegrate."

In *Dialogue,* Buber wrote:

> A time of genuine religious conversations is beginning—not those so-called but fictitious conversations where none regarded and addressed his partner in reality, but genuine dialogues, speech from certainty to certainty, but also from one open-hearted person to another open-hearted person. Only then will genuine common life appear, not that of an identical content of faith which is alleged to be found in all religions, but that of the situation, of anguish and of expectation.

These dialogues of open-hearted persons meant responsibility in the face of the "claim" of reality, answering a real address unmediated by any conceptual worldview. "The first person whom I thought of in this connection was you," Buber wrote Albert Schweitzer when he invited Schweitzer to a conference in Karlsruhe. "You have for a long time been exemplary for me of the direction that I mean."

Although Buber was widely accepted by the Christian world as apostle and spokesman for Judaism, he made no claim to be representative either of rabbinical Judaism or of any synagogue or official group. Similarly, he was not himself interested in dialogues with official Christians but with committed persons. Often the two were at variance.

There is a significant parallel between the correspondence of Buber with the young theologian and Semiticist Hans Kosmala, who wrote Buber in 1932 in deep distress over the invitation of the distinguished Bible scholar Alfred Jeremias to be the director of a mission to the Jews, and "Two Foci of the Jewish Soul"—the speech that Buber gave in 1930 to one of the four German-Christian missions to the Jews. To Kosmala, who confessed himself at home in Buber's sphere of thought, Buber wrote that it depended upon his own inner strength and the conditions that he set whether he could take on a missionary position such as this and remain spiritually alive. To the German mission, Buber declared that he was opposed to their cause as a Jew who waits for the kingdom of God and regards missions such as theirs as springing from a misunderstanding that hinders the coming of the kingdom. Buber saw the first focus of the Jewish soul as faith—not in the sense of the belief that God exists but in the sense of *emunah,* the trust that though God is wholly raised above man and beyond his grasp he is present in immediate relationship with human beings and faces them. The biblical "fear of God" is the creaturely awareness of the darkness out of which God reveals himself, the dark gate through which man must pass if he is to enter into the love of God. If one tries instead to construct a theological image of God as simply love, one runs the risk of having to despair of God in view of the actualities of history and life, or of falling into self-deception and hypocrisy. The fear of God is merely a gate, however, not a dwelling in which one settles down, as some of the Barthian and neo-Orthodox theologians who emphasized the "wholly otherness" of God seemed to feel. This also means that no primordial "Fall," or original sin, can abridge man's power to turn to God and imitate him. Because this is so, we cannot do God's will by beginning with grace but by beginning with ourselves—with our will, which, poor as it is, leads us to grace.

The second focus of the Jewish soul is the corollary of the first: the recognition "that God's redeeming power is at work everywhere and at all times, but that a state of redemption exists nowhere and never." While the Jew experiences the touch of God's nearness that comes to him from above, he also experiences, more intensely than any other, the world's lack of redemption and feels the burden of the unredeemed world on him. Redemption means to the Jew not the individual soul but the soul and the world inseparably bound together. As a corollary to this attitude toward redemption, Buber articulated here for the first time the distinction between the "prophetic" and the "apocalyptic" that became the cornerstone for all his later understanding both of biblical Judaism and of early Christianity. Prophetic faith preserves the oneness of God and the world, whereas the apocalyptic belief falls into an essentially Manichean dualism:

> The prophetic promises a consummation of creation, the apocalyptic its abrogation and supersession by another world, completely different in nature: the prophetic allows "the evil" to find the direction that leads toward God, and to enter into the good; the apocalyptic sees good and evil severed forever at the end of days, the good redeemed, the evil unredeemable for all eternity.

The prophetic is the call to man to turn back to God in the present, for "those who turn cooperate in the redemption of the world." "Man cannot bring down grace by magic or any definite act; yet grace answers deed in unpredictable ways."

The Jewish belief in the *non*incarnation of God and the unbroken continuity of human history means that premessianically the destinies of Judaism and Christianity are divided. "To the Christian the Jew is the incomprehensibly obdurate man, who declines to see what has happened; and to the Jew the Christian is the incomprehensibly daring man, who affirms in an unredeemed world that its redemption has been accomplished." But when both Christian and Jew care more for God than for our images of God, "there are moments when we may prepare the way together."

In 1926, Martin left it to Paula, who was with their daughter in Düsseldorf, to communicate to their son-in-law Ludwig Strauss how he felt about the question of the circumcision of Ludwig's and Eva's first child,

Martin Emmanuel. "I have learned in the course of my life," Martin wrote Paula, "that we in exile may not forgo the original authentication of our belonging, no matter how we may feel personally. It is the only one given to us. Through it we personally carry forward the 'covenant,' which in exile does not have the community as its bearer." In 1961, Buber said to Hugo Bergmann almost the identical thing concerning the Jew living in the Jewish community in Israel. Inconsistent as this might seem with Buber's position toward the Jewish law, this attitude should dispel the common notion that Buber was simply an *"apikoros,"* as Rosenzweig jokingly called him, who was as a matter of principle and practice totally nonobservant. The biblical covenant between God and Israel became more and more the center of Buber's understanding of Judaism.

The Kingship of God, a book that had gestated for many years in Buber's mind, was particularly significant because it was the first completely scholarly interpretation of the Bible that Buber had written and as such was the foundation for all the later scholarly interpretations that followed, such as *Moses, Prophetic Faith,* and *Two Types of Faith.* More specifically, it was published as the first of three volumes on the origin of the concept of messianism in the Hebrew Bible, even though the later volumes were never published as such but only in a fragment on the anointing of Saul by the prophet Samuel.

Buber believed that this book would establish him in the scholarly world in a way that none of his other books had. The heart of *The Kingship of God* lies in its repeated theme that the human being must enter into the dialogue with God with his whole being: It must be "an exclusive relationship which shapes all other relations and therefore the whole order of life." The failure of the kings in the dialogue with YHVH resulted in the mission of the prophets. The "theopolitical" realism of the prophets led them to reject any merely symbolic fulfillment of the divine commission, to fight the division of community life into a "religious" realm of myth and cult and a "political" realm of civic and economic laws.

Buber's approach to the kingship of God as a direct theocracy, or a "theopolitical state," is itself a striking example of walking the narrow ridge. The highest binding, which by its very nature knows no compulsion, is not, of course, realized in any actual state, since every state rests, more or less, upon compulsion. Therefore, every fight for the realization of the rule of God in political life contains the lasting danger of erring on the side of compulsion or of freedom. The narrow ridge between these two abysses is the drawing of the demarcation line in each hour in such a way as to approach as nearly as possible to making real the kingship of God in the human community.

The Swiss theologian Emil Brunner wrote Buber in June 1932: "Your book seems to me to be the first to have really broken through the comfortless schematism of objectivizing history with its evolutionary waltz which flattens everything to the same level." Years later, in his book *Man in Revolt,* he wrote that Buber's *Kingship of God* contained more real philosophy of history than any book on the philosophy of history. Gershom Scholem, in the course of a long letter with penetrating critical questions, said that the principles to which Buber had given a concrete application in *The Kingship of God* opened up a wholly new line of Bible scholarship, the significance of which for every level of Jewish reality was incalculable. The fact that Gershom Scholem had moved to Palestine and was doing active research on Hasidic materials there, to which Buber did not have access, occasioned a good deal of correspondence between them.

For Buber, even more than for most authors, events in a distant past germinated in his mind, took on tentative form and shape, were tested, thought through, and postponed for a time when he could sufficiently free himself from other commitments to give them the concentration they deserved. This is certainly true of *The Kingship of God,* but it is also true of many other of his lifelong concerns, such as Judaism, Hasidism, socialism, education, art, and the theater. What is more, what appears to be a simple continuity of interest, as with the Bible and Hasidism, was for Buber, again and again, a rediscovery and fresh beginning in response to the events of that particular period of his life.

An important concern for Buber during the years of the Weimar Republic was the shape that the Hebrew University, now at last becoming a reality, should take when it was founded in Jerusalem. To Buber, the choice was essentially between the traditional European university and a *Volkshochschule,* a folk school after the model of Grundtvig in nineteenth-century Denmark. One part of the problem was how to combine knowledge of the latest scientific methods with a grounding in Jewish knowledge and Jewish cultural life, undisturbed by alien methods and disciplines. Another was how to provide the satisfaction of the deep spiritual and intellectual needs of the new pioneer workers in the Jewish settlement (Yishuv). At the invitation of the Executive Committee in London, Buber declared himself ready to draw up a public presentation of the folk-school plan, for which purpose he would make a study of Palestine during the coming year. Buber wrote Rosenzweig about the Zionist Executive Committee's action on the issue of the folk school versus the university: "My youthful years return again with force, if without song." Yet his dream did not approach fulfillment until Buber himself established schools for the teachers of the new immigrants in 1949 and educational work rose among the kibbutzim themselves during the last decades of his life.

A paradigm of the educator of character whom Buber had in mind was Siegfried Lehmann, who directed the Volksheim for Eastern European Jews in Berlin during the First World War and who founded the Jewish Youth Village Ben Shemen near Lydda in Palestine in 1927. Lehmann's conception of education of the youth in the Land of Israel envisaged their preparation for rural life in a village. To achieve this, a children's village and a farm school were set up, followed by an open-air theater, children's homes, and a library. Coeducation of boys and girls of all ages in the village, and the combination of academic lessons in the primary and secondary schools with manual work in the field and workshop, facilitated the achievement of these goals. From the beginning Lehmann placed particular emphasis on understanding the Arab world—its history, religious tradition, language, and art—and on meetings of the community with neighboring Arab villages. During the years of Arab revolt against the British administration (1936–1939), Jewish settlements were constantly subject to attack. Yet no attack was ever made on Ben Shemen, owing to the friendship that Siegfried Lehmann had established with surrounding Arab villages.

Buber also maintained an active interest in the political life of Palestine during this period. During the First World War, the British openly proclaimed the Balfour Doctrine, which promised the Jews a homeland in Palestine but secretly wooed the Arabs in and outside of Palestine. When the Arab masses were incited to riot during the Jewish Passover in 1920, the Russian-born Zionist writer and leader Vladimir Jabotinsky (1880–1940) organized the Haganah (a Jewish defense army) and led them to confront the rioting Arabs. During the 1920s and 1930s Buber and his circle fought a behind-the-scenes battle against Jabotinsky's revisionists and their demand for a Jewish Legion, but it was a battle that was not often successful.

Buber himself no longer looked to Zionist majority politics to further his goals but instead joined forces with Brit Shalom, or Covenant of Peace, a group characterized by its concern for Jewish-Arab understanding in Palestine and by its advocacy of a binational state with population parity. The persons who were predominant in Brit Shalom until the 1929 disturbances were men who had immigrated into Palestine before the First World War, and two of these remained central in the years to come—the agronomist Chaim Kalvarisky (1868–1947) and the religious socialist Zionist Rabbi Binyamin (the pen name of Yehoshua Radler-Feldman [1880–1957]). The second group, which became predominant after 1929, were intellectuals of a central European liberal background, three of whom in particular, Hugo Bergmann, Hans Kohn, and Robert Weltsch, had all been Bar Kochbans in Prague and were all disciples of Martin Buber. There were also Ernst Simon and Gershom Scholem and a group of pacifists, such as Nathan Hofshi, the non-Zionist Werner Senator, and Orientalists. Lord Edwin Samuel, son of the first high commissioner to Palestine, and Norman Bentwich, attorney general during this period, were both sympathetic to Brit Shalom, as was Judah Magnes, who did not belong to it because of his position as chancellor of Hebrew University but who was in many ways a leading spirit of the group, as of later groups of a similar nature. "*Brit Shalom* had no ideology," writes Susan Hattis, in her perceptive study of the binational idea in Palestine.

They simply realized that the Arabs were justified in fearing a

Zionism which spoke in terms of a Jewish majority and a Jewish state. Their belief was that one need not be a maximalist, i.e., demand mass immigration and a state, to be a faithful Zionist.... What was vital was a recognition that both nations were in Palestine as of right.

What is not recognized today, even by most people in Israel, is how widespread the idea of binationalism was at that time. Hapoel Hatzair, the left-wing Zionist group that joined with Achdut Haavoda (United Workers) in 1930 to become the dominant Mapai party, counted quite a number of Brit Shalom members and supporters in its ranks, including Buber, Kohn, Weltsch, Bergmann, Hofshi—and even many of its other members were not opposed to the binationalist principle, such as Joseph Sprinzak, one of the leaders of the party. Chaim Weizmann, president of the Zionist Organization and first president of the State of Israel, was a staunch and unswerving supporter of binationalism, or "parity," as he preferred calling it, even when this position made him most unpopular and led to his resignation from the presidency of the Zionist Organization.

When Brit Shalom was founded, Buber identified himself with its principles, for they were identical with the ones that he had himself espoused for many years. The third part of Buber's book *Kampf um Israel* (Fight for Israel, 1932) was devoted to Arab-Jewish problems in Palestine and was dedicated to the "friends from Brit Shalom." The Jews are not merely stateless, Buber declared in 1926, but also unprotected by the states in which they live (a fact that most of us have long denied knowing). But this protection cannot come about through turning the tables and becoming the majority in Palestine, who might then treat the Arab minority as they had been treated (even if more humanely). Buber feared that "Zion" might turn out to be "the great Galut-Hotel," the comfortably fixed-up replication of the exile: "It belongs to the signature of our splendid and humane age that the dreams of mankind are fulfilled in it—in caricature."

In 1927, Buber met and came into close contact with the great fighter for Zion and for peace Judah Leib Magnes, a rabbi and conscientious objector in America during the First World War, the founder of the Jewish National Fund, the founder of Hebrew University when it opened in Jerusalem in 1925 and its first president, and, for the rest of his life, its chancellor. Magnes has been described as an "incorrigible idealist." Buber was a realistic meliorist, whose teaching of the "demarcation line" marked out the narrow ridge between a relativism that simply conforms to the situation and an absolute idealism that remains irrelevant to it. The difference between the two men is shown by Buber's response to the language used in a proposal to found a religious association that would confront the interlocking social-political and religious problems facing the Jewish people in Zion, most particularly Arab-Jewish relations. After an enthusiastic response by Hugo Bergmann and Hans Kohn, Magnes had them send his five-page program to Buber. Buber approved of Magnes's description of the proposed members of the association as social radicals who wanted to follow the justice and righteousness of the Hebrew prophets, but he took exception to Magnes's speaking of "the mandate of the 'God within' each" and of "absolute ethical or metaphysical values." In its place, Buber offered a formulation that spoke of a believing attitude that is the genuine ground of human life, one which obtains a relation to the truth of existence through one's entire being. "Such a sensibility can not only be constituted by the inwardness of one's soul: it must manifest itself in the entire fullness of personal and communal life, in which the individual participates."

In 1929, two leading German Zionists, Georg Landauer and Gershom Chanoch, informed Buber that he had been chosen by the Hitachduth, the Labor Zionists in America, and by the German Labor Zionists, as their representative to the Sixteenth Zionist Congress to be held in August in Basel, Switzerland. The Zionist leader Joseph Sprinzak held Buber's appearance at the congress to be absolutely imperative for the floor debate, where Buber's words and presence would in themselves constitute a fight against Jabotinsky's Revisionists. Buber yielded to these urgent pleas and went to Basel for the last Zionist congress in which he actively took part.

In his speech to the Sixteenth Congress, Buber rejected the ordinary contrast between the anti-Zionist who sees Israel as less than a nation and the Zionist who sees Israel as a nation. He favored a third category: those who see Israel as more than a nation—meaning everything by which a nation is defined but rejecting the "sacred egoism" that makes the nation an end in itself. Nor can the goal of Zion—the beginning of the kingship of God for all human people—be postponed until the life of the nation is secure: "If we do not will more than life, we shall also not win life." Speaking in Berlin in October 1929, Buber emphasized again the inseparability of land, people, and task and pointed to the small experiment of the kibbutz as more important than the enormous Russian state centralism: Only in the kibbutz was there really *topos*, place—concreteness of a social transformation not in institutions and organizations but in the interhuman immediacy itself.

"To those who say one must do wrong to live as a people," Buber replied, "yes, as long as one does only so much in every hour that one may be truly responsible for it." He defined true responsibility as that genuine actual imagining, or inclusion, that would enable the Jews in Palestine to imagine what it would be like if *they* were the people already living in Palestine and the Arabs were the newcomers who came there to colonize it. "Only when we know how we would react to that can we learn to do no more injustice than we must in order to live. We have not lived *with* the Arabs in Palestine but *next* to them," Buber said, and added that if this continued to be the case, the situation in Palestine would inevitably deteriorate to the place where the Jews would find themselves living *against* the Arabs. It is characteristic of Zion that it *cannot* be built with every possible means but only *bemisphat* (Isaiah 1:27), only "with justice," Buber said in Antwerp in 1932. If the goal is to be reached, the way must be as just as the goal.

From 1927 on, there were continual correspondence and efforts on the part of Magnes, Gershom Scholem, and many others to bring Buber to Hebrew University, if a position could be found for him which would be approved by the faculty and board of governors. The first attempt was a plan for an Institute of the History of Religions, which Buber would direct. Buber himself was amenable to this. However, in 1929 Buber's chair for the study of religion fell through, partly because of the opposition of the Orthodox, who rejected unconditionally Buber's teaching the subject of religion. Magnes then proposed to create a position for Buber as life rector of the Hebrew University. This offer greatly excited and pleased Buber. "The bomb is planted," he wrote to Rosenzweig. To Paula, Buber wrote, "His offer surprised me; it means a partial abdication in my favor." For Paula, who had given up her religion, her family, and her city to marry Buber, this meant a still greater sacrifice. Philo-Zionist though she was, she knew no Hebrew and could not but miss her beloved mountains and forests, the source of many of the stories she had written and published. "I understand well, dear heart, how difficult a decision that means for you," Buber wrote her. "Yet here I am offered for the first time in my life an office that at once demands greatness and makes greatness possible." As Adam said to Eve at the end of Milton's *Paradise Lost,* Buber concluded, "You must know that I would rather be a vagabond with you than the academic overseer of this planet without you." Whatever happens, Buber added, "I propose to make possible a broader and more active way of life for us. You must feel yourself freer to do your work and to move about more in the world. You must be able to give up part of the housework, and that means we must make the necessary changes in the house."

Magnes's dream of Buber's being the life rector of the Hebrew University did not materialize because of opposition such as met all of Magnes's later proposals on Buber's behalf.

In 1929, in a letter to his friend Robert Weltsch, Hugo Bergmann made a perceptive comment concerning Buber's difficulties in coming to Palestine:

> I am compelled to think of the different legends of how the devil hindered the Baal Shem from coming to Palestine because if he reached it it would mean the coming of redemption. If Buber should find the strength to come to Palestine and to overcome all that stands between him and Palestine, if he would actually realize in himself the meaning of the reality that he preaches, we would experience in ourselves together with him a new Aliyah, and a kind of redemption. But the devil will probably know how to hinder that too.

Through his close bond with Hermann Gerson, the leader of the "Work

Folk," Buber had a dramatic impact on one segment of the Jewish Youth movement in Germany and its transformation into an actual kibbutz in Palestine. "Folk Education as Our Task," an address that Buber gave at the twenty-first meeting of the delegates of the German Zionists in 1926, the very year in which he met Gerson, affords us an insight into the deep significance of Buber's master-disciple relationship with Gerson for Buber's own under-standing of his place in the Zionist movement. Buber portrayed his under-standing of the Jewish settlement in Palestine as a colonization continued over many generations, "allowing the participation in the generation-work of the community to be included in the atmosphere of a new normality." This colonization was to be carried out by an elite of Jewish youth who already had a firm foundation in the folk education of their former homeland. But Buber asserted that two basic human types were needed for this task—the Halutz, or pioneer, and the helper. Here there becomes visible, as Grete Schaeder has pointed out, not only Buber's conception of the way in which Palestine should develop, but also the role that he intended for himself while he ever again postponed his own immigration: that of the helper. Corresponding to the folk schools in Palestine, there must exist institutions in the Diaspora that will teach what Buber called the "Seinstradition"—the handing down of values, the *institutional* linking of the generations through teaching, as opposed to anything occasional, provisional, and temporary.

The Jewish Youth movement cannot fulfill this task, Buber said, because its leaders are not persons who hand down existence and teaching. The succession of its generations are not included in the great connection of the generations. "That is also the reason why we see the often gloriously liv-ing generations of the Youth Movement—the Jewish as much as the German—disappear one after the other, as though they had never lived in an inspired present."

Clearly, Buber felt in some measure called upon to turn to the youth and help them become the pioneers who would enregister themselves in an organic succession of generations. With the emergence of Hermann Gerson as one of his staunchest disciples, the way seemed to open for Buber to do just that, since Gerson was already one of the acknowledged leaders of the Jewish Youth movement in Germany. Through Gerson, Buber might hope to help found a genuine "Youth School."

Gerson came from a very assimilated family. At eighteen, he decided that he wanted to be a Jew—a decision that his friends in the youth move-ment thought insane. During this period, Gerson encountered Buber's writ-ings, especially his essays on Judaism. Gerson began studying at the Jewish Hochschule in Berlin in 1926, and, that same year, Buber came to Berlin to give a lecture, which Gerson attended. As if struck by lightning, Gerson knew that Buber was the person he had been seeking to guide him, and he wrote to ask Buber to be his spiritual mentor. Buber invited Gerson to meet him when he next came to Berlin, and, from then on, they were master and disciple. In many respects, Gerson became something of an envoy for Buber, conveying to him much of what was happening in Berlin. Buber's most important help to Gerson came when he was establishing the Werkleute branch of the Jewish Youth movement in Germany. Gerson's theory was that the ideals of the youth movement need not vanish when the period of youth fades and that one can continue to attempt to realize those ideals throughout one's entire life. Buber gave his wholehearted support to this original approach. The growing consciousness of the task facing him led Buber to the lasting resolution never to evade a call that came to him from the youth.

The synthesis of non-Zionist Jewish nationalism, non-Orthodox enthusiasm for Judaism, and noncommunist revolutionary socialism, which Gerson combined with Buber's religious socialism, his existentialist religion, and his Hebrew humanism, was "so complex," Grete Schaeder opines, "that it could only find a resonance among the bourgeois intellectuals in Germany." Gerson's total acceptance of Buber's language and thought was accomplished by a determined effort to look, speak, and act like Buber, down to the beard, the diction, and the pronunciation. At the same time, as Gerson admitted in 1966, he was so concerned with his role as charismatic leader of his circle that he was chary of bringing Buber together with his followers too often, lest his own position be in some way threatened. "To be prepared means to prepare," Gerson quoted from one of Buber's first "Three Speeches on Judaism."

In the light of the development and radical change of the Werkleute, we cannot help wondering whether the thoughts, speech, and mannerisms that Gerson had "made his own" and the *way* in which he had appropriated them had really prepared him for the unforeseeable new situations that he and his circle had to confront.

In September 1932, Buber wrote Gerson that, in his opinion, Gerson was too preoccupied with the conscious task of "being-in-the-world" and serving God, instead of just being in the world spontaneously and serving God as he happened to at any given time. "You are still too much of a 'billiard player' and too little a 'tennis player.' I know exactly how that is; for at your age (aside from the fact that I was more light-hearted than you) it was just the same with me." In the same letter, Buber spoke of Gerson's forthcoming marriage:

> Naturally one does not know when one "marries" whether one "will remain ready to involve his existence where necessary." But what is important is precisely that one does *not* know; that one remains uncertain, that when one moves to meet someone one has to withstand the test in its whole burden, unmitigated by any simplified life-style. To remain truly insecure is to remain insecure in the face of this test.

In a remarkable anticipation of the blessing that Elijah was to give to Elisha in Buber's "mystery play" of a quarter of a century later, Buber wished that Gerson and his fiancee might "experience the true blessing of life, that which comes out of contradiction."

Much later, looking back on his relationship with Buber during those early years, Gerson wrote:

> He was a master of conversation—and each conversation with him reached its high point when his partner in conversation shared with him the central problems which beset him in the intellectual, political, or personal sphere. When I got to know him in 1927, he had already made it a rule to answer personally every letter that he received; and when he accepted a young person as his personal disciple, then he shared in all that person's joys and sorrows. This great capacity to listen, to conduct a dialogue with individuals and with historical happenings—this rare capacity is that which determined Buber's person and made every conversation with him into a life-experience in which clarification, deepening, and encouragement wonderfully united.

At Gerson's request, Buber married him and his first wife, since it was possible at that time for anyone in Germany to perform a marriage ceremony. In April 1933, Buber wrote to Gerson, "Naturally it is right that you marry" and added that he was ready to perform a religious ceremony provided that he might somewhat modify the ritual.

At Gerson's request in 1932, Buber wrote his essay "Why Study Jewish Sources?" for the syllabus of the School of Jewish Youth that Gerson and Moritz Spitzer directed in Berlin.

In the spirit of this essay, Gerson wrote a circular letter to his circle on April 15, 1933, recognizing that the place of realization may change—more specifically, that the task of the Werkleute now lay in Palestine and not Germany—but that the work on the Bible and Jewish history should not be forsaken in favor of swelling the ranks of the already numerous party Jews who had no historical vision. With the rise to power of the Nazis in 1933 and the anti-Jewish boycott and restrictions that went into effect in April 1933, the foundation for the Jews' identification with German culture was swept away and with it all their vacillations about their relationship to the Halutzim. In April 1933, the decision to establish a Werkleute-Kibbutz in Palestine was unanimous. Buber wrote to Arthur Ruppin and Chaim Weizmann about acquiring land for the Werkleute in Palestine. He also wrote to rich Jews in Germany who could contribute to the fund for buying land. In his letter to Ruppin of November 1933, Buber warmly recommended the Werkleute.

> In the years that I have known them they have developed under the leadership of Hermann Gerson and under my influence into a group of serious Jewish consciousness and strong feeling of responsibility. At the same time their relation to Palestine has

grown ever deeper and more all-embracing so that by now it has won an active form. I am convinced that the Land will receive from them a worthwhile support for its building up and its moral status.

Although in his circular letter of April 1933, Gerson wrote at length of the innumerable tasks and difficulties and the social, pedagogical, cultural, and political problems that lay ahead of them, the radical changes that in fact awaited them far outstripped his imagination and that of the other members of the Werkleute. Gerson became a Moses who entered the Promised Land, but no longer as Moses. His charismatic leadership ended in a tragic way that he could not have anticipated.

◆ 11 ◆

Nazi Germany

(1933-1938)

"Of all the Jews in Europe," writes Nora Levin, "the dazed and bewildered Jews of Germany were most unprepared for the fate that was to engulf them." When the state abruptly prohibited them from describing themselves as "members of the German Folk," the shock "deprived them of the moral and cultural essence of their life." On March 30th, 1933, Buber wrote to Hermann Gerson, "As far as I am concerned—just in these days strangely enough faith has enclosed me as in a snakeskin." Shortly after the Nazis took power, they declared a Boycott Day on April 1, 1933, against the buying of goods from any Jewish store. At Buber's house, too, there appeared an S.A. man (a member of the Storm Troops that helped bring Hitler to power), who lifted his hand in a Nazi salute and announced to Buber that a boycott march would take place in front of his house. Buber observed mildly that he probably could not change anything, but the S.A. man turned to him with a question: "Herr Professor, we have different signs: 'Jewish Business,' 'Jewish Law Office,' 'Jewish Doctor,' but none of these fit you. What sort of sign shall we put in your window?" At this, Buber observed laconically that the choice must be left to the S.A. officer, for he himself had no label. The S.A. man looked about critically at Buber's study and observed the impressive library that lined the walls. Finally, an illumination came to him. "I have it," he announced happily, and drew from his briefcase a sign: "Jewish Bookdealer." "We shall put that in the window," he decided, and that is what happened. Buber never discussed politics, but once admitted to the parents of a former schoolmate of his son, Rafael, that he did not hate the Nazis, but merely scorned them.

Hedwig Straub, the Buber maid from 1930 to 1936, recalls that, in 1933, Albert Einstein was a regular visitor at the Buber house, as was the mayor of Jerusalem, and that they were always discussing the possibilities of emigration, which, when it happened, took Einstein to America and Buber to Palestine. Only in 1952, three years before Einstein's death, did the two friends meet again.

In the autumn of 1933, the very time when Buber was ousted from his position at the University of Frankfurt, such luminaries as Professor Ernst Ferdinand Sauerbruch, the surgeon; Martin Heidegger, the existentialist philosopher; and Wilhelm Pinder, the art historian, took a public vow to support Hitler and the National Socialist regime. When Heidegger came to lecture at Heidelberg, the faculty, assembled on the stage, had agreed in advance to get up and leave as soon as he got up to speak. When Heidegger arose, one young professor, Arnold Bergstraesser, stood up, but no one else did. Then he in turn sat down while Heidegger subjected the professors who had not yet become Nazis to a tongue-lashing such as had never before taken place in a German university!

In October 1933, Buber resigned his professorship, correctly anticipating the official dismissal. He received many expressions of sympathy from German professors. In Heppenheim, Buber remained in connection with the intellectual world, which had fallen into consternation and confusion. His house became a kind of shrine for Jews and Christians seeking advice and help. Scholars and spiritual personalities of Germany, who had formerly stood in academic or even friendly relations with Buber, sought to justify themselves to him when they joined this or that form of the National Socialist movement. In the first years, many "Aryans" showed their defiance by visiting Buber and expressed in person or in letters, sometimes intentionally on open postcards, their misgivings about what was happening in Germany.

The Nazi search of the Buber home in Heppenheim, in March 1933, was actually quite uneventful. As Buber himself said, the respect of the ordinary German for books and authority prevented their resorting to any violence—in the face of a library of twenty thousand books. What happened was simply that two young men in brown uniforms appeared unannounced before him to conduct a search of the house, without knowing what to look for. Buber was suspect as a famous Jew. They dimly sensed that his spiritual resistance represented a danger for their "new order" without knowing what form that danger might take. When they came on Buber, he was sitting at his desk working on the translation of the Bible. The one in charge demanded, "What are you doing here?" "I am translating the Bible," Buber answered. The brown-clad man looked mistrustingly at the long sheets of paper covered with Buber's clear, beautiful handwriting and observed skeptically that that was much too long for the Bible; it was the Talmud. Buber denied this and pointed to the already printed volumes of his translation. This in no way convinced the literal-minded S.A. man. "The Bible," he said, "is only just *one* book that one receives at confirmation." Finally Buber proposed that a Protestant pastor be fetched as an "expert" on the matter. The latter testified that this really was the Old Testament. Because he appeared credible in the eyes of the S.A. officer, the house search ended there.

During the ravages and brutality of the *Kristallnacht* in November 1938, when Buber had already emigrated, the Nazis destroyed all the furniture in the house in Heppenheim, which still belonged to Buber, and the three thousand volumes that still remained in his library, and then sent him a bill, demanding that he pay them twenty-seven thousand marks! By this time, the respect for books was no longer in evidence.

One of the most ironic touches of the Nazi accession to power equaled only by Rosenberg's quoting Buber's *Speeches on Judaism* at the Nuremberg trials because of Buber's emphasis on the importance of "blood" for the people was the fact recorded by Agnon that Goebbels, Hitler's propaganda minister and, along with Göring, the number two man, praised Hitler as a *Künder,* or Proclaimer, the special German translation of the Hebrew *nabi,* or prophet, that Buber and Rosenzweig used in their Bible translation.

A colleague of Buber's at the University of Frankfurt was Ernst Krieck. Buber himself described Krieck, after he turned Nazi, as having too much sense of responsibility to be appointed by the Nazis as the minister of culture of Prussia, even though he was the only man whom they might have seriously considered. In a periodical that he edited Krieck published an anti-Semitic essay on "the Jewish God." Buber offered him through a third party a statement clarifying only those things that were factually incorrect. Krieck replied to this third party that he had great respect for Buber, but that the latter was still too naive, because he did not understand at all that this was a *political* journal!

It was Nahum Glatzer who in a letter to Buber from London, dated April 27, 1933, spoke the truly prophetic and pathetic words of the situation of the Jew in Germany. Dismissed by the Nazis from his position at the University of Frankfurt, as Buber had not yet been, Glatzer foresaw, because he thought ghettos no longer possible, not the confinement of the Jews but their destruction. "The question of how much can be borne can only be tested practically," Buber responded. "For my part I shall now seek whether I can bring something about for the community." Buber was not dismissed at this time, but he had a letter from the rector of the university warning him against giving his lectures and seminars in the summer semester of 1933, which also meant that there would be no publicity surrounding it, unlike the dismissal of Glatzer and others that was reported in the *London Times.* "I do not believe that I shall still lecture in Frankfurt," Buber concluded.

In April 1933, Buber wrote the first of his great responses to the "judgment" of the hour, "The Jewish Person of Today." "The Jewish man of today is the inwardly most exposed person in our world," Buber declared. "The tensions of the ages have selected this point in order to measure their strength on it. They want to know whether man can still withstand them and they test themselves on the Jews.... They want to learn through his destiny what man is." At that time, the other children started to curse Barbara and Judith and to throw rocks at them in the street. Buber summoned them to his study and explained to them what anti-Semitism is, what is important in Judaism, and why their classmates and other people acted toward them in this manner. When all Jewish pupils were excluded from schools in Germany in 1936, Buber hired a special teacher for them, who was also his part-time secretary and who started to prepare them for the transfer to Israel. The most famous of Buber's responses to the situation, appropriately, was the essay "The Children":

> The children experience what happens and keep silent, but in the night they groan in their dreams, awaken, and stare into the darkness. The world has become unreliable. A child had a friend; the friend was as taken for granted as the sunlight. Now the friend suddenly looks at him strangely, the corners of his mouth mock him: Surely you didn't imagine that I really cared about you?

The world's familiar smile has turned into a grimace, and there is no one to whom the child can tell his anxiety, no one he can ask why everything is the way it is. The child's rage can find no outlet but smolders inside and turns into *ressentiment*: "This is how a child becomes bad." The judgment of the hour is not only that against the Nazis but also that against Israel.

> ..."Israel" means to practice community for the sake of a common covenant in which our existence is founded; to practice in actual living the community between being and being, person and person, toward which end creation was created. And today this means to preserve directness in a world which is becoming more and more indirect, in the face of the self-righteousness of collectivities to preserve the mystery of relationship, without which a people must perish in an icy death.
> But have we not started out ourselves on the road toward becoming a self-righteous collectivity?

Cruelly difficult though it is, "human openness is a dire need."

"Things do not look so good in Germany," Buber wrote Hans Trüb in June 1933. He doubted whether he could complete his work there: "The atmosphere has a constricting destructive effect on one's soul." Yet Buber's need to work was greater than ever: "I have begun to bring in the harvest of a great piece of my life." Despite all that was taking place, Buber did not falter in his own work during the five years that he still remained in Germany. This is all the more remarkable because, in the course of the year that followed, he took up an enormously demanding task of Jewish education that occupied him until his departure from Germany.

Neither did Buber falter in his prophetic task of speaking to the German-Jewish community in its time of crisis. In the summer of 1933, he wrote a "theological note" entitled "In the Midst of History". Resuming his preoccupation with the Servant and the hidden history, Buber declared that history is a dialogue between the Deity and mankind in which often the person who does not succeed is the one who has been faithful to the dialogue, and, as Buber said of Davis Trietsch after his public shaming by Herzl, secretly confirmed. From this standpoint, history can be understood only when we are the ones addressed and to the degree that we make ourselves receptive. We are flatly denied the possibility of making an objective judgment concerning history's meaning, but we are permitted to know history's challenge to and claim on us. This is not a "subjective" meaning, but one that can be caught only with one's personal life.

The "judgment" that Buber perceived for German Jewry in that hour of crisis was that everyone perceived his own need *and* that of those close to him.

> But who of us suffers the need of the Jewish people as a whole whose very existence is being put to the test through the destruction of that symbiosis with the German people which has been, up till now, confirmed through life and work? Who recognizes his own guilt in all this and turns from it in such a way that through him the turning of the whole people takes place?

In a January 1934 address to the Frankfurt Lehrhaus entitled "The Jew in the World," Buber characterized the Jew as the insecure person pure and simple. Such partial security as other peoples have enjoyed, he has been deprived of. Living on ground that may at any moment give way beneath its feet, the Jewish people has experienced every symbiotic relationship as treacherous, every alliance or union as temporary. This is why the Jewish Diaspora is characterized by Jews as the *galut,* or exile. This wandering, forsaken community has had for the peoples in whose midst it has lived something ghost-like about it, something uncanny *(unheimlich),* homeless *(heimlos)* that cannot be assimilated into the majority culture. The Jews were always the first victims of fanatical mass movements, such as the Crusades of the eleventh century, and were blamed for mass misfortunes, such as the "Black Death." Even when they tried to adjust to their environment, like the Marranos who converted to Christianity in Spain and remained secretly Jewish, that adjustment failed, and the Inquisition followed upon Marranism. Only in being faithful to the prophetic call to realize community can the Jewish people attain its own unique security, asserted Buber.

Buber was not only concerned with the Nazi threat to the Jewish people, but also with its threat to Christianity. In 1934, when Buber attended the Eranos Conference at Ascona, Switzerland, centering on the analytical psychologist C. G. Jung, he found himself compelled to respond publicly to the vicious attacks on Christianity by a number of Nazis who were present. "It is not usually my role to defend Christianity," said Buber as he rose to his feet, "but in this case I must do so."

It is easy to understand why the well-known German novelist, writer, and pastor Albrecht Goes declared that, at that time, Buber's books— Dialogue, I and Thou—were as important to us as bread." At that time, too, witnessed Goes, "it counted for not little that the man who wrote these words was still among us, that his lamp burned at night in Heppenheim on the Bergstrasse."

In 1936, Schocken Verlag published in its "Library of Little Books" a selection of twenty-three psalms in the original Hebrew with Buber's translation. In his Foreword to this selection, which he titled "Out of the Depths I Call unto Thee," Buber seemingly dealt with the psalms but actually, existentially, spoke, to the great need of his time. There is no sharp line to be drawn, he asserted, between the psalms of personal need and those expressing the hope for rescue of the community. In conversation with Schalom Ben-Chorin in 1956, Buber said: "The time of Hitler was the most terrible that I have lived through, but even in that time there was a holy meaning in history, there was God... only I cannot say how and where."

In early October 1936, Buber reported to Trüb the unexpected cancellation of his passport, and, by the end of October, this vexation continued. With the remarkable courage that was typical of him, Buber went by himself to Gestapo headquarters and asked them why they had taken away his passport. They thought that he was insane in coming to them, but he got the passport back. In December 1936, Buber turned to Hermann Hesse for advice as to a Swiss publisher who might publish a new novel by his wife Paula. She had been excluded from the Reich's Chamber of Writers because of her "Jewish marriage." An inkling of the toll that living in Nazi Germany took on Buber's spirit is given us by a letter of January 1937 to Hermann Gerson, who was now settled in a kibbutz in Israel. "I can well imagine," Buber wrote,

> that now in this difficult time of your life you had expected more support from me and rightly so. The worst of it is that it has also been for me a difficult time, perhaps the most difficult (if not the most violent) of my entire previous life, a time of heavy threat to soul, spirit and survival. If not needing any earthly help (for there is no help for that), I have been still less able to help, less able to be there than at any time during the past twenty years.

On November 26, 1938, Gandhi published a statement in his paper, the Harijan (The Untouchable), in which he suggested that the Jews in Germany use satyagraha, or soul-force, as the most effective reply to Nazi atrocities. In a public reply, which Buber wrote and published along with one by Judah Magnes, Buber took Gandhi to task for his statement that these persecutions were "an exact parallel" to those of the Indians in South Africa in 1905. In so doing, Buber revealed the full pathos of what he and his fellow Jews had been through in Nazi Germany. "What the rage of the enemy could not bring about, the friendly address has effected," Buber wrote. "I must answer."

> ...But, Mahatma, are you not aware of the burning of synagogues and scrolls of the Torah? Do you know nothing of all the sacred property of the community—in part of great antiquity, that has been destroyed in the flames? I am not aware that Boers and Englishmen in South Africa ever injured anything sacred to the Indians.... Now, do you know or *do you not* know, Mahatma, what a concentration camp is like and what goes on there?... And do you think perhaps that a Jew in Germany could pronounce in public one single sentence of a speech such as yours without being knocked down?... In the five years which I myself spent under the present régime, I observed many instances of genuine *satyagraha* among the Jews.... Such actions, however, apparently exerted not the slightest influence on their opponents.... A diabolic universal steam-roller cannot thus be withstood.... Testimony without acknowledgement, ineffective, unobserved martyrdom, a martyrdom cast to the winds—that is the fate of innumerable Jews in Germany. God alone accepts their testimony, and God "seals" it, as is said in our prayers.... Such martyrdom is a deed — but who would venture to demand it?

Writing on the first anniversary of *Kristallnacht,* Buber declared that the German state, in annihilating a minority that had not transgressed against it, was shaking the foundations of its own existence. Buber spoke of the state, to distinguish it from the German people who concurred with or tolerated it but who did not act on their own initiative.

> What happened in Germany a year ago was not an outbreak of a nation's passion, of widespread Jew-hatred, nor was it so in any action committed against us in these seven years. It was a command from the upper level and was executed with the precision of a dependable machine. For two weeks during the preparation of the Nuremberg Laws, school children came by the windows of my house in Heppenheim every morning at six o'clock and sang the pretty song "Only when the Jew's blood squirts from the knife."... On the next morning we waited in vain for the procession. In Poland I saw what elementary Jew-hate is—an outbreak of instinctual drives; I have never seen it in Germany.

Buber did not exempt the German people from culpability. On the contrary, he suggested that it was an old habit of the German people to obey those in power and see them as God-sent. "It is apparently quite difficult for a German to distinguish between God and success and to imagine a God who does not go forth with strong battalions, but rather dwells 'among the bruised and downcast' (Isaiah 57:15)." Even the true intellectuals in Germany seemed "inclined to believe in everyone who takes over the business of politics and carries it by force with uninhibited harshness." Even those who helped persecuted and suffering Jews were often inwardly in basic agreement with the tendency of the persecutors, although regretting their grossness.

Buber's greatest fear was that people in Palestine might learn the wrong lesson and imitate in the name of the Jewish cause that "golem on whose brow the name of Satan is inscribed," that "cruelty that functions like a machine" and that "seizes, desecrates, and destroys our communities one after the other."

The Nazis called Buber the "arch-Jew," a designation that he quoted with pride in his address on the occasion of his receiving the Peace Prize of the German Book Trade in 1953.

To Buber, Hitler was only the caricature of Napoleon, the "demonic Thou" toward whom everything flames but whose fire is cold, the man who was Thou for millions but for whom no one was Thou. The only remarkable thing that Buber saw in Hitler was his being possessed—in the literal sense of the term—as the consequence of his impotence. Hitler's idea of the higher race was not really biological, Buber held. It stemmed from Nietzsche.

In my essay "The Bases of Buber's Ethics" in *The Philosophy of Martin Buber* volume of the Library of Living Philosophers, I wrote, "One's antagonist may, indeed, be the devil or Hitler, but even such a one must be faithfully answered, contended with." In his "Replies to My Critics," Buber commented that he held no one to be "absolutely" unredeemable—by God. But speaking not "of God, but solely of myself and this man," he felt constrained to reject my interpretation:

> Hitler is not my antagonist in the sense of a partner "whom I can confirm in opposing him," as Friedman says, for he is incapable of really addressing one and incapable of really listening to one. That I once experienced personally when, if only through the technical medium of the radio, I heard him speak. I knew that this voice was in the position to annihilate me together with countless of my brothers; but I perceived that despite such might it was not in the position to set the spoken and heard word into the world. And already less than an hour afterward I sensed in "Satan" the "poor devil," the poor devil in power, and at the same time I understood my dialogical powerlessness. I had to answer, but not to him who had spoken. As far as a person is part of a situation, I have to respond, but not just to the person.

As important as the prophetic demand and comfort that Martin Buber brought to German Jewry during the first five years of the Third Reich was his leadership in spiritual resistance against the Nazis. (Abraham Joshua Heschel, who was Buber's friend during the last thirty years of Buber's life, spoke often of his association with Buber during this period in the direction of the reopened Frankfurt Freie Jüdische Lehrhaus. "Buber gave me my first job," Heschel said and testified, "This was the period of Buber's true greatness.") This spiritual resistance to Nazism took two principal forms: Jewish-Christian "dialogues" and the organization of education for the Jews of Germany. The latter commenced only after the Nazi rise to power. The former began even before, when the coming upheaval could already be scented in the air.

In 1932, Buber wrote an essay for a volume published in 1933 by the German Fellowship of Reconciliation, which considered whether the group can relieve the individual of his responsibility. Buber distinguished between the genuine person of faith who "trusts" within a relationship of faith, and the one who "believes in" a leader. People readily declare today that they believe in the Führer, Buber said,

> but the idols with human bodies are still worse than those in the form of ideas because they can counterfeit reality more effectively. With my choice and decision I answer for my hour, and this responsibility my group cannot take from me. My group concerns me enormously in my decision, [but] no program, no tactical resolution, no command of a leader can say to me how I, making my decision, must do justice to my group in God's sight. It may even be that I shall have to oppose the success of my group's program and carry into my group itself that "inner front" which can run as a secret unity across all groups and become more important for the future of our world than all the lines drawn today between group and group.

All this has nothing to do with "individualism." "I hold the individual to be neither the starting point nor the goal of the human world. But I hold the human person to be the unalterable center of the struggle between the movement of the world away from God and its movement to God." This struggle takes place to an uncannily large extent in the realm of public life, yet the decisive battles are fought out in the depths of the person. "The dizziness of freedom of the generation that has just passed has been followed by the search for bondage of the present one, the unfaithfulness of intoxication by the unfaithfulness of hysteria." This essay was used by Buber as an integral part of his book *The Question to the Single One*—published in 1936—a time when it had still greater relevance, if only as a voice crying in the wilderness.

Gerhart Kittel, the New Testament scholar, despite his evangelical piety and his emphasis on the Old Testament–Jewish roots of Christianity, affirmed National Socialism and represented a "Christian" anti-Semitism. In June 1933, Kittel wrote Buber that he was sending him a little book that he had written entitled *The Jewish Question,* some passages of which must seem inimical to Buber as a Jew. Yet he honestly wished to do justice to Judaism, he claimed, and reminded Buber of the high esteem in which he held his lifework, as shown by what he had written about it. Buber replied that he had read the book carefully and had found much in which agreement between them did or could exist. But, when he read the whole, he could not affirm that Kittel had done justice to Judaism. Buber objected to his speaking of *the* Jewish doctor, *the* Jewish lawyer, and *the* Jewish merchant, as if they could all be dealt with as a single class (the very stuff of prejudice), and he objected even more to Kittel's using the fact that the Jews were strangers in the land as a basis for discrimination. "Would you want this conclusion to apply to the German minorities in the world?" Buber asked Kittel, and cited passages from the Hebrew Bible about having one standard and one justice for host and guest alike. Acknowledging the "obedience" that Kittel cited as one part and one part only of the awakening of a new covenant of faith in the Jewish people, Buber asked Kittel whether such "obedience" means that we should regard our defamation not only as God's just judgment but also as men's just deed? Buber concluded by pointing out that Kittel wrote his message to a public to which Buber, as a Jew, had no access.

As it turned out, in July 1933, Buber was enabled to reply publicly to Kittel through the courage of his former partner in Jewish-Christian dialogue Karl Ludwig Schmidt, editor of *Theologische Blätter,* and this reply and a further reply were reprinted in Buber's book *The Hour and Its Judgment* (1936). To Kittel's statement that true Jewishness remains with the symbol of exiles wandering over the earth without rest or home, Buber responded that the "wandering Jew" is a figure from Christian, not Jewish, legend. True Judaism is always ready to see the promise fulfilled *in the next moment* and its wandering come to an end. The "historical givenness" of being strangers is a question addressed to the peoples and to Israel, not a solution to a problem. "If God were ever to judge between Israel and the nations of the world, he would not fail to look at the guilt of the nations," Buber declared. To Kittel's strong denial that he defamed Judaism, Buber cited, as one example out of many, Kittel's claim that *the* Jewish lawyer obeyed the letter of the law but acted directly contrary to the German consciousness of law. If this statement that the Jewish lawyer perverts the law *as a Jew* is not defamation, Buber asserted, "then I do not know what in the world deserves such a name." To publish these responses to Kittel was not without its dangers for a Jew in the Third Reich. But, as Schalom Ben-Chorin has observed, a civil courage was always characteristic of Buber, outwardly so tender a man but one who could become hard and severe where right and wrong, justice and injustice, were involved. From Jerusalem, Gershom Scholem wrote Buber that he had read Kittel's brochure with disgust and revolt and that, of all the shameful works produced by a well-known professor, this was certainly among the most shameful.

After the Nuremberg Laws of 1935, Julius Streicher's depraved journal *Der Stürmer* filled the minds of millions of readers with hatred and fear of Jews. In 1936, a delegation of German Protestant ministers, mostly village pastors, asked Buber for material against Streicher's falsifications, which he, of course, supplied. A still more significant spiritual resistance to nazism through Jewish-Christian dialogue was Buber's publication of his book *The Question to the Single One* in 1936. Taking off from a critique and redefinition of Kierkegaard's central concept of the "Single One" *(Einzelne)* and, to a lesser extent, of the nineteenth-century German philosopher Max Stirner's radical individualism, Buber, in fact, used this book as an occasion for a radical criticism of collectivism and, in connection with this criticism, of those persons, such as the Christian theologian Friedrich Gogarten and the University of Berlin professor of constitutional law Carl Schmitt, who interpreted Christianity in such a way as to lend theoretical support to collectivism. In particular, Buber contrasted Gogarten's affirmation of the radical and unredeemable evil of man with the Jewish position, which recognizes no "original sin." In a highly sympathetic reply to Buber's critique of Gogarten, Karl Ludwig Schmidt suggested that Buber write to the great systematic evangelical theologian Karl Barth for his views on the subject. Barth replied that the concept of "radical" evil was valid in Protestant Christianity *coram Deo* (before God) but not among human beings, and that this confrontation of the whole person with the demand and judgment of God in no way affected the command to love God and to love one's neighbor. "Were it otherwise," Barth concluded, "then the whole confessional church might have remained peacefully at home in these days or exactly in that place—where Gogarten stands!" Buber concurred that man might stand as evil in the sight of God but not in the sight of a human community or institution.

In his 1948 Foreword to *Between Man and Man,* Buber stated that its publication in Germany in 1936 was astonishing, "since it attacks the very foundation of totalitarianism." "The fact that it could be published with impunity is certainly to be explained from its not having been understood by the appropriate authorities." "I really wonder," Hermann Herrigel wrote to Buber, "that you publish a book today that... must bring you into the position of expressing yourself directly on the present political situation."

When the individual who is joined to a whole is denied his personal voice, human perception ceases, human response is dumb, and "the immeasurable value which constitutes man is imperiled." "In order that man may not be lost there is need of persons who are not collectivized, and of truth which is not politicized,... of the person's responsibility to truth in his historical situation," of the Single One who confronts and guarantees all being which is present to him, including the body politic.

The Question to the Single One represents a new emphasis upon the importance of saying "I," necessitated by the collectivist and totalitarian trends of the time. To those who have coupled Buber with George Herbert

Mead as an exponent of the "social self" or with Harry Stack Sullivan as an exponent of the "interpersonal" in general, Buber says here in unmistakable terms, "Not before a man can say I in perfect reality—that is, finding himself — can he in perfect reality say *Thou*.... And even if he does it in a community he can only do it 'alone.'"

"Creation is not a hurdle on the road to God, it is the road itself." Creatures are placed in my way so that I may find my way with them to God. The real God is the Creator, and all beings stand before him in relation to one another in his creation. "The real God lets no shorter line reach him than each man's longest.... Only when all relations, uncurtailed, are taken into the one relation, do we set the ring of our world round the sun of our being." In order to bring all our finite *Thous* into our dialogue with the "eternal Thou" we must create for ourselves an inner-worldly "monastery" that will prevent our bonds with the world from being dissipated. This loneliness in the midst of life, in which we take refuge as "retreats," is imperative if we do not wish to see our participation in the Present Being dying off. Kierkegaard is an image of the human condition for us—for he is, like us, isolated and exposed, and this is the fate of man as man. But he is not a human image that can give us meaningful direction for personal and social existence. Buber's "narrow ridge" is not on the fringe of life but precisely at its center: "We, ourselves, wandering on the narrow ridge, must not shrink from the sight of the jutting rock on which he stands over the abyss; nor may we step on it. We have much to learn from him, but not the final lesson." Kierkegaard's view is acosmic; it denies the creation. But God the Creator does not hover over his creation as a chaos; he embraces it. "He is the infinite I that makes every It into his Thou," and we imitate God when in our human way we embrace the bit of world offered to us by saying Thou with our being to the beings who surround us, loving God's creation in his creatures.

What is most remarkable is that, living in Nazi Germany, Buber could still affirm the body politic as the human world that seeks to realize in its genuine formations our turning to one another in the context of creation. If Kierkegaard, in his horror of the perverted forms social life takes, turned away, Buber, a century later, had far more reason to do so. But Buber, who confessed himself in one of his Hasidic writings as one ineluctably destined to love the world, pronounced, "The person who has not ceased to love the human world in all its degradation is able even today to envision genuine social form." The form to which Buber pointed in particular was the very one that Kierkegaard shunned—marriage. In true marriage, the confrontation with the body politic and its destiny can no longer be shirked. In this witness to marriage, Buber demonstrated once again how important his own marriage with Paula was to the development and continuance of his philosophy of dialogue. To enter into the sacrament of marriage is to take seriously the fact that the other is, the fact that I cannot legitimately share in the Present Being without sharing in the being of the other. If I do this, I have decisively entered into relation with otherness, "and the basic structure of otherness, in many ways uncanny but never quite unholy or incapable of being hallowed, in which I and the others who meet me in this life are interwoven, is the body politic." The persons with whom we have to deal have not merely a different way of thinking and feeling, a different conviction and attitude, but also

> a different perception of the world, a different recognition and order of meaning, a different touch from the regions of existence, a different faith, a different soil: to affirm all this... in the midst of the hard situations of conflict, without relaxing their real serious-ness, is the way by which we may... be permitted... to touch on the other's "truth" or "untruth", "justice" or "injustice".

The Single One meets God by putting his arms around creation and faces the biographical and historical hour that approaches him in its "apparently sense-less contradiction, without weakening the impact of otherness in it." The situ-ation in which Buber stood, the situation in which Hitler, in Martin Heidegger's words, was "the lord of the hour," Buber recognized as "God's question" to him. Human truth is bound up with the responsibility of the person. It becomes existentially true only when we stand the test in hearing and responding.

A pregnant example of such personal responsibility was Buber's leader-ship in Jewish education during the time of the Nazis. On March 22, 1933, Robert Weltsch wrote Buber from Berlin that most of the German Jews had not yet realized that most probably the complete establishment of a Jewish system of schools and culture would be necessary. "The monstrous difficulty in this undertaking lies in the fact that an abrupt impoverishment of German Jewry is taking place." On March 24, Buber wrote to Hermann Gerson that if the core of German Jews (with the exception, of course, of the separatist movement of the extreme Orthodox) put their trust in him, he would be ready to take over the responsible leadership of Jewish education in Germany.

On April 1, the boycott was imposed upon all Jews in Germany, even those of one-quarter Jewish blood, although the wearing of the yellow badge with the Star of David on it was not made mandatory until September 19, 1941. It was this identification, as Nora Levin has pointed out, that made it possible later to begin the mammoth task of the systematic extermination of six million Jews. On April 4, Robert Weltsch published an editorial in the *Jüdische Rundschau,* which was itself a high mark of spiritual resistance to the Nazis and saved many Jews from suicide. "Wear the Yellow Badge with Pride!" was its title, recalling the church's forcing the Jews to wear this badge in the medieval ghettos. "The Jews can only speak today as Jews," it read. "Anything else is totally senseless."

It was Martin Buber, more than any other single person, who taught the assimilated German Jews why they were suffering and by reawakening their Jewish consciousness gave them a counterweight against total despair. Before 1933, Menachem Gerson has pointed out, Buber's influence upon German Jewry was profound but not widespread. After Hitler's rise to power, many who had not formerly concerned themselves with Buber, or had dismissed him as an esoteric, incomprehensible prophet, now discovered in him their pathfinder and comforter. Surprised and unprepared and lacking any clear sense of Jewish identity, they suddenly found in Buber's teaching what they needed to withstand the cruel demands of the hour. He awakened many to a meaningful Jewish existence and prepared them spiritually for Aliyah (emigration to Palestine). By his personal engagement in every type of course, program, and lecture, and by his direction of cultural and educational activities, Buber quickly became famous, along with the great Rabbi Leo Baeck, as the fearless spokesman for the German Jews. During the time of his people's greatest trial and suffering since the beginning of the Diaspora, Buber provided leadership of a rare quality, teaching them to face their fate with courage and faith through a deeper affirmation of their Jewishness. "None of those who heard Buber's lectures at the college of Jewish Education in Berlin will ever forget them," writes Dr. Bertha Badt-Strauss. "It was like an island of peace in the daily-renewed flaring-up of the Nazi persecution of the Jews." Perhaps even more important was Buber's organization of small groups of teachers and disciples who toiled and lived together in work communities. Through these activities, by counseling, comforting, and raising their dejected spirits, he saved countless numbers from spiritual despair.

Moritz Spitzer relates a striking incident from the time shortly after the Nazis came to power:

> On May 1, 1933, we were sitting in Buber's house in Heppenheim. It was very hot. There was a May Day parade organized by the Nazis, and since the windows were open we saw and heard parts of it. After the parade ended, a maid came to Buber and said that a man wanted to speak to him. They went into Buber's study, and after a few minutes the young man left. Buber emerged from his study very excited. He said that the young man was an employee of the government and had been ordered to participate in the parade. It had made him disgusted with himself, and he felt that he couldn't come home to his wife and child without expressing this disgust to Buber. He said to Buber, "I lifted my hand to say 'Heil Hitler,' and I feel that the hand is filthy. Please shake my hand and I promise that I will never again raise my hand in such a salute." We later learned that he resigned from his government post and opened a private firm as a lawyer. His name is Ludwig Metzger. After the war he

became mayor of Darmstadt and was also a member of the Bundestag and was active in support of Israel.

Spitzer also testifies that, after Hitler came to power, Buber made an exception to his long-standing policy and went to the synagogue to give a sermon.

At the end of May, Buber invited Otto Hirsch, coleader of the Reichsvertretung, and Max Gruenewald, rabbi and communal leader at Mannheim, to his home to discuss his ideas about Jewish education, and, two days later, he wrote Ernst Simon in Jerusalem, asking him to consider working with him in these undertakings. He also went to Berlin to take part in meetings of the Reichsvertretung. Though he wrote Gerson at the time, "this hecticness is not for me," it became a necessary life-style for the five years that he was to remain in Germany. Gerson himself later described this period of Buber's life as one of "tireless activity undertaken in an atmosphere of insecurity and anxiety." Buber wrote Otto Hirsch that he had not been able to answer a letter from Hirsch's son. "Everything crowds together, as you can imagine. One can no longer enter personally into that which strongly touches one personally and may only hope for a future in which one again has leisure and immediacy." In this same year, Buber answered a circular question concerning Jewish youth by saying, "In order to be upright, it is not enough that one means what one says, and not even that one expresses what one means. More than that, one must really mean what one 'means,' that is, with the whole person. Otherwise only the understanding is upright and not the heart or vice-versa."

Meanwhile, in Berlin, the liberals and the Orthodox squabbled as to whether some more neutral person could not be found to lead the reconstruction of Jewish education, while Leo Baeck testified that Buber was "uniquely qualified" to do so. Buber had presented the leadership of the Reichsvertretung with two proposals for educational programs in which he stated that such a great communal work could be carried out only in a unified spirit and under a unified leadership. The task of this educational leader (Buber himself) would be to establish schools for the Jewish children who had been excluded from the public schools by Nazi laws, schools that would inculcate into the new generation the living substance of Judaism and create a human type capable of enduring under the most difficult conditions of the struggle for existence. At the end of his address, "Our Educational Goal" (June 1933), Buber stated: "We educate for Palestine, for those for whom it may be the land; for some strange country, for those for whom it must be the land; for Germany, for those for whom it can be the land. It is *one* human image, *one* goal, *one* education."

In November 1933, Buber reopened the Frankfurt Lehrhaus, which he directed until his departure for Palestine in 1938. The method characteristic of the Lehrhaus, that of intensive interchange between teacher and students, a community in which there is a transaction between teachers and students, in which both groups learn and teach, is necessary, Buber asserted, in order to arm young Jews to meet the situation and to meet it as Jews. To do this, it was not necessary to separate themselves from the German part of their heritage that was theirs, whatever the attitude of the Nazis, but to strengthen and renew the Jewish by becoming a *people* of God. This meant, said Buber, an education toward a community of memory, immediacy of living together with one another, and a community of work. Eric Weniger testified that, in the few years that it lasted, the reopened Lehrhaus became under the influence of Buber a unique place for the fostering of the spirit. In fact, from 1933 to 1937, it was one of the two places of refuge in Frankfurt that allowed for the working of the *German* spirit. "Martin Buber's lectures were historical events," Weniger testified, as did many others in memoirs of the time.

At about this time, Buber's disciple and friend, and Rosenzweig's faithful follower, Ernst Simon returned from Palestine to help with the Lehrhaus and with the broader tasks of Jewish adult education that Buber undertook. Simon provided a rare example of a German Zionist who had "ascended to the Land," yet was able to respond to the summons of the hour by voluntarily returning to a Germany shrouded in the dread darkness that had not yet descended when he left.

In March 1934, Buber wrote Otto Hirsch, suggesting a central office for adult Jewish education organized along the lines of the folk schools in which he had long been interested. The task of the central office, which Buber proposed to locate in Frankfurt, would be to erect adult schools, houses for learning, "Schools for Youth," courses of different kinds. This proposal served as the model for the "Central Office for Jewish Adult Education," which Buber directed for the Reichsvertretung. Through this position, Buber exercised an enormous influence on every aspect of Jewish education and culture in Germany during the next five years.

One of the men to whom Buber became closest in the course of his work at the Mittelstelle was Otto Hirsch, a Swabian of deep-rooted Jewish piety. Hirsch responded to Buber's teaching and character not only by placing at his disposal the services of the Reichsvertretung, but also, together with his friends Leopold Marx and the great choirmaster Karl Adler, by creating in the Stuttgart Jüdisches Lehrhaus a center from which Buber's personal influence could radiate far beyond Frankfurt. Of a number of Lehrhäuser that arose in Germany at this time, including some in Berlin and Mannheim, the Stuttgart center was the closest successor to the parent organization in Frankfurt. Hirsch's selfless activities on behalf of his fellow Jews exposed him to the wrath of the Nazis. Frequently arrested, he endured his periods of imprisonment "exceedingly well"—in his own opinion because of his "soldierly bearing and experience" but, in Ernst Simon's judgment, even more because of "the inflexible nobility of his character whose obvious qualities must have made an impression on the very torturers themselves." Simon also said of Buber's spiritual resistance to the Nazis through education: "Anyone who did not see Buber then has not seen true civil courage." "If a man wishes to bring his 'personality' through the crisis intact," Buber told his fellow educators, "then it is bound to crumble for then the crisis has what it wants—an object that is brittle enough to be cracked by it." Only through a new response could the German Jews retain their community and dignity in the face of the Nazi desire to atomize and destroy them.

In bringing together formerly conflicting Jewish youth groups, Buber rejected the language of "tolerance" and "neutrality" in favor of that of "making present the roots of community and its branches" and of "solidarity, living mutual support and living mutual action." In these designations, he saw the "model of the great community," the "community of communities." Thus, in his work as director of the Mittelstelle, Buber set as the goal of its educational program bringing groups with different worldviews into contact with one another in the experience of community. The great community "is no union of the like-minded," Buber wrote, "but a genuine living together of men of similar or of complementary natures but of differing minds. Community is the overcoming of *otherness* in living unity." This is not a question of some formal and minimal understanding but of an awareness from the other side of the other's real relation to the truth—"inclusion." "What is called for is... a living answering for one another... not effacing the boundaries between the groups, circles, and parties, but communal recognition of the common reality and communal testing of the common responsibility." Vital dissociation—the sickness of the peoples of our age—is only seemingly healed through crowding men together. "Here, nothing can help other than persons from different circles of opinion honestly having to do with one another in a common opening out of a common ground." This is the andragogy (the adult pedagogy) of our educational work. "We live—one must say it again—in a time in which the great dreams, the great hopes of mankind, have one after another been fulfilled—in caricature!" This massive experience Buber saw as caused by the power of fictitious conviction, the uneducated quality of the man of this age. "Opposed to it stands the education that is true to its age and adjusts to it, the education that leads man to a vital connection with his world and enables him to ascend from there to faithfulness, to standing the test, to authenticity, to responsibility, to decision, to realization."

In opposition to the spirit of the time, Buber taught the art of reading slowly, treating the meaning and content of holy text in a spirit that was far from orthodox yet possessed maximum fidelity to letter and word, particularly in sound and rhythm and the choice and repetition of words. Thus, Buber brought to many who had never before been face to face with the Bible the fruit of his years of work in translating the Bible in the way that he and Rosenzweig pioneered. "It was an experience that has lived with them for decades," testified Simon. Buber's most important achievement was changing the Bible for his hearers—from a book to a spoken teaching: "The biblical word cannot be detached from its spokenness. Otherwise it loses its concreteness, its corporality. A command is not a sentence but an address." "My Bible course was received downright enthusiastically." Martin wrote Paula from Lehnitz, where a Teachers Training Week took place in the summer of 1934 under the guidance of Buber and Ernst Simon.

Despite schools suffering from lack of facilities and crowded classrooms of more than fifty children, the system of Jewish education in Nazi Germany succeeded in molding the whole existence of the individual and thereby laid the foundations for the growth of a generation of Jews capable of striking roots in Palestine or in the countries of the Diaspora. Thus, Buber did find support from the Jewish youth of Germany, and his expectations of the Jewish schools were to some extent fulfilled. Commenting on this process, Buber wrote that a generation can receive the teachings only by renewing them, for in a living tradition it is not possible to draw a line between preserving and producing. Only when the older generation time and again stakes its existence on the act of trying to teach, waken, and shape the young, does the holy spark leap across the gap.

The noted German scholar Heinz Politzer tells how he first met Buber in 1934 in Prague, where Buber had come to address a meeting of young Zionist socialists agitated by Hitler's rise to power. Politzer had come for comfort, but instead of the sermon that he anticipated, Buber talked about the *kvutzot,* the village communes established by the pioneers in Palestine, and the relation of utopian socialism to the biblical teachings about social justice. Although there was neither comfort nor religious fervor in Buber's words, Politzer witnessed "the application of a living belief to the immediate needs of an existential situation."

> ...[T]here was... his voice, scooping the speech, as it were, from the depth of an ever present memory, and audibly reflecting the weight of responsibility which supported the speech without straining the words. Listening, I felt questions as well as objections arise in my mind, and I would like to think that they were not of the most obvious kind. Yet during the very time it took them to arise, Buber had already answered them in his speech. Similar experiences were had by several friends in the audience. This kind of rapport between Buber and his listeners has turned many of his lectures into dialogues with persons who were unknown to him, silent dialogue.

The situation of the dwindling minority of German Jews made impossible both active resistance (revolution) and passive resistance (noncooperation), but there existed a third way of seemingly invisible resistance, and this is the one that Buber adopted. It was the resistance of the spirit that took inventory of itself and thus unfolded its own powers in confrontation with the power of the Nazis. Both praying and learning could embody such resistance.

In 1934, Buber was invited to give a speech on the *Weltanschauung* of
the *Chalutz* (pioneer) at the convention of the Hechalutz movement. In his
speech, Buber attacked the Jewish Revisionists. But he did it in a philosophical manner, while hinting that he was also attacking the Nazis. There was a
clerk from the Gestapo at the meeting, who sent a note to the chairman, saying that Buber's speech was political and against the law. The chairman sent
back a note, saying that Buber was only talking philosophy, and the Gestapo
clerk let it pass. But all those present knew that the speech had political
implications and were impressed by Buber's courage in giving it. Aliza Ziv
Or, a teacher living in Jerusalem who was a student of Buber's in Palestine,
testified that, at the time of the Nazis, Buber's writings gave the Jews much
more help in responding to anti-Semitism than the writings of Herzl or
Pinsker: "One might say that he helped us to straighten our back." Benjamin
Uffenheimer, today professor of biblical studies at Tel Aviv University, says
that he first heard Buber's name and started reading his books at the age of
sixteen, when a group of Jewish students from Freiburg, who were traveling
through all the small towns, reached his town and started speaking with the
young people about Zionism. Buber's books, Uffenheimer told Haim
Gordon:

> ...enchanted me, and moved me so deeply that I could never fin-
> ish a book—it aroused such a storm of emotions in me. Buber's
> writings were for me a response to Nazi propaganda. They helped
> me decide to leave Germany and come to Israel—I had no Zionist
> education at home. When I was in *Hachshara* [training camp for
> those coming to Israel] we would read Buber together. We read
> him as a great teacher.

In 1934, Salman Schocken told Hugo Bergmann that he held Buber's presence in Germany to be uncommonly important for the German Jews because
he was the only personality who had authority. "Being a community official
Baeck does not even come into consideration next to Buber."

After Hitler came to power, related Moritz Spitzer, the Jews were seeking for a message like the one that Buber was conveying—that there is a way
back to Judaism—and they flocked to hear him. Buber received many letters
from students, some of which Spitzer answered (especially those written by
women!). Buber was open to people who approached him, but he had to
protect himself because at that time many people wanted to consult him,
including Spitzer himself, when the woman Spitzer had recently separated
himself from came to Heppenheim.

In October 1934, Buber gave a lecture entitled "The Power of the
Spirit," at the Frankfurt Lehrhaus. Later, he repeated this lecture at a large
public gathering in the Berlin Philharmonie. Although the audience was predominantly Jewish, there were also quite a number of non-Jews, including
some two hundred S.S. men, dispersed throughout the hall and especially in

the gallery. In this remarkable setting, Buber delivered an unmistakable challenge to the gods of the time by distinguishing among Christianity, which holds the elemental powers in subjection; paganism, which glorifies them; and Judaism, which sanctifies them. "Spirit is not a late bloom on the tree, Man," Buber stated, "but is what constitutes man." But this is so only if spirit is understood not just as one human faculty among others but as man's totality, "the totality which comprises and integrates all his capacities, powers, qualities, and urges." The spirit, therefore, has three possible relationships to the elemental forces: their glorification, their conquest, or that hallowing through which they are transformed. "Neo-paganism," by which Buber meant Nazism, couples Judaism with Christianity, arguing that both of them deny the great vital powers. Neo-paganism declares these powers holy as they are, thus creating a dualism between a spirit alien to the world and world alien to the spirit. "Blood and soil," the Nazi slogan, with which the Nazi leader Alfred Rosenberg at the Nuremberg trials sought to link Buber, is actually opposed to the true spirit of Judaism, which proclaims: "Blood and soil are hallowed in the promise made to Abraham, because they are bound up with the command to be 'a blessing' (Genesis 12:2). 'Seed' and 'earth' are promised but only in order that... a new people may 'keep the way of the lord to do righteousness and justice' (Genesis 18:19) in his land, and so begin building humanity." The Christian desanctification of hunger, sex, and the will to power left the spirit holy and the world unholy. "Even when Christianity includes natural life in its sacredness, as in the sacrament of marriage, the bodily life of man is not hallowed but merely made subservient to holiness."

Buber closed his speech with a ringing and unmistakable challenge to Nazism. If this spirit of Judaism that hallows the elemental urges "is given a new shape, it will be able to resist even in areas where the barely tamed elemental forces and urges are supreme." As a result of this speech in the presence of the S.S. men, even after the lifting of the ban on Buber's teaching on February 21, 1935, he was no longer allowed to speak in public. When a ban on Buber's speaking at public functions and in closed sessions of Jewish organizations was announced, the Frankfurt Quaker Rudolf Schlosser offered Buber the opportunity to continue his lectures at closed sessions of non-Jewish organizations, and in particular at the meetings of the Quakers, an invitation that Buber repeatedly accepted. In March 1935, another teaching ban was announced, although it was later qualified through the intervention of the Reichsvertretung so that Buber could continue his teaching, even if only on a limited scale.

When Buber published his talks on education in a collected volume, he described the task of Jewish adult education as a task of spiritual resistance to the Nazis: "What was at stake in the work performed under such great difficulties was to oppose Hitler's wish to wear down Jewry; to give the Jews, and especially the young people, unshakable support."

Moritz Spitzer, the editor of the Schocken Almanac, had been connected with Buber since 1919. On May 1, 1932, he moved from Berlin to work with Buber as his personal secretary, and he remained there until late in 1934. Although the Nazis feared Buber in the beginning, they searched his house only once, at which time they received a spirited tongue-lashing from Paula Buber, and the foreign press reported the event. But they searched Spitzer's house in nearby Benz five or six times, trying to find something incriminating on Buber. They even put Spitzer in solitary confinement and later issued a deportation order. He protested to the ministry, and they let him stay until 1939. In 1934, Spitzer, who had been working part-time with Buber for the Schocken Verlag, left Heppenheim and went to Berlin to take over full charge of the publishing firm. Buber was closely connected with the Schocken Verlag, and he always gave Spitzer his advice. At a Jewish gathering at which Buber spoke in 1937, a gentleman arose at the beginning and disclosed, in a somewhat embarrassed tone, that he was an official of the Gestapo, a remarkable occurrence at the very least. He was invited to take a seat and participate in the proceedings. Buber and the other people present spoke for three hours about religious questions. The Gestapo official dutifully made notes, but he also gave Buber the impression that he listened with personal interest. At the conclusion, he said, "We Christians can subscribe to that word for word." After further speech and answer, he seized Buber's right hand with both his hands and said: "Stay well!" On the journey from Leipzig back to Heppenheim, Buber asked Paula about her impression of this man and his parting words. "That was just a euphemism!" she replied. Buber translated this euphemism as "God grant that we do not have to kill you!"

At another time, Buber went walking in Heppenheim. A man stood on the path before him and said, "Na, you Jew!" "Na, you oaf!" Buber retorted, without hesitation. The man was nonplussed. "I admired his presence of mind," comments Werner Kraft, to whom Buber told this story. We can also admire his courage. Many Germans of high standing were, unfortunately, cowardly, Buber remarked to Kraft, and he added, "I do not understand how one can live at all without courage."

On his sixtieth birthday in February 1938, Buber received a great many testimonials from those with whom he had worked in Jewish adult education during those years. The presidium of the Reichsvertretung, Leo Baeck and Otto Hirsch, personally presented Buber in his house in Heppenheim with congratulations in the name of the Jewish community of Germany. One of these, written on parchment and bound in leather, was a statement making Buber an honorary member of the Zionist Union of Germany. "Zionism in Germany in its development and at its height is unthinkable without you," it read. "You have taught us that to be a Zionist, to be a Jew, and to be a human being are for us a single unity.... Your call to awake is equally valid for the Zion of the world and the Zion of the soul.... Three generations of German Zionists are bound to you in love and gratitude."

In 1943, on the occasion of Leo Baeck's seventieth birthday, Buber published in Palestine a tribute titled "In Theresienstadt." "In night hours of a most intensive wakefulness between light sleep and light sleep, it becomes at times uncannily present to me that he is there and I am here. Ah, you who are at ease in Zion and who imagine all the virtues of the nation are concentrated here, cast your glance there toward where those in the innermost vortex stand true!" In conversation with Kraft, Buber asked whether the Nazis would also have sent him, Buber, to Theresienstadt and added, "If they did not, I would have had to go there when Baeck went." "A remarkable question to which I could not respond!" Kraft commented and added, "It sounded like a belated shudder."

Buber wrote to Albert Schweitzer on the occasion of Schweitzer's sixtieth birthday, that for many years the knowledge that Schweitzer existed in this world had strengthened him, and in recent years had consoled him: "I am concerned about the helper, and you have been at all times and in many ways a great helper." Schweitzer responded by telling Buber how often and with what love and respect he had thought of him since they had last met, adding with pathos, "Ah, I had so much to do and was so dreadfully fatigued that I did not exist for acquaintances and friends." Buber received another sad letter in August of the previous year from his father, Carl, who said that if the present uncertain times did not come to an end, there would be nothing left for Martin to do but go to Palestine: "I have grown very old and cannot avoid discomforts. I understand that it cannot be otherwise and do not complain." In April 1935, Carl Buber died. Martin went to Poland for the funeral. He inherited one-third of his father's wealth, a considerable sum. But the government of Poland did not allow the money to leave the country, and it remained in a closed bank account. Replying to Max Brod's letter of consolation, Buber wrote that he had acquired a new feeling of being bound to others "despite all." In the same letter, Buber commented on the collected edition of Kafka that Brod had edited: "It shows how one can live with all honesty on the edge without falling into the abyss. The real refutation of Ivan Karamazov is hidden in it." Leo Baeck also wrote expressing his sadness for the death of Buber's father: "The flowing line between past and present becomes a decisive demarcation when one loses one's father."

The end of 1936 was a period for Buber remarkably like the years immediately preceding his death, and for the same reason: the expectation of an imminent end to his creative and scholarly labors. In this period, he completed book after book, even in the midst of the enormously demanding work for Jewish adult education. Yet he also found time to strengthen the bonds of friendship with many to whom he remained close.

Buber's interest in psychology and psychiatry also persisted during this period, particularly through his friendship with Hans Trüb and Ludwig Binswanger. The impact of Buber on Trüb was shown by the latter's remarkable 1935 essay "Individuation, Guilt, and Decision: Beyond the Boundaries of Psychology." In this essay, Trüb described how he went through a decade-long crisis in which he broke with his personal and doctrinal dependence on the great psychologist Carl Jung in favor of the new insights that his relationship with Buber had given him. The greatest influence on Trüb, according to his own testimony, was not Buber's philosophy but the personal meeting with him, and it was from this meeting that the revolutionary changes in Trüb's method of psychotherapy proceeded. Trüb found himself fully disarmed by the fact that in conversation Buber was not concerned so much about his partner's ideas as about the person himself. In such unreserved interchange, it is simply not possible to pursue any hidden intention, wrote Trüb. One individuality did not triumph over the other, for each remained continually the same. Yet Trüb emerged from this meeting "'renewed for all time,' with my knowledge of the reality of things brought one step nearer to the truth." "What gives Buber his imperishable greatness and makes his life symbolic," declared Trüb, "is that he steps forth as this unique man and talks directly to other persons."

> Martin Buber is for me the symbol of *continually renewed decision*. He does not shut the mystery away in his individuality, but rather from out of the basic ground of the mystery itself he seeks binding with other persons. He lets a soft tone sound and swell in himself and listens for the echo from the other side. Thus he receives the direction to the other and thus in dialogue he finds the other as his partner. And in this meeting he consciously allows all of his individuality to enter... for the sake of the need and the meaning of the world.

In September 1935, Buber responded to Trüb's question of what meaning the principle of "individuation" had for him by suggesting that it is a false term: "We *arise* as individuals, but we become *persons.*" The existential problem of becoming a person, which Kierkegaard had discussed, is dealt with by Jung as a problem of *psychological development*. It does not at all set foot upon the dimension of existence.

Buber always organized a Passover Seder for the entire family until 1938, when his granddaughters were seventeen or eighteen. Buber would read most of the Passover Haggadah, but he would leave out the chauvinistic sections such as the one asking God to pour out his wrath upon non-Jewish nations. Buber would also discuss certain passages that were not clear or that he felt were noteworthy. In those years, Buber did not walk much around the town, except when he went to the post office. He had a habit of reading while he walked, so that people used to say, "Professor Buber thinks even when he walks." The relations between Martin and Paula were very good, but she could be a rather strong-minded woman. Once, when Moritz Spitzer was riding with Martin and Paula on a train, Martin showed Paula a copy of a new book of his he had received that morning. In it, he had written a dedication to her, apparently without her permission. Paula got very angry and scolded him right there, in the train compartment, making him promise that the dedication would not appear in subsequent editions. The fact that Spitzer was present gave Paula no qualms.

In June 1937, Buber wrote Hermann Hesse, saying that he would not speak of what Hesse's lifework meant to them,

> from which we have received joy and consolation, against which our children in their younger years measured and formed themselves, and which we now page through to select the right passages for our young grandchildren. Rather we would say to you something that does not easily let itself be communicated, namely, how fond we both are of you, how often you visit us in our thoughts and speech, how glad we are—despite all—to exist with you in this time, and how we could not do without you in our world.

In 1939, Buber sent a similar message to the German poet Karl Wolfskehl, telling him how good and necessary it was that he exist in just this world with all its cruelty: "It is not the face but just the person that is the ever open gateway to the eternal." Buber held it a duty, indeed, in a time such as that to send wishes to one whom he loved and honored.

In the Schocken Almanac of 1938, Buber published an essay entitled "The Election of Israel," in which he declared that Jewish faith "teaches the mysterious *meeting* of human turning and divine mercy." Israel is elected only when it realizes its election, yet the Rejector can never cease being the Elector. The God who turns away in response to *our* turning away awaits our turning back. This is "the consoling paradox of our existence." In the everdarkening time in which Buber wrote this, these words may have consoled those who later found their way to Palestine and those others whose way led only to the gas chambers.

Prewar Palestine and the Early Years of the State

(1938-1953)

❖

CHAPTER

♦ 12 ♦

Ascent to the Land: Prewar Palestine

(1934-1939)

Even apart from his own negotiations with Hebrew University, an increasingly important part of Buber's attention during his last years in Germany was focused on Palestine. The immigration to Palestine of Hermann Gerson and his *Werkleute* (Work Folk) circle, of Buber's son Rafael, of his daughter Eva and her husband the poet Ludwig Strauss—and of many others to whom Buber was bound—made this inevitable, as well as the fact that much of the work of Jewish adult education in Nazi Germany was oriented toward preparation for settlement in Palestine.

With the rise of the Nazis to power, it became impossible for the Werkleute to believe any longer that they could meaningfully live and work in Germany. In April 1933, they unanimously decided to emigrate to Palestine and to establish a Werkleute kibbutz. By April 1934, they had raised enough money to buy land in Palestine, and, by the end of the month, they set out without waiting to actually complete the purchase of the land.

In a letter to Buber from Palestine, Hermann Gerson announced the stunning news that his wife Lo intended to leave him for another member of the kibbutz. In the first despair over this, Gerson left the kibbutz and considered taking his own life. In his reply, Buber comforted and scolded Gerson at the same time:

> Your letter has disturbed me, I am with you with my whole heart, but I do not merely grieve over you; I am also angry at you. This will not do, not for you! You have sworn yourself to a group of

235

persons. All possible personal disappointments and defeats must be included and anticipated in your oath. Nothing that befalls you may any longer liberate you to dispose of yourself like a private individual. I know what it means when dying becomes easier for one than living, but responsibility is greater than death and life, and you have one that today you cannot yet fully comprehend but about which you know....

As to what is happening between you and Lo, you have spoken most harshly, almost too harshly I feel. You are simply (I do not forget why, but that does not change anything) too bound to your I, and for your sake it is essential that you free yourself from this.... Open yourself to the world.... I embrace you, dear friend, I am vexed and pleased with you as never before.

After four years of intensive discussion, Kibbutz Hazorea decided to join Hashomer Hatzair. In the process of doing so, they adopted a Marxist ideology, looked back on their earlier position as bourgeois rationalization, and dismissed their ideals of religious socialism and community as "ideology" in the Marxist sense: a spiritual disguise for a materialistic interest. Gerson now rejected Buber and his teaching as sentimentally idealistic, unsuited to the harsh realities of kibbutz life. Gerson complained that Buber used overblown words that did not always appear compelling and necessary. "I often ask myself: 'Is that really spoken seriously in the face of the reality such as I have come to know it in the last years?'"

During this same period, the life of another kibbutznik from Germany, Buber's son Rafael, underwent profound changes. Separated for some time from his wife Margarete, who was later interned in a Nazi concentration camp and, despite her communism, in a Soviet slave-labor camp, Rafael remarried and, in 1934, immigrated to Palestine, where he worked in Kvuza Geva, near Ain Harod. There, he worked twelve hours daily in great heat, but, as he wrote to his grandfather, Carl, he was very happy, in fact, downright delighted. Rafael intended to bring over not only Ruth, his second wife, but also Barbara and Judith, the children of his first marriage who had been living with Martin and Paula, as soon as he had successfully made it through this transition. "For you this will undoubtedly mean a great sacrifice," Carl Buber wrote his son Martin of the possibility of Barbara and Judith joining their father, concluding, "But it must be." Despite this, the girls' move did not come to pass. In response to a long letter that Rafael sent his parents in August 1936, Martin wrote:

> Your letter has done your mother and me much good, above all because one constantly sees in it, joyfully, what one already knew, of course: what an excellent fellow you have become. Apart from you personally, this is for me a comforting sign in regard to your whole generation: it has had a difficult time of it and it has also gone seriously astray, but it is still granted to it to find the way.

Buber's son-in-law Ludwig Strauss had a more difficult time getting settled in Palestine. Buber was continually interested in Ludwig Strauss's poetry, but he was also constantly concerned with Strauss's financial situation. He advised him against taking publishing positions that were risky, and he was active again and again in finding him employment. He was not, however, in a position to give the Strauss family much financial aid; therefore, Eva's grandfather, Carl, provided a monthly subvention until his death. When Strauss announced his intention of emigrating to Palestine in 1934, Eva's parents were against it. This might at first seem strange, because Buber and Strauss originally met through their common interest in Zionism. Yet Martin and, even more powerfully, Paula, doubted that Eva would be up to the physical demands of life in Palestine, a view, according to Martin, that Eva herself shared. Strauss's concern was for his two young sons, for whom he foresaw, quite rightly, a dubious future in Nazi Germany. Only with difficulty did Strauss obtain Buber's approval.

In 1936, a similar but even greater conflict erupted between Ludwig and his parents-in-law, one that Ludwig saw as endangering his long friendship with Martin. After a painful inner struggle, Ludwig decided in, January 1936, to join the Werkleute at Kibbutz Hazorea. He informed Buber of this decision in a long letter, to which Buber did not respond until he learned from a letter from his daughter Eva that Ludwig had taken Buber's silence badly. In March, Buber wrote him a long letter in which he explained, in effect, that he had not written him because he could not confirm him in his decision.

> Try to imagine that I have a strong feeling against it that seems to be connected with something basic in me, something that is mysterious even to myself. How shall I translate into argument what can in no way be put into words?... What can I legitimately do other than with a loving but silent heart let you try what you want to!

There could be no question of trying to dissuade him, but Buber added a word of caution to make him particularly aware of a reality that he perhaps had not fully considered even though he wrote about it: "I take you quite seriously as an intellectual and spiritual person—but when you wish to take root in a kibbutz, you must forget to some extent who you are and take upon yourself the law of the commune, that of the full participation of everyone in manual labor. That will be more onerous than you imagine." Though Hermann Gerson and his circle would try to make things lighter for him, as a new member of a kibbutz he himself would not be able to allow that during the first years. This was not a question of the goodwill of the comrades but of an objective statement of facts.

> You will no longer be able to hold fast to the rhythm of activities and the leisure that you as a poet need. If you join a kibbutz, you

must let yourself be swallowed hide and hair by the equal-and-
common, by the command of the earth that needs to be plowed
and only accord yourself the poet's breath when and if the situation of the kibbutz frees you for it.

Buber was by no means as lacking in a concrete and realistic understanding
of the worker's life as the disaffected Gerson liked to think!

Ludwig held his ground, proceeding to join the Werkleute kibbutz and
writing Buber that their views indeed differed. This difference again came
into sharp focus at the time when Ludwig, unable to stay at the kibbutz,
nonetheless sought to remain close to the land. Buber exercised himself to
find literary employment for Ludwig in Jerusalem and, judging from his own
experience, suggested to Ludwig that precisely having to overcome the oner-
ousness of two kinds of intellectual work—editing and his poetry—might be
the breakthrough that he needed for his own creativity. Ludwig replied that
Buber had failed to see the situation from Ludwig's side. Putting it in Buber's
own terminology, Buber failed in "inclusion," or "imagining the real," and he
did so precisely through assuming that his own experience held for Ludwig,
too. Buber himself had no experience of working with his hands and could
not make present to himself what it meant to Ludwig. It was not another
kind of intellectual work that Ludwig needed for a breakthrough to his own
creativity but manual work on the land.

What accounted most for Buber's failure to see through Ludwig's eyes
and experience his side of the situation was the fact that when Paula visited
Palestine in 1937, she concluded that conditions on the land were too hard
for Eva and worked energetically to get the Strausses to relocate in the city.
Despite this, Ludwig moved with Eva and the two boys to the children's village at Ben Shemen, where Ludwig assumed a position. Only a few years
later did he, in fact, take up publishing work in Jerusalem, as Martin had
urged him to do.

In 1936, Buber published the book *Zion as Goal and Task,* in which
such admonitory essays as "And If Not Now, When?" appeared. In his
Foreword to this book, Buber spoke of the sick understanding of the age
that thought it necessary to "howl with the wolves" and expected to attain
the building of Zion through the devious means common to the world. The
genuine Zion can be attained as a goal only if one has brought into the way,
into the task, as much as one can of the goal itself. No way leads anywhere
else than to its own completion. Zion as a goal cannot be reached if the
means to that goal are utterly unlike the end.

In August, Rafael wrote his parents, describing the Arab attacks on his
kibbutz and two other settlements in the Plain of Jezreel and of the measures
taken by the settlers to defend themselves, including placing a special police
guard in the fields that they were cultivating. By day, Rafael worked on the
tractors, but, at special times and at night, he served as a guard for his own

and neighboring communities. In Palestine in general, the Arabs had attacked the Port of Haifa, the petroleum pipelines, and the trains, which had ceased to run between Haifa and Tel Aviv. Although the tension among the Jewish settlers was greatly heightened, the danger at that point did not seem serious. What gave Rafael particular cause for joy was the fact that, although they had to work their fields with weapons in their hands and almost every night had to fight against the Arabs who hid behind the rocks, no feeling of hatred for the Arab peoples existed. There were many men on both sides who wanted peace. His father responded, "Unfortunately, I do not see how in the immediate future the grave conflict can be overcome satisfactorily. What one might propose in this direction would not find a hearing with either of the two parties."

Like Raffi, Ludwig, and Hermann Gerson, Buber was to have uninterrupted years of continual work in Palestine. But like Jacob toiling for Rachel, his was a long period of waiting, frustration, and disappointment before he could arrive there. It took eleven years of negotiations plus years of complications with the Nazis and the British authorities in order for Martin Buber, co-originator of the movement to found the Hebrew University and world-famous scholar and philosopher, to take up residence in Palestine as professor at the Hebrew University! The negotiations with the university began in 1927 and repeatedly bogged down, despite every effort on the part of Judah Magnes, Hugo Bergmann (who became the rector of the university during this period), Gershom Scholem, and many others.

In reply to a letter from Gerson, Buber wrote: "I cannot concern myself at all with whether I shall be 'effective' somewhere. Something like that would go against modesty. When I think of a life in Palestine, I think only about whether I can live and work there, not whether I can have influence there (about which I have never had illusions)." Despite this, Gerson's questions would seem to have been prophetic *in the short run,* though not, it can be said, in the long. Buber then informed Gerson that he had accepted the position, even though serious private difficulties of an economic nature might affect the time of his going. He hoped to go in the beginning of March 1935. But less than a week later, Buber learned that the board of governors of the university had rejected the recommendation. The narrowly clerical clique did not find him Jewish enough, Magnes explained, and the specialists did not find this "gifted writer" scholarly enough!

It is an interesting comment on Buber's supposed lack of scholarship that he was ready and able to take on three different chairs in three quite different departments—history of religions, education, and social philosophy—and that, in fact, the position he finally held was the chair in sociology and the chairmanship of the Department of Sociology at Hebrew University. In a letter congratulating Hugo Bergmann on being selected for the new position of rector of Hebrew University, Buber also commented on the sacrifice entailed in his (Buber's) switching over to a discipline that, although it had for many years been very important to him, was not in the final sense "his" discipline. He would have to spend so much time working up independent points of view and methods that he would have little time for scholarly work in areas with which he was more personally concerned. "I have the feeling that, with two or three exceptions, no one there knows how hard this decision is. Such a feeling had never been able to disturb me all my life; now for the first time I feel a burden laid upon my heart."

Buber was not "driven out" of Nazi Germany. The Nazis did not even want to let Buber emigrate, because he could not pay twenty-five percent of the value of the land that he at that time possessed in Poland. Only after all sorts of intervention did they agree to his spending two-thirds of the year in Palestine on the condition that he live the rest of the time in Germany and maintain his house in Heppenheim in "inhabitable" condition. Paula took this condition so seriously that there really were possessions in the house for people to plunder in the *Kristallnacht* the following November, at which time all of the furnishings of Buber's Heppenheim house were destroyed, together with the three-thousand volumes remaining in his library there. As previously mentioned, the Nazi Office of Finance demanded twenty-seven thousand marks from Buber, which he could not, of course, pay.

A bizarre incident at the very end provided a comic relief to this fantastic affair. The most difficult part of the moving itself was packing Buber's library of twenty thousand volumes into boxes and crates. The officials of the Third Reich were mistrustful and sent a Gestapo official to oversee the packing of the library. The officer stood inactive and bored in the midst of the chaos of books and finally turned to Buber to request a book that he might read. Buber invited his uninvited guest to choose any book that he wished. But the Gestapo official replied, "Herr Professor, I should like to read one of your books." Buber hesitated, because he was not at all clear about which of his books would be appropriate for this minion of the Nazis. Finally, he gave the official of the secret state police the collected edition of his Hasidic books. For three days, the Nazi read with fascination the more than seven-hundred-page book until he had completed the whole thing. He then asked Buber if he might keep the book as a memento. When Buber assented, the Gestapo man asked him for a personal inscription. "I could not very well inscribe it, 'To my dear Gestapo man,'" commented Buber in telling this story. He solved the dilemma by simply writing his name in the book.

The task of packing the books also had an ironic twist. It was there alone that Buber's ideal of the family as a small society with many mutual goals was fulfilled, because the whole family worked together as a team to pack and move those thousands of books. As they worked, Martin would smile and comment, "Here I see a family working together." But he would not help Paula with all the household utensils, sheets, and other things that she had to pack! After they left, Buber agreed not to sell the house in Heppenheim and to return every year for a few months to teach adults in

Frankfurt. In 1937, the family arrived in Israel, where the children were signed up for school and an apartment rented, and then returned to Germany. In the spring of l938, they came back to Israel, and much of the furniture and many of the books were transferred to Israel without the house in Heppenheim being sold. Buber traveled to Europe in the summer of 1939 with the intention of going to Germany. When he reached Switzerland, he was warned not to dare crossing the border into Germany, as a result of which he returned to Israel.

During these years, Buber continued the study of modern Hebrew that he had begun under the tutelage of Abraham Heschel and in which he made such remarkable progress that Heschel could not avoid wondering whether Buber had not sought help elsewhere as well. The difference between the biblical and Talmudic Hebrew, with which Buber was familiar from child-hood, and the modern, especially in its spoken form, was so great that he could envisage the first semester of his teaching as consisting only of reading from written texts and he would not venture on engaging in Hebrew conver-sation except with his close friends.

On their arrival in Palestine, the Bubers found a house in Talbiyeh, one of the sections of the "new" (as opposed to the *really* old) city of Jerusalem. It was in the new sections of Jerusalem that the recent Jewish emigrants from Europe had mostly settled. The transition was a difficult one, but by May they were sufficiently settled so that Paula could get some rest after all the efforts and vexations that she had undergone. Buber described himself as, if not tumbling in the ocean, at any rate still swimming in it with the aid of a life jacket. "Life here suits me well," he wrote Scholem. "I let the winds blow about my ears, and the atmospheric pressure that accompanied me every-where in Europe I am free of—a proof that, despite all, there really is 'com-munity.'" Both Paula and Martin suffered from the heat, which was bearable except during the notorious *hamsin,* or desert wind, the equivalent of the French mistral and the California Santa Ana. This was a dry, oppressive heat that Buber never got used to. In response to Eduard Strauss's question of whether they were "safe," Buber replied that bombs (from the Arab terrorists) went off continually and in all parts of the city, including the part where they lived. "But with *this* unsafeness one can live remarkably well," he added, in an unmistakable contrast with the Nazi nightmare from which he had so recently emerged.

Buber found life in Palestine difficult but more meaningful than in Europe. He experienced an incredible spate of creativity, both as a teacher and as a writer. Although he had written an enormous amount, it was only now that he settled down to being a writer in the real sense of the term. Before this, his writings were more occasional, with the exception of the Bible translation; snake skins that he needed to shed, as he expressed it. There could no longer be a question of German publications, and even Schocken wanted to continue only the Bible translation but did not want to take on anything new of his. However, Buber was already reaching out to Switzerland, England, and America, an effort that bore great fruit in the war years and after.

The good spirit in the Buber household was his wife Paula, who determined the life-style of the house to a large extent, even when she remained somewhat unaware of the outside world. Buber preferred Arabic architecture, and all three of his houses in Jerusalem had high ceilings and thick walls that provided protection from heat and cold. The old European mahogany furniture in his relatively new Oriental house gave the impression of a synthesis of Orient and Occident. In his study, there stood large glass cases in which, next to scholarly works, stood art books with reproductions of the old masters. There were also individual pieces of art from his early years in Florence and a splendid edition of Dante in the original Italian, which Buber loved to read. The study was dominated by a large, foreign desk, on which there was always a large collection of pens but never a typewriter. The desk was covered with books and manuscripts and, above all, the notebooks in which Buber jotted down ideas that occurred to him from wholly different spheres, systematically entered into one notebook or another, according to the topic. Buber did not smoke, but he always had pieces of sugar at hand, which served to increase his energy and concentration when he was fatigued. In his first house in Jerusalem, he kept a complete edition of Goethe near his desk.

Buber always knew exactly where to go in his library to find the precise book or passage that he needed. He was able to read any book in a few hours and remember its contents entirely. Along with books, his study was never lacking in cats, which entered freely through the open window and lay on the sofa in his study. Buber spoke to the cats as if they were human beings, and they minded him in the same way. If he said to a familiar cat, "Ja, what are you doing? Lie down in the corner and don't disturb me," the cat obeyed.

By the time that Buber settled in Palestine, he had already mastered spoken Hebrew. At first, he wrote his lectures in German and then worked them through in Hebrew with the Hebraist Fritz Aronstein, with whom he also studied conversational Hebrew. In Hebrew as in German, his handwriting was almost sheer calligraphy, so that he often gave his written manuscripts to the printer. When he gave his inaugural lecture in the great auditorium in Hebrew University on Mount Scopus overlooking Jerusalem, his Hebrew was so clear and rich that his hearer often did not know where Buber was citing the Bible or Plato and where he was speaking for himself.

Over the next few years, when most of his writing was in Hebrew and not in German, Buber became a unique Hebrew writer. He tried to do in Hebrew what he did in German. The result was somewhat strained because the language was not suited for such a close transposition. He had to create his own Hebrew as he had created his own German. But he expressed himself very forcefully in Hebrew nevertheless. It was not at all true, as his detractors were wont to say, that he could not write a good Hebrew. When Theodor Heuss, the president of the West German Republic, came to Israel in 1960 for a lecture sponsored by Buber, Bergmann, Scholem, and Ernst Simon, David Ben-Gurion, the premier of Israel, approached Buber in the lobby of a hotel where a banquet was being given for Heuss. Ben-Gurion sought to relieve his own embarrassment at feeling constrained to honor a high-minded statesman, who was nonetheless a German, by attacking Buber. "How is it that you have never written your books in Hebrew?" Ben-Gurion demanded. "I have written many in Hebrew," Buber replied, "including *Gog und Magog [For the Sake of Heaven]*, which was published serially in your own party's newspaper!"

In abstract thinking and in poetry and drama, Buber continued to rely on German. Yet in important spheres of his life, such as the Hasidic, he became one of those "men who spontaneously thought in Hebrew." It was a work of the most intense concentration to write book after book for many years in both German and Hebrew. This was especially so because, as Buber himself pointed out, the two languages were not suited to say the same things. Only in his last years did Buber undertake to correct the translations into the Hebrew and into English, and he often succeeded in finding more exact words than the translators. Buber's inaugural lecture "The Demand of the Spirit and Historical Reality" was a remarkable combination of the old— Plato and Isaiah—and the new—the modern science of sociology—the academic and the spiritual, the timeless and the topical. Isaiah had no blueprint of a perfect and just state. He had only a message, a proclamation that was both criticism and demand. He was the powerless prophet who reminded both the people and the government of their *common* responsibility toward God's will for true community. His criticism was directed toward the lives of men in a society in which social inequality and the distinction between the free and the unfree split the community and made it impossible that there could be a true people able to fulfill the demands of the covenant. Isaiah, in his very failure in his historic hour, instilled his vision in the people for all time so that that spirit is still effective in any new situation in which there is once again a chance to translate it into social reality. Just because he received a message for a particular situation rather than a universal and time-less ideal truth, his word still speaks after thousands of years to manifold situations in the history of peoples. He cannot withdraw into Plato's attitude of a calm spectator when he feels himself surrounded by wild beasts. He must speak a message that will be misunderstood, misjudged, misused, yet whose sting will rankle forever.

In an uncanny way, with these words, Buber charted his own lonely and painful course in the years to come in Palestine and the State of Israel. If he might humorously be spoken of as the rebbe of Zehlendorf or Heppenheim while he was in Germany, the image that fits his life in the

Land is not that of the Hasidic leader surrounded by his community but of the lonely prophet bringing the hard word of the hour to deaf ears and hardened hearts. Not that Buber was a biblical prophet, but, rather, a philosopher. He did not have a divinely inspired message, but a teaching. Yet he, too, intended what was decisive for the transformation of social reality— the reality within the society and the reality between society and society. He, too, carried forward the prophetic task of criticism and demand within the present situation. He did not see the future on the basis of inspiration, as did Jeremiah, but of understanding, as did Isaiah.

Buber's inaugural core of lectures as professor of social philosophy at the Hebrew University represents — under the title "What is Man"—a decisive step forward in the development of his philosophical anthropology, his most significant contribution to philosophy and the history of Western thought. Although seemingly an objective survey of the history of philosophy from the standpoint of the problem of the human, there is much in "What Is Man?" that reveals its lived historical grounding in Buber's life.

Even more than in *The Question to the Single One,* Buber stressed the importance of solitude in *The Problem of the Human*—a solitude that he himself was to experience ever more keenly during the remaining years of his life. Only in a strict and inescapable solitude does the human problematic present itself as an independent reality to the thinker. "In the ice of solitude man becomes most inexorably a question to himself," and it is in the most solitary persons that anthropological thought has become fruitful in human history. Buber distinguishes here between epochs of habitation in which the human being lives in the world as in a house or a home and epochs of homelessness in which the person "lives in the world as in an open field and at times does not even have four pegs with which to set up a tent." Strikingly, Buber, who had experienced the threat of the infinity of space and time so keenly at fourteen that he had almost committed suicide, had settled into the macrocosmic security of Cusanus by the time he wrote his doctoral dissertation—only to lose it again and forever with the First World War.

After the discoveries of Copernicus and Einstein, the universe can still be thought—in mathematical theorems—but it can no longer be imaged or lived in as a home. The crisis of Nazism is what Buber is referring to when he speaks here of "a moment in history in which the problematic of human decision makes itself felt to a terrifying degree." A new anthropological dread has arisen: "[T]he question about man's being faces us as never before in all its grandeur and terror—no longer in philosophical attire, but in the nakedness of existence."

To an important extent, *What Is Man?* or *The Problem of the Human* represent Buber's own dialogue with thinkers who exercised a decided influence on him in his youth: Kant, Feuerbach, Kierkegaard, and Nietzsche. Buber's critique of Nietzsche's doctrine of "the will to power" as sick is not surprising in a philosopher who from his earliest writings stressed the necessity of making power responsible to meaningful personal, social, and national *direction*. What is new is what Buber says here about real greatness in the history of the spirit and of culture, as well as in the history of people and of states, for, in this characterization, we can perhaps glimpse something of Buber's insight:

> Greatness is an inner powerfulness, which sometimes grows suddenly and irresistibly to power over men, sometimes exerts its effect quietly and slowly on a company that is quietly and slowly increasing, sometimes, too, seems to have no effect at all, but rests in itself, and sends out beams which will perhaps catch the glance only of some far time.... The great man, whether we comprehend him in the most intense activity of his work or in the restful equipoise of his forces, is powerful, involuntarily and composedly powerful, but he is not avid for power. What he is avid for is the realization of what he has in mind, the incarnation of the spirit.

Only in our time has the anthropological problem reached maturity and come to be treated as an independent philosophical problem, because only in our time has homelessness in the universe been combined with the homelessness caused by the increasing decay of the old organic forms of the direct life between person and person. This double homelessness is intensified by man's lagging behind his works and finding himself dominated by the Frankenstein monsters that he himself has created in the form of machines, the economics of production, and incomprehensible political powers.

In spite of his uniqueness, man can never find, when he plunges to the depth of his life, a being that is whole in itself and as such touches on the absolute. Yet two limited and conditioned beings can experience the absolute in being together in genuine dialogue. In an essential relation, the barriers of self-being are breached and one experiences the mystery of the other being in the mystery of one's own. The two participate in each other's life existentially, not merely psychically. When we do not use the opportunities that come our way to open ourselves to another, we "squander the most precious, irreplaceable and irrecoverable material." Our lives pass us by.

"A *great* relation exists only between real persons. It can be strong as death, because it is stronger than solitude, because it breaches the barriers of a lofty solitude, subdues its strict law, and throws a bridge from self-being to self-being across the abyss of dread of the universe." Buber was not afraid of the nightmare any more than of the solitude or the abyss of dread. But, walking his narrow ridge, he went forth again and again to encounter the other that came to meet him, and this encounter on the narrow ridge was the starting point for his anthropology as for his life. When Buber met Max Scheler a few years after the war, after they had not seen each other for some time, Scheler had, unknown to Buber, passed through a phase of

Catholicism. Scheler surprised Buber by saying, "I have come very near your narrow ridge." If there was anything that Buber did not expect from Scheler, it was that he would forgo the security provided by the sure knowledge of the ground of being. Yet this is exactly what the "narrow ridge" had come to mean to Buber since his own thoughts about ultimate concerns reached in a decisive turning point in the First World War. When he described his standpoint to his friends as the narrow ridge, he meant that he did not rest on the broad upland of a system that includes a series of sure statements about the absolute, but on a narrow, rocky ridge between abysses, where one cannot have the certainty of metaphysical truths yet can have confidence in the genuineness of a meeting that yields the knowing of mutual contact without the certainty of objective knowledge. His second statement to Scheler was "But it is not where you think it is," for, in the meantime, he had understood that Scheler had confused the concept of the narrow ridge with Buber's early philosophy, influenced by German mysticism, in which he held that man is the being through whose existence the Absolute, while remaining eternal truth, can attain reality in time. Scheler's new philosophy of the becoming God was close, in fact, to this concept of the realization of God through man. Scheler, too, had had a shattering experience during the war, one so radically different from Buber's that, instead of bringing him to a meeting with otherness and the recognition of the spirit as existing in the realm of the between, he became convinced of the essential powerlessness of the spirit.

The central position that Freud gives repression and sublimation, their dominant significance for the whole structure of personal and communal life, is not based on the general life of man but on the situation and qualities of the typical man of today who is sick, both in his relation to others and in his very soul. Although the individual must often adapt his or her wishes to the commands of the community in any society, only if the organic community disintegrates from within and mistrust becomes life's basic note does the repression acquire its dominating importance. "The divorce between spirit and instincts is here, as often, the consequence of the divorce between man and man." In earlier ages, man thought with his whole body to the very fingertips; now he thinks only with his brain. For ours is the age of the sick man, cut off from the world and divided into spirits and instincts. Individualism, which understands only a part of man, and collectivism, which understands man only as a part of a larger entity, can neither one give us the wholeness of the human, for they are the conclusion or expression of the same human condition, at different stages. "This condition is characterized by the union of cosmic and social homelessness, dread of the universe and dread of life, resulting in an existential constitution of solitude such as has probably never existed before to the same extent." And collectivism means a more terrible isolation than individualism. The collective whole aims logically and successfully at reducing, neutralizing, devaluating, and desecrating every bond with living beings: "That tender surface of personal life which longs for contact with other life is progressively deadened or desensitized." But the solitude takes vengeance in the depths and rises secretly to a cruelty that will become manifest with the scattering of the illusion. "Modern collectivism is the last barrier raised by man against a meeting with himself."

Buber detected on the horizon, "moving" with the slowness of all events of true human history, "the great disillusionment with modern collectivism" and the recognition of the "between" as the sphere of genuine community, "the real place and bearer of what happens between men." In the most powerful moments of dialogue, where "deep calls unto deep," the narrow ridge, on the far side of the subjective "inner" impression and on this side of the objective "outer" event, is the place where I and Thou meet, the realm of "between." Only from this knowledge of the eternal meeting of the one with the other can we recover the genuine person again and establish genuine community.

> In the deadly crush of an air-raid shelter the glances of two strangers suddenly meet for a second in astonishing and unrelated mutuality.... In the darkened opera-house there can be established between two of the audience, who do not know one another, and who are listening in the same purity and with the same intensity to the music of Mozart, a relation which is scarcely perceptible and yet is one of elemental dialogue.

The true teacher, for Buber, like the true sociologist and the philosophical anthropologist, is not a "value-free" scholar and imparter of knowledge. "Education worthy of the name is essentially education of character," Buber said at the opening of the address he gave to the National Conference of Jewish Teachers in Palestine at Tel Aviv in 1939. Today, host upon host of people have everywhere sunk into the slavery of collectives, and each collective is the supreme authority for its own slaves. This is true not only of the totalitarian countries but also for the parties and partylike groups in the so-called democracies. No reference to absolute values can rescue a person from such slavery. Only that pain experienced in the hours of utter solitude can lead to a rescue of one's real personal self from the enslavement of collectivism. In this connection, Buber referred for the first time to what he later called the "eclipse of God": "To keep the pain awake, to waken the desire— that is the first task of everyone who regrets the obscuring of eternity. It is also the first task of the genuine educator in our time." The way that he or she can fulfill this task is, again, not to aim at, but to have as a final goal, the education of great character, for only through pointing to the great character can the educator awaken or keep alive the pain in the individual pupil, who becomes aware of the contrast between what she is and what she might be. The "great character" forms the link between the "great person" and the "great relationship" as Buber treated them in *What Is Man?* The great character responds with the whole of her or his being to the uniqueness of every situation that challenges her or him as an active person. The great character is thus one who lives the life of dialogue in the face of the utter newness of every moment:

> In spite of all similarities every living situation has, like a newborn child, a new face, that has never been before and will never come again. It demands of you a reaction which cannot be prepared beforehand. It demands nothing of what is past. It demands presence, responsibility; it demands you.

"No responsible person remains a stranger to norms," but the norms do not operate through maxim or habit but through those commands that remain latent until they reveal themselves to us concretely. As illustration, Buber told of a man whose heart was struck by the lightning flash of "Thou shalt not steal" in the very moment when he was moved by a very different desire from that of stealing, and whose heart was so struck by it that he not only abandoned doing what he wanted to do, but with the whole force of his passion did the very opposite. *"I* was that man," Buber told me, "only the command to me was not, 'Thou shalt not steal,' but 'Thou shalt not kill'!'" "I was not about to kill anyone," he added; yet, in this prohibition, Buber discovered the positive direction that he had to take. In a similar way, the prohibition of Buber's conscience against telling the teacher about the sexual pantomime of his schoolfellows in his childhood experience described in "The Two Boys" contained a direction, a "yes," that made him put aside the teacher's maxim "A good boy is one who helps *us"* in favor of the command of the situation that addressed him as a unique *Thou.* Maxims, in contrast, command only the third person, the each and the none.

The teacher can awaken in young persons the courage to shoulder life again by bringing before them the image of a great character who denies no answer to life and the world, but accepts responsibility for everything essential that he or she meets. Today the great characters are still "enemies of the people," whose love for society includes the desire to raise it to a higher level. "Tomorrow they will be the architects of a new unity of mankind," born from the longing for personal unity. This is a reciprocal process. A great and full relationship can exist only between whole and responsible persons, but they become this precisely through the life of dialogue.

Buber criticized the Hebrew University chiefly because it did not fulfill the original aim of being a center for adult education, and he repeated this criticism and demand again and again after he came to Palestine. But when he himself taught at the Hebrew University, he was a professor and not in very close contact with his students. Distinguished students, like Samuel Eisenstadt, have attested to the reality of dialogue that Buber evoked in the classroom. Buber raised issues and got the students to ask questions, but he was too "charitable" to students who would break in, Eisenstadt reported. "He was a great stage actor in the best sense of the word. He could listen within the framework of the drama he was directing." Eisenstadt also greatly admired Buber's knowledge of the whole range of modern sociology, in which he had read everything important, including what did not particularly interest him. "He could read three hundred to four hundred pages in an hour, could do in an afternoon what it would take an ordinary person a week to read." According to Eisenstadt, who later succeeded Buber as chairman of the Sociology Department at the Hebrew University, the atmosphere in Buber's class was open and informal. Buber taught in a well-organized manner and encouraged discussion and dialogue, both of great importance in his seminars. Buber, however, had too much patience and allowed people to take up class time with foolish questions. Asked whether Buber educated his students' character, Eisenstadt replied that he did not do so formally. "But he had an image that educated... whoever was impressed by it."

Another student of Buber, Joseph Ben Dov, who is today a professor at the Hebrew University, was impressed by Buber as a person—by his politeness and his attempts to relate personally to his students. Although Buber gave lectures and taught seminars as other teachers did, he gave the impression of presence. "He was less of an intellectual than other teachers and more of an educator." On rare occasions, Buber would mention personal encounters, such as an argument he once had with Max Weber. Occasionally, however, the students felt that Buber was behaving like a Polish nobleman:

> Buber always met with pupils at his home, which was what most teachers did at that time. His attitude toward students was good, but he kept his distance. Worse, Buber had very little sensitivity to the fact that he was very affluent while most of his students were poor. He would sit behind his desk and every so often take a piece of chocolate from his drawer and pop it into his mouth without ever offering a piece to the student, who, being poor, could not afford to spend money on chocolate.

Ben Dov also felt that Buber was less a sociologist in the technical sense than one who used sociological writings to express himself.

Yonina Talmon, who wrote her Ph.D. dissertation under Buber, was very vehement about how insensitive Martin and Paula were. At times, she would come to Buber for a morning meeting after spending the entire night on guard duty at the Hebrew University. During the meeting, Paula would enter and bring Martin coffee and cake, yet neither of them would offer Yonina anything. Another graduate student of sociology, who later became a professor of sociology before her early death, turned bitterly against Buber and accused him of not living his own teaching of dialogue.

Aliza Ziv Or, a teacher living in Jerusalem, reports that although students admired Buber's wealth of knowledge and acknowledged the greatness of such works as *I and Thou,* they were put off by his style and personality and, in her case at least, by how he expressed his Judaism. Once, she even felt uncomfortable about having Buber's books in her house and gave them all away. "Now I read his books with less anger, I seem to forgive him. I also came to his eightieth birthday party." Buber wanted to touch deep levels and to arouse his students, but he did not reach her. When he taught a class on Isaiah's vision, the students argued with him. Buber answered every question and made a point of honoring everyone there, even if what they said was stupid. All of this led to the lesson losing a clear sense of direction. The students' excitement was not about learning but about having someone to attack. In her conclusion, Aliza Ziv Or looks back from a sad, chastened, and mature point of view:

> I believe that we were rather unfair to him. He wanted to be close to us, and we rejected him because he seemed to touch points that were tender, and we wanted to be strong and tough. To some extent his greatness can perhaps be seen in the strong responses that he aroused. Yes, at times we acted like pigs. We were not honest enough to learn to be against Buber, so we found ways of evading him and his thoughts.

Ernst Simon said of Buber that he was not successful because he taught without a method. The distinguished biblical scholar Benjamin Uffenheimer was also not overly impressed by Buber as a teacher. Buber did not mind being attacked, even by a communist woman, in response to whose attacks Buber would smile, stroke his beard, try to understand her, and relate her arguments to what appeared in the text. Buber never got angry, and his seminars were more lively than those of some of his colleagues, which were "downright boring," testifies Uffenheimer.

> In those days... it was normal for there to be a distance between teacher and student. Most of us came from Europe, where distance between student and teacher was natural.... Buber contributed a great deal to the curriculum of the Hebrew University by teaching those philosophers who were central to German sociology, something that is hardly taught now when experimental sociology reigns.

Aside from Buber's natural aristocracy, to which Arnold Zweig referred when Buber was fifty, the lack of intimacy with his students arose, most likely, less from any incapacity (because Buber had had many close relationships throughout his life, including those with younger disciples) than from a residue of the European conception of what it meant to be a professor, something shared by most of his colleagues at the Hebrew University. When Walter Goldstein remarked to Buber in 1942 that he saw something tragic in the life of Hermann Cohen, Buber smiled and said, "What do you expect? The man was for forty years a professor!"

When the Buber family moved to Palestine, Paula was cut off from all her previous connections and literary life. Her German did not help her much in Palestine. She attempted to learn Hebrew, but, not being as good at languages as Martin, she failed, and that led to many frustrations. Being in charge of the house in Palestine was much more difficult. She had fewer servants than in Germany, and doing anything in Palestine demanded more of her time. She was greatly interested in life and in stories arising from life, but, living in Palestine, she was limited in her contacts to people who came from Germany or knew German. Martin tried to encourage her. In particular, he encouraged her to continue her own writing, which she did. This made him very happy. He suggested changes in her novel and helped her get it ready for publication.

Paula in turn helped Martin in every way, but at times she would speak out against him. Once, when Martin scolded Judith for not finishing her master's thesis, Paula remonstrated, "And don't you remember that when you were in the same situation, you only read English novels?!" Paula was interested in her neighbors in Palestine, but hardly ever went out of her house. Barbara and Judith would take her shopping at times but, after she came to Palestine, she never went anywhere alone.

In Palestine, Martin presided at the family Seder. He would read the entire Hagaddah, interpret sections of it, and add stories. Then he would hide the Afikoman (the piece of matzos for which children search) in a dramatic way. At times, he told stories that were linked to the exodus from Egypt. At other times, he would read from Hasidic tales. Eventually, however, he discovered that Barbara and Judith were unhappy with his religious approach. From that time on, he canceled the family Seder because he did not want to impose his views on his grandchildren.

In Palestine, Buber's grandsons Emmanuel and Martin (Mischa) lived close to Martin and Paula and often visited them. They were comfortable in their house and would consult with Buber about their problems. When Emmanuel decided to become an arts and crafts teacher, Buber encouraged him to do that. Buber told his grandson of his regret that he had not learned to work with his hands when he was young. Later, he would ask Emmanuel if he was happy with his marriage and would look deep into his eyes to see if the answer was sincere. His grandchildren found it difficult to lie to him, for they saw him as one who had the power of penetrating one's soul as no ordinary person could. When Emmanuel would come to Buber for advice, Emmanuel was always a bit tense until he heard what Buber had to say. Emmanuel felt the radiance of Buber's personality and felt secure because he had such a grandfather. When he had problems in school, he would come to Buber without setting up a meeting in advance, and Buber would always put aside his work and see him. At times, he would find Buber sunk in thought, but, after a while, it would pass and Buber would be fully present to him. He never said to Emmanuel that he had no time to see him. Rather, he would ask him, "How are you?" and when Emmanuel would answer, "Fine, thank you," he would say, "No, I really want to know how you are. Tell me in detail." Then they would talk at length.

Emmanuel experienced Paula as a very demanding woman who often voiced her criticism because she wanted to get things done. If Martin ever demanded something from Emmanuel, it was because Paula influenced him to do so or because he wanted to support her demands. Paula was a very strong person. She admired Martin, but she was often aggressive and impulsive, with a sharp tongue that she used against him and everyone else. Martin was more of an expressive person, testifies Emmanuel, while Paula was more of an instrumental person.

When Hermann Gerson decided to undergo psychoanalytic treatment, Buber was very unhappy with his decision and reminded him of the German legend wherein a person took out someone's living heart and replaced it with a heart of stone (an image Buber later used in discussing the case of Melanie). Gerson sees Buber's response as responsible for their relations cooling until they finally broke off. According to Gerson, Buber did not understand what was essential to Freud's thinking—that people have desires—an attribution that seems strange for a man who was concerned all of his life about giving direction to the "evil urge." Buber, on his part, was unhappy that Gerson saw what he wrote him as negative. He also insisted that he did not write him as a "teacher" to a "pupil." Buber added, somewhat humorously, that although he was able to teach his university seminar something from Marx and from Sorel (whom they could understand only out of the reality of the *tradition*), he could not work up Freud for his lectures but might write something about him.

When Gerson visited Buber in Jerusalem after their relations had been renewed, Buber asked Gerson how he had influenced life in Kibbutz Hazorea, Gerson answered, "Consideration for the individual." They learned from Buber that the kibbutz must be considerate toward its individual members, and they conveyed this important message to the coming generation. Unlike other kibbutzim, they strove to leave a private realm around each individual where kibbutz interest and gossip did not enter. They left the individual room to live.

Not long after Buber's long-delayed Aliyah, Buber's European-based religious socialism and the American Social Gospel from which Magnes drew his inspiration were joined in the foundation of a religious society in Jerusalem in 1939 called *Ha-'Ol* (the Yoke, or the Bond). Taking their name from the rabbinic midrash, which enjoins us to take upon ourselves the Yoke of the Kingdom of Heaven and act toward one another in loving kindness, the society put forward responsibility to mankind in general and the life of Israel in particular—a commitment to social action and practical political work that rejected any attempt to separate the dominions. Like Rosenzweig, both Magnes and Buber affirmed *faith* in contradistinction to religion. In a discussion of messianic politics in July 1939, Buber emphatically rejected the proposition that politics per se could effect the redemption. The most we can do is to *prepare* the way for redemption, and even here we are never sure which of our deeds may *have* messianic significance. Redemption itself is a matter of God's grace, but it also depends on us.

Buber came to Palestine in a time of great unrest. For two years, there had been continual attacks by Arab terrorists on out-of-the-way Jewish settlements, on travelers in autos and trains, and on solitary walkers. The press carried almost daily accounts of bloodletting. Whereas Haganah, the organization of Jewish self-defense, continued to follow its policy of self-restraint and refused to carry out reprisals on those who did not take part in the terror, the radical Jewish groups, such as the Stern Gang and the Irgun Zvai Le'umi, who stood outside the discipline of the Haganah, believed it necessary to fight terror with terror.

Buber raised his voice against this policy in the first article that he published in Palestine, "Against Betrayal" (July 1938). "The confusion in the country has intensified to an unbearable degree," Buber began. Buber called on his fellow Jews in Palestine to unite against the internal treason of those who did not want to obey the authorities of the Jewish settlement and attacked both British and Arabs.

> Factions which cannot reach power as long as confidence exists stimulate this betrayal in order to win through it. We should have supported those among the Arab population with good intentions, thus isolating the Arab terrorists. If blind violence replaces the fulfillment of justice on which the Zionist movement was built, contradiction, the wretched daughter of exile, will aspire to the status of the ruling law of Zion.

By "blind" violence," Buber meant the Jewish terrorists' professed principle of killing any Arab, no matter how innocent, in reprisal for the murder of Jews by Arab terrorists. "In the life of our nation there has never been an hour of affliction or of temptation like the present one."

In the same month, Buber joined the League for Human Rights in its appeal against the death sentence for Arab terrorists. They were particularly grateful for Buber's support, because they suddenly found themselves accused of being a "small band of traitorous Jews." In August, he wrote Hans Trüb, "Here all is more frightening, confused, crueler, and more innocent than one could imagine.... What one can experience here of human reality and of the indwelling [of God] 'in the midst of our uncleanness' [Isaiah] can perhaps be experienced nowhere else."

In Nazi Germany, Buber had awakened the Jews to faithfulness to Jewish peoplehood. In the reverse situation in Palestine, where the politically overheated atmosphere favored a fanatical nationalism, he tried to awaken them to humanity. Nowhere is this walking of the narrow ridge clearer than in Buber's famous letter to Gandhi, in which, in order to remain faithful to his witness to the covenant of peace *and* to Zionism, Buber took to task the man he admired more than any living person in public life.

In the November 26, 1938, issue of his paper *Harijan*—the same issue in which he counseled the Jews of Germany to use *satyagraha,* nonviolent resistance, against the Nazis—Gandhi said that Palestine belonged to the Arabs and that it was therefore "wrong and inhuman to impose the Jews on the Arabs." Declaring sympathy with the Jews as "the untouchables of Christianity," Gandhi set in opposition "the requirements of justice" and the Jewish cry for a national home, which "does not much appeal to me." "Why should they not, like other peoples of the earth, make that country their home where they are born and where they earn their livelihood? What is going on in Palestine today cannot be justified by any moral code of conduct," Gandhi pronounced in a curiously one-sided assessment of the situation on the part of the great exponent of a nonviolent direct action that meets the opponent with love and understanding. The nobler course, Gandhi suggested, with equally remarkable naiveté considering the situation of the Jews at that very moment, "would be to insist on a just treatment of the Jews wherever they are born and bred." "Surely it would be a crime against humanity to reduce the proud Arabs so that Palestine can be restored to the Jews partly or wholly as their national home." Gandhi imagined that as a consequence the Jews might be forced out of other parts of the world where they were settled and suggested that "this cry for the National Home affords a plausible justification for the German expulsion of the Jews." "The Palestine of the biblical conception is not a geographical tract," he added, "it is in their hearts." If the Jews must look to the geographical Palestine, they should realize, as Buber himself had often said, that "it is wrong to enter it under the shadow of the British gun." But Gandhi proposed that they should win Arab hearts and goodwill and the sympathy of world opinion by offering themselves to be shot or thrown into the Dead Sea without raising a finger against the Arabs. "There are hundreds of ways of reasoning with the Arabs, if the Jews will only discard the help of the British bayonet. As it is, they are co-sharers with the British in despoiling a people who have done no wrong to them."

In April 1939, "The Yoke," or "The Bond," published, as the first of a proposed series of pamphlets, two letters to Gandhi from Martin Buber and Judah L. Magnes, together with Gandhi's statement from *Harijan.* Buber began with "Mahatma," the expression of a reverence that took birth in Buber when he read Gandhi's statement in 1922 that "our nonviolence is skin-deep.... due merely to our helplessness." This reverence remained so great in Buber that even Gandhi's injustice to the Jews in Palestine could not destroy it. For this reason, Buber's reply to Gandhi is a deeply personal response as well as a political action, one written slowly, with repeated pauses, days sometimes elapsing between short paragraphs:

> Day and night I took myself to task, searching whether I had not
> in any one point overstepped the measure of self-preservation
> allotted and even prescribed by God to a human community, and
> whether I had not fallen into the grievous error of collective ego-
> ism. Friends and my own conscience have helped to keep me
> straight whenever that danger threatened.

In his reply, Buber pointed out that the 150,000 Indians in South Africa were
nourished by the more than 200 million in India, and he asked Gandhi
whether "the India of the Vedic conception is not a geographical tract but a
symbol in your hearts?" A land is in men's hearts because it is in the world; it
is a symbol because it is a reality. A mere idea cannot be holy, but a piece of
earth can. Dispersion is bearable, even purposeful, if somewhere there is an
ingathering, a growing home center where there is the life of a community
that dares to live today because it hopes to live tomorrow. Otherwise, dispersion becomes dismemberment. But, as in *The Kingship of God* and later in
Israel and Palestine, Buber insisted on the indissoluble unity of people, land,
and task.

> Decisive for us is not the promise of the Land—but the command,
> the fulfillment of which is bound up with the Land, with the exis-
> tence of a free Jewish community in this country. For the Bible
> tells us, and our inmost knowledge testifies to it, that once, more
> than three thousand years ago, our entry into this Land was with
> the consciousness of a mission from above to set up a just way of
> life through the generations of our people, such a way of life as
> can be realized not by individuals in the sphere of their private
> existence but only by a nation in the establishment of its society. I
> speak only for those who feel themselves entrusted with the com-
> mission of fulfilling the command of justice delivered to the Israel
> of the Bible.

In order to clarify his own position to Gandhi in the Arab-Jewish conflict,
Buber told him that he belonged to "a group of people who, from the time
when Britain conquered Palestine, have not ceased to strive for the concluding of genuine peace between Jew and Arab." In his explanation of what he
meant by this statement, Buber gave classic expression to the life of dialogue, the "community of otherness," and to the encounter on the narrow
ridge that eschews all either/ors in favor of holding the tension of both
points of view in any conflict:

> By a genuine peace we inferred... that both peoples should
> together develop the Land without the one imposing its will on
> the other.... Two vital claims are opposed to each other, two
> claims of a different nature and a different origin, which cannot
> be pitted one against the other and between which no objective

decision can be made as to which is just or unjust. We considered... it our duty to understand and to honour the claim which is opposed to ours and to endeavor to reconcile both claims. We cannot renounce the Jewish claim; something even higher than the life of our people is bound up with the Land, namely the work which is their divine mission.... Seeing that such love and such faith are surely present also on the other side, a union in the common service of the Land must be within the range of the possible. Where there is faith and love, a solution may be found even to what appears to be a tragic contradiction.

A note that already appeared in *The Question to the Single One* and that appeared increasingly in Buber's thought and utterances in the years to come was the "politicization" that exaggerates the real needs of people into claims of principle and political watchwords. The serpent of politics "conquers not only the spirit but also life." That was certainly Buber's own experience and fate in the highly charged political atmosphere of Palestine, and later, Israel, from his immigration there in 1938 to his death in 1965. Yet this never deterred him from holding to the "lived concrete" as much as possible in any given situation. Though he had protested from the beginning against the tie between Zionism and British imperialism implicit in the Balfour Declaration, he pointed out to Gandhi that the Jews began to settle in Palestine anew thirty-five years before the "shadow of the British gun" was cast upon it and that this shadow appeared and remained to guard British interests and not Jewish ones.

"We have not proclaimed, as you do and as did Jesus, the son of our people, the teaching of nonviolence," Buber added.

We believe that a man must sometimes use force to save himself or, even more, his children. But from time immemorial we have proclaimed the teaching of justice and peace; we have taught and we have learned that peace is the aim of the world and that justice is the way to attain it.... No one who counts himself in the ranks of Israel can desire to use force.

Although Buber would not have been among the crucifiers of Jesus, he would also not have been among the supporters of his absolute nonviolence. "I am forced to withstand the evil in the world just as the evil within myself," and although he strove not to have to do so by force, if there were no other way of preventing the evil destroying the good, he trusted that he would "use force and give myself up into God's hands." In an echo of his 1926 poem "Power and Love," Buber confessed: "We should be able even to fight for justice—but to fight lovingly."

✦ 13 ✦

The Second World War

———

(1939-1945)

Buber experienced the Second World War with all its drama and tragedy in the relative isolation of Palestine. The Nazi invasion of Poland in 1939 resulted in the final loss of Buber's Polish possessions. This made it impossible for him to repay in the foreseeable future a loan from Hans Trüb that had enabled him to sell his house in Heppenheim. In the face of this situation, Buber fell into a depression that for a long time prevented him from writing personal letters. Although outer circumstances occasioned the depression, by Buber's own testimony to Trüb, it reached deep within. His not being able to take care of his debt to Trüb was "a burden that not only bowed the neck but also choked the throat." "You must try to imagine," Buber wrote Trüb, in a play on the story of Jonah, "that for seven months I have lain in the belly of the monster and only just now have been spewed forth onto land."

While Ludwig Strauss was working at Ben Shemen Youth Village, Buber came and organized a joint Bar Mitzvah for his grandson and other boys his age. Buber wrote Ludwig that he would gladly give the Bar Mitzvah speech, not only for the sake of his grandson but also because it would be an opportunity to present the concept of *Mitzvah* quite simply and clearly, without ballast. In October 1939, when the news came that Ludwig's sister had killed herself, Buber wrote him that he sensed directly what that meant to him and knew that one could no longer offer consolation, only sympathy, "and that I do with my whole soul, with its poor knowing about our living and dying, and with my whole friendship for you." Ludwig replied that his sister's suicide was no "free death," as the Germans call voluntarily taking one's own life. His sister had been sick for some time and tormented to the point of despair by maddening anxieties and guilt feelings.

At various times, Buber's friends would come to his house for coffee. Among them was Shmuel Agnon. Buber and Agnon would tell each other stories and discuss them. But also, inevitably in Palestine, there would be much discussion of politics. Judith and Barbara would discuss politics with their grandfather and at times got very excited, whereas Buber himself never became excited. When Barbara and Judith started believing in Marxism in the 1940s, Buber called both of them to his study and explained why their approaches were wrong, especially their belief in the good emanating from what was being done in the USSR. In support of his view, Buber read to them impressions of many persons who had visited the Soviet Union. At the end of the eleventh grade, Judith received a low grade in Arabic. She decided not to make up the grade during the summer vacation and went to work at Kibbutz Dalia. After a month of clearing the fields of rocks, she received a letter from her grandfather, as a result of which she came home to study. Later, Judith became a student at the Hebrew University, where she took some courses from her grandfather, who would discuss with her the papers that she had submitted.

As Barbara and Judith grew up, they began to see that Martin's relations with them, and even more so, with their children, were much more spontaneous than with his son, Raphael, and his daughter, Eva. From her grandfather, Judith learned the importance of acquisition as a value—"something with which I'm not especially pleased."

> "You may be right in wanting to contribute to political developments in Israel," Buber argued, "but you can contribute much more if you first become a somebody. For instance, get an M.A. in some field...." Being somebody for Buber was not necessarily confined to the academic realm. My sister [Barbara] was a painter. She did not finish high school, but went to study at Bezalel Art School. Buber supported her: "She will be a somebody in the realm of arts."

Eva meanwhile audited some courses in psychology at the Hebrew University and began working with problem children under the guidance of her psychology professor. This was a vocation that she continued until she retired. When Eva's son Emmanuel was in basic training in the British army, he encountered some problems that he shared with his grandfather. Buber listened and suggested how he should behave with people. He told him not to be hurt by the behavior of some of his commanders, because they were merely doing their job. In general, he would not tell others how to respond, but only how he would respond. This way of listening gave Emmanuel a feeling of security, a feeling that there was a solution to his problem.

In February 1940, Buber wrote his old friend Eduard Strauss, who was living in America, complaining about how they had drifted apart. Buber had been unable to write to Strauss since September because he had been robbed of the land that he possessed, and he could not as a result pay any of his friends what he owed them. That gnawed at him and made it difficult for him to speak. In November 1941, Buber again complained in a letter to Strauss that the external connection between them had been interrupted and laid the guilt on himself, who had for long been unable to write his friends who lived outside of Palestine because of a heavy burden that he felt. Strauss's report of his illness had broken through this, prompting the letter.

Joseph Bentwich, principal of a high school in Israel and editor of a journal on contemporary Judaism, first met Buber during the Second World War. From 1941 to 1945, a group for the study of religion met once a month at Bentwich's home in Jerusalem in order to discuss religious texts. Buber frequently came to their meetings, but when the group adopted a formal constitution indicating that members of the group should be people who lived their faith through *Mitzvot*, Ernst Simon pointed out that Buber probably would refuse to join because he did not observe the commands of the Jewish law. Bentwich suggested that Buber come and participate without being a formal member of the group, and that is what happened. The group also included Julius Gutmann and Cecil Roth, both well-known professors of philosophy.

Buber's approach to dialogue could sometimes be humorous. Once, when Buber responded to a question in theology in a way that Shalom Ben Chorin did not understand, Buber rejoined, "All right, now I'll answer you in non-Buberian language!" When someone did not understand him, Buber had great patience. But he had no patience at all for intellectuals who paraded high-flown language in front of him. When a worker or a housewife did not understand him, then he took pains to help them understand.

Avraham Tsivion, an educator who lived in Jerusalem and came to see Buber, once asked him for a formula that would ensure that he did not fail when he went to England on a mission to educate young Zionists in the Diaspora.

> A smile spread on Buber's face, and he spoke almost in a whisper: "You're a young man and you want a formula? Let me tell you something. When I was young I liked to be in touch with great people, and to know their views on two matters: truth and religion. But that was worthless and faded like smoke. In those days I often used to walk along Unter den Linden in Berlin with my friend Albert Einstein…. 'Einstein, my friend, what are you looking for in your work?' I asked him. Einstein answered, 'Here is the face of the cosmos. I want to cover it with transparent paper and draw on that paper the coordinates of the universe. I lack only one thing, and that is what I am seeking: the formula.'" Buber sat up in his chair and continued with his eyes wide open:

"I answered him, You're asking for too much, Einstein,' and in my heart I thought 'Chutzpah.'"... Finally Buber turned to me and said, "You want a formula? What a person can do in this world is to struggle to move it just one inch in the right direction, and if he succeeds, he's done much. I wish you success."

In November 1942, Buber was very upset by the sickness of his half sister, who was brought, more dead than alive, from Teheran to the Hadassah Hospital in Jerusalem. Seeing her after all those years greatly excited Buber. The following month, he was forced to move from his dwelling in Talbiyeh, which belonged to a consulate. Not only was the task of packing the more than twenty thousand books an overwhelming one for Buber, but there was also the difficult problem of where to move. Paula preferred the far-lying hill of Dir Abu Tor. The fact that this was a purely Arab neighborhood at the time did not disturb Buber, but he would have preferred a house somewhat less far removed from the university. At the end of the year, the Bubers settled on a place in Dir Abu Tor known as the house of Jussuf Wahab Dajani. Dir Abu Tor is a hill exactly opposite Mount Moriah, divided from it only by the valley of Kidron. The house has old-fashioned timbering and large rooms with high ceilings, and it is situated high up on the hill, visible from afar. Especially from the roof, it has a fantastic view of the Temple Square, which is almost never the case in new Jerusalem. The El Aksa Mosque is also visible, and even the Dome of Rocks above the stone on which Abraham is supposed to have been ready to sacrifice his son Isaac until the divine command prohibited it. The view from the study was "truly worthy of a Martin Buber," as Walter Goldstein put it. This house was the most beautiful and spacious, if also the most old-fashioned, in which Buber lived in Jerusalem.

The Hebrew poet Lea Goldberg, who translated much of Dostoevsky into Hebrew, tells of how she met Paula Buber in this house in Dir Abu Tor. She had already come to know Eva and Ludwig Strauss at Ben Shemen, where she came to lecture, and she spent three months with the Strausses every summer in Beit Hakerem, a kibbutz on the northern side of Galilee that is a center for music and the arts. But she came to know Eva's father through her book on the Russian writer Nikolai Gogol. Buber was particularly interested in Gogol's pilgrimage to Jerusalem, and she had translated a chapter from the Gogol book for him. After this, he invited her to visit him in his house on a hot summer day. When she arrived, she had the impression that Paula Buber was not particularly happy about her presence. "She was very suspicious of Buber's friends," Professor Goldberg commented, in addition to which she was tired and did not like all the people who came to see him. To Lea Goldberg she was not at all friendly and, in fact, was highly reserved. Buber spoke of the view from their window and said to Paula, "Please open the door to show Miss Goldberg the view." "No," Paula replied, "it is too much bother." Then she remarked to Goldberg, in the presence of

Eva and Ludwig, about how large the house was. "My children think I should have a smaller one." To this, Goldberg responded, "I cannot imagine you in a smaller house." At that, Paula suddenly became most friendly and proceeded to open the window and show her the view. This friendship lasted until the end of Paula's life. "Paula Buber was a very difficult, unbalanced person," Lea Goldberg has said of her friend. "She was very hard on her children and her grandchildren. I used to call her Maria Theresa."

Martin Buber had a special relationship to the landscapes of Jerusalem, especially the Old City. The new one, he said to Eugenia* and me, "is only a suburb." Although he once referred to it as asymmetrical, he called the Temple Square the finest square that he knew: "Rome cannot compare to it."

Although Buber had written a great deal in the first half of his life, it was only in the second half that he settled down and became an ordered and disciplined writer. In 1942, the original, Hebrew, edition of his important book *Prophetic Faith* appeared, which carries forward the study of the origins of messianism of *The Kingship of God* and *The Anointed.* He also worked at that time on the Hebrew originals of *Israel and Palestine, Paths in Utopia,* and *The Origin and Meaning of Hasidism.*

In September 1941, Buber appealed to Thomas Mann, the great German writer who, as a representative of the free and liberal Germany, immigrated to Switzerland in 1933 and to the United States in 1939. Mann, at this time, was traveling around the United States, giving a talk entitled "The Coming Victory of Democracy." Buber wrote, "I am turning to you with an extraordinary request, unique in my life, as the bearer of the true German spirit in the present world." The request was to help find a publisher for Paula's novel *Muckensturm*, which Buber characterized as extraordinarily, comprehensive. "In this swarm of gnats the great community with its pathology is mirrored. This work, in which the pain and rebellion of a strongly rooted German has found expression, directly concerns the present world, but it is also an historical novel which preserves the meaningful connection of a place and an hour." As it turned out, the novel was not published until 1951 and then only in Germany.

One of the more difficult friendships that Buber carried on in Palestine was that with Walter Goldstein, a German-writing philosopher who eventually wrote several volumes on Buber's thought as well as one on Buber and Sartre. In March 1943, Buber took Goldstein to task for wishing to approach his work and thought through a psychological-anecdotal method rather than in terms of the general-human through which alone his motives could be understood. Buber's cause, his "word," could not be furthered through the expanded psychophysical image of him that Goldstein wished to portray.

In the years of the Second World War, Buber held an "open forum" devoted to questions and issues of the time on Saturday afternoon in the

(*My wife from 1947 to 1974.)

Jerusalem synagogue of German Jews, Emeth v'Emunah. The occasion for these discussions was the threat in 1942 of the Nazis' breaking through the line at El Alamein, in which case there was no way Britain could defend Egypt or Palestine. As a result, the atmosphere of the time was marked by defense measures, discussions among the Jews of mass suicide, and proposals that the British remove all the Jews from Palestine to India.

Buber used the first meeting of the "Open Forum" to discuss issues of the world war, about which both he and his hearers were intensely concerned. The satanic quality of the ruling Fascist systems already documents itself in their speech, Buber said. Speech should primarily serve dialogue, but the speech of the dictators is a monological bellowing that expects and allows no reply at all, seeking only to be accompanied by a chorus of enthusiasm. But where speech is devoid of its dialogical character, the lie becomes a system, and the possibility of protest is eliminated à priori. The lie holds itself to be the truth and seeks to suffocate the conscience (that "Jewish invention," as Hitler said in a conversation with Hermann Rauschnig). But even Hitler could not suffocate his conscience entirely, Buber held, and in his most lonely hours was surely exposed to its judgment.

Hitler is no pathetic cynic, like Mussolini, nor is he an actor. "He is honest before the microphone and honest in intimate conversation, but the contents of the two honesties contradict each other." When he surrenders to the intoxication of public address, he is a possessed man, but when he explains himself to an intimate, he can lay bare motives of which he is not conscious when in the grip of the hysterical muse that inspires his raging rhetoric. Mussolini is a consummate actor of the demonic; Hitler really becomes demonic. "When one considers Mussolini, one can be astonished and frightened by what man is; but when one looks at Hitler, one is seized by dizziness."

Like most of the other Jews in Palestine, Buber could not at that time credit the reports of the mass murder of Polish Jews. He conceded that ten to fifteen percent of what was reported might be true, which was frightful enough, but he saw that as a consequence of the war and deplored any political exploitation of these reports. "For a long while afterward he did not perceive the cruel reality," comments Goldstein. "His whole being resisted 'accepting' what exceeded his imagination and was incompatible with any of his basic views." When verified reports of the extent of the Holocaust began to arrive in Palestine in 1945 and 1946, he finally had to believe, even though he still could not picture the unimaginable horror. For the rest of his life, he once said, not an hour passed in which he did not think of the Holocaust.

In his 1942 poem "Rachman, A Distant Spirit, Speaks," which he selected just before his death to be preserved in his "Gleanings," Buber likens the conflict between the powers in the Second World War to the opposition in ancient Germanic mythology of the Ases, the light, heavenly Nordic gods, and Hel, the shelter place of the world of the dead, and he sees "trembling

Israel" as caught up in their conflict, and himself, in a striking image, as holding it in his hands like a wounded bird, a responsibility he did indeed feel. In Hermann Hesse's last great novel *Magister Ludi,* the rainmaker sacrifices himself because he is unable to bring rain and save his people. After the war, Buber confessed to Hugo Bergmann that he felt compelled to identify himself with this rainmaker!

By 1944, the reality of the extermination of the European Jews was beginning to be known among the Jews of the Yishuv. Buber's impassioned article "Silence and Outcry," appearing in the spring of 1944, showed that he was fully capable of responding to what was happening despite his inability to grasp it fully. Worst of all were the particular political parties that tried to exploit the catastrophe in order to radicalize the situation, knowing full well that this would not help the rescue. "I have sometimes wondered," wrote Buber, "whether a front could be formed in some extraordinary hour which might cut across all party lines—the front of those who want the salvation of their people with all their hearts and who want to work together for that worthy cause." The lives of the nameless ones to be saved should not be jeopardized by partisanship and playing politics. What is needed, at this late hour, Buber contested, is "to save as many Jews as possible by treating realistically the various practical questions with all means at our disposal, wherever and whenever there is still someone to be saved."

It was his strong personal response to the Second World War that enabled Buber finally to write the Hasidic chronicle-novel *For the Sake of Heaven,* which he had tried unsuccessfully to complete for more than twenty years. In his early work of retelling Hasidic tales and finding the right form for them, Buber came upon a powerful complex of stories that were connected by content. Together, they formed a great cycle, although they were narratives from two different traditions and tendencies that were in opposition to each other. This complex of stories could not be ignored; the events that stood at their center were especially significant. They were often looked at from a legendary perspective, but their real substance was unmistakable. Some *zaddikim* had tried through theurgical acts (the so-called Kabbala) to make Napoleon into the "Gog of the Land of Magog" from the Book of Ezekiel, whose war, as some eschatological texts announce, will be followed by the coming of the Messiah. Other *zaddikim,* opposed to these attempts, warned that the advent of redemption is not to be prepared through external actions, but only through the turning of the whole person. What was most remarkable was that all—those who dared and those who warned—died within a single year.

The only satisfactory approach was that of tragedy, where two persons oppose each other, each just as he or she is, and the true opposition is not one of the "good" will and the "bad" will but the cruel antitheticalness of existence itself. "Certainly, I was 'for' Pshysha and 'against' Lublin; from my youth on, the life and teaching of Rabbi Bunam had won my sympathies for

Pshysha." This approach was what Buber needed in order to write the novel. "My whole writing experience has taught me that books that are conceived by one ripen slowly, and then most strongly if one does not concern oneself with them, and that they finally announce their inner completedness to one so that, so to speak, one only needs to transcribe them."

What finally brought this book to its maturity was the beginning of the Second World War, "the atmosphere of the tellurian crisis, the dreadful weighing of forces, and the signs both on the one side and the other of a false messianism." What gave Buber the decisive impetus was a half dream in which unexpectedly there appeared that false messenger, of which the first chapter tells, as a demon with bat wings and the traits of a Judaized Goebbels (Hitler's propaganda minister). "I wrote—now no longer in German but in Hebrew (the German version was written only later)—very quickly, as though I really needed only to transcribe. Everything now stood clearly before my eyes; the interconnections came to view as though of themselves."

It is clear from the above that *For the Sake of Heaven* was tied up profoundly with Buber's concerns with tragedy, with messianism, with the Nazis, and with the Second World War. This link is reinforced by Buber's view of Hitler as a would-be Napoleon. In his story of Herzl's attack on his friend and fellow Zionist Davis Trietsch, Buber spoke of how at the age of twenty-four he stood for the first time on the soil of tragedy. His years of searching for the proper standpoint from which to tell the story of *For the Sake of Heaven* were deeply connected with what he came to understand then about "the grave of right and wrong," with his much later understanding of how, out of the grave of right and wrong, the right is resurrected, and, perhaps most significant of all for Buber's own life, with his personal opposition to Theodor Herzl—the leader to whom he nonetheless remained loyal in his heart—as the Yehudi remained faithful to the Seer. The Yehudi's affirmation of the oneness of God, in his refusal to cut himself off from the Seer entirely or to see him as simply evil and wrong, has a powerful association with one of the most painful events of Buber's early life, as with his understanding of genuine dialogue as confirming the other in a human way even in opposing him.

Buber told me that he regarded *For the Sake of Heaven* as his most important book. By this, he did not, of course, mean the most influential, like *I and Thou,* or the most culturally significant, as one might say of his translation of the Bible, but the book in which his heart had found its fullest and most significant expression in response to the world in which he lived. In his first telling of Hasidic tales, he was, as he later recognized, too free. In the form of the "legendary anecdote" that he developed for the later telling of the Hasidic tales, he found the proper format for the crude originals. But only in *For the Sake of Heaven* did he discover how to combine freedom and faithfulness to the spirit of the tales.

"Every controversy that takes place for the sake of heaven will endure," we are told in the "Sayings of the Fathers" in the Talmud. Even though the opponents in such a controversy present irreconcilable convictions, both are witnesses for the only human truth we have, that of our relation to the reality that accosts us at any concrete historical moment. Just such a controversy stands at the core of Buber's Hasidic chronicle-novel. Although it is set in the time of the Napoleonic wars and focuses on the struggles of obscure Hasidic communities, *For the Sake of Heaven* is in many respects Buber's most profound and concrete image of the human. The heart of the novel is the simultaneous closeness and conflict between Jaacob Yitzhak of Lublin, the "Seer," and his namesake, the "holy Yehudi" or "holy Jew." Here is a concrete embodiment of the tension between the "prophetic," which calls the hearer to turn with his whole being, and the "apocalyptic," which predicts a fixed future that needs only to unfold. This tension runs throughout the novel and forms its core.

The Yehudi's struggle with the Seer is a part of affirmation of the one-ness of God—his insistence that redemption must be *of* evil and not just *from* it. This affirmation prevents us from seeing the conflict of the story as one between good and evil. Rather, it is tragedy in that special sense in which Buber defines it—the fact that each is as he or she is and that there are not sufficient resources in the relationship to bring the opponents into genuine dialogue so as to prevent the relationship from crystallizing into fixed opposition. Though the Yehudi cannot remove the tragedy itself, he brings it into his relationship with God. He refuses to allow the contradictions of existence to cut him off from a faithful relationship with the teacher whom he acknowledges even while he opposes him.

The Seer asks the Yehudi to die so that through him the Seer might learn from the upper world what next step to take in the great messianic enterprise. Despite its unusual nature, the reader is not unprepared either for this request or its fulfillment. Although the Seer knows well that the Yehudi is following an entirely different spiritual path from his own, he demands of him his life, and the Yehudi, through a loyalty to the Seer that transcends the merely personal, complies.

The conflict between the "prophetic" and the "apocalyptic," between the Yehudi's way of working for redemption and the Seer's, has behind it the tragic fact that our human existence is compounded of hope for man's turning and despair over his being able to turn. "The cruel antitheticalness of existence itself" is inherent in the fact that in order to communicate we must be "over against" each other—distant from and opposite to, and only then and through that "face to face." Tragedy arises from the fact that we do not and often cannot respond to the address that comes to us from what is over against us. We thereby crystallize this over-againstness into simple opposition and prevent the realization of its possibilities of relationship. "We cannot leave the soil of tragedy," Buber said in 1951 when he first visited America.

"But in real meeting we can reach the soil of salvation after the tragedy has been completed." Tragedy can be experienced in the dialogical situation; the contradiction can become a theophany.

According to Karl Kerényi, the Swiss classicist and authority on myth, *For the Sake of Heaven* stands on the peak of epic prose, next to such masterworks as Thomas Mann's *The Holy Sinner* and Pär Lagerkvist's *Barabbas.* Buber's great achievement in his Hasidic chronicle-novel is "the evocation of fighters of the spirit who are without comparison in the whole of epic world literature in the ardor and exclusiveness of the unfolding of their religious powers." "Martin Buber has also accomplished this great achievement," concludes Kerényi: "[He] has allowed the good *and* the evil, the holy *and* the dangerous to appear in his own and his most beloved sphere. His 'Chronicle' transcends time and people as does every work which is a 'classic.'"

In the Buber volume of the Library of Living Philosophers, Rivka Schatz-Uffenheimer, a disciple of Scholem, devoted the last part of a long critique of Buber's interpretation of Hasidism to *For the Sake of Heaven.*

> Every conversation in *For the Sake of Heaven* is a chapter of life in the spiritual world of Hasidism, a chapter sifted free of all banality and sentimentality, all of it polished by the masterful use of adumbration, so that if you have not read it several times, you have not read it at all. Here we are taught by Buber how man should face the world and God.

In his "Replies to My Critics" in the same volume, Buber reasserted his claim that "the 'holy Yehudi,' without giving up the basic Kabbalistic teaching, essentially set a simple human 'existence'" in opposition to the magical actions of the Seer in behalf of Napoleon. In so doing, the Yehudi "reaches back to the cry that one can already hear in the prophets of Israel, that we must first 'turn' before God 'turns' from the 'flaming of his wrath,'" and to the Talmudic teaching that all eschatological combinations have passed by and it now depends on the human turning alone.

In contrast to Baruch Kurzweil's criticism that Buber stood outside of the world from which he brought his mission, Buber asserted that he stood at a point of very vital oneness with those men. "When, in my youth, I came in contact with my earliest Hasidic document, I accepted it in the spirit of Hasidic enthusiasm. I am a Polish Jew." His background was that of the Enlightenment, of course, "but in the most impressionable period of my boyhood a Hasidic atmosphere had a deep effect on me." This we already know, but nothing in Buber's earlier Hasidic writings prepares us for the statement that follows: "Had I lived in that period when one contended concerning the living Word of God and not concerning its caricatures, I, too, like so many others, would have escaped from my paternal home and become a Hasid." Although this was forbidden in the epoch into which Buber was born "according to both generation and situation," Buber identified himself with those in Israel who, equally opposed to blind traditionalism and blind rebellion, continue the Hasidic striving to renew the forms of both faith and life. Only now this striving "takes place in an historic hour in which a slowly receding light has yielded to darkness." Although Buber's entire spiritual substance did not belong to the world of the Hasidim, his foundation was in that realm and his impulses were akin to it.

"He who expects of me a teaching other than a pointing to realities of this order will always be disillusioned," Buber stated. What is crucial in this hour of history, which Buber in *For the Sake of Heaven* explicitly called that of the "eclipse of God," is not possessing a fixed doctrine but recognizing eternal reality and out of its depth facing the reality of the present. "No way can be pointed to in this desert night." All that one can do is "to help men of today to stand fast, with their soul in readiness, until the dawn breaks and a path becomes visible where none suspected it."

◆ 14 ◆

Jewish-Arab Rapprochement and Conflict

(1939-1949)

During the years of the Second World War, fighting never actually reached Palestine, and the Arabs, though sympathetic to the Nazis as enemies of the Jews, let their revolt against the British Mandate and the Yishuv become relatively inactive during the war. As a result, the war provided a background for Jewish-Arab cooperation, short-lived as that was, and in this movement Buber was fully active.

Early on Buber found himself compelled to take sides in the conflict between the more "political" Zionists and the more "practical" ones, between those who wanted to begin by acquiring political concessions and then build the settlements and those who felt that the actual work of settlement must precede the aspiration to legal rights. His identification with the latter stemmed, he said in 1958, "from the insight that the tremendous double work of completing the rebirth of the Jewish people and its becoming a member of the world of the Near East cannot be accomplished through a sudden, insufficiently prepared mass settlement, but only through the preparing activity of generations in the land." This meant a pioneering of work and peace, a selective, organic principle of development that would produce a core of Jewish community that could serve as the base for the rebirth of the people. It also meant practical economic and social cooperation with the Arabs, a solidarity founded on trust and working together. He knew that the Jewish settlement was not a henchman of British imperialism, but he lamented that the way in which the Jews came to Palestine made it possible and in many cases inevitable that the Arabs would think this. Even after the British

Empire was replaced by a Commonwealth, the Yishuv was still falsely considered the agent of British imperialism. Instead, there should have been a comprehensive plan that could make the Jewish settlement the organic center not only of the Jewish people but also of the rising Near East, a great plan that would have made the Arabs of Palestine partners in the work of building the land. This could have led to a cooperation between the two nations in which the question of numerical proportions would no longer be of decisive importance. Although a thousand buds of Arab trust that were beginning to grow had been destroyed, it was still possible to move in the direction of an alliance and a comprehensive bond between two brother nations.

Underlying Buber's approach to Jewish-Arab rapprochement was his Zionism and his Hebrew humanism. Buber found the basis for this Hebrew humanism in the humanism of the Bible. This was not for Buber a matter of the ideal versus the practical, but of the whole versus the part. "The men in the Bible are sinners like ourselves, but there is one sin they do not commit, our arch-sin: they do not dare confine God to a circumscribed space or division of life, to 'religion....' To divide life into a private life of morality and a public one in which any means can be used to the end is to invite destruction of the people's existence." This is not a matter of absolute pacifism or some impossible total justice but of drawing the demarcation line anew in every situation.

> It is true that we are not able to live in perfect justice, and in order to preserve the community of man, we are often compelled to accept wrongs in decisions concerning the community. But what matters is that in every hour of decision we are aware of our responsibility and summon our conscience to weigh exactly how much is necessary to preserve the community, and accept just so much and no more.

In 1939, a loose working community of those concerned about bettering Jewish-Arab relations was formed under the name of the League for Jewish-Arab Rapprochement and Cooperation. In the early 1940s, former members of Brit Shalom began to meet for discussion in each other's homes—Buber, Simon, Magnes, and Henrietta Szold, the founder of Hadassah. In the spring of 1942, they began a series of regular meetings at Magnes's house to discuss the visit to America by David Ben-Gurion, chairman of the Jewish Agency Executive, who aimed to generate American support for the transformation of Palestine into a Jewish state, or commonwealth. Magnes and Buber believed that such a program would inevitably lead to war with the Arabs, and they also held that the Zionist establishment had by no means exhausted all paths to Arab-Jewish rapprochement.

The call for the creation of a Jewish State with an eventual Jewish majority resulted in the consolidation of all the binationalist groups, left, right, and center. The leftist Hashomer Hatzair joined the League for Jewish-Arab Rapprochement and Cooperation, and, on June 23, 1942, the organization issued a comprehensive counterproposal. It recognized the right of the Jews to immigrate to Palestine up to its full economic absorptive capacity and of the Yishuv to become a complete and autonomous economic, cultural, social, and political entity. But it also recognized the right of the Arabs of Palestine to a national autonomous life and to relations with other sections of the Arab people; it affirmed nondomination of one people over the other, regardless of the numerical relationship, and a binational regime that would participate in a federation with the neighboring Arab countries when conditions permitted. The little circle of friends called a meeting in August 1942 of some one hundred believers in binationalism and Arab-Jewish rapprochement, in order to discuss the founding of an organization that they would call Ihud, or Unity. Most of the members belonged to the league but preferred to do so as a bloc rather than be referred to as "the intellectuals." Judah Magnes, who had never belonged to any binationalist organization before, was finally induced to participate in Ihud, which thereafter recognized him as its founder, even though he insisted that there simply be an executive committee and that he not be its head. This committee was composed of Buber, Kalvarisky, Magnes, Smilansky, Henrietta Szold, and Justice Valero, and its first meeting took place on August 11, 1942. It called for a revival of the whole Semitic world through Jewish-Arab social, economic, cultural, and political cooperation; a binational government; and participation in a larger Near Eastern federation.

In 1944, Robert Weltsch's failing journal *Problems of the Day,* was taken over by Ihud and called simply *Problems (Ba'ayot),* with Buber as the editor in chief and Ernst Simon as the editor.

Although Ihud included members of the left wing of the Labor Federation, members of the Third Aliyah, the new immigrants from Germany, members of the former Brit Shalom and of the League for Arab-Jewish Rapprochement and Cooperation, and religious Halutzim, as well as Buber, Simon, Hugo Bergmann, and Magnes, it remained a limited circle without strong impact on public life, making its appeal to the people more by the written than the spoken word. Ihud was also fatally divided on the question of immigration—the Marxist "Young Guard" demanding free and unlimited immigration of Jews, and Magnes and Buber advocating immigration up to numerical parity but not to a majority.

In the past, Buber had long spoken for and believed in unlimited immigration for the Jews and had held that an understanding with the Arabs could be reached on this basis. But four years in Palestine were enough to convince him of his error. The Zionist majority was ready to renounce the unity of Palestine in order to get a Jewish state. The binationalists, on the other hand, were ready to renounce the Jewish State in order to preserve the unity of Palestine. Commenting on this, Buber wrote: "Many is a concept from the very reality of life; whereas majority is a purely political concept. We strive towards having as many Jews as possible immigrate to Israel, whereas Ben-Gurion strives towards their attaining a majority in the country." When they learned that their beloved founder Henrietta Szold was one of the leaders of a binationalist group that opposed Ben-Gurion's Biltmore program, the reaction of Hadassah in America was embittered. In Palestine, some of the Ihud leaders were assaulted with stink bombs, threatened with violence, and denounced in newspaper headlines.

In 1944, Buber published in Hebrew an ironic dialogue about "Biltmore," between a "Loyal One" and a "Traitor". The "Traitor," Buber himself, asks the "Loyal One" why there is so much talk in the streets about the Gibeonites, the non-Jewish people who were allowed to live by Joshua in biblical times but were forced to live only as hewers of wood and drawers of water. The "Loyal One" denies that the Biltmore plan intends to degrade part of the population of the country to the status of second-class citizens, but the "Traitor" points out that if a people is deprived of political, collective equality, then it naturally follows that it will soon assume second-class status. This prophecy is one that even Ernst Simon objected to in the editorial meeting of *Ba'ayot* at which Buber proposed to publish this article. "Surely we who have been so terribly used by others would never treat our minorities in the same way?" Simon protested. But Buber refused to yield, and, seventeen years later, in Simon's Introduction to the collection of Hebrew essays by Buber *People and World,* in which this essay was reprinted, Simon acknowledged, with bitterness, that Buber had been right. Through military and employment restrictions, the Arabs in Israel had been reduced—in fact, even though not legally—to the status of second-class citizens.

Buber's relation with Judah Leib Magnes was one of the remarkable dialogues of this period of Buber's life, even apart from the political activities that they shared. This dialogue was founded on a great deal of mutual respect, despite the differences in their personalities. Although both men were eminently practical, Buber's interests were almost universal in their scope, whereas Magnes had restricted himself in his concerns. Buber was much more flexible in tactics than Magnes, who, even in his personal life, remained the president with the personality of a president. As a result, few persons were able to enter into the sort of give-and-take with him in which they might offer advice. But Magnes was able to accept advice from Buber on many things, even though there was much about which they did not agree. Magnes had something of the austerity of the Quaker in his personality, whereas Buber had a great deal of warmth and humor. Buber often visited Magnes at home for discussions, both alone and with others.

Buber gave Hans Trüb a full picture of his life at that time. His university work had been satisfying, but he had rejected the position of rector that had been offered to him because he did not wish to interrupt his own work. Although the housework in wartime had absorbed Paula's energies in a way hardly to be imagined, she had also been able to do important work. They had gone on their first two-week holiday to the sea since 1939 and that had done them good, especially Paula. "Bärbel," their granddaughter Barbara, who had gone to a trade school, had married a colleague of hers and lived in Haifa as a teacher of drawing. Judith, the younger granddaughter, was living with Martin and Paula and studying at the university. "She too wants to become a teacher." (She became a professor of political science.) "Eva lives with her husband and younger son in the great children and youth village Ben Shemen, where Ludwig teaches.... Rafael has already for a long time left the kibbutz where he had lived, bought himself a truck and drives it since then (mostly military transports) with great virtuosity and discretion."

Albert Einstein wrote Buber from America, reporting on his testimony in Washington before the Anglo-American Committee of Enquiry regarding the problems of European Jewry and Palestine. With remarkable frankness, Einstein spoke to the committee, composed of six Englishmen and six Americans, of how the British Mandate government had from the beginning sought to sabotage the realization of the Balfour Declaration by making immigration difficult, limiting the landholding Jews, and systematically inciting the Arab masses, along with arranging for riots in which the mandate government systematically cooperated. Einstein proposed, like Magnes, a binational government directly under United Nations supervision, because there was no hope for betterment of conditions as long as the British retained the mandate, and the erection of a Jewish State with division of the existing populations seemed to him impracticable. This was hard for the British half of the committee to take, as Einstein himself reported, though he gave his testimony quietly and amiably, without any passion. "I almost forgot that I shared with them my conviction," wrote Einstein, "that from the standpoint of the British government the Commission was a sort of 'smoke-screen' and that they did not have the slightest intention of letting themselves be influenced by its recommendations and proposals." At this, some of the British members of the committee became heated, and Einstein responded, "I would be delighted if I am proved to be wrong."

From Washington, the Anglo-American Committee proceeded to Palestine. The Jewish Agency wanted the Jewish case to be presented by a single front of those favoring a Jewish state, but Ihud insisted on giving its independent testimony for a binational state. This took the form of a written statement asking for the immediate admission of 100,000 Jews, whether or not the Arabs consented, a Swiss-model federation, two national communities with powers of taxation for cultural purposes, a gradual plan leading to binational independence, and an eventual Middle East federation, and an attack on the discredited notion of self-determination by tiny nationalist sovereign units, such as Woodrow Wilson had hoped for at the end of the First World War. Israel's ability to form ties of cooperation and partnership with the Arabs, who were also struggling for national liberation and spiritual renaissance, was the test of the dream of Zion. If a successful solution could be found to the Palestine problem, then a first, pioneer step "will have been taken toward a more just form of life between people and people." Magnes claimed that "a large part of the inarticulate section of the population believes more or less as we do."

The report of the committee in May, after it had retired to Palestine to ponder the evidence, represented something of a victory for Ihud. It recommended the immediate immigration of 100,000 Jews; repeal of discriminatory legislation about land transfers, which kept Jews and Arabs separate; and the establishment of a Trust Administration of the United Nations, which should take the form of neither a Jewish nor an Arab state but a binational country moving toward binational independence. This report was unanimous, but the British government, as Einstein had predicted, paid no attention to it, and instead put forward a plan of its own that was immediately rejected by both Jews and Arabs.

After the Anglo-American Commission's report, Magnes went to America for half a year in order to plead his cause before the American public and to remove delusions and false accusations concerning binationalism. During his absence, Buber and Moshe Smilansky wrote to General Sir Evelyn Barker, commander in chief of the British army in Palestine, pleading with him to commute the death sentence for Joseph Simhon and Michael Ashbel, two Jewish youths who had taken part in the terrorist activities of the revisionist Irgun Zvai Le'umi, a national military organization outside of Haganah that had made an armed attack on the military airfield at Kastina. Buber and Smilansky pointed out that they had taken the same position in the case of Arabs sentenced to death during the riots and that, as persons who had worked tirelessly for peace in Palestine, they were obliged to remind Barker that carrying out death sentences could only heighten the tension and make the attainment of peace more difficult. The two youths were subsequently pardoned. Buber's intervention on behalf of these terrorists, whose own position and activities he opposed with all of his being, is important for understanding Buber's encounter on the narrow ridge. Those who are themselves polarized tend to see others in the same way. There have been Jewish groups in and outside of Palestine who have mistakenly maintained that Buber pled for the lives of Arab terrorists sentenced to death but refused to plead for the lives of Jewish terrorists. One such case was that of the Jewish terrorist Dov Gurner. Here, too, the persistent rumor that Buber did not intervene for him is mistaken. Gavriel Stern, editor at that time of *Ba'ayot,* assures us that Buber and Henrietta Szold wrote a letter in common, which is reported in *Ba'ayot.*

Buber met Gavriel Stern, who interviewed him several times for *Ba'ayot,* through the Jewish-Arab Friendship League .When Buber felt that Stern's work was slipshod, he was very unhappy about it and let Stern know it. Later, Buber would invite Stern to his home, where, his initial hesitation overcome, Stern would talk with Buber at length. He characterized Buber as a person who really knew how to listen, who was always trying to get to the truth of a matter, and who was even willing to nag in order to do so. Finally, Stern saw Buber as a practical man, especially with money.

In 1945, Buber took part in the preparation of a ten-page "plea, at a very late hour, for Jewish-Arab cooperation in Palestine and the Middle East." The paper attacked the British White Paper of May 1939, which limited Jewish immigration to 75,000, a figure that had already been reached, leaving thousands of homeless Jews from Europe with no place to go. Pointing out that the Jews had with intelligence and devotion demonstrated that the economic resources of Palestine could receive more immigrants, and could be made to receive even more, than had at one time been supposed, the paper called for increased Jewish immigration to Palestine. It recognized, however, that the negative attitude of the Arabs stood in the way and proposed to overcome that attitude through a systematic effort toward Arab-Jewish understanding and cooperation, based on the creation of a binational Palestine in which both peoples were to have equal rights and duties and on the reinforcement of the international character of Palestine by bringing it under the trusteeship of the United Nations. It proposed an immigration of 100,000 Jews with the clear understanding that no Jewish State was intended.

In May 1946, Buber wrote an article entitled "A Tragic Conflict?" in which he created the important concept of "a political surplus conflict" to describe the difference between the real conflict and the politically induced, imagined conflict. He suggested that "the present Jewish-Arab situation, which appears to be without solution," emerged from political "surplus" conflicts developed in both camps. Here, too, he emphasized the need to combat the politicization of reality, which became such a frequent note in his later writings:

> We must do political work in order to induce a cure of the present sick relation between life and politics.... The only hope is to establish institutions which accord supremacy to the demands of life over the demands of politics and which thereby provide us with a real and substantial base from which to explain the truth.

The tension in Palestine reached a new height when, on July 22, 1946, the Irgun, acting alone, blew up the central government offices in the King David Hotel in Jerusalem, resulting in the death of eighty government officials and civilians, Britons, Jews, and Arabs alike. The appalled Jewish Agency ordered a halt in armed operations against the British. But Buber did not find that sufficient, as he suggested in an article in the Tel Aviv Hebrew daily *Ha-Aretz* on July 26, 1946. Buber felt that the leadership of the Yishuv was implicated in the Irgun's murderous attack, through its support of the Jewish Resistance movement:

It is a false teaching that the rebirth of a people can be accomplished by violent means. The way of violence does not lead to liberation or healing but only to renewed decline and renewed enslavement.... Criminals exiled to Australia become responsible human beings with a sense of social justice, while the people who come to Zion under a holy banner have become criminals.

On August 12, 1946, Buber, D. W. Senator, and Moshe Smilansky sent to the high commissioner a protest from Ihud concerning the interruption of refugee immigration, which they held did not fall within the category of security measures and which could mean only further suffering for the innocent victims of Nazi persecution. At the same time, they carefully distinguished their plea from the efforts of terrorists to gain similar concessions through violence.

On August 16, 1946, the British military court sentenced to death a gang of eighteen members of the Irgun caught earlier in the month. On August 21, Buber and six other members of Ihud appealed to the high commissioner for commutation of the sentence, underlining their own constant opposition to terrorism and pointing out that in 1930 some of the undersigned made a similar appeal on behalf of twenty-three Arabs sentenced to death for the murder of members of the Palestinian Jewish community. "Education and persuasion are more likely to bear fruit in the long run, whereas capital punishment creates 'martyrs' in the eyes of the surviving members of the offending groups and of some elements of the community as a whole."

The high point of cooperation between Jews and Arabs in Palestine at this time also turned out to be the most poignant and tragic. The League for Jewish-Arab Rapprochement and Cooperation in Palestine found an Arab counterpart in the body known as Falastin el-Jedida (The New Palestine). The founder and leader of this organization was Fauzi Darwish El-Husseini, a cousin of the bitterly anti-Zionist mufti of Jerusalem and himself an active Arab nationalist who had been jailed for his part in anti-Jewish riots. At a public meeting in Haifa on June 22, 1946, Fauzi had endorsed the essential Ihud position of a binational state supervised by the United Nations, with the problem of immigration to be worked out within the framework of a general agreement and on the basis of the economic absorptive capacity of the country. At the end of August 1946, Fauzi spoke at the home of Chaim Kalvarisky, urging an active Arab counterforce against the "Arab party" led by his cousin, the mufti. He attacked the official policy of both Arabs and Jews as producing only damage and suffering, and called on Arabs and Jews to unite and work hand in hand against the imperialist policy that played them off against each other.

On November 11, 1946, five members of Falastin el-Jedida signed an agreement with the League of Jewish-Arab Rapprochement and Cooperation, calling for cooperation, political equality, Jewish immigration according to the country's economic absorptive capacity, and a future Near Eastern federation. This agreement had been prepared by an active campaign on the part of Fauzi and his supporters, which reached out to Muslim and Christian teachers, journalists, businessmen, and workers among the Arabs. Their activities extended to publishing an Arab organ, *El-Akha* (Brotherhood), and acquiring a club room. These activities were accompanied by Arab warnings and threats, but Fauzi, undeterred, replied, "History will judge which of us followed the right path." On November 23, less than two weeks after this agreement was signed, with the promise of the league to support the activities of Falastin el-Jedida, Fauzi was murdered by unknown Arab extremists. A few days after his murder, his cousin Jamal Husseini, coleader of the Arab party with the mufti, said: "My cousin had stumbled and received his proper punishment." No Palestinian Arab politician had ever before openly negotiated with the Jews and signed an agreement with them. Fauzi's friends came to see Buber and other leaders of the League for Jewish-Arab Rapprochement and Cooperation, declaring that they were not afraid to carry on and asking advice as to what they should do now that Fauzi was dead. "Go home in peace," Buber and his friends told them. "They will kill you as they killed Fauzi." The Jewish and the Arab men of peace parted in sadness, and no similar counterthrust of Arab moderates against the extremists arose to deflect the onrush of events toward war.

In June, 1947, Buber presented a comprehensive picture of his vision of Jewish-Arab rapprochement in a talk over Dutch radio entitled "Two Peoples in Palestine." There he warned once more against the insidious effect of the domination of politics, which is not always recognizable because it has insinuated itself into every area of life in a different disguise.

Specifically, Buber saw the demands for an Arab state or a Jewish state in the entire Land of Israel as falling into the category of the political "surplus." "The evil does not lie with politics as such, but with its hypertrophy," Buber wrote in another 1947 article, "The Bi-National Approach to Zionism." The power of such fictitious political thinking over the Yishuv was increasing continuously—in part from a genuine despair "brought on by an action of extermination never before experienced by any other nation, as well as by the indifference of the world in the face of this action.... After an act of extermination of this kind, the poor human soul is inclined to see extermination lurking everywhere."

In June 1947, there began what R. M. Graves, the mayor of Jerusalem, described in a book as an "experiment in anarchy": a war of all against all in which three peoples—the British, the Arabs, and the Jews—raged against one another. Through Ben-Gurion's personal intervention, the overwhelming majority of Hadassah in America delivered a stinging rebuff to their founder Henrietta Szold, a staunch leader of Ihud, and voted for the partition of Palestine, leaving only the league and Hashomer Hatzair in favor of a binational state.

D. W. Senator informed Buber that Magnes was seriously ill with a strained heart and told him how much it would mean to Magnes if he were to receive a letter from Buber on the occasion of his seventieth birthday (July 8, 1947). Buber wrote Magnes a letter that was at once intensely personal — "It [Magnes's seventieth birthday] touches the depths of my soul"—and at the same time a public tribute published in the summer issue of *Ba'ayot*. Essentially, Buber wrote that he had received from Magnes a great gift: the possibility of again being politically active within the framework and in the name of a political group without sacrificing the truth in so doing.

In the report that the Special Commission made to the United Nations Assembly in the fall of 1947, the majority went on record for partition of Palestine into a Jewish and an Arab State, with Jerusalem under an international trusteeship. In the debates at the United Nations leading up to the two-thirds vote for partition on November 29, binationalism was not even mentioned as an alternative to partition. "One after the other get up and declare that they would like to vote for a federal plan, but that unfortunately no such plan exists," Magnes wrote Hugo Bergmann the day before the vote.

On November 29, the United Nations Assembly decided by a two-thirds vote in favor of the partition of Palestine. The next day, a party of Jews driving in Palestine was ambushed and killed. A day later, serious rioting occurred in Jerusalem, and the war that Buber and Magnes had consistently warned would accompany partition broke out. Summing up the situation ten years later, Buber wrote: "Since a Jewish-Arab solidarity had not been instituted,… the Arab peoples received the mass immigration as a threat and the Zionist movement as a 'hireling of imperialism'—both wrongly, of course. Our *historical* reentry into our land took place through a false gateway." Of the outbreak of war, he said: "Everything proceeded with frightening logical consistency and at the same time with frightening meaninglessness." A personal remark that Buber added at this point again showed the utter concreteness and realism of his encounter on the narrow ridge: "I am no radical pacifist: I do not believe that one must always answer violence with nonviolence. I know what tragedy implies; when there is war, it must be fought." This remark in no way means that Buber gave up his concern for doing whatever possible *in each situation* for Jewish-Arab relations. In January 1948, Buber, Magnes, and Senator sent a letter to the Hebrew and English press, appealing to public opinion and to the Jewish leadership to take steps to prevent vicious mob attacks by Jews: "Let recent regrettable incidents serve as a warning not to let the mob rule us, not to destroy with our own hands the moral foundations of our life and of our future."

"Next to surrender of the soul to the irreconcilable contradiction, everything that I have experienced before, for example in Hitler Germany, was a gentle idyll." Nazism was organized terror, which had by no means reached its height; the situation in Palestine was simple anarchy. What was and was not happening and what threatened to happen in the Old City of Jerusalem, the actions of the mob that seemed to be particularly ferocious in Jerusalem and that matched "ever more successfully" those of the Arab counterpart, and the decisions and nondecisions of "our current [local] 'leadership,'" which in any case more and more resemble those of the opposition"—all these added up to that totally absorbing claim on Buber's attention exercised by the city of Jerusalem, in which he continued to live throughout the war.

When the battle over Jerusalem could no longer be avoided and the United Arab armies' invasion practically cut the city off from the rest of the country and besieged it, Buber remained in the threatened city, although the possibility had been offered him of saving himself and Paula by going to Tel Aviv. Once, during the worst days of the siege, Buber encountered Schalom Ben-Chorin on Ben-Yehuda Street in the center of the city and said to him, "Even if they were to send an airplane to my doorstep, I would not leave this Jerusalem in which what I wanted to avoid is happening." In February 1948, when the English, in response to Jewish acts of terrorism, indulged in their own terrorist act by destroying Ben-Yehuda Street, Buber was extremely depressed. A distinguished Arabic family, that of Jussuf Wahab Dajani, tried in vain to protect Buber and his family in their Arabic quarter. Before the war, many of the Arabs in Dir Abu Tor had great respect for Buber and called him "the old saint" and "the old man." After the Jewish-Arab war broke out, the Arabs in the neighborhood divided, according to Buber's own testimony, into one faction that was for the Bubers and one that wanted to kill them. The Haganah made use of Buber's house, even using his books as a protection against Arab bullets, so that many of his books bear bullet marks. Finally, it became too difficult for the Bubers to stay on, and they moved with such of their belongings as they could take to the Grete Ascher Pension in Rehavia, a modern quarter of Jerusalem bordering on the new campus of Hebrew University, established after Mount Scopus became inaccessible. Buber went out in the car of Dr. Graham Brown, an Anglican archdeacon.

After the Bubers left, Dajani closed off the room in which Buber's library was housed. A few days later, Iraqi troops came to the house. "Where are the Jews who lived here?" they asked. "They are no longer here," Dajani replied. A house search followed. "What is this closed room?" an Iraqi soldier asked. "Stop!" said Dajani. "Behind this door there is the great library of Professor Buber on the history of religions. You will have to kill me if you want to get into this room." "Now, what do you take us for?" asked the Iraqi captain. "Do you think we are barbarians?" He promptly withdrew. In a speech about Buber over a West German radio station in 1962, Albrecht Goes said that in light of what the Nazis did during the *Kristallnacht* in November 1938, no German could hear this story without shame!

In the Arabic village, they had decided not to kill Buber, but the roads lending out of the country were dangerous because of the "unofficial war" that began in December and lasted until May 15. Once, when Gavriel Stern—

who took responsibility for Buber's house after he left, along with the Dajanis, who protected it from plundering—went on one of many trips to the Buber's house to bring out their furniture and equipment, there was a terrorist incident against the Arabs. As a result, the Arabs surrounded Stern's car, and he and his companions thought that they were lost. But the Arab officials said, "We know who you are and who your friends are," meaning the Bubers. The place was without any police, and so this moving of books and furniture was an act of courage on Stern's part. It took six weeks, but they were never harmed. The Arabs plundered and destroyed everything in the house of Buber's neighbor, but the Bubers' house was excellently looked after and its possessions remained completely untouched during the whole Arab occupation. There was even a saying among the Arabs that Buber was still living there, writing and thinking. Even among his "enemies," Buber was a living legend.

In 1948, Buber wrote Salman Schocken:

> When a week ago during my course (in the Rehavia Gymnasium where the lectures now take place) an English bullet passed over my head and into the wall, I and the students remaining to me experienced that barely as a disturbance, rather as a natural event and accepted it with the requisite humor. But just therein lies the absurdity of our present situation.

Buber wrote Heinz Politzer that there existed no more communication between Dir Abu Tor and Jewish Jerusalem, but that he had heard that, amid the utterly chaotic shooting, thirteen English cannonballs had penetrated his house and had among other things bored through the oil portrait of Buber painted by Emil Rudolf Weiss. To Ernst Simon, Buber wrote that the hourly reaction to the unimaginably cruel and senseless events there placed a great inner and outer demand on everyone and especially on "so routineless and disoriented a man, abandoned without defense to every situation, as I still always am and clearly must also remain." Buber also reported to Simon that they were working intensively in Ihud and that "a not insignificant number of the much afflicted people of Jerusalem openly profess our cause, in contrast to which, of course, *those who are at ease in Tel Aviv* (a play on Amos 6:1) want to know nothing further of us."

To Hugo Bergmann, Buber confided that in those hours or quarter hours of philosophizing that were, despite all, still afforded him, he was occupying himself more intensively than ever "with the category of the human (I really mean category), with its possibility, and all that I have learned about the human in the months of disorder, flows into it." Thus, "Distance and Relation," which is Buber's most abstract piece of philosophical writing and the cornerstone of his most mature philosophical work, *The Knowledge of Man,* had its origin not in the serenity and contemplation traditionally associated with philosophers, but in the midst of what Buber later called the most dreadful year of his life. Similarly, Paula, no less a titan than her husband, wrote what Buber considered her most important work, the epic novel *Am lebendigen Wasser* (By Living Waters) during the siege of Jerusalem, when she was under the strain of caring for the whole household, including Buber himself, several grandchildren, and nine cats, with very little resources of any kind. From that time on until Buber's death seventeen years later, there emerged a note that one was to hear again and again in the years to come: his need to expedite his publishing affairs in a way that he had not done until then.

On April 13, a convoy, carrying doctors and nurses to the Hadassah Hospital and professors and workers of the university to Mount Scopus, was ambushed by Arab bands and for hours left a helpless victim of savage onslaughts, while British forces were stationed within a mile, and Magnes and others vainly besought their aid. Ten of the university staff and the director of Hadassah Hospital were among the seventy killed. On May 14, the executive committee of the Jewish Agency and the Jewish National Council proclaimed in Tel Aviv the independence of Israel, which was immediately recognized by Harry Truman for the United States and shortly afterward by the Soviet Union. That marked the end of the "unofficial war" and the beginning of the official one. In the Foreword to *Two Types of Faith,* which Buber wrote "in Jerusalem during the days of its so-called siege, or rather in the chaos of destruction which broke out within it," he confessed that the work involved had helped him "to endure in faith this war, for me the most grievous of the three." On May 28, the Old City was surrendered to the Arabs and remained in their hands until two years after Buber's death.

In May 1948, the very time in which the State of Israel was declared and the official war began, Buber wrote his essay entitled "Two Kinds of Zionism." When the illusion that the Arab majority would consent to become a minority was shattered, official Zionism consented to split the very land it was to "redeem" in order that it might be a majority. It substituted for true independence the watchword of "sovereignty" "in a time in which the sovereignty of the small states is disappearing with ever increasing speed!" "Instead of striving to become the community of initiative within the framework of a Near Eastern federation," Buber added in truly prophetic words, "one set as one's goal a little state that runs the danger of living in constant antagonism to its natural, geopolitical surroundings and to have to devote its best forces to military instead of social and cultural values."

Buber concluded "Two Kinds of Zionism" with a sad personal confession:

> Fifty years ago when I joined the Zionist movement for the sake of the rebirth of Israel, I did so with a whole heart. Today my heart is torn. A war concerning political structure always threatens, in fact, to degenerate into a war concerning the national exis-

tence. Therefore, I can do nothing other than to take part in it with my own existence, and my heart trembles today like the heart of every Jew. But I cannot rejoice even at a victory; for I fear that a victory of the Jews means a defeat of Zionism.

In June 1948, Ludwig Strauss wrote Buber, asking him if there was no possibility of his leaving Jerusalem, since the university was closed for the time being and no duty bound him to the place. Recognizing that there was no security in the whole land, Strauss pointed out that Jerusalem was relatively less secure than anywhere else. Eva worked eight hours a day in the dining room — hard work—but her state of health in Kfar Vitkin where they lived now was better than it had been in Ben-Shemen. Ludwig's own blood pressure had dropped, which he attributed to the sea climate of this new village commune. He also reported how closely they were touched by "the sad events of the previous weeks," the fight between Ezl (a terrorist group) and the regular Haganah. Despite Ludwig's pleas, Martin did not even consider leaving Jerusalem. By July, with enormous expenditure of effort and money, the Bubers had rescued most of their belongings, with the books lying in sacks in various places. Buber had to give up the lecture that he had planned to give for the plenary session of the International Philosophy Congress in Amsterdam in August 1948.

In August 1948, Buber wrote Ernst Simon, who was in America, that the "Jerusalem" that Simon conceived of in his current situation was thoroughly unreal. It was present, so to speak, only in his inner dialectic. Only a Jerusalem visited by tribulation could lay claim to the hours of liberation and serenity of which Simon spoke. Buber pointed instead to an astonishing and unforeseen presence and to becoming aware more deeply than ever before of the contradictory character of human existence, bearing it with greater reality, that is, in daily life, and only thereby attaining a downright practical freedom and serenity at the price of great suffering. Buber had no reproach for those who were not present, but he confessed to a great sadness about the fate of a truth that did not stand the historical test.

Buber responded to a question of Simon concerning the sharing of guilt that there exists again and again a point where one is certainly not "liberated," but "absolved," from collective responsibility: One must bear it but not atone for it. (Many years later, Abraham Heschel was to say about a different collective situation: "Some of us are guilty, all of us are responsible.") This is exactly the same as how one balances accounts as one who is personally guilty, that is, according to the measure of one's powers. Second, Buber asserted that there are unwritten, untraditional, and accordingly still inexpressible *mitzvot*. "More is not to be said," Buber concluded. "But that I had to say to you, for where does friendship lie if one is remiss in answering?"

In late summer of 1948, Count Folke Bernadotte, president of the Swedish Red Cross, came to Palestine as mediator in the Arab-Jewish war and as the director of the U.N. Armistice Commission. On September 17, this highly revered figure was assassinated by Jewish terrorists. Werner Kraft brought the news to Buber, who had not yet heard it. Buber was speechless with shock. Buber wrote an essay on the assassination of Count Bernadotte that he did not publish. In it he said:

> These acts of vile murder will bring our people nothing but damage and contempt. They will not frighten a people so proud that no enemy ever intimidated it; they will only provoke it and incense it against us.... Murder from an ambush is vile and abominable; all murder is wicked and criminal, and murder in the name of a people only shatters that people's life and hope for life. In the commandment "Thou shalt not kill" can also be heard the commandment "Thou shalt not kill the soul of your people."

Many years later, when a concerted effort was made to raise support from influential world thinkers for a Nobel Prize in literature for Buber, Ernst Simon said that the Swedish ambassador in Israel had told him that because of the murder of Count Bernadotte, it was still impossible for an Israeli—even one like Buber who had steadfastly opposed all acts of terrorism—to receive the Nobel Prize.

In October 1948, Buber published in *Ba'ayot* an article entitled "Let Us Make an End to Falsities!" in which he characterized the feelings of both sides concerning the Arab-Jewish war in terms of the "mass psychology" and "hypnosis" that made each feel that it was the injured party—the very terms that he rejected so bitterly when Frederik Van Eeden used them about Germany at the beginning of the First World War! In opposition to the simplistic statement that the Arabs started the war by attacking the Jews, Buber added a historical *aperçu,* asserting, "When we started our infiltration into the country we began an attack 'by peaceful means.'" Everything then depended on convincing the other people that was already there—the Arabs—that the attack was not an attack at all, by awakening in them the belief in "our community of interest." On the positive side, this meant developing a *genuine* community of interests by including the Arabs in their economic activity. On the negative side, it meant holding back all proclamations and political actions of a unilateral nature. It was evident that neither of these things had been done.

The impact of such a statement in wartime can be only scarcely imagined. Gideon Freudenberg, a Nahal educator who later worked with Buber in the School for the Education of the Teachers of the People, wrote him that "Let Us Make and End to Falsities!" would only repel the thousands of Jews who cherished peace and whom Buber could have welded together under his guidance. Freudenberg recognized the danger to the soul of Zionism from the spirit of violence, nationalism, and militarism, and remonstrated with Buber for wanting a confession of guilt before calling "us to battle against... Jewish expansionism, against robbery and plunder, against anti-Arab discrimination, against the destruction of their villages, and for the return of the refugees." Freudenberg saw the way clear, despite obstacles, for building a land of peace for the Jews and Arabs who wanted to live within its borders, and he saw Buber as destined to be a guide and leader to all the thousands who wanted to help build it.

In his reply, Buber asked where those thousands were when he published his protest against the bombing of the King David Hotel. "If they exist, let them come," he added, and "we will examine the bitter reality...—as painful as this will be—and together we will search for a way out, if such a way exists. 'Redemption' of an external kind can be paid for with the blood of our sons. Internal redemption can only be bought by gazing directly at the brutal face of truth."

The "brutal face of truth" that Buber set forth in this essay was probably altogether unpalatable to his fellow Jews in the Yishuv; yet it proved starkly prophetic:

> We face the danger that peace, when it comes, will not be... real peace.... And when this hollow peace is achieved, how then do you think you'll be able to combat the "spirit of militarism?... Won't we be compelled, and I mean really compelled, to maintain a posture of vigilance forever, without being able to breathe? Won't this unceasing effort occupy the most talented members of our society?

In January 1949, Buber confided to Walter Goldstein something more of the toll that the Arab-Jewish war, which had finally come to a halt, had taken of him. The confusion of this most dreadful year of his life had deprived him, he felt, of his power to counsel people. Before that, whenever he saw a person, he saw the person's whole life at once. "Now that is no longer so." The depth of Buber's feeling about the war is reflected in a poem, "November," in which the association between the violence that the Nazis perpetrated on the Jews and that in which the Jews were now taking part in the name of Zionism is gently but unmistakably made:

> The scrolls burned slowly and long.
> I saw from the distance the sparks scatter,
> I saw how the parchment burst open,
> And when I forced my glance to continue,
> I saw: the ashes sank.
> Only the Word is left.
>
> The destroyers are now long since disposed of,
> A vile band of hangmen and thieves.

With them went the rage and the madness
And the cold greed for the plan of plunder.
I saw: the path has become empty.
Our Word has remained.

But we, are we speakers of the word?
Are we able to proclaim it and to love it?
I see us struggling—for the sake of what hoard?
Powerful the arm—and the heart withered?
O homeless Voice
In which the Word remained!

In 1946, after his release from the Jewish Brigade of the British Army, which he had joined two years before, Buber's grandson Emmanuel Strauss lived for a year and a half with Martin and Paula Buber in their house in Jerusalem. During the War of Independence, Paula washed his uniform for him. He felt at home and close to his grandparents, whom he knew were worried about the situation. Once, when a counselor of Emmanuel said that there was no way to talk to the Arabs and that the Jews must take back the land by force, Emmanuel disagreed, even though all the other members of the group agreed with the counselor. When, in the course of the argument, he mentioned a book that he had read in German, the counselor forbade him to continue reading in German. To this, Emmanuel responded that his grandfather wrote in German, and the counselor told him to spit in his grandfather's face. Buber found it unfortunate that a counselor would bring parents and grandparents into his arguments, but he did not get agitated about the counselor's statement.

Buber's granddaughter Barbara married Zeev Goldschmidt. Goldschmidt was sick for almost a year in a hospital in Jerusalem, while Barbara lived and worked in Haifa. After that, they decided to move to Jerusalem. In 1946, Martin and Paula decided to spend some time abroad and asked the Goldschmidts to live in and tend their house while they were out of the country. When the Buber's received a new house from the neighborhood committee in Talbiyeh, it was on the condition that they live in it together with another family. As a result, Buber suggested that Barbara and Zeev move into the house in Talibyeh. Because of this, they were in a position to help Martin and Paula when they became older. But it was Buber who paid the rent and the utilities and fixed up the house.

♦ 15 ♦

Biblical Judaism, Hasidism, and Adult Education

(1943-1959)

Buber's productivity during this period of anarchy, confusion, and war was no less astonishing than that during his five years in Nazi Germany. In addition to continuing the translation of the Hebrew Bible, he wrote three important books of biblical commentary—a book on the historical relationship of Israel and Palestine, a book on the history of utopian socialism, and a book of interpretations of Hasidism—and he revised and rewrote his whole corpus of Hasidic tales. In 1949, Buber wrote to his translator Ronald Gregor Smith:

> You are right in saying that I am "writing so much." But do you want to know why? Because I am copying here, so to say, from my mind the books I have composed but not written in the course of many years before coming to Palestine, and here I simply have to write them. As you know, all of them deal with one subject, only in different ways.

In *Moses* and *The Prophetic Faith,* Buber continued his documentation, begun in *The Kingship of God,* of the messianic demand of biblical Judaism for justice, righteousness, community, and peace. "Though something of righteousness may become evident in the life of the individual, righteousness itself can only become visibly embodied in the structures of the life of a people.... Only life can demonstrate the absolute, and it must be the life of the people as a whole." In the best decades of this settlement, "generations who discovered within themselves an undreamed-of working power and efficiency set the tablets of social justice up over their work." But in recent years the work of those generations has been inundated by a life that knows no tablets of social justice. The Yishuv was to be the center of the Jewish people, but what is the spiritual center of this center? Buber's biblical work over a forty-year span can be looked upon as an untiring effort, despite the increasingly deteriorating political situation, to try to restore the covenant to the heart of this center.

In *Moses,* Buber again held steadfast to the narrow ridge between the traditionalist's insistence on the literal truth of the biblical narrative and the modern critic's tendency to regard this narrative as of merely literary or symbolic significance. The traditionalist tends to regard the events of the Bible as supernatural miracles, and the attempt to equate them to our own experiences as illicit. The modernist sees them as impressive fantasies or fictions, interesting from a purely immanent and human point of view. Between these two approaches, Buber set down a third:

> We must adopt the critical approach and seek reality, here as well, by asking ourselves what human relation to real events this could have been which led gradually, along many by paths and by way of many metamorphoses, from mouth to ear, from one memory to another, and from dream to dream, until it grew into the written account we have read.

Buber called his treatment of biblical history "tradition criticism" as distinct from "source criticism." Tradition criticism seeks to penetrate beneath the layers of different redactions of tradition to a central unity already present in the first and developed, restored, or distorted in the later ones.

> Tradition is by its nature an uninterrupted change in form; change and preservation function in the identical current. Even while the hand makes its alterations, the ear hearkens to the deeps of the past; not only for the reader but also for the writer himself does the old serve to legitimize the new.

The Bible as "literal truth" and the Bible as "living literature" are thus supplanted in *Moses* by the Bible as a record of the concrete meetings in the course of history between a group of people and the divine. The Bible is not primarily devotional literature, nor is it a symbolic theology that tells us of the nature of God as he is in himself. It is the historical account of God's relation to man seen through man's eyes. "Miracle," to Buber, such as the parting of the Red Sea that enabled the Israelites to escape from the pursuing Egyptians, is neither an objective event that suspends the laws of nature and history nor a subjective act of the imagination. It is neither "supernatural" nor "natural," but a third alternative: an event that is experienced by an individual or a group of people as an abiding astonishment which no knowledge of causes can weaken, as wonder at something that intervenes fatefully in the life of this individual and this group. Thus, it is an event of dialogue, an event of the *between*.

> The real miracle means that in the astonishing experience of the event the current system of cause and effect becomes, as it were, transparent and permits a glimpse of the sphere in which a sole power, not restricted by any other, is at work. To live with the miracle means to recognize this power on every given occasion as the effecting one. That is the religion of Moses, the man who experienced the futility of magic, who learned to recognize the demonic as one of the forms by which the divine functions,... and that is religion generally, as far as it is reality.

Perhaps the most powerful example of what the "narrow ridge" meant for Buber's approach to the Bible is the autobiographical fragment that he told concerning "Samuel and Agag." Once, when he was riding in a train in Germany, Buber met Markus Cohn, a Swiss solicitor and Zionist and a pious and observant Orthodox Jew. They fell to discussing the Bible and in particular that passage where the prophet Samuel tells Saul that he has lost the succession to the kingdom because, after conquering the Amalekites and killing them and their animals, he spared the life of Agag, the prince of the Amalekites. The Amalekites were the people who swooped down upon the Israelites in the rear as they marched forty years through the wilderness. The Amalekites wantonly killed all they could, as a result of which Moses declared eternal war between Israel and Amalek, and Amalek became a symbol in Jewish history from Hamann to Hitler. According to the story in First Samuel 15, Samuel then called before him Agag, who said, "Surely the bitterness of death is over." "As you have made other mothers childless, so I shall make your mother childless," responded Samuel, "and hewed him into pieces before the Lord in Gilgal."

When he first read this story as a boy, it profoundly troubled him, Buber confessed to his traveling companion, and even now he could not believe that it was the will of God. His companion's brow darkened and his eyes flamed. "So you do not believe it?" he asked. "No, I do not believe it," replied Buber. Then, his eyes still more threatening and his brow still darker, the man pressed, "So, you do not believe it!" "No," Buber maintained, "I do not believe it." Then, pushing the words out, one in front of the other, the man said, "What, what then do you believe?" "I believe," Buber answered without thinking, "that Samuel misunderstood God." Then something extraordinary happened: The angry brow cleared, the eyes became positively gentle and radiant. Then the man said, "I think so, too."

In the end, it is not surprising, Buber reported, that if a really pious Jew of this sort has to choose between God and the Bible, he chooses God. But in the years since that happened, Buber asked himself again and again if he had given the right response, and again and again came up with a yes and a no. Yes, insofar as this particular dialogue was concerned, "so that the dialogue might not come to naught." But no, insofar as one might think that he meant that only this one interpretation of God's will had been a misunderstanding.

> God does not abandon the created man to his needs and anxieties; He provides him with the assistance of his word; He speaks to him, He comforts him with His word. But man does not listen with faithful ears to what is spoken to him. Already in hearing he blends together command of heaven and statute of earth, revelation to the existing being and the orientations that he arranges himself. Even the holy scriptures of man are not excluded, not even the Bible.

We have no objective criterion for distinguishing between that which is manufactured and that which is received from the voices and pens out of which the text of the Hebrew Bible has arisen. We have only faith—when we have it. "Always when I have to translate or to interpret a biblical text, I do so with fear and trembling, in an inescapable tension between the word of God and the words of man," Buber declared. The orthodox and the fundamentalist escape this tension through a bibliolatry that tries to freeze the word of the Bible into an objective statement handed down by heaven—as if words meant something in themselves without their being spoken and heard. The liberals try to escape it by approaching the Bible with the touchstone of the "progressive" and the "universal," accepting what they feel fits the most "modern" morality and rejecting what does not. Buber preserved the tension and, with it, the encounter on the narrow ridge.

The first answer that Moses receives to the question "Who shall I say sent me?" is the God of your fathers, the God whom you *recognize*. The second is "I shall be as I shall be": "He who promises his steady presence, his steady assistance, refuses to restrict himself to definite forms of manifestation." This God does not need to be conjured, for he is always with you, but this God also cannot be conjured.

The importance of Moses for our time Buber also found in the Ten Commandments, the soul of which he saw in *Moses* and the word *Thou*. This Thou means the preservation of the Divine Voice. "At all times,... only those persons really grasped the Decalogue who literally felt it as having been addressed to them themselves." How autobiographical this statement is we already know from "The Education of Character," in which the lightning flash of "Thou shalt not" strikes the heart of a "man," Buber himself, so that he does the exact opposite of what he was going to do with all the passion he was going to bring into that action. Of equally modern relevance in Buber's *Moses,* because it goes against the universalist approach to comparative religion, is his insistence on the atypical and the unique as having a central place in the history of the spirit just because it is *history,* not timeless truth. Buber stressed that the "firm letter" ought not be broken down by any general hypothesis based on the comparative history of culture as long as what is said in that text is historically possible. Those who reject Moses's God as a patriarch will find a modern, if unwelcome, relevance in Buber's insistence that the unity and imagelessness of God places God above sex: "A sexually determined God is an incomplete one, one who requires completion; it cannot be the one and only God."

Perhaps most remarkable, given Buber's earlier statements about his relationship to the *mitzvot,* or commandments, of Jewish Law, is Buber's discussion in *Moses* of the rebellion of Korah against Moses. Korah, claiming that everything is already holy and does not need to be hallowed, leads a band against Moses and the "law" that Moses is imposing upon the people. Because the whole work of the covenant between God and people is threatened, Moses must now doom the rebels to destruction. Buber comes down on the side of "law" against lawlessness, although he still means by "law" the Torah, or instruction of God in the dialogue with him, rather than any fixed universal that can be detached from God's address and man's response:

> Without law, that is, without any clear-cut and transmissible line of demarcation between that which is pleasing to God and that which is displeasing to Him, there can be no historical continuity of divine rule upon the earth.
>
> ...As against this comes the false argument of the rebels that the law as such displaces the spirit and the freedom, and the false conclusion that it ought to be replaced by them.

The false would become true as soon as the presence of God comes to be fulfilled in all creatures, but those eschatologies, like the pseudomessianism of the followers of Sabbatai Zvi (the seventeenth-century Kabbalist and "mystical messiah" of Palestine) and Jacob Frank (eighteenth century), that proclaim that to be already the case cannot withstand the realities of history. "The 'Mosaic' attitude facing this is to believe in the future of a 'holy people'; and to prepare for it within history."

The Prophetic Faith completes and crowns Buber's years of concern for the origin of messianism in the Bible, and in many ways it is his most impressive book of biblical exegesis. In it, he resumes the thesis of *The Kingship of God* that there can be no split between the "religious" and the "social," that Israel cannot become the people of YHVH without just faith between men. To recognize YHVH as Lord of the world means that man cannot establish in earthly life his own regime and satisfy the power above by cult. "The God of the universe is the God of history." He is the deity who walks with his creature and with his people along the hard way of history.

Our path in the history of faith is not a path from one kind of deity to another but from the "God Who hides Himself" (Isaiah 45:15) to the God of history that reveals himself.

The prophet of Israel is a partner in this revelation. Contrary to the popular conception, he hardly ever foretells an inevitable future but speaks to an actual and definite situation in the present. Even his message of disaster is meant to awaken man's real power of decision so that he may turn back to the covenant—the fulfillment of the kingship of God. Human and divine turning correspond, not as if man's turning brings about God's, but God responds to man's turning back, even as he responds to man's turning away. The Israelite prophet "knows" God not as a subject knows an object but in the intimate contact of the two partners of a two-sided occurrence. He does not seek God in order to hear future things but for the sake of this contact which, like that of Adam knowing Eve, is fully mutual and fully real. Thus, the name YHVH, which was disclosed at the revelation to Moses in the thornbush, is unfolded in the "righteousness" of Amos, the "loving kindness" of Hosea, and the "holiness" of Isaiah. "Only all together could express what is meant by the being present of the ONE Who is present to Israel. Who is 'with it.'" This revelation of God's presence is also a demand placed on man, for there is something essential that must come from him. This prophetic situation of reciprocal dialogue carries over to the messianic, for the messianic prophecy, too, conceals a demand and an alternative. It is not prediction, but a conditional offer. "The righteous one, whom God 'has,' must rise out of this historic loam of man."

The Messiah of Isaiah is not a divine figure who takes the place of man's turning or brings about a redemption that man has merely to accept and enter into. The belief in the coming of a messianic leader is the belief that at last man shall, with his whole being, speak the word that answers God's word. Through the nucleus of Israel that does not betray the covenant and the election (Isaiah's "holy remnant"), the living connection between God and the people is upheld, and from their midst will arise "the perfected one." Through his word and life, Israel will turn to God and serve as the beginning of his kingdom.

> The Messiah—whether he is regarded more as the man whom God has found, or as the man whom God has sent... is anointed to set up with human forces and human responsibility the divine order of human community.... The Messiah of Isaiah is godlike, as is the man in whom the likeness has unfolded, no more and no less. He is not nearer to God than what is appointed to man as man; nor does he pass over to the divine side; he too stands before God in indestructible dialogue.

When Isaiah's hope for the true king is disappointed, the hopes of his successor, the anonymous prophet known as Deutero-Isaiah, turns to the prophet, the *nabi*; here, not as a success story, but out of the depths of history and of the suffering of the "servant," the messianic task is continued. The word is spoken to the prophet as between person and person, and it is left to him to translate it into a human language and to answer, lamenting, complaining to God, disputing with God about justice, praying. In Jeremiah, the dialogue of Israel's faith has reached its pure form. If man only speaks truly to God, there is nothing that he may not say to him. And to man, to Israel, Jeremiah places God's demand not for religion, but for community, in order that God's kingdom shall come. "Therefore here, where He blames a people for not having become a community, man's claim upon man takes precedence of God's claim." God leaves to man the choice of opening his heart to the hard truth or of accepting the easy lie as truth. "This God makes it burdensome for the believer and easy for the unbeliever; and His revelation is nothing but a different form of hiding His face." All that can help man here is the force of extreme despair, a despair so elemental that it saps the last will of life or renews the soul by prompting it to turn with its whole being. The faith relationship has to stand the test of an utterly changed situation and be renewed, if at all, in a different form.

The God against whose remoteness Job struggles, the deity who rages and *is silent,* who "hides his face," brings Job and Deutero-Isaiah to the despair arising from the eclipse of the divine light. Only when God draws near Job again, when he *sees* God, is this despair lifted. In the midst of precisely *this* eclipse of God, Buber made one of his most remarkable statements of faith: "The creation itself already means communication between Creator and creature. The just Creator gives to all His creatures His boundary, so that each may become fully itself." The meaning of this faith can be understood only in terms of the succession of God's "servants": Job the faithful rebel, Abraham, Moses, David, and Isaiah, a succession that leads to Deutero-Isaiah's servant of the Lord, whose sufferings especially link him with Job. Only in the depths of suffering does the servant discover the mystery of "the God of the sufferers" in which, in the communion with God, he knows that God is eternal and that God is his "portion."

"The *zaddik,* the man justified by God, suffers for the sake of God and of His work of salvation, and God is with him in his suffering." Deutero-Isaiah's "suffering servant of the lord" voluntarily takes on himself all the griefs and sicknesses of the people's iniquities in order to bring them back to YHVH. The "servant" cannot be identified either with Israel or with Christ, as is traditionally done. According to *The Prophetic Faith,* the servant is not a corporate but a personal being that takes shape through the generations in many likenesses and paths of life.

In suffering for the sake of God, the servant comes to recognize that God suffers with him and that he is working together with God for the redemption of the world. The servant thus completes the work of the judges and the prophets, the work of making real God's kingship over the people.

Although he is a prophet, he is no longer a powerless opposition to the powerful, for it is laid on him to inaugurate God's new order of peace and justice for the world. This kingdom now signifies in reality all the human world. Yet there remains a special tie between the personal servant and the servant Israel. Through his word and life, Israel will turn to God establishing God's sovereignty upon itself and serving as the beginning of his kingdom.

There are three stages on the servant's way: first, the futile labor of the Israelite prophet in Israel; second, the work of suffering, when the servant not only endures but suffers willingly; and third, that of fulfilled messianism, the stage which to Buber was clearly unthinkable in an unredeemed world. The stage in which Israel and mankind persistently live is the second one. Here the unity between personal servant and the servant Israel passes over to their unity in suffering. Living and writing in a time just after the greatest suffering that the Diaspora, the galut, had ever known, Buber undoubtedly had the extermination of the Jews in the Nazi Holocaust in mind when he spoke of this unity of the personal servant and the servant Israel in the willing acceptance of suffering:

> As far as the great suffering of Israel's dispersion was not compulsory suffering only, but suffering in truth willingly borne, not passive but active, it is interpreted in the image of the servant. Whosoever accomplishes in Israel the active suffering of Israel, he is the servant, and he is Israel, in whom YHVH "glorifies Himself."

"Only a viewpoint that is Biblical in a very profound sense," writes the eminent Old Testament scholar J. Coert Rylaarsdam in a discussion of *The Prophetic Faith*, "could so consistently illuminate every part of the Bible it touches." "Professor Buber," says Rylaarsdam, "is in a unique way the agent through whom, in our day, Judaism and Christianity have met and enriched one another."

As if anticipating the "eclipse of God," which was more and more to become a central theme in Buber's thought in that year and those that followed, Ewald Wasmuth wrote him in 1951 that after all the noise about the death of God, he could imagine people losing touch with the Bible for some centuries and then someone's reading Buber's *The Prophetic Faith* and finding in it such power that his heart would beat and he would seek again the sources, and the breath of God would return into a godless world.

In 1943, Buber wrote to Lina Lewy, the Jewish disciple of Leonhard Ragaz,

> I may not believe in a Messiah who has already come, so and so many years ago; because I sense the unredeemedness of the world all too deeply to be able to agree with the conception of a completed redemption—even if it be only of the 'soul' (I will not live with a "redeemed" soul in an unredeemed world). God is our help in all need and none outside of him. But this was also—of

this I am certain—the faith of Jesus himself. I do not believe in Jesus, but I believe *with* him.

In a memorial address for Ragaz in Kurt Wilhelm's synagogue in Jerusalem, Buber made his most concise and impassioned statement on the place of Jesus in the Jewish community, a statement that shows at once the sympathy and the "otherness" that have marked his dialogue with his Christian friends. It also shows, as does the letter to Lina Lewy, the indelible impact of the Holocaust on Buber:

> I firmly believe that the Jewish community in the course of its renaissance, will recognize Jesus; and not merely as a great figure in its religious history, but also in the organic context of a Messianic development extending over millennia, whose final goal is the Redemption of Israel and of the world. But I believe equally firmly that we will never recognize Jesus as the Messiah Come, for this would contradict the deepest meaning of our Messianic passion.... In our view redemption occurs forever, and none has yet occurred. Standing, bound and shackled, in the pillory of mankind, we demonstrate with the bloody body of our people the unredeemedness of the world. For us there is no cause of Jesus; only the cause of God exists for us.

Ragaz was a genuine friend because, in opposition to those who hold that the election of Israel has passed over to Christianity, he held that Judaism and Christianity are the two living streams of Israel and that each must become itself in order to be able to come to the other.

Even when he conducted his Open Forum "experiments in dialogue" in the Jerusalem synagogue of Rabbi Kurt Wilhelm, Buber refused to take part in the service beforehand. Most religious people, and not only Orthodox, could not understand Buber's "religious abstinence." Buber's living faith was an unmediated and thereby a primal Jewish one, Ben-Chorin explains, adding that it is often overlooked that the Jewish Law has taken on the function of a mediator between God and the people of Israel. Buber's total rejection of mediation, his direct dialogue with God, caused him also to renounce for himself all covert Jewish forms of mediation. More radically than the Hasidim, Buber rejected every division of life into holy and profane spheres. Buber forsook the rituals that designated set days and hours, circumstances and spheres, as holy in order to bring into the light of God those wide stretches of everyday life that the Jewish rituals leave in the darkness of profanity.

In 1954, Hugo Bergmann noted in his diary how moved he was in conversation with Buber by Buber's positive attitude toward the land of Israel:

> Only with us is there continuity from generation to generation. Along with all the stupidity that takes place here and all the sins

there still grows here something that works in the heart of those who live here, despite all their disappointments, receives them and bears their working further. There in Europe everyone is isolated. Here and there there is a small group that lives as a sect, but over all the persons of faith live *next* to life.

In 1959, Buber wrote to his old friend Nahum Goldmann, who for years was president of the World Zionist Organization, that it would not be possible for him to treat the theme that Goldmann had proposed, namely, how Jewish life is possible. "In the last years this theme has become for me, especially in its general formulation, ever more problematic, and I do not believe that I have something positive to say about it, particularly before such a public audience."

Buber's interest in psychology continued during these years, and with it the development of his philosophical anthropology. In 1946, in reply to a question from Hans Trüb, Buber declared that the world is clearly, first of all, that against which the soul "pushes." For the infant, the world is not the mother's breast, which belongs to him, but the table corner that causes him pain. Thus, world is first of all what presents itself emphatically as "other than I," which I do not include in my soul and cannot enter into. The perception of world *as world* takes place ever again through vexation, resistance, contradiction, absurdity—which must be overcome before one can come to an understanding or even to a friendship with or love for the world. This conception of the world led Buber to a critique of the modern misuse of the concept of the "unconscious."

The world is not mine, Buber wrote Trüb, but it can "become" mine again and again in genuine meetings, not mine as *in* me, but mine as *with* me. This fact has become obscured by the modern conception of the "unconscious." The unconscious is to be acknowledged as a psychological auxiliary—to be treated with foresight and restraint, to be confronted ever again with reality, always to be grasped dynamically and not statically, as process and not as something that can be fixed as an object. But it pretends to be immensely more. Through the fiction of the "world in the soul," therefore of a world that is mine in me, it wants to conceal the possibility of the "life of the soul with the world." This was one of Buber's clearest statements on the danger of "psychologism," to which he had pointed at length a quarter of a century before in his address to Jung's and Trüb's Psychological Club in Zurich on "The Psychologizing of the World."

In 1949, Ernst Michel wrote to Buber of the "painful event of the departure of our beloved friend Hans Trüb," whose posthumous book *Healing through Meeting* he and Arie Sborowitz edited and Buber introduced. This book was an *Auseinandersetzung*, or discussion, of the dialectical psychology of Jung against which Trüb developed his own dialogical-anthropological approach to psychotherapy. In his Introduction to *Healing through Meeting,* Buber did not mention Jung, but in a letter to Trüb in 1946, Buber anticipated his own famous controversy with Jung five years later. Commenting on the *Introduction to Mythology* by Jung and Karl Kerényi, Buber said that seemingly the two authors deal with the same subject from different sides. But, in truth, Kerényi means by myth something that arises *out of contact with the world*, as the disclosure and shaping of the mysteries of this reality; Jung, in contrast, understands by myth what arises of its own *in the soul* and what ultimately cannot express or mean anything else than the mysteries of the soul itself.

In 1947, Buber went to Europe, where he gave more than sixty lectures at universities in Holland, Belgium, Sweden, Denmark, France, and England. The enthusiastic reception that he received in England and Holland surprised him and made clear to him that he was more in touch with the intellectual, cultural, and spiritual life of Europe than he had thought.

The beautiful little essay "Books and Men," which Buber wrote in 1947 and privately printed and distributed to his friends, is a personal confession that crowns Buber's development from the "easy word" to the "hard word," and from the spiritual and cultural preoccupations of his youth to his later unwavering commitment to the "lived concrete."

> If I had been asked in my early youth whether I preferred to have dealings only with men or only with books, my answer would certainly have been in favour of books. In later years this has become less and less the case. Not that I have had so much better experiences with men than with books; on the contrary, purely delightful books even now come my way more often than purely delightful men. But the many bad experiences with men have nourished the meadow of my life as the noblest book could not do, and the good experiences have made the earth into a garden for me. On the other hand, no book does more than remove me into a paradise of great spirits, where my innermost heart never forgets, I cannot dwell long, nor even wish that I could do so.
>
> For (I must say this straight out in order to be understood) my innermost heart loves the world more than it loves the spirit. I have not, indeed, cleaved to life in the world as I might have;... again and again I remain guilty towards it for falling short of what it expects of me, and this is partly, to be sure, because I belong so to the spirit.

This is the testimony welling up from the soul of the man who knew early that he was destined to love the world!

The renunciation of all the literary possibilities and means at his disposal that accompanied Buber's move from the "easy word" to the "hard word" also entered into his retelling of Hasidic legends, which moved from the multicolored fabrics of his earlier books to the rough, crude, and fragmentary events that he later called "legendary anecdotes." Buber himself described his first attempts to testify to the great reality of faith that he encountered in

Hasidism as the work of "an immature man" who did not yet know how to hold in check his inner inclination to poeticize the narrative material. Although he knew from the beginning that Hasidism was a way of life to which the teaching provided the indispensable commentary, it was only through the First World War that it became overwhelmingly clear to Buber that his life was involved in a mysterious manner in the task that had claimed him. The young litterateur who began the task in 1905 would never have dreamed of the existential claim that the Hasidic material would place on him and with it the possibility of making dialogue fully concrete and serious:

> Since I began my work on Hasidic literature, I have done this for the sake of the teaching and the way. But at that time I believed that one might relate to them, merely as an observer. Since then I have realized that the teaching is there that one may learn it and the way that one may walk on it. The deeper I realized this, so much more this work, against which my life measured and ventured itself, became for me question, suffering, and also even consolation.

The two volumes of *The Tales of the Hasidim (The Early Masters and The Later Masters)*, which Buber published originally in Hebrew under the title *Or Hagganuz* and later in German, English, and French, among other languages, crown Buber's lifetime of retelling Hasidic legends and stories. In them, two earlier German works, written since Buber rejected his original overly free poetic re-creations for ones that remain closely faithful to the simple, rough originals, are included, and even these were totally reworked. By far the greater part of them were written after Buber's arrival in Palestine in 1938. In his Preface, written in the summer of 1946, Buber credited "the air of this land" with the urge to this new and more comprehensive composition. The Jewish sages of old said that it makes one wise, but to Buber it granted a different gift: the strength to make a new beginning even after he had regarded his work on Hasidic legends as completed. The form that Buber found for these tales was that of the "legendary anecdotes", which reconstruct the events that lie at the heart of the tales. "They are called anecdotes because each one of them communicates an event complete in itself, and legendary because at the base of them lies the stammering of inspired witnesses who witnessed to what befell them." The Hasidim believed that telling stories about the *zaddikim* was in itself a real event that carried to future generations the power that once was active by propagating it in the living word. This quality of story as event is beautifully captured by a story within a story that Buber told in the Preface:

> A rabbi, whose grandfather had been a disciple of the Baal-Shem, was asked to tell a story. "A story," he said, "must be told in such a way that it constitutes help in itself." And he told: "My grandfather was lame. Once they asked him to tell a story about his

teacher. And he related how the holy Baal-Shem used to hop and dance while he prayed. My grandfather rose as he spoke, and he was so swept away by his story that he himself began to hop and dance to show how the master had done. From that hour on he was cured of his lameness. That's the way to tell a story!"

In 1949, Hermann Hesse, who had himself received the Nobel Prize for literature the previous year, nominated Buber for this same prize. In his letter to the Swedish Academy, Hesse spoke of Buber as "the great teacher and leader of the spiritual elite among the Jews." "As translator of the Bible, as rediscoverer and interpreter of Hasidic wisdom, as scholar, as great writer, and finally as a wise man, as teacher and representative of a high ethic and humanity, he is, in the opinion of those who know his work, one of the leading and most valuable personalities in the present day literature of the world." In a letter that Hesse wrote to a friend explaining his nomination of Buber for the Nobel Prize in literature, it was to *The Tales of the Hasidim* in particular that he pointed:

> Martin Buber is in my judgment not only one of the few wise men who live on the earth at the present time, he is also a writer of a very high order, and, more than that, he has enriched world literature with a genuine treasure as has no other living author—*The Tales of the Hasidim....* Martin Buber... is the worthiest spiritual representative of Israel, the people that has had to suffer the most of all people in our time.

These letters, Buber confided to me later, were written with "a sympathy that I know is deep." Writing to Hesse himself after he had received from friends in Stockholm the wording of Hesse's letter of nomination, Buber said, "I have once again felt, and with a forcefulness as never before, how unimportant 'fame' is and how important is confirmation by those to whom our trust belongs. We mortals need to be confirmed by our mortal brothers." This theme of confirmation was to be central to the philosophical anthropology that Buber set forth in *The Knowledge of Man* in the years immediately following and particularly in "Distance and Relation," which concludes with the sentence: "It is from one man to another that the heavenly bread of self-being is passed."

In his contribution to *The Philosophy of Martin Buber,* Walter Kaufmann says of Buber's *Tales of the Hasidim* that they are definitive in their simplicity. In *Tales of the Hasidim,* "Buber presents gem upon gem without mounting each in a setting of inferior quality. Buber's stories cannot be improved by cutting. That is more than one can say of the art of any of the four evangelists."

> What saves Buber's work is its perfection. He has given us one of the great religious books of all time, a work that invites compari-

son with the great Scriptures of mankind.... The rank of such works does not depend on their positivistic accuracy but on their profundity. And that is true also of the Tales of the Hasidim.

Buber saw the truth of Hasidism as vitally important for persons of *all* faiths, "for now is the hour when we are in danger of forgetting for what purpose we are on earth, and I know of no other teaching that reminds us of this so forcibly." "Hasidism has never set foot in the world of man as Christianity has done," Buber concluded, but "because of its truth and because of the great need of the hour, I carry it into the world against its will." Just how much this was against the will of Hasidism was illustrated all too clearly in June 1965, when the young men of the Hasidic Bratslaver Seminary in the Mea She'arim in Jerusalem spoke of Buber's death with the Yiddish phrase that one uses for the death of an animal!

Buber never wanted to propagate Hasidism as such, but Hasidism was for him an impressive example of a kind of piety that is tied to life and that has overcome the unholy division into sacred and profane spheres by the hallowing of the whole of life. Nowhere is this clearer than in the little book *The Way of Man,* (according to the teachings of the Hasidim), which was originally given by Buber as a series of lectures in Holland. In 1948, Hermann Hesse wrote Buber that *The Way of Man* "is probably the most beautiful of your works that I have read." *The Way of Man,* writes Gershom Scholem, "is not only a gem of literature but also an extraordinary lesson in religious anthropology, presented in the language of Hasidism and inspired by a large number of authentic Hasidic sayings."

The Way of Man is an entirely different kind of work from any of Buber's other Hasidic writings. It consists of six sections, each in the form of a commentary on a Hasidic tale, supplemented by other tales and sayings. Yet it is far more than a mere interpretation or summary of Hasidic teaching. No other of Buber's works gives us so much of his own simple wisdom as this remarkable distillation. It ranks with *I and Thou, For the Sake of Heaven,* and *Tales of the Hasidim* as one of the great and enduring classics. Even more than between the separate tales in each section of *Tales of the Hasidim,* the sections of *The Way of Man* are organically linked so that it is, in itself, a way of wisdom, which no philosophical statement, however profound, can be.

Along with *What Is Man?,* two other expressions of Buber's activity as professor of social philosophy, and later as chairman of the Department of Sociology at the Hebrew University, were, his important theoretical essay "Society and the State" (1951) and his book *Paths in Utopia,* published in Hebrew in 1947 and in English translation in 1949. While the former represents a far-reaching distinction between the "political principle" and the "social principle," the latter is a history of decentralistic socialism, including separate chapters on Proudhon, Kropotkin, Landauer, Marx, and Lenin, as well as one on the kibbutzim of Palestine. To Lambert Schneider, to whom he wished to entrust the German edition of *Paths in Utopia,* Buber wrote: "The book has had a strong success in England; in the Sunday Times it was characterized as the most important book of the year. I believe that it has a special task to fulfill in Germany—as an intellectual-historical presentation of 'utopian socialism' and criticism of the teachings of Marx and Lenin."

What sets Buber apart from men like Reinhold Niebuhr, Bertrand Russell, and other contemporary political thinkers, and what brings him into fellowship with men like A. D. Gordon, Albert Camus, Carlo Levi, and Ignazio Silone, is the basic distinction that he makes between the "social principle" and the "political principle." The "social principle" is the concrete principle of real fellowship and real community. The "political principle," on the other hand, is a basically abstract principle that sacrifices the social reality of fellowship to the domination of government. The latent crisis that exists between nation and nation makes the political surplus above what is necessary for order inevitable, but a social restructuring toward maximum decentralization compatible with given social conditions is possible and necessary if mankind is not to be swallowed by the political principle. The social vitality of a nation, its cultural unity and independence, depends on the social spontaneity to be found in it. Social education and a concern for real social change are necessary if this spontaneity is to be preserved and enhanced.

To create new fellowship and social spontaneity in a world in which capitalism has left man lacking in organic social structure and in which communism has lost sight of social regeneration in favor of a rigid political centralism, Buber proposed a federalistic communal socialism. Buber distinguished his socialism from theoretical utopian socialism, which he characterized as a schematic fiction that contrives systems of absolute validity on the basis of an abstract notion of human nature. Topical socialism begins with the diversity and contrariety of the trends of the age and grows out of the needs of a given situation. At the same time, this local and topical realization must be nothing but a point of departure for the higher goal of an organic society: a community of communities eventually broadening to a world confederation of commonwealths, a grouping of nations that, like the individual commune, will preserve the maximum social spontaneity compatible with the situation and the given time.

The most important vehicles for social restructuring, Buber announced in *Paths in Utopia,* are the full cooperatives, or village communes, which combine production and consumption, industry and agriculture, in a cooperative community revolving around commonly held land. The most promising experiment in the village commune, in Buber's opinion, has been that of the Jewish collective settlements in Palestine. These have been based on the needs of given local situations combined with socialistic and biblical teachings on social justice. The members of these communes have combined a rare willingness to experiment and unusual critical self-awareness with an "amazingly positive relationship—amounting to a regular faith—... to the inmost being of their Commune." The communes themselves, moreover, have worked together in close cooperation and at the same time have left complete freedom for the constant branching off of new forms and different types of social structure, the most famous of which are the kvutza and the kibbutz. The rapid influx of Jewish refugees from the Nazis into Palestine during the years of the Third Aliyah in many cases resulted in the rise of a quasi-elite who were not able to provide true leadership for the communes and came into conflict with the genuine *halutzim*. Despite this fact and the politicization that in recent years had split kibbutzim along party lines, Buber felt that the Jewish communes were of central significance in the struggle for a structurally new society in which individual groups would be given the greatest possible autonomy and yet would enjoy the greatest possible interrelationship with one another. In America in 1952, Buber reaffirmed his conviction that the most important decision of the next generations is that between a socialism of power and a spontaneous socialism springing up from below, between the "political principle" and the "social principle." "The coming state of humanity in the great crisis depends very much on whether another type of socialism can be set up against Moscow, and I venture even today to call it Jerusalem."

Buber saw his image of the socialist restructuring of society as based on an eternal human need:

> The need of man to feel his own house as a room in some greater, all-embracing structure in which he is at home, to feel that the other inhabitants of it with whom he lives and works are all acknowledging and confirming his individual existence. If the world of man is to become a human world, then immediacy must rule... between house and human house.

The principle of mutual confirmation, which Buber expanded in much more abstract terms in "Distance and Relation" (1951), was stated with clarity, concreteness, and conciseness as Buber pointed to the significance of the attempt of architects to build surroundings that invite meeting and centers that shape meeting:

> The unavowed secret of man is that he wants to be confirmed in his being... not merely in the family, in the party assembly or in the public house, but also in the course of neighborly encounters, perhaps when he or the other steps out of the door of his house or to the window of his house and the greeting with which they greet each other will be accomplished by a glance of well-wishing, a glance in which curiosity, mistrust, and routine will have been overcome by a mutual sympathy....

When Buber came to Palestine in 1938, he continued the demand that adult education be placed in the center of the activities of the Hebrew University. After the war, however, the Jews in Morocco, Algeria, Egypt, Lebanon, Syria, Yemen, Saudi Arabia, and elsewhere were dispossessed of their property and forced to leave homes where their ancestors had lived in many cases for two thousand years. It was this mass immigration of Oriental Jews into the new State of Israel that occasioned the great, unforeseen problem of education and finally brought into being the institution that Buber envisaged, the Beth Midrash l'Morei Am, the School for the Education of Teachers of the People. Buber was invited by the Hebrew University Adult Education Center, the government, and the Jewish Agency to set up a center that would train teachers who would themselves go to live in the camps and hostels for immigrants as well as in settlements established by the newcomers. Gideon Freudenberg became the director of action, or principal, Buber the director of ideas and president of the school, in daily contact with the students. The people in the provisory camps were fifty percent Oriental Jews and fifty percent from European detention camps and, before that, Nazi concentration camps. It was agreed that the teachers to be trained should themselves be new immigrants. At first, the institute was established for a year and then extended because of its great success. The new school was to train a small group every year, the number to be kept limited so that the teacher might get to know the students individually and establish contact with every one of them.

It is not question and answer, Buber pointed out, but the dialogue between person and person that lies at the heart of education.

> The people's school is based upon the encouragement of contact between teacher and students—upon the principle of dialogue; dialogue of questions from both sides, and answers from both sides, dialogue of joint observation of a certain reality in nature, or in art, or in society, dialogue of joint penetration into one of the problems of life, dialogue of true fellowship, in which the breaks in conversation are no less of a dialogue than speech itself.

The school also became an *ulpan*—a place for the intensive learning of Hebrew where students and teachers were in contact from morning to night and talked over things that they had heard during the day. In this way, it was possible to influence not only the minds but also the hearts of the students. The ages of the students ranged from seventeen to fifty, their education from below high school to university graduation with many years of teaching experience abroad, their understanding of Judaism from shallow to profound. Because of the pressing demand the course had to be limited to one year and students had to work at least fourteen hours daily to complete the work. "In the course of my life, I have not seen such intensity of learning from morning until midnight," Buber reported. The six hours of daily lessons took the form not of lectures but of seminars in which all the students took as active a part as possible. This allowed for individual attention to the student, because the classes were of thirty or fewer. The teachers, who were brought from the Hebrew University and elsewhere, had to be ready to give the students whatever assistance was necessary, advising them and, in many cases, even consoling them because they had suffered so much. Those who came from the detention camps brought with them a stress that the teachers and the directors had to help them overcome. But Buber and Freudenberg also felt responsible for their future existence and advised them as to how they could solve their financial problems and how they could marry and build a family. Freudenberg, who lived with them, told them that his office was always open, and Buber himself was always ready to receive them when they wanted to speak with him.

By now, Buber had been living for some time in his third and last home in Jerusalem, the beautiful Arab-style house in Talbiyeh at 3 Chovevei Zion (most appropriately, "Lovers of Zion" Street). The hostel on Jabotinsky Street was around the corner. Buber gave Freudenberg a call at ten every evening, and they sat together until very late hours to speak on the problems of the day and on the whole philosophy of mankind. When a prospective teacher of the people came, Buber and Freudenberg sat together in the office of the school and talked with the candidate about his or her interests and intentions. In this way, they gained impressions about the personality of the candidate and his or her qualifications for this type of demanding work. "Buber knew if this man or this woman was apt for the work," Freudenberg has said. "We had very, very few disappointments." Almost every evening, Buber would call Gideon Freudenberg to discuss some minor problem or suggestion. Buber agreed to accept people to the seminar as students only on the basis of an interview, and not on the basis of certification. He participated in all the interviews. Buber's name helped establish and support the seminar, especially in coping with budgetary problems. Once, when the Jewish Agency did not proffer its share and Freudenberg had to pay out of his own pocket, Buber went to the agency and refused to leave their office until they gave him one thousand pounds! In the third year, the Ministry of Education requested that the number of students be doubled.

Buber himself taught a course on the Bible, one time spending three months on the meaning of the Hebrew word *re'ah* in *ahavta l're'ah cmocha*, usually translated as "Love your neighbor as yourself." When Buber taught, he did not read from notes but would just speak. He gave every pupil an opportunity to interrupt and ask questions, after which he would continue his talk. Buber's influence on the students was very great, according to Freudenberg, not because of the content of his teaching but because of his personality. "When he read from the Bible and the prophets, it was as if the prophets themselves came into the room." Thus, Buber himself embodied the aim of the school, which was, primarily, addressing the wholeness of the person, because "only whole persons can influence others." What he had spoken of ten years before in his address to the teachers of Tel Aviv he now was able to make a reality—the conjunction of situation and person in the education of character. "Character is not above situation," Buber stated in his discussion of the school in America in 1951, "but is attached to the cruel, hard demand of this hour."

After Buber's death in 1965, the Hebrew University announced plans for the establishment of an ambitious and extensive "Martin Buber Center for Adult Education and Continuing Education" in a large building to be constructed for this purpose "in grateful recognition of Buber's pioneering work." The Martin Buber Center for Adult Education was opened in 1972 on the new-old Mount Scopus Campus overlooking Jerusalem in an impressive building that includes a Martin Buber room, in which Buber's study is preserved exactly as it was in his house in Talbiyeh, with his desk, the picture of Paula, the pictures of Florence and Rome, the art history books in the old bookcase, his magnifying glass, and his pen. The director of the Martin Buber Center is Dr. Kalman Yoran, a graduate of the Beth Midrash I'Morei Am. Dr. Yoran hopes to revive Buber's and Freudenberg's School for Educating Teachers of the People in order to train adult education teachers to work in all the communities of Israel. At the same time, the center does impressive work in continuing education and is in touch with the local developments in adult education throughout Israel in exactly the way that Buber proposed.

In August 1953, Ludwig Strauss died. When Buber learned the news of Ludwig's death, he sent Eva a remarkable letter of comfort:

> My beloved Evie, since the news came yesterday afternoon I have several times had the impression that Ludwig's soul-image was near me, and just now, before I took up this piece of paper, it seemed as if he stood next to me, each time without concerning himself about me, but also without strangeness. But it was not at all the Ludwig whom I had seen when I took leave of him and have since borne in mind, nor was it an earlier Ludwig, and yet it was not shadowy and indistinct: I mean that it was the completed image, the gestalt in its completion, such as a person can achieve only through the deepest suffering. And it seems to me that the peace of his last days has to do with that completion in a manner that no survivor can understand; it seems to me that the great weakness of the dying earthly being was only the visible in it, the invisible was the presentiment of becoming complete that overcame all infirmity.
> God comfort you and bless you and your sons!

◆ *Martin Buber in the 1920's*

◆ *Franz Rosenzweig in 1920.*

◆ *Rosenzweig at the writing desk (1928)*

◆ *Buber on his first trip to Palestine (1927).*

◆ *Buber around 1930.*

◆ *Buber with his German publisher, Salman Schocken.*

◆ *Buber with Leo Baeck, leader of the German Jews under the Nazis.*

◆ *Buber in his study in Jerusalem.*

◆ *Buber at the summer camp for Jewish teachers in Lehnitz, Germany (1934).*

◆ *Buber in Palestine.*

◆ *Buber with Leo Hermann of the former Prague Bar Kochba Union in Jerusalem in the 1940's.*

◆ *Buber with students at the Hebrew University on Mr. Scopus in Jerusalem (1940).*

◆ *Buber at his Jerusalem bookdealer's (March 1946).*

PART IV

Postwar Germany and America: Replies to Critics

(1945-1963)

❖

· IV ·

Postwar Germany
and America:
Replies to Critics

(1945 1963)

♦ 16 ♦

Dialogue with German Christians

(1945-1961)

The resumption of Buber's interrupted dialogue with German thinkers and friends in Germany after the defeat of Hitler and the end of the Second World War was an important part of a whole new phase of his involvement in Jewish-Christian dialogue. It centered on *Two Types of Faith,* the book on Jesus and Paul that Buber wrote during the siege of Jerusalem and published in Germany, England, and America in the early 1950s. In its paperback edition, *Two Types of Faith* is subtitled "A Study of the Interpenetration of Judaism and Christianity." It is also a study of their fundamental divergence and, in particular, of the messianism of biblical Judaism that Buber felt was continued and reinforced by Jesus as opposed to the altogether different messianism of Paul and John that revolved around the belief in the risen Christ rather than around the biblical *emunah,* or trust, that Jesus preached.

In the essay with which he introduced his collection of Hasidic books in 1927, Buber said that the meaning of Jesus' appearance for the Gentiles "remains for me the real seriousness of Western history." But from the standpoint of Judaism, Jesus is the first of those men who stepped out of the hiddenness in which God has left the Servant and have acknowledged their Messiahship in their souls and in their words. "That this first one in the series was incomparably the purest, the most legitimate, and most endowed with real Messianic power—*as I experience ever again when those personal words that ring true to me merge for me into a unity whose speaker becomes visible to me*—alters nothing in the fact that he was the first in this series; indeed it undoubtedly belongs... to the fearfully penetrating reality that has characterized the whole series of those who proclaimed themselves the Messiah [italics added]." It was an astonishing fact that for Buber the dialogue with Jesus (as with Plato and a few others that he had read) was not a metaphorical but an actual dialogue with the person of Jesus, who became present to him in the merging of various of his sayings. *In Two Types of Faith,* Buber seriously questioned the implication that Jesus saw himself as the Messiah. But he retained the dialogue with the person who reached him through the voice:

> From my youth onwards I have found in Jesus my great brother.
> That Christianity has regarded and does regard him as God and
> Saviour has always appeared to me a fact of the highest impor-
> tance which, for his sake and my own, I must endeavour to
> understand.... My own fraternally open relationship to him has
> grown ever stronger and clearer, and today I see him more
> strongly and clearly than ever before.

Two Types of Faith is the last in that series of biblical studies in which Buber dealt with the origin of messianism, and in that sense represents the completion of the foundation Buber laid seventeen years before in *The Kingship of God.* Jesus stood in the shadow of the Deutero-Isaianic suffering servant of the Lord, but he stepped out of the real hiddenness that is essential to the servant's work of suffering. Even then, however, Buber did not believe that Jesus held himself divine in the sense in which he was later held. Furthermore, whatever was the case with his "messianic consciousness," Jesus, insofar as we know him from the synoptic tradition, did not summon his disciples to have faith in Christ but in God. The faith that he preached was the Jewish *emunah*—"that unconditional trust in the grace which makes a person no longer afraid even of death because death is also of grace." Paul and John, in contrast, made faith in Christ *(pistis)* the one door to salvation. This meant the abolition of the immediacy between God and man, which had been the essence of the covenant and the kingship of God. "'I am the door' it now runs (John 10:9): it avails nothing, as Jesus taught, to knock where one stands (before the 'narrow door'), it avails nothing, as the Pharisees thought to step into the open door; entrance is only for those who believe in 'the door.'"

Buber saw Jesus as demanding that the person go beyond what would ordinarily be his full capacity in order to be ready to enter the kingdom of God that draws near. But Jesus follows biblical Judaism in holding that God has given man the Torah as instruction to teach him to direct his heart to God. The Torah is not an objective law independent of man's actual relationship to God, Buber declared here. It bestows life only on those who receive it for the sake of God so that something of hearing still clings to the divine command. "Fulfillment of the Torah means to extend the hearing of the Word to the whole dimension of human existence."

Paul, in contrast to Jesus, posits a dualism between faith and action based on a belief in the impossibility of the fulfillment of the law, which he conceived as an independent objective set of rules that made all men sinners before God and their salvation dependent upon accepting the proposition that God suffered, died, and ascended in Christ. Trust in the immediacy between man and God is further destroyed through Paul's strong tendency to split off God's wrath and his mercy into two separate powers, with the world given over to the power of judgment until the crucifixion and resurrection of Christ bring mercy and redemption. He sees man as vile by nature and incapable of receiving pardon from God until the advent of Christ. Paul's God has no regard for the people to whom he speaks but uses them up for the higher ends of his divine plan. God alone makes man unfree and deserving of wrath, while in the work of deliverance God almost disappears behind Christ. As compared to Paul, the Christian Paulinism of our time does not emphasize the demonocracy of the world, but it, too, sees existence as divided into an unrestricted rule of wrath and a sphere of reconciliation. "De facto the redeemed Christian soul stands over against an unredeemed world of men in lofty impotence."

Buber contrasted the modern Paulinism of the Protestant crisis theologians with Franz Kafka's "Paulinism of the unredeemed." Kafka knew from within the "eclipse of God" that, in the years immediately following, Buber himself was to put forward as the character of this hour of human history. Kafka's "unexpressed, ever-present theme is the remoteness of the judge, the remoteness of the lord of the castle, the hiddenness, the eclipse, the darkness." He describes most exactly, from inner awareness, "the rule of the foul devilry which fills the foreground." But Kafka, the Jew, also knows that God's hiding himself does not diminish the immediacy: In the immediacy, God remains the redeemer and the contradiction of existence becomes for us a theophany.

> Kafka depicts the course of the world in gloomier colours than ever before, and yet he proclaims Emunah anew, with a still deepened "in spite of all this," quite soft and shy, but unambiguous…. In all its reserve, the late-born man, wandering around in the darkened world, confesses in face of the suffering peoples of the world with those messengers of Deutero-Isaiah (45:13): "Truly Thou art a God Who hides Himself, O God of Israel, Saviour!" So must Emunah change in a time of God's eclipse in order to persevere steadfast to God, without disowning reality.

If Buber concluded that Paulinism cannot overcome Marcionite dualism, he also anticipated for Christianity "a way which leads from rigid Paulinism to another form of *Pistis* nearer to *Emunah.*" Judaism and Christianity will remain different until mankind is gathered in from the exiles of the religions into the kingship of God. "But an Israel striving after the renewal of its faith through the rebirth of the person and a Christianity striving for the renewal of its faith through the rebirth of nations would have something as yet unsaid to say to each other and a help to give to one another—hardly to be conceived at the present time."

Buber did not mean that *emunah* belongs exclusively to the Jews. He declared that in the course of his life he had come to know a succession of Christians who had an ideal relationship of trust in God that could not be injured through any failure or misfortune and this trust did not originate in *faith that* God was made man in Christ. The latter was only an aid to comprehension.

> I experienced this most strongly several years ago in conversation with the leading personality of an important Christian sect. It was one of those conversations that is conducted between two persons without reservation. We spoke of the readiness, common to both of us, to be overtaken by "eschatological happenings," in an entirely unexpected manner contradicting all previous conceptions. Suddenly I heard my partner say the words: "If God should then demand it of me, I am ready, even to give up..." Where I have here placed three periods, the center of the Christian dogma was stated. Even now, while I write this, I feel the emotion of that moment.

The person Buber referred to was the English Quaker Joan Fry. To understand the importance of this testimony, we must bear in mind that English Quakers, in contrast to many American members of the Society of Friends, do believe in the divinity of Christ.

For many Christians, Christ is not the "I" of the I-Thou relationship with God, but the "Thou." *In Two Types of Faith,* Buber declared that insofar as Christianity fixes God in the image of Christ, it prevents God from hiding and therefore from revealing himself ever anew, and he pointed out that what was explicitly said by the theologian Nathan Söderbloom, and by Shatov in Dostoevsky's novel *The Devils* or *The Possessed,* is true for many Christians—that Christ remains real for them even when God becomes uncertain or unreal.

Through faith in Christ, the Gentiles "found a God," Buber stated in *Two Types of Faith,* "[W]ho did not fail in times when their world collapsed, and further, One Who in times when they found themselves sunk under guilt granted atonement." What was evil to Buber was "not expressing reality in the form of myth and thereby bringing the inexpressible to speech but turning myth into universal gnosis and tearing it out of the historical-biographical ground in which it took root." Myth is still compatible with existential reality because it is bound to faith; gnosis is not. In this connection, Buber summed up concisely his own approach to the content and manner of faith of Jesus: not to cling to any image ("even memory mythicizes, particularly memory that wishes to hand itself down"), but to the one voice, "recognizable ever anew, that speaks to my ear out of a series of undoubtedly genuine sayings." "The image of the speaker may be indistinct," Buber added, "but the voice is distinct enough," and so, too, is the central significance to Jesus of persevering in immediacy with God, the great *devotio.*

The Protestant biblical scholar James Muilenburg makes a surprisingly affirmative assessment of Buber's contribution to the Jewish-Christian dialogue in his essay "Buber as Interpreter of the Bible." He not only sees Buber as "the greatest Jewish thinker of our generation" and a "profoundly authentic exponent and representative of the Hebrew way of thinking, speaking, and acting," but also as "the foremost Jewish speaker to the Christian community."

> He, more than any other Jewish writer, tells the Christian what is to be heard in the Old Testament, what the Old Testament is really saying and what it certainly is not saying.... What is more, he has a deep interest in and sure grasp of much of the New Testament, a warm appreciation of the historical Jesus, and a recognition of the place where Jew and Christian go different ways. More than any other Jewish thinker of our time, he stands at the frontier which separates Christianity from Judaism. He is the best contemporary corrective to the persistent Marcionism of large segments of the Christian Church. He gives Jewish answers to Christian questions, the kind of answers Christians must have if they are to understand themselves.... He, more than any other Jewish scholar of our time, has opened the Scriptures of the Old Covenant for the Christian community.... Without an understanding and appreciation of the Old Covenant, the Scriptures of the New Covenant must remain forever closed.

The assessment of the German Jesuit theologian Hans Urs von Balthasar was very different. "If the mystery of Christ is not visible in the background," von Balthasar wrote, then Buber's "dialogue moves relentlessly forward to Job's question to God... eating down deeper and deeper with the passage of time, like a cancer." What von Balthasar meant by this last statement was that Buber's biblical dialogue with God must founder on the problem of evil if it does not have the transcendent solution to this problem offered by the advent of Christ. Buber, in his response, claimed Job as his father and squarely as his own in that combination of trusting and contending that marked the biblical figure and that marks the "Modern Job," that second type of modern rebel that I designate in *Problematic Rebel* and *The Hidden Human Image.* In so doing, Buber reaffirmed the biblical *emunah* against the *pistis* that lies at the heart of von Balthasar's Christianity:

> Without Christianity, so von Balthasar says to me, the dialogical leads inevitably to Job's question to God. Yes, that it does, and God praises "His servant" (Job 42:7). My God will not allow to

become silent in the mouth of His creature the complaint against
the great injustice in the world, and when in an unchanged world
His creature nonetheless finds peace, it is only because God has
again granted him His nearness and confirms him. Peace I say;
but that is a peace compatible with the fight for justice in the
world.

Buber believed in both the future perfection of society and a future transformation of the world:

> Only in the building of the foundation of the former I myself may
> take a hand, but the latter may already be there in all stillness
> when I awake some morning, or its storm may tear me from
> sleep. And both belong together, the "turning" and the "redemp-
> tion," both belong together, God knows how, I do not need to
> know it. That I call hope.

In 1961, Buber took part in a Church Day in Berlin devoted to creating a
working community of Jews and Christians that might create a new relation
between the German Evangelical church and Judaism. In his address to this
group, Buber declared that such Jewish-Christian dialogue was possible only
if the church would give up its claim to superiority. Some Evangelical theologians were, in fact, ready to give up this claim, but the church would not.
Buber realized the task to be a difficult one, because, even where the church
does recognize Israel, it is with considerable reservation. The church, in
Buber's view, would need to give up its missionary posture toward Israel and
to substitute genuine love for "tolerance." Buber was deeply moved when
the spiritual founder of the Reconciliation Action (*Aktion Sühnezeichen*) in
Berlin wholly spontaneously offered to build a synagogue for the Reform
Jewish community in Jerusalem, a project that did not materialize because of
the Jerusalem community and not through the fault of the Reconciliation
Action, which was free of every vestige of missionary intent.

Once, while Buber and Ben-Chorin were speaking in Buber's home,
Buber's great-grandchildren were building a booth, or tabernacle, for the
Jewish feast of Succoth in front of Buber's study. Ben-Chorin mentioned the
vision of the prophet Zechariah (14:16–18), in which the Feast of Booths
would be extended to include all peoples and asked Buber why just this
national festival of Israel, which reminds the Jewish people of the forty years
of wandering in the wilderness, should become a festival for all peoples.
"Because the peoples of the 'Cross' must take upon themselves the homelessness of Israel," Buber remarked.

In 1947, Judith accompanied Martin and Paula to Europe on a lecture
tour that Martin gave in Denmark, Sweden, England, France, and
Switzerland. Judith found her grandfather charming and eloquent, with a
grace to his speeches and extremely well-prepared lectures, including the

dramatic moments. She was particularly impressed by his command of so many different languages and his ability to keep large audiences in many countries enthralled with his presentation. These languages included not only German and Hebrew, but French, English, and even Polish, not to mention Latin, Greek, Yiddish, and Italian!

In the summer of 1948, Hermann Hesse sent Buber a copy of a letter that he had written to a Protestant minister in which he made it abundantly clear that he did not share the minister's view either of the Old Testament as merely the container of a few pearls and mostly a forestage of the New, or as merely for the Jews. "I would gladly give up the letters of Paul or the Apocalypse for many chapters of the later Prophets," Hesse wrote, and added that the Old Testament teaching of loving one's neighbor was equal in value to any word of Jesus or the Apostles. "I hold the old Jew-baiting by the collective guilt of the Jews in the death of Jesus to be unallowable today in the mouth of a Christian, and certainly a German," Hesse concluded, in unmistakable reference to the Nazis and the Holocaust. Buber responded that he was especially struck by the letter to the pastor, since he was engaged in writing the first part of *Two Types of Faith*. Four years later, Martin and Paula sent Hesse an eight-line poem that they had written together as a message of friendship to him.

In 1949, Josef Minn, a director of studies in Bonn, wrote Buber, suggesting that he return to Germany. "What is now happening in Germany concerns me directly despite, indeed because of, its chaotic nature," Buber replied, "and in the question that so strongly grips me of what now will become of man this element is an important one." But, he added, he did not feel himself called to return to Germany and give direction. In this connection, "something has happened." "But do not misunderstand me, my friend," Buber added;

> it is altogether desirable that what I have thought and put into words during the more than a hundred months since I have been gone (far more than in any earlier corresponding time-span of my life) should reach the Germans to whom it is accessible in a near or distant future, if possible in a near one. But collectively I cannot single them out and talk with them, other than to individuals (as just now to you).

In December 1949, the Evangelical theologian Karl Heinrich Rengstorf, professor of New Testament and of the history and literature of Judaism in Münster and director of the Institutum Judaicum Delitzschianum, wrote Buber, urging him to complete the translation of the Hebrew Bible into German so that they might not be left with a "torso." He predicted, quite rightly, that this piece of work would be greeted with enthusiasm in Germany. Buber did, indeed, complete this lifework with his remaining energy.

In March 1950, Rengstorf encouraged Buber to follow Leo Baeck, who had come to them in 1948, and Alfred Wiener, who had come in 1949, and lecture at the two-day student conference called "Church and Judaism," sponsored by the Evangelical church in Germany, on the subject of "Israel— Our Land." "You will grant that I have some impression of what it would mean for you to come to Germany after you had to leave this land of your decade-long activity under such shameful circumstances," Rengstorf wrote. "But in view of the intensity of our desire (of how close it is to our heart) and of the importance of our work for the future of our nation and our church, I dare ask, despite all that has happened and despite your age, that you not refuse our request."

In a personal letter to his old friend Alfred Döblin, who had invited him to become a corresponding member of the Mainz Academy of Sciences and Literature, Buber confided that, since the end of the war, he had given all kinds of help and advice to a growing number of persons from Germany who had turned to him for assistance, including participants in denazification proceedings. "I have also proclaimed publicly my undiminished interest in Germans of good will," he averred. "But I cannot bring myself to take part in the activity of German public institutions; for this demands a degree of association of which I do not feel myself capable." "But," he concluded, "I greet all that exists and occurs in Germany that is of genuine spirituality and genuine humanity with a deep and unreserved sympathy."

In May 1950, Karl Rengstorf repeated his invitation, despite Buber's refusal and because of the very reason that Buber gave: that there were persons there who, because of their participation in the Nazi extermination of the Jews, no longer had faces for him. "I dare do so because I struggle with my whole heart and all my might that the people here shall again have faces. I dare it so much the more because I know that the destruction of their faces is connected with what has been done to you and yours." But, as their experiences with Leo Baeck and Alfred Wiener had shown and as Buber could show even more clearly "they can only recover their faces or come to a new face if one again meets them." Rengstorf assured Buber that his invitation to Buber to give the Münster lectures in 1951 was also an invitation from the rector and the senate of the University of Münster.

In July, Rengstorf wrote Buber that Buber's latest letter of refusal had shamed him. "Naturally I understand you," he added, "but what helps in these matters is not understanding but love. There lie the missed opportunities of the past and there too the roots of German guilt and the basic reasons why we have lost our faces. Without love man cannot live." When Buber declared himself ready to talk to a small circle of especially invited persons, Rengstorf no longer dared to ask him to. But he wanted Buber to know how many of his colleagues and students loved him, diligently studied his books, eagerly wanted to see his face, hear his voice, and meet him. Buber then informed Rengstorf that he planned to spend December in Germany and would at that time gladly meet with him and those colleagues and students of whom he had spoken.

"At such gatherings instead of lecturing I am ever more inclined to answer without reservation every genuine question." "It is as you say," Buber concluded. "Without love man cannot live—not truly, not as man. But love today more than ever before seems to be grace—felt out of grace, received out of grace. Thank God, I know it when I meet it." After his month in Germany, Buber wrote Rengstorf that he had learned much "and, God willing, something will come of it."

In 1961, in a conversation with Werner Kraft, Buber spoke of Oskar Loerke, Viktor von Weizsäcker, and Hans Corossa as persons who literally died of Hitler. In his essay "Guilt and Guilt Feelings" (1957), Buber spoke of these same three men, but not by name: "I have seen three important and, to me, dear men fall into long illnesses from their failing to stand the test in the days of an acute community guilt." It was certainly the German doctor, poet, and novelist Hans Carossa (1878–1956) whom Buber had in mind when he spoke of the third of these men as not letting "himself be forgiven by God for the blunder of a moment because he did not forgive himself."

Hans Carossa made a remarkable confession of guilt to Buber personally and to the world at large through his autobiographical novel *Unequal Worlds,* published in 1951. Carossa was elected against his will to membership in the Prussian Academy of Writers and later, under pressure, elected to the Nazi-dominated European Association of Writers, of which he became president in 1942. Afterward, he grieved for many years, right up to his death, over this and over his failure to offer resistance early enough. What moved Buber in Carossa's novel was not just the inner history of the Nazi years alone, but also what he saw as an important contribution to the understanding of the destiny of the spirit in our time. "The might of the vile does not come from below alone," Buber wrote Carossa. "The good works in it as well as the evil—only it is not a passionate good. Is the passion of the good… only to be found outside of public life, which is, therefore, abandoned to the other passion, the one without grace?"

Some time before Carossa's death in 1956, when they were taking leave of each other after spending some time together, Carossa seized Buber's arm and said, in an unforgettable tone of voice, "Is it not true that one cannot do evil with the whole soul?" Buber had stated in his book *Good and Evil,* which Carossa had recently read, that while good can be done only with the whole soul, evil is never done with the whole soul. Carossa was not asking a theoretical question but the most essential personal question of his life. Buber looked at Carossa and confirmed both his statement and Carossa himself by saying, as answer and farewell, "Yes."

In 1961, Buber wrote Eugen Rosenstock-Huessy that he was shaken by what Rosenstock-Huessy had written him about Viktor von Weizsäcker, even though he did not understand it. Although it is not clear what that was, one imagines some connection between von Weizsäcker's death and his guilt over his participation, in however small a degree, in the collective actions of Nazi Germany. "When I saw him the last time, his sickness seemed to me to stand in a dreadful, by me hardly graspable, antithesis to that of Franz [Rosenzweig]."

In December 1951, Dr. Bruno Snell wrote to Buber, informing him that he had been awarded the 1951 Goethe Prize of the University of Hamburg. The annual prize, established the preceding year, had been awarded then to Professor Carl Burckhardt, Swiss historian, writer, and diplomat, and president of the International Red Cross. In awarding the Goethe Prize to Buber, the university wished to honor his great scholarly activities, but, above all, his work for genuine humanity that serves the mutual understanding of men and the preservation and continuation of a great spiritual tradition. Snell invited Buber to come to the University of Hamburg in February to receive the prize and to lecture to the academic youth of the university. Buber was fully aware that in accepting a prize from a German university, no matter how humane and noble its purpose, he would deeply offend Jews throughout the world, and particularly in Israel, who felt that no Jew should have anything to do with Germany in a public capacity. Nonetheless, Buber accepted it "as one of the first few signs of a new humanity arising out of the antihuman chaos of our time." He saw it, moreover, not, as in old times, in the great vision of individuals, at times scholars and philosophers, but in the fight of every people with itself, and, as such, he regarded and accepted it as a more than personal confession—an institutional one. He could not come to Hamburg in 1952, however, because of his commitments in America, which would occupy him until his return to Israel.

Buber donated the proceeds of the Goethe Prize to *Ner* (Light), the monthly journal that after the establishment of the State of Israel had replaced *Ba'ayot* as the official organ of Ihud. On January 25, 1952, Buber advised Bruno Snell from New York that he could not fulfill Snell's renewed invitation to give a lecture at a celebration, not only because of technical difficulties but also for more essential reasons, which he did not want to withhold from Snell personally:

> As much as it has been granted me in every genuine meeting with a German to accept him without reservation as a person and to communicate with each circle made up of such persons, it has still not been possible for me up to this time to overcome the facelessness of the German public, which has persisted for me since the events of 1938 and after. A public that is not made up of persons each of whom has been selected, as is the case with the student body of a school of higher education, cannot fulfill the indispensable presupposition for my speaking publicly: being able to regard every face that I turn toward as my legitimate partner.

Among the burdens which the history of this age has laid on me,
I experience this as one of the most difficult.

In December 1952, Buber wrote to Romano Guardini, the distinguished
German-Catholic theologian whom he had known since 1918, thanking him
for a printed copy of Guardini's lecture at the University of Munich entitled
"Responsibility: Thoughts on the Jewish Question." "While reading it, I
noticed that something had changed for me," Buber said. "It was again possible for me to speak publicly in Germany." This letter marked a turning point
for Buber, because, as will be seen, the following year he was awarded and
accepted the Peace Prize of the German Book Trade, which had been awarded to Romano Guardini himself in 1952. It also opened the way for Buber to
come to Hamburg in June 1953, where he belatedly received the Goethe
Prize and gave a lecture entitled "The Validity and Limitation of the Political
Principle."

Although Buber clearly had in mind Nazi Germany when he wrote
What Is Man? (1938), as we have seen, the section of the book that he devoted to a critique of Heidegger in no way alluded to Heidegger's own activities
as a Nazi. Because of the wide influence of Heidegger's thought on philosophy, theology, and existential psychiatry and psychology in Europe and
America, many influential thinkers have either ignored or soft-pedaled this
aspect of his career, which he himself never in any way disowned before his
death in 1976. The fact is that from 1933 until around 1942, Heidegger was
an active member of the Nazi party who identified himself with Hitler and
the Nazi cause and who took part during his time as rector of the University
of Freiburg in all the S.A. activities that led to further persecution of the Jews
and of dissidents and to the exclusion of Jewish professors, including fellow
disciples of his own Jewish teacher Edmund Husserl.

In 1951, Buber wrote a critique of Sartre, Heidegger, and Jung, entitled
"Religion and Modern Thinking," which he later included in his book *Eclipse
of God*. Buber spoke of Heidegger as one "who undoubtedly belongs to the
historical rank of philosophers in the proper sense of the term." As an integral part of his discussion of Heidegger's thought on religion, Buber spoke of
Heidegger's devotion to Nazism and Hitler. There can be no doubt, Buber
said, that it was current history that had led to Heidegger's belief in an entirely new "Coming One," to be distinguished from all previous images of the
divine. In his rectoral address in May 1933, Heidegger praised in general
terms "the glory and the greatness" of the successful "insurrection." The title
of this address, in which Heidegger embraced Nazism, was "Die
Selbstbehauptung der deutschen Universität," and *Selbstbehauptung*, as
Walter Kaufmann has pointed out, is the very term that Buber used in the
second part of *I and Thou* to refer to that "false drive for self-affirmation [I
should prefer to translate it as 'self-assertion'] which impels man to flee from

the unreliable, unsolid, unlasting, unpredictable, dangerous world of relation into the having of things"! In his manifesto to the students on November 3, 1933, Heidegger proclaimed Hitler "the present and future German reality and its law." "Here history no longer stands, as in all times of faith, under divine judgment," commented Buber, "but it itself, the unappealable, assigns to the Coming One his way." Buber recognized that by history Heidegger did not mean a list of dated events. "History exists," wrote Heidegger, "only when the essence of truth is originally decided." But, commented Buber,

> it is just his hour which he believes to be history in this sense, the very same hour whose problematics in its most inhuman manifestation led him astray. He has allied his thought, the thought of being... to which he ascribes the power to make ready for the rise of the holy, to that hour [of Hitler's Nazism] which he has affirmed as history. He has bound his thought to his hour as no other philosopher has done...

Before "Religion and Modern Thinking" was published in *Merkur* in 1952, the editor wrote Buber, pleading with him to delete or modify his criticism of Heidegger's nazism. "The wounds of the post-war era are already great," he declared. "Must we make them worse?" "He is talking about metaphorical wounds," Buber said to me, "but I am talking about real wounds, millions of them." A few years later, however, Buber agreed to speak with Heidegger on the subject of "Speech" at an event planned by the Bavarian Academy of Fine Arts, and Martin and Paula Buber met with Heidegger and his wife in a castle in Germany in preparation for this event. "I have already said what I have to say against him," Buber explained to me. The meeting took place at the end of May, together with Carl Friedrich von Weizsäcker, the noted physicist, in Altreuthe at the castle of Count Schaumburg-Lippe, at the invitation of Count Podewils, general secretary of the Bavarian Academy of Fine Arts. Buber wrote me that Heidegger "is more to my taste than his writings."

In June 1953, Buber wrote to Albrecht Goes that, prior to his next trip to Europe, he had been going through letters that he had received since 1933, and he had come across Goes's letter of August 1934, in which he asked Buber about the attitude of responsibility. This letter affected Buber in a special way. "I now felt the inquiring spirit of the then young... man more strongly than I did at that time," Buber admitted. "The world today is so constituted that one may not remain silent concerning any experience of genuine closeness," Buber went on to explain why he was writing: "I do not know to what extent you are still identical with the writer of the letter (I am today more receptive than I was at that time) but you surely still stand in such an intimate relationship to him that you can give him my greeting directly." Goes responded warmly that Buber had always remained with him as one of his two or three most important life masters and that his letter had touched "all the roots of life." This was the beginning of a close relationship that lasted until Buber's death.

On June 17, 1953, Arthur Georgi wrote Buber from Hamburg, saying that the Peace Prize of the German Book Trade, which had been awarded in 1951 to Albert Schweitzer and in 1952 to Romano Guardini, was now being awarded to him, and inviting him to speak at a ceremony at St. Paul's Church in Frankfurt on September 27. Buber, who was in Germany at the time, wrote Georgi, accepting the prize and agreeing to give a lecture in Frankfurt entitled "Genuine Dialogue and the Possibility of Peace." The ten thousand German marks that Buber received for the prize he donated to the cause of Jewish-Arab understanding.

On Sunday, September 27, 1953, while tens of thousands listened through loudspeakers, Buber was awarded the prize by Arthur Georgi, who characterized Buber as a "man of truth who proclaims and fashions a humane spirit suffusing all living things; interpreter of his people's destiny in history, philosopher of dialogue, theologian and educator." Albrecht Goes then gave an address entitled "Martin Buber: Our Support." In spelling out what he meant by "our support," Goes made the identical distinction between "leader" and "teacher" that Buber had made years before in his essay on Ahad Ha'am: "The truth which is directed at me and to which I owe an answer does not come from a Führer's command to me, no matter what kind it may be. He who lives by fiat does not live as a personality. A bonds-man does not listen." Through Buber, in contrast, said Goes, "we were not instructed but shown a direction; life-masters, not school-masters, spoke to us...." "The trust which Martin Buber radiates is the trust of the true zaddik," including the readiness to be sad with others and to keep silent "because we are united by the insight that it is hard really to love one's fellow men."

Before an audience that included Theodor Heuss, president of the West German Republic, and many of the most distinguished politicians and thinkers of Germany, Buber gave his own address, "Genuine Dialogue and the Possibilities of Peace." In language stronger than had ever been used in Germany from such an elevated rostrum, he called to account those who took part in the Nazi Holocaust:

> About a decade ago a considerable number of Germans—there must have been many thousands of them—under the indirect command of the German government and the direct command of its representatives, killed millions of my people in a systematically prepared and executed procedure whose organized cruelty cannot be compared with any previous historical event. I, who am one of those who remained alive, have only in a formal sense a common humanity with those who took part in this action. They have so radically removed themselves from the human sphere, so transposed themselves into a sphere of monstrous inhumanity

inaccessible to my conception, that not even hatred, much less an overcoming of hatred, was able to arise in me. And what am I that I could here presume to "forgive"!

At the same time, Buber clung to his lifelong conviction that a people ought not be judged as a whole, and he distinguished between the different and even contending impulses within the German people:

> When I think of the German people of the days of Auschwitz and Treblinka, I behold, first of all, the great many who knew that the monstrous event was taking place and did not oppose it. But my heart, which is acquainted with the weakness of men, refuses to condemn my neighbor for not prevailing upon himself to become a martyr. Next there emerges before me the mass of those who remained ignorant of what was withheld from the German public and who did not try to discover what reality lay behind the rumors which were circulating. When I have these men in mind, I am gripped by the thought of the anxiety, likewise well known to me, of the human creature before a truth which he fears he cannot face. But finally there appears before me, from reliable reports, some who have become as familiar to me by sight, action, and voice as if they were friends, those who refused to carry out the orders and suffered death or put themselves to death, and those who learned what was taking place and opposed it and were put to death, or those who learned what was taking place and because they could do nothing to stop it killed themselves. I see these men very near before me in that especial intimacy which binds us at times to the dead and to them alone. Reverence and love for these Germans now fills my heart.

Buber regarded the youth of Germany who had grown up since these events as probably the essential life of the German people, and he saw them caught in a powerful inner dialectic—a part of "the great inner struggle of all peoples being fought out today... in the vital center of each people." He had found in the German youth, despite their being rent asunder, more awareness than elsewhere of "the struggle of the human spirit against the demonry of the subhuman and the antihuman." "The solidarity of all disparate groups in the flaming battle for the rise of a true humanity," laid on Buber, "the surviving Jew chosen as symbol," the obligation to "obey this call of duty even there, indeed, precisely there where the never-to-be-effaced memory of what has happened stands in opposition to it." In giving thanks, Buber expressed his solidarity with the battle of the fighters for humanity among both Germans and Jews against the contrahuman.

In 1958, in a discussion of his attitude toward postwar Germany, Buber had quoted a favorite saying of his grandmother: "One never knows in advance how an angel will look." On this occasion, as Buber certainly anticipated, the "angel" bore two quite different aspects. The unique and unprecedented homage of the prohuman element in Germany was accompanied by bitter and often vicious attacks on Buber in the Israeli press and in the Yiddish, German, and English Jewish newspapers in Switzerland, England, and the United States.

In Israel, Buber was totally isolated by this action. Even his closest friends, such as Hugo Bergmann, advised him against accepting the Peace Prize. When Buber returned to Israel, he said to Bergmann, "Ich muss die Reifeprüfung bestehen"—"I must withstand the test of maturity" (literally, "matriculation examination"). In a speech over the Israeli radio Station Kol Yisrael (Voice of Israel) a year after Buber's death, Bergmann offered this whole story, including his own opposition to Buber's action, as evidence that Buber was the conscience and sentinel of mankind!

"I cannot condemn a people as a people," Buber said, "as the Christian church has so often done in branding the Jewish people as murderers of the Messiah," for one must distinguish between the actively guilty, the passively guilty, and the not guilty ("I do not say 'innocent' because there is none"). Far from having the German listeners regard Buber's speech as an exoneration of themselves, every serious public reference to that speech showed that it had brought about severe self-appraisals. Buber reported that, after some of his university lectures, leading German scholars, "at times in a manner without precedent in Western civilization, confessed that their share in the guilt of nonresistance was the greatest burden of their lives and described their complete transformation in the most vivid terms." Buber also pointed to what he said in his widely disseminated address "The Validity and Limitation of the Political Principle": "We saw people, who were of the most scrupulous honesty in their private lives, as soon as their party had indicated to them who the (in this case inner) 'enemy' was, day after day, undoubtedly with peaceful consciences, lie, slander, betray, rob, torment, torture, murder."

In July 1953, Buber wrote me that he had given his speech "The Validity and Limitation of the Political Principle" in seven German universities (Heidelberg, Frankfurt, Bonn, Münster, Hamburg [at the prize ceremony], Tübingen, and Göttingen) "and was surprised by the strong response. In Göttingen, after the lecture many hundreds of students assembled before the university to give me an 'ovation.'" In his last letter to Ludwig Strauss, Buber also wrote that this radical-critical lecture, despite or because of its character, had had a stronger and even purer effect than he had expected. A real resistance was noticeable only in Bonn, but it was drowned out by the positive responses of the other cities.

In 1953 or later, Buber wrote a remarkable response to a statement of his German friend Ewald Wasmuth. Wasmuth wanted to make a historical dialectic out of the alternation that Buber pointed to in *What Is Man?*, between epochs of being at home and epochs of homelessness. But the Copernican eruption of the infinite had the effect that it did because up till that time man had only set over against it the Kantian antinomy of space-time infinity and finitude but not yet a greater image of God than the traditional one, "one that is greater and *still not expressible,* the image of the God that out of his eternity has set this infinite-finite space-time world into being, embracing and overwhelming it with his eternity."

When Buber spoke at a German university during his visits in the 1950s, reports Albrecht Goes, he was concerned neither to please nor to shock but, going straight to his subject, engaged in his own patient monologue and dialogue, distributing before thousands "the bread of being together." "I have never known anyone who was less concerned about supplying material with which to ignite the flammable part of an audience." Goes also described his personal dialogues with Buber or with Martin and Paula together. Buber, over seventy-five, exactly thirty years older than Goes, was in no way impeded by any signs of weakness. "His eyes were clear, his hearing excellent; a soft tone of voice was just as likely as an animated outburst. His stupendous memory never lapsed, and this venerable personage hardly seemed to know what fatigue meant." On one occasion, after a more than four-hour conversation, Goes, concerned that he had wearied Buber beyond all propriety, stood up and mumbled an apology. "But what do you expect?" Buber asked. "A good conversation must be long, it must be possible for it to be long."

In 1960, when German students were asked to name the greatest spiritual figures of our time, Buber was placed third, along with Pope John XXIII. That same year, a German-Israeli student group from a church college in Berlin came to see Buber in Jerusalem and asked him what hope there was in a superficial, meaningless world. There is hope, Buber answered. The real happening takes place in the stillness, unnoticed by anyone. In response to Buber's request that they be concrete, the students spoke of the guilt of their parents, the crime of the older generation against the people of God. One cannot ask anyone to be a martyr, Buber replied, but where there is sin, there is hate, and where there is hate, there must be reconciliation. Yet true reconciliation is possible only where the person who is guilty turns to a better way. "In this, Germany is lacking," said Buber, meaning not only the Nuremberg trials, at which every one of the accused answered "Not guilty," but also the whole older generation in Germany. But the younger generation, too, will be guilty if they do not seek a better way, for, as in a Greek tragedy, they bear the sins of their parents.

In December 1961, Heinz Kremers asked Buber what he thought concerning the development of the relation of the West German Republic to Israel. Buber replied that he saw it first of all as a relation of the republic to itself. For centuries the republic had been burdened by a geographical situation that gave Germany few political successes. This situation led the Germans to accept uncritically successful politics and successful politicians and to surrender themselves to political "charismatics." As a typical example, Buber told of how he and Paula, when they first came to Jerusalem from

Germany, could find no place to live in the overflowing city. A German Evangelical pastor took the Bubers in with open arms and gave them a beautiful place to live. Buber was deeply moved by the love that this German showed him, coming as it did just when they had left Germany for good. He was deeply shocked, therefore, when the pastor said, "One may think of Hitler what one will. One thing is for me certain: God has visibly blessed him"!

In 1958, on the occasion of Buber's eightieth birthday, Hans Kohn published an article in an important German journal in which he spoke of the great crowds that attended Buber's lectures in Germany, most of which were composed of young people.

> Drawing from biblical and Hasidic sources, he was still deeply rooted in that—intellectually so fruitful and existentially—so rich in tension, so creative and so fragile and, because of that, wholly unique—German-Jewish dialogue that, like so much else in Germany, came to an end and disappeared with Hitler's rise to power. The changed, post-Hitler Germany rightly greets in Buber a venerable figure that reminds it of the greatness of its own past. To the world Buber signifies one of the essential thinkers and persons of our time. To Germany he means more.

What Buber represented to postwar Germany was precisely the courage and strength with which he walked the narrow ridge and encountered the Germans on it. In July 1960, Buber received a letter from the Society for Christian-Jewish Cooperation of Darmstadt, informing him that the administrative head of the county of Bergstrasse wanted to place a plaque on his house in Heppenheim, commemorating the long years that Buber lived there, and that the society would like to sponsor a ceremony on that occasion at which Buber himself might speak if he planned to be in Germany the following year. Buber responded:

> I believe I may say that I have served the cause of the reconciliation of peoples to the best of my abilities. But that is a cause which can only thrive under the sign of truth. It would not do justice to the truth, in my opinion, if a plaque were erected on the house in which my family and I lived during the years 1916–1938 which only commemorated the fact of this dwelling but left unmentioned the fact that it was plundering and expropriation which marked the end of our connection with this dwelling. A commemorative plaque such as you plan would, to be sure, mean a high honor for my person, but it would not thereby show the honor due the historical truth which should serve the coming generations as admonition and warning.

In 1975, I sent a letter to the mayor of Heppenheim at the request of a German committee fighting the plans to demolish the "Buber house" in favor of a freeway and received a long but negative reply. However, in March 1978, a letter arrived from Margarete Exler of this same committee, saying that Buber's house in Heppenheim had been saved after all:

> The government of the Federal State of Hessen will take care of it and it shall in future be the quarters of the International Council of Christians and Jews (ICCJ) connected with a meeting-room for different purposes, not only to keep the memory but also the ideas of Martin Buber alive, so that people may be enabled to practice them in their daily life.

The letter had on it a commemorative stamp with a picture of Buber and the dates of his life, and it was postmarked "Martin Buber 1878–1978 / in Heppenheim 1916–1938."

♦ 17 ♦

Dialogue with Americans

(1951-1956)

In November 1948, Louis Finkelstein, chancellor of the Jewish Theological Seminary of America, the institution that trains Conservative rabbis, asked Buber to come to America to lecture at the seminary. Buber responded warmly that he would like to meet the next Jewish generation in the immediacy of life, face to face, and not just through his books, for he was more than ever convinced of the significance of that generation "for our future." Because of his work in the School for the Teachers of the People, Buber twice had to postpone coming, so that his first visit to America did not take place until the academic year 1951–1952.

The American philosopher Michael Wyschogrod tells how Buber showed his respect for the Conservative, and therefore observant of Halakhah, seminary that brought him to America:

> On the first Friday evening, the Jewish Theological Seminary organized a Sabbath meal in Buber's honor. After the meal, Buber was supposed to get to his hotel, which was about fifty blocks from where we were. It was ten o'clock at night, and a cold rain was falling. None of us would ride or drive on the Sabbath, and we did not know how Buber would get to his hotel. We knew that he didn't mind riding on the Sabbath and asked him if we should hail him a cab. We were quite unhappy to do this, because we are not supposed to encourage another Jew to ride on the Sabbath, but since Buber was an elderly man and the weather was bad, we felt that it was all right. But Buber answered, "No, I'll

walk." And so all of us decided to accompany him. We all walked along Broadway with him for fifty blocks and arrived at the hotel wet. He was wet also, but he had felt that it was not appropriate to ride in a cab.

In reply to the question of whether Buber personally realized his thought, Wyschogrod testified that as a person he was often greater than his books. "When he sat with you he gave you his full attention. Only you existed. This ability to listen and to give you the feeling that he was waiting for you, as you are, influenced people." This also carried over to the way in which Buber created a dialogue with anyone who asked him a question after his lectures. "He was willing to listen and respond on the deepest level that the question required."

I first met Buber on October 31, 1950, after six years of immersion in his work. The Jewish Theological Seminary had put him up at the Hotel Marcy on 96th Street and West End Avenue, where he resided throughout his stay in New York. This meeting was perhaps the most memorable of our many meetings over nine years. Buber welcomed me into his hotel suite and looked me searchingly in the eyes while taking my hand. My first response was to feel how totally "other" this man seemed after I had felt such kinship to him through his writings and letters. He was less than five feet tall. I am five feet ten. His eyes were of a depth, gentleness, and directness that I have never before or since encountered. He asked me to sit down. "You must not think that I am interested in you mostly because you have written a book on me," he said, and he added, speaking of himself, "My books are not what is important to me. They are like snake skins that I shed when I need to."

Buber told me of his meeting with T. S. Eliot five days before in London. They were brought together by Ronald Gregor Smith, translator of *I and Thou* and *Between Man and Man*. There were only two other persons present. Eliot was very shy but directly frank, which Buber did not usually find with persons when they first met him. Having constructed a scale of attitudes toward evil in connection with my doctoral dissertation and having just planned a year course on "Philosophy and Literature" at Sarah Lawrence College that would include Buber's *I and Thou* and T. S. Eliot's *Four Quartets,* I asked Buber whether he did not find his opinions very different from those of Eliot. "When I meet a man I am not concerned with opinions but with the man," said Buber. I took this response as a reproach, and it was. I had turned Buber and Eliot into positions in a dialectic within my own mind and lost the reality of their dialogue as persons meeting each other! Fifteen years later, when I wrote T. S. Eliot to ask his support in nominating Buber for a Nobel Prize, Eliot confirmed Buber's sense of the rareness of the meeting between them. "I only met Buber once," Eliot wrote me, in agreeing to support the nomination, "but I felt then I was in the presence of greatness."

Buber's first visit to America was also the occasion for his official retirement from the Hebrew University. Now that he had retired, he had been asked to teach a seminar in biblical faith when he got back, something that had been strictly forbidden to him as long as he was serving officially. "I am just the same person as I was before," Buber complained to me. "Why can I do it now when I could not then?" The answer, of course, was that same opposition by the Orthodox that had originally prevented his teaching religion in any official capacity in the university. Actually, I doubt if he ever taught a seminar in biblical faith even after his retirement. Later, he informed me that he had been asked to teach a seminar in comparative religion, and he had accepted.

I never took a note during or even after my many conversations with Buber, so what has remained of them is only what Buber himself called the work of the "organic selective memory." At his public lectures and in seminars and discussion groups, I did take notes. One of these was a small group who met with Buber in his hotel suite at the Marcy. Buber did not lecture to us; he simply answered questions. Asked what proof he could offer for his religious attitudes, he answered,

> The "man of faith" (I prefer not to say "believing man") has decided for faith without objective proof and precisely this is his situation. What I mean by religion is just one's personal life. One usually does not dream of putting his personal life at stake—of really meeting abyss with abyss. I must by violence of the spirit bring the person I meet to deal with his personal life. I must not show him that his arguments are wrong by their content but that argument—argumentation as such—is wrong. I must break down his security by driving him to confront his self. He puts me in a situation of responsibility for him... struggling with him against him—using as allies the forces deep within him. I can venture this only if he comes in utter sincerity without any restraint. It is just a question of personal relationship—nothing else.

One sympathetic but ambivalent young man questioned the relevance of Buber's books to life. "If my books do not speak to you, burn my books!" responded Buber without a trace of anger or irony. Malcolm Diamond of Princeton, who was also doing his dissertation on Buber, raised the question of "subjectivity" in Buber's thought. "Subjectivity always means opinion, reflection," said Buber. "I don't speak of this at all—only about being, existing." But he was also not talking about "objectivity," he explained. "God has to do with every living being but not with ideas. Philosophical thinking is a transposition of reality to another plane altogether."

"On the Suspension of the Ethical" is the first of the essays that I translated for *Eclipse of God*. Like all the others, although starting from a scholarly standpoint, it ended with a fervent statement about our time. To

Kierkegaard's claim that the "knight of faith" must suspend the ordinary ethical in favor of the "absolute duty to the Absolute," Buber posed the question "Are you really addressed by the Absolute or by one of his apes?" Although the voice of Moloch prefers a mighty roaring to the "voice of a thin silence," in our age it appears to be extremely difficult to distinguish the one from the other. In the past, images of the Absolute, "partly pallid, partly crude, altogether false and yet true," gave men some help against the apes of the Absolute which bustle about on earth. But now that "God is dead," in Nietzsche's words, and the eye of the spirit "can no longer catch a glimpse of the appearance of the Absolute," false absolutes rule over the soul and the suspension of the ethical fills the world in a caricaturized form. Well-conditioned young souls sacrifice their personal integrity in order that equality or freedom may come (originally Buber also wrote "or the kingdom may come" but deleted it because of the sensitivity of Christian theologians). "In the realm of Moloch honest men lie and compassionate men torture," really and truly believing "that brother-murder will prepare the way for brotherhood!"

It is striking to compare Buber's impassioned critique of Kierkegaard's "suspension of the ethical" with the very different emphasis of a statement that he made to Hugo Bergmann in 1940:

> God is not moral.... God is not good in the sense of the moral, and we may not carry the moral into faith, as Augustine has done. The moral is a shelter that faith shatters. The situation of Abraham, twice: ("Go out of your country," Gen. 12:1) and the sacrifice of Isaac—in all such cases the moral decision is the lighter one. One who has not experienced that does not know what heavy is. It is a narrow way between two abysses, such as I once encountered in the Dolomites.

In "Religion and Reality," Buber characterized the thinking of our time as aiming to preserve the idea of the divine as the true concern of religion while destroying the reality of the idea of God and of our relation to him. "This is done in many ways, overtly and covertly, apodictically and hypothetically, in the language of metaphysics and of psychology." Specifically modern thought can no longer endure a God who is not confined to man's subjectivity. Whenever man has to interpret encounter with God as self-encounter, his very structure is destroyed. "This is the portent of the present hour." In contrast to the "death of God," Buber set forth the metaphor of the "eclipse of God" as a real happening that does not take place in God or in the human spirit but between us and God. "Eclipse of the light of heaven, eclipse of God—such indeed is the character of the historic hour through which the world is passing." If one insists, like Heidegger, that it is within earthly thought that we discover the power that unveils the mystery, one denies the effective reality of our vis-à-vis and contributes to the human responsibility for the eclipse. We can do away with the name God, which implies a possessive, but "He who is denoted by the name lives in the light of His eternity" while "we 'the slayers,' remain dwellers in darkness, consigned to death."

Asked about the Jewish Law, or Halakhah, Buber conceded that his position might be mistaken for antinomianism, or lawlessness, and that it might be misused by an irresponsible person to confirm him in his irresponsibility. But, for the responsible person, Buber saw the *personal* as the only way. "In three hundred years there may be a new Halakhah. But now this is just the way of modern man. I am only against life becoming rigid. I want to warn man against *anticipated* objectivation." Of course, objectivation will come again and again, and when it does the tradition can be renewed only through the personal way. "On this personal way one may discover things that are not only true for oneself but for others. One cannot live without danger, without risk—the question is to choose between risks." "There are things in the Jewish tradition I cannot accept at all," Buber said,

> and things I hold true that are not expressed in Judaism. But what I hold essential has been expressed more in biblical Judaism than anywhere else—in the biblical dialogue between man and God. In Hasidism this is developed in a communal life. I want to show that Judaism can be lived. It is most important that the Jews today live Judaism.

We can gain some notion of Buber's incredible expenditure of energy during this first trip to America just from the itinerary of the first two months, which Buber shared with me. Between November 8 and December 21, he delivered twenty lectures in New York, Cleveland, Chicago, and Detroit, at such colleges and universities as Dartmouth, Haverford, Brandeis, Yale, Columbia, the University of Chicago, and the University of Wisconsin. In addition to these lectures, Buber received a stream of visitors, met with publishers, carried on an active correspondence with people all over the world, worked with me on the translations of his lectures, and worked with Professor Seymour Siegel of the seminary on the pronunciation of English (*thou* was the one word Buber could never master: it always came out "vow"!).

In his second seminary lecture, "The Silent Question," Buber presented Judaism via a critique of two modern French-Jewish thinkers who turned away from it—Simone Weil and Henri Bergson. Both Bergson and Weil saw Israel as an embodiment of a principle of social life that was either a stage to be surpassed, as for Bergson, or the great obstacle, the "Great Beast" of the Apocalypse, according to Weil. In opposition to the dualism both posited between that spiritual interior in which they found their touchstone of reality and the external, social world, Buber portrayed Judaism as according inwardness its rightful place but contesting the self-sufficiency of the soul: "Inward truth must become real life, otherwise it does not remain truth. A drop of Messianic consummation must be mingled with every hour; otherwise the hour is godless, despite all piety and devoutness." He who loves brings God and the world together—this Hasidic teaching is the consummation of Judaism, and in it is realized, if anywhere, that "active mysticism" for which Bergson called. In an impassioned statement, Buber characterized the Hasidic message to all as "You yourself must begin": "Existence will remain meaningless for you if you yourself do not penetrate into it with active love and if you do not in this way discover its meaning for yourself. Everything is waiting to be hallowed by you.... If you wish to learn to believe, love!"

The third seminary lecture, "The Dialogue between Heaven and Earth," reveals the coming together of Buber's interpretation of the Hebrew Bible and his philosophy of dialogue with an explicitness that cannot be found in any of his other writings: "To God's sovereign address, man gives his autonomous answer." Even man's silence is an answer. Lamenting, supplicating, thanks and praise-giving man experiences himself as heard and understood, accepted and confirmed. "The basic teaching that fills the Hebrew Bible is that our life is a dialogue between the above and the below."

> What happened once happens now and always, and the fact of its happening to us is a guarantee of its having happened. The Bible has, in the form of a glorified remembrance, given vivid, decisive expression to an ever recurrent happening. In the infinite language of events and situations, eternally changing, but plain to the truly attentive, transcendence speaks to our hearts at the essential moment of personal life. And there is a language in which we can answer it... our actions and attitudes, our reactions and our abstentions.

This understanding of the totality of our responses as our responsibility in the dialogue with transcendence is almost identical with what Buber wrote in 1957 in the Postscript to the second edition of *I and Thou*, without referring at all to the Bible. Warning that we be careful not to understand the conversation with God as something happening solely outside the everyday, Buber declared that God's speech penetrates everything biographical and historical in our lives "and makes it for you and me into instruction, message, demand." "Happening upon happening, situation upon situation, are enabled and empowered by the personal speech of God to demand of the human person that he take his stand and make his decision."

In "The Dialogue Between Heaven and Earth," the real heart of Buber's understanding of this hour as one of the "eclipse of God" is laid bare. He does not use this language here, but rather the biblical language of God's hiding his face, yet he inserts into it an unmistakable autobiographical confession. When God seems to withdraw himself utterly from the earth and no longer participates in its existence, the space of history is full of noise but empty of the divine breath. "For one who believes in the living God, who knows about Him, and is fated to spend his life in a time of His hiddenness, it is very difficult to live." After this confession, Buber went on to speak about Psalm 82, but he ended the essay with the question of how a Jewish life or, more correctly, a life with God is still possible in a time in which there is an Auschwitz. Elie Wiesel, himself a survivor of the Holocaust, has said, "With the advent of the Nazi regime in Germany, humanity became witness to what Martin Buber would call an eclipse of God." It was above all, in fact, in the name of the "Job of Auschwitz" that Buber called this an age of the "eclipse of God." In language reminiscent of his interpretation of Kafka, Buber said in "The Dialogue Between Heaven and Earth": "The estrangement has become too cruel, the hiddenness too deep," and he asked whether we can still speak to God, hear his word, call to him, or, as individuals and as a people, enter into dialogue with him. "Dare we recommend to the survivors of Auschwitz, the Job of the gas chambers: 'Give thanks unto the Lord, for He is good; for His mercy endureth forever'?" The only answer that the biblical Job received was God's nearness, that he knew God again. "Nothing is explained, nothing adjusted; wrong has not become right, nor cruelty kindness." And how is it, Buber asked, with "all those who have not got over what happened and will not get over it?" Buber revised his original response to his own question, writing a new and more powerful ending, one that shows, if anything does, the trust and the contending that mark "the Modern Job":

> Do we stand overcome before the hidden face of God like the tragic hero of the Greeks before faceless fate? No, rather even now we contend, we too, with God, even with Him, the Lord of Being, whom we once, we here, chose for our Lord. We do not put up with earthly being; we struggle for its redemption, and struggling we appeal to the help of our Lord, who is again and still a hiding one.... Though His coming appearance resemble no earlier one, we shall recognize again our cruel and merciful Lord.

One of Buber's most memorable lectures in America was at the Park Avenue Synagogue in New York City. There, he presented an interpretation of the Psalms from his small book *Right and Wrong*. When he said, in the words of the psalm, "I shall not die but live," it seemed the most personal declaration conceivable and, at the same time, a statement made for all Israel. After the lecture, Buber answered questions informally. "Professor Buber, why have you had such an influence on the Protestants?" asked one man, clearly implying, in this Jewish setting, that Buber must not really be a good Jew if he could have had great influence on Protestants. "Ask the Protestants!" Buber responded. Another posed a query that made Buber ask, "Have you really lain awake at night thinking about this question?" Unlike the public's ordinary conception of a lecturer, Buber never dealt with general cultural questions. In the most public of settings, he would answer only "real questions," questions in which the questioner staked herself or himself. "This is really pilpul," Buber said of another question that night, "pilpul" being the name for the type of hair-splitting that became common when the study of the Talmud had degenerated into sterile casuistry. What was most impressive, however, was that although not an observant Jew himself, Buber at seventy-three walked miles across Central Park on a cold winter's night, coming home from the synagogue, rather than ride on the Sabbath and thereby violate a religious law important to the Conservative Jewish seminary that had been his host!

Among the old friends with whom Buber made contact again while he was in America was Albert Einstein, who spent many years at Princeton University before his death in 1955. Einstein and Buber were delighted to discover that they both liked Ellery Queen mystery stories! Later, Buber confided to me that Einstein was very depressed over the atomic bomb, which his own researches had helped bring into being, and that, as a result, he refused an operation that might have saved his life. After the scientist's death, Buber wrote Rudolf Kayser, Einstein's son-in-law: "I think of Einstein often and from the depth of my heart. It was at that time [of Einstein's death], despite the rareness of our personal contact, as if a support had been torn away from me." "Father Einstein told me with great enthusiasm of your visit in Princeton," replied Kayser. "He felt such closeness and admiration for you that each new meeting was a great joy for him."

In "Man and His Image-Work," Buber told of a conversation that he had had forty years before with Einstein, in which he had been pressing him in vain with a concealed question about his faith. Finally, Einstein burst forth: "What we [and by this "we" he meant "we physicists"] strive for is just to draw his lines after *Him.*" Einstein meant by "draw after" what one does in retracing a geometrical figure. At that time, Einstein's desire seemed to Buber an innocent hubris. But in light of the new physics that came to light since then, Einstein's strivings began to seem more and more seriously questionable. "The fundamental impossibility of investigating the electron, the 'complementarity' of contradictory explanations — and the lines of being that God has drawn! And nonetheless we must proceed from this unimageable, unrealizable, uncanny, unhomelike world...."

In the lecture entitled "Religion and Philosophy" that Buber gave before a large audience at Columbia University, he stated that the highest certainty in every religion is "that the meaning of existence is open and accessible in the actual lived concrete, not above the struggle with reality but in it." At a luncheon at the Cathedral of St. John the Divine in New York City with Bishop James Pike, Reinhold Niebuhr, and others, I asked Buber how he could make this statement about all religion in the face of the Hindu Vedanta, which, in its nondualistic tradition, rejects the duality of I and Thou in favor of the One without Second, the identity of Brahman and Atman.

"That is its philosophy," Buber replied; "its religious reality is still the lived concrete." The religious must struggle to protect the lived concrete as the meeting place between the human and the divine, against all those forces that threaten its quality of presentness and uniqueness—metaphysics, gnosis, magic, politics. It must also reject the historicizing of the moment into the merely past or technicizing it into a means to a future end. But the meaning is not to be won through any type of analytical, synthetic, or phenomenological investigation of and reflection upon the lived concrete, such as modern existentialist philosophies are given to, but only in the unreduced immediacy of the moment.

> Of course, he who aims at the experiencing of the experience will necessarily miss the meaning, for he destroys the spontaneity of the mystery. Only he reaches the meaning who stands firm, without holding back or reservation, before the whole might of reality and answers it in a living way. He is ready to confirm with his life the meaning which he has attained.

For man, the existent is either face-to-face being or passive object (*Gegenüber oder Gegenstand*). The child who silently speaks to his mother by merely looking into her eyes, and the same child who looks at something on the mother as any other object, shows these two basic modes of relating to existing being. A few months after Buber's granddaughter Barbara gave birth to Buber's first great-grandchild, Tamar, Buber remarked to me, "When I became a father, I was a mere boy. I saw nothing. When I became a grandfather, I saw a little something. Now that I am a great-grandfather I really see." What Buber saw as already present in embryo form in the infant of six months, he also traced in its full development to the heights of human existence. I-Thou finds its highest intensity and transfiguration in religious reality, in which unlimited Being becomes, as absolute person, my partner.

I-It finds its highest concentration and illumination in philosophical knowledge, in which the subject is extracted from the immediate lived togetherness of I and It and the It is detached into contemplated existing beings, or contemplated Being itself. "The religious reality of the meeting with the Meeter, who shines through all forms and is Himself formless, knows no image," yet God suffers that we look at him through all these necessarily untrue symbols until, as happens again and again, they swell up and obstruct the road to God by claiming to be reality themselves. Then comes round the hour of the philosopher, like Socrates, who destroys the untrue images in his prayer to the again unknown God and by so doing arouses the religious person and impels him to set forth across the God-deprived reality to a new meeting with the nameless Meeter.

In the discussion that followed the delivery of "Religion and Philosophy" at Columbia University, Buber said that he had been more often criticized for the I-Thou relationship with nature than for any other part of his philosophy. But when he looked at the great tree outside his window, he could not deny the reality of the meeting with it.

In 1961, I sent Buber a copy of the baccalaureate address that I gave at the University of Vermont, in which I pointed for the first time to that common attitude of Buber and Camus that in *Problematic Rebel* (1963) I was to identify as that of the "Modern Job"—the attitude in which dialogue and rebellion, trust and contending, are inseparably coupled. "It need not matter whether this rebellion be expressed in terms of the 'atheism' of a Camus or the 'theism' of a Buber," I said in *Problematic Rebel*. But in my baccalaureate address, I referred to Camus as an atheist, without quotation marks. Buber replied, "I would not call Camus an atheist. He was one of the men who are destroying the old images. You know how I feel about them." Buber was referring to the conclusion of "Religion and Philosophy." When symbols tend to become more than signs and pointers to God and claim to be reality itself, then the philosopher comes who rejects both the image and the God which it symbolizes. To the image, the philosopher opposes the pure idea, which he even at times understands as the negation of all metaphysical ideas. This prayer of the philosopher to the again unknown God Buber identified, with true insight, as the attitude of Camus. In 1958, in a panel that we shared on Buber and literature at a University of Michigan intercollegiate conference, the distinguished American literary critic R. W. B. Lewis told me that, at the Salzburg Festival in Austria, Camus had said to him that he did not mind being called religious in Buber's sense of the term. As Lewis later expressed this in *The Picaresque Saint,*

> Camus acknowledges a profound respect for Buber.... And Camus is even willing to say that, for himself, "the sacred" is just that presence felt in the silence during a moment of genuine awareness.... Only in what Buber calls the condition of being aware is even a transitory moment of communion accomplished.

Buber remarked to me that people in America were "very polite," by which he did *not* mean "in genuine dialogue." "There are some cities," Buber said to me, "that we call *'nachtschöne,'* beautiful at night. New York is one of them." On the way to Los Angeles, Martin and Paula stopped to see the Grand Canyon, and this made an enormous impression on them both. "Los Angeles is indeed 'as unusual' as New York," Buber wrote me,

> but not by far as important. Since yesterday we are living on the roof of this hotel and on a night like this we are looking down on all the singularity of the town—utterly unable to see it as a single entity, it is an agglomeration of agglomerations. But of course seeing these mountains and this ocean together was a unique experience.

Once in Los Angeles, when Buber was traveling some distance in a taxi, the taxi driver suddenly turned toward him and said, "Mister, I've got something to ask you. The other day I read that you don't have to get mad at people right away. What do you think about that?" Buber agreed and asked him where he had read it. "In a magazine," the taxi driver replied. "Don't laugh, but the guy who said that is seven hundred years old." "You mean, he lived seven hundred years ago?" Buber asked. "Yeah, that's what I said…. Name of Francis." "Francis?" "Oh, yes, Francis of Assisi." "Oh, then you have read something good," said Buber and told the taxi driver about St. Francis of Assisi. After Buber had paid his fare and left, he missed his eyeglass case and decided that the handsome case must have fallen out of his pocket in the cab. Twenty minutes later, when he came out of the building, he encountered the cab driver walking toward him, with the case in his hand. As Buber himself pointed out in telling the story, for such a driver, time is money and gasoline is more money. Recognizing that, Buber said to him, "Thank you. That was good of you. You are a nice man." At this, this giant of a man put his arms around the diminutive Buber and declared, "Nobody has ever said that to me!" In January 1952, Buber wrote to Hermann Hesse from Los Angeles, "The American impressions have been important for both of us. I have learned to know the human in a new way—in its contradictory nature."

Many of Buber's lectures in America were later collected into *Eclipse of God.* In *I and Thou,* Buber had written, "Of course, God is the Wholly Other, the Mysterium Tremendum that appears and overthrows, but He is also the wholly same, nearer to me than myself." At that time, Buber was trying to correct the overemphasis of Karl Barth and Rudolf Otto on the transcendence of God. In *Eclipse of God,* his emphasis was the reverse, because meanwhile the situation had reversed: "Those who restrict God to the transcendence limit Him unduly," he wrote, "but those who make God wholly immanent mean something other than God." Because those who deny our relation with transcendence contribute to the human responsibility for the eclipse of God, Buber felt it necessary to attack the highly influential philosophies of Sartre, Heidegger, and Jung in "Religion and Modern Thinking."

Sartre's statements about the silence of the transcendence combined with the perseverance of the religious need in modern man may have an entirely different meaning than Sartre imagines, Buber suggested. If God is silent toward man and man toward God, "then something has taken place, not in human subjectivity but in Being itself. It would be worthier not to explain it to oneself in sensational and incompetent sayings, such as that of the 'death' of God, but to endure it as it is and at the same time to move existentially toward a new happening, toward that event in which the word between heaven and earth will again be heard." Sartre's conclusion that it is up to us now to give life meaning and value "is almost exactly what Nietzsche said, and it has not become any truer since then," Buber ironically remarked.

In his critique of Heidegger, Buber's main thrust was against Heidegger's theses concerning the "appearance" of the divine. Heidegger's view is incompatible with the real transcendence of the divine: Being or Beings have always stepped into relation with us *of their own will* and allowed us to enter into relation with them. "Being turned toward us, descended to us, showed itself to us, spoke to us in the immanence.... That has always distinguished religion from magic." God wills to need man as an independent partner in dialogue, as comrade in work. "God does not let Himself be conjured, but He also will not compel." Through man's giving or denying himself, "the whole man with the decision of his whole being" may have an immeasurable part in the actual revelation or hiddenness of the divine.

> But there is no place between heaven and earth for an influence of concept-clarifying thought. He whose appearance can be effected or co-effected through such a modern magical influence clearly has only the name in common with Him whom we men, basically in agreement despite all the differences in our religious teachings, address as God.

In the concluding essay entitled "God and the Spirit of Man," which Buber wrote for *Eclipse of God,* he pointed to two stages in philosophizing—one in which the human spirit fuses its conception of the Absolute with itself "until, finally, all that is over against us, everything that accosts us and takes possession of us, all partnership of existence, is dissolved in free-floating subjectivity," and one in which the human spirit annihilates conceptually the absoluteness of the Absolute and in so doing destroys its own absoluteness. Now the spirit can no longer exist as an independent essence but only as a product of human individuals "which they contain and secrete like mucus and urine."

Buber also pointed to two pseudoreligious counterparts of the reality of the relation of faith—controlling and unveiling, magic and gnosis. In magic, one celebrates rites without being turned to the Thou and without really meaning its Presence. Magic wishes to control the power that it conjures up. "Instead of understanding events as calls which make demands on me, one wishes oneself to demand without having to hearken." In gnosis, the power of the intellect is used to unveil and display the "divine mysteries," the holy It. In many theologies, as well as theosophies, "unveiling gestures are to be discovered behind the interpreting ones."

Genuine prayer, in contrast, asks that the divine Presence become dialogically perceivable. The simplest presupposition for such prayer—"the readiness of the whole man for this Presence, simple turned-towardness, unreserved spontaneity" — is destroyed today by overconsciousness that I am *praying,* that *I* am praying. He who is not present perceives no Presence, and modern man cannot be spontaneously present so long as he holds back a part of his I which does not enter into the action of prayer with the rest of his person, an I to which the prayer is an object—"the subjective knowledge of the person turning-toward God *about* his turning-toward."

What is in question with both modern philosophy and modern religion is not the choice between I-Thou and I-It, but whether the I-Thou remains the architect and the I-It the assistant, the helper. If the I-Thou does *not* command, then it is already disappearing. Yet precisely this disappearance of "I-Thou" is the character of this hour:

> In our age the I-It relation, gigantically swollen, has usurped, practically uncontested, the mastery and the rule. The I of this relation, an I that possesses all, makes all, succeeds with all, this I that is unable to say Thou, unable to meet being essentially, is the lord of the hour. This selfhood that has become omnipotent, with all the It that surrounds it, can naturally acknowledge neither God nor any genuine Absolute which manifests itself to man as of non-human origin. It steps in between and shuts us off from the light of heaven.

Buber's last statement on the "eclipse of God" was his reply to Emil Fackenheim's assertion in *The Philosophy of Martin Buber* that the silence, or eclipse of God, is a "most troubling question":

> One may also call what is meant here a silence of God's or rather, since I cannot conceive of any interruption of the divine revelation, a condition that works on us as if it were a silence of God.... These last years in a great searching and questioning, seized ever anew by the shudder of the now, I have arrived no further than that I now distinguish a revelation through the hiding of the face, a speaking through the silence. The eclipse of God can be seen with one's eyes, it will be seen.
>
> He however, who today knows nothing other to say than, "See there, it grows lighter!" he leads astray.

At the request of the Jewish Peace Fellowship to which I belonged, I asked Buber whether he would meet with its members when he returned to New York. Buber wrote me in March 1952 from Los Angeles:

> I am no pacifist; for I do not know at all whether in a given situation in which fighting had become necessary, I would not fight. ["One must choose between 'ism' and situation," Buber once said to me, "including pacifism," and he also said, "I could not have been a conscientious objector, like you, in the face of Hitler."] Of course, I am with my whole heart for peace, but not for the usual peace which only continues and prepares for war in a veiled form.

Buber said he had nothing at all against discussing this with a small group in unreserved openness and proposed the evening of April 12. We met, accordingly, with a few members and leaders of the Jewish Peace Fellowship. One member asked Buber why Israel did not unilaterally disarm. "Because the first day the Bedouins would look on in amazement," responded Buber, "and the second they would ride in."

On April 28, I wrote Buber about his book *Images of Good and Evil*, which he had sent me in manuscript in his own handwriting in the German and which I had now read again in the English translation. "I shall never cease to be astonished," I confessed to Buber, "at how each of your works expresses something really new and yet remains within the unity of your thought." In this book, Buber designated two stages of evil—a first in which evil grows directly out of "decisionlessness," the failure to find the direction to God through responding with one's whole being to the concrete situation, and a second in which evil takes the form of a decision, but not with the whole being. The first stage looks back to Buber's teaching of "Direction" in the first dialogue of *Daniel* (1913). In the first stage, unable to bear the tension of possibility and to go through the difficult path of bringing itself toward unity, the soul clutches at any object past which the vortex happens to carry it and casts its passion upon it, grasping, seizing, devouring, compelling, seducing, exploiting, humiliating, torturing, and destroying. This vision of man as bowled over by possibility as by an infinitude is very similar to Kierkegaard's concept of the origin of sin and the fall in *The Concept of Dread*. More important, it stands in a direct line with that threat of infinity that brought the fourteen-year-old Buber close to suicide; with the temptation of the creative man to lose himself in the infinity about which Buber wrote when he was twenty-five; with "The Day of Looking Back," in which he recalled at fifty how Paula Buber had set a limit to delusion and madness and helped him make a real decision as a young man; and with the "fiery stuff" of one's possibilities that circles around the person who must give direction to the "evil urge" *(I and Thou)*.

In the second stage of evil, the repeated experiences of indecision merge into a fixation that produces a crisis of confirmation. That yes which others spoke to him and which he could speak to himself "to liberate him from the dread of abandonment, which is a foretaste of death," is no longer spoken. In a pinch, one can do without the confirmation of others but not of oneself. Those who do not then make the remarkable turning back to the good or become pathologically fragile in their relationship to themselves extinguish the image of what they are intended to be in favor of an absolute self-affirmation which holds that what I say is true because *I* say it and what I do is good because *I* do it. It was undoubtedly Buber's experience with the Nazis and with the war in Palestine that led him to deepen his view of evil to include this second stage.

In July 1955, Buber wrote to me concerning the writer "Georg Munk": "My wife does not like at all that people write about her *person*. Just to avoid it she chose the pseudonym." Buber's old publisher, the Insel Verlag, accepted for publication Paula's epic novel *By Living Waters*, and she spent the next summer revising it. It is striking that this story of German-Catholic families recaptures down to the minutest details what must have been Paula's life in Munich before her marriage and reflects nothing of her forty-five years of life with Martin in Berlin, Heppenheim, and Palestine. The two of them planned to go to Italy after the award of the Peace Prize in Frankfurt on September 27. "We shall not go to the Dolomites," Buber advised me; "in contrast to former times there is now too much noise there in summertime. On the first of September, Buber reported from Amsterdam that he had lectured in a circle (in the Oüde Loo, the charming Old Castle) in which the "Queen of Holland was the most interesting person." "The Queen I meant is Juliana," he later explained. "Her mother is a very different person." He added that a new edition of the Buber-Rosenzweig translation of the Hebrew Bible was coming out in four volumes from Jakob Hegner Verlag in Cologne (Köln). He also expressed his pleasure that the University of Chicago Press finally accepted *The Life of Dialogue* for publication in cooperation with Routledge & Kegan Paul: "I am afraid the cutting will cost you a lot of work." To my report that Will Herberg claimed that the decisive change in Buber's philosophy was due to Rosenzweig's essay entitled "Atheistic Theology," Buber responded, "I have been influenced decisively not by men but by events, particularly in the years 1916–1919," and added, "I am somewhat astonished that H. thinks such a change can be effected by other persons instead of life itself." In January 1954, Buber told me that he had written in "these last weeks a Biblical mystery-play." In March, he said that the title of his mystery play was *Elijah*. "I have wrestled with the subject a great part of my life.... No plan to publish." He also declared that he could not say *anything* about finishing his anthropology: "It is a question of pure grace."

My simultaneous friendship with both Buber and Heschel placed me under great tension concerning the question of the observance of the Jewish Law, or Halakhah. While Heschel never demanded of me that I become Orthodox, he made it very clear that fulfilling the Law was the way to real participation in Judaism or, as he was to write in *God in Search of Man*, "the holy dimension of existence." When I learned from a disciple of Heschel that Buber did not observe Jewish Law and ritual (I had assumed he did because of his beard!), I experienced great, but only temporary, relief. In 1954, I wrote to Buber about this problem, and he responded in March from Heidelberg that he could not see such a question independent of personal existence: "For me I know that I try to do what I experience I am ordered to do; but how can I make this into a general rule about ritual being right or wrong?" What he then asserted gave me more insight into his attitude toward the Jewish Law than anything that he had written since his correspondence with Rosenzweig on the subject thirty years before:

> I open my heart to the Law to such an extent that if I feel a commandment being addressed to me I feel myself bound to do it as

far as I am addressed—for instance, I cannot live on Sabbath as on the other days, but I have no impulse at all to observe the minutiae of the Halakhah about what work is allowed and what not. In certain moments, some of them rather regular, partly on occasion I pray, alone of course, and say what I want to say, sometimes without words at all, and sometimes a remembered verse helps me in an extraordinary situation; but there have been days when I felt myself compelled to enter into the prayer of a community, and so I did it. This is my way of life, and one may call it religious anarchy if he likes. How could I make it into a general rule, valid for instance for you! I cannot say anything but: Put yourself in relation as you can and when you can, do your best to persevere in relation, and do not be afraid.

I was particularly struck by Buber's last remark to me, for I had said nothing about being afraid, yet he had sensed the anxiety that lay beneath my questions regarding what was the right course and how I could find it. Years later, when I read Albrecht Goes's essay on Buber, in which he said that every person has something written on his face and on Buber's it was "Do not be afraid!," I thought of this letter. "Religious anarchy" is exactly what Gershom Scholem later accused Buber of, but when he wrote that Buber had never once set foot in a synagogue during his thirty years in Israel, I judge from this letter that he was mistaken.

In 1955, when I was writing on Buber's exchange with Rosenzweig in connection with the Jewish Law, I asked Buber whether one could not be open to the Law just as one was to the teachings. "Of course, one may be 'open to all of the Law,'" he responded, "but not by *doing* anything before being 'touched.' I can learn tentatively, but I cannot act tentatively. I do not need decision in order to perceive but I need decision in order to act." "By opening my heart I cannot find 'historical revelation,' only personal," he added in response to another question.

> I do not distinguish between me as a mere individual and as a member of Israel, but I am utterly unable to accept anything as God's commandment that I do not hear as such, and I can hear only through this person that I am. Every historical document is the work of transformation, but the Voice in the dialogue itself is not.

In reply to a sharp letter from the English Jewish educator Emil Marmorstein, Buber pointed out, "In all the years no one has ever heard a single critical word from me about the tradition, and when someone tells me that he lives his life according to the Torah in your sense of the term, I answer him: that is your good fortune."

In "The Validity and Limitation of the Political Principle," which I trans-

lated for Buber at about this time, Buber resumed in more concrete form
what he had said about the distinction between the social and the political
principles in "Society and the State." Starting from Jesus' saying "Give to
Caesar that which is Caesar's and give to God that which is God's," he
sought to demonstrate that what Jesus meant was not a dualistic division of
life between the spiritual and the material, as is commonly thought, but the
distinction between the indirect aspects of society, which are the means, and
the direct, which give these means meaning. The human person, ontological-
ly regarded, constitutes a union of two spheres—that of wholeness and that
of separation or division. "What is legitimately done in the sphere of separation receives its legitimacy from the sphere of wholeness." Giving to the state
what is due it in the sphere of separation is authorized by the sphere of
wholeness in which we give God what is due him: ourselves. Give to God
your immediacy in direct relationship with him, as Jesus' saying about the
taxes says to us, and from so doing you will learn ever anew what you shall
give to Caesar in the indirect relations of politics, money, and the structure of
society.

In the opinion and attitude of a very great part of the modern world, in
contrast, public regimes may legitimately determine human existence, "since
the political environment constitutes the essential condition of man, and it
does not exist for his sake but he for it." Whether the remainder that is left
after the abstraction of the essential part for Caesar can still be booked to the
account of "God" is hardly of importance. In the modern world, to discuss
the validity and limitations of the political principle means to criticize at the
decisive point the one absolute that has not been relativized—the political
archons of the hour. Proceeding from a discussion of Hegel, Marx, and
Heidegger, Buber pointed out that, if historical time and history are absolu-
tized, in the midst of present historical events, the time-bound thinker may
easily ascribe to the state's current drive to power the character of an absolute. "After that, the goblin called success, compulsively grinning, may occupy for a while the divine seat of authority." Here, too, Buber was talking
about a direction of movement, not an either/or but an ever newly drawn
demarcation line, the *"quantum satis"* of "as-much-as-one-can." "If the political organization of existence does not infringe on my wholeness and immediacy, it may demand of me that I do justice to it at any particular time as far
as, in a given conflict, I believe I am able to answer for." He was well aware
of the cruel conflicts of duties and in no way implied that under *all* circumstances the interest of the group is to be sacrificed to the moral demand. "But
the evident absence of this inner conflict, the lack of its wounds and scars, is
to me uncanny." "I want to tell you," Buber wrote me at this time, "that I am
not on principle opposed to 'security'; what I am opposed to is sacrificing
the very meaning of life (not less than that!) to security."

It was at this time that Buber sent me, in response to my own deep concern, the answer to my questions concerning meditation and mysticism. What replaced the spontaneous meditations that occurred in his early days, Buber said,

> is something very different, something always bound to a reality, to a situation. I cannot but think all this talk about meditation rather exaggerated. The term "mysticism" has become more nebulous since the days of my youth, and therefore I do not like to use it without explaining thoroughly what I mean. Of course, you may call it mysticism if something is "told" me through a situation; I do not call it that, because this "being told" is simply the minimum of revelation, the elemental form of universal revelation, and revelation has nothing to do with mysticism. As for "meditation," as far as I can see people mean by it absorption in the absolute Self, more or less by the "inner" way; this is very far from what I mean by a religious attitude.

In December 1953, the German original of "Prophecy, Apocalyptic, and the Historical Hour" was published in *Merkur*. In this essay, Buber set forth one of his last sets of polar opposites, two ideal types held in tension with each other, that characterized his thinking from its earliest to its most mature stages. These polarities give Buber's thought elasticity and subtlety, but, for the same reason, they are often the occasion of misunderstanding and confusion. "Letting go and deciding," "orienting and realizing," "I-Thou" and "I-It," person and ego (individual), dialogue and monologue, *emunah* and *pistis, gnosis* and *devotio,* are not so much resumed as given historical depth and dimension by this last set of terms: prophecy and apocalyptic. Unfortunately, many readers are not trained to think either dialectically or phenomenologically, and for this reason they want to read Buber's polar terms as incompatible opposites, as either/ors between which one must choose. This has been as great an obstacle to the understanding of his thought, even by scholars, philosophers, and theologians, as any other single factor.

Buber began "Prophecy, Apocalyptic, and the Historical Hour" by contrasting two different ways of responding to a crisis: drawing on one's primal resources and contributing to the decision about the next hour or "not letting oneself be fooled," that is, fatalistically resigning oneself and letting oneself be carried along. The soul's innermost question of trust is: "Do I dare the definitely impossible or do I adapt myself to the unavoidable?" Prophecy arises out of a time of strength, apocalyptic out of decadence. The one is *spoken* to the *present.* The other is *written* for the *future.* "Wherever man shudders before the menace of his own work and longs to flee from the radically demanding historical hour, there he finds himself near to the apocalyptic vision of a process that cannot be arrested." Like the "modern Paulinism" of *Two Types of Faith,* there prevails a completely secularized, thoroughly disenchanted apocalyptic attitude that has no hope for the future but preserves the character of the present as being all-too-late. The irremediable old age of the world is accepted as self-understood. This new apocalyptic no longer says, "One cannot swim against the stream," because the image of the stream, to which an outlet belongs, is already too full of pathos. Rather, it says, "An old period must behave like an old period if it does not wish to be laughed at." Its only poetry is one of self-directed irony, its only art is one that atomizes things, and faith has become altogether unseemly. Buber's own personal experience in trying to rebel against this indirectness that has penetrated all human relationships, and in being upbraided as a romantic full of illusions, is clearly mirrored in his description of the present hour:

> If he resists the flagging of the dialogical relationship between men, he is forthwith reproached with failing to recognize the fated solitude of present-day living.... If one declares that one of the main reasons why the crisis in the life of the peoples appears hopeless is the fact that the existential mistrust of all against all prevents any meaningful negotiation over the real differences of interest, he is set right by a smile of the shrewd: an "old" world is necessarily shrewd.

Buber *did* rebel in favor of the depths of history, which he saw as continually at work to rejuvenate creation and therefore in league with the prophets, in favor of the risk of inner transformation, which transfigures the "customary soul" into the "surprise soul." Turning does not mean a return to an earlier, guiltless stage of life, but swinging around to where the wasteful aimlessness becomes walking on a way, and guilt is atoned for in the newly arisen genuineness of existence.

> As in the life of a single person, so also in the life of the human race: what is possible in a certain hour and what is impossible cannot be adequately ascertained by any foreknowledge.... One does not learn the measure and limit of what is attainable in a desired direction otherwise than through going in this direction. The forces of the soul allow themselves to be measured only through one's using them. *In the most important moments of our existence neither planning nor surprise rules alone*: in the midst of the faithful execution of a plan we are surprised by secret openings and insertions. *Room must be left for such surprises*, however; *planning as though they were impossible renders them impossible.* One cannot strive for immediacy, but one can hold oneself free and open for it. One cannot produce genuine dialogue, but one can be at its disposal. Existential mistrust cannot be replaced by trust, but it can be replaced by a reborn candour. [Italics added]

This passage makes incontrovertibly clear what should have been clear all along: that Buber never put forward ideal types in order to affirm one and reject the other but as part of a lifelong struggle that there should be *room* in the modern world for realization, I-Thou, person, *emunah, devotio,* freedom, surprise, dialogical immediacy, and the courage to trust.

In 1955, the American Protestant theologian Reinhold Niebuhr wrote *The Self and the Dramas of History,* based on Buber's philosophy of dialogue, and Will Herberg sent Buber his review of the book. In his Preface to his anthology *The Writings of Martin Buber,* Herberg claimed that *for Buber* God is always I and man always Thou. "Against Herberg's view of man 'being the Thou simply,' the Bible brings two great arguments," Buber rejoined: "the book of Job (who only at the end gets an answer) and the book of Psalms (nearly all of them asking for a dialogue or thanking for an answer)." But Herberg, under Niebuhr's influence, felt so strongly that Buber *should* hold God to be always I and man always Thou that he could not bring himself to change his Preface to what Buber really thought!

Buber asked me to give Niebuhr his essay "The Validity and Limitation of the Political Principle," commenting:

> It is obvious he does not know it. I have never been antipolitical, neither in theory nor in practice, but I think it vitally important to fix the boundaries of politics, at least as long as it is not possible to put the power of decision in the hands of the best men (not the philosophers, as Plato thought, but the best men indeed), a thing that would increase the tragedy in the life of those men but would diminish the tragedy in the life of mankind. Herberg, like Niebuhr, has not grasped why my "social philosophy" is as it is: because I do not see any salvation, any true help coming from the non-personal. What they think to be "practical" is nothing but theory of a practice (just as is Marx's philosophy) and never becomes, never became real *praxis,* real act. What is done in the social field is done out of personal relation, out of "decrowding the crowd." To show this I have written (to match *Paths in Utopia*) the third part of "Dialogue" and "Society and the State," and I would go on, if I were only asked real questions on the subject.

Both Herberg and Niebuhr accepted Buber's I-Thou philosophy on the level of interhuman and divine-human relationships, but, in the realm of the social and the political, they held him to be "utopian."

In October 1955, Buber dictated two pages on revelation in reply to questions that I asked him. This later became one of the fragments on revelation that he preserved in "Gleanings," thus providing a striking illustration of how his thought at times came into being in response to "real questions." As in his reply to Jung, he here used the simile of "a divine fire seizing a lump of ore, entering it, melting it, transforming it," so that the flame of God dwells in it, never to be distinguished from it. Buber saw himself as speaking for those persons for whom the distinction between the divine and human part in revelation had become a personal problem that they could neither ignore nor overcome:

> These cannot go back on their knowledge, which is an organic part of their personal faith. But neither can they renounce the historical tradition that has molded them religiously. What they can and must do is to listen again and again, in order to learn which of the commandments of tradition can be heard by them as being commanded by God to them, and of course to live accordingly. This can be done only in the stern responsibility of faith.

In 1958 and 1959, Reinhold Niebuhr, Buber, and I corresponded on the subject of social philosophy and the relation of the social and the political. Niebuhr's comments on Buber's social philosophy and Buber's replies I later incorporated into the Buber section of *Philosophical Interrogations*. Buber's summation of the issue between him and Niebuhr is perhaps the most concrete single expression in Buber's social philosophy of his teaching of the "demarcation line":

> What he calls the basic structure of society is historically and even pre-historically (this is my opinion against the prevailing opinion of ethnologists) based on personal relations, and where it subdues them it becomes wrong. As to modern technical society, of course it depends upon "artfully constructed equilibria of power," but what depends on them is its order and not its justice. If Niebuhr cannot concede it, then obviously we shall have to distinguish carefully between two very different kinds of "justice," and I for myself am harassed by the thought that the concept of justice must be split in two, bearing even different names. I cannot see the God-willed reality of justice anywhere than in "being just," and this means of course: being just as far as it is possible here and now, under the "artful" conditions of actual society. So in my opinion it is not the justice that depends upon them, but ever again the realisable "how much" of it. *Sometimes, striving to be just, I go on in the dark, till my head meets the wall and aches, and then I know: Here is (now) the wall, and I cannot go farther. But I could not know it beforehand, or otherwise.* [Italics added]

"Niebuhr is interested in society as an institutional reality and I as… built upon personal human relations," Buber commented in 1959.

After I had translated *The Tales of Rabbi Nachman,* Horizon Press postponed its publication of the book in order to ask the painter Marc Chagall to illustrate it. Buber was not at all pleased by this: "You must understand, my dear [Maurice], that I am not as young as you are and so time has for me a somewhat different significance than for you. I want to settle things." In May, Chagall told Buber in Paris that he had been asked to illustrate *Nachman,* but Buber did not ask him his decision. "Entre nous," Buber wrote me from Heidelberg, "his daughter wanted me to ask him to make illustrations to the *Tales of the Hasidim,* but I did not want to. He is a very remarkable artist, and his new illustrations to the Bible are beautiful, but I rather prefer the tales to remain unillustrated." In July, Buber added in a letter from Zurich, "I appreciate him highly, but his 'Hasidism' and mine are different and should better not be mixed."

In October 1956, Buber painted a picture of what was, without question, a typical work day, day in and day out, year in and year out until his final illness:

> I have to deal now with (1) re-writing the guilt lectures, (2) preparing the dream lecture, (3) reading proofs of the Bible translation, Vol. 3, and (4) comparing the French translation of *Tales of the Hasidim,* Vol. 2. If you add to all this the daily business (editorship of the Pedagogic Encyclopedia, correspondence, serious talks with visitors every day, Ihud affairs, etc.), you will get a nice day's work.

The most remarkable thing was that despite this crushing load of work, Buber was *fully* present for every person who came to see him!

✦ 18 ✦

Encounter with Psychotherapy and Paula's Death

(1951-1958)

One of those who took part in Buber's week on Taoism in the Netherlands in 1924 was Carl Jung's wife, Emma, who sent Buber New Year's greetings in 1925 "in thankful remembrance of Amersfort." In August 1932, Buber wrote to Hans Trüb that, in the past few years, he had read a few essays of Jung that had made a positive, "nearer" impression on him, and, in March 1933, Buber wrote Trüb that when he went to take part in the Eranos meetings at Ascona, he hoped, among other things, to get together with Jung. In 1947, however, in a letter to Trüb, Buber singled out the Hungarian mythologist Karl Kerényi as the only person of all Jung's circle whom he would really like to get to know. "I have read almost all of his books in the last years and with especial profit. He is today the person in Europe who carries forward the great line of Usener."

In June 1952, Buber brought to my attention the June issue of the *Neue Schweizer Rundschau* with the "beautiful article by Kerényi, 'Martin Buber as a Classical Author.'" "It is interesting also as a fine sign of moral independence, Kerényi being one of the teachers in Jung's institute and Jung being the autocrat he is," Buber added. This last remark was not a reference to Jung's thought but to his personality as Buber knew it from the many disciples of Jung with whom he associated in the 1920s and 1930s. It is interesting in this connection to reflect how Hans Trüb's moving toward Buber and away from Jung must have affected Jung, because Trüb had been so close to Jung that Jung had asked Trüb to treat his own wife, Emma.

In 1934, Buber took part in the Jungian Eranos Conference at Ascona,

Switzerland, and he would have done so again in 1935 had it not been for the Nazi restrictions on his lecturing. In addition, he had for many years had close relations with many Jungian analysts, the chief of which was Hans Trüb. Yet, in 1951, Buber devoted the second half of his sharply critical essay "Religion and Modern Thinking" to Jung. Jung's gnostic transformation of faith seemed to Buber to contribute far more in actuality to the human responsibility for the "eclipse of God" than Heidegger's thought-magic. The part of Heidegger's thought that deals with the coming appearance of the divine has been less influential, in fact, than that part of Jung's thinking which transmutes faith into *gnosis,* for the latter is central to Jung's highly popular philosophy of individuation. This same issue of *gnosis*—knowing *about* faith—versus *devotio*—*actually living faith* in the dialogue of address-ing and being addressed—lies at the heart of the other famous controversy that has lasted beyond the 1950s and beyond Buber's death—the controversy with Gershom Scholem over the interpretation of Hasidism, though in this case the controversy was initiated by Scholem and not by Buber.

When the controversy between Buber and Jung came into the open in 1951, many people in Europe, America, and Israel were shocked. The tradi-tional enemy of religion was Freud, while Jung was hailed as its great friend. Many of Jung's followers were close to Buber and vice versa, and not a few considered themselves disciples of both men, who, ostensibly, shared a com-mon concern with "modern man in search of a soul." What is more, Jung's "collective unconscious," or "objective psyche," has an unmistakable transpersonal, objective, and numinous, or awe-inspiring, nature which led Jung to identify it with Rudolf Otto's *Mysterium Tremendum.* In "Religion and Modern Thinking," Buber himself called Jung "the leading psychologist of our day" and pointed out that he had made religion, in its historical and biographical forms, the subject of comprehensive observations.

However, Buber criticized Jung because, for all his disclaimers, "he oversteps with sovereign license the boundaries of psychology" by defining religion as "a living relation to psychical events which... take place... in the darkness of the psychical hinterland" and conceives of God in general as an "autonomous psychic content." That these are not merely psychological state-ments, as Jung would claim, but metaphysical ones, Buber showed by quot-ing Jung's statements that otherwise "God is indeed not real, for then He nowhere impinges upon our lives" and that God is "for our psychology... a function of the unconscious" as opposed to the "orthodox conception" according to which God "exists for Himself," which means psychologically "that one is unaware of the fact that the action arises from one's own inner self." Psychology becomes to Jung the only admissible metaphysic while remaining, for Jung, an empirical science. "But it cannot be both at once," commented Buber.

Modern consciousness, with which Jung clearly identifies himself, "abhors faith and... the religions that are founded on it" and turns instead with its "most intimate and intense expectations" to the soul as the only sphere that can be expected by man to harbor the divine. The new psychology thus "proclaims the new religion, the only one which can still be true, the religion of pure psychic immanence." What is more, it turns to the soul, in Jung's own words, "in the Gnostic sense," as the new court which replaces conscience by the unity of good and evil. This union of opposites is, Buber pointed out, the mature expression of a tendency characteristic of Jung from the beginning of his intellectual life: "In a very early writing, which was printed but was not sold to the public, it appears in direct religious language as the profession of an eminent Gnostic god [Abraxas], in whom good and evil are bound together and, so to speak, balance each other." In modern mandala dreams, "the place of the deity," Jung explains, "appears to be taken by the wholeness of man," which Jung calls the Self. Although Jung avoids the suggestion of the deification of man in some places, in others the Self, the marriage of good and evil, is elevated by Jung to the highest possible place as the new "Incarnation," whose prospective appearance Jung repeatedly intimates. "If we should like to know," says Jung, "what happens in the case in which the idea of God is no longer projected as an autonomous essence, then this is the answer of the unconscious soul: the unconscious creates the idea of a deified or divine man." "This figure," commented Buber, "is the final form of that Gnostic god, descended to earth as the realization of the 'identity of God and man,' which Jung once professed."

What concerned Buber was not questions of creed or belief or metaphysics but what happened to the relationship of faith itself in actual human existence. "Whatever may be the case concerning God," Buber paraphrased Jung, "the important thing for the 'man of modern consciousness' is to stand in no further relation of faith to God." When one knows oneself called to a particular work and has not fulfilled a task that one knows to be one's own, one knows what it means to say that one's conscience smites one: for conscience is the voice that compares what one is with what one is called to become. This court of conscience is dispensed with by Jung in favor of the soul, which is integrated in the Self as the unification, in an all-encompassing wholeness, of good and evil. Jung sees the Self as including the world, to be sure, but "the others," declared Buber, "are included only as contents of the individual soul that shall, just as an individual soul, attain its perfection through individuation." All beings who are "included" in this way in my self are, in fact, only possessed as an It. "Only then when, having become aware of the unincludable otherness of a being, I renounce all claim to incorporation it in any way within me or making it a part of my soul, does it truly become Thou for me. This holds good for God as for man." Buber characterized the way which he advanced in opposition to Jung's as one that "leads from the soul which places reality in itself to the soul which enters reality."

"Jung has sent *Merkur* an answer and *Merkur* asks me for an answer to it," Buber remarked to me at this time. "I will write a very short one—it is a hopeless matter: two different spheres, I seeing his and he not seeing mine." The strangest thing about Jung's reply was that he ascribed Buber's criticism of him to Buber's "orthodoxy," a statement the irony of which no one could be unaware who knew what Buber had had to live through for fifty years, and particularly in Palestine and Israel, from the constant attacks of the Orthodox Jews on his conceptions of Judaism and Hasidism.

In his reply to Jung, which was published as a supplement to *Eclipse of God*, Buber remarked that as a rule he did not bring his own beliefs into the discussion but held them in check for the sake of human conversation.

> But it must be mentioned here for the sake of full clarity that my own belief in revelation, which is not mixed up with any "ortho-doxy," does not mean that I believe that finished statements about God where handed down from heaven and earth. Rather it means that the human substance is melted by the spiritual fire which vis-its it, and there now breaks forth from it a word, a statement, which is human in its meaning and form, human conception and human speech, and yet witnesses to Him who stimulated it and to His will. We are revealed to ourselves—and cannot express it oth-erwise than as something revealed.

Why Buber saw Jung's modern Gnosticism as more dangerous than Heideggers's modern magic is made unmistakably clear in Buber's final para-graph of his reply to Jung:

> The psychological doctrine which deals with mysteries without knowing the attitude of faith towards mystery is the modern mani-festation of Gnosis. Gnosis is not to be understood as only a his-torical category, but as a universal one. It—and not atheism, which annihilates God because it must reject the hitherto existing images of God—*is the real antagonist of the reality of faith*. Its modern manifestation concerns me specifically not only because of its massive pretensions, but also in particular because of its resumption of the Carpocratian motif. This motif, which reaches as psychotherapy, is that of mystically deifying the instincts instead of hallowing them in faith. [italics added]

The issue Buber put before Jung, at its simplest, was this: Either truth is reduced to the psychic and becomes mere tautology or the psychic is elevat-ed to Truth and becomes a false hypostasizing. For Jung is not a Gnostic, who traditionally believed in a totally transcendent God, but a *modern* Gnostic, whose touchstone of reality is the collective psyche, or Self. For all the numinous, guiding quality of Jung's collective unconscious, it is still an It and not a Thou. It can neither be addressed as Thou nor can one live in real dialogue and contending with it, as could man with the transcendent yet pre-sent God of the Hebrew Bible. It certainly has a quality of overagainstness; it can never be identified with the conscious person, or even with the personal unconscious. But there is no mutuality, no give and take, no sense that Jung's God needs man for the very purpose for which he created him. Indeed, Jung's God is not the Creator, but a demiurge finding his place within a larger order as Zeus did within the Greek cosmos, for Jung's ultimate touchstone of reality is not the autonomous content of the unconscious psyche that he calls Self but the unconscious psyche itself. The placing of the divine in the unconscious, however archetypally and universally conceived, still psychologizes God *and* reality, robbing our meeting with "the things of this world" of any revelatory power other than the mimetic reflection of our forgotten and buried inner truths. If Jung had not asserted the psyche as *the* exclusive touchstone of reality, he could have bestowed great honor upon a realm that undoubtedly has profound meaning, whether that of the shadow, the anima, the animus, the Great Mother, or any of the other life symbols that slumber in our depths, without hypostasizing that realm into an inverted Platonic universal and elevating this larger-than-life-size sphere to the now empty throne of the Absolute.

Buber's critique of Jung's modern gnosticism is closely linked to the contrast between *devotio* and *gnosis* that Buber stressed in his mature presentation of the teachings of Hasidism. Common to the ancient Christian and non-Christian Gnostics, and to the more recent gnostical movements in Judaism associated with the pseudomessiahs Sabbatai Zvi and Jacob Frank, is the substitution of the doctrine that, within the community of the "elect," everything already *is* holy for the task of hallowing an as yet unhallowed creation. Although antinomian gnosticism rejects creation in general as radically evil and incapable of being hallowed, it views its members, particularly the so-called perfect or elect, as so holy that they not only are allowed to sin but positively should do so in order to raise sin to holiness. Revolting against the distinction between good and evil, the radical Sabbataians and the Frankists believed that they could redeem evil by performing it as if it were not evil, that is, by preserving an inner intention of purity in contrast to the deed. This illusion, divested of the exotic costume of the Sabbataian and Frankist orgies, has a decidedly modern ring.

This demonic "lust for overrunning reality," as Buber puts it, is not simply a product of unbelief but a crisis within persons' souls, a crisis of temptation, freedom, and dishonesty. The fascination with the demonic in modern literature, the tendency of many to turn psychoanalysis or "psychodrama" into a cult of self-realization, the illusory belief that personal fulfillment can come through "release" of one's deep inward energies, and the more specific forms of modern gnosticism, such as the analytic psychology of Carl Jung, which advocates taking part in evil as the road to the integration of the self and to "individuation"—all these show the peculiarly modern relevance of this "crisis of temptation and dishonesty."

Buber saw Hasidism as the antidote to the messianic poison of Sabbatai

Zvi and Jacob Frank, precisely because of its message of "hallowing the everyday"—working for a redemption that could not come at all at any fixed hour but only through persevering in an unsentimental life with the concrete reality of everyday. In so doing, Buber increasingly sharpened the contrast between Hasidism and the Kabbalistic mysticism on which it was based, and laid the groundwork for the ideal types of *gnosis* and *devotio*. Frank wanted to penetrate into the very depths of the kingdom of sin in order to overpower it, to fill the impurity with the strength of holiness until it burst from within. Buber understood what was at issue in Frank's revolt in thoroughly modern terms. The Frankist doctrine of "strange actions" and the Hasidic doctrine of "alien thoughts" proceed from the same common presuppositions:

> The abyss has opened, it is not for any man to live any longer as though evil did not exist. One cannot serve God merely by avoiding evil; one must engage with it. The seeds of disintegration have penetrated into the furthest reaches of the people so that even those who fiercely fought the evil had to withstand its assault in the dark depths of their own soul, in the turmoil of dreams.

Buber described this poison as "the lust for overrunning reality."

> Instead of making reality the starting point of life, reality that is full of cruel contradictions but for that very reason calling forth true greatness, namely the quiet work of overcoming the contradictions, one surrenders to illusion, intoxicates oneself in it, subjugates life to it. To the degree that one does this, the core of his existence becomes at once completely agitated and crippled in his power to give direction to its impulses.

The Sabbataian notion that one could redeem evil by doing it without intending it as evil Buber branded as "an illusion, for all that man does reacts on his soul, even when he imagines that his soul floats above the deed. The realms are overturned, everything encroaches on everything else, and possibility is more powerful than reality."

The Hasidic teaching that Buber opposed to this "lust for overrunning reality" was not new, but it took on a different and deepened, fully modern significance. The Hasidic hallowing of the world is not "an isolated Messianic action, but a deed of the everyday that prepares the Messianic completion."

> The great *kavana* is not joined to any particular selection of the prescribed: everything that is done with kavana can be the right, the redeeming act. Each action can be the one on which all depends; what is decisive is only the strength and concentration of hallowing with which I do it.

"We must transform the element that wants to take possession of us into the substance of true life." Buber distinguished this Hasidic teaching from the psychoanalytic theory of "sublimating the libido," pointing out that the latter is limited to psychic events alone, whereas the former means real contact with other beings. Buber translated the language of the "evil urge" into modern language of fantasy and imagination, but imagination here is "no free play of the soul but a real meeting with real elements of being who are outside of us." "What we suppose we effect merely in our souls, in reality we effect on the destiny of the world."

Although Hasidism, like Sabbataianism, based itself on the Kabbala, it took from the Kabbala only what it needed "for the theological foundation of an enthusiastic but not overexalted life in responsibility" for the piece of the world entrusted to one. From being unbinding spirituality, gnostic teachings become an integral part of authentic life. "In the place of esoterically regulated meditations has stepped the task of endowing each action with strength of intention, not according to any prescriptions but in response to the moment." The holy no longer appears in the seclusion of ascetics, but in the joy of the Hasidic leaders and their communities, and—what was unthinkable in the circles of the old Kabbala—the "simple man," the man of the original *devotio,* who possesses neither rabbinic nor Kabbalistic learning, is held in honor because he serves God with his whole being: "Where the mystic vortex circled, now stretches the way of man." "In Hasidism *devotio* has absorbed and overcome *gnosis,*" Buber concluded. "This must happen ever again if the bridge over the chasm of being is not to fall in."

In March 1957, Leslie H. Farber, chairman of the faculty of the Washington (D.C.) School of Psychiatry sent Buber a formal invitation to give the Fourth Annual William Alanson White Memorial Lectures, asking him to center them on his philosophical anthropology and its contributions to psychology. He described the Washington School as an eclectic group open to every criticism and particularly interested in Buber's criticism of Freud's theories of the unconscious and dreams, about which I had told Farber. Farber also described at length Harry Stack Sullivan, the founder of the Washington School, and his theory of interpersonal psychiatry, which Farber rightly thought might be close to Buber's own approach.

In February 1957, Farber informed Buber that a private foundation had agreed to provide the money ($25,000) to film the seminar meetings if Buber agreed. In the most tactful manner possible, Farber suggested that, although he was aware of the possible inconveniences, such a record might be of great value to many seminaries and universities around the world that otherwise would never have the opportunity to see and hear the seventy-nine-year-old Buber. "Too, I believe such a film would have historical significance." Farber had found Willard Van Dyke, maker of the documentaries *The River* and *The City,* who was willing to make the film. Buber responded that, to his very great regret, he would have to say no this time:

My experience is (at any rate my experience with myself) that being filmed injures the spontaneity of the dialogue, and this is what I need most: full spontaneity. This was my motive when some days ago I declined the proposal of Dean Pike that a television film of a dialogue with me be made. I am sure you understand that the rejection of certain modern technical contrivances is necessary *in this connection.*

When Leslie Farber, Eugenia, and I went to the airport to meet Buber in New York, he said that he would not even agree to having the seminars taped and added, "In twenty-five years no one will even know what I am talking about!"

At Chestnut Lodge, Buber met Frieda Fromm-Reichmann, whose illness had prevented her from taking part in the seminars. She asked Buber if she could talk with him alone and, when she did so, confided in him her great, almost despairing loneliness. A year later, she died. When Leslie Farber gave a memorial lecture for her a year or two later, he entitled it "The Therapeutic Despair." The main activity at Chestnut Lodge was listening to a long case report given by one of the psychiatrists who was himself of Hasidic ancestry. He had picked for his case a young woman of mystical and poetic leanings, clearly assuming that this was what would interest Buber. But Buber, without commenting on her poetry or mysticism, said only, "I do not see the line of therapy in this case." Was it merely an adjustment to society, or did real healing through meeting take place?

The overall title of Buber's four lectures at the Washington School was "What Can Philosophical Anthropology Contribute to Psychiatry?"

Buber began "Elements of the Interhuman," his second lecture, by distinguishing between the *social* in general and the *interhuman*; the latter term he had used fifty years before for the social psychological. Now, in contrast, he singled out the "interhuman" as the sphere in which persons are really present, or ready to be present, for each other. In pointing to this sphere, Buber rejected those existentialists who assert that the basic factor between men is that one is an object for the other, and he also stressed that the psychological is only the hidden accompaniment to the dialogue, whose meaning is found in the "between." The most important new contribution of this lecture was the distinction that Buber made between "being" and "seeming," the duality of which he saw as the essential problem of the sphere of the interhuman. These two are ideal types, commonly found mixed together, but needing to be distinguished conceptually to recognize their anthropological importance. In both "being" and "seeming," one is concerned with influencing the other, but in "being" one proceeds from *what one really is,* whereas in "seeming" one proceeds from the *impression one wishes to make* on the other person by what one seems to be. Truth in the interhuman does not depend upon persons letting themselves go before each other or saying everything that comes to mind, but it does depend upon not letting seeming creep in between oneself and the other, upon communicating oneself to the other as what one is. "This is a question of the authenticity of the interhuman, and where this is not to be found, neither is the human element itself authentic." The temptation to seeming originates in our need to be confirmed by one another, our wish that the other approve of what we think, what we do, and what we are. To yield to this temptation is our essential cowardice, to resist it our essential courage.

What Buber did *not* accept was that anyone is "seeming" by nature, neither the child—"I have never known a young person who seemed to me irretrievably bad"—nor the older person, who may have layer upon layer of seeming, which can be penetrated only with great difficulty, if at all: "Man as man can be redeemed." That this is no easy optimism is shown by Buber's statement that the greater part of what is today called conversation among men would be more properly described as speechifying, as powerfully illustrated by Chekhov in his play *The Cherry Orchard*. Responding to Sartre's attempt to brand every thought of a breakthrough as reactionary romanticism, Buber gave an impassioned personal testimony:

> He who really knows how far our generation has lost the way of true freedom, of free giving between I and Thou, must himself, by virtue of the demand implicit in every great knowledge of this kind, practise directness—even if he were the only man on earth who did it—and not depart from it until scoffers are struck with fear, and hear in his voice the voice of their own suppressed longing.

Modern man tries to take apart not only the so-called unconscious but the psychic stream itself, which can never, in fact, be grasped as object, to reduce the multifaceted person to a manageable equation, and to derive the dynamic central principle from some genetic formula. "An effort is being made today to destroy the mystery between man and man. The personal life, the ever near mystery, once the source of the deepest meanings, is leveled down." Buber was not attacking the analytical method indispensable to the human sciences, but the overstepping of the boundary that impairs the essentially different knowledge of the uniqueness of the human person. The antidote to this modern attitude Buber found in "imagining the real"—"a bold swinging—demanding the most intensive stirring of one's being—into the life of the other."

The turning to the partner is frustrated when some of those present do not take an active part, as Buber illustrated with an anecdote about a conversation that he had with two friends: Two of the men engaged in the conversation fell into a duel because of the silent, but influential, presence of the three wives. The first man abandoned the usual composure and strength with which a "master of conversation" speaks and instead scintillated, fought, and triumphed, while the other friend, a man of noble nature and objective fairness, "lost." The "performance" may have been a success, but the dialogue was destroyed.

Buber's distinction between existential guilt and neurotic guilt in his third William Alanson White Lecture, "Guilt and Guilt Feelings," was also a division into ideal types of two phenomena that in our everyday life are usually profoundly and even bewilderingly mixed. Neurotic guilt is identical with the taboos about which Freud and others spoke, whether they can be those of a culture or those internalized under the influence of the Oedipus complex. Such "guilt" is repressed into the unconscious, whereas existential guilt is remembered, but not as guilt for which one is now responsible. Buber defined existential guilt as the guilt that one takes on oneself as a person in a personal situation—in other words, as the injury that one inflicts on the common order of existence. This "objective" guilt cannot be understood as long as one thinks in the ordinary terms of individual versus society. Most people in our culture are so recently "freed" from the guilt imposed by social taboos that they tend to resist Buber's existential guilt as just another guise for the old restrictions that they feel they have thrown off. This is why Buber's lecture "What Is Common to All" is essential to understanding "Guilt and Guilt Feelings." That objective order that one injures—"the order whose foundation we know and recognize as the foundation of our own and of all common human existence"—is nothing other than the common world built out of the common speech-with-meaning of which Buber speaks in "What Is Common to All." Existential guilt, therefore, is the result of a violation of the common, which is also, and by the same token, an injury to the authenticity of one's own personal existence. That is why it is not a question of any society or religion or Platonic ideals being imposed on a person from without, but of the very meaning of interhuman personal existence. We know this from the smaller groups to which we belong, such as the family and the community, for we know what it means to injure such a group by what we do or what we fail to do. The interhuman is not Harry Stack Sullivan's "interpersonal," which is as much I-It as I-Thou, as much impersonal social sense as meaningful reciprocity and partnership, but neither is it just the dyad of I and Thou. It is the group whose members are there for one another.

The therapist must recognize that there exists real guilt, "fundamentally different from all the anxiety-induced bugbears that are generated in the cavern of the unconscious." He must come to this knowledge not out of any religious tradition, but must allow it to arise anew from the historical and biographical self-experience of the generation living today, which knows in what measure we have become guilty. "Under the schooling of this knowledge, which is becoming ever more irresistible, we learn anew that guilt exists." Injuring our relationship to others means injuring at this place the human order of being. It also means that we remain responsible for this injury, for "no one other than he who inflicted the wound can heal it."

The seminars were held in the Cathedral School next to the Washington (Episcopal) Cathedral. Participating in the group were prominent psychoanalysts from the Washington School as well as from as far away as San

Francisco, plus one or two theologians, such as Bernard Mollegan of the Virginia Theological Seminary, and some philosophers. During the intermission on the last evening, the noted neuropsychiatrist David Rioch said, "Now I'm going to get Buber. I'm going to ask him about God." When the seminar resumed, David Rioch asked, "What can you say about God in healing?" Buber walked over to Rioch, faced him, and said:

> In that moment when the name of God is mentioned, most human circles break asunder as persons without knowing it. In that moment the commonness of thinking—the fact of thinking together—is disrupted. The difference between the world with God and without is so enormous that a discussion of God must be divisive except in a group united by a real common faith. People say God without meaning reality, merely as a sublime convention of the cultured person.

Of all Buber did and said during his whole stay in Washington, his refusal to speak about God was what impressed David Rioch most!

Buber accepted what modern psychology meant by the unconscious insofar as it is taken literally as a hidden sphere that has real effects. But he rejected the understanding of the unconscious by Freud, Jung, and most other psychoanalysts—namely, that the unconscious is psychic in nature. Instead, he put forward the idea that it may be just the wholeness of the person before the separation and elaboration into the physical and the psychic, the "body" and the "soul," the outer senses and the inner sense. This implies that the unconscious is not just a psychic deep freeze in which dreams and ideas dwell in already psychic form, ready to float up to the surface when the repression is overcome. A dream is an elaboration by the psyche of an event in the unconscious that we can never know in itself. What is more, its form and meaning are primarily formed by our interpersonal and interhuman relationships, the most important of which, for the patient in therapy, is the relationship with the therapist. Buber related a dream in which at one moment he walked forward and a wind was blowing into his face. In his dream, he said to himself, "Ah, this is the other time." "I felt not only the one line of time going on from birth to death," he explained, "but also as if there were another line of time coming toward me, striking me. Upon reflection I thought, 'Oh, this is the same thing with space as with time.'" In dreams that we remember, Buber claimed, there is sometimes an interposition of spaces, meaning that here things are going on and here there are other things, without intermingling. Here they are, so to speak, two planes, two space dimensions going on, one in the face of the other. Even more curious are appearances in time. Buber also told of a dream that went on until at one moment he felt in the dream, "It is not as it should be—what now?" It was as if he were writing a story and thought of changing it. "From this moment on the same scene occurred again and again with some variants. Finally, I succeeded in changing the last scene and it continued. This recurred many times." "There was a time in my life when I knew very much of dreams and then less and less," Buber said, "so now it is only remembering."

Buber also spoke of lying awake in a state of unusual lucidity after being asleep. "I remember... nights of extraordinary lucidity without sleep." In these nights, the sort of problem solving takes place that also occurs in sleep. "It is an extraordinary wakefulness—much more than in the common world. This is not dream or sleep." This may be a hint of what replaced the mystic hours for Buber after he gave them up. David Rioch asked Buber if he knew anyone who had had a night of lucidity without having worked diligently on a problem beforehand. "Yes, myself," Buber responded, "once or twice as a surprise, as a continuous surprise, and it determined the course of my other thought afterward."

Buber told of a schizophrenic friend whose illness he followed for years. The man had a wife with astonishing willpower who wanted to see him recover once and for all. She visited him in those catatonic moments when he assumed attitudes, positions, and movements that are generally not possible to a normal person, and she actually succeeded in making the same movements as he. He let her into his particular world, and she left the world that is common to all. To the same degree that he let her in, he came out. Twenty-five years later, the man came to visit Buber and told him that he had been normal for a series of years—a professor in the university respected by all—whereas his wife no longer ventured to go out of her house or even leave her bed by day. They talked together for hours, but when Buber left, the professor told Paula that he had been very useful to the British during the war because his connection with the stars enabled him to tell them when Nazi war planes would come over! His seeming normality was only adjustment, and not the healing of the "atrophied personal center." Later, he became a professor in the Soviet Union. One thing Buber said then, which has always remained with me, is that the so-called normal person does not prefer the real world to the world of the schizophrenic because it is a *better* world—the world of the schizophrenic may be better—but because it is real.

Buber looked forward to a new, more musical type of therapist who would not simply follow the theories of his or her school but would practice "obedient listening" and discover the right method and response for each particular person and each particular dream. You would not interpret a poem by the same method as a novel or the poems of Keats by the same method as those of Eliot, Buber observed. "The real master responds to uniqueness."

In the strongest illness manifesting itself in the life of a person, the highest potentiality of this person is manifesting itself in a negative form. If this is so, confirming the person *as he is* is only the first step for the therapist. She must also take the other person in her dynamic existence, her specific potentiality. In the present lies hidden what *can become*. The patient's potentiality makes itself felt to the therapist as that which the therapist would most confirm. Trying to understand the implications of his new approach to the unconscious, I asked Buber whether, if the unconscious is not a psychic sphere *within,* it might not have *more* direct contact with and part in the interhuman than the psychic. If that were so, there would be an immediate relationship between two unconsciouses rather than one filtered through the psyche of each person, as we usually imagine. Buber's response confirmed my insight:

> If the unconscious is that part of the existence of a person in which the realms of body and soul are not dissociated, then the relationship between two persons would mean the relationship between two nondivided existences. The highest moment of relation would be what we call unconscious. The unconscious should have, may have, will have, more influence in the interhuman than the conscious. For example, in shaking hands, if there is real desire to be in touch, the contact is not bodily or psychic, but a unity of one and the other. The unconscious as such does not enter easily into action.... The unconscious sometimes leads to a half-articulated exclamation which all the prepared words cannot, however. The voice becomes the direct instrument of the unconscious in this case.

Buber told Farber that as a young man he wanted to be a therapist, but he found the psychiatric clinics of that time, where the patients were displayed before an audience, abhorrent. Although Buber took a different vocational path, he acquired over the years a deep insight into psychotherapy. Farber himself testifies that he has never read a better description of mania than that "flight into pseudo-decision" of which Buber wrote in *Good and Evil.* "Social puberty" lasts much longer than people think, Buber remarked to Farber— sometimes into middle and old age. Buber also told Farber that he found Sullivan's approach to guilt superficial. "I have been concerned with guilt all my life while he treats guilt just as a form of anxiety." Freud struck Buber as a person temperamentally given to silence, and this is how Buber struck Farber.

Buber spoke of Jung as assuming a nonphenomenological yet psychic reality in his treatment of the unconscious. This seemed to Buber illegitimate. We know from continuous life experience only about being, which embraces the physical and the psychic. "The assumption of a psyche that exists as something exists in space should be either a metaphor or an entirely metaphysical thesis about the nature of being for which we have no basis at all in experience." But if Jung dealt wrongly with the problem of the unconscious, Freud did not deal with it at all. Buber saw Freud, like Marx, as one of the great simplifiers, that is, as "one who places a general concept in place of the ever-renewed investigation of reality." He treated a new aspect of reality as if it were the solution of one of the riddles of being. "Fifty years of psychotherapeutic thought have been based on this dangerous manner of thinking. Now this period is at an end." When we drove together on the way to Chestnut Lodge, Buber said to me, "If you live long enough, and I hope you will, for I love life, you will see a time when Freud is no longer held to be important." He predicted that, by the twenty-first century, there might no longer be "psychiatrists" and the separation of mind and body implicit in that designation.

A number of notable scholars took part in the panels on Buber at the University of Michigan in April 1957, among them Kenneth Boulding, the economist; Ross Snyder and Perry LeFevre of the Divinity School of the University of Chicago; and R. W. B. Lewis, who was then at Rutgers. The most notable event at this conference was the dialogue between Buber and the noted American psychologist Carl R. Rogers, founder of the "nondirective" or "client-centered" approach to psychotherapy. There were a number of striking resemblances between him and Buber, and, during the dialogue, these resemblances emerged, but along with them some important differences.

The dialogue took place in the Rackham Auditorium at the University of Michigan in front of an audience of four hundred, with the understanding that there would be no question period. Buber consented to its being taped, as a result of which the text is preserved verbatim as the Appendix to *The Knowledge of Man*. Rogers's opening question was amusing: "How have you lived so deeply in interpersonal relationships and gained such an understanding of the human individual, without being a psychotherapist?" Buber answered Rogers's question autobiographically, telling about the time he had studied psychiatry at the Psychiatrische-Klinik. But what was most important was his inclination to meet each person, to change something in the other, and also to let himself be changed by him. In 1918, when he was forty, he realized how the war had influenced him through compelling him to "imagine the real," and he gave as his main illustration of this his response to Landauer's death. From then on, especially in his meetings with young people, he felt that he had to give something more than just his inclination to exchange thoughts and feelings. "I had to give the fruit of an experience."

What emerged most clearly in Buber's dialogue with Rogers was his concern with situation and with limits, even the limits of genuine dialogue. This led to the first issue between them. Rogers insisted that there was a complete mutuality between him and his clients. "I see you *want* to be on the same plane," Buber said. "But there is also a certain situation which may sometimes be tragic and even more terrible than what we call tragic. You *cannot* change this." "Out of a certain fullness," Buber said to Rogers, "you give him what he wants in order for him to be, just for this moment, so to speak, on the same plane with you." But this is a situation that lasts not even for an hour but for minutes, minutes made possible by the therapist. At one point in this interchange, Rogers remarked, "Now I'm wondering who is Martin Buber, you or me," to which Buber responded, "I am not 'Martin Buber' in quotation marks!"

In the Postscript to the second edition of *I and Thou,* which Buber wrote the following year, he explained more fully the "normative limitation of mutuality" in the helping relationships. If the genuine psychotherapist is satisfied merely to "analyze" his client, "i.e., to bring to light unknown factors from his microcosm, and to set to some conscious work in life the energies which have been transformed..., he may be successful in some repair work." He may help a diffused and unstructured soul collect and order itself, but he will not achieve the regeneration of an atrophied personal center. "This can only be done by one who grasps the buried latent unity of the suffering soul with the comprehensive glance of the doctor." This is possible in the person-to-person attitude of a partner who experiences the effect of his own action by standing both at his own pole and, "with the strength of his ability to make his partner present," at the other. "But again, the specific 'healing' relation would come to an end the moment the patient" practiced "inclusion" and experienced the event from the doctor's pole as well. This does not mean that the student, client, or parishioner does not glimpse anything of the other as a person. There is mutuality of contact and mutuality of trust and *some* sense on both sides of where the other is coming from. But the responsibility and concern is focused by both partners on the education or healing of the one who is helped and not on that of the helper.

"When you get to what is deepest in the individual, that is the very aspect that can most be trusted to be constructive or to tend toward socialization or toward the development of better interpersonal relationships," said Rogers, continuing the dialogue. "What you say can be trusted... stands in polar relation to what can be least trusted in this man," said Buber. "When I grasp him more broadly and more deeply than before,... I see how the worst in him and the best in him are dependent on one another... I may be able to help him just by helping him to change the relation between the poles. The poles are not good and evil, but yes and no, acceptance and refusal. Perhaps we can even strengthen the force of direction in him because this polarity is very often directionless." All existential relationship begins with accepting the other as he is, said Buber. For that reason, it *cannot* be an "unconditional positive affirmation of everything he says, does, and is." But confirming means accepting the whole potentiality of the other and even making a decisive difference in his potentiality. We can recognize in the other the person he has been *created* to become and confirm him in relation to this potentiality that is meant by him so that it can answer the reality of life. "Just by my accepting love, I discover in you what you are meant to become." Buber said that he experienced cases where he had to help the other against himself, help him to find his unique personal direction.

> The first thing of all is that he trusts me. Yes, life has become baseless for him. He cannot tread on firm soil, on firm earth. He is, so to speak, suspended in the air.... What he wants is a being not only whom he can trust as a man trusts another, but a being

that gives him now the certitude that there *is* a soil, there *is* an existence. The world is not condemned to deprivation, degeneration, destruction. The world *can* be redeemed. *I* can be redeemed because there is this trust. And if this is reached, now I can help this man even in his struggle against himself. And this I can do only if I distinguish between accepting and confirming.

After the dialogue, Buber said to me, "I was very kind to him. I could have been much sharper." But he also said that Rogers had really brought himself as a person and that it was because of this that there had been a real dialogue. In fact, as a result, he canceled the last paragraph in the manuscript of "Elements of the Interhuman," in which he had stated that it was impossible to have a public dialogue.

The last major event in Buber's second visit to the United States was a seminar on biblical faith at Columbia University, arranged by Jacob Taubes for May 1957. The seminar was restricted to the faculties from a number of universities and colleges in the area around New York City. Reinhold Niebuhr, James Muilenburg, Joseph Campbell, Walter Kaufmann, Malcolm Diamond, Michael Wyschogrod, and quite a number of other eminent scholars from different fields were present. Buber dealt with the interpretation of a number of verses, particularly from the New Testament. At one point, he remarked that the passage in Matthew directly following "Since the days of John the Baptist men have tried to take the Kingdom of Heaven by violence" did not seem to him genuine. When asked for his reason, Buber said, "It is merely my own subjective feeling." After several continued to press him, he finally stated, "I do not hear the voice of Jesus in it." At this, James Muilenburg became very red in the face and pounded the table, saying, "That's pure subjectivity!" "But I told you," said Buber mildly.

Michael Wyschogrod, an Orthodox Jewish professor of philosophy who was very much concerned with Kierkegaard and Heidegger, suggested a connection between the Holocaust and the spiritual break that arose in Judaism since the Enlightenment and that produced such a terrible falling away. Buber went over to Wyschogrod and said to him, with utter sincerity, emphasizing every word, "I could not believe in a God who would condemn six million people to death because of their sins." At another time during the seminars, Joseph Campbell asked Buber, "Is this God of Israel the same as Shiva?" Buber, who did not know Campbell and his interest in universal mythological motifs, responded that only God can liberate the religions from their exile and melt down all the images of God into the one imageless God. Later, I told Buber about Campbell's universalistic approach to religion (he had not yet written *The Masks of God,* but his approach was well known to me from his book *The Hero with a Thousand Faces* and from my years of association with him as a colleague at Sarah Lawrence College) and that Campbell had edited some of the books of Heinrich Zimmer, the German scholar on Indian religion. "Ah, I knew it," Buber exclaimed, meaning that he sensed where Campbell was coming from. He and Paula talked warmly of Zimmer, whom they knew and who had married the daughter of Buber's friend Hugo von Hofmannsthal.

Buber was invited to Princeton in the spring of 1958 on a research fellowship, an invitation that led to his third and last trip to America. In December, he responded to the numerous invitations to lecture and give seminars while he was in Princeton: "I have to do a tremendous lot of work in Princeton and cannot go away for a week of seminar or the like. Princeton means for me quiet and work with very few and short interruptions." He agreed to give a public lecture for Princeton and one at the Union Theological Seminary in New York, but, aside from that, he refused all other invitations. One invitation that Buber accepted came from me in the name of the American Friends of Ihud, a group that I had chaired since 1956.

In August 1956, I wrote Buber and Ernst Simon, expressing my anxiety at what seemed to me a predominantly anti-Zionist tone within the Executive Committee of the "American Friends" of Ihud, an Israeli organization all of whose adherents had been and were staunch Zionists. This was of particular concern to me, because from the outset I had been asked to be the chairman of the organization and had accepted this position. The program of the American Friends of Ihud was unexceptionable. But the workings of the organization in practice, including our executive committee, at times made me feel as if we were closer in fact to the American Council of Judaism, with its strong anti-Zionist position, than to Ihud, something that was perhaps inevitable because of the politicization and polarization of the issue in America, where it seemed unthinkable, in 1956, that people could be both Zionist and concerned with Arab-Jewish rapprochement, as were Magnes, Buber, Smilansky, Simon, Henrietta Szold, and other leaders of Ihud in Israel. Buber's response was unequivocal:

> The problem you put before me has only one possible solution. The Friends of Ihud, as such, cannot differ in their political declarations from those of Ihud. An American society for promoting friendship between Jews and Arabs, or the like, may publicly say what they want to say, but a society using the name of Ihud is particularly bound and particularly responsible. For me at least no discussion is possible on this point. I shall raise it expressly in the next meeting of our board.

In his next letter, after the meeting of the board of Ihud, Buber wrote me that Ernst Simon would communicate with me when in New York: "What he says will be said in my name too."

The American Friends of Ihud decided to hold a great celebration in memory of the tenth anniversary of the death of Judah Magnes, and in honor of Buber's eightieth birthday, while Buber was in America during the spring of 1958. The purpose of the meeting was to raise money for *Ner*. Buber agreed to speak, although he wrote me in January 1958: "I have the impression you think I can give a lecture on the *Ner* meeting. I cannot prepare anything, but I am willing to answer freely what you or anyone may say or ask." This was not possible, because the meeting was held at the Community Church in New York before several thousand people. Roger Baldwin spoke, as did Erich Fromm, both members of our board of directors.

Buber's speech lasted for almost an hour and was an ambitious attempt to present an overview of the whole Zionist movement, which was split between those who wanted to achieve Zion by diplomatic means and those who, like Buber and his friends, believed in organic colonization *and* in Jewish-Arab good-neighborliness and cooperation. In the course of this overview, Buber suggested that *some* of the Jews in Palestine had chosen to use Hitler's methods—to place their trust in power, rather than in the spirit, in their attempts to build Zion. This passage was picked up by the Jewish press in America and in Israel, and was severely criticized. From Soglio, Italy, on his way back to Jerusalem, Buber informed me in July 1958:

> I have been vehemently attacked by some Israeli newspapers because of the Hitler passage in my speech and it has even been misquoted. But I have seen now—too late, this is my own fault—that the text in the Newsletter is somewhat misleading. How could "the majority of the Jewish people" think, even after Hitler's defeat, that he did what he did "with impunity"? It makes no sense. In my notes I find the following sentence: "In the days of Hitler the majority of the Jewish people saw that millions of Jews have been killed with impunity, and a certain part [of the Jewish people] made their own the doctrine that history does not go the way of the spirit but the way of power."

Buber sent a "rectifying communication" to the editor of *Ha-aretz*, which had not criticized him, in which he also said: "I must add now that that part of the Jewish people did not change this opinion even after Hitler's defeat. I oppose now as I opposed then, with all my force, those who believe in the doctrine of 'Not by the spirit, but by power' and act upon it."

Later, Buber, on further reflection, felt himself obliged to write down, for the American Jewish press, "a clear and precise exposition of my views on the problems of the evolution of the Zionist movement and especially of its crisis in the days of Hitler and the consequences of this crisis up to the present." How deeply Buber felt this mistake about the Hitler reference, and how personally he took it, he expressed in this same letter in which, poignantly, he saw it as the first real failing of old age:

> I am sorry for the confusion I have caused concerning the Hitler passage, I do not exactly understand how I did it. My heart cannot recover from it, because here, as far as I see, is the first nega-

tive sign of old age, and I had hoped to be spared. I like to be old, I like the strange experiences of old age, I like even the burden and the difficulties, but I hate causing confusion.

After the American Friends of Ihud eightieth birthday meeting, I naively imagined that I could raise what had increasingly seemed to be a central issue (the growing predominance of anti-Zionists on the Executive Committee) by resigning as chairman. I mentioned this informally to Don Peretz, who reported it to the Executive Committee and got himself elected chairman in my place at a meeting held without me. Simon remonstrated with me, saying that he had worked for Ihud and its predecessor for over thirty years, and Buber himself said that it was an irrational act on my part. It was certainly a naive one, but within a few months Ihud formally communicated with the American Friends of Ihud and demanded that they desist from using the name of Ihud since, after my departure, the organization became more and more openly anti-Zionist. It is not easy in America (or in Israel or anywhere else) to walk the narrow ridge!

During 1956 and 1957, I worked with Buber, editing and translating *Pointing the Way,* which included most, but not all, of the essays in his German collection *Hinweise* and some others besides. One of the essays was "The Teaching of the Tao" (1911), which was discussed in Chapter 3. The Foreword to *Hinweise* contained the statement, "I have included only those essays that I can stand behind today." I pointed out to Buber that he could not really say this of "The Teaching of the Tao," because it still stressed a "unity" that was not really compatible with his philosophy of dialogue. I suggested to him that he write an addition to the Foreword to explain why he nonetheless felt that he had to include this essay. "The Foreword shall indeed explain what you hint at," Buber wrote me in August 1956. "The 'unity' of which the Tao essay speaks, is not the unity of Being, but that of 'the one thing that is necessary,' but you are right that the essay is too 'mystical.'" Buber did, in fact, write a whole new Foreword in which he explained that he could not affirm all of "The Teaching of the Tao," yet he had included it because it belongs to that "mystical... stage that I had to pass through before I could enter into an independent relationship with being."

The genuine ecstatic experience that usually underlies the belief in a union of the self with the all-self leads the person who has that belief to regard everyday life either as an obscuring of or a preparation for the true life. Instead of bringing into unity his whole existence as he lives it, from the hours of blissful exaltation unto those of hardship and of sickness, he constantly flees from it into the detached feeling of unity of being, elevated above life. In these "higher hours," the great dialogue between I and Thou is silent; "nothing else exists than his self, which he experiences as *the* self. That is certainly an exalted form of being untrue, but it is still being untrue." Now Buber pointed to the "one thing needful" not as the unified life of the "central man" of "The Teaching of the Tao" but "being true to the being in which and before which I am placed."

Ursula Niebuhr, the wife of Reinhold Niebuhr, told me an amusing sequel to these events. On the very morning in which Reinhold Niebuhr's review of *Pointing the Way* appeared in *The New York Times Book Review* (in the spring of 1958), Martin Buber happened to be coming over to the Niebuhrs, for breakfast (Niebuhr was then at the Institute for Advanced Studies). In the generally favorable review, Niebuhr went out of his way to attack "The Teaching of the Tao" as evidence of a lingering mysticism that Buber had not been able to overcome. When Martin Buber entered, holding the review in his hand, he turned immediately to Niebuhr, who towered above him. Buber put his index finger against Niebuhr's stomach and said accusingly, "You did not read my Foreword!" "That is right," Niebuhr admitted. "I did not read the Foreword."

When Martin and Paula arrived in New York at the beginning of March 1958, Eugenia and I went to meet them in a car driven by my Sarah Lawrence student Kitty McCaw. Kitty, who later became one of the leading graduate students in philosophy at Northwestern University, asked Buber to meet with her and some other members of the philosophy seminar that she chaired and for which I was the faculty adviser.

I met regularly over two months with six young women from the philosophy seminar, all of them excellent students whom I had known and worked with in my classes for one, two, or even three years. I tried to impress upon them that Buber would answer only "real questions," and they tried conscientiously to prepare themselves for the meeting. Despite this, they could not really understand just how concrete Buber meant for their questions to be until they had been with him for a while. Occasionally, I interpreted a question, because these were students whom I knew extremely well and I was fearful lest a misunderstanding get the discussion going on a wrong track. Buber did not particularly want this help, and I learned something totally unexpected about dialogue and dialectic at a deeper level than I could have anticipated. Each of the six, without Buber's in any way asking for it, not only told him the question that she had prepared but told him the concrete experience that lay behind the question and gave rise to it. Although I knew them well (many of them were my "données," or advisees, as well as my students) and I knew their thinking, these experiences were totally new to me. One of the answers that Buber gave provided a whole deeper insight into the problem of temptation and guilt. "When one is tempted," he said, "the choice is not between becoming guilty and not becoming guilty but between giving in to the temptation or reaching a whole new stage where one has never been."

Paula was a strong woman, given to an enormous amount of physical and intellectual work. "She was too strong. She was a Viking!" Buber's secretary Margot Cohn said to me. Once when Paula had injured her shoulder moving a heavy trunk, Buber told me, she had refused to see any doctors because she did not believe in them. When Buber wrote me from Soglio, Italy, in July 1958, about the essay correcting the Hitler passage in his American Friends of Ihud speech, he said that they hoped to be home by August 4, after staying at Zurich and Venice. "When we arrive in Israel, the danger of war may have become imminent," he added. On August 2, he reported from Venice: "My wife took ill here a few days ago (a thrombosis, but seemingly not a very grave one) and we, I and my daughter, who came from a journey to Greece to meet us here, have brought her to a hospital on the Lido. My daughter stays here with her, and I stay in a nearby hotel." He also said that the next ship from Venice to Haifa left on August 30, "and we think to go with it." "I will try as best I can to go on with the work." On August 13 he wrote from Venice:

> My wife died two days ago. Her strong heart resisted at first the new hemorrhaging and then the pulmonitis for days and days, till it could not resist any more. We have buried her, I and my children, in the old cemetery of the Jewish community here on the Lido, full of old trees. Some days before her death she had uttered suddenly: "...The grave of Platen [the German poet] in Syracuse...."
> We are returning Friday 15, to Israel.

In August 1958, Hugo Bergmann published in the magazine of the German-speaking Jews in Israel from central Europe an article about Paula Buber, in which he spoke of her great influence in helping Buber to escape the overly aesthetic and uncommitted life of his youth. He concluded:

> Paula Buber was other than we are. But when she, as she often did in her speech, said, as a matter of course, 'we Jews,' then we felt ourselves confirmed. We did not make it easy for her among us. We did not always learn what we had to learn from her great, pure, solid, astringent, critical, but always deeply genuine figure. She walked her separate way unerringly.

In September, Buber wrote, thanking Eugenia and me "for your good words that have done me good. The structure of my life has been broken up so thoroughly that I have given up all plans for lectures abroad, including Munich." The reference to Munich concerned the lectures on speech with Martin Heidegger at the Academy of Fine Arts, which had been planned for more than a year. "I have not been able to work till now, but I have in mind to begin again the day after to-morrow," Buber added. "I mean to begin with re-writing the seven chapters of the responses for the *Living Philosophers* I have drafted in Princeton, and I will send you a copy." He also needed to write the last chapters, including the one on the Bible, as well as the answers for the *Review of Metaphysics* and, after finishing all the responses, "the Autobiography, a rather brief one." Six more letters followed in the next twelve days, in the last of which he said, "Work is the only earthly help in my present situation." In October, Buber wrote, "My work now is a kind of 'walking against the wind.'"

From New York, the philosopher Hans Jonas wrote Buber after he had learned of Paula's death: "Never have I seen a more perfect community of two who remained what they were while affirming the other. That the choice of youth can so prove itself and become ever more true in the course of time—such success is the highest tribute to the good fortune of the original meeting.... It was always beautiful to see you two together.... The blessing of that infinite communion which the two of you shared must penetrate your present aloneness."

In February 1959, Buber sent out from Jerusalem to the thousands of people who had written him about Paula's death a printed statement that said he had been ill and only now was able to follow the longing of his heart and thank all the friends and intimates

> who, in this darkest hour of my life, have bestowed on me their comfort, yes their consolation. For it was a comfort: to learn how the great presence of the one to whom I have vowed myself forever really wove itself and endured in all the souls. She spoke at times of this earthly immortality and it is indeed the only one that can be grasped by our earthbound imaginations. All of you who have given me news of it receive the thanks of one who is alone but not abandoned!

In 1961, Buber wrote, as a Foreword to *Spirits and Men,* his own selection from three of Paula's books of tales, a short essay in which he described her as "'the blessed woman,' who ventured upon the brokenness of the human house." She was a narrating person for whom images became events and who "imparted our human time to the elemental spirits, who know only cosmic, destinyless time. She brought them into that time into which the dark threads of our afterknowledge of our birth are interwoven with the still darker threads of our foreknowledge of our death."

♦ 19 ♦

Replies to Critics:
Buber versus Scholem

────────

(1956-1963)

In 1956, I received a letter from Paul Arthur Schilpp, founder and director of the famous Library of Living Philosophers, asking me if I were ready, as "a labor of love," to take on the work of editing a *Philosophy of Martin Buber* volume for the series. At the same time, I agreed to conduct a "philosophical interrogation" of Buber for a series edited by the philosophers Sydney and Beatrice Rome and destined, originally, for publication in an issue of *The Review of Metaphysics*. In the *Review of Metaphysics* "interrogation" series, a variety of philosophers addressed short questions to a philosopher; the conductor chose the contributors and edited and forwarded their questions.

Fritz Kaufmann, a phenomenologist from Freiburg who now taught at the University of Buffalo, was my chief adviser in editing the former work, until his untimely death in 1958. In April, Fritz Kaufmann had given a beautiful speech in German entitled "Baeck and Buber" at the Congregation Habonim in New York, which I later translated into English for publication in *Conservative Judaism:* "In the sea of suffering that surrounded Jewry, Baeck and Buber have become and remained, particularly for the German Jews, the firm pillars of a community consecrated in suffering." Kaufmann characterized Baeck and Buber as *zaddikim,* each in his way guardian and representative of the Covenant. Most precious in Kaufmann's speech was the honesty with which he cut through the public image to Buber the man, recognizing that loneliness became his fate, much more so than it did for Baeck. "The silver beard of the sage covers the wounded streak of the mouth. The nocturnal wrestling is taken for a success story. But as far as it is a victory, it is a

victory in tension with defeats." Buber has taught us to endure, forever insecure and uncertain. But Buber himself, Kaufmann implied, is lonelier than
those he taught. "He is walking on a narrow ridge, the path illuminated only
in unexpected, lightning flashes by meetings with the eternal Thou.... This is
necessarily a hard, essentially lonely path." In the incorruptible gaze of
Buber's searching eyes is the composedness of him who cannot conform to
the established law because he wants to be open and obedient to the
demand of the hour. "But in it too is the sadness of abandonment felt by one
who is resigned to others' being essentially just different—already
Rosenzweig was frightened by this feeling of distance—and who is attacked
by those close to him with a kind of tragic love-hate, while those far
removed are his adherents."

Early in 1957, Buber began preparation for a new German and English
edition of *I and Thou.* Buber asked me to draw up for him a list of the questions that I felt most often occurred to people concerning *I and Thou,* and to
address these questions, he wrote what he originally conceived of as a preface but later changed to a postscript, or afterword. Although Buber was not
willing to give up the I-Thou relationship with nature, he recognized that it
was confusing to the reader and even said to me that if he were to write *I
and Thou* again, he would try to find some different vocabulary to make the
distinction. In his Postscript, he divided the relationship with nature into a
liminal, or threshold, relationship with the animals, who share with us the
quality of spontaneity, and a preliminary, or prethreshold, sphere stretching
from stones to stars to planets. Man wins from tamed animals, and occasionally nontamed ones, an often astonishing active response to his addressing
them "which in general is stronger and more direct in proportion as his attitude is a genuine saying of *Thou."* Although plants cannot "respond" in this
same sense, there is a reciprocity of being in its course *(seiend).* "Our habits
of thought make it difficult for us to see that here, awakened by our attitude,
something lights up and approaches us from the course of being." This is
that "bestowing side of things" that Buber spoke of in "With a Monist" and
that I referred to as the impact of otherness in my chapter on Buber's
"Theory of Knowledge" in *The Life of Dialogue.*

The Postscript to *I and Thou* included a very important paragraph
about the relation between our relationship to the "absolute Person" and our
relationship to one another:

> As a person God gives personal life, he makes us as persons
> capable of meeting with him and with one another. But no limita-
> tion can come upon him as the absolute Person, either from us or
> from our relations with one another; in fact we can dedicate to
> him not merely our persons but also our relations to one another.
> The man who turns to him therefore need not turn away from any
> other I-Thou relation; but he properly brings them to him, and
> lets them be fulfilled "in the face of God."

God is not a person in his essential being but, nonetheless, is *also* a person in that he "enters into a direct relation with us men in creative, revealing, and redeeming acts, and thus makes it possible for us to enter into a direct relation with him." "This ground and meaning of our existence constitute a mutuality, arising again and again, such as can subsist only between persons." God is not a limited person, however, but the *absolute* Person whose speech to us penetrates what happens in the life of each one of us "and transforms it for you and me into instruction, message, demand." "The existence of mutuality between God and man cannot be proved, just as God's existence cannot be proved," Buber concluded, and added, with a clear thought of those readers who would come to *I and Thou* after his own death, "Yet he who dares to speak of it, bears witness and calls to witness him to whom he speaks—whether that witness is now or in the future."

In December 1960, two years before the publication of the German volume of the Library of Living Philosophers, Buber's "Autobiographical Fragments," finally completed, were published in a separate German Christmas publisher's edition under the title *Begegnungen,* or *Meetings,* by which title they are now also available in English. They quickly took their place as one of Buber's enduring little classics. In the Library of Living Philosophers volume on Karl Jaspers, the autobiography ran to some 250 pages of a closely knit personal-intellectual history. Buber's, in contrast, came to less than fifty pages, even with three appendices. "These 'events and meetings' are in the fullest sense of the term 'teaching' and perhaps, in the end, the most real teaching that Martin Buber has left us," I wrote in my Introduction to the English-language edition of *Meetings.* "Some of the most profound of Buber's hard-won insights are contained within them like a vein of gold in marble. They await extraction by those who wrestle and contend with them until they are compelled to divulge their secret." In March 1961, Hermann Hesse notified Buber of "the great participation, joy and excitement" with which he had read and reread *Meetings.* "In your life I found some figures and experiences of the same streaming and convincing power as those in Frankenberg's *Life of Jacob Boehme.*" In September 1963, on the initiative of Hans Fischer-Barnicol, Buber recorded a series of "Autobiographical Fragments," which were broadcast by many German radio stations and rebroadcast after Buber's death. In addition to the German and American editions, editions of *Meetings* have been published in Holland, Israel, and Japan.

Although Buber appreciated the contributions to the Library of Living Philosophers volume, answered them as faithfully as he could, and conscientiously sought to clear up any misunderstandings, he once remarked that the essays in the volume represented the whole range of possible misunderstandings of his thought! One of the saddest "mismeetings" was that between Buber and Charles Hartshorne, the famous American process philosopher, who wrote the essay on "Buber's Metaphysics" for the volume. Hartshorne *used* to say that Buber was no metaphysician, yet he decided that he was one of the "good guys" (that is, the panentheists), and put him in that category in his book *Philosophers Speak of God.* In the tradition of Plato and Whitehead, Hartshorne maintained that if God is absolute, he is not in relation, and if he is in relation, he cannot be absolute. Halfway through the essay, he remarked that he liked Buber's metaphysics very much and added, with candor, "I ought to. I have remade it in my own image." But Buber's "absolute Person" stuck in his throat. When Buber wrote his reply, he said that he could not acknowledge as his own Hartshorne's interpretation of his metaphysical position and added:

> Because I say of God, that He enters into a relationship to the human person, Hartshorne says that this makes God relative! He thinks that is proved by the sentence: the relative depends for being what it is upon some relation to another. As if an absolute being had to be without relationship!
>
> I confess that I do not know what to do with Hartshorne's concept of a relative perfection; it affects me on each new examination as equally unacceptable. And when I hear, besides, "the divine essence is nothing else than God's idea of his individuality," I mark once again how difficult it is for me to find a common language with a modern metaphysician.

"You begin, dear Hartshorne, with the sentence, I am no metaphysician and I am one of the greatest metaphysicians," Buber wrote in the conclusion to his short reply. "After attentive reading of your essay, I am far more strongly convinced than I was at the beginning of the reading, that we can make only the first half of your sentence the basis for an understanding." Thus, Buber decisively distanced himself from all metaphysicians who imagine that God must be subsumed under Aristotle's law of noncontradiction, as Buber's friend, the philosopher Lev Chostov, so aptly puts it.

In the Editor's Preface to *The Philosophy of Martin Buber,* I pointed out that the form of Schilpp's Library of Living Philosophers is particularly congenial to Buber's philosophy of dialogue, because it gives other philosophers the opportunity to question and criticize the philosopher while he is still alive, and it gives the philosopher the opportunity to respond.

> Thus it introduces into the critical dialectic that has traditionally constituted philosophical interchange the basic elements of a dialogue in which really different points of view may come into fruitful contact. The philosopher must endeavor to understand the points of view from which he is questioned while at the same time pointing out to his critics those misunderstandings in their criticism that arise from seeing his philosophy from the outside rather than from within.

It was appropriate that editors Walter Kegley and Charles Bretall, who had once approached Buber but did not follow through, devoted a volume of their series, the Library of Living Theologians, to Paul Tillich, whereas Buber appeared in the Schilpp series. Although Tillich's thinking was systematic, as Buber's was not, there is no doubt that Tillich was basically a theologian, whereas Buber was a philosopher and philosophical anthropologist.

The Buber section of *Philosophical Interrogations* forms an invaluable supplement to the longer essays and *responsa* of *The Philosophy of Martin Buber*. In fact, the short question and direct answer of the interrogations made for much more genuine dialogue than the traditional essay form and systematized *responsa* of the larger volume.

The "Philosophical Accounting" that Buber placed at the beginning of his "Replies to My Critics" is an important general response and testimony that could not have been invoked by the more specific questions of the *Interrogations*. Rejecting those who wished to see him as a philosopher, a theologian, or in terms of any other traditional category, Buber declared himself "an atypical man" who, because he matured to a life lived on the basis of his own experience during the years 1912—1919, "had the duty to insert the framework of the decisive experiences that I had at that time into the human inheritance of thought, but not as 'my' experiences, rather as an insight valid and important for others and even for other kinds of men." This communication had to be a philosophical one that would relate the unique and particular to the "general," discoverable by every person in his or her own existence. "I had to make an It out of that which was experienced in I-Thou and as I-Thou." Buber was convinced, moreover, "that it happened not otherwise with all the philosophers loved and honored by me. Only that after they had completed the transformation, they devoted themselves to the philosophy more deeply and fully than I was able or it was granted to me to do."

Buber saw reason as included in the great experience of faith which he had, one of bearers of faith which can function as a trustworthy elaborator: "It is incumbent upon reason to apply logic... to avoid inner contradictions; but it may not sacrifice to consistency anything of that reality itself which the experience that has happened commands it to point to." This refusal to go along with the autocratic form in which reason usually appears in no wise meant that Buber's communication of faith might properly be called a theological one, for theology is a teaching about God, even if a negative one. "But I am absolutely not capable nor even disposed to teach this or that about God. I cannot leave out of consideration the fact that man lives over against God," Buber added, "but I cannot include God himself at any point in my explanation, any more than I could detach from history the, to me indubitable, working of God in it, and make of it an object of my contemplation. As I know no theological world history, so I know no theological anthropology in this sense; I know only a philosophical one." Buber's thinking did not derive from anything traditional, as important as the theological element had been in his scholarship and reporting, but from his own experience of faith. His philosophy did not serve a series of revealed propositions but "an experienced, a perceived attitude that it has been established to make communicable. I am not merely bound to philosophical language, I am bound to the philosophical method, indeed to a dialectic that has become unavoidable with the beginning of philosophical thinking." If he did not replace the name God by a general concept, that was not because he disagreed with Heraclitus, who held it to be inadmissible to say only "Zeus," but because, unlike Tillich, he had no doctrine of a primal ground (*Urgrund*) to offer. "I must only witness for that meeting in which all meetings with others are grounded, and you cannot meet the Absolute."

Buber also pointed out in his "Philosophical Accountings" that he had never held that inner life and thinking are exclusively composed of I-Thou and I-It: "Every essential knowledge is, in its origin, contact with an existing being and, in its completion, possession of an enduring concept." But the continuum between origin and completion cannot be divided up into one or the other, for it is a noetic movement from a personal meeting to a factual knowledge-structure in which the two primal words [I-Thou and I-It] cooperate:

> Authentic philosophizing originates ever anew in contacts born of the I-Thou relationship that still affords no "objective" knowledge. Now the transposition into the structured order of It takes place, and, if a real workman is at work, there may stand at the end the freestone structure of a system.... The fiery track of the original contacts is inextinguishable.... To the penetrating genesis-glance each bold metaphysical setting manifests its origin in a meeting of the knowing person with an element of being that manifests itself through what meets him in a living way.

Buber did not claim for himself, however, "the freestone structure of a system," for the theme that he had to develop was not suited to development into a comprehensive system. He had to make visible a neglected, obscured, primal reality and to restrict his teaching to that which would point to it. He could not philosophize about being, but only about the human twofold relationship to being. Therefore, his philosophizing had to be essentially an anthropological one, starting with the question of how man is possible. For this, a compact structure was suitable, but not one that joined everything together. Even Buber's philosophy, therefore, must be subsumed under that pointing that he spoke of in the Foreword to *For the Sake of Heaven*. In this vein, Buber stated in his "Replies," "I point to something in reality that had not or had too little been seen. I take him who listens to me by the hand and lead him to the window... open the window and point to what is outside. I have no teaching, but I carry on a conversation." Unlike the great systematizers, Buber did not claim that the experience on which he based his philosophy was other than a limited one. But he rejected any attempt to designate that experience as "subjective."

Buber's refusal and incapacity to construct a total philosophical system marked his essential modernity, for it grew out of his recognition of the validity and limitations of his philosophy as a pointer to reality. In both *The Philosophy of Martin Buber* and *Philosophical Interrogations,* Buber acknowledged the continuity between the I that detaches itself from the other and the I that turns to it, but he would not recognize this self-consciousness as "an isolated I that stands over against neither a Thou nor an It." Whereas the distinguished French philosopher Emmanuel Levinas saw this self-identification as the source of "happiness," Buber also saw it as the source of "the deepest suffering of which we are capable" and hinted darkly that this polarity of feelings "points us back to a deep duality of which... my philosophy perhaps merely makes manifest the foreground that we can grasp." Buber made a distinction that he regarded as of fundamental importance between the first "lightning flash" of self-consciousness and the second "elaborated" one in which the self becomes an object to itself. He denied the Israeli philosopher Nathan Rotenstreich's claim that the first emerging of the I is the center of existence, and instead regarded it as an aura about the center, and saw reflection, which Rotenstreich also emphasized, as the play of a searchlight that shines upon the aura. Reflection, like the It, is necessary, but not sufficient, for full human existence: "Without it the human being known to us would not exist, yet it does not belong to its primal phenomena." Persons must be present for a personal meeting to take place, but developed consciousness of the I and its reflective elaboration is not essential: "I see that Socrates reflects, I do not see that Francis does so; the relation of both men to their disciples is genuinely personal."

In his "Replies," Buber commented ruefully on "the psychology of misunderstanding," which he illustrated by Rotenstreich's claim that Buber's statement in "Dialogue," that "in real faith the dictionary is put down," means that he advocated an empty, formal dialogue with no real content. "It is for me of the highest importance that the dialogue have a content," Buber responded; only this content does not belong to the isolated word in the dictionary, where speech shows us only its general applicability, but, rather, to the word in its living context in conversation, poetry, prayer, and philosophy. The more concrete and concretizing the word, the more it does justice to the unique, the coming to be, the formed. Buber did not deny that contents in general allow valid and binding propositions to be transmitted, "but in so doing the peculiar, that which by its nature is unique, is lost." These latter contents are not codifiable; even the most universal commands attain unforeseen interpretations, which the situation itself furnishes.

Buber's response to criticisms of his category of "the between" was that it will have to remain for a long while within the unaccustomed—"but I do not believe that the human spirit can do without it in the long run." But this, too, is only a pointing. Asked how he could speak of love as attesting to the existence of the beloved, Buber could only testify from direct and indirect experience, that the great love for an actually existing being is qualitatively different from the most poetically compelling fantasy or image, because it accepts the other wholly just as she is, which the latter cannot do. In philosophical interchange as in theological, Buber's witness remained a passionate one.

Buber's replies to his critics took on an important historical overtone when Ernst Simon quoted approvingly Franz Rosenzweig's criticism of *I and Thou* as not doing justice to the It for here Buber gives us in writing the response that he probably made to Rosenzweig orally: "Indeed it does not do justice to it. At another time, it would perhaps have been granted to me to sound the praises of the It; today not so: because without a turning of man to his Thou no turn in his destiny can come." This in no way meant that Buber did not prize science, with its so-called objective knowledge. Science gives us our orienting connection with the space-time sphere in which we live, and, without it, no handing down of an organized body of knowledge from generation to generation would be possible. Our current worldviews are built on science's current "position." What is more, Buber recognized a relation—"one that remains ever mysterious to me"—between the basic knowledge of mathematics and being itself, upon which the triumph of inherited knowledge of the human race from Euclid to Einstein is founded. But he refused to see science as exclusively the province of the It. What an original investigator discovers in his contacts with the unique still has the essential structure of the I-Thou relationship: a person and a presence that that person stands over against—not yet object, the contact of the unique with the unique, still prior to all transposition into the general. The investigator must from time to time radically remain standing before concrete reality in order to attain general insights or exact formulae. "But at the beginning of his way he is ever again led by the genius of meetings until that genius can safely deliver him to the reliable spirit of objectification."

Science, however, is only an aid, not a reliable objective technique, in the work of the true therapist or educator. In the hands of a person without a true vocation, psychology or pedagogy will be deceptive and misleading. The methods developed by the different schools of therapy can be used to heal or destroy, depending upon the therapist. "Outside of the responsibility practiced by a responsible person, 'normative' generalizations that are made in the name of science have no real meaning for me."

This qualification in no wise meant that Buber sought some hypothetical perfect I-Thou relationship unmixed with I-It. "I am not at all concerned about perfection," Buber replied to a question from Malcolm Diamond, but the I-Thou relationship must be realized where it can be and the life of man determined and formed by it. "For I believe that it can transform the world... into something very much more human... than exists today." Real persons can participate in one another's lives not only in space but in time, as when they think of each other at the same time. But they do so only by means of their difference, by means of the uniqueness of each person.

Even in dealing with the theory of knowledge, Buber managed to remain quite concrete. Thus Buber used the example of a child who looked an English sheepdog in the eyes: the child remained standing, laying his hand on the dog's head and calling him by a name that he invented on the spot. "When later at home the child sought to recall what had been special about the sheepdog, he managed without ideas or categories; he needed them only when he had to relate the occurrence to his best friend." The "truth" that one attains through such conceptualization and dialectical reasoning is only a preparation and a practice. It attains its authenticity only when it steps out of the realm of concepts into that of meeting.

> Inner contradictions are no less possible here than in a Socratic philosophy, and with him who seriously seeks to point out to me such a contradiction, I go seriously into it. In no way, therefore, do I reject consistency. But where I am compelled to point to "paradoxes," there are none that are meant as being beyond possible experience; rather a silent understanding is again and again established between me and those of my readers who are ready, without holding back, to make their own the experiences that I mean.

The corrective office of reason is incontestable, Buber said at another point, and it can be summoned at any moment to set right the incongruity between my sense of perception and what is common to my fellow men. In the I-It relation, what is received in the I-Thou is elaborated and broken up, and here "errors" are possible that can be corrected through "objectively" establishing and comparing what has passed and passes in the minds of others. But in the true I-Thou relationship, there is no knowledge of objective facts, hence nothing that can be corrected as an "error" by comparison with the data of the I-It. Reason, with its gigantic structure of general concepts, "cannot replace the smallest perception of something particular and unique, cannot by means of it take part in the grasping of what here and now confronts me."

To Buber, Socratic teaching meant dialectic but not dialogue: "I know of very few men in history to whom I stand in such a relation of both trust and veneration as Socrates." But Socrates overvalued the significance of abstract general concepts in comparison with concrete individual experiences. He "treated them as if they were more important than bones—that they are not." What is more, the questions that he posed were not real ones but merely moves in a sublime dialectical game that had as its objective revealing the person whom he questioned as one who did not really know.

The real teacher, in contrast, awakens in the pupil the need to communicate of himself and at the same time learns to know ever more concretely the particular, the individual, the unique.

Buber's unvarying insistence on the concrete shone through in the way that he again and again based his responses on actual personal observation rather than on some logical extension of his own views. To Paul Pfuetze's question of why, "even at his best, man feels an inordinate tug of self-interest," Buber responded that this in no way accorded with the actual lives of persons, whom he knew, of whose inwardness he could perceive something:

> I see how they concern themselves, each in his own way, the one noisily or awkwardly, the other goodnaturedly and at times even tenderly, with their family, comrades, passers-by with open spirit for what takes place, and, not infrequently ready with participation, information, and help.... I sometimes watch boys playing. What really concerns the individual is just the game itself, and that means, of course, before all, his share in it; but I see such a boy, often, also really concern himself about... the other's fortune and misfortune, and at times I see such a young heart, as it were, fly across to where the other stands, with the wish that he could help there where, according to the rules of the game, no help at all is possible.

Buber could not acknowledge theology's claim for exclusiveness, and therefore he could not take seriously Hans Urs von Balthasar's reproach that he was see-sawing between theology and philosophy of religion. "The categories themselves have fallen into see-sawing before my eyes, and they are not to be halted. Where I may draw out of primal depths that had opened to me as he who I am, I must acknowledge it." But he had to deal with the plurality of religion in all its reality, and not merely historically or psychologically, recognizing that he was not within that reality. "I pursue no theology as theology and no philosophy of religion as philosophy of religion," he asserted. "Honor to those who can still today bind these categories with all their strength to the strong bough of a revelation; I have not been able to go their way."

What Buber could and did affirm was a vibrant connection between the moments of Thou and the presence of the eternal Thou as primarily real for the man of genuine faith. Precisely this was the meaning of *emunah* to Buber: These are the moments in which the I, present in its wholeness, speaks into the distance of all distances the Thou of the greatest nearness. Just from addressing the "eternal Thou," the I knows itself as Thou. Those moments flash up out of a darkness rich with possibility, a darkness in which we perceive nothing "and in which we nonetheless trust as the ground and meaning of our existence." That the lines of I-Thou relationships "intersect in the eternal Thou is grounded in the fact that the man who says Thou ultimately means his eternal Thou." The legitimately religious existence of man consists in genuinely accepting and mastering the discontinuity that is basic to human life. Remaining open to the lead of the I-Thou, "the grace that appears ever anew in earthly material," is the only way in which the existence of man can become whole, and it is to this theme that Buber dedicated his work in all spheres. In this sense of the concern for the *wholeness* of life, Buber acknowledged that his thought might be called religious, but not in the sense that he started from a religion, as did Pascal, Hamaan, and Kierkegaard—three thinkers from whom Buber learned things that he could not forget, while pursuing a course fundamentally different from theirs.

I asked Buber whether his words in *I and Thou* concerning that pure relation in which potential is still actual being and "the unbroken world of Thou which binds up the isolated moments of relation in a life of world solidarity" meant that we relate to the actual and present eternal Thou even when the temporal Thou has again become only past and potential. In response, Buber resolutely distanced himself from the metaphysics into which an answer to my question would have drawn him:

> I perceive in this question, from words of mine which have been quoted here, that I have already come close to the limit of what is accessible to our experience. I hesitate to go a step further with words the full responsibility for which I cannot bear. *In our experience* our relation to God does *not* include our I-It relations. What is the case beyond our experience, thus, so to speak, from the side of God, no longer belongs to what can be discussed. Perhaps I have here and there, swayed by the duty of the heart that bids me point out what I have to point out, already said too much.

Totally consonant with this position was Buber's reply to Pfuetze that if there were a cogent proof of God's existence, there would no longer be any difference between belief and unbelief: "I have no metaphysics on which to establish my faith, I have created none for myself, I do not desire any, I need none, I am not capable of one."

"When I speak of the exclusion of the world from the relation to God," Buber declared in the *Interrogations,* "I do not speak of the *hour* of man, but of his *life.*"

> I regard it as unqualifiedly legitimate when a man again and again, in an hour of religious fervor, adoring and praying enters into a direct, "world-free" relation to God; and my heart understands as well the Byzantine composer of hymns who speaks as "the alone to the Alone," as also that Hasidic rabbi who, feeling himself a stranger on earth, asks God, who is also, indeed, a stranger on earth, to grant him, just for that reason, his friendship. But a "life with God" erected on the rejection of the living is no

life with God. Often we hear of animals who have been loved by holy hermits, but I would not be able to regard anyone as holy who in the desert ceased to love the men whom he had left.

Some of Buber's responses in the *Interrogations* were delightful on a purely personal level, as when Arthur Cohen prefaced a question by saying, "If you will excuse a direct question," and Buber replied, "I do not have to excuse direct questions, I prefer them." And when asked by Rollo May to what extent he was an existentialist, Buber replied: "I cannot, of course, be particularly pleased when, instead of paying attention to what I directly have to say, a questioner furnishes me with the label of an 'ism' and then wants to know concerning it." Then there is Buber's response to William Ernest Hocking, who said that if there is an absolute good, there must also be an absolute evil: "We become acquainted day after day with all degrees of relative stupidity; shall we conclude from that there exists an absolute stupidity?"

Buber acknowledged the reality of the evil to which Hocking pointed: There are many in our time who would not have believed themselves capable of wanting to save someone like a Goebbels before themselves, said Buber. Yet he refused to reject the possibility, almost incomprehensible though it is, that we can help the man who has apparently completely succumbed to arrogant self-affirmation to find the way out: "I confess that I can hold no one to be 'absolutely' unredeemable." Even the person who says that he will sin and then repent may, in a later hour, be seized, "like a heart-purifying lightning flash," by the insight that he cannot be forgiven. "What can transpire between the real God and a real man is of so paradoxical a nature that no saying, be it ever so 'true,' is equal to it." Evil radicalizes itself, but it is granted us to cooperate in its deradicalization. "It is easy to pronounce me a romantic optimist because I have always clung to the messianic belief in redemption," said Buber to Pfuetze, "but that charge is false because I have never and nowhere asserted that man can overcome the inner conflict of human existence through his own power and 'good will.'" "I am a realistic meliorist," Buber claimed. Human life approaches its fulfillment and redemption in the measure that the I-Thou relationship becomes strong in it.

Buber's faith was not based on a biblical theology. Rather, his insight into the Bible was based upon his experience of faith, including that threat of infinity that brought him close to suicide as a boy of fourteen. In "What Is Man?," Buber asserted that the present epoch of "homelessness" has proceeded out of the Copernican invasion of the infinite. But in *Philosophical Interrogations,* he added that "this invasion has had the effect that it had only because man has merely opposed to it the Kantian antinomy of the infinity and finiteness of space and time." What Buber now pointed to as transcending this antinomy is precisely that sense of the eternal that he attained when he surmounted this crisis of his youth: So far man has not opposed to this invasion "a greater image of God than the traditional one, a greater one *and yet one that can still be addressed,* the image of a God who out of his eternity has set in being this infinite-finite, space-time world, and who embraces and rules over it with his eternity." The awful silence in the spaces between the stars that terrified Pascal and the "indefiniteness that shadows forth the heartless voids and immensities of the universe and stabs us from behind with the thought of annihilation when beholding the white depths of the Milky Way" (Melville), Buber encompassed, at the end of his life as at the beginning, with a renewed and deepened existential trust.

Buber's reply to Gershom Scholem's critique of his interpretation of Hasidism could be a chapter in itself.

Scholem was nineteen years old when he first met Buber. Buber immediately appreciated his talents, as did Paula, who said that he would be an important man. In November 1935, Buber wrote Scholem, congratulating him on his volume on the Zohar, which Buber held to be a breakthrough. Buber was surprised by the atmosphere of clarity that permeated the book because, until then, the Zohar had so successfully resisted being grasped in clear concepts that its inaccessibility had been mistakenly accepted as part of its essential nature. At the same time, Buber raised important questions concerning some of Scholem's presentations of the oneness of God and the independent origin of primal evil, and his attempt to build a theology on the inner drama of the divine and the dialogue of the "middot" (the walks of God between mercy and strict justice).

When Scholem published the English edition of his book *Major Trends in Jewish Mysticism* in 1946, at a time when he had already done a great deal of his research on the Kabbala and Sabbataianism, his final chapter on Hasidism not only contained no criticism of Buber's interpretation, but agreed with it in almost every important respect. According to Scholem, Hasidism "neutralized" the messianic element in Jewish mysticism without renouncing the popular appeal of later Kabbalism, hence achieving what Buber called "the messianism of the everyday." Its heroic period, during the first fifty years after the death of the Baal-Shem, was characterized by a spirit of enthusiasm based on the idea of the immanence of God in all that exists.

Although the continuity of Kabbalistic thought was not really interrupted, the Kabbala was used as an instrument of mystical psychology and self-knowledge rather than a penetration of the upper worlds for their own sake. In this "mysticism of the personal life," "almost all the Kabbalistic ideas are now placed in relation to values peculiar to the individual life, and those that are not remain empty and ineffective." "The originality of Hasidism lies in the fact that mystics who had attained their spiritual aim... turned to the people with their mystical knowledge, the 'Kabbalism become Ethos' [a quotation from Buber's introduction to *The Tales of Rabbi Nachman*]. "The existence of the *zaddik* was the actual proof of the possibility of living up to the ideal: The life of the Hasidim centers on the personality of the *zaddik*. His opinions are less important than his character. The *zaddik* becomes the center of the new myth, and the Hasidic tale about the *zaddik* is the religious carrying forward of that myth.

> The revival of a new mythology in the world of Hasidism to which attention has been drawn occasionally, especially by Martin Buber, draws not the least part of its strength from its connection between the magical and the mystical faculties of its heroes. When all is said and done it is this myth which represents the greatest creative expression of Hasidism.... Not a few great Zaddikim... have laid down the whole treasure of their ideas in... tales. Their Torah took the form of an inexhaustible fountain of story-telling. Nothing at all has remained theory, everything has become a story.

Hasidism, Buber claimed, freed the myths that it took over from the Kabbala from their gnostic nature and restored them to their original condition. This mythical essence of Hasidism "has entered into the lived life of seven generations, as whose late-born interpreter I function." This interpretation had such an impact on the non-Jewish world that Buber was often urged to liberate Hasidism from its "confessional limitations" as part of Judaism and proclaim it as an unfettered teaching of mankind. Buber's response to this demand is one of the finest illustrations of how the life of dialogue meant for him meeting the other and holding one's ground in that meeting: "Taking such a 'universal' path would have been for me pure arbitrariness. In order to speak to the world what I have heard, I am not bound to step into the street. I may remain standing in the door of my ancestral house: here too the word that is uttered does not go astray."

At the dinner following the eightieth birthday celebration for Buber at the Hebrew University, Agnon and Scholem both spoke. Buber responded to all of Scholem's criticisms with humor. Ernst Simon has testified that, in general, Buber was very patient with Gershom Scholem. Buber was, in general, open to criticism from his students, asserted Simon, as a result of which some of them became his friends. Buber always behaved with composure, even in the face of those who hated him.

In 1960, when Eugenia and I went for four months to Jerusalem, I visited Scholem and asked him personally whether he would reconsider his decision not to contribute an essay on Buber's interpretation of Hasidism to *The Philosophy of Martin Buber*.

"Don't you have something already written?" I persisted.

"I do, but I wouldn't give it to you," he answered.

"Besides I don't believe in the principle of the Library of Living Philosophers," he asserted. When I asked, "Why not?" he replied, "Because it gives the philosopher the last word." This reply, as Scholem was later to say of one of Buber's remarks, was unforgettable.

He did recommend one of his disciples, Rivka Schatz-Uffenheimer, as an alternate contributor, and she agreed to write an essay on the subject.

Schatz-Uffenheimer's essay, entitled "Man's Relation to God and World in Buber's Rendering of the Hasidic Teaching," begins and ends with a paragraph of praise, in between which are forty pages of solid Scholemite criticism. "There is no doubt that Buber has done more than any other scholar to open men's hearts for a profound understanding of Hasidism," she wrote. "And even if portions of his teachings appear to me open to question on essential points, it remains true that these questions grew on that soil which Buber had prepared and sowed." Although Buber insisted in conversation with Rivka Schatz-Uffenheimer that he had no system in his representation of the Hasidic world, she stressed that his synthetic tapestry was woven of selected strands, and it was he who determined the hue of the cloth. Schatz-Uffenheimer portrayed Buber as full of enthusiasm for the very concrete reality that Hasidism saw as problematic, as boundlessly loving that very "world" whose whole ontic existence is set at naught in the eyes of Hasidism. "In the eyes of the Hasidim the greatness of the Zaddikim lay in their knowing how to turn... the divine 'being' that has fallen into the world back to its 'nothing,' which is the true being." Man's contact with creation is an ideal mission that demanded of man the nullification of creation and of the concrete as such. Life in the world was transformed into life in God because Hasidism developed an indifference to the concrete. Hasidism held that God speaks to us also in corporeal reality and that we must serve God in that reality by redeeming it. But it did not hold that every action is of equal worth and equally endowed with "sacramental possibility," a view that Schatz-Uffenheimer sees as originating in Buber's own antinomian relation to the Torah, whose claims set prior limitations on the extension of the holy over the profane.

Agreeing with Schatz-Uffenheimer's view that his tapestry of Hasidic interpretation is woven of elective strands, Buber stated that since 1910, when he completed a basic study of the sources, his aim had not been to present a historically comprehensive picture of Hasidism but only a selective one. But the principle of selection that ruled here, as in his work on Judaism in general, was not a subjective one. "I have dealt with that in the life and teachings of Judaism which, according to my insight, is its proper truth and is decisive for its function in the previous and future history of the human spirit." This involves evaluation from its base up, Buber conceded, but this evaluation had its origin in the immovable central existence of values. "Since I have attained to the maturity of this insight, I have not made use of a filter; I became a filter."

Scholem rightfully designated *devekut,* the "cleaving" of the souls to God, as the central tendency of the Hasidic teaching. But Buber in his reply distinguished between two kinds of *devekut,* as neither Scholem nor Schatz-Uffenheimer did:

Among the zaddikim who sought... to elaborate the Kabbalistic doctrine, there predominated the view, already familiar to us from Gnosis, that one must lift oneself out of the "corporeal" reality of human life into the "nothing" of pure spirit in order to attain contact with God.... But opposed to them—without a contest between the two taking place—is the view that this "constant being with God"... is rather reached through man's dedicating to God all that is lived by him.

Devekut as a Gnostic spiritualization of existence is first found in Hasidism in its great thinker the Maggid of Mezritch. But before that, *devekut* as the hallowing of all life originated with his teacher, the Baal-Shem-Tov. Thus, the teaching of *hallowing* is the original thesis of Hasidism and *not* that of spiritualization.

Asked by the author of Kabbalistic writings about the secret *kavanot* or "intentions" that entered into Hasidism through the Kabbalistic prayer book that it took over, Rabbi Moshe of Kobryn warned:

You must keep in mind that the word Kabbala is derived from *kabbel:* to accept; and the word kavana from *kavven:* to direct. For the final meaning of all the wisdom of the Kabbala is to take on oneself the yoke of God's will and the final meaning of all the art of kavanot is to direct one's heart to God.

Here, according to Buber, the life of devoted cleaving to God (the primal faith of Israel) opposes itself to the hypertrophy of mystical-magical doctrine. The Baal-Shem included everything corporeal, without exception, in the sphere of what can be hallowed through *kavana,* or intention, *not* excluding the coupling of man and wife. "Of a 'nullification' of the concrete there is in *this* line of Hasidism—which begins with its beginning—nothing to be found." It is not "Hasidism" that was faced with the "critical problem" of "life split apart into external action and inner intention," but its spiritual coinage and extension, which won the upper hand in the school of the Maggid of Mezritch. What ultimately concerned Buber was not an act for its own sake, as Schatz-Uffenheimer imagined, but "the restoration of the immediacy between God and man for the sake of overcoming the eclipse of God."

Therefore, Buber's selection "necessarily directed itself to the unjustly despised "anecdotes'—stories of lived life—and 'aphorisms'—sayings in which life documents itself," for both expressed with great pregnancy the life of the *zaddikim.* Some *zaddikim* were predominantly teachers of future *zaddikim;* others, like Levi Yitzhak of Berdtichev, R. Zusya, and R. Moshe Leib of Sasov, are popular figures who help the broad circle of relatively unschooled followers among the Hasidim. These latter represent that which is simply unique in Hasidism. The relationship of the master to the relatively educated disciples has also perhaps taken exemplary shape in the writings of

Zen Buddhism, but that of the master to ignorant people is nowhere in the world expressed as it is here.

At another place in the "Replies," Buber addressed himself to a criticism of Hugo Bergmann, also made by Schatz-Uffenheimer and Scholem, that his presentation of the Hasidic conception of a "messianism of all times" had weakened the messianic belief. The ever-recurring event of redemption preceding the, ultimate messianic fulfillment in no way injures the devotion to the *eschaton,* the final redemption, Buber asserted:

> Just as I believe not merely in the creative act in the beginning, but also in the creation at all times, in which man has a share as "God's comrade in the work of creation."... so I believe in the redeeming act poured forth over the ages, in which man again has a share. These events do not add themselves to one another, but all together they cooperate secretly in preparing the coming redemption of the world.

Norman Podhoretz, the editor of *Commentary,* heard about Scholem's views on Buber's Hasidism and asked him for a critical essay, which Scholem gave him, thus fulfilling his own desire to have the last word rather than let the philosopher have it. This essay was published in the October 1961 issue of *Commentary,* and later in Scholem's *Messianic Idea of Judaism.*

Like Schatz-Uffenheimer, Scholem began with words of praise: Buber "has that rare combination of a probing spirit and literary elegance which makes for a great writer."

> When an author of such stature and such subtlety set down with untiring seriousness what to him seemed the very soul of Hasidism, it was bound to make a deep impression on our age. In one sense or another we are all his disciples. In fact most of us, when we speak about Hasidism, probably think primarily in terms of the concepts that have become familiar through Buber's philosophical interpretation.

A critical analysis of Buber's interpretation of Hasidism is made exceedingly difficult, Scholem added, because "Buber, to whom no one denies possession of an exact knowledge of Hasidic literature, does not write as a scholar who gives clear references to support his contentions." Because the creative impulse in Hasidism was what really mattered to Buber, he felt justified in almost completely ignoring its Kabbalistic or "gnostic" element, which he saw as "a kind of umbilical cord which must be severed as soon as the new spiritual creation exists in its own right."

Of the two types of Hasidic literature—the teachings that embrace well over a thousand volumes and the legends that have adorned every single leading Hasidic personality—Buber based his presentation and interpretation almost exclusively on the legends, claiming that they and not the theoretical literature are our chief source of knowledge of Hasidism. But, said Scholem, the teachings were the first and most authoritative presentation of the meaning of Hasidic life, whereas the legends were not written down until nearly fifty years later. "The Hasidic authors obviously did not believe they had in any way broken with the gnostic tradition of the Kabbala and, little as Buber wants to admit it, they wrote clearly and plainly as Gnostics."

At this point, the divergence between Scholem as an intellectual historian and Buber as a filter of Hasidic life and spirit becomes most evident. For Scholem identified the "real doctrines" of Sufism and Catholicism with their dogma, and he put forth the theoretical teachings of Hasidism as the primary source for what Hasidic legends and sayings "really meant." In striking contrast to his statement in *Major Trends,* Scholem now claimed that the Baal-Shem's reinterpretation of individual Kabbalistic concepts as key words for the personal life of the pious did not deprive these concepts of their original meaning. Scholem agreed with Buber that Hasidism teaches that man meets God in the concreteness of his dealings with the world, and that Hasidism's transformation of simple and insignificant action into vehicles for the sacred was one of the most original aspects of the movement. But, like Schatz-Uffenheimer, he asserted that this contact was for the sake of annihilation. The undaunted and enthusiastic joy that Hasidism demanded of its adherents is not a joy in the here and now but in what is *hidden* in the essentially irrelevant garment of the here and now. In fact, Buber's existential interpretation to the contrary, the classical literature of Hasidism consistently treats the individual and concrete existence or phenomenon quite disdainfully and disparagingly. "The concrete in Buber's sense does not even exist in Hasidism." Scholem's corrective to Buber's interpretation is as one-sided as what he set out to correct: "If we want to understand the real phenomenon of Hasidism, both in its grandeur and in its decay (which are in many ways connected), we shall have to start again from the beginning."

Buber's reply to Scholem appeared in the September 1963 issue of *Commentary* and began with a long section on the "two different ways in which a great tradition of religious faith can be rescued from the rubble of time and brought back into the light"—that of historical scholarship and that of faithfully and adequately communicating the vitality and power of this faith. The latter "approach derives from the desire to convey to our own time the force of a former life of faith and to help our age renew its ruptured bond with the Absolute." For this approach, it is necessary to have an adequate knowledge of the tradition in all its spiritual and historical connections, but it is not necessary to present all of them—only a selection of those elements in which its vitalizing element was embodied, a selection based not upon objective scholarship but "upon the reliability of the person making the selection in the face of criteria; for what may appear to be mere 'subjectivity' to the detached scholar can sooner or later prove to be necessary to the process of renewal." Second, this person "should not be expected to turn away from the traditional reports concerning the life of the pious in order to give primary emphasis to the theoretical doctrine to which the founder and his disciples appealed for their authority." Even in the founding of the great world religions, what was essential was not a comprehensible doctrine but an event that was at once life and word. And when, as in Hasidism, religious life reaches back to a much earlier doctrine in order to establish its legitimacy, it is not the old teaching as such that engenders the new life of faith in a later age, but rather the context of personal and community existence in which a far-reaching transformation of the earlier teachings takes place.

To Scholem's objection that his interpretation rested largely upon legends written down fifty years after the theoretical writings produced in the age "in which Hasidism was actually productive," Buber replied that the genre of writing in question, the "legendary anecdote," was fully developed only in the literatures of Sufism, Zen Buddhism, and Hasidism, and that, in all three, it is not theoretical works, but legendary tales that stand at the center of their religious-historical development. This is not true for all kinds of religious mysticism, but for the kind whose essential development can be seen most clearly in the *mode of lived realization,* in that of the event. In all three movements, the legends were first transmitted orally and recorded only much later, whereas their theories were set down by those who originated them or by their immediate disciples. In Hasidism, this oral transmission was aided by recording, wherever possible, the names of earlier figures who relayed the legends along with the legends themselves. Eventually, to preserve them from too much corruption, the legends were written down and collected. The fact that this took place later, fifty-five years after the death of the Baal-Shem, in no way invalidates their authenticity as sources.

"Both are right," Agnon said to me concerning the Scholem-Buber controversy. It should be said, rather, that both are right *and* wrong: that is, both are one-sided. Until Scholem and his disciples began publishing, Buber was looked to by the Western world as *the* interpreter of Hasidism, just as D. T. Suzuki used to be looked to as *the* interpreter of Zen. Thus, it was indeed a scholarly deficiency on Buber's part that he did not indicate more clearly in his interpretations of Hasidism that he was presenting only one of the two major streams of Hasidic tradition, as he later did say in reply to Scholem. On the other hand, Scholem's failure to recognize the stream stemming from the Baal-Shem, and his total rejection of the "hallowing of the everyday" as a valid interpretation of Hasidism is even more misleading, for nearly everyone now thinks of Scholem as *the* scholarly interpreter of Hasidism, and few recognize *his* one-sidedness.

Addressing the Central Conference of American Rabbis in 1961, the distinguished American philosopher and Jewish theologian Emil Fackenheim remarked that he found most of the criticisms directed against Buber's interpretation of Hasidism unimpressive:

> The most common criticism is that Buber, instead of writing the kind of history which separates sources in painstaking analysis,

has given the kind which is a creative synthesis. But the preju-
dices of positivistic scholarship to the contrary notwithstanding,
there is always need for the latter as well as the former type of
history, unless one is to be left, not with the spirit of the age or
movement one seeks to understand, but merely with its dead
bones. Moreover, while Buber's kind of history has great dangers
of subjectivity and distortion—which incidentally, Buber himself
has been the first to admit—Buber would seem to have coped
with these with extraordinary success. His treatment of Hasidism
shows him to be capable of practicing the emphatic openness
which he preaches.

In 1966, at the annual Eranos Conference in Switzerland, Scholem broadened
his attack on Buber into a full-scale polemic against Buber's treatment of
Judaism. Passages in this long essay give us insight into layers of the Buber-
Scholem controversy that lie deeper than questions of scholarship. The first
of these reads, in fact, like a personal confession:

> No one who has known Buber could escape the strong beams
> that radiated from him and that made controversy with him dou-
> bly passionate. To enter into controversy with Buber meant to be
> thrown back and forth between admiration and rejection,
> between the readiness to hear his message and the disappoint-
> ment over this message and the impossibility of realizing it.

Scholem recognized Buber's creative transformation of Judaism:

> From the hour when as a twenty-year-old he attached himself to
> the just emerging movement of Zionism to the end of his days he
> tirelessly sharpened, preserved, and developed the meaning of
> the creative transformation in the phenomena closest to his heart.
> The provocative in his conception of Judaism and its history...
> was unmistakable, and Buber, to whom neither self-awareness
> nor courage can be denied, was ready to pay the price for this...
> new vision.

Visiting Buber in Germany in 1932, Scholem asked, "Why do you not write
finally a presentation of the theology of Hasidism?" "I intend to do that," he
answered, "but only after you have written a book on the Kabbala." "Is that a
promise?" asked Scholem. "Perhaps," Buber replied. "I did not understand at
that time that he could not have any scientific attitude toward this theme,"
asserted Scholem. In 1943, two years after the appearance of Scholem's book
on the Kabbala, he laid before Buber the fundamental criticisms of Buber's
interpretation of Hasidism, which Scholem had formed during long years of
continual study of the texts. Buber listened with great interest and unicharac-
teristic tension.

When I had finished, he was silent for a long time. Then he said slowly and with emphasis on every word: "If what you have said be true, dear Scholem, then I have occupied myself with Hasidism for forty years wholly in vain, for then it would indeed not at all *interest* me." It was the last conversation that I had with Buber over the factual problems of Hasidism. It closed speech for me. I understood that there was nothing more to say.

Buber said to Simon "I do not care what Scholem says about me. We all have disciples; some of us have produced schools; but only Scholem has created an academic field." By saying this, Simon pointed out, Buber renounced any suggestion that he himself had created a new field through his work on Hasidism. "If Scholem was Joshua, Buber was Moses," Walter Kaufmann remarked in a speech at the Buber Centennial Conferences in Israel and America. The value of Scholem's scholarly contributions for the generations to come is incontestable. But if anything in this analogy could be regarded by Jew and non-Jew alike as "the Promised Land," it would not be Scholem's destruction of the Jericho walls of all previous scholarship on the Kabbala, but Buber's *Tales of the Hasidim, For the Sake of Heaven,* and *The Way of Man.*

A number of years ago, a group of African students met with Abraham Joshua Heschel and Heschel's own student of twenty years before, Rabbi Arnold Jacob Wolf, Hillel chaplain at Yale University. "How should we begin the study of Hasidism?" they asked Heschel. Forgetting the Talmudic dictum that one should not speak in the presence of one's teacher, Wolf responded, "We now have Scholem in English. Read him." But Abraham Heschel, the direct descendant of a long line of distinguished *zaddikim* reaching back to the Maggid of Mezritch, and a scholar whose knowledge and understanding of the theoretical teachings of Hasidism was second to none, said, "No, if you want to know Hasidism as it was, begin with Buber."

Like the relationship between Buber and Herzl and that between the Yehudi and the Seer, the controversy between Buber and Scholem touches on "the cruel antitheticalness of existence itself," where just because each is as he is, different life stances, instead of contributing to dialogue, are crystallized into fixed opposition. If "every controversy that takes place for the sake of heaven endures," as the Talmud says, then this controversy, too, will endure in its profound two-sidedness and not, as many people suppose today, with a decision *for* Scholem and *against* Buber.

◆ *Buber and Leslie H. Farber, chairman of the faculty of the Washington School of Psychiatry, 1957.*

◆ *Buber and Prime Minister David Ben-Gurion at a celebration in honor of Buber's eightieth birthday at the Hebrew University, Jerusalem, Israel, February 1958.*

◆ *Martin Buber and Naemah Beer-Hofmann, in July of 1963.*

◆ *Paula Buber*
in her last years.

◆ *Portrait of*
Buber by a
photographer who
came to Israel to
take pictures of
flowers, with an
inscription to the
author.

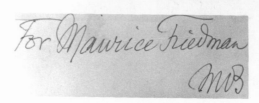

◆ *Buber reading in his study in Talbiyeh, Jerusalem*

◆ *Buber talking with United Nations Secretary General Dag Hammerskjold in the philosopher's study in Talbiyeh, Jerusalem, 1959.*

◆ *Buber in his house in Talbiyeh with his great-granddaughter Tamar Goldschmidt.*

◆ *Buber, Ernst Simon (left), and Hugo Bergmann (center) — his two closest friends and disciples — together on the porch of Buber's home in Jerusalem.*

◆ *Buber at around eighty.*

◆ *Martin Buber in the jeep of his granddaughter Barbara's husband.*

◆ Torchlight parade of Hebrew University students in front of Buber's home in Talbiyeh on the occasion of Buber's eighty-fifth birthday, February 8, 1963.

◆ Buber delivering his speech "A Believing Humanism" as part of the Erasmus Prize ceremony in Amsterdam, summer 1963.

◆ *Buber receiving the Erasmus Prize — Queen Wilhelmina (left), Barbara Goldschmidt, Buber's granddaughter who accompanied him on the trip (immediate left), and Prince Bernhard (right).*

◆ *Buber with Princess Beatrix at dinner.*

◆ *Martin Buber in 1962 at the sanitarium in Switzerland where he spent the summers.*

Hammarskjöld, Ben-Gurion, and Last Years

(1949-1965)

❖

CHAPTER

♦ 20 ♦

Buber and Dag Hammarskjöld: The Covenant of Peace

(1952-1963)

The address that Buber gave at his farewell celebration in April 1952 at Carnegie Hall, New York City, was titled "Hope for This Hour." In it, he confronted the situation created by the "cold war" between America and the Soviet Union, a war in which he refused to take sides: "...Each side has assumed monopoly of the sunlight and has plunged its antagonist into night, and each side demands that you decide between day and night." Not only is the opponent seen as false, as in former ages, but as fundamentally out of order, its "ideas" mere ideologies masking selfish interest. As a result, genuine dialogue between persons of different kinds and convictions is becoming ever more difficult and rare: "The abysses between man and man threaten ever more pitilessly to become unbridgeable." Buber saw this inability to carry on a genuine dialogue from one camp to the other as the severest symptom of that existential mistrust which is the sickness of present-day man, and this in turn stemmed from the inner poisoning of the total human organism by the destruction of trust in human existence: "At its core the conflict between mistrust and trust of man conceals the conflict between the mistrust and trust of eternity."

Beyond this, Buber called for the true representatives and spokesmen of the peoples—"independent persons with no authority save that of the spirit"—to come together to sift out of the alleged antagonisms the real conflicts between genuine needs. Only after this was done could the consideration of the necessary and possible settlements between them begin. The hope for this hour depends, Buber concluded, upon those who feel

409

most deeply the sickness of present-day man and who speak in his name the word without which no healing takes place: *I will live*. It depends upon the renewal of dialogical immediacy between persons. "If our mouths succeed in genuinely saying 'thou,' then, after long silence and stammering, we shall have addressed our eternal 'Thou' anew. Reconciliation leads towards reconciliation."

In "The Validity and Limitation of the Political Principle," the speech that he gave at the German universities in 1953, Buber spoke of a front that cuts across all the fronts of the hour, the front of all those engaged in the one fight for human truth. The experienced administrators of the political principle are unable to meet the problem of common human destiny that confronts mankind at this juncture. In the face of this impotence of the politicians, those who stand on the crossfront and have the common language of faithfulness to the human truth that they cannot possess, must unite "to give to man what is man's in order to rescue him from being devoured by the political principle."

"Genuine Dialogue and the Possibility of Peace," the address that Buber gave when he received the Peace Prize of the German Book Trade in September 1953, continued the concern of "Hope for This Hour"—the effect of mistrust in preventing genuine dialogue.

> The debates between statesmen, which the radio conveys to us, no longer have anything in common with a human conversation: diplomats do not address one another but the faceless public. Even the congresses and conferences which convene in the name of mutual understanding lack the substance which alone can elevate the deliberations to genuine talk: candour and directness in address and answer.

The crisis of speech is bound up with this crisis of trust in the closest possible fashion, "for I can only speak to someone in the true sense of the term if I expect him to accept my word as genuine."

Despite all this, Buber reaffirmed his belief that the peoples in this hour could enter into true dialogue with another. "In a genuine dialogue each of the partners, even when he stands in opposition to the other, heeds, affirms, and confirms his opponent as an existing other. Even though conflict cannot be eliminated from the world, through genuine dialogue it can be humanly arbitrated.... Let us dare, despite all, to trust!"

In August 1957, Buber received a letter from the American Committee on Africa, signed by Eleanor Roosevelt, Bishop James A. Pike, and Martin Luther King, appealing for his cooperation in a worldwide protest against the organized inhumanity of the government of the Union of South Africa. In the letter, they referred to the policy of apartheid and to the totalitarian force brought to bear on all the "non-whites" of South Africa in almost every sphere of human life. They asked Buber to join them as a leading member of an international committee that would set aside December 10, 1957, as a day of protest and demand that South Africa fulfill its obligations under the Charter of the United Nations. In October, Eleanor Roosevelt wrote to Buber personally, thanking him for his splendid response to their invitation and informing him that leaders from eighty-three nations were ready to take part in the day of protest. "Surely the South Africans of good will, who work on for justice and freedom, regardless of the danger to their lives, freedom and future, are thankful for your announcement of support and participation," she concluded.

After reading my translation of *Pointing the Way,* Dag Hammarskjöld initiated communication with Martin Buber on April 15, 1958, just five days after his reinduction for a second term as secretary-general of the United Nations: "I wish to tell you how strongly I have responded to what you write about our age of distrust and to the background of your observations which I find in your general philosophy of unity created 'out of the manifold.' Certainly, for me, this is a case of 'parallel ways.'"

After writing to Buber in Jerusalem, Hammarskjöld read that Buber was in Princeton and warmly invited Buber to visit him at the United Nations on May 1. Hammarskjöld's secretaries were "under strict instructions that under no circumstances were he and his guest to be interrupted," reports Henry Van Dusen. "Several important messages were impatiently brushed aside as the two men continued in intense conversation for more than two hours." In a speech over the Swedish radio in 1962, Buber himself described this meeting and commented on its significance:

> ...We were both pained in the same way by the pseudo-speaking of representatives of states and groups of states who, permeated by a fundamental reciprocal mistrust, talked past one another out the windows. We both hoped, we both believed that, still in sufficient time before the catastrophe, faithful representatives of the people, faithful to their mission, would enter into a genuine dialogue, a genuine dealing with one another out of which would emerge in all clarity the fact that the common interests of the peoples were stronger still than those which kept them in opposition to one another....

In an address at Cambridge University in England on June 5, 1958, Hammarskjöld analyzed the world situation precisely in the terms of Buber's own approach to the "covenant of peace" in the concluding essays of *Pointing the Way,* and he explicitly quoted "Hope for This Hour":

> In an address in Carnegie Hall in New York, in 1952, Martin Buber had the following to say: "One no longer merely fears that the other will voluntarily dissemble, but one takes it for granted that he cannot do otherwise.... The other communicates to me the perspective that he has acquired on a certain subject, but I do

not really take cognizance of his communication as knowledge.... Rather I listen for what drives the other to say what he says, for an unconscious motive.... Since it is the idea of the other, it is for me an 'ideology.' My main task in my intercourse with my fellow-man becomes more and more... to see through and unmask him.... It is no longer the uprightness, the honesty of the other which is in question, but the inner integrity of his existence itself.... This game naturally only becomes complete as it becomes reciprocal.... Hence one may foresee in the future a degree of reciprocity in existential mistrust where speech will turn into dumbness and sense into madness." ...Out of the depth of his feelings Martin Buber has found expressions which it would be vain for me to try to improve.

Hammarskjöld visited Jerusalem in September 1958, after which he reported at a press conference "one out-of-the-way [incident of tourism] with a strong personal accent. I had the pleasure of paying a personal call on Professor Martin Buber for whom I have a sincere admiration." In his next and last visit to Jerusalem in January 1959, he and Buber had their longest and most intimate conversation over dinner in Buber's home. Speaking of this meeting at a press conference in January 1959, Hammarskjöld confirmed "that the moment I get the time for it, I would like very much to translate not the whole volume of *Pointing the Way*—I would never find time for that—but some three or four essays."

In June 1959, Hammarskjöld submitted to the Nobel Prize Committee in Sweden a four-page memorandum nominating Buber for a Nobel Prize. Van Dusen describes this document as "a characteristically detailed, discerning and scrupulously objective account of Buber's work and influence which reveals as much about its author as about his subject." One might also characterize it as an ambivalent document, because it spends most of its time on Buber's qualifications as candidate for a Nobel Prize in literature, yet concludes by recommending him for a Peace Prize instead! Although it could not have done Buber's hopes much good, this ambivalence undoubtedly arose from Hammarskjöld's bending over backward to be fair, and probably also not to influence the Nobel Prize Committee unduly. Hammarskjöld referred to Buber as "the spokesman of humanistic internationalism, based on elements of Jewish thought." Hammarskjöld also stated that Buber's "literary work is closed to us (only a small part of it was made public)" and that "after the war he has become to an ever-growing extent an active force in the international discussion, e.g., in the Anglo-American world." Then Hammarskjöld discussed the surprising (to him) fact that, despite his great name, Buber did not occupy as important a place in Jewish thinking as an outsider would have expected. To account for this he cited Buber's position as spokesman for Israeli-Arab "friendship," as well as Buber's religious and philosophical convictions, which he saw as alien to contemporary Jewry:

> The mysticism of personality... that Buber has developed, under the influence of Hasidism but also under that of the Christian-medieval mysticism, sets itself in the sharpest opposition to the rationalistic materialism which especially characterizes Ben-Gurion, for example, as also to the formalistic Orthodoxy and religious intolerance which is just as often present in Israel.

Hammarskjöld concluded, "Although Buber's position within the Jewish people is thus controversial, he appears nonetheless, to everyone who has plumbed his work, as an interpreter of genius of some of the most prominent and purest elements in Jewish tradition and Jewish spiritual life."

Discussing Buber's work with Hasidic legends, Hammarskjöld claimed that Buber had "endowed Western literature with something stable and rich" and characterized Buber as "an outstanding storyteller whose linguistic ability puts him in line with the greatest masters of prose of the first part of this century."

After an interval of two years, Hammarskjöld wrote to Buber in August 1961 that he had been reading the essays in *Between Man and Man,* which he had not seen before. What Buber wrote about "signs" in "Dialogue" and, in the essay that followed, about the responsibility of the "Single One" in the political sphere, so remarkably formulated shared experiences that they made Buber's writings themselves "very much what you would call a 'sign'" for Hammarskjöld himself. "It is strange—over a gulf of time and a gulf of differences as to background and outer experience—to find a bridge built which, in one move, eliminates the distance." Hammarskjöld reiterated his idea of translating Buber into Swedish, but it was increasingly difficult to choose among Buber's works, and the nuances of Buber's German made him shy.

Buber responded at once, thanking him for his letter as "a token of true understanding—rather a rare gift in this world of ours." Buber recommended that Hammarskjöld translate *I and Thou,* the most difficult of all his works, "but the most apt to introduce the reader into the realm of dialogue," and Hammarskjöld wrote Buber in turn that he saw this as a silent summons "to try a translation of this key work, as decisive in its message as supremely beautiful in its form." "If all this works out," he added, "may I tell you how much it would mean to me also by providing me with justification for a broadened and intensified contact with you personally." Hammarskjöld got in touch with his Swedish publishers and in less than two weeks had a favorable response; on September 12, 1961, the day that he left New York for the Congo, Hammarskjöld informed Buber of this, in what must have been one of the last letters that he ever wrote. Aside from Thomas à Kempis's *Imitation of Christ,* the only book that Hammarskjöld took with him on the plane was the new German edition of *I and Thou* that he had just received from Buber, and en route to and during his stay in Léopoldville, where he tried to stop the fighting between Moise Tshombe's army in Katanga and the United Nations force, he translated twelve pages. Thus, on his way to his final mission as a "servant of peace," Hammarskjöld worked toward the completion of a cherished dream that would bring him closer to Buber.

The book and manuscript were not with Hammarskjöld on his fatal flight to Ndola, on January 18, where he had arranged to have face-to-face talks with Tshombe about the secession of Katanga, but were found among his effects in the home of the head of the United Nations mission to the Congo in Léopoldville, of which Hammarskjöld's nephew Knut informed Buber in a letter of October 5.

Buber received Hammarskjöld's last letter an hour after he had heard over the radio about the latter's death in the plane crash in the Congo. Thus, the dialogue between the two men was a present reality from both sides even after Hammarskjöld's death. In Hammarskjöld, Buber saw a man of goodwill who tried to do something but who had been abandoned. "Doing his utmost," Buber said to Meyer Levin, "Hammarskjöld still lacked the technical means to carry out his peace mission, and so he was martyred in his death." On September 28, Buber sent me the German translation of an article from the Stockholm paper *Dagens Nyheter* about Hammarskjöld's plan to translate *I and Thou* and the intention of Stockholm's leading publishing house, Bonnier, to continue with plans to publish a translation of it in Hammarskjöld's honor.

Buber's answer to a peace questionnaire from the Novosti Press Agency in Moscow about what the world will be like in twenty years was hopeful, though only cautiously so. Even if one assumed that war will have been averted, everything depends, responded Buber, upon whether world peace signifies mere cessation of the cold war or real coexistence. The former could lead only to a new and still more dangerous cold war. But real cooperation for mastery of the common problems of the human race is possible, Buber maintained, "despite the fundamental differences of views of social justice and individual freedom... if in direct, unprejudiced, and comprehensive discussion qualified, independent, and realistically thinking men from both camps succeed in recognizing the urgency of vital common interests."

Although Buber was active in the cause of peace, he was not unaware of the political implications of what he did. Buber quoted approvingly a statement of Jesus that one should be as innocent as a dove and as cunning as a snake. Buber once told A. Elhanani, a journalist for the Israeli newspaper *Davar,* that after the Soviet Union had exploded its megaton nuclear bomb, a rich man in Switzerland asked Buber to organize a meeting of intellectuals from around the world, including the Soviet Union, to respond to this development. That person was willing to pay all the expenses for such a meeting. Buber agreed on the condition that the meeting be kept secret, but it did not work out.

But Buber was not at all afraid to stick his neck out for unpopular causes. Convinced of the innocence of Morton Sobell, who was sentenced to a thirty-year prison term for spying at the time that Julius and Ethel Rosenberg were executed, Buber and Bertrand Russell appealed to the president of the United States for clemency. In making their appeal as persons "of independent political views and in the interest of justice and humanity only," they pointed out that, to many legal authorities, the charges against Sobell appeared flimsy at best. The careful wording of this appeal suggests that they did not want to be seen as taking sides in the cold war or as acting from political motives. In March 1960, Buber wrote to the president of Rumania on behalf of two friends of his, an elderly couple who had immigrated to Israel and whose daughters had remained in Rumania. Despite repeated requests, one of these daughters had not been able to join her husband and parents in Israel and was in addition condemned to three years in prison. "It is as an old champion of the difficult causes of humanity that I address myself to you, Monsieur le President," Buber wrote, "with the fervent hope that my appeal will find an echo."

In June 1960, Buber wrote to Bertrand Russell, urging him to join a number of distinguished figures from around the world at a conference in Paris to study the present situation of the Jews in the Soviet Union: "We cannot speak today of actual physical persecution as at the time of Stalin, and not even of legal discrimination. However, discrimination is, in fact, being exercised against the Jewish population in the Soviet Union," who, unlike other minorities, were not permitted any positive national expression (such as Jewish schools, books or journals in the Hebrew or Yiddish language, or even appropriate means of expressing religious feeling—the few synagogues in the Soviet Union were continually under attack and no central Jewish religious organization was allowed for the three million Jews living in Russia).

During this period, Albert Schweitzer and Buber cooperated several times on appeals against the spread of nuclear weapons. In October 1961, abortive demonstrations were called by the Israeli Public Committee against Nuclear Tests. The committee was formed spontaneously by a group of intellectuals, including Buber and Hugo Bergmann. In November, Buber joined Pablo Casals, Albert Schweitzer, Bertrand Russell, François Mauriac, Brock Chisholm, and Max Born in appealing to President John F. Kennedy to abstain from nuclear testing.

In the fall of 1960, Buber attended the Mediterranean Colloquium in Florence, sponsored by Giorgio La Pira, the mayor of Florence and professor at the University of Florence. This conference consisted of a number of well-known persons from Mediterranean countries, including Israelis and Arabs, and was thus the *only* place where the latter met face to face. Buber had been urged to go by Joseph Golan, at that time the political adviser of Nahum Goldmann, president of the Jewish World Congress. Golan told Buber that the Egyptians set great store on his coming, and Buber wrote to

Simon Shereshevsky, fellow leader of Ihud, that he would be very happy to be allowed to do something "for our cause." Buber, who was in close touch with the Israeli Committee for a Nuclear-Free Zone in the Middle East, discussed the differences between a small peace and a great peace. "After the lecture of a very gifted Egyptian," Buber reported in November, "I invited him to sit with me at the presidential table and to talk the problems over before everyone and we did it thoroughly and directly; it was a rather symbolic moment." To Meyer Levin, he later said of this discussion of Arab-Israeli problems with George Henein: "It was a real talk, in which we tried to pierce the hard core of the political sphere. Yes, I say it is still, it is always possible in human terms."

In May 1961, the Soviet Union reinstated the death penalty for economic offenses, and a high proportion of those sentenced to death proved to be Jews. Bertrand Russell was known to be in good standing in the Soviet Union and was in touch with Premier Nikita Khrushchev, as a result of which Buber decided in March 1962 to ask Russell to intervene on behalf of Soviet Jewry. Buber pointed out that capital punishment for economic crimes had not existed in the Soviet Union since the days of the revolution forty years before, and declared that all enemies of capital punishment must energetically protest the reinstitution of the death penalty for such crimes as being incompatible with the role of a great and progressive nation. He also pointed out that, since most of those sentenced to death were Jews, though his own attitude would not be one whit different if those sentenced were non-Jews, he also saw it as a grave threat to the whole Jewish community in the Soviet Union, if the general population should come to think that Jews figured prominently in economic crimes. "We should do our utmost to struggle against such a danger," said Buber, undoubtedly thinking of how precisely such measures in Nazi Germany eventually led to the total dispossession and extermination of the Jews. Buber proposed that Bertrand Russell, Eleanor Roosevelt, and the distinguished French Catholic writer and Nobel Prize winner François Mauriac should telegraph a request to Khrushchev to commute the sentences.

Aubrey Hodes reports that Russell's intervention with Khrushchev on behalf of the Soviet Jews was one of the reasons that the Jerusalem Municipality awarded him its first Literary Prize for Human Freedom in the spring of 1963. Ralph Schoenman, Russell's secretary, who accepted the prize for Russell, joined Hodes, Ernst Simon, Shereshevsky, the leaders of the Israeli Committee for a Nuclear-Free Zone in the Middle East, and Simcha Flappan of *New Outlook* at Buber's home for an evening devoted to discussing how the danger of introducing nuclear weapons into the region might be averted. These discussions resulted in a private appeal by Russell to the heads of eleven states and later in a public declaration in *New Outlook* by ten eminent scientists and moral leaders, including Max Born, Danilo Dolci, Martin Niemöller, Linus Pauling, Eugene Rabinowitsch, Jean-Paul Sartre, and

Albert Schweitzer. In connection with Buber's deft informal chairing of this meeting, Hodes writes:

> When a knotty point arose, or the discussion strayed from the main issue, it was Buber who, with a phrase that did not order or insist but suggested, proposed, hinted almost, led the group skillfully back to the main flow of the talk.... Buber was the perfect chairman of a committee composed of factions hostile to one another, or a delicate international conference. He had all the tact, composure, and rapier-like subtlety of a first-class statesman. If anyone could have brought Arabs and Israelis around a table to a common understanding, Buber could have—if he had been given the opportunity.

In fact, such differences as those between the Arabs and Israelis can foster a "community of otherness." As Buber asserted, the I-Thou relationship

> seems to me to win its true greatness and powerfulness precisely there where two men without a strong spiritual ground in common, even of very different kinds of spirit, yes of opposite dispositions, still stand over against each other so that each of the two knows and means, recognizes and acknowledges, accepts and confirms the other, even in the severest conflict, as this particular person. In the common situation, even in the common situation of fighting with each other, he holds present to himself the experience-side of the other, his living through this situation. This is no friendship, this is only the comradeship of the human creature, a comradeship that has reached fulfillment.

In his attitude toward civil disobedience, Buber was close to Martin Luther King. As King was the disciple of Gandhi on the path of nonviolent resistance, so Gandhi in his turn was deeply influenced by an American of the century before—Henry David Thoreau. Writing on the centennial of Thoreau's death, Buber testified in 1962 that reading Thoreau's classic tract "Civil Disobedience" had had a strong impact on him in his youth, but that it was only much later that he understood why.

> It was the concrete, the personal, the "here and now" in the writing that won my heart for it. Thoreau did not formulate a general principle as such; he set forth and grounded his attitude in a particular historical-biographical situation. He spoke to his reader in the realm of this situation common to them so that the reader not only learned why Thoreau at that time acted as he acted, but also—provided that this reader was only honest and unbiased—that he himself, the reader, must act, should the occasion present itself, in exactly that way if he were seriously concerned about making his human existence real.

Because Thoreau, Gandhi, King, and Buber spoke as concretely as they did from the standpoint of their historical situation, each expressed in the right way what is valid for all human history.

In 1963, Buber applied his view of civil disobedience to the international situation of the day. Civil disobedience, if it is to be legitimate, must be obedience to a higher authority than the one that we here and now obey. But there is no general way of demonstrating the legitimacy of this higher authority or of setting the limit to what we have to give to Caesar. Not at all times and places but only in the particular situation, in the here and now, can this question be answered. In our present situation, however, it is easier to reply than ever before, Buber declared, for we are today on the point of letting the determination of our fate slip out of our hands. The universal military preparations and the bellicose surprises, one outstripping the other, on all sides in the cold war may reach such a point of automation as to transform the human cosmos "into a chaos beyond which we can no longer think." If the rulers of the hour cannot wake up before it is too late, command a halt to the machinery, and learn to talk *to* instead of *past* one another, then who will come to the rescue while there is still time but the "disobedient," those who personally set their faces against the power that has gone astray? "Must not a planetary front of such civil disobedients stand ready, not for battle like other fronts, but for saving dialogue? But who are these if not those who hear the voice that addresses them from the situation—the situation of the human crisis—and obey it?"

In 1962, Reinhold Niebuhr and I wrote secretly to a number of prominent men throughout the world, supporting the nomination of Martin Buber for a Nobel Prize in literature. The letter began with a statement by Reinhold's brother, the eminent theologian H. Richard Niebuhr, on the occasion of Buber's eightieth birthday celebration in America: "More than any other person in the modern world, more even than Kierkegaard, Martin Buber has been for me, and for many of my companions, the prophet of the soul and the witness to that truth which is required of the soul not as solitary but as companionable being." Unfortunately, Professor H. Richard Niebuhr died of heart failure at the very time that Reinhold's and my letter was sent to him. The responses from the others, however, were immediate and wholehearted. Of these, the most astonishing and heartwarming was the response from the Lebanese statesman and philosopher Charles Malik. In 1960, Buber told Eugenia and me how Malik had wandered by mistake into the Israeli pavilion at the Brussels Exposition and signed his name to the guest register. The newspapers picked this up, and Malik as a result lost his position as ambassador to the United Nations and any possibility of holding public office in Lebanon. It would not have been at all surprising if he had declined to sign the letter to the Nobel Prize Committee. Instead, Malik not only signed the letter but added under his signature an eloquent statement:

Buber is one of the important influences for my thought, especially through his "Ich und Du." I also conceived a high regard for him and the late Dr. Magnes in connection with the Palestine Question. I always felt that he and I would agree on many things, spiritual and political. The type of spirit he represents could still help in bringing about a reconciliation, in God's own time, between Arab and Israeli. If only political passion on both sides would make it possible to "meet," in Buber's sense of the term, in an atmosphere of Christian love and forgiveness! But man is so limited and history is so tragic and the mystery of God is so unfathomable. I trust the Swedish Academy would give this matter their most serious consideration, for no living man, in my opinion, deserves the Nobel Prize for literature more worthily than Martin Buber.

In a separate letter that was not forwarded to the academy, Malik wrote: "It gives me the greatest pleasure to join you and Dr. Niebuhr in this most worthy endeavor. I wish there was something else I could do for this noble soul. Buber is greater than even the fine eulogy you compiled for him in your draft letter."

Aside from Charles Malik, Reinhold Niebuhr, and myself, the signatories to the letter to the Swedish Academy included W. H. Auden, T. S. Eliot, Emil Brunner, Albrecht Goes, Victor Gollancz (the English writer and publisher), Hermann Hesse, Gabriel Marcel, Sir Herbert Read, Ignazio Silone, and the German philosopher Wilhelm Szilasi. In his letter to me, T. S. Eliot confirmed the sense of real meeting that Buber had told me about when he and I first met in person in 1951: "I once had a conversation with Dr. Buber,... and I got the strong impression that I was in the company of a great man. There are only a very few men of those whom I have met in my lifetime, whose presence has given me that feeling." After Buber's death, the reporter from *Newsweek* took this statement, which I gave them along with a great deal of other material, as the title of their story on Buber: "In the Presence of Greatness."

CHAPTER

♦ 21 ♦

Buber versus Ben Gurion

(1949-1964)

When I was in Jerusalem in 1960, a doctor from Hadassah Hospital said to me, "we have two 'B's' in Israel—Buber and Ben-Gurion. We wish the former would stick to philosophy and the latter to politics!" Buber was, in fact, always enormously concerned with politics and, as everyone who knew him testified, surprisingly well informed about what was going on in Israel and in the world in general. Nahum Goldmann used to come to see him regularly whenever Goldmann was in Israel, to brief him on local, national, and international developments, and Buber followed them with keen interest, concerned not only about their immediate effect, but also about what they might mean a generation or two hence.

The conflict between Buber and Ben-Gurion was not based on their differing attitudes toward the Arab-Jewish question alone. Buber was a social anarchist in the biblical sense. He was very distrustful of the state organization, whereas Ben-Gurion was *the* representative of the cult of the state and of *Realpolitik.* This does not mean that Buber opposed the state as such, as does the traditional anarchist. In his American Friends of Ihud speech in 1958, Buber said:

> I have accepted as mine the State of Israel, the form of the new Jewish Community that has arisen from the war. I have nothing in common with those Jews who imagine that they may contest the factual shape which Jewish independence has taken. The command to serve the spirit is to be fulfilled by us today in this state,

420

starting from it. But he who will truly serve the spirit must seek to make good all that was once missed: he must seek to free once again the blocked path to an understanding with the Arab peoples.

No one can be blamed for the thwarting of the hopes for an organic development of the Yishuv, Buber remarked, for the hordes of homeless and displaced people created a psychological pressure that Zionism was unable to withstand. The state was not built on the basis of mutual trust in the Middle Eastern area, as Buber's group had hoped. But what they could do now was to recognize that they did not yet have a living culture of high quality: "We have a great tradition and people endowed with abilities, authors, poets, artists, philosophers, scientists and research workers. We also have excellent educational and cultural institutions. But a culture whose influence is felt in all walks of the nation's life—that we do not have." A "Jewish Renaissance" no longer was enough for Buber. As long as there was no decisive order of justice and truth which determined the course of life, there could be no true culture.

On March 10, 1949, David Ben-Gurion, who led the provisional government of the State of Israel, became its first elected prime minister. Two weeks later at his home in Tel Aviv, he called a score of the country's most prominent intellectuals to confer on what should be the moral and spiritual direction of the newborn state. Buber, one of the first to speak, challenged Ben-Gurion's assertion that the government per se had no direct role in shaping the moral character of the state. This was the beginning of a series of confrontations between Buber and Ben-Gurion that lasted as long as the latter was in office.

According to Michael Keren, author of *Ben-Gurion and the Intellectuals,*

> the ideology of political messianism in Israel in the 1950's had its roots not only in ancient biblical thought but also in modern theological and intellectual works—especially those by Martin Buber.... Political messianism could not have flourished were it not for the depth and meaning Buber's philosophy gave to messianic thinking. This is perhaps the reason that no other relationship—on both a theoretical and practical level—was as complex as the relationship between Buber and Ben-Gurion.

In March 1953, Buber sent a letter on behalf of Ihud to Joseph Sprinzak arguing against proposed legislation for expropriation of Arab land, contesting that, in numerous cases, land had been expropriated not on grounds of security but for expansion of existing settlements: "In some densely populated villages two-thirds and even more of the land has been seized." Owners should be left enough land to support themselves by cultivation even when it is seized for security reasons, and such land should be fully returned to its owners within a maximum term specified by law. "We fail to understand why... hardly a single Jewish member of the Knesset has raised his voice against a law intended to give the stamp of legality to acts and deeds which he would consider a grave injustice if they were directed against himself or against Jewish property."

In January 1955, in response to Hans Blüher's expression of concern about Buber's isolation in Israel, Buber denied feeling isolated, and painted a picture of his life in Israel that showed he clearly understood his position in his adopted home:

> I have enough friends and disciples. I am unpopular, to be sure, and for a nonconformist such as I have been from my youth... and remain in my old age, it could not be otherwise. What the "broader circles" mostly reproach me for is that since 1917 I have expressly come out for cooperation with the Arabs—until 1947 in the form of a bi-national state and, since the victory of Israel over the seven states that attacked it, in the form of a Near-Eastern federation of peoples—and have led political actions supporting Jewish-Arab rapprochement. Secondly, that I have... opposed confounding the German people with the murdering insects of the gas chambers organization.

When a group of Israeli soldiers killed sixty men, women, and children in a reprisal action in the Jordanian village of Kibya in 1953, Buber and his political friends openly protested. He also attacked the Israeli rabbinate because it said not a word against the Kibya incident. A rabbinate that concerned itself only with rituals and ignored transgressions against humanity would itself be ignored, Buber felt. Buber later expressed indignation over the Kfar Kassem massacre in October 1956, in which forty-seven Arabs were shot down as they returned from the fields because of a curfew about which they had not been informed. In his 1958 speech for the American Friends of Ihud in New York, Buber expressed his sorrow in unmistakable terms:

> Often, in earlier times, Arab hordes had committed outrages of this kind, and my soul bled with the sacrifice; but here it was a matter of our own, or my own crime, of the crime of the Jews against the spirit. Even today I cannot yet think about this without feeling myself guilty. Our active faith in the spirit was too weak to prevent the outbreak and spread of the demonic false teaching.

Buber was equally opposed to the invasion of Sinai that Ben-Gurion undertook in the fall of 1956 with the cooperation of France and England. When Werner Kraft asked Buber whether he meant this opposition politically, strategically or morally, Buber responded that he did not recognize any isolated morality. He held the "right" politics to be "moral." Buber deemed Ben-Gurion's politics false, and Ben-Gurion himself a "dreamer" who had not rightly estimated the powers with which he leagued himself. As a result of the Sinai invasion, America's position was totally reversed and the Russians finally brought into the closest proximity.

At the Jerusalem Ideological Conference in August 1957, the opposing positions of Ben-Gurion and Buber received almost classic expression. In his speech "Vision and Redemption," Ben-Gurion seemed at first to be entirely in accord with Buber in viewing the revival of the Jewish people as based upon a vision of the Jewish State as a moral state: *"Anyone who does not realize that the Messianic vision of redemption is central to the uniqueness of our people, does not realize the basic truth of Jewish history and the cornerstone of the Jewish faith."* But Ben-Gurion's messianism was not Buber's, for Ben-Gurion was able to see in the *State of Israel* not only the *greatest* but also the *only* common asset of the entire Jewish people, divided in values and disintegrated in structure. "The rise of Israel... straightened the back of every Jew wherever he lived" and "restored to the people living in its midst their wholeness as Jews and human beings." The professed liberal values that Ben-Gurion ascribed to the state were not, in fact, being applied to the Arab minority.

The real issue between the two men—their difference in the estimate of the state—Ben-Gurion expressed in words again addressed entirely to Buber:

> Professor Buber says that the State is only an instrument. Of course it is an instrument—but it is a precious instrument without which there can be no freedom and independence, no possibility of free, creative activity, suitable to our needs, our aspirations and our values.... The miracle that has taken place in our generation is that there has been established an instrument for the implementation and realization of the vision of redemption—and the instrument is the State of Israel, in other words the sovereign people in Israel. For that reason, give honor to the State of Israel. It is not merely an instrument.... It is the beginning of the redemption, a small part of the redemption.

Just as Ben-Gurion's second speech was addressed exclusively to Buber, so Buber's speech was throughout an explicit reply to Ben-Gurion. In Buber's speech, the classic opposition between king and prophet in ancient Israel is given a modern context.

> Ben-Gurion is right in saying that youth in Israel is very much interested in certain parts of the Bible, especially in the stories about the conquest of the land, in the stories of the hero-kings and also in some words of the prophets. But on no account are the prophets to be regarded apart from their historic mission

which sent them to those men who had seized the reins of power
in order to summon them to stand in judgment before their God
who had made them king provisionally.

It is not enough to set the redemption of Israel side by side with the redemption of the human race, as Ben-Gurion did. The destiny of Israel depends
upon the fulfillment of the demand that Israel "make an exemplary beginning in the actual work of realization, that it be a nation which establishes
justice and truth in its institutions and activities." To Buber, the prophetic
demand applied not only to the generations of the Bible, but to all the generations since and especially to our own, which, for the first time in two millennia, "has the prerequisite for fulfilling its task,... the power to determine
for itself in no small measure its institutions, its modes of life and its relations
to other nations." The sharpness of the words that Buber now addressed to
Ben-Gurion reflects the concern that led him during these same years to see
the "politicization" of the relations between nations as leading to the "techni-
cally perfect suicide of mankind":

> Behind everything that Ben-Gurion has said on that point, there
> lies, it seems to me, the will to make the political factor supreme.
> He is one of the proponents of that kind of secularization which
> cultivates its "thoughts" and "visions" so diligently that it keeps
> men from hearing the voice of the living God. This secularization
> takes the form of an exaggerated "politicization." This "politiciza-
> tion" of life here strikes at the very spirit itself. The spirit with all
> its thoughts and visions descends and becomes a function of poli-
> tics.

Buber went on to point out that this phenomenon, "which is supreme in the
whole world at present," has roots that reach back to the biblical times, in
which some kings in Israel (King Ahab for one) "employ false prophets
whose prophesying was merely a function of state policy."

In his concluding words, Buber answered Ben-Gurion's claim that the
messianic idea is alive and will live with the question, "In how many hearts
of this generation in our country does the Messianic idea live in a form other
than the narrow nationalistic form which is restricted to the Ingathering of
the Exiles?"

> A Messianic idea without the yearning for the redemption of
> mankind and without the desire to take part in its realization, is
> no longer identical with the Messianic visions of the prophets of
> Israel, nor can that prophetic mission be identified with a
> Messianic ideal emptied of belief in the coming of the kingdom of
> God.

Buber considered both utopianism and politics to be false relationships
between the spirit and everyday life, the former being a spurious idealism

"toward which we may lift our gaze without incurring any obligation to recover from the exigencies of earth" and the latter being a spurious realism "which regards the spirit only as a function of life." Ben-Gurion's messianism, in contrast, represented the combination of both utopianism and politics. As Michael Keren has pointed out, "To Buber, redemption lay in the yielding of earthly life (through its true self-fulfillment) to a meeting between earth and heaven, life and spirit, while to Ben-Gurion it lay in the application of heavenly ideals to the tasks on earth." Buber demanded that the state be evaluated in the broader societal and human context, but he rejected any idealization of that context beyond the meeting between human beings. What is needed, Buber asserted, was neither a morality that serves the life of the nation nor a morality based on general principles that disregards the conditions of each day but "a conscience that is not readily deceived and a trustworthy view of reality."

For Buber's eightieth birthday in 1958, there was a celebration in the Aula of the Hebrew University. When Buber entered the auditorium, the five to six hundred persons present spontaneously rose from their seats in a great ovation. Ben-Gurion came to honor Buber on this occasion and sat in the front row next to Paula Buber, which pleased Buber greatly. Three generations of Buber's pupils spoke in his honor, recalling a memorable past to those who had felt the power of his spirit and leadership in Germany, central Europe, and, since 1938, in Palestine and Israel. For many of the young sabras who came out of curiosity or out of pride in their university, this was the first real introduction to the man who occupied the anomalous position of being the best-known Israeli scholar and philosopher to the world at large and yet, up to that time, a man known more to the older Zionists and the European Aliyah than to the new generations. With the picture of Herzl on the wall behind him and Ben-Gurion in the front row before him, Buber was very likely thinking of both men when he recounted how Herzl asked him not to resign as editor of *Die Welt* and added, "I refused because the spirit should not surrender to a statesman."

In this same year, 1958, the conflict between Buber and Ben-Gurion broke out afresh over the indictment of Aharon Cohen for meeting a Soviet agent in his kibbutz and not reporting it to the authorities. Cohen, an authority on the Arab world and on Jewish-Arab relations in Palestine, was a member of the Mapam (Labor Zionist) kibbutz, Sh'ar Ha'amakim, and was Mapam's chief representative in the League for Jewish-Arab Understanding and Cooperation. Although Aharon Cohen was a Marxist to the left of Mapam, Buber was impressed by Cohen's energy, dedication, organizational ability, voluminous knowledge about Jewish-Arab relations, and his enthusiastic belief in the possibility of improving them. Buber, in fact, wrote the preface to the third volume of Cohen's trilogy, *Israel and the Arab World,* which he described as an objective and extremely important scientific work based on an inner knowledge of the events and written with fervor and love of the cause.

Cohen's trouble arose in connection with this very trilogy, which narrated the history of the relations between Zionism and the Arabs of Palestine and neighboring lands from the late nineteenth century to the present—a book, not at all incidentally, highly critical of Ben-Gurion's attitude toward the Arabs. Unable to obtain from the Hebrew University and the National Library Russian-language periodicals on the Middle East dating back to before the Russian Revolution, Cohen got in touch with the Russian Scientific Mission in Jerusalem, and, in the course of meetings with them, not only expressed openly his critical views on Israel's Middle East policies but also wrote down the names of the Mapam leadership in a personal code in order to conceal the visits of the Russians from the leaders of Mapam, who preferred to conduct all talks with Russians themselves and who had criticized Cohen for his overemphasis on Marxist theory. By Israeli law, anyone meeting a "foreign agent," the definition of which was unclear, could be accused of passing information if he could not satisfactorily account for the meeting, even if there was no evidence that he had in fact done so. Cohen was arrested under this law in 1958, at the very time that his book was being prepared for publication. Cohen believed that this was done to stop the publication of his book, parts of which were impounded to be used at the trial, which was not held until 1962. Buber took Cohen's side without a moment's hesitation, and he did not relax his efforts on Cohen's behalf from the day of his arrest until he was released from jail. Buber was the first to declare himself willing to testify before the Haifa District Court, and, when the trial opened, the eighty-four-year-old Buber, ignoring all medical considerations, made the strenuous trip to Haifa, testifying for three hours in Cohen's favor. Buber testified before the crowded courtroom that he had known Cohen since 1941, when they had both been among the first members of the League for Jewish-Arab Rapprochement, along with Henrietta Szold and Judah Magnes. Buber met frequently with Cohen (who became secretary of the league at the end of 1941), particularly after Cohen's visit to Syria and Lebanon in 1942 and his testimony, together with Ernst Simon, before the Anglo-American Commission of Enquiry in 1946. Buber appeared as a character witness, and he did not hesitate to claim that he was, indeed, a judge of character who had founded his entire philosophical thinking from the time of his youth on a study of actual human beings.

"For nearly three hours he remained there," reports Aubrey Hodes, "replying patiently to all the queries leveled at him, his voice clear and unhurried, explaining in an almost fatherly way his conviction that a man such as Cohen could not possibly have acted deceitfully in the way the prosecution claimed." In a relationship of over twenty years, Buber could not recall a single incident that would contradict his conviction that Aharon Cohen was a man who meant what he said.

Buber's words made a profound impression upon the judges, none of whom believed that Cohen had given any information to the foreign agents whom he had met. Nonetheless, they did not find his explanation of his contacts convincing and sentenced him to five years in prison. Ben-Gurion was pleased with the verdict and the sentence as well as with the court's arguments, praising privately the wisdom of the Israeli judiciary. He was not so pleased when the Israeli Supreme Court took a different line, one justice wanting to quash the verdict and release the prisoner immediately and the other two, including the chief justice, reducing the sentence by half, not joining their colleague only because they felt that the law, highly dubious and draconic though it was, still was binding upon them and left them no other choice. "Public opinion in Israel generally regarded this as the vindication of Aharon Cohen which Buber and his friends had demanded from the first," reports Simon.

In February 1963, on the occasion of Buber's eightieth birthday, Ben-Gurion sent him best wishes—"the wish of a friend, an admirer and opponent."

> Your deep and original philosophy, your faithful participation in the work of the rebirth of Israel from your youth to the present day, your deep ideal and existential relationship to the vision that the prophets of Israel had of national and universal redemption and a reign of righteousness, peace, and brotherhood in the world, the total agreement between your strivings and demands and the conduct of your life—for all these you are entitled to praise and fame in the history of our people and our time.

Ben-Gurion signed this letter "in love and veneration," and Buber replied that he had been made truly happy by this letter, which touched on a complicated realm of interhuman relationships—the type of opposition that does not exclude personal closeness. "I may say to you that I agree with you in this, and that, with all factual reservations, I could characterize my position toward you in words similar to the friendly ones that you have used in writing me." But Buber went on to say that he saw in this letter a sort of continuation of Ben-Gurion's previous exchange of letters with him in February 1962, regarding Buber's request that he pardon Aharon Cohen: "Allow me on this occasion to make an observation concerning our controversy. Some time has elapsed meanwhile, and perhaps you now see a possibility, in the framework of your authority, to pardon and to release the ailing Aharon Cohen from prison. That would make me very happy." Ben-Gurion immediately replied to Buber's letter, once more refusing to pardon Cohen. One of the first actions of Buber's friend Zalman Shazar, when he became president of Israel, was to fulfill Buber's wish and pardon Cohen, an action that he communicated personally to Buber.

In September 1959, the executive committee of Ihud decided to bring its position on the Arab refugees to the attention of the Israeli public by holding a press conference in Buber's home. Nearly all of the Israeli newspapers gave a prominent place to reports on this press conference, and many wrote special articles expressing appreciation of the meeting and of Buber, in particular, who took the central role. Buber shook hands warmly with each of the dozen journalists who were introduced to him and, with a degree of alertness and liveliness difficult to find even among the young, directed the conversation. He began by pointing out that the refugee problem would be given more serious and realistic treatment at the forthcoming General Assembly of the United Nations and that the meeting between Eisenhower and Khrushchev in Washington might also result in a relaxation of tension in the Middle East that would make it possible to do something about this problem. The time had perhaps come, he thought, for Israel to take the initiative on the Arab refugee problem, which he had suggested to Ben-Gurion in his talk with him ten years before. Such an initiative Buber saw as an unconditional moral-political duty in the present situation, independent of a peace treaty with the Arab states. "I am doubtful," Buber added, "whether after the U.N. General Assembly session the matter will still remain in our hands."

In October 1961, Buber issued a statement on the Arab refugee problem for Ihud, expressing "deep sorrow at the Prime Minister's statement of October 11, 1961, in which he firmly rejects 'the insidious proposal for freedom of choice for the refugees' between returning to Israel and accepting compensations and resettlement elsewhere," a proposal which reiterated the belief that the means could be found to have hundreds of thousands of refugees transferred to a productive life as peace-loving citizens in the Arab States and in the State of Israel. Buber called for a cooperation among Israel, the Arab States, the refugees, and the United Nations in which joint committees of experts should devise "projects for rehabilitation of the refugees and methods of carrying them out 'in a constructive spirit and with a sense of justice and realism' (Hammarskjöld), taking into account the economic, demographic, humanitarian and, particularly, security conditions involved in this operation." It would be the special task of these committees "to ensure that the choice of the refugees will really be a free one, based on objective information of the conditions prevailing in Israel and in the Arab States." Thus, Ihud coupled an awareness of problems concerning security with a deep humanitarian concern over the refugees' plight.

The next clash between Buber and Ben-Gurion came in connection with the "Lavon affair," a political thicket with roots that reached back to the formation of the state. Pinkas Lavon, a former minister of defense involved in a spy scandal in Egypt that rocked the government of Israel, had now become secretary-general of the powerful labor organization Histadrut, which he used to build up his power; he demanded that Ben-Gurion exonerate him. Ben-Gurion decided that Lavon had to go, and he resigned his position as prime minister in order to force him out.

In December 1960, a number of intellectuals issued a manifesto entitled "The Danger to Democracy," specifically protesting against Ben-Gurion's intervention. This statement was signed by fifty professors and by some of the most prominent persons in the country, calling on the leaders to take action to clear the atmosphere and regain the confidence of the people.

> The greatest danger to a democratic regime and its values is from a scorn of criticism and an attitude of contempt towards the opponent. This danger is many times greater in a society which is still in the process of crystallizing its political and social regime, and in which large parts of the population lack the experience of democratic government and a sense of proportion to distinguish between the important and the subsidiary in a controversy between the parties.

Buber's name led the list of those who signed the manifesto. Ben-Gurion was furious, and he was particularly offended that Buber, for whom he had great respect, should take sides against him. Up to this point, Ben-Gurion belonged to the Mosad Bialik committee that Buber headed for the translation of the classics into Hebrew and had visited Buber in his home to discuss the translation of Spinoza, in which he was very much interested. Now Ben-Gurion publicly resigned from this committee. At the end of January 1961, Raphael Bashan published a long interview with Buber in *Ma-ariv*, with the title "Why Did I Sign the Professors' Manifesto?" Buber believed that this was precisely one of those times in which a person is obliged to raise his voice. When Bashan asked him exactly what danger he had in mind, Buber showed that he was totally conversant with everyday problems down to the last detail, that he knew the inmost intrigues of the political parties and the way an army is run. "He suddenly impressed me as a most mysterious man, pulling a hundred strings of secret information," Bashan confided. But what Buber said during that hour he asked Bashan not to publicize. Bashan concluded from this long talk that Buber believed unconditionally that the Middle East was on the eve of radical political and social changes that might bring about a sharp turn in Israel's international relations. "If renunciations are imposed upon us from without, this will be a catastrophe," Buber said. "But if we renounce willingly, this will be politics."

In his response, Ben-Gurion denied that intellectuals had anything of special weight to say in security matters. "If I need an expert opinion in godly matters I shall gladly refer to Professor Buber," Ben-Gurion said. This statement led Ernst Simon to counter that, although Ben-Gurion went to greater extremes than Buber in the authority that he granted the intellectuals in principle, he played down every attempt on their behalf to voice their opinion on crucial matters. Ben-Gurion's rejoinder to Simon led an opposition newspaper to comment:

> One person in the country has a monopoly over everything: over truth and righteousness, justice and morality, over the kingdom of

the spirit and over democracy. Not only does he have a monopoly, he is the one and only in charge of determining what is truth, who can talk in the name of truth, what is intellectual and who is entitled to be called an intellectual.

Buber's most famous conflict with Ben-Gurion concerned the trial and execution of Adolf Eichmann, an issue that reached far beyond internal Israeli affairs to postwar Germany and the modern world in general.

Although by no means the person most responsible for the Holocaust, Eichmann had been entrusted with the organization and to some extent the execution of the "final solution." As a result, his capture and kidnapping by Israeli police in Argentina in 1961, and his subsequent prosecution by Gideon Hausner before a court of Israeli judges, was a sensational series of events that aroused great controversy regarding international law, war crimes, and the justice of Eichmann's being tried and executed by an Israeli court. Buber believed that Eichmann should be tried in Israel, but by an international court, because he did not believe that the Jews, who were the victims of the Holocaust, should also be the judges.

On December 15, Eichmann was sentenced to death by the Israeli court. Buber telephoned Ben-Gurion and asked to meet with him. Ben-Gurion replied, "I am younger than you. I shall come to you." The two men talked for two hours at Buber's home in Talbiyeh, where Buber pleaded with the other to commute the sentence to life imprisonment. Ben-Gurion, who earlier had said that he was concerned about the trial and not about the sentence (in *Eichmann in Jerusalem,* Hannah Arendt characterized Ben-Gurion as the "invisible stage manager of the trial"), said that he himself was not intent upon the execution. But President Ben-Zvi was determined that Eichmann be executed. In a Histadrut convention in the 1930s, Ben-Zvi was the only member who did *not* want capital punishment abolished, although it was, in fact, abolished with the foundation of the state, except in cases of high treason in wartime and for war crimes against humanity in general or against the Jewish people in particular. Buber also appealed directly to Ben-Zvi, but here, too, his plea was unsuccessful. "Indirectly, Ben-Gurion gave a public answer to Buber," reported *Time* on March 23, 1962. "As the Israeli Supreme Court prepared to consider Eichmann's own appeal before handing down a verdict, the official government gazette published a regulation authorizing the appointment of 'a man to execute a death sentence.'" The principal reason for Buber's opposition to the execution, which was the identical position taken by Hugo Bergmann, was that the commandment, "Thou shalt not kill" applies with equal force to the state and the individual. Buber stated to *Newsweek:* "The death sentence has not diminished crime—on the contrary, all this exasperates the souls of men.... Killing awakens killing."

The other reason for Buber's opposition to Eichmann's execution was the fear that the German youth might take the execution for a symbolic justice that would relieve them of the burden of German guilt for the Holocaust. This seemed to be particularly so because of the enormous worldwide attention that the trial had received, which raised it far beyond *any* other trial of an individual. No punishment could really expiate Eichmann's crimes, Buber declared. What he had done went far beyond any human punishment that could be devised. To oppose his execution had nothing to do with clemency or mercy. Buber had no feeling of compassion or pity for Eichmann, for whom, as Hodes recounts, "Buber felt nothing but distaste and horror." Buber proposed instead that Eichmann should be given life imprisonment— not in a cell like an ordinary criminal but, as a symbol of the Holocaust, put to work on the land in a kibbutz, farming the soil of Israel. When the Israeli newspapers reported Buber's plea not to execute Eichmann, public reaction was overwhelmingly against him.

After Eichmann's hanging on May 31, 1962, Buber gave an interview to The *New York Times* in which he called the execution a "mistake of historical dimension."

On January 17, 1962, Buber gave an interview to Lawrence Fellows, the same correspondent of The *New York Times* who later interviewed him about the execution of Eichmann, in which he took Ben-Gurion to task for having said that most of the Israeli Arabs, "if given the opportunity, would help destroy Israel." This is the kind of expression that would make bad citizens of the Arabs, Buber said to Fellows, and is unworthy of the early ideals of the founders of the Jewish state. Appalled by the bias expressed in Ben-Gurion's statement, Buber and two other members of Ihud issued a statement pointing out Ben-Gurion's failure to imagine the nationalistic feelings of the Arabs, which paralleled those that he felt as a Zionist:

> Mr. Ben-Gurion has, apparently, forgotten what we have learned from the history and ideology of the Zionist movement, namely, that one should not forego a life of equality and dignity—personal and national—for the sake of superior economic, social, and educational conditions. When the State of Israel was established, the Arab population was promised full equality, without discrimination. During the last thirteen years, however, the government of Israel has neglected many opportunities [to improve the civic and political situation of the Arabs] and has committed acts which have engendered in the Arab inhabitants of the State a feeling that they are but second-class citizens.

As a result of the publication of the Fellows interview in The *New York Times,* the American Council for Judaism, the last stronghold of anti-Zionism among the Jewish community in America (because they hold Judaism to be a religion and not a nation) asked Buber to write an article for its journal *Issues* on the Arab refugee problem and to propose measures that could lead to peace between Israelis and Arabs. They were afraid that Ben-Gurion's remarks about the Arabs in Israel would increase the hostility that many American Jews already felt toward the Arabs. Buber replied that he could not fulfill their request, for this would mean in some respect identifying his standpoint regarding the great problem of Zionism with theirs.

> But in reality they are far apart. Ihud's criticism of the Israeli government's Arab policies comes from within, yours from without. Our program for Jewish-Arab cooperation is not inferior to what is called official Zionism; rather it is a greater Zionism. We would like to bring the Jewish people to understand this greater Zionism and make it their own.

Once again, Buber walked the narrow ridge with measured certainty.

The last action that Buber engaged in for Ihud with regard to Jewish-Arab relations in Israel was no longer addressed to Ben-Gurion but to his successor, Prime Minister Levi Eshkol. After a meeting of the Ihud executive committee at his home in October 1964, Buber wrote personally to Eshkol to communicate to him their conclusions. Buber added a personal word that was clearly meant as a contrast between Eshkol's regime and that of Ben-Gurion. "Since you have taken office as Prime Minister, a clear change in tone and to a certain extent also in the political lines is to be felt in important spheres, including the attitude toward the Arab citizens of Israel."

Buber could not subscribe fully to any Israeli party, but neither did he abstain totally from participation in them. According to the situation, he would at times support the left-radical socialists of the Mapam or the Liberal Progressives, who consulted him as a mentor. In his 1960 autobiography, *A Life of Strife,* Max Brod expressed great admiration for Ben-Gurion's politics and said that he had often been the pathbreaker and leader of the people: "His enormous service in the founding of the State in a most difficult time and in overcoming a series of crises has a firm place in history." At the same time, he expressed regret concerning Ben-Gurion's attitude toward the Arab refugees and his failure to make use of Buber's political talents:

> But [what is] incomprehensible to me is that Ben-Gurion and the representatives of the great parties have until now not considered that a man like Martin Buber belongs in the government of this young state. For such a uniquely qualified man of great wisdom, power of action, and international fame not to serve in the time of the historical transformation... of our people—that downright borders on mad wastefulness.

Brod had observed Buber's political activity at Zionist congresses, such as Karlsbad; he had noted Buber's breadth of vision, his spiritual presence and

adroitness in action, his warmth and openness in conversations, to say nothing of his scholarship and his religious depth. "Martin Buber is, among other
things, also a great politician. It should not have been allowed to happen
that at critical times he stood aside. In the future, in historical retrospect, this
will be adduced as our most serious error, as a sad curiosity." Brod called on
the government to remedy this error but, of course, that did not happen.

In February 1966, *New Outlook, The Middle East Monthly* ran as its lead
article an essay by Ernst Simon, published in *Ner* shortly after Buber's death,
entitled "Buber or Ben-Gurion?" "The tragic circumstances of Israel's birth
brought the Statesman to the fore and left the Philosopher in the shade,"
reads the summary at the top. "Israel's future depends on a more fruitful dialogue between the two." The opening paragraph of the article, however,
does not take so moderate or well balanced a position:

> It seems that these two, the thinker and the statesman, have to
> share the honor of being the most famous Jews of the middle of
> the twentieth century. Some would say that they complement
> each other, that each has what the other lacks; others see them as
> the personifications of an extreme contrast between two wholly
> irreconcilable attitudes. I intend to show that Buber and Ben-
> Gurion cannot exist in one and the same spiritual and moral cli-
> mate, and that we must make a deliberate choice between them.

Simon acknowledged that Ben-Gurion showed more respect for Buber than
for perhaps any other figure in the world of the spirit, but he attributed this
not to what Buber stood for but to Ben-Gurion's "well-developed and sure
instinct for discerning power in general, and Jewish power in particular,
wherever it might be located."… But, said Simon, there was no true respect
between the two, because their common ground was too narrow to provide
a basis for their being willing to learn anything from each other. Simon then
proceeded to demonstrate this at length in separate sections devoted to the
Arab question, the Aharon Cohen case, and the endeavors to make the
Middle East a nuclear-free zone. Buber helped in every way that he could,
including giving advice and using his home as a meeting place for consultations, from the day the Committee for Nuclear Disarmament of the Israeli-
Arab Region was established, all in opposition to the expressed views and
determined wishes of Ben-Gurion—who, in demanding total disarmament or
nothing, made sure that nothing would be done and made impossible the
first step of nuclear disarmament.

In the final section of his article, Simon modified this strict disjunction
in favor of a possible future situation in which the image of the history of
Israel would look as follows: "The establishment of the state was not possible otherwise than under the aegis of Ben-Gurion, but the fact that it could
continue to exist can only be explained by its being penetrated by Buber's

spirit to the extent where [that spirit] informed its leaders and most of its people." This must happen, said Simon, if Israel is not to live forever by the sword—under the sign of Mars. "That is the hope which never left Buber, almost to his last day, and for the sake of which he kept faith with the State of Israel which is so largely the handiwork of Ben-Gurion."

Just as the Second World War enabled Buber to complete *For the Sake of Heaven,* it seems probable that this very opposition between himself and Ben-Gurion enabled Buber to go back to the theme that had fascinated him as a young man and complete in 1956 his one piece of drama, *Elijah: A Mystery Play.* The way in which Buber portrayed the opposition between King Ahab and the prophet Elijah in his play is itself an essential part of the understanding of dialogue as a way to peace. Ahab is not pictured as a "wicked king," as Melville puts it in *Moby Dick,* but as someone who, even in his failure to decide, remains bound up in dialogue with God, from whom he has turned. Elijah does not see himself as Ahab's enemy, nor does Elijah's God. For this reason, too, *Elijah* is a great statement of existential trust, precisely where it departs from the Hebrew Bible with its starker story of Elijah killing the four hundred priests of Baal after they are defeated on Mount Carmel.

Buber's mystery play *Elijah* contains in dramatic form all the central motifs in Buber's understanding of biblical and Jewish existence: the demand that the Covenant which Israel places on the people and the king make real the kingship of God through justice, righteousness, and loving-kindness; the task of building the Covenant of peace with other nations and of building true community; the attack on all forms of dualism that relegate religion to the cultic and the "spiritual" and place no demand on everyday life; the biblical *emunah* or unconditional trust in the relation to the imageless God who offers no security or success yet who will be with us *as* he will be with us; the summons and sending of the prophet to whom God calls but whom he does not compel; the call of the prophet for real decision in the present—the peoples turning back to God with the whole of their existence—rather than the apocalyptic prediction of a fixed future; evil as the failure to make real decision; the king as the viceroy of God, who is anointed to realize God's kingship but who has no "divine right" to rule in God's stead; and the suffering servant" as the messianic figure who will lead the "holy remnant" of those who remain faithful to the Covenant to set the dialogue right through free and wholehearted response.

Nothing so characterizes Buber's own life as the blessing that Elijah gives to Elisha in this mystery play. When Elijah takes final leave of Elisha, he tells him that no one ripens into a prophet who does not learn to bear loneliness. Elisha asks for the blessing of Elijah's spirit, but Elijah replies that he has never possessed the spirit, that it has come and gone. He blesses Elisha with obedience to the spirit and the ability to withstand the Lord.

These two together—"obedient listening" and contending—make up the very heart of *Elijah*, as they do of Buber's philosophy of dialogue. *Elijah* not only summarizes the motifs of Buber's biblical Judaism; it speaks to us of the concerns that lay closest to Buber's heart and of the attitudes that were embodied in his life, including his own dialogue with Ben-Gurion.

♦ 22 ♦

Surfeited with Honors

(1958-1964)

During his last years, Buber once described himself to Werner Kraft as "surfeited with honors." To Hugo Bergmann, Buber, the "wise man of the mountain," as Bergmann's wife called him, had once said, "Fame is an empty nut that he who can cracks" ("Der Ruhm ist eine taube Nuss, die knacke wer sie knacken mag"). Buber's eightieth birthday was celebrated at special meetings in Israel and America, where Buber himself was able to be present, and by Festschriften in Germany. The Israeli newspaper *Davar* printed a special interview for the occasion, in which the interviewer described Buber as easy in manner, alert in his movements, and full of youthful energy, causing the questioner to wonder at the hidden springs from which Buber drew his power. "I work from twelve to sixteen hours a day," Buber said and then, lest it sound like bragging, added shyly, "I am no longer bothered by sleep." "His eyes are open, big, shining," the interviewer said, "as if celebrating the fact that the years could not defeat or dim them." Hermann Hesse sent Buber a particularly beautiful letter on this occasion, and Albert Schweitzer conveyed his condolences, noting that from eighty on everything becomes more difficult from year to year! The Sorbonne gave Buber an honorary doctorate, and Emmanuel Levinas and Wilhelm Szilasi wrote special evaluations of Buber's place in European culture for a series of radio programs on "The World of Martin Buber" that I conducted for the Pacifica Radio stations in New York, San Francisco, and Los Angeles. Buber's old friend Nahum Goldmann sent him a telegram that read, "May your example and your wisdom contribute to showing our generation a way out of the chaos of the present." In January 1959, Simon Halkin, professor of Hebrew Literature at the Hebrew University, nominated Buber for the Nobel Prize in literature with the concurrence of the senate of the Hebrew University.

To the many persons who wrote him from around the world, Buber sent an expression of thanks, "directed to each individual," in which he said that the older one becomes, the more grows the inclination to thank—that which is above us, for the unearned gift of life, and especially each entirely good hour that one receives like an unexpected present—and also to thank one's fellow man "for really meeting me, seeing and hearing me and not another, and opening what I really addressed, his well-closed heart."

In 1960, a long-standing dream of Eugenia and mine was fulfilled: We went to spend four months in Jerusalem, near Buber. For two evenings a week, Eugenia and I spent four hours with Buber in the relaxed atmosphere of his study, in welcome contrast to his more pressured visits to America. We talked about everything from Israel and Jerusalem, politics, literature, and religion, to Buber's personal life as we sat together on the couch, having wine, tea, and cookies that were brought in by his granddaughter Barbara at some point every evening. (I can still hear the way Barbara said to us, "He was always lovable," when we went to visit her in Talbiyeh in 1966 after Buber's death.) The Buber household cats now numbered only three, and they came in and out through the window of his study as they pleased. Sometimes we talked about the difficulty of translating his works into English, and Buber remarked, "Some of these words do not even exist in German!" At other times, Buber and Eugenia would read passages from the New Testament in the original koiné Greek that they both loved. Occasionally, Buber would tell stories, such as the time that the people in the hometown of the great Italian composer Rossini decided to build a statue in his honor. Rossini, who was himself living in near poverty, offered to stand on the pedestal for several hours each day if they would give him the money instead! Then there was the story of the elderly Jew who sat in the front row at Hitler's lectures, laughing until Hitler could bear it no more and asked him, "Why do you laugh?" "There was a man called Hamann, and he wanted to do in the Jewish people," the elderly man replied, "and later there was another man, and now there is you!" During the evenings, Buber would try to tend the big stove that kept his room warm and added light to boot, though his eyes were bad, and he could not in fact see well (he had to use a magnifying glass for most of his reading). We had the impression that he did not want us to observe too much these weaknesses of age, and still more, on the rare occasions when he spoke in public, he did not want it noticed that he had a hard time finding his way.

Buber possessed enormous energy. He would still be going strong at midnight while Eugenia and I would be drooping. On his desk was a huge pile of unanswered mail from all over the world. "It is a terrible thing to be this thing called famous!" Buber remarked to me. Once Buber told me of a man who came to visit him who made him extremely uncomfortable, and he did not know why. As he got up to go and Buber walked with him to the door of his study, the man, himself older than Buber, said to him, "You are the Messiah!" Then Buber understood. "I cannot talk with someone from above to below," Buber said. "I am only someone who has seen something and who goes to a window and points," he said at the eightieth birthday celebration that the American Friends of the Hebrew University held for him in New York. "I am really not a saint," Buber said to Eugenia and me in Jerusalem. "During the first half of my life I had to refrain from pushing myself and other people over into evil. Only in the second half of my life did I master this tendency."

Our conversation also included amusing anecdotes about Buber's life. Buber once told us that when he had gone to an Israeli hotel for a rest, he wrote the hotel a check with an extra zero on the end. "An absent-minded professor!" exclaimed the desk clerk. "No," replied Buber, "present elsewhere." Actually, what struck me most about Buber, and more during the four months of this visit than ever before, was that he, more than anyone I knew, was fully present at each moment and situation. Once I asked myself whether Buber was charismatic and decided, "No, it is just that he is really present when he is with you, and most of us, including myself, are not." That made his presence sometimes uncomfortable, for it demanded of you that you be present, too. I found Buber every time I met him not only the most *concrete* person I knew and the most insistent on the concrete, but also the most *objective*, dispassionately *interested* person I had met, and there seemed to be no limit to what interested him.

During our last meeting in Jerusalem, I went to see Buber alone at night. I asked him a question about his translation of two key passages in the Book of Job for the section on the "Biblical Image of Man" in my book *Problematic Rebel*. He showed me the original and went over the text with me. Instead of "Though he slay me, yet will I trust in him" from the King James Version and "He will slay me; I have no hope" from the Revised Standard, Buber translated the familiar passage "He may slay me, I await it," expressing being in God's hands and yet trusting at the same time. Regarding the second passage, instead of translating it "I know that my redeemer lives and in my flesh I shall see God," he rendered it "I know that my redeemer lives and that when my skin has been stripped away, I shall see God." This, to Buber, meant no reference to a life after death but to the progressive deterioration of his body which Job was experiencing and expected.

Buber was in Munich in July 1960 to present the paper "The Word That Is Spoken" at the Bavarian Academy of Fine Arts, where he spoke in clear, firm tones of "the fruitful ambiguity of speech and language." It was a great occasion. More than a thousand people filled the hall of the University of Munich. On this occasion, Buber was also given the Culture Prize of the City of Munich, and the newspapers and journals were full of accounts of the happenings. The prize of fifteen thousand marks had before then been awarded only to the physicist Werner Heisenberg and the conductor Bruno Walter. Buber thanked the officials of Munich, saying that the ceremony had a special significance for him because he had close and long-standing ties with Munich, where Paula grew up and Gustav Landauer was murdered for his part in the revolution.

Buber's speech before the academy proved to be his final contribution to his anthropology volume *The Knowledge of Man* (1965). What makes designations problematic, Buber said, is not that there are no single, agreed-on definitions, but that they do not show a concrete context that can be controlled. Every abstraction must stand the test of being related to a concrete reality without which it has no meaning. We do not clarify designations in order to reach agreement or unanimity, but in order to discuss them and relate to each other in terms of them, whether in cooperation or opposition. Useful as precision and definition are for the exact sciences, the true humanity and the very meaning of language depend upon its being brought back to the fruitful disagreement of lived speech between persons, whose meanings necessarily differ because of the difference of their attitudes and situations.

Buber did not follow Heidegger in seeing the truth of lived speech as the *aletheia* of the Greeks—"the sublime 'unconcealment' suitable to Being itself." Instead, he saw it as "the simple conception of truth of the Hebrew Bible whose *etymon* means 'faithfulness,' the faithfulness of man or the faithfulness of God." "This concrete person, in the life-space allotted to him, answers with his faithfulness for the word that is spoken by him."

In December 1960, Buber was awarded the Henrietta Szold Prize for his work in education, and, in May 1961, he was the first Israeli to be elected to honorary membership in the American Academy of Arts and Sciences. In December 1961, Buber received the Bialik Prize of the City of Tel Aviv for his contribution to Jewish Studies. In October 1964, the Albert Schweitzer Medal for "having exemplified the spirit of reverence for life and other tenets of the philosophy of Dr. Schweitzer" was bestowed upon him. One of the most interesting of the many awards and honorary doctorates that Buber received was the honorary doctor of medicine conferred on him in 1962 by the University of Münster for the contribution of his philosophy of dialogue to the relationship between doctor and patient. In fact, in the award ceremony, Buber was called a "doctor of souls."

In 1960, Buber told Schalom Ben-Chorin that, although he had perhaps not had success in any other sphere, he could claim some success in combating the Marcionite trend within the Christian church and in helping create a more positive attitude toward the Hebrew Bible and Judaism. Buber held that participation of Jews in the Second Ecumenical Council in Rome, such as had been suggested in America, was a questionable concept, because creating an "Una sancta" of the church with Israel was impossible. When Buber was in Florence in September 1960, Mayor La Pira wanted to set up an audience for him with Pope John XXIII, but Buber declined the offer, because he did not care for representative conversations at a distance and he did not believe a simple human dialogue possible with a pope, not even with such a human pope.

In March 1961, Buber admitted that reasons of health had induced him to give up much work, including the (yet unwritten) essay on the unconscious in the anthropology volume. "By the way," he added, "it was assuming in my mind the size of a little book by itself rather than that of one of those essays." (While at the Hebrew University in 1966, I copied more than forty pages of his notes from two folders in the Martin Buber Archives on the unconscious and dreams, which would, indeed, have provided the basis for a most important book.)

In October 1961, Buber reported a German governmental grant that would make possible the publication of his works in three large volumes, about four thousand pages in all, by Kösel Verlag in Munich and Lambert Schneider in Heidelberg. The first volume, *On Philosophy,* appeared the following year. When I asked why the essays from *Ereignisse und Begegnungen* (Events and Meetings), most of which had been translated for the first part of *Pointing the Way,* did not appear in it, Buber replied that it was "because they belong more to literature than to philosophy."

The poet and translator Ruth Finer Mintz told of a young man who asked Buber whether he should marry a girl who was not an intellectual. Buber said, "Why not?" "But what could she teach me?" complained the young man. At this, Buber's eyes flashed and he said, "She might teach you what it is to be a woman!" To the end of his life, Buber remained a teacher. He was editor in chief of Israel's Encyclopedia of Education and also himself wrote a long article for it in 1961 entitled "The Aims of Adult Education." He was also very much interested in the work of the journalist Alissa Levenberg, who was the first to really live with and teach the Oriental Jews in the new city of Dimona in the Negev. Also, through the publication of *Am v'Olam* (People and World) in 1961, Buber's political and social thought and his views on education became known to many sabras who did not have access to them before. Buber felt a strong kinship with the generation of his grandchildren that he did not feel at all with that of his own children, and, in the last few years of his life, young people came more and more to see him, vaguely dissatisfied with those political goals that before had been everything to them.

Buber's most important impact during the last five years of his life was on the young people of the kibbutzim and on the active kibbutz education movement in Israel. Menachem (Hermann) Gerson was active at this time in kibbutz education work. But it was a much younger kibbutznik, Avraham Shapira of Kibbutz Jezreel, who spearheaded the most fruitful contacts between Buber and the kibbutz education movement.

On July 26, 1963, members of Kibbutz Afikim met with Buber, and the

transcript of this meeting was later published in full in the Israeli journal
Sdemot. One young man asked Buber how a feeling of community can be
created in a large kibbutz (Afikim, with more than two thousand members, is
the largest kibbutz in Israel). Buber distinguished between *closeness* and
relation and declared any kibbutz of six or seven hundred members, much
less two thousand, to be a social monster that needed to be broken down
into smaller, interlocking groups in which each person could feel a part of
the group. He also emphasized the need for enough space for each individual to have some distance from his comrade through which alone he might
choose to enter into relation with him, and there should be the opportunity
for meditation and contemplation as well. Asked about religious observance,
Buber said that one thing that the kibbutz and Hasidism should have in common is *kavana,* doing what one does wholeheartedly. "Human life deserves
this name if and only if a person does everything out of *kavana*—for its own
sake—but this is not necessarily a religious affair. In my opinion in a kibbutz
one could live the life of *kavana* without religious concern." He stressed the
influence the kibbutz educators could have, not through their theories but
through their personal lives, through the power of human example. This
power is effective even when one must live contrary to the principles of
one's own kibbutz. "Real influence is slow. A man lives and actualizes what
he intends to teach others. Sometimes he must devote the whole of his life to
this, but such a life is worth living."

During the last five years of Buber's life, many leaders and educators of
kibbutzim came to see him and discuss kibbutz problems with him. Many of
these discussions were published and aroused echoes in other kibbutzim.
"Every time Buber astonished those whom he met by the freshness of his
thought and by the way he entered in as soon as it became concrete,"
Avraham Shapira reported in a long essay entitled "Meetings with Buber." By
the same token, Buber eschewed ideas and ideologies in favor of considering whether the young have a real trust in the person to whom they listen.
"That and not the idea is the alpha." Shapira gave a clear picture not only of
what Buber said but of the way in which he said it:

> His words were spoken in a very clear-cut fashion, emphasizing
> each letter and word. When he finished his short answer, he used
> to wait for a sign that he was understood. When he told a story,
> he finished it with a caesura, as if allowing a certain amount of
> time for his listener to absorb his words, and then he used to look
> down, to lean over his desk or to sit back in his chair, but without
> relieving himself of the tension of the conversation. Only in his
> last years at the end of the conversation I noticed how concentrat-
> ed he had been in them and how exhausted he was by them.

In all these meetings, Buber never consented to start the conversation: "I
came only to answer the questions of the comrades." Only when questions

were asked did the conversation begin. "It was marvelous to see how young comrades who came with hesitation and awe became in one evening inter-locutors of Buber. After sitting tensely in the beginning, they relaxed in their chairs. It was as if the scales of armor fell."

Buber's eighty-fifth birthday was an even greater event than his eighti-eth one. He was honored in Israel and throughout the world. The Hebrew University had a special ceremony for him and announced its intention to reprint the original 1902 pamphlet, by Buber, Chaim Weizmann, and Berthold Feiwel, in which the establishment of a Hebrew University was first proposed. But perhaps the most remarkable event of all and, to judge by the picture that we have of it, the most gratifying to Buber personally, was a spontaneous torchlight parade of the students from Hebrew University to his home in Talbiyeh. Something of the charm of this occasion was captured by *Time*:

> Bedtime for Israel's most distinguished philosopher, Martin Buber, is 10 o'clock. But his 85th birthday was an exception. At the stroke of 11, some 400 students from the Hebrew University... paraded up Jerusalem's Lovers of Zion Street to the door of Buber's villa, carrying torches and singing in Hebrew "For Martin's a jolly good fellow." On the veranda, a pretty coed garlanded the white-whiskered Hasidic sage with flowers and soundly bussed his cheek. "What?" asked Buber with a merry twinkle. "Is there only one girl student here?" Then the students presented him with honorary membership in their student union. "I have a drawer full of honorary degrees, in everything from theology to medicine," said Buber. "But this is the first time I've been made an honorary student. This is a great honor for me."

Although this custom was followed in some European universities, it is the first time it had ever been done in Israel. Buber saw in this occasion the pos-sible signing of the pact between himself and the generation of his grandchil-dren and their children, and was "radiantly happy," as Hodes reports. If to be a student means to be a person who naturally studies, as John Huizinga spoke of the natural playing man *(homo ludens)*, "someone for whom learn-ing and study are equally an expression of human freedom," then he was delighted to be a partner in it! Asked if he had ever taken part in such a torchlight parade as a young man, Buber said that he had, but only a few times, because he had not liked most of his professors! Buber was delighted by the event.

Buber also heard at this time of the intention of founding a Martin Buber Chair of Judaica at the University of Cologne in Germany and of the Martin Buber Forest, which a group of his well-wishers in Germany, led by Romano Guardini, who composed the summons for this appeal, had funded in his honor. The forest was later planted at Kibbutz Hazorea.

In January 1963, Buber received a letter from the business director of the Erasmus Prize Foundation (established in 1958 on the initiative of Prince Bernhard of Holland), announcing that he had been chosen for the 1963 award of the prize, which had been given to the Austrian people in 1958, to the French statesman Robert Schuman and the German philosopher Karl Jaspers in 1959, to the painters Marc Chagall and Oskar Kokoschka in 1960, and to Romano Guardini in 1962. The Erasmus Prize was to be given to Buber to honor the significance of his work in furthering the spiritual life and consciousness of the peoples of Europe, above all in reference to the dissemination of his own philosophy and for the general awakening of an interest in, and an understanding of, Hasidism. Buber accepted the prize of 100,000 Dutch guilders on the understanding that three-fourths of it would go to the Leo Baeck Foundation for a scholarly anthology entitled "Judaism and the European Crisis" (the Hitler period).

The Erasmus Prize was intended, in principle, to be comparable to the Nobel Prize, to act as a stimulus to individuals or institutions whose work is considered of outstanding merit for the spiritual and cultural resurgence of an integrated Europe. Unlike the Nobel Prize, it was to be partially expended in grants for cultural, social, or social-scientific projects for unifying European spirit and culture. The year 1963 was the first time that the prize was awarded on Dutch soil. On July 3, 1963, seven hundred prominent invited guests filled to capacity the hall of the Royal Institute for the Tropics in Amsterdam to watch Prince Bernhard award Martin Buber the Erasmus Prize in the presence of Queen Juliana. Yehudi and Hepzibah Menuhin played Ernst Bloch's *Baal-Shem* Suite. In the Erasmus Prize booklet, there are charming pictures of Buber with the Menuhins, a delightful picture of Buber with Princess Beatrix, and an image of an altogether different Buber—serious and even stern—delivering his own speech, "Believing Humanism."

The believing humanism of Erasmus meant two separate spheres in the life of the human person, neither of which limited the other and to each of which belonged special times and activities, said Buber. In contrast, Buber put forth a believing humanism in which humanity and faith penetrate each other and work together so fully that "we may say our faith has our humanity as its foundation, and our humanity has our faith as its foundation." Then, elaborating, Buber pointed to two separate answers to the modern question of what *humanum* in its most positive sense is. The one answer is that stream of German philosophy from Hegel to Heidegger that sees man as the being in whom Being attains to consciousness of itself and hence regards "reflexion," bending back on oneself, reflecting on oneself, as the preeminently human activity. The other answer is that which finds the *humanum* in the fact that "in the history of the world it is first through man that 'meeting' has become possible, as meeting of the one with the other." In the former definition, humanity and faith necessarily exclude each other in our lives because we can "meet" this empty Being in all metaphysics, but not in the lived life of the human person for whom faith means trust in the God that is *there.* "A genuine believing humanism can no longer grow from this soil." For the latter, the true *humanum* and the experience of faith are rooted in the same soil of meeting. "Indeed, the fundamental experience of faith itself may be regarded as the highest intensification of the reality of meeting." Although very little of such a believing humanism is to be discerned in our age, in which the observing and exploiting type of man predominates, nonetheless, a powerful education toward a new and genuine believing humanism has arisen in the present in the crisis that threatens the human race with extinction—leaderless technology, unlimited mastery of means without any end, voluntary enslavement of man in the service of the split atom. The growing awareness of this crisis in the still malleable generation summons the only counterforce that can again elevate great clear ends above rebellious means—the new believing humanism. "From the land of Erasmus I greet the believing humanists in all the world," Buber concluded, "—those who are already active and those who are only ripening."

The Erasmus Prize was the last high point for Buber, reports Grete Schaeder, and, for his gradually waning powers, it was an elixir whose effects continued through a cure in Sonnmatt over the rest of the summer. The pictures in the prize booklet show the great earnestness of his audience, the liveliness flaming up in conversation, the concentrated spiritual force of his lecture and, always, the shining of the dark eyes. "Taken together they are a mirror of the intensive presentness that revealed itself in such high points of experience as the expression of a deep and shy piety." This was Buber's last trip to Europe.

In 1963, Buber sent me a statement on my book *Problematic Rebel,* which expressed in new form his opposition of the "eclipse of God" to the "death of God":

> *Problematic Rebel* is... especially important because its theme is not expounded through the discussion of concepts but through representative figures of the narrative literature of two generations—that of Melville and Dostoievsky and that of Kafka and Camus. The theme is the revolt of man against an existence emptied of meaning, the existence after the so-called "death of God." This emptying of meaning is not to be overcome through the illusionary program of a free "creation of values," as we know it in Nietzsche and Sartre. One must withstand this meaninglessness, must suffer it to the end, must do battle with it undauntedly, until out of the contradiction experienced in conflict and suffering, meaning shines forth anew.

In January 1964, I received a remarkable letter from Ruth Warshaw, a Manhattan woman who had listened to the series of programs that I had conducted on Pacifica Radio Station in honor of Buber's birthday:

> I am a voluntary reader at the Guild for the Blind. I read *I and Thou* to a woman who is totally blind.... I read "with" her, at the rate of one hour a week.
>
> The spirit within the covers of the book became virtually illuminated. Her response developed to the point where deep problems and tense family relationships were brought to the surface, struggled with, and gradually brought into a state of reconciliation.... More than a year has elapsed during which period the benefits have appeared to be lasting. I witnessed a self-analysis. To quote my friend, "You became only a voice—it was just Martin Buber and myself." I also discovered that reading Buber in this way reveals the deeper layers—it is a realization of Dialogue. The ideas expressed in the book leap into a living reality.

In February 1964, Buber had to have a dangerous eye operation. The operation was successful, but an inflammation of the nerves developed afterward. By July 1964, complications had developed in the eye that had been operated on, and his doctors decided that they could not allow him to go abroad that year. In March 1964, Heinrich Ott, who had succeeded Karl Barth as professor of Systematic Theology at the University of Basel, notified Buber that he was writing a work entitled "Faith and Reality," one volume of which he wanted to dedicate to Buber's thought, and he indicated his desire to come to Jerusalem in the course of the year to talk with Buber. In September, after their meeting, Ott wrote Buber that his talk with him in Jerusalem had helped him to a clear understanding of his own problem: how we can understandably and credibly talk of God so that the reality of human existence is encountered in doing so. Just after talking with Buber, Ott read the Postscript to *I and Thou* and was strengthened in his conviction that

> we must apply your thinking and the experience out of which you think to the present situation of Christian theology. I have long held the existential interpretation of the talk of God to be a necessary path in our thought, but in the way that this path is mostly followed today I see the danger of an "ideologization" of faith, i.e., the danger that the character of faith as a personal meeting will be darkened. Out of your thinking, a priceless auxiliary may grow for Christian theology.

To this, Ott added a remarkable personal witness:

> What you said to me about your position toward Christianity remains to me unforgettable. But I must say to you that as a Christian I must agree with you, and that I have never been able to understand my Christianity otherwise than as solidarity with the whole world that is to be redeemed—never as merely private certainty of salvation. I believe that this universalist trait has existed

in Christianity from the beginning, and that today the world hour begins in which it must wholly unfold.

In July 1964, Buber expressed to Lambert Schneider how happy he was that the three volumes of the *Werke*—Philosophy, Hasidism, and the Bible—were now completed. "One can really say now that 'the corn is in the barn.'" In September, Hermann Levin-Goldschmidt asked Buber from Zurich why his monumental volume of essays *The Jew and His Jewishness* was a separate volume and not included with the works: "Your effort has been just to bring Judaism into the world, to make the world conscious of it. Now it is again stuck in the ghetto." Buber replied that he had not included *Der Jude und sein Judentum* in the *Werke* because his writings on Judaism, Zionism, and the like did not have the character of "works" in the strict sense of the term but of occasional writings. They were, indeed, "Words to the Time."

✦ 23 ✦

On the World's Edge

(1959-1965)

In April 1959, Buber wrote to Ewald Wasmuth, "Brother Body is a wonderful companion along the way for me at this time. One can never know with any certainty what he has in mind for one in the next hour, and a real continuity in work is not yet to be thought of."

Buber also wrote to the American philosopher Walter Kaufmann in 1959. not only agreeing with his critique of Paul Tillich but going beyond it: "To me 'being itself' as a predicate appears highly questionable. The verb 'being' abstracted into a noun from Parmenides through the Scholastics to Heidegger has ever more lost in substance." In March 1961, Hermann Hesse wrote Buber, expressing his delight in the autobiographical legends and fragments contained in his book *Meetings*. Buber and Hesse corresponded and even planned meetings at Hesse's home, Montagnola in Switzerland, but Buber's illness and Hesse's death brought these plans to naught. But even at the end and at a distance, these friends remained poignantly close.

A good picture of Buber's day-by-day life during his last years is given us by a letter that he wrote his friends Ewald and Sophie Wasmuth in November 1961:

> One does not feel oneself "really ill," but if one behaves as though one were well, dares perhaps to go out for an evening in order to hear Casals play, then the next day one must do penance. So one sits at one's desk and reads the latest pageproofs of the latest volume of the "Bible"—and between times one sits on the terrace and does oneself good by breathing. One has to be

sure, God be thanked, one's faith on one's right, but without humor on one's left, one cannot manage. There is thinking of all kinds, also young people come ever again with questions, among them not a few from Germany.... And in the middle of all this one feels again and again memory weave around the forehead, and the living friends with whom one has them in common, are not anywhere else than here, in this moment wholly here.

In October 1963, Paul Tillich visited Buber at his home in Talbiyeh, and they shared " a great evening of reminiscences and exchanges." When Tillich left Buber, he asked him whether he would come again to Europe or America. "He answered with a clear 'No,' and he looked at me with an expression in his eyes which said unmistakably: 'This is a final farewell.' It was." Not long after that, Buber sent me a reprint inscribed simply. *"Ave et Vale!"*

Two months before Tillich's visit, Buber reported from the Kurhaus in Sonnmatt near Lucerne, where he had gone after the Erasmus Prize ceremonies: "I am feeling rather well. Our family friend, Naemah Beer-Hofmann (younger sister of Miriam B-H), is very helpful not only in matters of health but in work too." Naemah, younger daughter of Buber's friend, the poet and playwright Richard Beer-Hofmann, was a gifted physiotherapist who was able to do much for Buber during the summers of 1962 and 1963 at the sanitarium Sonnmatt. In August 1962, she came to Israel to accompany Buber back to Lucerne. By help in his work, Buber meant in part the Introduction that he wrote to Richard Beer-Hofmann's collected works, published in Germany in 1962, in which Buber wrote: "The world stands on trust," the trust that is part of a love for God "as He is, cruel and merciful, " and of "the sun of love that warms throughout the world: the love of God for his creatures... from the grace of the election through sin to that higher grace which is granted only to those who have turned."

Through her warmth and friendship and almost childlike spirit of openness (to which many have touchingly testified), Naemah Beer-Hofmann helped to heal in part the great wound of Paula's death and the lifelong wound of Martin's mother's desertion. Naemah spoke of how happy and relaxed Buber was during those summers at Sonnmatt, and some of her pictures of him there bear striking testimony to his happy frame of mind at this time.

Yet the concern with death remained with him, too, as an ever-present theme. Naemah told of one young nun who was shocked to discover that Buber was afraid of death. "But, Professor Buber," she remonstrated, *"you* should not be afraid of death." When Buber did have fear, he himself said on another occasion, it was not psychological: It was because of physical deterioration. Even in the face of this fear, Buber still retained his trust. When Buber went to sleep at night, he often prayed, "Into thy hands I commit my spirit."

In the recollections that she recorded after being with Buber in Zurich in the summer of 1962 at his beloved Park Hotel, Naemah told how both of them were so overcome with emotion at having to separate that they could not eat and went into the garden. Buber fell to his knees and clasped Naemah around the legs. "I then take leave of my life, my breath," he said to her.

> Promise me that you will never change. Don't let other people tell you how important I am. People make me that. They suffocate me with it. I was a prisoner before you came to me. If I should reach my eighty-fifth birthday, what sort of an achievement (*Wirbel*) will that be?... You will hear again that one should venerate me. No, one must *love* me. Think only that this day belongs to you; for you I was born once, as you for me... and by you, through you I am a second time born anew.
>
> He trembled. I bade him to stand up; his knees did not seem to feel the hard gravel. He hugged me around my legs, his head on my knees. "You give me ever new strength. You are my real mother; now I no longer have a place where I can lay my head.... Everything that one says and writes is lies. Only the body of a young woman protects one from death...."
>
> Dr. Lion's words came to me when he gave me a tranquilizer before my departure from Israel: "When someone so suddenly gains new strength, when one becomes so young again as he has become since you came, then he will devour you."

Shulamit Katz-Nelson, the director of Ulpan Akiva, came to know Buber through Hugo Bergmann and went to see Buber regularly during the last ten years of his life. Shulamit testified that, in his early years, Buber helped build the image that people had of him and then found himself imprisoned in it. He needed someone who would reach out to him and meet him as a person and not just as a famous man or a fount of wisdom and knowledge.

Another person who spent some time with Buber during the last few years before his death was the American psychologist Katherine Whiteside Taylor. "Have you ever thought of life after death? she asked Buber. "Who has not? he replied. "Do you believe in life after death? she persevered. 'After' is the wrong word," he replied. "It is an entirely different dimension. Time and space are crystallizations out of God. At the last hour all will be revealed."

Buber was very clearheaded until the age of eighty-five, said Ernst Simon, after which it was difficult for him to concentrate. As Buber aged, he said, "I have only one prayer to God, that he won't take my spiritual integrity from me as I grow older." In April 1962, Buber complained to Werner Kraft about his memory: "The old things I see quite clearly, but I forget much of the new," to which Kraft replied that the same was true of him. "But you are still a young fellow!" Buber exclaimed to the sixty-six-year-old Kraft. In March 1963, Kraft noted in his journal: "The verve of this man who is becoming ever older is wonderful. He may have anxiety about death, but he is free from all melancholy. His desires are as intact as those of a young man. He lives." Kraft found in Buber an example of his own dictum that at each stage of life the person has his whole life before him. In December 1963, before Buber had his cataract operation, Schalom Ben-Chorin found him buried deep in the task of correcting proofs. "I want to bring everything into the barn before the operation," he said to Ben-Chorin, almost as if excusing himself. When Kraft went to visit Buber in January 1964, he found that he listened and spoke as always, but, for the first time, he gave Kraft the impression of being *spiritually* tired. "He lives now in a kind of timelessness," Kraft entered in his journal, "often no longer knowing what day of the week it is." Yet, a week later, Kraft wrote: "He is now almost eighty-six years old. He speaks freely. His spirit affected me this evening like that of a young man." In March 1964, Kraft reported that Buber was sick again, in bed with a high fever. "The doctors have decided to know nothing about my sickness," Buber said in the five minutes Kraft was with him. "That is already a resignation close to death," Kraft commented. But Barbara said to Kraft that he was better at times and would speak of plans to travel. "This uncanny affirmation of life up to the end is of overwhelming grandeur," Kraft added. "Although the spirit is present in Buber in the highest degree, it has nothing to do with this affirmation of life." Other times, Kraft found Buber lively or tired but fresh. Kraft once left, saying Buber was perhaps tired, and Buber responded, "I am always tired." "He is still himself, " Kraft commented, "but fading." In March 1965, Kraft found Buber sitting on the floor amid a gigantic pile of papers. "What are you doing?" Kraft asked. "Don't you know what that means: to put one's house in order? replied Buber. Isaiah said that, Kraft recalled: "Put your house in order, for you are going to die."

A person who played a major role in Buber's last years was Grete Schaeder, who spent much time with him between 1961 and 1965. Thanks to her, we have a remarkable poem that Buber wrote in February 1964, at the time that he had to have the dangerous cataract operation. This poem expresses with poignant immediacy the continued ascetic discipline and sacrifice that Buber had to make to renounce, for the love of the world, that mystic ecstasy that came to him so naturally:

A strange (loud) voice speaks:
A rope is stretched across the abyss,
Now set your foot on it
And, before your step awakens the contradiction,
Run!
A rope is tightly strung across the abyss,
Renounce on the wall all that is here!
Already there beckons to you from over there a hand:
"To me!"

The familiar (soft) voice speaks:
Follow not the demanding call!
He who created you
Intended for you: "Be ready
For every earthly time!"
Already his hand ever holds you—
Remain turned toward the world in love!

The figure of the rope stretched across the abyss was one that Buber had already used in *The Legend of the Baal-Shem* in 1908, where he wrote of that *hitlahavut* or ecstasy, that dropped out of sight almost entirely in his later interpretations of Hasidism, with the exception of *For the Sake of Heaven*. The sentence in the second stanza, "Already his hand ever holds you," is an unmistakable reference to a passage from Psalm 73:

And nevertheless I am always with you,
You have taken hold of my right hand,
You guide me with your counsel
And afterward you take me into honor.

In the second volume of Buber's collected works, the one, in fact, last completed, Buber writes of Psalm 73:

I return today once again to this psalm that I once, in accordance with Franz Rosenzweig's wishes, spoke at his graveside.

What is it that so draws me to this poem that, pieced together out of description, report, and confession, it draws me ever more strongly the older I become? I think it is this, that here a person reports how he attained to the true sense of his life experience and that this sense touches directly on the eternal.

Psalm 73 is not only Buber's "death poem," as Schaeder puts it, but also his "life poem," for it captures the trust and the remarkable intuition of the eternal that accompanied him on his way from the time of the crisis over the infinity of time and space that brought him close to suicide at the age of fourteen. It was Psalm 73 that Buber read at Franz Rosenzweig's funeral, and it was these four lines from Psalm 73 that were inscribed on Buber's tombstone at his own request. Psalm 73 thus embodies, as no other traditional literature, Buber's own deepest attitude toward death.

Happily, Buber himself left us a key to this attitude in his interpretation of Psalm 73 in his *Good and Evil*. What is remarkable about Psalm 73, Buber stated at the outset, is that a man tells how he reached the true meaning of his experience of life, and that this meaning borders directly on the eternal. We tend to turn the decisive experiences of our life to use without penetrating to their heart. It requires deeper experience to teach us to do this latter.

The speaker of the psalm, like Buber himself, "is a man of Israel in Israel's bitter hour of need, and in his personal suffering the suffering of Israel has been concentrated, so that what he now has to suffer he suffers as Israel. In the destiny of an authentic person the destiny of his people is gathered up, and only now becomes truly manifest." Insofar as the Psalmist becomes pure in heart, he experiences God's goodness, not as some reward, but as the revelation of what he cannot know from his side of the dialogue— that he is continually with God. This is not a pious feeling, Buber cautioned. "From man's side there is no continuity of presence, only from God's side." The psalmist cannot say "Thou art with me," like the speaker in Psalm 23— "Though I walk through the valley of the shadow of death / I shall fear no evil / For thou art with me." Rather he says, "I am continually with thee." But he does not know this from his own consciousness and feeling, for no human being is able to be continually turned to the presence of God. "He can say it only in the strength of the revelation that God is continually with him" and this revelation is expressed not as a word of God but as a gesture—the very one that Buber inserted into his poem on mystic ecstasy: that God has taken his right hand. Despite all his own personal experience of the prosperity of the wicked, of which the speaker of Psalm 73 complained, Buber compared this dialogue with God to the way in which in the dark a father takes his little son by the hand, only partially to lead him "but primarily in order to make present to him, in the warm touch of coursing blood, the fact that he, the father, is continually with him."

> The guiding counsel of God seems to me to be simply the divine Presence communicating itself directly to the pure in heart. He who is aware of this Presence acts in the changing situations of his life differently from him who does not perceive this Presence. The Presence acts as counsel: God counsels by making known that He is present. He has led his son out of darkness into the light, and now he can walk in the light. He is not relieved of taking and directing his own steps.

This revealing has not only changed the life and the meaning of life of the speaker. It has also changed his perspective on death, and we cannot doubt that what Buber now put forward, written in 1951 after his own experience of the Nazis and of the war in Palestine, represented Buber's own deepest attitude toward death: For the "oppressed" man death was only the mouth towards which the sluggish stream of suffering and trouble flows. But now it has become the event in which God—the continually Present One, the One who grasps the man's hand, the Good One—'takes' a man." The "honor" (kavod) into which one is afterward taken is not some glorious afterlife, but, rather, from man's point of view, the fulfillment of existence, and from God's, the entrance into God's eternity. The psalmist neither aspires to enter heaven after death nor to remain on earth, and he imagines no personal immortality, no continuation in time's dimension.

It is not merely his flesh which vanishes in death, but also his heart, that inmost personal organ of the soul, which formerly, "rose up" in rebellion against the human fate and which he then "purified" till he became pure in heart—this personal soul also vanishes. But He who was the true part and true fate of this person, the "rock" of his heart, God, is eternal. It is into His eternity that he who is pure in heart moves in death, and this eternity is something absolutely different from any kind of time.

In the end, therefore, the dynamic of farness and nearness from God is broken by death when it breaks the life of the person. With death, there vanishes the heart, that human inwardness out of which the "pictures" of the imagination arose, the heart that rises up in defiance but that can also be purified. Separation, separate souls, and time itself vanish. Only the rock in which the human heart is concealed does not vanish for it does not stand in time: "The time of the world disappears before eternity, but existing man dies into eternity as into the perfect existence."

Grete Schaeder has given us a perceptive picture of Buber in the last year of his life. Buber continued, with great energy, improving his translation of the Bible. In the winter of 1964–1965, he assembled the material for "Gleanings." Meanwhile his works on philosophical anthropology, dialogical thought, Jewish and Zionist humanism, and interpretation of the Bible were brought to the attention of the younger generation of Israel for the first time through their publication in Hebrew translation. Buber's work discipline, a fixed division of each day, was admirable. Also, a certain amount of time was reserved daily for answering correspondence, which continued to flow in from all countries, from persons known and unknown, consisting of letters, publications, demands. Buber fought tirelessly against the flood and took pains to give an answer to each one: a few words of thanks of encouragement, of personal advice. Schaeder further comments:

> But it is shattering how a man who was ever an opponent of fixed forms and a champion of spontaneous utterance at the end ever more frequently employed the same turns of speech, phrases which *sounded* as if they were unique and personal, as he got caught in the net of his own formulas. Very often he pointed out in his short letters that the problem that the other brought before him could only be clarified through conversation. Precisely his letters of old age show that the written expression was not a form of communication that was really suited to Buber, only a substitute for the conversation that was so often not possible.

In personal conversation, aside from the times when he was very weak, Buber's spontaneity was preserved until the last. "It was," says Schaeder, "the enlivening element for him," bringing powerfully to mind the statement that a friend of Rabbi Moshe of Kobryn made about the rabbi after his death: "If there had been someone to whom he could have talked, he would still be

alive." Buber had daily visitors, often several a day, from near and far, including an increasing number from Germany. As usual, Buber tolerated no small
talk and forced the persons who came to see him to carry on a real dialogue.
What he liked best was that his guests should bring him burning problems,
which enabled him to unfold the richness of his thoughts and his feelings. At
these times, even his memory and the presence of his knowledge were
remarkable. Buber particularly liked the visit of young persons, even of whole
groups who posed questions and told him of their lives. He liked persons
with an original gift for narration and communicating themselves. With them,
he forgot his age and felt himself alive. When they were shy, he encouraged
them with turns of phrase that gradually took on a somewhat formal character. They should speak to him of what kept them awake in the gray of dawn.
When his carefully weighed balance of work and relaxation, fellowship and
rest, was disturbed, as it often was by pain, he was helped over it by his
undaunted will to live and by his humor, which he called the "milk-brother of
faith." Barbara would try to limit his callers, but Buber insisted,"If they seek
me out, I must see them," Once however, Buber groaned to Hugo Bergmann
about his many visitors and asked, "Am I then a sight worth seeing?"

The last letter that I received from Buber was dated April 14, 1965. "It is
with a feeling of true sympathy I learned from your letter about the death of
your father," he wrote. "I know well by my own experience what it means to
lose a loving father. It is now just forty years since I lost mine. He was then
as old as I am now."

In 1965, two months before Buber's death, a young friend of mine
went to Israel and talked with him. Upon his return, he expressed disappointment in his talk with Buber but did not say why. The following year, I
learned the reason when I was in Jerusalem, from the assistant to Buber's
photographer, Alfred Bernheim. She told me of the young American who
had come to Israel just to see Buber and who had become part of their
German-Jewish group because of his excellent command of German and his
understanding of German poetry. "What will you ask Buber when you go to
see him," she had asked my young friend. "I don't need to think about that,"
he replied. "You are mistaken," she said. "You ought to have a question in
mind." Not heeding her words, the young man went to see Buber. Buber
received him at the door of his study, took his hand, looked deeply into his
eyes, and asked him to sit down. "I wrote a master's thesis on Whitman and
you." The young scholar said. "Oh," said Buber, "I didn't know that." Then
they sat in total silence for eight minutes, until the young visitor could bear it
no longer, seized Buber's hand, and departed.

At first glance, this incident seems like a repetition of that earlier mismeeting in which Buber failed to be present for Herr Mehé during the First
World War because he failed to guess the questions that the other did not
ask—the only difference being that that was two months before Mehé's

death, this two months before Buber's own. But the similarity is merely superficial, masking a deeper contrast. My friend's life question was a *real* one, but he left it to Buber to carry on both sides of the dialogue, assuming that Buber would understand the question without his having to ask it. The young man in "The Conversation," in contrast, did not look to Buber as the magic helper who would reach into his soul and extract his question. He did not simply *have* a question: He concentrated his whole being into *becoming* a question. It was the address of this unuttered question that Buber might have heard behind every spoken question that Herr Mehé *did* ask, if Buber had been "present in spirit—if he had brought himself into the dialogue with the whole of his being, rather than with the intellectual and social fragments left over from his preoccupation with that morning's mystical experience. What Buber learned from this earlier mismeeting is exactly what he brought to the later one: to be wholly present but also *not* to take over for the other, not to handle *both* sides of the dialogue. In his old age, Buber was no longer "an oracle who would listen to reason." but he was a person who confirmed the other by contending with him or her, as well as by accepting and affirming.

Schaeder does not agree with Kraft's judgment that Buber did not experience that lowering of spirits that comes to most persons when age and illness attack them.

> Behind his well-guarded façade melancholy often hid, but not his mouth, only the darkness of his eyes, expressed it. Persons came and went; there was always leavetaking and often the death of those younger than he; but weariness remained and increased, which was in itself a little death. With it there overtook him a... reality no longer heightened by the intensity of the life-stream.

One of the very few poems that Buber selected to be preserved in his "Gleanings " is "The Fiddler," which Buber wrote in October 1964 and dedicated to Grete Schaeder, indicating, as nothing else could, how much her relationship to him meant in these last months of his life. It expresses with great poignancy what it meant to Buber to live "on the world's edge" during this final stage:

> Here on the world's edge at this hour I have
> Wondrously settled my life
> Behind me in a boundless circle
> The All is silent, only that fiddler fiddles.
> Dark one, already I stand in covenant with you,
> Ready to learn from your tones
> Wherein I became guilty without knowing it.
> Let me feel, let there be revealed

To this hale soul each wound
That I have incorrigibly inflicted and remained in illusion.
Do not stop, holy player, before then!

What is so deeply moving about "The Fiddler" is that Buber prayed before death to be given to know and to face his guilt.

Buber sent a copy of this poem to his friend Naemah Beer-Hoffman, who replied with concern about what she took to be a morbid or melancholy mood. Buber's rejoinder to Naemah on November 15, 1964, made it clear that this poem was more than an expression of feeling, such as was perhaps the case with his poem on "Melancholy" written shortly before:

> I answer you immediately, and I do so without any holding back: in face of a being to whom one is open in body and soul one must also be wholly true, otherwise life would be senseless:
>
> The poem that I sent you was not the expression of a passing mood or one that might be overcome. Certainly I love life after it as before and hope that I may still be permitted to live on for a while, perhaps even for a long while. But the hour has come for me—that I have experienced unmistakably—which bids, "Set your house in order!" I must set my house in order from my side, and that is a command that will tolerate no postponement. Love cannot overcome it—but it also may not want to overcome it—for even the most heartfelt love between person and person may not place itself between a person and God.
>
> It is probably the first time, Naemah, that I speak to you of these matters. This one time I must do so; for without absolute candour love also would become meaningless, meaningless and unreal.
>
> I would like to end this letter with a blessing—and know no better one than just this one of daring to be true, being able to be true. For, believe me, the crown of life is not being happy but being true.

This letter shows that there was a depth of relationship that Buber shared with Grete Schaeder that he had not shared with Naemah, even though they had been intimate and loved each other deeply.

On the evening of April 26, 1965, Buber broke his right leg in a fall and had to be operated on that same night. The break and the wound from the operation healed satisfactorily, and Buber insisted on coming home, because he did not want to die in the Hadassah hospital. In the next weeks, Buber's chronic nephritis grew steadily worse, producing uremic poisoning.

As Buber lay dying a shameful battle was being fought out in the Jerusalem City Hall. The mayor of Jerusalem, Mordecai Ish-Shalom (Hebrew for Friedman), fought to have Buber awarded the "Freedom of the City," an honor that had been given to Chaim Weizmann, President Itzhak Ben-Zvi, and Shmuel Joseph Agnon, among others. Ish-Shalom was supported in the council by the other members of Mapai and by the Mapai and Liberal representatives, but he was opposed by the rightist Herut, who could not forgive Buber for opposing the execution of Eichmann, and by the Orthodox, who bitterly resented Buber's interpretation of Judaism in general and of Hasidism in particular. According to Albrecht Goes, in the face of this stalemate, someone came to Buber, to ask whether he would accept the Freedom of the City in case they mustered a majority in favor of granting it to him. Buber replied "I do not know yet, but first let them fight it out." The most beautiful thing about this story is not that the majority finally came around, comments Goes, but Buber's composure, humor, and wisdom in those all too human circumstances. Finally, the resolution was adopted ten to six, with two abstentions and two absences.

Thus, Martin Buber, the most famous inhabitant of Jerusalem in the world, became the fifteenth Freeman of the City! Mayor Ish-Shalom and Agnon, himself an Honorary Citizen of Jerusalem, rushed to Buber's bedside. Buber listened intently for a few minutes, but could no longer reply. Adding to the irony, no one on the Jerusalem Council had read one of Buber's books, according to Shereshevsky. Two days before Buber's death, Shulamit Katz-Nelson told Hugo Bergmann that she wanted to see Buber. "If you go, I will come too," said Bergmann. When they arrived, they found that Buber had shrunk to the size of a child. Bergmann could not bear to come near, but Shulamit took Buber's hand. "You are coming straight from life," said Buber, looking directly at Bergmann. "I have been for so long so far from life. Tell me something about life." Shulamit thought to herself, What would I want to hear if I were dying? That people still loved and cared for me. So she told Buber that, in the latest *Pendle Hill Bulletin*, there was an announcement of a course on *I and Thou* to be given by Dan Wilson, the director. "That is not life," said Buber. Then she told him that the Israeli news magazine *Davar* had announced that still another of his books would be translated into Hebrew. "That is still not life," Buber complained. Finally, she said, "My husband passed the Israel bar exam." "Shulamit, *that* is life!" said Buber. This was the nearest that Buber came to dying "With a human hand in my own," as he wrote in "Books and Men". Shortly before the end, Buber said to Ernst Simon, "I am not afraid of death but of dying."

On June 13, 1965, Martin Buber died, At his bedside were Eva, Rafael, Barbara and Zeev Goldschmidt, and all his great-grandchildren. After Buber died, the first person to come to the house in Talbiyeh was Zalman Shazar, the president of Israel. Ben-Gurion insisted on accompanying the body to the Hadassah hospital. That evening over Kol Yisrael, Israel's national radio station, Ben-Gurion spoke of Buber's death as " a great loss to Israel's spiritual life," and of Buber himself as "a metaphysical entity in his own class, a true man of the spirit." Buber was given a traditional Jewish funeral, without a coffin, and Rabbi Aharon Phillip of Simon's Emet Ve-emuna congregation performed the funeral service. He was buried in the "Hill of Rest" at the place reserved for professors from the Hebrew University. At ten o'clock on the morning of June 14, Buber's body was brought from the Hadassah hospital covered by a *talit*—a black and white prayer shawl—and carried by President Eliahu Elath of the Hebrew University, Nathan Rotenstreich, the rector, Ernst Simon, Benyamin Mazar, Alexander Dushkin, and Zwi Werblovsky. Together with Agnon and a representative of the students, they formed a guard of honor, which was changed every fifteen minutes until noon. Classes were canceled from twelve to two in Buber's honor, but from ten in the morning, hundreds of students lined up to file slowly past Buber's body, along with friends, kibbutznikim, Christian monks, Arab Moslems and Christians, representatives of foreign embassies, and hundreds of others. Levi Eshkol, prime minister of Israel, began the eulogies:

> The passing of Mordecai Martin Buber marks the end of an era in the annals of the spiritual and territorial resurgence of the Jewish people in modern times. The Jewish people today mourn a luminary and a teacher, a man of thought and achievement, who revealed the soul of Judaism with a new philosophic daring. All mankind mourns with us one of the spiritual giants of this century. I do not know whether there is anyone else in our midst in the sphere of spiritual life, who was so much a part of the heritage of the entire world; but he was deeply anchored—to a depth that few could reach—in his Jewishness, in the Jewish people, in the resurgence of Israel and the love of Jewry.

Overcome with emotion, Hugo Bergmann cried out the words of Elisha when he saw Elijah taken up to heaven in a whirlwind: "My father, my father, Israel's chariot and its horsemen!" Bergmann finished his speech, Hodes tells us, "with a cry from the heart, an outpouring of personal grief and loss which moved all of us": "You have done your share. We shall try to follow in your footsteps.... We thank you, dear Martin Buber." Rafael Buber recited the Kaddish—the traditional prayer for the dead—and the body was carried to the hearse by President Shazar, Prime Minister Eshkol, Agnon, President Elath of the Hebrew University, the Speaker of the Knesset, Yigal Allon, Scholem, and Simon, among others. At the graveside, Gershom Scholem spoke of Buber as a man of true dialogue, of advice and action, and of hope and optimism, a great speaker and listener, and a teacher who wanted his pupils to be rebels who would follow their own paths (like Scholem himself). Ernst Simon spoke of Buber as an envoy and emissary to the Gentile world who had never been summoned by his people, a man who was alone when he fought, with even smaller support in times of peace than in times of crisis and disaster. Avraham Shapira spoke some words for the members of the kibbutz movement; the Independent Liberals and Mapam laid wreaths on Buber's grave; and three Arab students, representing all the

Arabs at the Hebrew University, placed a wreath of roses, carnations, and gladioli on the freshly turned earth.

The Israeli Knesset had a memorial session for Buber while eulogies and messages of condolence poured in from all over the world—from the West German president and the chancellor, from former chancellor Konrad Adenauer, from Giorgio La Pira, the former mayor of Florence, from the mayor of Vienna, from American Secretary of State Dean Rusk and the permanent U.S. Ambassador to the United Nations Adlai Stevenson. Senator Abraham Ribicoff of Connecticut and Senator Jacob Javits of New York entered statements in the *Congressional Record,* along with the long obituary from The *New York Times.*

Abraham Joshua Heschel, in Jerusalem but unable to get in to see Buber before his death, told the local *Newsweek* reporter:

> I know of no one with a life as rich with intellectual adventures or who so strongly responded to their challenges as Martin Buber. His greatest contribution was himself, his very being. There was magic in his personality, richness in his soul. His sheer presence was joy.... He loved to listen and to talk, and our conversations sometimes lasted twelve to thirteen hours. "I am not a Jewish philosopher," he once told me. "I am a universal philosopher." Buber spoke to Jews in a way that all men found relevant. There were no apologetics, no parochialism.... He exposed the challenges of modern society, and at the same time insisted upon loyalty to Jewish insight.

The "national universalism" that Buber saw in the prophets he, too, espoused. As he himself said, he did not need to leave his ancestral house of Judaism in order to speak to those outside it. The word that Martin Buber uttered standing in the doorway of that house and speaking into the street of mankind has not gone astray. It has spoken into the street of mankind has not gone astray. It has spoken into the very life of our time, and it will continue to speak to that of the generations to come. Even more important is the image of authentic human existence that Buber has left us—that of a person whose very life was an "encounter on the narrow ridge."

Martin Buber withstood the thousandfold questioning glance of countless persons and measured hourly the depths of responsibility with the sounding lead of his presence, his decision, his words. He gave to the problematic person for whom life had become baseless "the certitude that 'there *is* a soil, there is an existence.... The world *can* be redeemed. *I* can be redeemed because there is this trust.'" "Trust, trust in the world, because this human exists"—that was Martin Buber's most precious gift to the persons of our age and the ages to come. Martin Buber was our comrade. He lived with us, won our trust through real-life relationship, and helped us to walk with him the way of the creature who *accepts* the creation. The innermost core of

Buber's teaching and of his existence was the combination of this existential trust with the mystery of suffering—of our suffering for the sake of redemption and of God's suffering with us. "Man penetrates step by step into the dark which hangs over the meaning of events, until the mystery is disclosed in the flash of light: the *zaddik*, the man justified by God, suffers for the sake of God and of His work of redemption, and God is with him in his suffering."

No one has joined trust and contending in his life and thought more clearly than Martin Buber—in his spiritual leadership of the German Jews under Hitler, in his lonely stance in relation to postwar Germany and Eichmann, in his lifelong fight for Jewish-Arab rapprochement and understanding, in his insistence that the State of Israel and the reality of Zion not be separated, in his opposition to the cold war and his call for genuine dialogue as a way to peace, in his fight for the becoming of one humanity. In an era of the "eclipse of God" Buber withstood and contended with meaninglessness, sustaining in the darkness the living substance of faith. In a time when we are in danger of losing our birthright as human beings, Martin Buber has given us again an image of the human. In a time when human thought preserves the *idea* of God but destroys the reality of our relationship to him, Buber has pointed us anew to the meeting with the "eternal Thou."

Sources

CODES:

EARLY YEARS = Maurice Friedman, *Martin Buber's Life and Work: The Early Years—1878–1923* (New York: E. P. Dutton, 1982; Detroit: Wayne State University Press, 1988, paperback).
MIDDLE YEARS = Maurice Friedman, *Martin Buber's Life and Work: The Middle Years—1923–1945* (New York: E.P. Dutton, 1983; Detroit: Wayne State University Press, 1988, paperback).
LATER YEARS = Maurice Friedman, *Martin Buber's Life and Work: The Later Years—1945–1965* (New York: E.P. Dutton, 1984; Detroit: Wayne State University Press, 1988, paperback).
MBA = In Martin Buber Archives, Jewish National and University Library, the Hebrew University, Jerusalem, Israel.

PREFACE

Maurice Friedman, *Martin Buber: The Life of Dialogue,* 3rd rev. ed. with new Preface and enlarged Bibliography (Chicago: The University of Chicago Press Phoenix Books (paperback), 1976), p. 3.
Martin Buber, *Die Legende des Baalschem* (Frankfurt a.M.: Ruetten & Loening, 1908). "The New Year's Sermon" was not included by Buber in the English translation that I made of *The Legend of the Baal-Shem in 1954.*

CHAPTER 1: CHILDHOOD AND YOUTH

EARLY YEARS, Sources for Chapters 1 and 2, pp. 375–77.
Haim Gordon, *The Other Martin Buber: Recollections of His Contemporaries* (Athens, Ohio: Ohio University Press), pp. 34, 40.

CHAPTER 2: ZIONISM

EARLY YEARS, Sources for Chapters 3 and 4, pp. 377–80.

Gordon, *The Other Martin Buber,* pp. 14, 21–23.
Letter from Martin Buber to Paula Winkler, August 16, 1899, MBA.

CHAPTER 3: MYSTICISM: THE DISCOVERY OF HASIDISM

EARLY YEARS, Sources for Chapters 5 and 6, pp. 383–86.

CHAPTER 4: PRE-WAR TEACHINGS OF "REALIZATION"

EARLY YEARS, Sources for Chapters 7 and 8, pp. 388–92.
Letter from Martin Buber to Sigmund Kaznelson, December 5, 1925, MBA.

CHAPTER 5: THE FIRST WORLD WAR AND
THE BREAKTHROUGH TO DIALOGUE

EARLY YEARS, Sources for Chapters 9 and 10, pp. 393–403.
Gordon, *The Other Martin Buber,* pp. 14, 18 f., 24, 31f., 42–44, 46–49, 130f.
General letter from Martin Buber, Nathan Birnbaum (Mathias Acher), Oskar Cohn, Josef Bloch, Kurt Blumenfeld, Julius Kaliski, Davis Trietsch for the Executive of the Jewish National Committee, Zehlendorf, Berlin, October 1914, MBA.
Letter from Martin Buber to Ludwig Strauss, August 14, 1917, MBA.
Letter from Martin and Paula Buber to Ernst Elijahu Rappeport, April 2, 1918, MBA.
Letter from Martin Buber to Ernst Elijahu Rappeport, April 20, 1918, MBA.
Letter from Martin to Paula Buber, October 10, 1918, MBA.
Ludwig Strauss, "Besuch in H. (Fuer Martin und Paula Buber)" (poem cycle) in Ludwig Strauss, *Der Flut, Das Jahr, Die Weg: Gedichte (1916–1919),* Berlin, 1921, pp. 61–69.

CHAPTER 6: COMMUNAL SOCIALISM AND REVOLUTION:
THE MURDER OF LANDAUER

EARLY YEARS, Sources for Chapter 11, pp. 403–05.

Eugene Lunn, *Prophet of Community: The Romantic Socialism of Gustav Landauer* (Berkeley: The University of California Press, 1973), pp. 9, 192f.

Martin Buber to Gustav Landauer, June 26, 1906, MBA.
Martin Buber to Gustav Landauer, January, 1911, MBA.

CHAPTER 7: POSTWAR ZIONISM, EDUCATION, AND POLITICS

EARLY YEARS, Sources for Chapter 12 and 13, pp. 405–08.
Martin Buber to Sigmund Kaznelson, May 13, 1922, MBA.
Martin Buber to Leo Hermann, July 21, 1922, MBA.

CHAPTER 8: ASCENT TO "I AND THOU"

EARLY YEARS, Sources for Chapters 15–20, pp. 412–33.

CHAPTER 9: FRANZ ROSENZWEIG AND THE BUBER-ROSENZWEIG BIBLE

EARLY YEARS, Sources for Chapter 14, pp. 410f.
MIDDLE YEARS, Sources for Chapters 2–5, pp. 331–50.
Gordon, *The Other Martin Buber,* pp. 7, 12–14, 22f., 49, 94f.

CHAPTER 10. THE WEIMAR REPUBLIC

MIDDLE YEARS, Sources for Chapter 1, 6–8, pp. 329–31, 350–59.
Statement by Martin Buber about *Die Kreatur,* Hans Trüb section of correspondence, MBA.

Martin Buber to Hans Trüb, September 19, 1925, MBA.
Poem from Martin Buber to Hermann Hesse, 1927 or 1928, MBA.
Martin Buber to Arthur Ruppin, November 2, 1933, MBA.
Shmuel Hugo, Bergman (sic), *Tagebuecher & Briefe,* Vol. I, *1901–1948,* ed. by Miriam Sambursky with an Introduction by Nathan Rotenstreich (Koenigstein: Juedischer Verlag bei Athenaeum, 1985), letter to Robert Weltsch, January 10, 1929, p. 280.
Shmuel Hugo Bergman (sic), *Tagebuecher & Briefe,* Vol. II, *1948–1975,* ed. by Miriam Sambursky with an Introduction by Nathan Rotenstreich (Koenigstein: Juedischer Verlag bei Athenaeum, 1985), diary, March 11, 1961, p. 363.
Gordon, *The Other Martin Buber,* pp. 3–5, 7–9, 11–14, 16–18, 27, 32, 43, 56, 97f., 102f.

CHAPTER 11: NAZI GERMANY

MIDDLE YEARS, Sources for Chapters 9–12, pp. 359–66.
Martin Buber to Hermann Gerson, March 30, 1933, MBA.
Martin Buber to Leo Beack (undated), MBA.
Martin Buber to Leo Baeck, February 23, 1934, MBA.
Martin Buber, "Hinweis—Antwort an Rundfrage," July 31, 1935, MBA.
Erich Weniger, "Ernst Kantorowics," *Die Sammlung* (Goettingen), Vol. 2, No. 12, 1947, pp. 719–22, MBA.
Gordon, *The Other Martin Buber,* pp. 3, 8, 109,115, 142, 149, 151–55.
Bergman (sic), *Tagebuecher & Briefe,* I, diary, January 20, 1934, p. 350.

CHAPTER 12: ASCENT TO THE LAND: PREWAR PALESTINE

MIDDLE YEARS, Sources for Chapters 13–15, pp. 366–71.
Gordon, *The Other Martin Buber,* pp. 13, 23, 29, 34, 36, 52–56, 101, 103.
Martin Buber to Ludwig Strauss, September 18, 1934, MBA.
Martin Buber to Ludwig Strauss, December 9, 1935, MBA.
Ludwig Strauss to Martin and Paula Buber, January 24, 1936, MBA.
Ludwig Strauss to Martin Buber, March 1, 1936, MBA.
Martin Buber to Ludwig Strauss, March 9, 1936, MBA.
Ludwig Strauss to Martin Buber, April 1, 1936, MBA.
Ludwig Strauss to Martin and Paula Buber, May 10, 1936.
Paul R. Mendes-Flohr, "The Appeal of the Incorrigible Idealist," Chapter 10 of William M. Brinner and Moses Rischin, eds., *Like All the Nations? The Life and Legacy of Judah L. Magnes* (Albany: State University of New York Press, 1987), pp. 142, 147–50.

CHAPTER 13: THE SECOND WORLD WAR

MIDDLE YEARS, Sources for Chapter 16, pp. 371–73.
Martin Buber to Eduard Strauss, February 7, 1940 and November 26, 1941, MBA.
Martin Buber to Walter Goldstein, March 28, 1943, MBA.
Ludwig Strauss to Martin Buber, October 27, 1939, MBA.
Gordon, *The Other Martin Buber* pp. 3f., 6, 8, 10, 23f., 45, 52–59, 88–90, 105, 115–18, 129f., 142–44, 159, 163, 172f.

CHAPTER 14: JEWISH-ARAB RAPPROCHEMENT AND CONFLICT

LATER YEARS, Sources for Chapter 1, pp. 451–53.
A Land of Two Peoples: Martin Buber on Jews and Arabs, ed. with commentary by Paul R. Mendes-Flohr (New York: Oxford University Press, 1983), pp. 188, 190f., 194f., 224–27, 234f., 238.
Plea for Jewish-Arab Cooperation, August 3, 1945, MBA.
Letter from Ichud Association signed by M. Buber, D.W. Senator, M. Smilansky to the High Commissioner, Government of Palestine, August 12, 1946, MBA.
Martin Buber to Ernst Simon, August 13 and September 18, 1948, MBA.
Gordon, *The Other Martin Buber,* pp. 35f., 55, 58, 168f.

CHAPTER 15: BIBLICAL JUDAISM, HASIDISM, AND ADULT EDUCATION

LATER YEARS, Sources for Chapter 2, pp. 453–55.
Martin Buber to Nahum Goldstein, March 3, 1959, MBA.
Gordon, *The Other Martin Buber,* pp. 174f.
Bergman *(sic), Tagebuecher & Briefe,* II, diary, December 12, 1954, p. 184; diary, March 22, 1960, p. 330 and p. 354, n. 9.

CHAPTER 16: DIALOGUE WITH GERMAN CHRISTIANS

LATER YEARS, Sources for Chapters 4–5, pp. 457–65.
Letter from Hermann Hesse to Stadtpfarrer, Summer 1948, MBA.
Martin Buber to Hermann Hesse, November 15, 1948, MBA.
Martin Buber to Eugen Rosenstock-Huessy, March 9, 1961, MBA.
Martin Buber on Ewald Wasmuth (undated), MBA.
Gordon, *The Other Martin Buber,* pp. 5f.

CHAPTER 17: DIALOGUE WITH AMERICANS

LATER YEARS, Sources for Chapters 6, 8, pp. 465–70.

Gordon, *The Other Martin Buber,* pp. 113f.
Bergman *(sic), Tagebuecher & Briefe,* diary, April 11, 1940, p. 520.

CHAPTER 18: ENCOUNTER WITH PSYCHOTHERAPY AND PAULA'S DEATH

LATER YEARS, Sources for Chapters 7, 9–10, pp. 468f., 471–73.
Emma Jung to Martin Buber, December 25, 1925, MBA.
Martin Buber to Hans Trüb, August 14, 1947, MBA.
Martin Buber, *I and Thou,* 2nd rev. ed. with Postscript by Author Added, trans. by Ronald Gregor Smith (New York: Chas. Scribner's, 1958), Postscript, pp. 131–34.

CHAPTER 19: REPLIES TO CRITICS: BUBER VERSUS SCHOLEM

LATER YEARS, Sources for Chapters 11-12, pp. 474-77.
Gordon, *The Other Martin Buber,* pp. 128f.

CHAPTER 20: BUBER AND DAG HAMMARSKJÖLD: THE COVENANT OF PEACE

LATER YEARS, Sources for Chapter 13, pp. 478–81.
Gordon, *The Other Martin Buber,* pp. 86f.
Martin Buber & Bertrand Russell, Appeal to President of the United States in behalf of Morton Sobell (undated) MBA.
Martin Buber to President of Rumania (in French), March 1, 1960, MBA.
Martin Buber to Bertrand Russell, June 20, 1960, MBA.
Bertrand Russel to Martin Buber, March 21, 1962, MBA.
Martin Buber to Bertrand Russell, March 23, 1962, MBA.
Eleanor Roosevelt to Martin Buber, March 23, 1962, MBA.

CHAPTER 21: BUBER VERSUS BEN-GURION

LATER YEARS, Sources for Chapter 14, pp. 482–92.
Michael Keren, *Ben-Gurion and the Intellectuals: Power, Knowledge, and Charisma* (DeKalb, Illinois: Northern Illinois University Press, 1983), pp. 75–80, 96–99, 175, 184, note 45, 185, notes 51–53.
Buber, *A Land of Two Peoples,* pp. 262f., 296f.
Gordon, *The Other Martin Buber,* p. 82.

CHAPTER 22: SURFEITED WITH HONORS

LATER YEARS, Sources for Chapter 15, pp. 495–99.

Mrs. Siegfried Kramarsky, National President and Mrs. Dorothy Gordon, Chairman, Henrietta Szold Centennial Awards Committee to Martin Buber, October 17 and November 17, 1960, MBA.

Bergman *(sic)*, *Tagebuecher & Briefe,* II, diary June 28, 1963, p. 436.

Ruth Warshaw to Maurice Friedman, January 3, 1964, MBA.

CHAPTER 23: ON THE WORLD'S EDGE

LATER YEARS, Sources for Chapter 16, pp. 502–05.

Martin Buber to Walter Kaufmann, January 6, 1959, MBA.

Martin Buber to Ewald Wasmuth, April 27, 1959, MBA.

Martin Buber to Hermann Hesse, end of March 1961, MBA.

Hermann Hesse to Martin Buber, July 30, 1962, MBA.

Recollections by Naemah Beer-Hoffman (summer 1962?) in Richard Beer-Hoffman Archives, Houghton Library, Harvard University, Cambridge, Massachusetts.

Martin Buber to Naemah Beer-Hoffman, November 16, 1964, in Richard Beer-Hoffmann Archives, Houghton Library, Harvard University.

Gordon, *The Other Martin Buber,* p. 133.

Bergman *(sic)*, *Tagebuecher & Briefe,* II, letter to Chawa (Eva) Bergman, May 6, 1973, p. 692.

Annotated Bibliography

BUBER'S MOST IMPORTANT WORKS IN ENGLISH

A Believing Humanism: My Testament, **trans. with an Introduction and Explanatory Comments by Maurice Friedman. Atlantic Highlands, New Jersey Humanities Press International, 1990.**

This book includes Buber's own selections made just before he died, of some of the poems and short writings on literature, philosophy, psychology, religion, and social problems that he wished to preserve.

Between Man and Man, **trans. by Ronald Gregor Smith with an Introduction by Maurice Friedman. New York: Macmillan, 1985.**

This is a book of essays on "Dialogue," "Education," "Education of Character," "The Question to the Single One" (on Kierkegaard), and "What Is Man?"—the last a book in itself on philosophical anthropology that lays the groundwork for Buber's mature anthropology *The Knowledge of Man*—and an important Afterword on "The History of the Dialogical Principle." It represents the next stage after *I and Thou* in the development of the philosophy of dialogue. Many will find the opening essay "Dialogue" the best introduction to Buber's philosophy.

Daniel: Dialogues on Realization, **trans. with an Introductory Essay by Maurice Friedman. New York: Holt, Rinehart, & Winston, 1964.**

This early book (1913) is out of print but is of importance to anyone interested in the development of Buber's thought, his early existentialism, his teaching of holy insecurity and realization, and his approach to drama and poetry. The dialogues are set in the mountains, above the city, in the garden, after the theater, and by the sea and deal with direction, reality, meaning, polarity, and unity.

Eclipse of God: Studies in the Relation between Religion and Philosophy, **trans. by Maurice Friedman and others, with an Introduction by Robert Seltzer. Atlantic Highlands, New Jersey: International Humanities Press, 1988.**

Eclipse of God is mostly made up of Buber's American lectures in the early 1950s. It is an important statement of philosophy of religion and contains an important critique of the various ways in which such contemporary thinkers as Heidegger, Sartre, Jung, and Bergson have contributed to the eclipse of God by their denial of the reality of transcendence.

For the Sake of Heaven: A Hasidic Chronicle-Novel, trans. by Ludwig Lewisohn. New York: Atheneum (Macmillan), 1969.

Buber considered this novel, built around the conflict of actual Hasidic rebbes, or *zaddikim,* in some ways his most important work. It combined the freedom of his early retelling of Hasidic legends with the faithfulness of his later Hasidic tales. It constitutes a powerful statement of *devotio* versus *gnosis* and a powerful response to the pseudo-messianic movements Buber encountered during the Second World War.

Good and Evil: Two Interpretations. New York: Scribner's (Macmillan), 1980.

Good and Evil consists of two little books originally published separately: *Images of Good and Evil* — an anthropological study of the two stages of evil based upon biblical and Zoroastrian myths — and *Right and Wrong* — an existential interpretation of six psalms. It is of great importance for the understanding of Buber's philosophy of dialogue and his philosophical anthropology.

Hasidism and Modern Man, ed. and trans. with an Introduction by Maurice Friedman. Atlantic Highlands, New Jersey: Humanities Press International, 1988.

This is the first of two volumes of Buber's interpretations of Hasidic life and teachings. This volume includes the classic little book *The Way of Man* and "The Life of the Hasidim," the famous and beautiful opening of Buber's early *Legend of the Baal-Shem,* as well as "The Baal-Shem-Tov's Instruction in Intercourse with God."

I and Thou, 2nd rev. ed. with Postscript by Author Added, trans. by Ronald Gregor Smith. New York: Chas. Scribner's, 1958.

I and Thou is Buber's classic work, to which everything written before moves and from which everything written after stems. Ronald Gregor Smith's translation is the best translation, much to be preferred to that by Walter Kaufmann, which is also published by Scribner's. Kaufmann changes I-Thou to I-You, "all real living is meeting" to "all actual life is encounter," and "the turning" to "the return."

Israel and the World: Essays in a Time of Crisis. New York: Schocken Books, 1963.

This is an important collection of essays, which for many will be the best introduction to Buber's approach to Judaism. It contains sections on Jewish religiosity, biblical life, learning and education, Israel and the world, and nationalism and Zion.

The Kingship of God, trans. by Richard Scheimann. Atlantic Highlands, New Jersey: Humanities Press International, 1990.

This book is the foundation stone for a series of biblical studies on the origins of messianism in biblical Judaism. It sets forth the true meaning of the covenant as making real the kingship of God in every aspect of communal life.

The Knowledge of Man: A Philosophy of the Interhuman, ed. with an Introductory Essay (Chap 1) by Maurice Friedman, trans. by Maurice Friedman and Ronald Gregor Smith. Atlantic Highlands, New Jersey: Humanities Press International, 1988.

This is the mature expression of Buber's philosophical anthropology and as such his most important philosophical statement after *I and Thou.* It explores the distancing and relating that underly the I-Thou and I-It relations and applies this to understanding the interhuman, the common world that we build together through speech-with-meaning, guilt and guilt feelings, the anthropology of art, and "the word that is spoken."

A Land of Two Peoples: Martin Buber on Jews and Arabs, ed. with Commentary by Paul R. Mendes-Flohr. New York: Oxford University Press, 1983.

From 1916 until his death in 1965, Buber was consistently and actively concerned with the relations between Jews and Arabs in Palestine and later Israel and in the Middle East. This book is the best single source in English documenting Buber's writings and setting them in the context of the events of the time.

The Legend of the Baal-Shem, trans. by Maurice Friedman. New York: Schocken Books, 1969.

This is the second of Buber's early books on Hasidism. Freer than the later tales, it remains a classic recounting of a legend which Buber has made his own. Of all his books, this is the one that sold the most in Germany, Buber told me. It established him as a German writer of the first rank and influenced such poets as Rainer Maria Rilke.

The Letters of Martin Buber, Edited by Nahum N. Galatzer. New York: Schocken Books, 1991 (forthcoming).

Meetings, ed. and trans. with an Introduction and Bibliography by Maurice Friedman. LaSalle, Illinois: 1967.

These are the "Autobiographical Fragments" that Buber wrote or collected for *The Philosophy of Martin Buber* (see at end).

Moses: The Revelation and the Covenant. Atlantic Highlands, New Jersey: Humanities Press International, 1988.

Moses can be regarded as the second of the volumes in Buber's study of the origin of messianism. It is also an important study in itself and, not incidentally, an answer to Freud's *Moses and Monotheism*. There is no natural and supernatural here, but the power of God speaking through the "wonder on the sea."

On the Bible, ed. by N. N. Glazter with an Introduction by Harold Bloom. New York: Schocken Books, 1982.

An important collection of eighteen essays of Buber's on the interpretation of the Bible that supplements his books on the subject.

On Judaism, ed. by N. N. Glatzer. New York: Schocken Books, 1972.

On Judaism contains Buber's early "Speeches on Judaism" through which he had an enormous impact on the Jewish youth of Germany and central Europe from 1909 to 1919, influencing many of them to emigrate to Palestine through a combination of an existential-personal approach to Judaism and Zionism. Also published here are the four lectures Buber gave on Judaism in 1951–1952, when he first visited America, the latter originally published as *At the Turning*.

On Zion. New York: Schocken Books, 1986.

On Zion was originally published under the title *Israel and Palestine: The History of an Idea*. More than a collection of essays, it is a history of some of the most important figures in the development of Zionism from the biblical seeds to Yehuda Halevi, Nachman of Bratzlav, Moses Hess, A.D. Gordon and Rav Kook.

The Origin and Meaning of Hasidism, ed. and trans. with an Introduction by Maurice Friedman. Atlantic Highlands, New Jersey: Humanities Press International, 1988.

This is the second of two volumes on Buber's interpretation of Hasidism, *Hasidism and Modern Man* being the first. These are more scholarly essays that draw on Gershom Scholem's interpretation of the Kabbalah but also contrast Hasidism with the Kabbalah *(devotio* versus *gnosis)* in a way that Scholem could not accept (See chapter 19 in *Encounter on the Narrow Ridge* on "Replies to Critics, Buber versus Scholem").

Paths in Utopia, trans. by R.F.C. Hull. New York: Macmillan, 1988.

Paths in Utopia is Buber's single most important contribution to the history of socialism and to social philosophy. Rejecting Marx's dismissal of "utopian socialists," Buber distinguishes between those that were merely theoretical and those that were topical. An important and careful study in its own right, the book has chapters on Proudhon, Marx, Lenin, Gustav Landauer, and Kropotkin among others and ends with a chapter on the Israeli kibbutzim—"an experiment that did not fail."

Pointing the Way: Collected Essays, ed. and trans. with an Introduction by Maurice Friedman. Atlantic Highlands, New Jersey: Humanites Press International, 1990.

The first, most poetic part of *Pointing the Way* is made up of essays from Buber's beautiful little book *Events and Meetings* (1918), plus "The Teaching of the Tao." Striking in themselves, these essays are also important in understanding the transition of Buber's thought from his early mysticism to his later philosophy of dialogue. The second part contains two of Buber's essays on the theater, plus essays on Goethe, Bergson, Rosenzweig, therapy, and education. The third and largest part is an important statement entitled "Politics, Community, and Peace," which forms, together with *Paths in Utopia,* Buber's most important contribution to social philosophy. This was the book that first attracted Dag Hammarskjöld to Buber.

The Prophetic Faith, trans. from the Hebrew by Carlyle Witton-Davies. New York: Macmillan, 1949.

This book may be regarded as a third in the series of Buber's studies of the origins of messianism. Although out of print at the moment, it is, in my judgment and that of many others, the most important of Buber's interpretrations of the Bible, one that links the original covenant with the prophetic demand placed on the present and with the messianic hope as making real the kingship of God by genuine response to that demand. Its section on the God of the Sufferers (Job and the suffering servant of the Lord) is a classic in itself.

Tales of Rabbi Nachman, **trans. by Maurice Friedman. Atlantic Highlands, New Jersey: Humanities Press International, 1988.**

This is the first of Buber's Hasidic books (1906) and also his first book. It retells some of the famous fairy tales and legends composed by the great Hasidic rabbi Nachman of Bratzlav as a way of teaching his disciples. Although in recent years other versions of Nachman's tales have appeared, Buber's formulation remains a contribution both to literature and to the understanding of Hasidism, as does his introductory essay on Jewish mysticism as the one mysticism in which ecstasy and revelation, timelessness and ethos, are combined.

Tales of the Hasidim: The Early Masters **and** *Tales of the Hasidim: The Later Masters,* **trans. from the Hebrew by Olga Marx. New York: Schocken Books, 1972.**

This is Buber's mature and faithful retelling of what he described as the "legendary anecdotes" of the great Hasidic *zaddikim,* organized according to the rebbes, each with a unique teaching of his own. Even the stories grouped under each rebbe are often subtly interconnected from story to story. In nominating Buber for the Nobel Prize in literature in 1947, the great Swiss writer Hermann Hesse declared that with *The Tales of the Hasidim* Buber had enriched world literature as had no other living author. The American philosopher Walter Kaufmann called Buber's Hasidic tales "one of the great religious books of all time, a work that invites comparison with the great Scriptures of mankind."

Ten Rungs: Hasidic Sayings, **trans. from the Hebrew by Olga Marx. New York: Schocken Books, 1962.**

This beautiful little books arranges Hasidic teaching by rungs ("For there is no rung of being on which we cannot find the holiness of God everywhere and at all times."): God and man, prayer, heaven and earth, service, teachings, the way, love, good and evil, pride and humility, and redemption. It is a book one can live with and meditate on.

Two Types of Faith, **trans. by Norman P. Goldhawk. New York: Macmillan, 1986.**

This is an impressive and highly controversial study of Jesus and Paul that ranges Jesus with the *emunah,* or unconditional trust in relationship, of the psalmist, the prophets, and Hasidism, Paul with the *pistis* or faith in a knowledge proposition which he shared with John and all those who turn faith into a possession or a gnosis. It does not deny trust to Paul, but sees its origin as lying in *pistis.* It is not, as some imagine, an apologetic for Judaism and against Christianity, but the endeavor of someone who saw Jesus as his "great brother" to understand Jesus from within in his Jewish soul and the New Testament, which Buber loved reading in the original coiné Greek.

The Way of Man. According to the Teachings of Hasidism. **Wallingford, Pennsylvania: Pendle Hill Publications, 1959 (with a Foreword by Maurice Friedman); New York: Carroll Publishing Group (formerly Citadel Press).**

Although it takes the form of commentary on Hasidic tales, *The Way of Man* is far more than an interpretation of Hasidism. No one of Buber's works gives us as much of his own simple wisdom as this remarkable distillation. I rank *The Way of Man* with *I and Thou* and *For the Sake of Heaven* as one of Buber's great and enduring classics. It is also printed as part of Buber's *Hasidism and Modern Man* and of Walter Kaufmann's *Religion from Tolstoy to Camus.*

BOOKS WITH IMPORTANT WRITINGS OF BUBER
THAT APPEAR NOWHERE ELSE

Martin Buber and the Theater, ed. and trans. with Three Introductory Essays by Maurice Friedman. New York: Funk & Wagnalls, 1969.

Although out of print and not likely to be reprinted, this book is an important source for those interested in Buber's relation to the theater, in the connection between his philosophy of dialogue and drama, and in a striking embodiment in fictional form of Buber's understanding of the Hebrew Bible. In addition to four essays by Buber on drama and the theater, it is the only place where one may read the English translation of Buber's "mystery play" *Elijah. Elijah* contains in dramatic form all the central motifs in Buber's understanding of biblical and Jewish existence: the demand that the covenant with Israel places on the people and the king to make real the kingship of God through justice, righteousness, and loving-kindness; the task of building the covenant of peace with other nations and of building true community; the attack on all forms of dualism that relegate religion to the cultic and the "spiritual" and place no demand on everyday life; the biblical *emunah,* or unconditional trust in the relation to the imageless God who offers no security or success yet who will be with us as he will be with us; the summons and sending of the prophet to whom God calls but whom he does not compel; the call of the prophet for real decision in the present—the people's turning back to God with the whole of their existence—rather than the apocalyptic prediction of a fixed future; evil as the failure to make real decision; the king as the viceroy of God who is anointed to realize God's kingship but who has no "divine right" to rule in God's stead; and the "suffering servant" as the messianic figure who will lead the "Holy remnant" of those who remain faithful to the covenant to set the dialogue right through free and wholehearted response. Although Buber did not intend *Elijah* to be performed, my translation of it was performed in 1967 at Manhattanville College of the Sacred Heart, where I was professor of Philosophy.

Sidney and Beatrice Rome, eds. *Philosophical Interrogations.* New York: Holt, Rinehart & Winston, 1964.

This book begins with a Buber section conducted and edited and Buber's Responsa trans. by Maurice Friedman. The Buber section contains questions by more than thirty philosophers, theologians, and psychotherapists answered by Buber and organized into seven parts: the philosophy of dialogue, theory of knowledge, education, social philosophy, philosophy of religion, the Bible and biblical Judaism, and evil. Since the questions and answers are short, it is often more truly dialogical than *The Philosophy of Martin Buber.*

Paul Arthur Schilpp and Maurice Friedman, eds. *The Philosophy of Martin Buber* in *The Library of Living Philosophers.* LaSalle, Illinois, and London: Cambridge University Press, 1967.

Actually edited by Maurice Friedman, this book opens with Buber's "Autobiographical Fragments" (published separately as *Meetings)* and closes with Buber's "Replies to Critics," both trans. by Maurice Friedman. The fragments are unique of their kind and show how Buber's thought develops as a response to the events and meetings of his life. The Replies, organized under such headings as "philosophical accounting," "I and Thou," theology, mysticism, metaphysics, ethics, the interpretation of the Bible, and Hasidism, contain invaluable material for anyone seriously interested in Buber's philosophy and its applications to many fields. The essays, ranging through every aspect of Buber's thought are by such eminent thinkers as Gabriel Marcel, Charles Hartshorne, Emmanuel Levinas, Emil Fackenheim, Hugo Bergman, Emil Brunner, Max Brod, James Muilenberg, Jean Wahl, and Ernst Simon, among others.

INDEX

Note: Italicized page numbers indicate illustrations

Abitur, 7

Absolute (Person), Buber on relationship of, 336, 378–379, 380

Abyss: Buber's experience of, 65; Buber's poem on, 450–451; Buber's use of, 43–44

Achdut Haavoda (United Workers), 201

Acher, Mathias, 22

Action Committee, 27

Adenauer, Konrad, 459

Adler, Karl, 223

Adult education, Buber's work with, 301–303. See also Education: Jewish Education

Afikoman, 251

"Against Betrayal" (Buber), 253

Agitation Committee, 30

Agnon, Shmuel Joseph, 191, 210, 258, 390, 457, 458; on Buber/Scholem controversy, 395

Agriculture, Carl Buber and, 9–10

Ahab, King, 434

"Aims of Adult Education, The" (Buber), 440

Albert Schweitzer Medal, 439

Aletheia, 439

Aliyah (emigration to Palestine), 119, 221

Allenby, Edmund Lord, 118

Allon, Yigal, 458

"Altat, The" (Buber), 50, 82

Altenberg, Peter, 14

Altneuland (Herzl), 33

Altreuthe, 326

Am lebendigen Wasser [By Living Waters] (P. Buber), 280

Am v'Olam [People and World] (Buber), 440

American Academy of Arts and Sciences, 439

American Committee on Africa, 410–411

American Council on Judaism, 371, 431

American Friends of Ihud, 371–373, 420–422

American Social Gospel, 252

Amersfoort, the Netherlands, 180, 193, 355

Andreas-Salomé, Lou, 71

Anglo-American Committee of Enquiry, 272, 426

Angst, Kierkgaard's, 64

Antinomianism (lawlessness), 337

Anti-Semitism: Christian, 216–217; and concept of the "blood," 58; German, 93; Hitler's, 171; and pogroms, 24; rising tide of, 91; and Zionism, 23–24

Apartheid, 410–411

Apikoros, 200

"Apollonian" limitation, 19

Apocalyptic attitude, 350–352

Arabs: Buber on, 121–124; emphasis on understanding, 200; expropriation of lands of, 427–428, 432–433; terrorist attacks of, 238–239, 253, 280

Arab-Israeli difference, 417

Arab-Jewish relations, 201–202, 283–284

Arch-Jew, Buber as, 215

Arendt, Hannah, 430

Aronstein, Fritz, 242

Ascona, conference at, 212, 355

Ases, myth of, 262

Ashbel, Michael, 273

Assimilation and Assimilationists: as crisis, 63; and intermarriage, 27–28; Jewish, 23; liberal tendency toward, 56
"Atheistic Theology" (Rosenzweig), 347
Auden, W.H., 419
Auseinandersetzung (discussion), 294
"Autobiographical Fragments" (Buber), 16, 17, 68, 379. *See also Meetings*
Avoda (service), 48

Baal-Shem, Israel, 34
Baal-Shem Suite (Bloch), 443
Baal-Shem Tov, 37, 394
Baal Teshuvah, 155
Ba'ayot, 270, 273
Bab, Julius, 100
Badt-Strauss, Dr. Bertha, 221
Baeck, Rabbi Leo, 175, 221, 222, 228, 229, *307*, 322
"Baeck and Buber" (F. Kaufmann), 377
Balaam, and Dubnow, 90
Baldwin, Roger, 372
Balfour Declaration, 117–118, 200, 256
Balthasar, Hans Urs von, 319–320, 386
Bar Kochba Association (Union) and Bar Kochbans, 52–53, 55–56, 61–62; Buber and, 57–58, 90
Barrabas (Lagerkvist), 266
Barker, Gen. Sir Evelyn, 273
Barth, Karl, 137, 140, 192, 218, 445; on transcendence of God, 343
Basel, Switzerland, 24, 29, 30
"Bases of Buber's Ethics, The" (Friedman), 215
Bashan, Raphael, 429
"Basic Forms of Religious Life, The" (Buber), 189
"Basic Principles" (Buber), 106
Bavarian Academy of Fine Arts, 326, 438
Beard, reason for Buber's, 3
Beatrix, Princess (Holland), *405*, 443
Bebel, August, 101
Beer-Hofmann, Miriam, 448
Beer-Hofmann, Naemah, *399*, 448–449, 456
Beer-Hofmann, Richard, 60–61, 448

Begegnungen [Meetings], 40, 362
Beit Hakerem, 260
"Belief in Rebirth, The" (Buber), 193
"Believing Humanism" (Buber), 443
Beltz, Hasidism of, 9
Ben-Chorin, Schalom, 213, 217, 259, 278, 320, 439, 450
Ben-Gurion, David, 243, 269, *399*, 457; and Buber, 420–435; and partition of Palestine, 276
Ben-Gurion and the Intellectuals (Keren), 421
Ben Shemen (Jewish Youth Village), 199–200, 238
Bentwich, Joseph, 259
Bentwich, Norman, 200
Ben-Zvi, Itzhak, 430, 456
Berger, Julius, 91
Bergmann, Hugo, 56, 119, 161–162, 200, 201, 203, 226, 239, 263, 280, 293–294, 336, 393, 415, 436, 449, 454, 457; on Buber as conscience, 329; at Buber's funeral, 458; on Eichmann execution, 430; and Ihud, 270; on Paula, 375
Bergson, Henri, 337–338
Bergstrasser, Arnold, 209
Bernadotte, Count Folke, 281–282
Bernfeld, Siegfried, 104–105
Bernhard, Prince (Holland), *405*, 443
Bernheim, Alfred, 454
Bertram, Cardinal, 194
Beth Midrash l'Morei Am (School for the Education of Teachers of the People), 301
Between: Buber on, 67, 77, 247, 383–384; realm of, 45; sickness of, 136
Between Man and Man (Buber), 126, 218, 413
Bezalel Art School, 258
Bialik, H. N., 92
Bialik Prize of the City of Tel Aviv, 439
Bible: Buber on, 286–288; Buber's translation of Hebrew, 128, 321; as spoken teaching, 224–225. *See also* Buber/Rosenzweig Bible; Hebrew Bible; Old Testament

Biblical Judaism, 285–292. *See also* Judaism

"Biblical Leadership" (Buber), 271

"Bi-National Approach to Zionism, The" (Buber), 276

Binationalism, in Palestine, 200–201, 270

Binyamin, Rabbi, 200

Binswanger, Ludwig, 229

Birnbaum, Nathan, 22

Bjerre, Poul, 75, 86, 87

Black path, 78–79

Blau-Weiss (Jewish youth movement), 97, 104

Blind violence, Buber on, 253

Bloch, Chaim, 27

Bloch, Ernst, 443

Blood: Buber on "community of," 58; concept of, 57, 59; emhasis on importance of, 210

"Blood and soil," as Nazi slogan, 227

Blüher, Hans, 422

B'nai B'rith Lodge, 175

Boehme, Jacob, 46; Buber essay on, 130; influence of on Buber, 47; and ternary of fire, 39, 83

Bonnier (publishers), 414

"Books and Men" (Buber), 295, 457

Born, Max, 415, 416

Borel, Henri, 75

Boulding, Kenneth, 368

Boycott Day, 208

Bratslaver Seminary, 298

Bretall, Charles, 380

Brit Shalom (Covenant of Peace), 200–201, 269

B'rith Shalom, 121

British: and Balfour Declaration, 256; and Jewish settlement, 268; and White Paper on immigration, 274

Brock, Elise (mother), 5. *See also* Buber, Elise

Brod, Max, 56, 229; on Buber, 432–433

Brown, Dr. Graham, 278

Brunner, Emil, 192, 419; on Buber's work, 198–199

Buber, Adele (grandmother), 4, 5, 95, *145*; communication skills of, 5–6

Buber, Barbara (granddaughter), 173, 236, 272; and anti-Semitism, 211; and life with grandparents, 179–184; marries, 284; and Marxism, 258. *See also* Goldschmidt, Barbara

Buber, Carl (father), *146*; death of, 229; influence of on Martin, 9–10; Martin on, 178; profile of, 9–10

Buber (nee Wurgast), Elise (mother), *146*

Buber [Martin] Emmanuel (grandson), 251–252, 258

Buber, Judith (granddaughter), 173, 236, 272; and anti-Semitism, 211; life of with grandparents, 179–184; and Marxism, 258

Buber, Margarete (daughter-in-law), 236. *See also* Buber-Neumann, Margarete

Buber, Martin, *147, 148, 304, 306, 307, 308, 309, 310, 311, 399, 400, 401, 402, 403, 404, 405, 406*

Buber, Martin [Misha] (grandson), 251

Buber, Paula (wife), *150, 151, 400, 425*; approach of to housekeeping, 182; and Buber/Roswenzweig Bible, 173; concern of for Eve, 237, 238; and custody of granddaughters, 179–184; death of, 374–376; and developement of I-Thou relationship, 132; excluded from Chamber of Writers, 213; Martin's reliance on, 197–198; in Palestine, 242, 251; as Philo-Zionist, 203; pseudonym of, 346–347; and Scholem, 389; strength of, 374; watchword of, 134; works of, 41, 116. *See also* Winkler, Paula

Buber, Rafael [Raffi] (son), 12, 28, 41, 97–98, 116, *151*, 272, 457; on Buber/Rosenzweig Bible, 171; in Communist youth organization, 178–179; at father's funeral, 458; in Palestine, 236, 238

Buber, Ruth (daughter-in-law), 236

Buber, Solomon (grandfather), 4, *145*; and Hasidism, 38; profile of, 8–9;

as scholar, 7, 22–23
"Buber as Interpreter of the Bible" (Muilenberg), 319
Buber Centennial Conferences, 397
Buber House, *151*
Buber-Neumann, Margaret, 180
"Buber or Ben-Gurion?" (Simon), 433–434
Buber/Rosenzweig Bible Bible, 155–177
"Buber's Metaphysics" (Hartshorne), 379–380
"Builders, The" (Rosenzweig), 162
Burkhardt, Carl, 324
Burkhardt, Jacob, 22
Burgtheater, 13
By Living Waters (P. Buber), 346–347. *See also Am lebendigen Wasser* (P. Buber)
Cambridge University, 411
Campbell, Joseph, 370
Camus, Albert, 299, 342
Carnegie Hall, 409
Capitalism, Buber on profit motive of, 105, 106
Casals, Pablo, 415
Cats, and Buber family, 130, 242, 437
Catastrophe, Buber's presentiment of American
Catholicism, 394
Cause, relation of to person, 35–36
Central Conference of American Rabbis, 395, 396
"Central Office for Jewish Adult Education," 223
Chagall, Marc, 353–354, 443
Chalutz (pioneer), 226
Chanoch, Gershom, 202
Charisma, Weber on, 174
Cherry Orchard, The (Chekhov), 363
"Children, The" (Buber), 211
"China and Us" (Buber), 174
Chisholm,   Brock,   415
Chostov, Lev, 380
Christian socialism, and religious socialism, 192
Christianity: aim of early, 141; Buber defends, 213; destiny of, 197; and Judaism, 192–193

Chuang-tzu, 104
Circumcision, 197–198
Civil disobedience, 417–418
Claudel, Paul, 69
Closeness, and relation, 441
Cohen, Aharon, 425–427
Cohen, Arthur, 388
Cohen, Hermann, 83; as Idealist, 190; as professor, 250; profile of, 91–92; and Rosenzweig, 156
Cohen/Buber debate, 91–92
Cohn, Margot, 374–375
Coincidentia oppositorum, 47
Collectivism, Buber on, 218, 246–247
College of Judaism, 60–61
Columbia University, 340, 341
"Coming Victory of Democracy, The" (Mann), 261
Commentary, 393, 394
Communal socialism, 118; and revolution, 99–115. *See also* Socialism
Communes, village, 299–300
Community: Buber on, 94, 99, 103–104, 247; Eastern Jews as, 26; God's demand for, 291; Jewish spirit of true, 142; and reality, 136–137
"Community" [Gemeinschaft] (Buber), 106
"Community of the blood," 58
Compulsion, vs. communion, 187
Concept of Dread, The (Kierkgaard), 346
Concrete, Buber's insistence on, 386. *See also* Lived concrete
"Confession of the Author" (Buber), 172
"Confessions of a Philozionist" (P. Buber), 28
Confirmation: crisis of, 346; principle of mutual, 300; theme of, 297
Congressional Record, 459
Conscience, Hitler on, 262
Conservative Judaism, 377
Contemporary, power of, 82
Contrasts, Buber's central, 79
"Conversation, The" (Buber), 455
Conversion: Buber's, 80, 82; and inclusion, 82
Corossa, Hans, 323

Corpus Hasidicum (Agnon/Buber), 191
"Consmopolitanism," 27
Covenant, Buber on, 198
Creation, Buber on, 143, 219
Creativity: Buber's longing for, 27; Nietzsche's celebration of, 20; and self-expression 20; and temptation, 20–21
Crossfront, Buber on, 114, 410
Culture, and religion, 19–20
Culture Committee, 30
Culture Prize of the City of Munich, 438–439
Cusanus. *See* Nicholas of Cusa

Dagens Nyheter, 414
Dajani, Jussef, Wahab, 260; family of, 278, 279
Daniel: Dialogues of Realization (Buber), 20, 50; appraisal of, 63–69; compared with *I and Thou*, 71–72; Landauer critiques, 102–103; realization of, 83
Danger, celebration of, 126–127
"Danger to Democracy, The," 428–429
Daniel, prophecy of, histomap of, 78
Dark charism, 114; Trietsch's 174–175
Das Jüdische Prag (Buber), 90
Das Verbogne Licht [The Hidden Light] (Buber), 190
Davar, 414, 436, 457
"Day of Looking Back" (Buber), 346
"Days of Awe" (Buber), 44
Death: Buber on, 65–66, 176–177, 452–453
"Death of God," 20
Death sentence, Buber on, 430
Decentralist socialism, 298–299. *See also* Socialism
Decisionlessness, Buber on, 346
"Demand of the Spirit and Historical Reality" (Buber), 245
Demarcation line, 114, 120, 201, 353; and quantum satis, 349
Democratic Fraction, 30, 56; and Herzl, 35
Demonism, Buber on, 85, 86
Der Grosse Maggid (Buber), 191

Der Jude: Buber editorship of, 190; founding of, 88; influence of, 89–90; on Jewish youth movements, 105; Landauer on, 89; Rosenzweig on, 158; Simon as editor of, 192
"Der Mensch als Weib" [The Human Being as Woman] (Andreas-Salomé), 71
Der Sozialist, 101
Der Stürmer, 218
Despair: Buber on, 66; and faith, 291; as gateway to reality, 137; Landauer on, 103; and suicide, 80
Deutero-Isaiah, 290–292; suffering servant in, 173, 175, 316
Devekut, kinds of, 391–394
Devils, The (Dostoevsky), 318
Devotio, 79: vs. gnosis, 356, 359, 361
Dialectic, Buber on, 385–386
Dialogue: with Americans, 333–354; Buber on, 45–46, 47, 68, 259; education as, 186–187; essence of genuine, 195–196; with German Christians, 315–332; Jewish-Christian, 77; vs. monologue, 36; principle of life of, 36; World War and breakthrough to, 73–98. *See also* Monologue; Philosophy of dialogue
"Dialogue" (Buber), 173, 195
"Dialogue between Heaven and Earth" (Buber), 338–339
"Dialogues on Realization" (Buber), 65–67
Diamond, Malcolm, 335, 370, 384
Die Gesellschaft (Society), 71, 75
Die Kreatur, 193–195
Die Rede, die Lehre, und das Lied (Buber), 130
Die unechten Kinder Adams [The Illegitimate Children of Adam] (Winkler), 26. *Die Welt*, 22, 28, 33; Buber as editor of, 30, 32, 425; Buber's poem in, 78
"Dionysian" energy, 19
Dir Abu Tor, 260
Direction: Buber on, 67, 346; and holy insecurity, 69; and inclusion, 69;

and kinesis, 85; need for, 20; and passion, 69; and polarity, 69–70; power responsible to, 245
Discours de la Methode (Descartes), 128
Dissociation, vital, 224
"Distance and Relation" (Buber), 279, 297
"Do You Still Know It?" (Buber), 41
Döblin, Alfred, 322
Dolci, Danilo, 416
Dostoevsky, F., 47, 318
Dov, Joseph Ben, 249
Drama, and theater, 68–69
"Drama and the Theater" (Buber), 69
"Dream, A: (Kafka), 90
Dreams, Buber on, 365–366, 440
Dreyfus, Alfred, 23–24
Du (Thou), Buber's use of, 167
Duality, inner, 59
Dualism: Marcionite, 317; new, 85; Paul's 316–317
Dubnow, Simon, 90
Dumont, Louise, 69, 113
Duse, Eleonora, 41
Dushkin, Alexander, 458
Düsseldorf Playhouse, 69
Dynamism, and form, 19
East European Jews, 83, 88, 93, 199–200
East Kenya, 31
Easy word, Buber on, 125, 172, 295
Ebner, Ferdinand, 128
Eckhart, Meister, 46
Eclipse of God, 336, 345; Buber on, 247, 267, 338–339, 460; vs. death of God, 444; Wasmuth on, 292
Eclipse of God (Buber), 325, 343
Ecstasy, Buber on, 48, 49–50
"Ecstasy and Confession" (Buber), 49, 129, 130
Ecstatic Confessions (Buber), 49
Editorial committee, 122–123
Education: as dialogue, 186–187; philosophy of, 124; and postwar Zionism, 116–124
"Education" (Buber), 115, 186–188, 195
"Education of Character, The" (Buber), 288
Eeden, Frederik Van, 74–75, 76, 86, 282

Eichmann, Adolf, 430–431
Eichmann in Jerusalem (Arendt), 430
Einstein, Albert, 209, 272, 340
Einzelne (Single One), 218
Eisenhower, Dwight D., 428
Eisenstadt, Samuel, 248–249
Eisik Scheftel (Pinski), 8
Eisner, Kurt, 107, 109, 112
Elath, Eliahu, 458
"Election of Israel, The" (Buber), 231
"Elements of the Interhuman" (Buber), 75–76
Elhanani, A., 414
Eliasberg, Ahron, 14–16, 21, 22
Eliezer, Israel ben, 37, 39, 41
Elijah: A Mystery Play (Buber), 347, 434–435
Eliot, T. S., 333, 419
Emunah (trust), 79; Buber on, 318, 434; faith as, 196, of Jesus, 315–316; meaning of, 386–387
Encounter on the narrow ridge, Buber's life as, 186–188. *See also* Narrow ridge
Enlightenment: Jewish, 26, negative effects of, 24. *See also* Haskalah
Epstein, Oskar, 60
Eranos conference, 212, 355–356, 396
Erasmus Prize Foundation, 443
Ereignisse und Begenungen [Events and Meetings] (Buber), 97, 440
Eriugena, Scotus, 68
Erotic, The (Andreas-Salomé), 71
Eshkol, P. N. Levi, 432, 458
Eternity, Buber on, 18, 19
Ethical Culture Society, 15
Ethnopsychology, 14
European Association of Writers, 323
Events and Meetings (Buber), 82
Evil: Buber on, 323; stages of, 346
Evil urge, 20, 39, 69, 346, 361
Existential guilt, vs. neurotic, 364
Existential thinking, 156–157
Existential trust, 132–133, 144
Exler, Margarete, 332
"Experience of faith," Buber on, 73–74
Ezl (Jewish terrorists), 281
Fackenheim, Emil, 345, 395–396

Faith: Buber on, 138, 388–389; as distinct from religion, 252–253; emunah as, 196; gnostic transformation of, 356; and humor, 176; prophetic vs. apolyptic, 197

Family life: Buber, 95–98, 116–117, 240; and Buber/Rosenzweig Bible, 173; as grandparents, 181–184

Farber, Leslie H., 361, 362, 367, *399*

Federalistic communal socialism, 299–300

Feelings: vs. institutions, 135; and involvement/otherness, 135

Feiwel, Berthold, 8, 32, 56, *148*, 442; and *Die Welt*, 30, 33; and Herzl, 35; and Jewish Renaissance, 29–30

Fellows, Lawrence, 431

Feuerbach, Ludwig, 45, 46

"Fiddler, The" (Buber), 455–456

Finkelstein, Louis, 333

Fischer-Barnicol, Hans, 7, 379

Flappan, Simcha, 416

Florence, Italy, 40–41, 415–416, 439–440

"Folk Education as Our Task" (Buber), 204

For the Sake of Heaven (Buber), 34, 159–160, 263–267, 382, 397

"For You" (Buber), 29

Force, Buber on use of, 256

Form, and dynamism, 19

Forte Kreis, 86, 88, 194

Four Quartets (Eliot), 334

Fox, Everett, 169

Francis of Assisi, 46, 343

Frank, Benno, 159

Frank, Jacob, 289, 359–361

"Free Jewish House of Learning," 155

Freedom, Buber on, 187

Freie Jüdische Lehrhaus, 126, 216. *See also* Lehrhaus

Freud, S., 71, 356; Buber on, 367–368; and concept of neuroses, 74

Freudenberg, Gideon, 282–283, 301–302

Friedman, Eugenia, 261, 362, 390, 418, 437, 438

Fromm, Erich, 372

Fromm-Reichmann, Frieda, 362

Fry, Joan, 318

Führer, German belief in, 216

"Für die Sache der Treue" [For the Cause of Being True] (Buber), 175–177

Gagern, Freiherr von, 112

Galut (exile) Judaism, 23

Gandhi, Mahatma, 75; advised Jews, 213–214; on Arab right to Palestine, 254; and nonviolence, 417

"Gandhi, Politics, and Us" (Buber), 195

"Genuine Dialogue and the Possibility of Peace" (Buber), 327, 410

Georgi, Arthur, 327

German Evangelical Church, 320, 322

German Jewry, 83, 88, 221

German people: Buber on, 322; contending impulses within, 328; culpability of, 214–215; facelessness of, 324; and political charismatics, 330–331

German Revolution, 106–107

German Youth Movement, 135–136

Germany: Buber's return to, 321–323; postwar, 315–406. *See also* German people

Gerson, Hermann (Menachem), 184, 208, 213, 221, 235–236, 440; and Jewish Youth movement, 203–207; and psychoanalysis, 252; and Werkleute, 207

Gerson, Lo, 235–236

Ghetto Judaism, 24–26

Glatzer, Nahum, 158–160, 191, 210

"Gleanings" (Buber), 25, 176–177, 352, 453

Gnosis, 79, 344; vs. devotio, 356, 359, 361; and myth, 318

Gnosticism, Jung's, 358–359

God: Buber's belief in, 78–79, 143; eternality of, 170; evolution of, 47–48; as Existing, 169; fear of, 196–197; immanence of, 68; kingship of, 198; as Mysterium Tremendum, 343; nonincarnation of, 197; "otherness" of, 137, 197; presence of, 139–140; stages of realization of,

61; transcendence of, 343; word to replace, controversy on, 192
"God and the Spirit of Man" (Buber), 344
God in Search of Man (Heschel), 347
Goebbels, Joseph, 210
Goes, Albrecht, 213, 278, 326–327, 330, 419, 457; on Buber, 348
Goethe, J. W., 133
Goethe Prize, 324, 325
Gog und Magog [For the Sake of Heaven] (Buber), 159, 243
Gogarten, Friedrich, 192, 218
Golan, Joseph, 415
Goldberg, Lea, 260–261
Goldmann, Nahum, 294, 415, 420, 436
Goldschmidt, Barbara, *405*, 454, 457. See also Buber, Barbara
Goldschmidt, Tamar, 341, *402*
Goldschmidt, Zeev, 284, 457
Goldstein, Walter, 250, 260, 261, 283
Golem, Buber on legend of, 90
Gollancz, Victor, 419
Golus (exile), 25–26, 31
Good and Evil (Buber), 323, 451–453
Gordon, A. D., 119–120, 299
Gordon, Haim, 98, 226
Göring, Hermann, 210
Grandchildren, Buber's kinship with, 440
Graves, R. M., 276
Greek, 7, 437
Grete Ascher Pension, 278
Gruenewald, Max. 222
Guardini, Romano, 325, 327, 442, 443
Guilt: Buber on, 281, 364; Sullivan's approach to, 367
"Guilt and Guilt Feelings" (Buber), 323, 364
Gundolf, Friedrich, 84
Gurner, Dov, 273
Gutkind, Eric, 75, 86
Gutmann, Julius, 259
Ha'am, Ahad, 33, 34, 119; Buber's criticism of, 59; vs. Herzl, 36
Ha-Aretz, 274, 372
Hadassah, 269, 276
Hadassah Hospital, 280, 420

Hagaddah, 251
Haganah (Jewish defense army), 200, 253, 278, 281
Halakhah, 333, 337, 347. *See also* Jewish Law
Halkin, Simon, 437
Halutz(im), 105, 119–120, 204, 206, 300
Hammarskjöld, Dag, *402*, 411–414
Hammarskjöld, Knut, 414
Hapoel Hazair (Young Workers), 119, 120, 122, 201
Harijan (The Untouchable), 213, 214
Hart, Heinrich, 46
Hart, Julius, 46
Hartshorne, Charles, 379–380
Hashomer Hatzair, 62, 270
Hasidism: as antidote, 359–360; Buber on, 19, 68, 105, 128, 141, 169, 266–267, 393–397; Buber/Scholem controversy on, 356; founder of, 34; and Haskalah, 26; history of, 37–38; and Jewish mysticism, 26; and Kabbala, 47, 361, 393–394; legends of, 295–296; literature of, 393–394; Scholem on, 389–397; teaching, 41–46
Haskalah (Jewish Enlightenment), 8, 26
Hattis, Susan, 200–201
Hausner, Gideon, 430
Healing through Meeting (Trüb), 294
Hebrew, modern, 241–243
Hebrew Bible: and philosophy of dialogue, 338; as theologoumenon, 170. *See also* Bible; Buber/Rosenzweig Bible; Old Testament
Hebrew University of Jerusalem, 12, 117, 201, 203, adult/continuing education in, 301–303; Aula of, 425; Buber's concept of, 199; Buber critizes, 248–249; Buber negotiation with, 239–240; Buber's part in establishing, 442; Buber retires from, 335; established, 30–31; torch-light parade, *404*, 442
Hebrew University Adult Education Center, 300
Hechalutz movement, 226
Hechler, Rev. William, 25, 77–78

Hegel and the State (Rosenzweig), 156

Hegner, Jakob, 69

Heidegger, Martin, 86, 191, 209, 375; Buber's critique of, 325, 343–344; and Hitler, 325–326; and Rosenzweig, 176; on truth of lived speech, 439

Heidelberg Conference, 186–188, 209

Heine, Heinrich, 34

Heisenberg, Werner, 439

Hel, myth of, 262–263

Hellerau Dramatic Union, 69

Hellerau Playhouse, 69

Henein, George, 416

Henrietta Szold Prize, 439

Heppenheim, 94, 96; Buber home at, 209–210, 331–332

Heraclitus, 18, 382

Herberg, Will, 347, 352

Hermann, Leo, 56, 57, 91, 118, *310*

"Hero Book, A" (Buber), 91

Hero with a Thousand Faces, The (Cambell), 370

Herrigel, Hermann, 218

Herzl, M. Jeannette, 35

Herzl, Theodore, 21–36, 119; and Buber, 30, 32–36, 425; contributions of, 34; death of, 32; and Nietzschean vitalism, 24; on Paula Winkler, 26; strength and weakness of, 34–36; and Trietsch, 212, 264; Zionism of, 25

"Herzl and History" (Buber), 34

Heschel, Abraham Joshua, 8, 216, 281, 397, 459

Hess, Moses, 22, 119

Hesse, Hermann, 194–185, 213, 343, 419, 436; Buber on, 231; on Buber/Rosenzweig Bible, 171; on *Meetings*, 379, 447; on Nobel Prize, 297; on Old Testament, 321

Heuss, Theodor, 243, 327

Hidden Human Image, The (Friedman), 319

Hiller, Kurt, 87

Hinweise (Buber), 373

Hirsch, Otto, 222, 223, 228

Histadrut, 428

History of Greek Culture (Burckhardt), 22

"History of the Dialogical Principle, The" (Buber), 45–46, 126

Hitachduth, 202. *See also* Labor Zionists

Hitlahavut (ecstasy), 48, 451

Hitler, Adolf: Buber on, 215; Heidegger and, 325–326; as Künder, 210; speeches of, 262, 437

Hitler passage, Buber's, 372–373

Hocking, William Ernest, 388

Hodes, Aubrey, 416–417, 426, 431, 458

Hofmannsthal, Hugo von, 13, 71, 371

Hofshi, Nathan, 200

Hölderlin, Friedrich, 127

Holocaust, 262; Buber on, 293, 327–328

Holy insecurity: Buber's, 64–65, 66, 67; and coming of Thou, 131–132; danger as, 126–127; of *Daniel*, 79; and inclusion, 69–70; and Presence, 73

Holy Sinner, The (Mann), 266

Holy Way, The (Buber), 118

Homelessness, Buber on, 245, 388

"Hope for This Hour" (Buber), 409–412

Horwitz, Rivka, 79, 126

Hour and Its Judgment, The (Buber), 217

Hovevei Zion, 32. *See also* East European Jews

Huizinga, John, 442

Humanism, Buber's, 269

Humanum, Buber on, 443–444

Humility, Buber on, 48, 49

Humor, faith and, 176

Husseini, Fauzi Darwish El-, 275–276

Husseini, Jamal, 276

Husserl, Edmund, 191, 325

I and Thou (Buber), 334, 413; ascent to, 125–144; compared with *Daniel,* 71–72; and dialogue, 45–46; first draft of, 94, 97; and need for decision, 20; over-againstedness of, 83; Postscipt to, 378, 445–446; on Presence, 73; Simon on Rosenzweig's criticism of, 384. *See also* I-Thou

Ich und Du, 106. *See also I and Thou*

Idealism and Idealists: Cohen as, 190; Rosenzweig and, 156, 159
Ihud (Unity), 121, 270, 276; on Arab refugees, 427–428; Buber on, 279; platform of, 272-273. *See also* American Friends of Ihud
I–It, 18. *See also* I-Thou
Illegitimate Children of Adam, The (P. Buber), 102
Images of Good and Evil (Buber), 346
Immigration, 270–271, 274
Imitation of Christ (à Kempis), 413
Inclusion, 6; Buber's use of, 67, 70-71, 188; expansion of concept of, 82, 115; and holy insecurity, 69–70; and imagining the real, 115; and nature, 67–68
Inclusiveness, 186. *See also* Inclusion
Individualism, 47, 216, 246–247
Individuation, 230, 359
Individuation, Guilt, and Decision: Beyond the Boundaries of Psychology (Trüb), 229–230
Infinity, 67, 388–389
Insel Verlag, 346
Insensitivity, Paula/Martin's, 249
Institute of History of Religions, 203
Institutions, and otherness, 135
Institutum Judaicum Delitzschianum, 321
Intention, Buber on, 48
Interhuman, and I-Thou relationship, 10, 135
Intermarriage: and assimilation, 27–28; as crisis, 63
International Council of Christians and Jews (ICCJ), 332
International Philosophy Congress, 281
International Work Circle for the Renewal of Education, 186
Internationalism, Buber's, 123–124
Interpersonal psychiatry, 361, 364
"In the Midst of History" (Buber), 212
"In Theresienstadt," 229
Introduction to Mythology (Jung/ Kerényi), Buber on, 295
Irgun Zvai Le'umi, 253, 273; bombs King David Hotel, 274, 275

Ish-Shalom, Mordecai, 456
Israel, Buber's attitude toward, 293–294; future State of, 31–33; independence of, 280; prophet of, 290. *See also* Palestine; State of Israel
Israel and Palestine: The History of an Idea (Buber), 22, 119, 255, 261
Israel and the Arab World (Cohen), 425
Israel Committee for a Nuclear–Free Zone in the Middle East, 416
"Israel—Our Land," 322
Israeli Public Committee against Nuclear Tests, 415–416
Issues, 431–432
It, role of in life, 132
I-Thou: and I-It, 345, 384, 385; and nature, 10; and religious reality, 341–342. *See also I and Thou*
Jabotinsky, Vladimir, 200, 202
Jacobson, Viktor, 91
Jakob Hegner Verlag, 20, 347
Jaspers, Karl, 379, 443
Javits, Jacob, 459
Jeremias, Alfred, 196
Jerusalem: Buber on, 281; Hammarskjold in, 412; international trusteeship, 277; siege of, 278–280
Jerusalem Ideological Conference, 423
Jerusalem Municipality, 416
Jesus: Buber on, 77, 140–142; faith of, 318–319; messianism of, 315–316; place of, 293
Jew and His Jewishness, The (Buber), 446
Jew-hate, Buber on, 214
"Jew in the World, The" (Buber) 212
Jewish Agency, 269, 280, 300
Jewish anti–Semite, 23
Jewish-Arab Friendship League, 273–274
Jewish-Arab rapprochement and conflict, 268–284
Jewish-Arab unity, 122–123
Jewish-British coalition, Gandhi on, 254
Jewish-Christian dialogue, 77; Buber on, 192, 216-218; Trüb on, 193
Jewish education: Buber's work in adult, 188–189; and Buber's break-

through to dialogue, 86; Buber on, 91, 128, 220–228; in Nazi Germany, 225

Jewish Law, Buber's attitude toward, 347–348. *See also* Sabbath

Jewish Legion, 200

"Jewish Mysticism" (Buber), 42–43

Jewish National Committee, 88

Jewish National Council, 280

Jewish National Fund, 201

Jewish Palestine, 104, 118–121

Jewish Peace Fellowship, 345–346

"Jewish Person of Today, The" (Buber), 210–211

"Jewish Religious Philosophy and Ethics," lectureship in, 161

Jewish Renaissance, 23: Buber's anticipation of, 25; Buber on, 56–58; cultural unfolding of, 29–30; and Zionist movement, 26. *See also* Zionism

Jewish Resistance movement, 274–275

Jewish Revisionists, 226

Jewish Socialists of Germany, 84

"Jewish Society for International Understanding," 123

Jewish State, visions of, 423. *See also* Israel; State of Israel

Jewish Theological Seminary of America, 333

Jewish World Congress, 415

Jewish Youth movements, 204-207; and Bible study, k173–172; Buber and, 104–105, 224

Jewishness, Buber on, 57

Jews: and Second Ecumenical Council, 439; in Soviet Union, 415, 416; as victims, 212. *See also* East European Jews; Judaism; Western Jews

Job, Buber on, 438; and Deutero–Isaish servant, 291–292. *See also* Modern Job

John: Buber on Gospel of, 140-141; messianism of, 315

John XXIII, Pope, 330, 440

Jonas, Hans, 376

Journey to the East, The (Hesse), 185

Judaism: basic tendencies of, 60; and Buber's breakthrough to dialogue, 86; Buber's concept of, 62; Buber on, 93, 337–338, 396; and Christianity, 192–193, 293; crises in, 62-63; destiny of, 197; and German Evangelical Church, 320, 322; and messianism, 60; Paula Buber's conversion to, 28; synthesis of national/social ideas in, 22. *See also* Biblical Judaism; Prophetic Judaism; Reform Judaism

"Judaism and Mankind" (Buber), 57, 60

"Judaism and the European Crisis," 443

Jüdische Rundschau, 220

Jüdische Verlag, 8, 30–32, 156

Jüdisches Lexicon, 160

Juliana, Queen (Holland), 347, 443

Jung, Carl G. 186, 212; Buber on, 294–295, 343, 352–353, 355–359; Trüb break with, 230

Jung, Emma (Mrs. C. G.), 180, 355

Kabbala, 263; and Hasidism, 261; influence of, 47; mysticism of, 360; and realization of God, 61; Scholem on, 389, 396

Kaddish, Buber's, 458

Kadosh, 169

Kafka, Franz, 5, 90, 317; and Buber, 80–81, 339

Kalvarisky, Chaim, 200, 270, 275

Kampf um Israel (Fight for Israel), 201

Kant, Immanuel, 16–18

Katz–Nelson, Shulamit, 449, 457

Kaufmann, Fritz, 377

Kaufmann, Walter, 127, 297–298, 325, 370, 397, 447

Kavana (kavanot), 42, 48, 394; Buber's formulation of, 85, 360

Kavod (honor), 452

Kayser, Rudolf, 340

Kaznelson, Sigmund, 63

Kegley, Walter, 380

Kennedy, John F., 415

Keren, Michael, 421, 425

Kerényi, Karl, 266, 295, 355

Kfar Kassem massacre, 422

Khrushchev, Nikita, 416, 428

Kibbutz, 300; and consideration for individual, 252; education in, 440–442; formation of, 119

Kibbutz Afikim, 440–441

Kibbutz Hazorea, 236, 442

Kibbutz Jezreel, 440

Kierkegaard, Soren, 45, 47, 137; Buber contradicts, 143; concept of Single One, 218; on crisis of Western man, 74; and Ebner, 128-129; and knight of faith, 44, 336

Kinesis, age of, 85

King, Martin Luther, Jr., 410, 417

King, vs. prophet, 423-424

King David Hotel, 274, 283

Kingship of God, The (Buber), 194, 198–199, 255, 285

Kiss of brotherhood, 77, 194

Kittel, Gerhart, 216–217

Knesset, on Buber's death, 459

Knowledge: Buber on, 144, 385; new theory of, 156–157

Knowledge of Man, The (Buber), 279, 439; taping of, 368

Koch, Richard, 159, 189

Kohn, Hans, 25, 56, 84, 200, 201, 331; on breakthrough, 73; on Jewish Renaissance, 29, 32; on youth emigration, 120

Kokoschka Oskar 443

Kol Yisrael 457

Kook, Rav, 119

Korah, and Moses, 289

Kösel Verlag, 440

Kosmala, Hans, 196

Kotzk, question of, 169

Kraft, Werner, 228, 282, 323, 422, 436, 449-450, 455

Kremers, Heinz, 330

Krieck, Ernst, 210

Kriegsbuber, 84

Kristallnacht, 210, 240

Kropotkin, P. A., 298

Kurhaus, 448

Kurzweil, Baruch, 266

Kvutza, 300

Kvutzot, 225

Kvuza Geva, 236

Labor Federation, 270

Labor Zionism and Zionists, 119–120, 202

Lachman, Hedwig, 87, 106, 109

Lagerkvist, Pär, 266

Landauer, Charlotte (Lotte), 97, 99, 113; funeral of, 114

Landauer, Georg, 202

Landauer, Gustav, 46, *152*, 298; as anarchist, 83, 99; on Buber, 62, 102–103; death of, 368; and Düsseldorf Playhouse, 69; on freedom, 187–188; friendship with Buber, 87–89; influence of on Buber, 76, 99; on Kriegsbuber, 84; murder of, 94, 99–115; obelisk to, 113; at Potsdam meeting, 75; spiritual power of, 101; writings of, 101–102

"Landauer and the Revolution" (Buber), 113

Languages, Buber's fluency in, 321

L'Announce faite à Marie (Claudel), 69

Lao–tzu the Old, 82, 174

La Pira, Giorgio, 415, 439–440, 459

Lassalle, Ferdinand, 15, 34, 101

Lavon, Pinkas, 428

Law: revelation vs., 163–164; Rosenzweig on, 162–164; Simon on, 190; tragedy of, 189

League for Jewish-Arab Rapprochement and Cooperation, 269, 426; and Falastin el Jedida, 275-276

League for Jewish-Arab Understanding and Cooperation, 425

Lecture tours: American, 337, 361-374, 409–411; European, 320–321

Lectures: filming of 361–362 taping of, 368

Le Fevre, Perry, 368

Legend, and myth, 45–46

Legend the Baal-Shem, The (Buber), 41–45, 48–49, 52–54, 56, 63, 85, 451

Legendary anecdotes, 295, 296, 395

Lehmann, Siegfried, 199–200

Lehrhaus: expansion of, 161, 223; method of, 222–223; Jewish adult education in, 188–189; leadership

of, 189–190; lectures, 79; unique-
ness of, 157–158. *See also* Freie
Jüdische Lehrhaus
Leib, R. Moshe of Sasov, 394
Leipzig, 15, 22
Lenin, V. I., 298
Leo Baeck Foundation, 443
"Let Us Make an End to Falsities"
(Buber), 282–283
Levenberg, Alissa, 440
Levi, Carlos, 299
Levin, Meyer, 414, 416
Levin, Nora, 208, 220
Levinas, Emmanuel, 383, 436
Levin–Goldschmidt, Herman, 446
Lewis, R. W. B., 342, 368
Lewy, Lina, 292–293
Library, Buber's, 240
"Library of Little Books," 213
Library of Living Philosophers, 215, 377,
379, 380, 390
Library of Living Theologians, 381
Life of dialogue, 47, 255-256. *See also*
Dialogue
Life of Dialogue, The (Buber), 347
Life of Jacob Boehme (Frankenberg),
379
Life of Jesus (Renan), 9
Life of Strife, A (Brod), 432
"Life of the Hasidim, The," *See Baal-
Shem, The*
Lilien, E. M. 29, 32, *148*
Literary Prize for Human Freedom, 416
"Literary Society," 15
Lived concrete, 83, 256; Buber on, 81,
114, 295
Living Philosophers, Buber's responses
to, 375
Loerke, Oskar, 323
Logoi, world of, 7
Logos, world of, 7
Lowe, Rabbi, 90
Löwit Verlag, 156
Luftmensch, 58
Lunn, Eugene, 100, 101
Lydda, Palestine, 199–200
Ma-ariv, 429
Mach, Ernst, 14

Maggid of Metzritch, 394
Magic, Buber on, 344
Magister Ludi (Hesse), 263
Magnes, Judah Leib, 200, 203, 213, 239,
252, 269, 269, 371; and Buber, 201-
202, 271, 277; on binationalism,
273
Mapai party, 201, 457
Mapam (Labor Zionist) kibbutz, 425
Mainz Academy of Sciences and Litera-
ture, 322
Major Trends in Jewish Mysticism
(Scholem), 389, 394
Malik, Charles, 418–419
"Man and His Image-Work" (Buber),
340
Man in Revolt (Brunner), 198–199
"Man of Today and the Jewish Bible"
(Buber), 172
Mann, Thomas, 261
Marcel, Gabriel, 419
Marcionite trend, Buber on, 439
Marmorstein, Emil, 348
Marranos and Marranism, 212
Marriage: Paula/Martin's, 94–98; and
philosophy of dialogue, 219–220
"Martin Buber: Our Support" (Goes),
327
Martin Buber: The Life of Dialogue
(Friedman), 125, 192
Martin Buber Archives, 440
"Martin Buber as a Classical Author"
(Kerényi), 355
Martin Buber Center for Adult Educa-
tion, 303
Martin Buber Chair of Judaica, 442
Martin Buber Forest, 442
Martin Buber's Path into Reality
(Michel), 191
Martin Buber's Way to I and Thou
(Horwitz), 126
Marx, Karl, 74, 298
Marx, Leopold, 223
Marxism, 106, 258
Masad Bialik committee, 429
Masken, 69
Maskil, defined, 38
Masks of God, The (Campbell), 370

Maugli, as pet name, 28, 41
Mauriac, François, 415, 416
Mauthner, Fritz, 93, 101, 106, 113
May, Rollo, 388
Mayer, Eugen, 167
Mazar, Benjamin, 458
McCaw, Kitty, 374
Mea She'arim, 298
Mead, George Herbert, 218–219
Meditation, Buber on, 51–52; and mysticism, 350
Mediterranean Colloquium, 415–416
Meetings (Buber), 18, 379
"Meetings with Buber" (Shapira), 441
Mehé, Herr, 80-81, 454–455
"Melancholy" (Buber), 456
Memory, Buber's, 449–450
Mendel, Rabbi, 169
Mendelssohn, Moses, 168
Menuhin, Hepzibah, 443
Menuhin, Yehudi, 443
Merkur, 357
Merleau-Ponty, Maurice, 191
Messianic Idea of Judaism (Scholem), 393
Messianic longing, 43
Messianism: as basic to Judaism, 60; Ben-Gurion's, 423; concept of, 44, 198, 264; fulfilled, 292; Hasidic conception of, 393; Jewish understanding of, 141; origin of, 316; and suffering servant, 173. *See also* Redemption
Metzger, Ludwig, 221-222
Mica, Buber's experience with, 66, 67, 130
Michel, Ernst, 294
Michel, Wilhelm, 191
Midrash, 8, 22
Mikva (ritual bath), 28
Minn, Josef, 321
Mintz, Ruth Finer, 440
Miracle, Buber on, 286
Mismeetings: childhood experience of, 131; with Hartshorne, 379–380; and Herr Mehé, 454-455
Misnagdim, 9
Mistrust, effect of on dialogue, 409, 410

Misunderstanding, psychology of, 383
Mittelstelle, 223
Mitzvah, Mitzvot, 181, 257, 259, 281, 289
Mixed marriages, 27
Moby Dick (Melville), 434
Modern Job, 318, 339, 342
Modern Judaism (Acher), 22
Mollegan, Bernard, 365
Monologue(s): Buber's, 68; and reflexion, 11. *See also* Dialogue
Moses (Buber), 71, 198, 285, 286–289
Moshe of Kobryn, Rabbi, 394, 453-454
Mother: disappearance of, 3-5; Martin's need for, 28
Movement, and direction, 85–86
Muckensturm (P. Buber), 261
Muilenburg, James, 319, 370
Munich: Buber's ties to, 438–439; revolution in, 107–113
Munich Academy of Fine Arts, 375
Munk, Georg, 102, 346–347. *See also* Buber, Paula
Mutuality: between God and man, 379; limitation of, 369
My Way to Hasidism (Buber), 105
Mysterium Tremendum, 356; God as, 137, 343
Mysticism: Buber's attraction to, 45–52; Buber renounces 81; and discovery of Hasidism, 37–54; Jewish, 26; medieval, 47; and meditation, 350; and myth, 52, 62
Myth: and gnosis, 318; Jung/Kerényi on, 295; and legend, 45; and mysticism, 52, 62
"Myth and Judaism" (Buber), 52

Nabi (prophet), 210, 291
Nachman, Rabbi, 41, 42–43. *See also Tales of Rabbi Nachman, The*
Narrow ridge: and Arab problem, 122; Buber's use of term, 43–45, 287. *See also* Encounter on the narrow ridge
Nation, Cohen's definition of, 92

National and University Library, 11
National Conference of Jewish Teachers, 247
National universalism, Buber on, 459
Nationalism: Arabs', 431; Buber's hostility to, 118–119; fanatical, 253–254; German, 93; legitimate vs. arbitrary, 120–121
"Nationalism" (Buber), 121
Nationality, Cohen's definition of, 92
Natorp, Paul, 139, 167
Nature: I and Thou relationship with, 378; relatedness to, 130
Nazi Germany, 208-231. *See also* Germany; Holocaust; Nazis and Nazism
Nazis and Nazism: Buber concern with, 264; Buber leads spiritual resistance to, 215–216, 218; Buber scorns, 208; and concept of "community of the blood," 58; Heidegger and, 325-326; Holocaust of, 73; threat of to Jewish and Christian people, 212–213; and use of Zionism, 24. *See also* Germany; Holocaust
Negev, 440
Neo-paganism, Nazism as, 227
Ner (Light), 324, 371
Neue Freie Presse, 26
Neue Schweizer Rundschau, 355
Neurotic guilt, 364
New Community, 46
New Outlook, The Middle East Monthly, 416, 433
Newsweek, 419, 430, 459
"New Thinking, The" (Rosenzweig), 156–157
"New Year's Sermon, The" (Buber), 44
New York Times, 431, 459
New York Times Book Review, 374
Nicholas of Gusa, 47
Niebuhr, H. Richard, 418
Niebuhr, Reinhold, 299, 340, 352, 353, 370, 418
Niebuhr, Ursula, 374
Niemöller, Martin, 416
Nietzsche, Friedrich Wilhelm: and
Andreas-Salomé 71; and Buber 15–20, 59; and God is dead, 336; influence of on Zionism, 23–25; mysticism of, 47; and will to power, 244–245
"Nietzsche and Life-Values" (Buber), 19
Nobel, Rabbi Nehemiah, 162
Nobel Prize for literature, 297; Buber recommended for, 412–413, 418–419, 437; Simon on bias against, 282
Nonaction, 68
Noncontradiction, law of, 380
Nonincarnation, of God, 197
Noninterference, 135
Nonresistance, guilt of, 329
Nonviolent resistance, 256, 417–418
Nordau, Max, 31, 33
Norlind, Theodor Gustav, 75
"November" (Buber), 283–284
Novosti Press Agency, 414
Nuclear weapons testing, 414–417
Nuremberg Laws of 1935, 218

Objective guilt, 364
Objectivation, Buber on, 337
Odenwaldschule, 95, 181, 186
"Old and New Community" (Buber), 46
Old City (of Jerusalem), 277–278, 280
Old-New Synagogue, 90
Old Testament, translated from Hebrew to German, 164–193. *See also* Bible; Buber/Rosenzweig Bible; Hebrew Bible
"On Direction" (Buber), 102
On Philosophy (Buber), 440
"On Polarity" (Buber), 67, 102–103
"On Polarity, Dialogue after the Theater" (Buber), 68–69
"On the day of Looking Back" (Buber), 133
"On the Suspension of the Ethical" (Buber) 335–336
Open forum, Buber's, 261–262
"Open Letter to Our German Friends" (Van Eeden), 86
Or, Aliza Ziv, 226, 249
Or Haggazuz (Buber), 190, 296. *See*

also Tales of the Hasidism, The
Oriental Jews, 301, 440
Origin and Meaning of Hasidism, The
    (Buber), 261
Origin of Species (Darwin), 9
"Original Forms of Religious Life"
    (Buber), 188–189
Original sin, 197; Kierkegaard on, 346
Orthodox tradition: Buber's, 358; influ-
    ence of on Martin, 38; opposition
    of to Buber, 335, 457
Otherness, 10–11; awareness of, 81;
    community of, 255–256; of God,
    197; in-rush of, 82
Ott, Heinrich, 445–446
Otto, Rudolf, 137, 343, 356
"Our Educational Goal" (Buber), 222
"Our People's Awakening" (Buber), 25
"Out of the Depths I Call unto Thee"
    (Buber), 213
Over-againstedness, 265–266; Buber on,
    77, 142; of *I and Thou*, 83
Overman, Nietzsche's concept of, 19

Pacifica Radio station, 436, 444–445
Palestine: binationalism in, 200–201;
    British conquer, 118; British sup-
    port Jewish Homeland in, 117–118;
    Buber against imperialism/mercan-
    tilism in, 104; Buber's life in,
    241–242; development of, 204; as
    Jewish state, 269; partition of, 277;
    prewar, 235-311; political life of,
    200–202; relation of Western Jews
    to, 57; youth emigrate to, 120; as
    Zionist settlement site, 31-33
Panentheism, 50, 380
Pantheism, 50
Parity, 201. *See also* Binationalism
Passover Seder, Buber organizes, 230,
    251
Paths in Utopia (Buber), 99, 261, 298
Paul: dualism of, 142; messianism of,
    315–317
Pauling, Linus, 416
Paulinism, Christian, 317–318
Peace Prize of the German Book Trade,
    215, 325, 327, 410

Pendle Hill Bulletin, 457
People, definition of, 92
Peretz, Don, 373
Person, relation of to cause, 35–36
Personal direction, Buber on, 65, 69.
    See also Direction
Pfuetze, Paul, 386–387, 388
Phillip, Rabbi Aharon, 457–458
Philosophers Speak of God (Hartshorne),
    380
"Philosophical Accounting" (Buber),
    381
Philosophical anthropology, Buber's,
    69, 244, 294, 361–368
Philosophical Interrogations, 353;
    Buber's responses to, 381, 383,
    387–389
Philosophical system, Buber's, 382-389
Philosophizing, stages of, 344
Philosophy of Martin Buber, The (ed. by
    Paul A Schilpp and Maurice Fried-
    man); Fackenheim, 345; Friedman,
    215, 377; Kaufmann, 297–298
Philosophy of dialogue: Buber on, 67,
    94; in Claudel Program Book, 69;
    essence of Buber's, 434–435; and
    Hebrew Bible, 338; and Library of
    Living Philosophers, 380-381; mar-
    riage and, Buber on, 219-220
Philozionist, Paula as, 28
Picaresque Saint, The (Lewis), 342
Pike, Bishop James, 340, 410
Pilpul, 340
Pinder, Wilhelm, 209
Pinsker, Leo, 119
Pinski, David, 8
Pistis, 79; vs. emunah, 316
Planning, Buber on, 351
Plato, 82
Podewils, Count, 326
Podhoretz, Norman, 393
Pogroms, 24, 63
Pointing the Way (Buber), 373, 374, 411
Polarity, 65, 67, 68–69
Polish language, 11
Polish Jews, mass murder of, 262
Political Committee, 121–122
Political principle, vs. social principle,

298-300

Political messianism, 421. *See also* Messianism

Political surplus conflict, Buber on, 274, 276

Politicization, Buber on, 424

Politics: boundaries of, 352; Buber's attitude toward, 134; discussion of, 258; and postwar Zionism, 118-124

Politzer, Heinz, 225, 279

Porges, Dr., 15

Potsdam meeting, 75, 86. *See also* Forte Kreis

"Power and Love" (Buber), 134–135, 256

"Power of the Spirit, The" (Buber), 226–227

Prague: Bar Kochba Union at, 52–58; Buber's walking tour of, 56–57

Prayer, Buber on, 344

"Prayer" (Buber), 189

Presence, and holy insecurity, 74

Princeton, 371, 411

Problematic Rebel (Friedman), 319, 342, 438, 444

Problems of the Day, 270

Professor, European concept of, 250

Prolegomena to All Future Metaphysics (Kant), 17, 18

Promised Land, Herzl vs. Buber concept of, 32–33

Pro–Palestine Committee, 88

Prophecy, Buber on, 351

"Prophecy, Apocalyptic, and the Historical Hour" (Buber), 350

Prophetic Faith (Buber), 198, 261, 285, 289–292

Prophetic Judaism, 59–60

Protestants, Buber's influence on, 339

Proudhon, Pierre Joseph, 298

Proust, Marcel, 5

Prussian Academy of Writers, 323

Psalm 72, 451–453

Pseudomessianism, 289, 358

Psychiatrische-Klinik, 368

Psychiatry: Buber's interest in, 229–230. *See also* Interpersonal psychiatry

Psychological Club, 294

Psychologism: Buber's opposition to, 135; danger of, 294; and self-contradiction, 136–137

"Psychologizing of the World" (Buber), 294

Psychology: Buber's interest in, 229-230, 294; Jung on, 356

Psychopathology, 136

Psychotherapy: Buber's encounter with, 355-370; nondirective approach to, 368–370

Quakers, and belief in divinity of Christ, 318

Question to the Single One, The (Buber), 216, 218, 256

"Rabbi and His Son, The" (Buber), 43

Rabinowitsch, Eugene, 416

"Rachman, A Distant Spirit, Speaks" (Buber), 262

Rackham Auditorium, 368

Radler-Feldman, Yehoshua, 200

Ragaz, Leonhard, 292, 293

Rang, Florens Christian, 75, 86, 167; and *Die Kreatur*, 193-194; influence of on Buber, 76

Rappeport, Ernst Elijahu, 83, 98, 116, 119, 181

Rashi, 7, 171

Rathenau Walter, 14-15; on Judaism, 93; and Landauer, 88; murder of, 94

Rauschnig, Hermann, 262

Read, Sir Herbert, 419

Reading, Buber teaches art of, 224

Re'ah, Buber on, 302

Reality: Buber on, 65, 70; and despair, 137, interhuman, 76; politicization of, Buber on, 274; Rosenzweig's relation to, 157

Realization: Buber's emphasis on, 85; Gordon as epitome of, 119-120; and orienting, 63; prewar teachings, of, 55-72

Reason, Buber on, 381

Rebbe, 38

Rebbe Martin, of Heppenheim, 54

Reconciliation, Buber on, 330, 410

Reconciliation Action, 320

Redemption: Buber on, 45, 141-142, 144, 253, 283; Buber/Ben-Gurion on, 425; meaning of to the Jew, 197; and suffering servant, 173

Reflexion, 195-196; Buber on, 443-444; and monologue, 11

Reform Judaism, 59

Reicnsvertretung, 222

Reichswehrtruppen, 112

Relating, as movement, 69

Religion: Buber on, 172; and culture, 19-20

"Religion and Modern Thinking" (Buber), 325, 343, 356

"Religion and Philosophy" (Buber), 340–341

"Religion and Reality" (Buber), 336-337

"Religion as Presence" (Buber) 126, 127

"Religion as Reality" (Buber), 138

Religion of Reason out of the Sources of Judaism (Cohen), 128

Religious abstinence, Buber's, 293

Religious anarchy, Scholem on, 348

Religious reality, and I-Thou, 341-342

Religious socialism: Buber's, 94, 105, 252; and Christian society, 93

Renaissance, defined, 25. *See also* Jewish Renaissance

Renan, Joseph-Ernst, 9

Renewal, Buber on teaching of, 59-60

Rengstorf, Karl Heinrich, 321-322

"Replies to My Critics" (Buber), 215, 266, 381-384

Repression, Freud on, 246

Resistance, Spiritual, 225

Responsibility: attitude of, 326-327; Buber on true, 202

"Responsibility: Thoughts on the Jewish Question" (Guardini), 325

Ressentiment, Buber on, 211

Revelation: Buber on, 352-353, 358; in Old Testament, 172-173; as summons and sending, 137, 143

"Revelation, The" (Buber), 44, 66, 83

Review of Metaphysics, 376, 377

Revisionists, Jabotinsky's, 202

Revolution: and communal socialism, 99–115; as religious tragedy, 114

"Revolution" (Landauer), 101

Right and Wrong (Buber), 339

Rilke, Rainer M., 71

Rioch, David, 365, 366

Rogers, Carl R., 115, 368-370

Rolland, Romain, 75, 86

Rome, Sydney and Beatrice, 377

Roosevelt., Eleanor, 410, 411, 416

Rosenberg, Alfred, 58, 59, 210, 227

Rosenberg, Julius and Ethel, 415

Rosenstock-Huessy, Eugen, 195, 323

Rosenzweig, Edith, 160

Rosenzweig, Franz, 39, 47-48, 54, 128, *305*; and Buber-Rosenzweig Bible, 155–177; on *Der Jude*, 89; and Freie Jüdische Lehrhaus, 126; on God as Existing, 169; influence of on Buber, 77; and Jewish Law, 347, 348; methods for nursing, 160; paralysis of, 159; thought of, 157

Rosenzweig, Rafael, 167-168

Rossini, G. A., 437

Rotenstreich, Nathan, 383, 458

Roth, Cecil, 259

Rotten, Elizabeth, 188

Routledge & Kegan Paul, 347

Royal Institute for the Tropics, 443

Rubicoff, Abraham, 459

Ruckbiegung (reflexion), 195-196

Rumania, Buber intervention in, 415

Ruppen, Arthur, 206

Rusk, Dean, 459

Russell, Bertrand, 299, 415, 416

Russian Revolution, Landauer on, 104

Rylaarsdam, J. Coert, 292

Sabbataianism, Scholem on, 389

Sabbath, Buber's observance of, 333-334, 340

Sadagora, 38

Samuel, Lord Edwin, 200

Sankt Getrauden Minne (P. Buber), 116

Santelli, Santina, 41

Sarah Lawrence College, 334, 370, 374

Sartre, Jean-Paul, 191, 343, 363, 416

Satyagraha (soul-force), 213-214, 254

Sauerbruch, Ernst Ferdinand, 209

"Sayings of the Fathers," 265

Sborowitz, Arie, 294

Schaeder, Grete, 27, 29, 83, 444, 450, 453, 455, 456; on Buber concept of education, 190; on Buber's insecurity, 132; and dedication to Paula, 133; on Gerson, 205

Schatz-Uffenheimer, Rivka, 266, 391-394, 393, 394

Schaumburg, Lippe, Count, 326

Scheler, Max, 245-246

Schilpp, Paul Arthur, 377

Schlosser, Rudolf, 227

Schmidt, Karl Ludwig, 217, 218

Schmitt, Carl, 218

Schneider, Dr. Lambert, 299, 440, 446; and Buber/Rosenzweig Bible, 164-193

Schocken, Almanac, 228, 231

Schocken, Salman, 226, *307*

Schocken Verlag, 213

Schoenman, Ralph, 416

Scholem, Gershom, 191, 200, 203, 239, 458; appraisal of Buber, 61-62; vs. Buber, 389-397; on Buber/Rosenzweig Bible, 168, 171; on Buber's impact on young people, 63; on Hasidism, 356; on Kittel, 217; on religious anarchy, 348; on *Way of Man*, 298

School for the Education of Teachers of the People, 300, 333

School of Jewish Youth, 206

Schopenhauer, Arthur, 15

Schuman, Robert, 443

Schweitzer, Albert, 196, 229, 327, 415, 417, 436

Science, Buber on, 384

Sdemot, 441

Sea, as symbol, 65

Seclusion, Buber's years of, 55

Second Ecumenical Council, 439

Second World War, 257–267

Seer, and Yehudi, 265, 266

"Seinstradition," 204

Selbstbehauptung (self-assertion), Nazism as, Heidegger on, 325-326

Self, Jung on, 357

Self and the Dramas of History, The

(Neibuhr), 352

Self-identification, 383

Seminars, impact of, 12

Senator, D. Werner, 200, 275, 277

Separation, sphere of, 349

Service, Buber on, 48

Shapira, Avraham, 440, 441, 458

Sh'ar Ha'amakim, 425

Shazar, Zalman, 427, 457, 458

Shekinah (God's glory), 48

Shereshevsky, Simon, 416, 457

Shiflut (humility), 49

Shmarsov, August, 15

Siegel, Seymour, 337

"Silence and Outcry" (Buber), 263

"Silent Question, The" (Buber), 337–338

Silone, Ignazio, 299, 419

Simhon, Joseph, 273

Simmel, George, 14, 58, 76, 158

Simon, Ernst, 183, 200, 222, 259, 279, 281, 371, 373, 397, 416, 426, 457, 458; and Ba'ayot, 270; Ben-Gurion's rejoinder to, 429-430; and Buber, 90, 118, 449; on Buber/Ben-Gurion, 433, 434; on Buber vs. Cohen, 91–92; Buber poem to, 172; on Buber's reputation, 191–192; on Buber-Rosenzweig Bible, 168-169; on Buber spiritual resistance to Nazis, 223-224; for Buber as teacher, 250; on *Daniel*, 63; on *Der Jude*, 89; and League for Jewish Arab Rapprochement, 269; and Lehrhaus, 189-190, 222, 223; on *Speeches to Judaism*, 62

Sinai, invasion of, 422-423

Sinclair, Upton, 75

Smilansky, Moshe, 270, 273, 275, 371

Smith, Ronald Gregor, 287, 334

Snell, Dr. Bruno, 324

Snyder, Ross, 368

Sobell, Morton, 415

Social philosophy, 353; Buber lectures on, 244

Social principle vs. political principle, 92, 298-300, 349, 353

Socialism: Landauer's, 99-100, 103; *See*

also Christian soci-communal socialisms; Decentralist socialism; Federalistic communal socialism; Religious socialism; Utopian socialism

Socialist party (Germany), 88

Socialist power-State, 105

Society, indirect aspects of, 349

"Society and the State" (Buber), 298, 349

Society for Christian-Jewish Cooperation (of Darmstadt), 331

Socrates, teaching of, 385-386

Soderbloom, Nathan, 318

Solitude, importance of, 244

"Song of Life" (Hofmannsthal), 13

Sonnmatt, 448; Buber at, 444, 448

Sophocles, Buber's knowledge of, 7

Soviet Union: Buber on Jews in, 414-417; recognizes Israel, 280

"Space Problem of the Stage, The" (Buber), 69

Space/time, finiteness of, 388-389

Spartacists, communist regime of, 112

Speech: Buber/Heidegger on, 326; God's, 338; as multiplicity, 126; truth of lived, 439

Speech-as-event, reality of, 13

"Speeches on Judaism" (Buber), 52-53, 57-58, 61, 90, 139, 145, 162; existential appeal of, 59, 62

Speech-with-meaning, 81

Spinoza, Baruch, 34, 429

Spirit, Buber on, 227

"Spirit of Judaism, The" (Buber), 88

Spirits and Men (Buber), 376

Spiritual realism, in *I and Thou*, 134

Spitzer, Morris, 118, 206, 221, 226, 228; on Buber personalities, 230-231

Sprinzak, Joseph, 201, 202, 421

Star of Redemption (Rosenzweig), 128, 156, 157, 175

State, Buber's attitude toward, 134

State of Israel: Buber on 420-421; early years of, 235-311. *See also* Israel; Palestine

Stefan Georg school, 84

Steppenwolf (Hesse), 184, 185

Stern, Gavriel, 273, 278-279

Stern, Gang, 253

Stevenson, Adlai, 459

Stirner, Max, 218

Straub, Hedwig, 219

Strauss, Edward, 189, 241, 258-259

Strauss, Emil, 69

Strauss, Emmanuel, 183, 184, 284

Strauss, Eva Buber, 272, 281, 457. *See also* Buber, Eva

Strauss, Ludwig, 83, 96-98, 281, 329; Buber consoles, 257-258; death of, 303; Eva marries, 117, 180; life on Kibbutz, 237-238

Streicher, Julius, 218

Stumpf, Carl, 14

Subjectivity, Buber on, 335, 336-337

Sublimation, Freud on, 246

Suffering, mystery of, 459-460

Suffering servant, 114; of Deutero-Isaiah, 290-292; Rosenzweig as, 115; stages of way of, 292; as symbol, 173

Sufism, 394, 395

Suicide, and despair, 80

Sullivan, Harry Staek, 219, 361, 364, 367

"Summons and sending," 68

Susman, Margarete, 76, 83-84; on Landauer, 113

Suzuki, D. T., 395

Szilasi, Wilhelm, 419, 436

Szold, Henrietta, 269, 270, 273, 276, 371

Tagore, Debendranath, 75

Talbiyeh, Buber home at, 241, 302

Tales of the Hasidim (Buber), 41, 397; Hesse on, 297; Kaufmann on, 297-298; as unillustrated, 349

Tales of Rabbi Nachman, The (Buber), 41, 42-43, 56, 63, 389; illustrations for, 353-354

Talit, 458

Talmon, Yonina, 249

Talmudic stage, of realization of God, 61

Tao, teachings of the, 104, 135, 174, 355. *See also* Wu-wei

Tao Te Ching (Lao-tzu), 180

Targum (commentary), 171
"Task, The" (Buber), 124
Taubes, Jacob, 370
Taylor, Katherine Whiteside, 449
Teaching, Freudenberg on Buber's, 302–303
"Teaching of the Tao, The" (Buber), 49–50, 68, 373
Teffillin (phylacteries), 38
Temple of Lemberg, 38
Temple Square, 260, 261
Temptation, Buber on, 20–21, 374
Ternary of fire, 39, 83
Ternary of light, 39, 83
Terrorists, Buber intervenes for, 273
Teshura, 61
Testament of Rabbi Israel Baal-Shem, The (Buber), 39, 41
Theater, and drama, 68–69
Theologische Blätter, 217
Theology, defined, 381
Theophany, Buber on, 127
Theologoumenon, Hebrew Bible as, 170
Theopolitical state, Kingship of God as, 198
"Therapeutic Despair, The" (Farber), 362
Third International Pedagogical Conference, 186
Thoreau, Henry David, 75, 417–418
Thou: eternal, 137–138, 460; meeting with, 131. *See also* I-Thou
"Three Speeches on Judaism" (Buber), 57–58, 205
Thuring, Margaret, 178–179. *See also* Buber-Neumann, Margarete
Thurneyson, Edward, 192
"Thursday Society," 69
Thus Spake Zarathustra (Nietzsche), 18-19
Tillich, Paul, 192, 381, 447, 448; Urgrund of, 382
Time: Buber's preoccupation with, 17–20; Nietzsche's interpretation of, 18, 19
Time, 430, 442
"To P." (Buber), 133

"To the Contemporary' (Buber), 82
Topos, (place), 202
Torchlight parade, Hebrew U. students, *404*, 442
Tradition criticism, vs. source criticism, 286–287
Tragedy, Buber's view of, 36, 189, 263–265
"Tragic Conflict, A" (Buber), 274
Trial, The (Kafka), 90
Trietsch, Davis, 32, 35, *148;* dark charisma of, 174–175; and Herzl, 174, 212, 264
Trotsky, Leon, 104
Trüb, Hans, 180, 185, 194, 211, 355, 356; Buber confides in, 271–272; Buber's loan from, 257; approach of to psychotherapy, 294; impact of Buber on, 229–230; on Jewish-Christian dialogue, 193
Trust, Buber on, 448, 459–460
Truth, Rosenzweig on, 156–157, 175–176
Truman, Harry S., 280
Tsivion, Aviaham, 259
Tshombe, Moise, 414
"Two Boys, The" (Buber), 248
"Two Foci of the Jewish Soul" (Buber), 196
"Two Kinds of Zionism" (Buber), 280–281
"Two Peoples in Palestine" (Buber), 276
Two Types of Faith (Buber), 198, 280, 315–319
"Twofold Future" (Buber), 19

Uffenheimer, Benjamin, 226, 250
Uganda, as Zionist settlement site, 31–32
Ulpan, 301
Ulpan Akiva, 349
Unconditionality, Buber, 85
Unconscious: Buber on, 365–366, 440; conception of, 294; Jung's treatment of, 367- 368
Under Two Dictators (Thuring-Buber), 178–179

Understanding the Sick and the Healthy (Rosenzweig), 156

Unequal Worlds (Carossa), 323

"Unfolding of Creative Forces in the Child, The," as theme, 186

Union of South Africa, 410–411

Union Theological Seminary, 371

Uniqueness, 81; concept of, Buber on, 47, 366; Jesus', 140

United Arab Army, 278-280

United Nations: and apartheid, 410–411; Armistice Commission, 282; supervises Palestine, 272; Trust Administration of, 273, 274

Unity: Buber on, 57, 65–67, 130, 255; grace of, 129–130; realization of, 68, 69–70; Taoist, 373–374

University of Berlin, 14

University of Buffalo, 377

University of Chicago, Divinity School of, 368

University of Cologne, 442

University of Frankfurt, 96; Buber and, 161–162, 209

University of Heidelberg, 96, 209; Conference at, 186–188

University of Leipzig, 14

University of Michigan, 368

University of Munich, 438

University of Münster, 322, 439

University of the Sorbonne, 7, 436

University of Vienna, 11, 14

University of Zurich, 14

Urgrund, 382

Utopian socialism, 299

Utopiainism, and politics, 424–425

Valero, Justice, 270

"Validity and Limitation of the Political Principle" (Buber), 325, 348–349, 410

Van Dusen, Henry, 411–412

Van Dyke, Willard, 361

Van Eeden. *See* Eeden, Frederik Van

Vedanta, nondualistic tradition of, 340–341

Vergegnung (mismeeting), 4–5

Verkündigung [The Annunciation]

(Claudel), 69

Vienna: culture of, 12–13; university studies at, 12–14. *See also* University of Vienna

Virginia Theological Seminary, 365

"Vision and Redemption" (Buber), 423

"Visit to H." (Strauss), 96–97

Vogeler, Heinrich, 179

Volksheim (for Eastern European Jews), 199

Volkshochschule, 199

Walter, Bruno, 439

Wandering Jew, 217

Wandervogel, 136; Arian clauses in, 105

War, Buber's growing alienation from, 90, 92–93

War diaries (Buber), 84–85

War Politics, Landauer on, 89

Warshaw, Ruth, 444–445

Washington (DC) School of Psychiatry, 361

Wasmuth, Ewald, 292, 329, 447–448

Wasmuth, Sophie, 447–448

Wasserman, Jakob, 93

"Watchword, The" (Buber), 88

Way of Man, The (Buber), 298, 397

Weber, Hans von, 15

Weber, Max, 249; and charisma, 174

Weil, Simone, 337

Weimar Republic, 187–207

Weiss, Emil Rudolf, 279

Weizmann, Chaim, 23-24, 32, *148*, 206, 442, 456; on parity, 201

Weizsäcker, Carl Friedrich von, 326

Weizsäcker, Dr. Viktor von, 159, 194, 323–324

Weltanschauung (worldview), 138, 139; Zionism as, 30

Weltsch, Felix, 56

Weltsch, Robert, 24, 56, 122, 200, 201, 203, 270; on need for Jewish education, 220

Weniger, Eric, 223

Werblovsky, Zwi, 458

"Werewolf, The" (Buber), 44

Werfel, Franz, 104 *Werke* (Buber), 446

Werkleute (Work folk) kibbutz,

206–207, 235; and Jewish Youth movement, 205

West German Republic, 327; relation of to Israel, 330

Western Jew: as divided person, 58; relation of to Palestine, 57. *See also* Jews; Judaism

"What Can Philosophical Anthropology Contribute to Psychiatry" (Buber), 361–368

"What Is Common to All" (Buber), 364

What Is Man (Buber), 247–248, 325, 388

Wholeness, sphere of, 349

"Why Did I Sign the Professors' Manifesto" (Bashan), 429

"Why Study Jewish Sources" (Buber), 206

Wiener, Alfred, 322

Wiener Rundschau, 13

Wiesel, Elie, 339

Wilhelm, Rabbi Kurt, 293

Wilhelmina, Queen (Holland), *405*

"Will to power," Neitzsche on, 19

William Alanson White Memorial Lectures, 361–368

Wilson, Dan, 457

Winkler, Paula, 24; and anti-Semitism, 28–29; profile of, 26–29. *See also* Buber, Paula

"With a Monist" (Buber), 70, 74, 81

Wittig, Joseph, 194–195

Wolf, Rabbi Arnold Jacob, 397

Wolf, Ernest M. 171

Wolfskehl, Karl, 84

Women's liberation movement, 101–102

Word, philosophy of, Buber on, 126

Word and the Spiritual Realities, The (Ebner), 128

"Word That Is Spoken, The" (Buber), 438

Words, linking of, in Hebrew Buber/Rosenzweig Bible, 170–171

Words to the Age (Buber), 106

"Word to the Times" (Buber), 172, 173

Work, tragedy of, 189

"Work Folk," 203–204

Worpswede, 179

World, psychologizing, 135

"World of Confusion," 20

"World of Martin Buber, The," 436

World War: and breakthrough to dialogue, 73–98; Buber on hopes for from, 86–87; and German/East European Jews, 83; problematic aspect of, 87; as term, 78; as turning point for Buber, 73–98

World Zionist Organization, 294

Writings of Martin Buber, The (Herberg), 352

Wundt, Wilhelm, 14, 15

Wu-wei, 48, 174

Wyschogrod, Michael, 333–334; 370

Yehuda Halevi, 158, 166, 167

Yehudi, and Seer, 265, 266, 397

Yellow badge, wearing of, 220

YHVH 289–290

Yiddish language, 8

Yishuv (Jewish settlement in Palestine), 118, 208

Yitzhak, Levi, of Berdtichev, 394

"Yoke, The" (Buber/Magnes), 254–255

Yoran, Dr. Kalman, 303

Young Guard, 270

Young Workers. *See* Hapoel Hazair

Young Zionist(s), 31; Buber as leader of, 55. *See also* Zionism

Youth: Buber's impact on 61–62, 63, 331; elements of call to, 105

Zaddik(im), 3, 38, 43; Baeck and Buber as, 377–378; Buber on, 52–54; Hasidic focus on, 389–390; life of, 394–393; role of, 53

"Zaddik of Zehlendorf," 3

Zans, Hasidim of, 9

Zehlendorf, 77–78, 94

Zen Buddhism, 393, 395

Zervana, 185

Zimmer, Heinrich, 370–371

"Zion and Youth" (Buber), 105

Zion as Goal and Task (Buber), 238

Zionism and Zionists, 21-36, 201; and Balfour Declaration, 256; biblical, 92; bourgeois, 56; Buber on, 57,

59, 62, 78; and Buber's break-through to dialogue, 86; Central Bureau, 32; characteristics of, 202–203; Congresses, 24, 29, 30, 32, 35, 56, 121–122; Cologne convention of, 22; cultural, 30, 33, 56; effect of war on, 88; Executive Committee, 199; and future State of Israel, 31–33; in German-speaking Europe, 32; of Herzl, 23–24, 33; influence of, 23, 25; as Jewish Renaissance, 23; overview of, 372; Palestinian, 26; Paula embraces 28; postwar, 118–124; sense of community in, 103–104; West and East, 29–30. *See also* Labor Zionism; Young Zionists

Zionist Union of Germany, 228
Zohar, 389
Zola, Émile, 23
Zurich Analytical Club, 185
Zusya, R., 394
Zvi, Sabbatai, 289, 359–361
Zweig, Arnold, 74, 250
Zweig, Stefan, 12, 104
Zwiesprache [Dialogue] (Buber), 195, 196